Thomas Stackhouse

A New History of the Holy Bible

From the Beginning of the World, to the Establishment of Christianity: Vol. I.

Thomas Stackhouse

A New History of the Holy Bible

From the Beginning of the World, to the Establishment of Christianity: Vol. I.

ISBN/EAN: 9783337169336

Printed in Europe, USA, Canada, Australia, Japan

Cover: Foto ©Lupo / pixelio.de

More available books at **www.hansebooks.com**

The Revd Mr THOMAS STACKHOUSE.

A

NEW HISTORY

OF THE

HOLY BIBLE,

FROM THE

BEGINNING OF THE WORLD,

TO THE

ESTABLISHMENT OF CHRISTIANITY,

WITH

ANSWERS TO MOST OF THE CONTROVERTED QUESTIONS, DISSERTATIONS UPON THE MOST REMARKABLE PASSAGES, AND A CONNECTION OF PROFANE HISTORY ALL ALONG.

To which are added,

NOTES, EXPLAINING DIFFICULT TEXTS, RECTIFYING MIS-TRANSLATIONS, AND RECONCILING SEEMING CONTRADICTIONS.

BY THE REV. THOMAS STACKHOUSE, A. M.
LATE VICAR OF BEENHAM IN BERKSHIRE.

VOL. I.

GLASGOW:

PRINTED BY JOSEPH GALBRAITH.

1795.

TO THE

RIGHT REVEREND FATHER IN GOD,

E D M U N D,

LORD BISHOP OF LONDON.

AND

One of his Majesty's Most Honourable Privy Council.

My Lord,

THAT a book of this size, by a person of my obscurity, should, in so short a space of time, after so large a number already printed off, come to its second impression, must be imputed very much to the influence of your Lordship's name in the front; which is of weight sufficient to stamp authority upon any thing, and to induce both clergy and laity to read what your Lordship has not disdained to approve.

There is something however, I hope, in the laudableness of my intention, which, in conjunction with your Lordship's influence, has been a means to conciliate the good opinion of the public, and to give the work a greater currency: For the defign of what I now prefent to your Lordfhip, is, fo to methodife, explain, and illuftrate the Hiftorical Part of the HOLY BIBLE, as to remove the difficulties in reading it, which fome have afferted, and others complained of, with an intent, I fear, to prejudice the world againft it. And were I under no previous obligations to your Lordfhip, the very nature of my fubject would remit me to one, who has always been a known encourager of works of this kind, and who has himfelf fo glorioufly maintained the truth and authority of thofe facred records, and both the evidences and excellency of the Chriftian difpenfation.

Since it is our fate, my Lord, to live in an age wherein divine revelation is rejected, the fenfe of ancient prophecies perverted, the miracles of our Bleffed Saviour degraded, the myfteries of our holy religion ridiculed, its laws and conftitutions flighted, and its guides and minifters treated with defpite; we ought to account it the peculiar bleffing of Heaven, that in this great metropolis we have one prefiding over us, who is fo well qualified to withftand this inundation of impiety, who is both able and willing to vindicate the caufe of God and religion, and, by his example and encouragement, to animate us in defence of it.

To you, my Lord, we owe a full confutation of infidelity, in your Lordship's most excellent Pastoral Letters; to you we owe that wife syftem of directions for our private conduct, and the honourable difcharge of our ministerial office, which, if duly obferved, would make *us unto God a fweet favour of Chrift*, and a glorious clergy indeed; to you we owe the knowledge of our ecclefiaftical laws and conftitutions, which your Lordship, with great care, and pains indefatigable, has digefted and explained; to you we owe the defence of thofe immunities and privileges, and the prefervation of thofe rights and poffeffions, with which thofe laws and conftitutions have invefted us; and, however other tongues may be filent, my gratitude, I hope, will always oblige me to declare, that to you I owe the prefent comfortable leifure I have for ftudy, and the generous encouragement your Lordship has always been pleafed to give to my weak, but well-intended labours.

Whatever then, my Lord, the perverfenefs of this prefent generation may be, future ages muft be told, what an exquifite judge and mafter of all ufeful learning, what a firm friend to men of merit, what a true patriot to your country, what a zealous defender of the Chriftian caufe, what a wife guide and governor of Chrift's church, what a kind protector of his minifters, and ftrenuous affer-

DEDICATION.

tor of their rights and privileges, you have all along been; in how large a sphere your Lordship, these many years has moved; and with what lustre you have always adorned it.

That the great *giver of every good and perfect gift* may long preserve your Lordship, a public blessing to this church and nation, is the daily fervent prayer of,

My Lord,

Your Lordship's

Most humble,

Obliged, and

Devoted servant,

THOMAS STACKHOUSE.

Beenham in Berkshire,
April 7, 1744.

THE APPARATUS TO THE HISTORY OF THE OLD TESTAMENT.

BEFORE we enter upon the history of the [a] Holy Bible, it may not be improper to enquire a little into the truth and authority, the perfection and excellency, the antiquity, style, and other properties of that Part of it which we call the *Old Testament*, (for what we have to say concerning the *New* must be reserved to another place,) the number and nature of the books whereof it is composed, and the several translations and other incidental changes, which, since the time of its publi-

---

[a] The books which we look upon as the foundation of our holy religion, go under different names. They are stiled *sacred* and *divine books*, *holy writ*, and *holy scriptures*, because they were wrote by persons divinely inspired, and do contain the commandments of God himself. Our Saviour calls them *the scriptures*, by way of eminence; because no other book is comparable to them. Several of the ancients gave them the name of *Pandect*, and *Bibliotheca Sancta*, as containing all the tracts which were wrote upon the same divine subject. Of later ages the word *Bible*, (which comes from the Greek *Biblia*, signifying *books*)

publication, it has undergone. And this we are the rather induced to do, because a bolder spirit of infidelity than usual, has, of late, gone out into the world; teaching some to look upon all religion as a mere trick, contrived by the arts of princes, and conserved by the interest of priests; others, to call in question the genuineness of some particular books of scripture, thereby to make way for the subversion of the whole; others, to disparage the whole, as a rude and immethodical, a flat insipid composition, unbecoming the Spirit of God to dictate, or men of letters to read; and others again, from the pretended sufficiency of natural religion, to deny the necessity of any divine revelation at all.

A divine revelation what. What we are to understand by a *divine revelation* needs no great pains to discover. [b] In the most simple and obvious sense of the word, *revelation* is the making that known, which was a secret before; and so, when applied to a religious use, "It is God's making known himself, and his will to mankind, over and above what he has made known by the light of nature and reason." To this purpose we may observe, that the objects of our knowledge are of three kinds: Some are discernable by the light of nature without revelation; such is the knowledge of God from the effects of his power and wisdom, as [c] the apostle argues: Others knowable, not at all by the light of nature, but by revelation only; such is the salvation of mankind

---

books) has universally prevailed. But how the word *testament* came to be applied to the holy scriptures, is not so easy a matter to define; only we may observe, that the Septuagint's using the word *Diatheke*, (which signifies a *testament*,) might probably induce the Latin interpreter to translate it by *testamentum*. But then we must remember, that this word must not be used in its ordinary sense, as it means a man's *last will*, that it is to be executed after his death; but, in a more general signification, to denote, a *solemn declaration* of the *will* of God towards men, containing his laws, his precepts, his promises, and the covenant which he has contracted with them. And for this reason it is likewise called by the Latins *instrumentum*, i. e. an authentic *deed*, containing solemn ordinances, or treaties, and compacts. The books which comprehend what God revealed to the Jews, are called *the Old*, and those which contain what he declared by Jesus Christ and his apostles, are titled *the New Testament*. Du Pin's hist. of the Canon, &c.

[b] Bishop Williams' sermons at Boyle's lectures.
[c] Rom i. 20.

mankind by the death of Jesus Christ, ᵈ *which (as the apostle expresses it) has, from the beginning, been hid in God*: And others, discoverable by the light of nature indeed, but very imperfectly, and therefore stand in need of a revelation to give them a farther proof and evidence; and of this kind is that ᵉ *life and immortality*, which (the same apostle tells us) our Saviour *brought to light by the gospel*. But now, be the revelation of what degree soever, whether partial or entire, whether a total discovery of some unknown truths, or only a fuller and clearer manifestation of them, it must be supernatural, and proceed from God.

That God can make a revelation of his will, either immediately to our minds and inward faculties, or mediately to our understandings, by the intervention of our outward senses, can never be questioned by any one who considers him as the author of his being, and therefore intimately acquainted with all the springs and movements of his soul. ᶠ We find ourselves capable of communicating our thoughts to one another, either by means of a sound of words, which strikes the ear, or by writing, or other signitures of our intentions, which effect the eye; and why cannot God make use of the like means to impress what idea he thinks fit on our minds, or to give such motions to the brain, as may occasionally excite whatever thoughts he designs to produce in us? or rather indeed, why may not he, without any intermediate or occasional cause at all, enlighten the mind by a direct and naked view of such truths as he desires it should know? for ᵍ *he that planted the ear*, and *he that formed the eye*, shall not he have access to them? or shall not he have the power of communicating his thoughts, *who teacheth man understanding?*

The possibility of God's making one.

Since therefore it cannot be denied, but that it is possible for God to reveal his will to mankind, let us, in the next place consider, which is most probable, which most agreeable to the notions we have of him, whether he should, or should not, make such a revelation. Now, if we may judge of this by the general sense of mankind, we shall hardly find any one, that believed the existence of a God, who did not believe likewise some kind of commerce and communication between God and men. ʰ This was the foundation of all the religious rites and ceremonies, which every nation pretended

The probability that he did.

Vol. I. No. 1.   B

ᵈ Eph. iii. 9. ᵉ 2 Tim. i. 10. ᶠ Fiddes's body of divinity, vol. 1. ᵍ Psal. xciv. 9. ʰ Dr. Sherlock's sermons.

pretended to receive from their gods: And, what gave birth to all their superstitious arts of divination, was the persuasion that their gods had a perpetual intercourse with men, and, by sundry means, gave them intelligence of things to come.

And indeed it is hardly to be imagined, that God should make reasonable creatures on purpose to know him, and to be happy in the knowledge, and love, and admiration of him, and yet withdraw himself from them, without giving them any visible tokens of his presence, or communicating any farther knowledge of himself to them, than what they might perceive in the reflection of his works. A desire to be acquainted with the will of the Supreme Being seems to be so connatural to the soul of man, that, in the more civilized parts of the world, we scarcely know any people of note, who had not their Sibyls, such as they accounted the mouth of their gods; and, without all doubt, none were without an oracle, to which, upon all exigencies, they had recourse, and to whose injunctions they willingly submitted. And if such a desire be implanted in us, the consideration of God's goodness will not suffer us to doubt, but that he has made a proper provision to answer this, as well as our other natural appetites. Whereupon we cannot but conclude, that the same power and wisdom which made man a reasonable and inquisitive being, and allowed him a world of wonders to employ his intellectual faculties in the contemplation of, has likewise taken care to satisfy that noble desire of knowing what the will of his maker is, and what relates to his own eternal welfare: And that is *revelation*.

Without this, indeed, the case is with him, as with one that is born blind, [i] who, whatever other evidence he may have of the being of a God, wants one, the most convincing of all, *i. e.* the wonders of an almighty power, and

[i] Our excellent Milton, in that episode upon light, wherein he bewails his own want of sight, very feelingly, has expressed this thought with a great deal of tenderness and beauty:

―――― Thus with the year
Seasons return, but not to me return
Day, or the sweet approach of ev'n or morn,
Or sight of vernal bloom or summer's rose,
Or flocks, or herds, or human face divine.
But cloud instead, and ever during dark
Surrounds me, from the chearful ways of men

and incomprehensible wisdom, conspicuous in the frame of nature, and the visible parts of the creation. And, in like manner, whatever sense such men as have only reason for their guide, may attain of the mercy and goodness of God; whatever they may observe, in the course of his providence, to confirm them in the belief of it; whatever hopes they may entertain of it from a general notion of the divine nature; whatever desire they may have for it from the sense of their own misery: yet they want that evidence of it, which alone can satisfy and compose their doubtful and distracted minds; and that is certainty, or, which is the same *revelation*, by which, and nothing less, that certainty is to be obtained.

The plain truth is, if there be no revelation, we are, as it were, *without God in the world;* and, considering the nature of some events, cannot assuredly say, whether the divine providence interferes in the government of it, or fate and chance happen to all things [k]. If there be no revelation, we are still in our sins, and have no sanctuary against the accusations of our enraged consciences, the fears of our guilty minds, or the justice of an incensed Deity. If there be no revelation, we have no hope, can have no comfort in our death, nor any assurance of immortality after it. In a word, if there be no revelation, we are in a perpetual maze, as if we were at sea, without star or compass, and knew not what course to take to gain our harbour. And therefore the same reason which we have to believe that God is good and gracious in all his other dispensations, we have to believe likewise, that, from the first creation of the world, he always vouchsafed mankind some revelation of his will, whereby to direct their conduct.

The necessity of his doing it

Adam, no doubt, was created, at first, in the full perfection of his reason; and yet, if we take a view of him in that state, we shall soon perceive, that he could not attain a competent knowledge of many things, without the assistance of divine revelation. [l] He felt indeed himself to

to the first man,

Cut off, and, for the book of knowledge fair,
Presented with an universal blank
Of nature's works, to me expung'd and raz'd,
And wisdom at one entrance quite shut out. *Book.* 3.

[k] Bishop Williams's sermons at Boyle's lectures.
[l] Milton, whom I take to be a good commentator upon what happened to Adam in his state of innocence, introduces him thus expressing himself:

to be, but how he came to be, he knew not; for he saw nothing about him, that could either be supposed to have given him that being, or could inform him how he came by it. He saw he had a body, but what that body was originally made of, he could not possibly tell; for how could he suppose, that such warm, soft, and tender flesh, such firm and well-compacted joints, such bright and radiant eyes, &c. were ever formed of cold shapeless, and unactive earth? He felt his body move obsequious to his will, but what that inward principle was, which moved it, he was wholly ignorant; nor could he possibly, of himself, conceive, that there was an immaterial spirit, of a distinct nature and subsistence, vitally united to it, and what gave the spring to all its motions. He cast his eyes up to the heavens, and there saw that glorious luminary, which gave light (as he perceived) to all about him; but whether it was an intelligent being or not, or, when it came to decline and set, whether it might not be inclosed in perpetual darkness, he could not understand. He found, towards the approach of night, an heavy stupidness begin to seize him, and that he was forced to submit to its power; but he did not know, but that it was to be the extinction of his being, and that he was to close his eyes and conclude his life together. This we may very well suppose to have been the case of Adam, at his first looking about him, immediately upon his creation. For though he had what we call reason, in a sovereign degree; yet even that reason must have been his torment for a while, when it made him inquisitive, but could give him no satisfaction: And therefore

> Myself I then perus'd and limb by limb
> Survey'd, and sometimes went, and sometimes ran
> With subtle joints, as lively vigour led.
> But who I was, or where, or from what cause
> Knew not. To speak I try'd, and forthwith spake:
> My tongue obey'd, and readily could name
> Whate'er I saw: "Thou Sun, said I, fair light!
> " And thou, enlighten'd earth, so fresh and gay!
> " Ye hills, and dales! ye rivers, woods, and plains!
> " And ye, that live, and move, fair creatures! tell,
> " Tell (if ye saw) how came I thus, how here——
> " Not of my self—by some great maker then,
> " In goodness, and in power pre-eminent.
> " Tell me how I may know him, how adore,
> " From whom I have, that thus I move, and live,
> " And feel that I am happier than I know." *Book* 8.

fore it is proper to believe, (the wisdom and goodness of God constrain us to believe,) that, in order to relieve him under this perplexity, God took care, either by the ministry of his holy angels, or by some immediate inspiration, and impression, to inform him of every thing, that was necessary for him to know, in the state wherein he had placed him.

He had placed him now in a beautiful garden, and given him great variety of fruits for his nourishment and support. But might not some of these fruits be designed for other purposes than food? or might they not have some bad and pernicious qualities in them, how apparently fair soever, and inviting? [m] Without making the experiment, it was impossible for Adam to know what food was proper for his constitution, which experiment (for ought he knew) might have proved fatal to him; and therefore we find God giving him this direction: [n] *Of every tree in the garden thou mayst freely eat, but of the tree of knowledge of good and evil, thou shalt not eat of it; for in the day that thou eatest thereof, thou shalt surely die.*

He had placed him, naked and defenceless, in the midst of savage creatures, all able and inclined to destroy him, had they not been restrained by some invisible power; and, in this condition, he must have been miserable beyond all imagination, and under perpetual apprehensions, that the first lyon or tyger he met would certainly devour him: but, to ease his mind in this particular, we find God giving him assurance to the contrary, and investing him with this authority: [o] *Have dominion over the fish of the sea, and over the fowl of the air, and over every living thing that moveth upon the earth.*

He had formed a woman, to be a consort and companion to him; but how he should know any thing of a future state of marriage, and the ties of conjugal affection among his posterity, [p] (as his words plainly indicate;) how he should have a perfect notion of *father* and *mother*, before there was any such thing as father and mother in the world; should have clear ideas of the affection and endearments arising from that relation, and yet, at the same time, should perceive, that the affection and endearments arising from marriage, would so far get the better of them, as to attach a man nearer to a stranger, taken into his bosom, than to those very parents whose blood ran in his veins;

[m] Revelation examined. [n] Gen. ii. 16, 17. [o] Ibid. i. 26. [p] Ibid. ii. 24.

veins; is a problem which cannot be refolved without having recourfe to divine revelation; and therefore we find our Saviour thus expounding it: *Have ye not read, that he who made them in the beginning, made them male and female: and faid, For this caufe fhall a man leave father and mother, and fhall cleave to his wife and they twain fhall be one flefh?* So that the words of Adam, upon this occafion, were the declaration of God himfelf, and only pronounced by Adam, in confequence of an exprefs revelation from God. And if a revelation, in thefe and fuch like inftances, was needful for the conduct of man in his ftate of integrity, much more was it neceffary in a ftate of defection and general depravity.

and his pofterity. Whether we believe, then, or not believe, the account which Mofes gives of the devil's deceiving our firft parents in the form of a ferpent; yet, unlefs we will deny the truth of all hiftory, we muft allow, that in procefs of time, (both before and after the flood,) the corruption of mankind became univerfal; and that their grand adverfary had fo enlarged his empire, as even to outvie the *God of heaven* in the fplendour of his temples, the number of his votaries, and the pomp and folemnity of his worfhip. *In this cafe, we do not indeed fay, that man had any right to the divine affiftance: that he had forfeited by his apoftafy; and where the neceffity is created by our own fault, there lies no obligation upon the Creator to provide a remedy. But though God was under no obligation to do it, yet, confidering the miferable circumftances mankind were in after the fall, more efpecially through want of a revelation, we may reafonably conclude, that the benignity of his nature would no lefs incline him to give them one, than if he had been obliged to it by a fpecial promife or covenant.

For how can we believe, that a being of infinite perfection, when he faw mankind under the deception of fin, and the delufions of Satan, fhould take no care to rectify their miftakes, and reform their manners? *Can we fuppofe it confiftent with infinite truth, to fuffer all nations to be expofed to the wicked defigns of feducing and apoftate fpirits, without ever offering them any means to undeceive them? Can we imagine, that a God of infinite majefty and power, who is a *jealous God*, and will not *give his honour to another*, fhould allow the world to be guilty of idolatry;

^q Matth. xix 4, &c. ^r Bifhop Williams's fermons. ^s Jenkins' reafonablenefs of the Chriftian religion, vol. I,

Idolatry; to make themselves gods of wood and stone; nay, to *offer their sons and daughters unto devils*, without concerning himself to vindicate his own honour, by putting a stop to such abominations? We have no true notion of God, if we do not believe him to be infinite in knowledge, holiness, mercy, and truth; and yet we may as well believe there is no God at all, as imagine, that a God of infinite knowledge should take no notice of what is done here below; that infinite holiness should behold the whole world overspread with wickedness, and find no way to redress it; and that superstition, and idolatry, and all the tyranny of sin and Satan, for so long a time, should enslave and torment the bodies and souls of men, and there should be no compassion in infinite mercy, nor any care over a deluded world in a God of truth. We may therefore justly conclude, that since a revelation, in the state of man's defection, was so necessary in itself, and so agreeable to the known attributes of God, there is abundant reason to be persuaded, that God was always inclinable to impart one to mankind, whenever their occasions required it.

"But what occasion could there be for any divine re- "velation, ᵗ when, by giving them the light of reason, "(that perfect and unerring guide, and implanting in them "the law of nature, God had made an ample and stand- "ing provision, both for the instruction of their minds, "and the direction of their lives? when, by a due at- "tention to these, they might, at any time, be enabled "to perceive all that was necessary for them to know, and "to practise all that was required of them to do, without "any supernatural intervention, which, in this case, seems "highly needless and superfluous?"

An objection.

We readily grant, indeed, that the great principle of action in human nature is reason; insomuch that to judge according to its directions, is not the privilege of the philosopher only, but a thing essential to our very beings, and as much inseparable from all persons, as is the sense of their own existence. But then we are to consider how small a portion of light any man's reason has, that he can properly call its own. For, ᵘ as we derive our nature from our parents, so that which we generally call *natural knowledge*, or *the light of nature*, is a knowledge and light,

Answered by shewing the imperfection.

ᵗ Christianity as old as the creation, *passim*.

ᵘ Law's Case of reason; or, Natural religion fairly and fully stated.

light, that is made natural to us by the same authority which makes a certain language, certain customs, and modes of behaviour, natural. Nothing, in this case, seems to be our own, but a bare capacity to be instructed, or a nature fitted for any impressions; as capable of vice as virtue; and as liable to be made an Hottentot, by being born among Hottentots, as to be made a Christian, by being born among Christians. So that our moral and religious knowledge is not to be imputed to the internal light of our own reason or nature, but to the happiness of having been born among reasonable beings, who have made a sense of religion and morality as natural to our minds, as articulate language is to our tongues.

We allow, again, that there is a moral distinction between good and evil, right and wrong, founded in the nature of things; but then we affirm, that this is not from a philosophical contemplation of the fitness of the one, and the unfitness of the other, that we prefer virtue to vice; but from the instruction of those who had the care of our education, and the formation of our judgements from our infancy. When we arrive at an age of more maturity, indeed, and happen to have a genius fitted for philosophical inquiries, we may then deduce proofs that will establish our notions of such a moral distinction; but these, we must allow, are an after-knowledge, not common to men, but accidental confirmations of that sense of religion and morality, which, more or less, was fixed in us by the institution and authority of those among whom we had the good fortune to live. Now, if this be the true state of reason, as it is originally in us; if this be all the light that we have from our own nature, *viz.* a bare capacity of receiving good or bad impressions, right or wrong opinions and sentiments, according to the particular country we chance to be born in; if we are nothing without the assistance of men; nay, if we are foolish and helpless animals, till education and experience have revealed unto us the wisdom and knowledge of other men; then are we but weakly qualified to assert and maintain the absolute perfection of human reason, in opposition to the necessity and advantage of a divine revelation. But this is not all.

and depravity of human reason. It is not only the imperfection of our reason, but its frequent depravity likewise that ought to abate our confidence in it; since, upon farther examination, we shall find, that all the mutability of our tempers, the disorder of our passions, and corruption of our hearts; all the extravagancies

OR PREPARATORY DISCOURSE.

travagancies of the imagination, all the contradictions and absurdities which are to be found in human life and human actions, are strictly and properly the mutability, corruption, and absurdities of human reason. We, indeed, in the common forms of speech, talk of our reason as a distinct principle from our passions, affections, and humours; but this is only a distinction of language made at pleasure, and without any real distinction in the things themselves. [x] The same principle, which is the agent of all that is good in us, must be equally the agent of all that is evil; for the action and power of reason are as much required to make any thing vicious, as to make it virtuous: and if so, reason is certainly the worst as well as the best faculty we have; and not only the principle of virtue, but the certain cause likewise of all that is base and shameful in human life.

Brutes, we know, are incapable of imprudence and immorality, because none of their actions are actions of reason; and therefore, if our reason be the only faculty which distinguishes us from brutes, it must certainly follow, that all the irregularities, whether of humour, passion, or affection, which cannot be imputed to brutes, must solely be ascribed to the faculty whereby we are distinguished from them; and, consequently, every thing that is vain, shameful, false, or base, must be the sole product of our reason; since, if they proceeded from any other principle, they could have no more vanity, falseness, or baseness in them, than we have in our hunger or thirst. And if the matter stand thus with our reason; if all that is wise or absurd, holy or profane, glorious or shameful, in thought, word, or deed, is to be imputed to it; then is it as gross an absurdity to talk of the absolute perfection of human reason, as of the unspotted holiness of human life,

or

---

[x] *Ibid.* St. Paul, indeed, in his epistle to the Romans, (ch. vii.) seems to speak of two distinct things, when he tells us of the *law in his mind*, and the *law in his members;* but in this he might accommodate himself, in some measure, to the known forms of diction, and yet possibly mean no more than one and the same principle, considered in different views, or acting differently. Without the will or choice, there can be neither virtue nor vice in any act we do; and yet it is a received maxim, that *voluntas sequitur ultimum intellectus practici judicium;* and though that *judicium* does not always happen to be right, yet still it is the spring and cause of our actions, be it right or wrong.

or the absolute infallibility of human conjectures; since, upon examination, it is found to be a principle of an ambiguous nature, productive of vice as well as virtue; and capable of leading us into error, as well as discovering truth.

The ignorance of the best philosophers.

It will be no disparagement, I hope, to the present age, to suppose that the ancient philosophers had as great strength of reason and judgement, as sincere a desire to find out truth, and as great diligence in inquiring after it, as any of our modern unbelievers; and yet, if we look into their writings, we shall find that they were utterly ignorant in many great and important points of religion, and strangely inconsistent with themselves in others.

They were ignorant of the true account of the creation of the world, and the original of mankind; and therefore [y] some of them held all things to be eternal, while others [z] imputed them to chance; and those who allowed them a beginning, knew nothing of the manner and gradations whereby they rose up into so beautiful an order.

They were ignorant of the origin of evil; whereupon they devised two contrary principles, in perpetual conflict with one another; and though they were sensible that human nature was strangely corrupted, yet they acknowledged that its corruption was a disease, whereof they knew not the cause, and could not find out the cure.

They were ignorant of any form of worship that might be acceptable to God, and of a proper way to appease his displeasure, when they were conscious of their offences against him; and therefore we find Cicero, the greatest and best philosopher that Rome, or perhaps any other nation, ever produced, [a] "allowing men to continue in the idolatry of their ancestors, and advising them to conform "themselves to the superstitious religion of their country, "in offering such sacrifices to different gods, as were by "law established."

They were ignorant, at least they taught nothing of the exceeding love of God towards us; of his desire of our happiness, and his readiness to conduct us in the ways

of

---

[y] Peripatetics. [z] Epicureans. [a] A patribus acceptos deos placet coli; *De leg.* l. 2. Item illud ex institutis pontificum et auspicum non mutandum est, quibus hostiis immolandum cuique deo. *Ibid.*

of virtue; and therefore [b] some of them made their supreme Jupiter a solitary kind of being, wholly taken up in the contemplation of his own perfections, and leaving the government (of all sublunary things at least) either to some inferior agents, or the guidance of a blind, unthinking, chance.

They were ignorant, at least [c] they taught nothing of divine grace and assistance towards our attainment of virtue, and perseverence in it; and therefore we find [d] others of them equaling themselves to the gods, and sometimes taking precedency; " because we have difficulties, " say they, to encounter, which make the conquest of vice, " and the improvements in virtue, more glorious in us, " than in the gods, who are good by the necessity of their " nature."

And as these great philosophers were utterly ignorant of some, so they were far from being clear and consistent with themselves in other great articles of religion. They had but dark and confused notions of the nature of God; and therefore the renowned Socrates ingenuously confessed, that all he knew of God was, that he knew nothing; and, for this reason, endeavoured to draw men off from divine and heavenly contemplations, (as being what he found too high for human reason to understand,) and to betake themselves to the study of civil life.

They had but dark and confused notions of the *summum bonum*, or *supreme felicity of man*: and therefore Cicero tells us, that there was such a dissention among them upon this head, that it was almost impossible to reckon up their different sentiments, even while himself is setting down the notions of above twenty of them, all equally extravagant and absurd.

They had weak and uncertain notions of the immortality of the soul; for however they might perceive it to have a spiritual existence, yet they could from thence deduce no argument, but that God might destroy it, if he pleased; And therefore

---

[b] Epicureans. ¹ Non quis, quod bonus vir esset. gratias diis egit unquam : Jovem optimum maximum ob eas res appellant, non quod nos justos, temperatos sapientes, efficiat, sed quod salvos, incolumes, opulentos, copiosos; *Cic. de nat. deorum*, *l*. 3.

[d] Stoics. Est Aliquid, quo sapiens antecedat deum; ille, naturæ beneficio, non suo, sapiens est; *Sen. epist*. 53.

therefore ᵉ Cicero plainly declares that, "which of the two "opinions" (that the soul is mortal, or that it is immortal) "be true, God only knows:" Which, among other declarations of the like nature, might probably induce Seneca to say, ᶠ "That immortality (however desirable in itself) "was rather promised than proved by these great men."

They had weak and uncertain notions of a future state; for, though their poets had prettily fancied an elysium and an hell; yet all sober men looked upon these rather as well-contrived restraints for the vulgar, than any matters of their own belief: and therefore Socrates is introduced, as saying, ᵍ "I hope there is a place where I and good men "shall meet; yet I cannot affirm it:" And ʰ "I wish," says Cicero, "that you could prove to me that our souls "are immortal;" so that, after all, they wanted arguments to convince themselves, and ended all their disquisitions in a peradventure, and a wish. But, what is more,

They had no notion at all of the resurrection of the body; for, though their poets made frequent mention of the ghosts of departed men appearing in a visible form, and retaining in the shades below their former shapes; yet by this (if they mean any thing) they mean no more, than that the soul, after this life, passes into another state, and is there invested with a body, made up of light, aërial particles, quite different from what it had before; but that the gross matter, which they saw laid in the grave, and turn to corruption, or burnt into ashes, or blown away in the air, should ever be raised, or collected again and revivified; of this the most speculative among them had no conception.

and their immorality and viciousness:

Thus ignorant, or thus doubtful at least, were some of the greatest names of antiquity, of these prime and fundamental truths, which must be acknowledged the great barriers of virtue and religion: And therefore we need less wonder, that we find so many of them abetting practices apparently flagitious; ⁱ that we find several sects esteeming revenge, not only lawful, but commendable; and the desire of popular applause the greatest incentive to all kind of virtue; That we find some of the greatest of them full of the praise of self-murther, and setting themselves for the example of it to their followers: That we find Cato

commending

ᵉ Tusc. Quæst. lib. 1.   ᶠ Epist. 100.   ᵍ Plato in Phæd. ʰ Tusc. Quæst.   ⁱ Vid. Bishop of London's second pastoral letter.

commending fornication as a proper remedy againſt adultery; Plato, aſſerting the expediency of men's having their wives in common; and Chryſippus, teaching the worſt of inceſt, that of fathers with their daughters, and pleading the lawfulneſs of unnatural luſt: That we find; in ſhort, whole fraternities degrading human nature into that of beaſts; the Cynics, laying aſide all the natural reſtraints of ſhame and modeſty, committing their luſts openly; and the Stoics affirming, that no words or ſpeech of any kind ought to be cenſured and avoided, as filthy and obſcene: So true is the obſervation which Quintilian makes of the philoſophers of his time, [k] "That the moſt notorious "vices were ſcreened under that name; and that they did "not labour to maintain the character of philoſophers by "virtue and ſtudy, but concealed very vicious lives under "an auſtere look, and an habit different from the reſt of "the world."

And if theſe men of ſpeculation, and profound reaſoners, were thus ignorant in their notions, and corrupt in their principles, what reaſon have any of our modern contemners of revelation to preſume, that, if they had lived in thoſe days, they would have acquitted themſelves better? What grounds to imagine, that they would have been wiſer than Socrates, and Plato, and Cicero? [l] Had their lot been among the vulgar, how are they ſure they ſhould have been ſo happy, or ſo conſiderate, as not to be involved in that idolatry and ſuperſtition, that wickedneſs and immorality, which then overſpread the world? Had they joined themſelves to the philoſophers, what ſect would they have followed, (for they were all erroneous,) or what book would they have made the adequate rule of their lives and converſations? Or had they ſet up for themſelves, how are they certain they ſhould have been able to deduce the ſeveral branches of their duty, or to apply them to the ſeveral caſes of life, by argumentation, and dint of reaſon? It is one thing to find out a rule at firſt, and another to perceive its agreement with reaſon; and the difficulty is not much (when once we know our duty) to begin and deduce its obligation from reaſon: But to begin and diſcover our duty in all points, with all its true motives, merely by the help of natural reaſon, is like groping for an unknown way in an obſcure twilight. It is

no

---

[k] Inſt. l. 1. præf. [l] Clarke's demonſtration of natural and revealed religion.

The best of their knowledge from tradition. no improbable opinion then, that the discoveries, which the wisest of the heathen world made (even in points of morality) were not so much owing to the strength of their own reason, as to certain traditions which they might either receive from their ancestors, or gain by the conversation they might have with the Hebrews, to whom God had committed the oracles of his will by the hand of his servant Moses. For this is certain beyond all controversy, that the most eminent philosophers, such as Pythagoras, Plato, Democritus, and others, finding a dearth of knowledge at home, travelled for improvement into other parts; and, as Egypt was accounted the chief seat of learning, there were few men of note, who went not thither to complete their studies; where, conversing with the Jews, (who were there in great numbers,) and having the opportunity of consulting the law of Moses in the Ptolemean library, they might from thence collect many remarkable doctrines, though when they came to publish them) they chose to disguise, and blend them with their own notions and inventions. However this be, it is manifest, that the philosophers, who have lived since the publication of the gospel, have, in their several systems, been much more clear and uniform, both as to the measures of human duty, and the motives requisite to the performance of it, than they were before; which clearness and uniformity are really owing to the help of revelation, that has given us a far more perfect and exact knowledge of the nature and attributes of God, from whence many of our duties immediately flow; a greater certainty of future rewards and punishments; and a clearer conviction of the necessity of sobriety, temperance, and other moral virtues, as preparatory to our happiness in the next life, by perfecting our nature in this.

This (as I take it) is the true state of human reason in its present ruinous and depraved condition: in its minority, equally capable of bad, as well as good impressions, and formed entirely by the examples we see, and by the institution of those who have the charge of our education: in our maturity, the source of our passions and desires, our humours and appetites, and the sole agent of all the evil, as well as all the good, we do: in the highest pitch of its perfection, unable to settle any certain rule of morality, and beholden to tradition or revelation for the chief and best discoveries which it makes: in the breast of the greatest philosopher, over-spread with error, ignorant in many,

many, and doubtful in all the great principles and motives of religion, and thereupon enfnared in divers hurtful lufts; and much more, in the breaft of the vulgar, funk into ignorance and ftupidity, and thereby fubmitted to the wiles of the tempter, and [m] *taken captive by him at his will.* And is this the faculty of which we hear fuch loud boafts, and to which the abfolute perfection of immutability and infallibility are afcribed? " Is this [n] the fundamental " law of the univerfe, that can tell us more than books " or mafters, more than the two tables of Mofes, or the " twelve tables of the Greeks, and of which all other laws " are but copies and tranfcripts?" Is this the only principle that is allowed us, to inform our minds in all religious truths, and direct our conduct in all our moral actings? This the only pilot, to fteer our courfe through this tempeftuous world, in the midft of fo many dangers, avocations, and fnares; with fo many lufts within, and temptations without, to carry us wrong; fo many Syrens to allure us, fo many rocks to dafh us, and fo many waves to fwallow us up quick? Whether God, in this method, would have made a fufficient provifion for man's falvation, we will not here difpute: But, to confider human reafon (as it is in fact) modified by the various difabilities, paffions, and prejudices, which will ever prevail among the greateft part of mankind; and then confider every man left, in this wild difconcerted ftate, without rule or guide, to fearch out truth and happinefs by his own collections; the diftractions and perplexities, which muft needs enfue, would make every wife man wifh for fomething better: And, if fo, what can we imagine more defirable, more appofite to the wants of human nature in fuch a cafe, than that God fhould interpofe, and by an authoritative declaration of his will, (committed to perfons ordained to that office) inftruct the ignorant, and reduce thofe that were going aftray.

" But fuppofe that God, in compliance to men's wants, *An objec-*
" fhould vouchfafe to give them a declaration of his will; *tion.*
" yet ftill the queftion is, Who are the perfons that are
" appointed to convey it? The pretence to revelation is fo
" common, and the number of impoftures fo great; the
" difference between a divine impreffion and a diabolical
" illufion, natural enthufiafm and fupernatural infpiration,
" is

---

[m] 2 Tim. ii. 26. [n] *Vid.* Chriftianity as old as the creation, p. 60, 61, &c.

"is so undistinguishable, and by us who live at such a dis-
"tance of time, so impossible to be adjusted; that the saf-
"est way is to suspend our belief, until we have a suffi-
"cient conviction, that what is offered as a message from
"heaven, infallibly comes from God."

<small>Answered by enumerating the different kinds of revelation.</small> The most usual ways wherein God of old was wont to communicate his mind to mankind, were by visions, by dreams, by voices, and by inspiration. The Jewish doctors, who treat of the subject, have many curious observations concerning the difference of these several kinds of revelation; but the most plain and obvious distinction seems to be this———That vision was the representation of some momentous thing to man, when they were awake, in opposition to dreams, which were representations made to them when their external senses were asleep; that voices were either God's calling to men from on high º (as he did to St. Paul) or his immediate conversing with them (as he did with Moses,) ᵖ *face to face, even as one man speaketh to his friend;* and that inspiration was an inward excitement of the soul of man, by the operation of the Holy Ghost, without any bodily perception or sensation.

These are the several sorts and degrees of revelation which have commonly been ascribed to God: And, what do we see in any of them, that he cannot, when he pleases, make use of, and that effectually? Cannot he, by some visible appearance, convince men of his immediate presence beyond the possibility of doubt? Cannot he, either with or without such visible appearances, talk as familiarly to them, as one man converses with another? Cannot he, who formed our minds, and knows of all the ways of access to them, draw such clear and bright scenes, and pictures of things on our fancy and imagination, whether sleeping or waking, as shall need no other proof of their divinity, but themselves; even as light is known by itself, and the first principles of reason by their own evidence? In short, why cannot he so clarify the understanding by a beam of light let in from above, as shall be as evident a proof of its divine original, as it is that the light proceeds from the sun, the fountain of it?

<small>How the persons inspired might judge of their own inspirations.</small> Whatever it may seem to us, who have not the sensation or experience of such divine representations as the prophets had, and therefore can no more describe them, than

º Acts ix 4.   ᵖ Exod. xxxiii. 11.

than the person who never had his eye-sight, can conceive what light and colours are; yet, as the blind man may be convinced, that there are such things as light, colour, figure, and sight, by what he hears and observes from those who are about him; so we may be assured, that there was in the prophetic schemes, that powerful representation, on the part of the divine agent, and that clearness of perception on the part of the person inspired, as would abundantly make good those phrases of vision and speaking, by which it is described in scripture; insomuch that such a person, after such illumination, might as well question what he heard and saw by the natural organs of sense, as doubt of what was revealed to him by the impressions made upon him through the agency of the divine Spirit.

"But do not we see enthusiastic persons as confident of "their inspirations and visions, and (according to their "persuasion) as much obliged to follow them as those that "are truly inspired? How then shall we find out the dif-"ference, and by what criterion shall we judge?" It is owned, indeed, that confidence in imaginary inspirations may be sometimes very great, but then the perception, and consequently the assurance arising from thence, cannot be equal, or any ways comparable to what is produced by a real one. For, though God Almighty can so communicate himself, as that the person inspired shall know most certainly that it is from him, and from him only, (in which case there is no absolute necessity for any farther evidence,) yet, that nothing might be wanting to the full conviction of him who had the revelation, God was frequently pleased to add some sign, or supernatural proofs, in order to satisfy the party of the truth of his divine mission. Thus Gideon, when required to go upon a difficult enterprise, was cured of his fear, and confirmed in his mind ⁹ *by the fire out of the rock, which consumed the flesh and the cakes*: as Moses, when sent to deliver the children of Israel from the Egyptian bondage, perceived that his commission was from God, upon seeing the *bush burn* without consuming, ʳ *and the rod* in his hand *turned into a serpent:* a course this, highly necessary to give the messenger full satisfaction, especially when the case is such as Moses seems to put it, ˢ *They will not believe me, nor hearken to my voice; for they will say, The Lord hath not appeared unto thee.*

"But suppose a person never so well satisfied in what "he calls a revelation, and that (in his own opinion) he

How to distinguish it from enthusiasm.

How we may judge when a person is inspired.

⁹ Judges vi. 20. ʳ Exod. iv. 3. ˢ Ver. 1.

"is as sure of it, as he is of his being and existence; yet what is all this to me, unless I am equally satisfied that he really had such a revelation; that his pretensions to a mission from heaven are true, and he far from being an impostor; but how shall I judge of this?" Why, the only way is, to consider with ourselves, what it is that we might expect from the person who pretends to be a messenger sent from God, and then observe whether he answers that character. Now, as a revelation is a divine communication, and a mark of divine favour, we may well expect, that the person who pretends to it should be a man of virtue, good sense, and known probity; cool and considerate enough, not to be imposed on himself, and too honest and upright ever to think of imposing upon others: one who has no trick, no crafty design, no secular ends to serve, no vanity or ambition to gratify; who disclaims all worldly greatness and emoluments, and intends nothing but the good of mankind, and the glory of God, who sent him: one, who by his whole behaviour discovers that he is in earnest, and really believes his own commission; is, consequently, deterred by no threats, discouraged by no opposition, but goes on with undaunted courage, still persisting in the same assertions, and ready to lay down his life in confirmation of what he says. So far then as the credibility of a person is the proof of a revelation, and so far as the wisdom, probity, and sincerity of a person is a proof of his credibility, we have an evidence to rest upon, and a character, whereby we may try the truth of his revelation.

viz. from his personal character;

As the revelation pretends to come from God, we may reasonably expect, that it should be consonant to the notions we have of the divine attributes, and conducive to the happiness and instruction of man; that therein we should find the most lively characters of the divine perfections, justice and power, set forth in all their authority, to administer matter of terror to the wicked; but so tempered with mercy and kindness, as to raise the hopes, and attract the love, and establish the comfort of the righteous: therein to find the mysteries of the divine counsels unfolded, and the beauty and harmony of divine providence displayed, as far as God's government of the world, and the condition of mankind in it will permit: therein to find the best principles and precepts to inform and direct us in what we are to know and do, the best arguments and motives for our encouragement, and the best means and expedients

from the subject-matter of his revelation;

expedients for the purifying and perfecting of our natures: therein, lastly, to find the chief subjects of human inquiry, and what is best and most necessary for mankind to know, the creation of the world, the origin of evil, the supervention of grace, the condition and certainty of a future state, and by what method God may be appeased, forgiveness obtained, and the heavy load upon human nature, arising from the sense and consciousness of sin, removed. So far then as its sublimity and usefulness are an indication of its divine original, we have another evidence to rest upon, and a farther character whereby we may try the truth of a revelation.

Once more, we may expect, that a person coming with such high pretensions, should give us some proof of his delegation from heaven, either by predicting events of a very uncertain contingency, or performing works of a very supernatural kind, in confirmation of it: and, since miracles and prophecies require a divine power, and are always looked upon as an authentic evidence of a divine commission, the man who does these, and does them fairly, without fraud or collusion, must certainly be a prophet sent from God; otherwise we must be reduced to the necessity of allowing, that God may sometimes employ his power for the confirmation of a falsehood, and set the broad seal of heaven, as it were, to a lie; which is confounding the notions we have of him, and inverting all his attributes. *and the miraculous attestations given to it.*

These then are the marks and tokens whereby we may judge of the truth of a revelation at any time: the credibility of the person who brings it; the excellency of the doctrine he teaches; and the divine attestation which he produces. Where these are concurring, and with one mouth, as it were, giving in their evidence, we cannot but say that it is the voice of God, and a revelation, which carries upon it the conspicuous stamp of his authority. And now, to try the pretensions of those in the Old Testament who claimed such commission from God by the foregoing marks and characters:

That there was really such a person as Moses is attested by many of the ᵗ heathen writers, who speak of him as an extraordinary man, and the founder of the Jewish laws and religion. That this Moses pretended to have this *Moses's personal character, as to his wisdom; religion*

ᵗ *Vid.* Grot. De veritate, lib. 1. where he enumerates several.

religion from God, and whatever he wrote or delivered to the people, to receive from him by immediate revelation, is plain to any one who looks into his writings. But that his pretensions in this respect were real; that he actually received what he delivered from the mouth or inspiration of God, and was neither capable of being deceived himself, nor desirous to impose on others; this will appear from the evidence we have of his wisdom and veracity; from the nature and tendency of his precepts and doctrines; and from the miraculous demonstrations he gave of his commission. In order to which it will be necessary for us to look a little into the sacred records: desiring, however, that no more credit may be given to them (as yet) than what is usually given to any other narrative of tolerable repute, concerning the actions of persons who lived in former ages.

Now, besides the account of his strange and miraculous preservation, the scriptures acquaint us, that he [u] *was brought up* in Pharaoh's court, educated in all princely qualities, and *skilled in all the learning of the Egyptians*. What the [x] learning of the Egyptians was, we need not here relate: if we will believe Macrobius, who, [y] in one place, makes Egypt the mother of all arts, and, [z] in another, the Egyptians the fathers of all philosophic sciences, there was not a nation under the sun that could compare with them. How can we then imagine, that a person bred up in all the polite literature of Egypt, and conversant amongst the wisest philosophers of Pharaoh's court, should not be able to pass a judgement between an imposture and truth, between a familiar converse with God, and a deception of his senses? Can we think that he, who had such opportunities of raising himself to the highest pitch of honour, should willingly forsake all his present pleasure and future advantages, had he not been fully persuaded of the certain and undoubted truth of the matters which he recorded? Is it possible, that a man of common sense and prudence should ever venture himself upon an affair so hazardous, and unlikely to succeed, as that which he undertook, had it not been by the instigation of that God who appeared to him, and promised him the assistance of his power, to enable him to accomplish his design? And what tolerable

[u] Heb. xi. 25. Acts vii. 22. [x] *Vid*. Stillingfleet's Orig. Sac. [y] Macrob. Saturn. lib. 2. cap. 15. [z] Som. Scip. lib. 1. cap. 19.

tolerable ground can we have to imagine, that a perfon, who really believed the truth of what God had revealed to him, fhould dare to write otherwife than it was revealed?

To extol himfelf, or agrandize his nation, may be and difinthought a probable inducement: but fo far is he from magnifying himfelf, that he omits no opportunity of recording ª his own failings and mifcarriages; paffes over in filence his own ᵇ qualities and ᶜ atchievements; and opens the account of his miniftry with the relation of a fact, ᵈ (the murther of the Egyptian,) which nothing but the prefumption of his being acted by a divine authority can juftify or excufe. Now, had it been any part of his aim to have raifed his reputation into a fuperftitious veneration among the Jews, or to have eftablifhed his family in any high degree of honour and authority, how eafily might he have done it? It was but concealing what might feem to deprefs the one, and ufing the power he had to advance the other: but inftead of that, we find him very fecure and carelefs in both refpects; relating to his own faults without difguife or extenuation; conferring ᵉ both the civil and ecclefiaftical power upon other families, and leaving his own in the meaneft fort of attendance upon the tabernacle. And fo far was he from aggrandizing his nation, that he fets forth the lefs, as well as the greater enormities of their firft progenitors; that he fpares not the ftock of his own family Levi, but records very punctually ᶠ his and Simeon's inhumanity to the Schechemites; and, through the whole courfe of his hiftory feems as if he were defcribing ᵍ the obftinacy, and unbelief, and unthankfulnefs, and difobedience of a people towards a gracious God, rather than any way enhancing their reputation in the world. Hitherto it appears, that Mofes acted like an honeft and fincere man let us, in the next place, make fome infpection into the revelation he makes, both as an hiftorian and a lawgiver.

As

ª Exod. iv. 10, 13. Num. ii. 10, 11. Chap. xx. 12.
ᵇ Heb. xi. 25. Acts vii. 22.   ᶜ Jofephus relates, that Mofes, for fome years, was general to Pharoah, and that he obtained a very fingular victory over the Ethiopians.
ᵈ Exod. ii. 12.   ᵉ Vid. Grot. De verit. and Shuckford's connect. of the facred and profane hift. lib. 12.
ᶠ Gen. xxxiv.   ᵍ Deut. ix. 7.

THE APPARATUS,

The subject he treats of as an historian.

As an historian then, what could he deliver to the world more becoming the Majesty of God to impart, and the necessities of men to know, than the origin of the universe, and the first beginning of all things; than the formation of man, his state of innocence at first, his fall, and the consequential evils of it; his redemption, and the glorious hopes and expectances of the new covenant; than the propagation of mankind, their general defection, the universal deluge, the confusion of tongues, and thereupon the plantation of families, and origin of kingdoms; than the selection of one particular family (of which Christ was to come in the flesh) from the rest of mankind, and the many wonderful works which God did to redeem them from bondage, and conduct them through the wilderness, until he had settled them in the promised land, and given them laws and ordinances, whereby they were to live?

Wherein other historians agree with him;

These are some of the great subjects which Moses has treated of in the Pentateuch; and it is no small confirmation of their truth and reality, that we find the same things related much in the same manner by the most ancient and best authors. What Moses says of the origin of the world is [h] recorded in the old histories of the Phœnicians and Egyptians. The formation of man according to the image of God, and his dominion over other creatures, is described by Ovid, who had it from the Grecians. The history of Adam and Eve, the tree of knowledge, and the tempting serpent, were found formerly among the Indians, as Maimonides tells us, and is still among the Brachmans, and inhabitants of Siam, as later voyagers report. The history of the deluge, of the ark, and of those who were saved therein, is recorded by Berosus, by Plutarch, and Lucian; nay, Abydenus as he is cited by Eusebius makes mention of the very dove which was sent out to explore the waters. The building of the tower of Babel, and the giants attempting to reach the height of heaven, is the common tale of every poet. The burning of Sodom is related by Diodorus, Strabo, and Tacitus. The account of Abraham, Isaac, Jacob, and Joseph, in the same manner as Moses relates it, was found in many ancient historians quoted by Eusebius, and is still extant in Justin, from Trogus Pompeius; and (to mention no more) the actions of Moses himself, how he led the people of Israel out of Egypt, received the two tables of the law from the hand of God, and instituted several

---

[h] *Vid.* Grot. de veritate.

veral rites and religious observances, are to be found in most of the same authors, but more especially in the verses which are ascribed to Orpheus, and in histories which treat of the affairs of Egypt.

Thus consonant to the greatness and majesty of God, as a law-giver. and the received opinions of the earliest ages of the world, are the historic facts which Moses relates. And to consider him in his legislative capacity, what can be more agreeable to the notions we have of God, than the prohibition of idolatry and polytheism, and the institution of his true religion and worship; than the prohibition of perjury and vain swearing, of theft, of murder, of adultery, of covetousness of all kinds; and the injunction of the contrary virtues, of justice and mercy, of chastity and charity, together with all due reverence to parents, both in a natural and civil capacity? What can be more becoming the character of a divine legislator, than his often inculcating upon the people (as we find almost in every page Moses does) the many obligations they had to God, and the innumerable favours they had received from him; his frequent and pathetic exhortations to obedience, and living answerable to the singular mercies conferred upon them; his constant reminding them of their former miscarriages, their murmurings and rebellions against heaven, and his compassionate forewarning them of the judgement of God, and of the various plagues and punishments which would certainly be the consequence of their persisting in their sins? Nay, the very ceremonial precepts which he enjoins to discriminate them from other nations, are a sufficient indication that he received them from God; since, had they been of his own invention, he would have consulted the people's ease, and his own popularity more; and * not imposed so many laborious and expensive ordinances, so many sacrifices, both stated and occasional, so painful an institution, as that of circumcision, and such annual and weekly cessations from labour, as were apparently against the interest of a nation, whose great subsistence was upon pasturage and agriculture. Nor can we conceive how any people would have submitted to such arbitrary injunctions, but that they were fully satisfied they came originally from God, and were only delivered to them by the hand of his servant Moses. And, for their farther conviction of this, they had all the evidence that could be required, the prediction of events, which none but God could

* Shuckford's connection. *Ibid.*

could foreknow, and the demonstration of miracles, which none but God could perform.

His miracles. For not to insist at present [1] on the several prophecies (contained in the Pentateuch) which Moses himself foretold, and accordingly came to pass; what can we account the whole method of his conducting the people of Israel out of Egypt, both in its progress, and in its execution, but one continued miracle? Nothing but a series of wonders, surprizing in their nature, and dreadful in their effects, could have prevailed with Pharoah to let the people go; and nothing but a divine power, which went out before the people, could have given them a free passage, and the Egyptians a total overthrow in the red sea. The wonderful support of so great a multitude in a waste and barren wilderness, when neither their raiment decayed, nor their bread and water failed, and the victories they afterwards gained in their way to the promised land, were both convictions of the Almighty's power, and a confirmation of the truth of the Mosaic revelation; since it would be impious to suppose, that providence would, in the sight of the heathen, have favoured Israel with such wonderful successes, under the conduct of a leader who only pretended to act and make laws by an authority which he was not really invested with. So that the whole turns ultimately upon the veracity of God. The constant apprehensions which both reason and religion give us of him, forbid us to imagine, that he will employ his power to deceive his creatures; and yet, if he should permit the same evidences to be produced for errors as for truth, this would be a way to put a deception upon them, as well as to cancel his own credentials, and make miracles of no significance at all.

A recapitulation of the argument. Upon a review then of what has been said in relation to Moses, *viz.* that he was a person of great wisdom and integrity, unlikely to be imposed on himself, and unwilling to impose upon others, and without any private designs of popularity, or self-exaltation in what he did; that, as an historian, he related facts necessary for man to know, and becoming the nature and majesty of God to reveal; as a legislator, gave laws and ordinances, which had a manifest stamp of divine authority; as a prophet foretold such things, as none but God (who has all events under his intuition) could know; and, as a worker of miracles, did

such

[1] *Vid.* Exod xxiv. Numb. xiv. Deut. xxviii. 53. compared with Josephus, De bell. Jud. lib. vii.

such things as had all imaginable evidence of an almighty power assisting him: it will necessarily follow, that, as sure as God is true, and cannot be an abettor of falsehood, what he did, was by the order and appointment; what he delivered, was expressly the will; and what he wrote (for the books that go under his name we shall hereafter prove to be his) was infallibly the word of God.

That there was to be a succession of prophets after Moses, is very plain, not only from the rules which God has [k] prescribed for the trial of them, but from that express promise likewise which Moses made to the people: *A prophet will the Lord thy God raise up to thee of thy brethren, like unto me, unto him shalt thou hearken.* For though the words, in their full and complete sense, relate to Christ, who is the great prophet of the church; yet, whoever attends to the main scope of them, will easily perceive, that their immediate aspect is towards an order of prophets who should succeed Moses, to instruct the people in the spiritual sense and true obligation of the law; and to make such farther discoveries of the Almighty's will, as he, from time to time, should give them commission and authority to do. And to this purpose we may observe, that the first schools of these prophets among the Jews, were in the cities of the Levites, which, for the conveniency of instructing the people, were dispersed up and down in the several tribes; that [l] the first institution of these schools seems to be about Samuel's time; and that he very probably was ordained president over one or more of them, and had the care and tuition of such as were to be trained up to the prophetic office.

the education of the prophets;

In what particular manner they were there trained up, in order to obtain a previous disposition to prophecy, the scripture is not express; but this we may suppose, that they were put upon such studies and spiritual exercises as had a tendency to improve their understandings and natural abilities, to regulate their passions and appetites, and to raise their affections to things sublime; that they were employed in searching out the hidden sense of the law, in contemplating the nature and attributes of God, in adoring him, and celebrating his praises. To which purpose, because there was a certain quality in it to allay the passions and elate the heart, they always made use of music, both vocal and instrumental; for so the first company of prophets [m] that we

VOL. I. No. 1.   E

[k] Deut. xviii. 21, 22.   [l] *Vid.* Stillingfleet's Orig. Sac. and Lewis's Or. Hebr. lib. 2, c. 15.   [m] Wheatly's School of the Prophets

we read of are described, [n] *coming down from the high place, with a psaltery, and a tabret, and a pipe, and a harp before them.*

their integrity;

Out of these seminaries, or colleges of prophets, God usually made choice of persons to be sent on messages; though he did not so strictly tie himself up to this method, but called sometimes one from the court, as he did Isaiah, and sometimes one from the herds, (as he did Amos,) and *bade them go, and prophesy to the house of Israel.* And whenever he made choice of any one, he always gave him such a full conviction, both of the reality of his own inspiration, and the importance of the message he sent him upon, as made it impossible for him to resist the impulse; for so Ezekiel tells us of himself: [o] *The Spirit lifted me up, and took me away, and I went in bitterness, and in the heat of my spirit; for the hand of the Lord was strong upon me.* And indeed, considering that the prophets were men of sober sense, and most of them of very liberal education, we can hardly believe that they would have ventured upon so hazardous an employ, where persecution was sure to be their lot, had they not been urged to it by an immediate and irresistible call from Heaven. The apostle has given us a very dolorous description of the many calamities which their profession brought upon them: [p] *They had trials of cruel mockings and scourgings, yea, moreover, of bonds and imprisonments: they were stoned, were sawn asunder, were tempted, were slain with the sword, &c.* Now, what men in their senses would have exposed themselves to these persecutions and sufferings, in the execution of an office, had they not been persuaded of the truth of their vocation, and under an indispensible necessity to pursue it, whatever penalties might stand in their way?

Nothing then can be more evident, than that the prophets (if we allow them to be men of common sense) were men of integrity likewise, and far from pretending to a commission which they had not; since (in accession to what has been said) the doctrines they taught, the predictions they gave, and the miracles they did, loudly proclaimed them to be sent from God.

the excellence of their doctrine;

For what can be more suitable to the nature of God, than those exprobations of superstition and idolatry, and those many exhortations to inward piety and real holiness,

so

---

[n] 1 Sam. x. 5.   [o] Ezek. iii. 14.   [p] Heb. xi. 36. 37.

so frequently, so kindly occuring in the prophets? ^q *Wherewithal shall I come before the Lord, and bow myself before the most high God? Shall I give my first-born for my transgression, the fruit of my body for the sin of my soul?* No. God requires nothing of thee, *but to do justly, and to love mercy and to walk humbly before him.* What can be more agreeable to the divine mercy and goodness, than those earnest calls and invocations to repentance? ^r *Turn ye, turn ye from your evil ways for why will ye die, O house of Israel? For, as I live, saith the Lord, I have no pleasure in the death of the wicked.* What is more conducive to the honour and glory of God, than those rapturous songs of praise wherewith the Royal Psalmist tunes his harp, and those tender strains of grief wherewith the mournful prophet wets his bed? ^s *Oh! that my head were waters, and mine eyes a fountain of tears, that I might weep day and night for the slain of the daughter of my people.* What discovery can be of such importance, as that of the birth and high character of the Saviour of the world? ^t *Unto us a child is born, unto us a son is given, and his name shall be called Wonderful Counsellor, the mighty God, the everlasting Father, the Prince of Peace:* as that of his death and vicarious punishment? ^u *He was oppressed, and he was afflicted, yet he opened not his mouth; he made his soul an offering for Sin, and for the transgression of my people was he stricken:* and lastly, as that of the happy effect which his religion would produce? when ^x *the wolf should dwell with the lamb, and the leopard lie down with the kid, and the calf, and the young lion, and the fatling together and a little child shall lead them:* as the avangelical prophet expresses it in that beautiful allegory.

That the prophets should be able to foretel things so many ages before they came to pass; that he who went from Judah to denounce God's judgements against the altar of Bethel, and against ^y Jeroboam, for setting it up, should make mention of the very name of Josiah (who was to be God's instrument in executing them) three hundred and sixty one years before the event happened: that ^z Elijah should denounce all the punishments which God would bring upon Ahab and his family for their great impiety, some years before the thing came to pass: that Isaiah should

their prophecies.

^q Micah vi. 6. ^r Ezek. xxxiii. 11. ^s Jer. ix. 1. ^t Isa. ix. 6. ^u Chap. liii. ^x Chap. xi. 6. ^y 1 Kings xiii. 2. ^z Chap. xvii.

should prophesy of Cyrus by name, [a] two hundred and ten years before the accomplishment of his prophecy; [b] foretel his rebuilding of the temple, and describe his conquests, in such full and expressive terms, that the history of Cyrus by Xenophon has hardly done it better: and (to mention but one prophet more) that Daniel should speak of the profanation of the temple and sanctuary by Antiochus Epiphanes, declare the manner of his death, and delineate the very temper and countenance of the man, [c] four hundred and eighty years before the accomplishment; this, and much more that might be mentioned, can be ascribed to nothing else but the inspiration of God, which made the same strong impression upon the minds of the prophets, and guided their tongues to the same words and expressions, as if the things had been actually presented before their eyes.

their miracles. The prophets indeed did not work many miracles, because there was not that occasion for them. The law of Moses, which they were sent to inforce, not invalidate, had been sufficiently confirmed by miracles before; and, as they were a standing order of men, which the people were well accustomed to, the people were inclineable enough to believe them, without a divine attestation. However, when they were employed upon great and important messages to persons who either believed not the God of Israel, or had revolted from his service, God was never wanting to accompany them with a power of working miracles, to be the credentials of their commission. Thus, upon the defection of the ten tribes, and when calves were set up in Dan and Bethel, in opposition to the worship at Jerusalem, the prophet, who was sent to denounce God's anger against such procedure, was enabled by a word's speaking, [d] *to rend the altar*, and both *to wither, and restore again Jeroboam's hand*. In the famous controversy between the priests of Baal and Elijah, the prophet was empowered [e] *to call fire down from heaven, which consumed his sacrifices*, and gained him the victory over his adversaries; and, to convince Naaman the Syrian of the true God's being in Israel, Elisha was directed [f] to cure him of his leprosy, by the simple prescription of dipping himself in the river Jordan. Upon these, and the like occasions, when the honour of God, or the truth of the prophet, seemed to be called in question, a power of working miracles was communicated

---

[a] *Vid.* Joseph. Antiq. l. 2. cap. 1. [b] Isa. xliv. 26. [c] Joseph. Antiq. lib. 12. cap. 11. [d] 1 Kings, xiii. 4, 5, 6. [e] Ch. xviii. [f] 2 Kings, v.

municated to him, as an evident demonstration of God's abetting his cause, and attesting the truth of what he pretended to reveal.

Putting all this together then, *viz.* that the prophets were men of sobriety and good education, but void of all craft and dissimulation; that they exposed themselves to infinite hazards and difficulties in the execution of their office; that they taught doctrines consonant to the divine attributes, and made discoveries of the greatest importance; foretold events which none but God could know; and performed works which none but God could do; gave all imaginable evidence of the truth of their commission, and sealed it very often with the testimony of their own blood: it will certainly follow, that we have all the reason we can desire (all indeed that the nature of the thing will bear) to believe, that they were messengers sent from God to supply the intermediate space between Moses and Christ; and consequently, that the revelation of God's will in the Old Testament (so far they are concerned in declaring it) is indubitably true. *A recapitulation of the argument.*

"But, be the character of Moses and the prophets (as "messengers sent from God to impart his will to mankind) "never so well established; yet what is that to us who "live in times so distant and remote from them, and have "only the tradition of men uninspired, and the testimony "of a set of books, (said indeed to be dictated by the Holy "Ghost, but how truly we cannot tell,) for the foundation "of our faith? Had we lived indeed in the days of Moses "and the prophets, when revelation was attended by signs "and mighty wonders, the testimony of many glorious mi- "racles, and the completion of many remarkable prophe- "cies, we should have then been inexcusable, had we re- "mained incredulous amidst these instances of divine power: "but since, in our present circumstances, we are reduced to "the bare letter of the scriptures, which, for ought we know, "may be spurious and corrupt; or, if genuine, seem to have "small signatures of a divine spirit in their composition; "which almost in every passage, are loaded with absurdi- "ties and contradictions, with mysteries and riddles, and "obscure passages; and, where they chance to be intelli- "gible, are so trifling in their narrations, so illogical in "their reasonings, so confused in their method, so insipid "in their style, so tedious in their repetitions, so ambiguous "in their various readings, and, in the whole, so barren of "any real entertainment to an ingenious reader, that, *An objection.*

"instead

"instead of poring in these musty and perplexed records, (and which perhaps too may not be so ancient as is pretended) we think it the easier and safer way to attend to the sentiments of our minds, and those plain and immutable laws which God has written upon the fleshly tables of our hearts."

<small>The state of the case between the contemporaries with the prophets, and those of after ages.</small> We allow indeed, that there is a great deal of difference between those who were contemporaries with Moses and the prophets, and us, who are at some thousand years distance. The completion of a prediction gave sanction to the prophets' pretensions, and miracles carried with them a clear and present conviction; they entered quick, and gained assent without any argumentation: whereas our faith now is founded on human testimony, and the evidences of our religion comprised in no very large volume. But then, we are to consider, that we give credit to the contents of other books upon no better grounds; that upon this very account we firmly believe, that Alexander, about two thousand years ago, conquered a great part of the world: and that there was such a person as Julius Cæsar, who, upwards of seventeen hundred years ago, conquered France, and came into England: and yet the authority of the sacred records has been more strictly examined into, and found to be better attested than that of any human composition. The contemporaries with inspired men were convinced by sense and ocular demonstration; but in this we have the advantage of them, that, having lived to see the whole scheme of revelation completed, and at once placed in our view, we can compare one part with the other, and thence observe how the mystery of man's redemption gradually advances; what harmony there is between the Old and the New Testament; and how the many prophecies in the one receive their accomplishment in the other; which cannot but give great comfort and satisfaction to an inquisitive mind.

It is not to be doubted then, but that *we, of after-ages, upon whom the ends of the world are come,* have sufficient grounds for our faith to rest upon, if we can but satisfy ourselves—that the persons by whom God made revelations of his will *at sundry times, and in diverse manners,* were directed by him to record them in certain books ---- That, in writing these books, they were assisted by the inspiration of his infallible spirit---That, according to the best computations, they were wrote by the very same persons to whom they are ascribed:---- That, at a proper period of time, they were compiled into one body by such as were authorised rifed and enabled fo to do:——That from them they have defcended to us, true and genuine, without any confiderable lofs or alteration:——That the books now extant, and received by the Chriftian church, are the very fame which were thus written by infpiration, and compiled by authority:——And that they are not liable to the foregoing objections, but deferve a better character, and better ufage, than fome in this age are pleafed to give them.

§ It is the opinion of fome learned men, that writing was an art cœval with mankind, and the invention of Adam himfelf. Jofephus indeed informs us, that it was in ufe before the flood; and from thence fome have conjectured, that the hiftory of the creation, and the reft of the book of Genefis, were (for the fubftance of them) delivered down to Mofes in verfe (which was the moft ancient way of writing) and that, from them, he compiled his book. This however can hardly be a probable conjecture, becaufe it is fcarce conceivable how men could have loft the fenfe of religion fo totally as we find they did, had there been any ftanding records of it at that time. The more probable opinion is, that it was the long-experienced infufficiency of oral tradition (the only way of conveyance then in ufe) that gave occafion to the general corruption; while fome forgot, and others perverted, the doctrines delivered to them by their anceftors, and, in compliance to their lufts, brought themfelves, by degrees, firft to believe a lie, and then to propagate it, having no written rule of truth to confront the error.

The objection anfwered by fhewing that revelations were recorded in books.

It can hardly be doubted, but that God vouchfafed frequent revelations to the patriarchs before the law, and fufficiently inftructed them in his will; nor can we queftion but that thefe holy men ufed their beft endeavours to propagate the doctrine they received, and to reform the manners of thofe at leaft who depended on them: And (what was a great advantage to them in this refpect) both their lives were fo very long, and the principles of their religion fo extremely few, that two perfons might have conveyed them down from Adam to Abraham. For Methufalah lived above three hundred years, while Adam was yet alive: Sem was almoft an hundred when Methufalah died; and when Sem died, Abraham was above an hundred, according to the Hebrew computation. Here is a great period of time filled up by two or three perfons; and yet,

Why God appointed it to be fo.

---

§ Jenkin's Reafonablenefs, and Stillingfleet's Orig. Sacr.

yet, in this time, the tradition of those few things wherein religion was then comprehended, was so totally corrupted, that idolatry was generally practised, and God was obliged to make a new and immediate revelation to the patriarch Abraham.

[h] The promulgation of the law on mount Sinai, was one of the most amazing things that ever happened; and, as the circumstances of the whole solemnity were very surprising, the commandments then delivered but few, the people all of one language, separate from the rest of mankind, and obliged to a constant commerce among themselves; so there seems to be in this case all imaginable advantages in favour of tradition: and yet, notwithstanding these, God would not trust his precepts to this uncertain way of conveyance, but [i] himself, *with his own finger*, twice wrote them upon *two tables of stone*. The historical transactions of the Jews, the many strange deliverances Heaven vouchsafed them, and particularly their signal victory over the Amalekites, God commanded Moses not to relate to posterity by word of mouth only, but *to write them for a memorial in a book*: [k] nay, the very ceremonial part of the law, though not intended to be of perpetual obligation, was not referred to this traditionary method, but, according to divine appointment, committed to writing, and reposited with the priests: and therefore we have less reason to wonder, that, in things which were to come to pass in future ages, (such as the predictions of the prophets were,) and whereon the fate of nations, as well as divine veracity, did depend, we always find God giving injunctions of this kind, [l] *to write their inspirations before the people in a table, and to note them in a book, that they might be for the time to come, for ever and ever.*

That these books were written by divine inspiration.

That the books which were successively wrote in this manner, were wrote by the order and assistance of God's blessed Spirit, no one can doubt, who either attends to the high sentiments which the Jews of old entertained of them, or to the testimony whereby both Christ and his apostles have given a full sanction to them. The law of Moses was to the Jews accounted the law of God himself, and the Pentateuch esteemed the foundation of their religion. The familiar converse he had with God, the wonders

[h] Burnet on the Articles. [i] Exod xxxi. 18. [k] Chap. xvii. 14. [l] Isa. xxx. 8.

ders and miracles that he wrought, and the divine wisdom and gift of prophecy which resided in him, put it beyond all dispute, that the books which he left behind him were penned by the inspiration of the Spirit of God, whereof he was full. The other canonical books which, in process of time, were collected into a body, the Jews always held in the like veneration; insomuch, that (as Josephus tells us) they were accustomed from their infancy to call them *the doctrines of God*, and were ready at any time, to lay down their lives in vindication of them: nor is it any bad argument to us Christians, that we find our blessed Lord quoting these books under the title of *The Scriptures*, and acquainting us with the common distribution of them, in his days, into the law, the prophets, and the psalms; because the book of psalms was placed in the front of that collection, which was usually styled the *Hagiographa*. It is upon the evidence of these books that he proves himself to be the Messias; it is by them that he confutes the Jews; and to them that he appeals both in the proof of his own doctrine, and in all his disputations with them: and therefore we need not wonder that we find both the apostle of the Gentiles assuring us, that [m] *all scripture is given by the inspiration of God*, and the apostle of the Jews asserting the same thing, viz. that [n] *no prophecy of the scripture is of private interpretation; for the prophecy came not in old time by the will of man, but holy men of God spake as they were moved by the Holy Ghost*. Upon the whole therefore we must conclude, [o] either that Moses and the other writers of the Old Testament were inspired, or that they were consummate cheats; and that not only Christ and his apostles by remitting us to them, and citing their writings as divine, did connive at the cheat, but that God himself likewise, by giving them the power of miracles and prophecy, did countenance the imposture; and by investing them with the characters of his authority, and all outward marks of his approbation, inevitably lead us into error; which is most impious to think, and most blasphemous to say.

Considering then that the divine intention in having the scriptures wrote, was to make them the standard of faith and rule of life in all future ages of the church, there was a strong reason why God should take care that the

and for what reason.

---

[m] 2 Tim. iii. 16. [n] 2 Pet. i. 20, 21. [o] Vid. Calmet's Disser. vol. 1.

the books which he designed to be the sole guide of mankind in matters of religion, and which he foresaw all posterity would appeal to as the great touchstone of truth, should not be liable to any errors; but that his Holy Spirit should so guide the hand of his penmen, (as it were,) and assist them in their compositions with such an infallible veracity, as might be of sufficient authority to silence all differences whenever they should arise. And accordingly we may observe, that, in all ages, both Jews and Christians have appealed to these books as to oracles, in order to decide all controversies in religion; that, in every general council, the Holy Bible was always placed on high as the directory and unerring compass whereby to steer in their debates; and that at the opening of such assemblies, each member was wont to declare himself much in the same sense with p the article of our church; "That the Holy "Scripture containeth all things necessary to salvation; "so that whatsoever is not read therein, nor may be prov- "ed thereby, is not to be required of any man that it "should be believed as an article of the faith, or be "thought requisite or necessary to salvation."

How far inspired. It is needless, and almost impossible for us to define precisely how far the Spirit of God was engaged in the composition of the Holy Scriptures. It seems more consonant however to the manner of the divine operations, which do not usually put any force upon human nature, but leave it in a great measure to the exercise of its faculties, to suppose, that the authors of them were something more than mere amanuenses to the Holy Ghost. The great diversity of style and diction which may be observed in several books, and sometimes the expressing one and the same thing in different terms by different authors, is almost a sure indication, that they themselves had some share in the composition, and that the Holy Ghost was not the sole author of every word and expression; for if this had been the case, the style of each book had been alike and uniform; at least there had not been that apparent difference in it which we now see, and which (taking in the holy penmen for a share in the composition) may not unfitly be ascribed to natural causes. If the Holy Ghost had dictated every word, I say, why should Isaiah, who was bred in a court, be more florid and magnificent in his expression than Amos, who had his education among the herds? It is a more easy supposition therefore of the two, that

p Article VI.

that God should suggest the matter of his revelation first to their minds, and then leave them to weigh it in their thoughts, (as they did other truths,) and so put it into such a form of words, as their own minds, or the tenor of their education, naturally inclined to.

The writings of the holy penmen are of different kinds: some of them are historical, some perceptive, some argumentative, some doctrinal, some poetical, and some prophetical; in all which the measure of the divine assistance seemed to vary in proportion to the nature of the subject whereof they treated. If they wrote historically of matters of fact, which either they themselves knew, or had received from credible witnesses, there was no reason that the substance of their history should be revealed again: all that seems requisite is, that the Holy Ghost should so far inspect them, as to prevent any error in the relation. If they delivered any moral precepts, or argued from any revealed truths, he then allowed them to employ their reasoning faculties as far as their arguments were suitable and solid; and at the same time cleared their understanding, and hindered them from writing any thing impertinent. If their compositions were of the poetic kind, he left them to follow the established rules of that art, and to scan out the metre by themselves; and all that he did, in this case, was to quicken their invention, and refine their fancy: But if they were to indite things of an higher nature, and such as were above their faculties; if they were either to predict some remarkable event, or declare some divine truth that was never revealed before; it seems reasonable to believe, that the whole of these was immediately inspired into their minds by the Holy Ghost; because they could be the result neither of their understanding nor memory; and consequently could come into their minds no other way but by immediate inspiration.

From the whole, then, it is reasonable to think, that the measures of divine inspiration varied according to the nature of the subject, or the exigencies of the penmen who recorded it: that, in the main, they pursued their own method and manner of expression; but on some important occasions had the words dictated to them: that in some subjects they had their memory refreshed; in others, their understanding enlightened; in others, their fancies elevated; in all, their wills directed to the discovery and declaration of the truth: and even in the least matter they wrote, were never so far left to their own discretion, as not to have the Holy Spirit presiding over them, and keeping them from expressing any thing contrary to the divine mind, or the dignity of the sacred subject.

The number, order, and authority of the books.

Now the books of the Old Testament, which, by the divine will and inspiration, were in this manner written, were by the Jews of old usually divided into three several classes, whereof the first comprehended the five books of Moses; the second, all the prophets; and the third, those writings which they called *Chetubim*, the Greek *Hagiographa;* or books that were written by holy men, but not with such fulness of spirit as to be ranked among the prophets. In this division they reckoned five books in the first class; eight in the second; and nine in the third; in all two and twenty; according to the number of the letters of their alphabet, and as fully comprehending all that was necessary to be known and believed, as the number of their letters did all that was requisite to be said or written; for in this method it is that they range them.

The books of Moses.
V.
- Genesis.
- Exodus.
- Leviticus.
- Numbers.
- Deuteronomy.

Four books of the former prophets.
IV.
- Joshua.
- Judges, and [q] Ruth.
- Samuel 1. and [r] 2.
- Kings 1. and [r] 2.

Four books of the later prophets.
IV.
- Isaiah.
- Jeremiah, and his [s] Lamentations.
- Ezekiel.
- [t] The books of the 12 lesser prophets.

And the rest of the holy writers.
IX.
- King David's Psalms.
- King Solomon's Proverbs.
- His Ecclesiastes.
- His Song of Songs.
- The book Job.
- The book of Daniel.
- The book of Ezra, and [u] Nehemiah.
- The book of Esther.
- The book of [x] Chronicles 1. and 2.

Which

[q] Which was put as an appendix to the Judges. [r] Counted them but one book. [s] Counted but one book. [t] Which were all put in one. [u] The Jews reckoned them both together for one. [x] And these two went with them for one book.

OR PREPARATORY DISCOURSE.

Which two books of Chronicles, containing the sum of all their former histories, and reaching from the creation of the world to the Jews return from Babylon, are a perfect epitome of the Old Testament; and therefore not improperly placed, as if they concluded and closed up their whole Bible.

The book of *Genesis*, which is an introduction to the rest of the Pentateuch, (and contains the history of about 2369 years, from the beginning of the world to the death of the patriarch Joseph) is so called, because it treats of the creation of the world, the beginning and generation of man, and all other creatures [y].

<small>Genesis.</small>

That of *Exodus*, which relates the tyranny of Pharaoh, and the bondage of the Israelites under him (and contains an history of near 145 years) is so called, because it comprehends the history of the departure of the Israelites out of Egypt, under the conduct of Moses [z].

<small>Exodus.</small>

That of *Leviticus*, (which contains about one month's time) has its name, because it gives an account of the Jewish service and worship, of the offices of the Levites, and the whole Levitical order [a].

<small>Leviticus.</small>

That of *Numbers*, (which contains the history of somewhat more than 38 years,) and relates several remarkable incidents in the Israelites passage through the wilderness, has its denomination from Moses's numbering the tribes of the people, [b] according to God's order and appointment [c].

<small>Numbers.</small>

That of *Deuteronomy*, which signifies *a second law*, (and takes up about the space of six weeks) is a summary repetition of the laws, both moral, civil, and ceremonial,

<small>Deuteronomy.</small>

---

[y] The Hebrews call it *Beresith, in principio, in the beginning*, because in their language it begins with that word. [z] The Hebrews call it *veele Schemoth*, because it begins with these words, *now these are the names*, &c. [a] The Jews term it *Vaicra*, because in Hebrew it begins with this word, which signifies, *and he called*. [b] For now that they are passing through the wilderness, wherein they were in danger of meeting with many enemies, it was highly convenient to take an account of their forces, and to put themselves in a posture of defence; Lewis, Antiq. Heb. l. 8. [c] The Jews term it *Vacdabber, and he spake*, because in Hebrew it begins with those words.

[a] This seems to be of absolute use, because the Israelites, who had heard them before, died in the wilderness; and as

monial, which Moses had given the Israelites in the former books; together with several kind admonitions and earnest exhortations to better obedience for the time to come, from the consideration of the many divine favours already received, and the promises that were in reversion. ᵈ

This is the scope of the Pentateuch, or five books of Moses: and that he, and none but he, was the writer of them, we have all the assurance that innumerable passages, in the Holy Scriptures, the joint authority of Christ and his apostles, the universal consent of all ages, and ᵉ the concurring testimony of the most ancient Heathen authors, can give us. Only it must be observed, that some part of the last chapter of Deuteronomy, wherein mention is made of the death of Moses, must have been added by some other writer, either by Joshua, his immediate successor, or (as others would have it) by Ezra, the great restorer of the Jewish canon.

Joshua. The book of *Joshua* (which contains the history of 17 years) is so called, not so much upon the account of its author, as of its subject-matter; since it contains the history of the wars, and other affairs which happened under the administration of that great captain: but since the author of the book of Ecclesiasticus gives him this character, ᶠ *that he was successor of Moses in prophecies*, i. e. the next inspired writer of scripture after Moses, we have no reason to oppose the judgement of the Jewish church, which ᵍ generally ascribed it to him.

Judges. The book of *Judges*, which relates the state of the Jewish people in the land of Canaan, in the time of the judges,

---

there was now another generation of men sprung up, it was highly requisite to have these laws promulged afresh, which Moses does in this book, and here and there intersperses both explications and additions; Lewis, *ibid.* ᵈ The Jews call it *Elle haddeburim, hæc sunt verba*, *these are the words*, because the Hebrew text begins in this manner. ᵉ Vid Grot de Verit. lib. 1. sect. 16. Du Pin's Canon, vol. 1. and Le Clerk's Prolegom. De scriptore Pentateuchi. ᶠ Ecclef. xlvi. 1.

ᵍ The Talmudists indeed make him the author of the book; but some of the ancients, and many modern writers, deny it: and accordingly we find Theodoret affirming, that this volume was collected a long time after Joshua's death; and that it was no more than an abstract of an ancient commentary, called *The book of just men*, whereof we find mention made in the tenth chapter of the said book of Joshua; Lewis's Antiq. Hebr. lib. 8.

judges, from Jushua's death until Eli, (i. e. about 300 years) is very ancient, as appears from a passage in a psalm of David, [h] *When thou wentest forth before the people, when thou marchedst through the wilderness, the earth shook, the heavens also dropped at the presence of God*; which words are an exact imitation of these in [i] Judges; *Lord, when thou wentest out of Seir, when thou marchedst out of the field of Edom, the earth trembled, the heavens dropped, the clouds also dropped water*. and that it was wrote by Samuel, as well as the book of Ruth, (which is an appendix to it,) the doctors of the Talmud agree, though others attribute it to Hezekiah, and many to Ezra.

The two books of *Samuel*, which are public histories of the transactions under the two last judges, Samuel and Eli, and under the two first kings, Saul and David, (comprising the compass of 100 years,) have likewise evident marks of their antiquity: and, though it be not absolutely certain who their author was, yet the generality of the Jews do, with great probability, assert, that the four and twenty first chapters were written by Samuel himself, and the rest by the prophets Nathan and Gad; which assertion they found on this passage of the Chronicles, [k] *Now the acts of David the King, first and last, behold they are written in the book of Samuel the seer, and in the book of Nathan the prophet, and in the book of Gad the seer*.

The books of Samuel.

The books of *Kings* [l] and the *Chronicles*, (for I take them in the order wherein they now stand in our Bibles,) which, taking in some part of the foregoing books, contain the history of the Jewish monarchy down to the captivity of Babylon (a space of above 500 years,) were compiled out of ancient records, which records were wrote by men of a prophetic spirit; and all that Ezra (or whoever their compiler was) added of his own, was only some genealogical observations at the beginning of the Chronicles, and some other passages of small moment, relating to the times after the captivity.

Kings and Chronicles.

The

---

[h] Psal. lxviii. 7, 8. [i] Judges v. 4. [k] 1 Chron. xxix. 29.
[l] Though it be a matter of great uncertainty, whether the book of the Kings or of the Chronicles were first written, yet it is evident, that this of the Chronicles is more full and comprehensive than that of the Kings: and from thence these books are called *Paralipomena, Remains, Supplements*, and *Additions*, by the Greek interpreters; because they contain some passages or circumstances that were omitted in the other historical writers; Lewis, *ibid.*

Ezra.

The book of *Ezra*, which is a continuation of the Chronicles, and comprises the history of the Jews from the time that Cyrus made the decree for their return, until the 20th year of Artaxerxes Longimanus, (which was about 100 years,) was all composed by him, except the six first chapters, which contain an account of the first return of the Jews upon the decree of Cyrus; whereas Ezra did not return until the time of Artaxerxes. It is of his second return therefore that he writes the account, and adding it to the other, (which he found ready composed to his hand,) he made it a complete history of the Jewish restoration.

Nehemiah.

Nehemiah, who was the son of Hilkiah, of the tribe of Levi, was advanced in Babylon to be cup-bearer or page to King Artaxerxes; and from him he obtained leave to return to Judea for 12 years, in order to rebuild the city of Jerusalem. He continues the history of Ezra from the 20th year of Artaxerxes to the reign of Darius Nothus, (about 40 years in all,) and is, [m] by the writer of the book of Maccabees, attested to be the author of that work.

Esther.

The history of *Esther*, a Jewish captive virgin, who, for her transcendent beauty, was advanced to the throne of Persia, and, by her interest with her royal husband [n] Ahasuerus, (who some will have to be the same with the above-mentioned Artaxerxes, and others with Darius Hystaspes,) procured to her countrymen a wonderful deliverance from Haman's intended massacre, by some is supposed to have been written by Ezra, and by others by Mordecai. But the more probable opinion of the Talmudists, is that the great synagogue (to perpetuate the memory of that remarkable event, and to account for the original of the feast of Purim) ordered this book to be composed, and afterwards approved, and admitted into the sacred canon.

Job.

Who the author of the book of *Job* was, is indeed uncertain: It is very probable however, that he was a person of great antiquity, and one who lived before the promulgation of the Jewish law; because there are no traces of that to be found in the whole compass of the book: and therefore the most general opinion is, that it was written by Moses, during his abode in Egypt, or in his flight into the land of Midian, with an intent to encourage the Jews

under

---

[m] 2 Mac. ii. 13.   [n] Vid. Prideaux's Connect. part 1. book 4.

under the severities of the Egyptian bondage. Though some will rather have it, that the materials of this book were drawn up first by Job himself, or some of his friends, the interlocutors; and afterwards coming into the hands of Moses, and thence into the possession of Solomon, were by him turned † into Hebrew verse, in the manner we now find them.

Some of the ancient fathers were of opinion, that the whole book of *Psalms* was written by David only; but in this they must be mistaken; because the titles of several psalms tell us, that they were composed by Moses. The Hebrew doctors do generally agree, that the 92 psalm was made by Adam. Solomon, no doubt, was the author of the 49th psalm, which is much of the same strain with his other nuptial song which is called *the Canticles;* and it is no improbable conjecture, that the 88th and 89th psalms were indited in the time of the Egyptian bondage; the former condoling the people's distress, and the latter prophesying their deliverance. However this be, it is certain, that David (who had an excellent gift of poetry and psalmody) was the composer of much the greater part of them; and therefore his name was thought proper to give title to the whole collection, which was undoubtedly made by Ezra.

That the book of *Proverbs, Ecclesiastes,* and *Canticles,* were written by King Solomon is the general opinion of the Jewish doctors, who pretend to tell us, that he wrote the Canticles in his youth, his Proverbs in his manhood, and his *Ecclesiastes* at the latter end of his life. There are, however, but 25 chapters in the beginning of the first, which are reputed the original collection

Psalms.

The Proverbs.

---

† St Jerome, in his preface to the book of Job, informs us, that, for the most part, it is in heroic verse; that, from the beginning of the book to the third chapter, it is prose; but, from the words *Let the day perish wherein I was born,* chap. iii. 3. to these, *Wherefore I abhor myself, and repent in dust and ashes,* chap. xiii. 6. all is hexameter verse, consisting of dactyls and spondees, like the Greek verses of Homer, or the Latin of Virgil. And Marianus Victorius, in his note upon this passage of St. Jerome, tells us, that he has examined this book of Job, and finds St. Jerome's observations to be true; Shuckford's Connection, vol. 2. chap. 9

THE APPARATUS,

tion of Solomon, the rest were compiled by other hands; only the last chapter (which bears the name of *Lemuel* is supposed to have been written by him under a borrowed name, and seems to be made up of some wise instructions which his mother Bathsheba had taught him when he was a child.

Canticles. The *Song of Songs*, (as it is called,) though it may relate to Solomon's marriage with the daughter of the King of Egypt, and is so far historical; yet the pious, in all ages, have ever esteemed it an allegorical dialogue between Christ *Ecclesiastes* and his church. And, though some passages in *Ecclesiastes* seem to express an Epicurean notion of providence: yet it is to be remembered, that the author (in an academic way) disputes indeed on both sides, but, in the conclusion, determines for that which is right, viz. ⁰ *To fear God and keep his commandments, which is the whole duty of man: for God,* says he, *will bring every work to judgement, and every secret thing, whether it be good, or whether it be evil.*

The Prophets. That the books both of the *greater* and *lesser Prophets* (for we have no need to consider them separately) have been always thought to belong to the persons whose names and inscriptions they bear, we have the universal consent of the Jewish church, several plain passages from Josephus, and a very remarkable testimony in the book of Ecclesiasticus to convince us, where, after many praises bestowed upon Ezekiel, and other prophets and worthies of Israel, there are these words: ᵖ *And, of the twelve prophets let the memorial be blessed: let their bones flourish again out of their place; for they comforted Jacob, and delivered them by a certain hope.*

The canon of the Old Testament compiled by Ezra. Thus it appears, that the books of the Old Testament were either the work of the men whose names they bear; or at least the compositions of persons assisted by the Holy Ghost; and how they came to be collected into a body; and, by persons who were duly qualified for the work, revised, and published in one volume, in the manner we now have them, is the next point of inquiry we are to pursue.

It must be acknowledged indeed that we cannot give an exact account of the settlement of the canon of the Old Testament, because we have no authors extant who professedly treat of this affair; but, if we may believe the concurring testimony of ancient writers, both Jewish and Christian, (who might probably have their opinions from

some

° Eccles. xii. 13, 14.   ᵖ Eccles. iv. 10.

some authorities that are now lost, we must allow, that Ezra, upon his return from the captivity of Babylon, undertook the work; and, after he had finished it, had it approved by the grand Sanhedrim, and published by authority. Only we must observe, ^q that the two books of Chronicles, and those of Nehemiah, Esther, and Malachi, were very probably afterwards added by Simon the Just; and that it was not till his time that the Jewish canon of the Holy Scriptures was fully completed.

That this canon began to be compiled soon after the return from the captivity, is pretty plain from the above-cited passage in Ecclesiasticus, which makes mention of the *twelve minor prophets*, and is an argument that they were then collected, and digested into one volume: and if we believe^r that the LXX interpreters translated all the Old Testament, (which is an opinion that many learned men do maintain,) then it is evident, that the canon must have been settled before the time that their version was made, which was done under Ptolomy Philadelphus, and not improbably at the beginning of his reign. The truth is, both the jewish history ends, and the spirit of prophecy ceased, much about this time: Nehemiah was the last historian, and Malachi the last prophet, both contemporaries with Ezra, and both assisting to him in publishing this new edition of the scriptures; and therefore, it is reasonable to suppose, after the race of such writers were extinct, and *all vision and prophecy sealed up* among the Jews, that this was a proper period for collecting the several copies, and adjusting the catalogue of their sacred books.

But Ezra did more than this: ^s He not only collected all the books whereof the Holy Scriptures did consist, and disposed them in their proper order, but, by comparing the several copies together, he corrected all the errors which had crept into them through the negligence or mistakes of transcribers. He changed the old names of several places that were grown obsolete, and, instead of them, inserted such new ones as the people were better acquainted with. He filled up the chasms of history, and added, in several places, throughout the books of this edition, what appeared to him to be necessary for the illustration, connection, and completion of the whole. And, lastly, he wrote every

What he did to make his edition perfect:

G 2   book

---

^q Vid. Prideaux's Connection, part 1. l. 5.   ^r Vid. Walton's Prolog. 9. in Bib. Polyg.   ^s Vid. Prideaux's Connection, part 1. lib. 5.

book in the Chaldee character, which, since the time of the captivity, the people understood much better than the old Hebrew. But whether, upon this review, he added the vowel points, as they now are in our Hebrew Bibles, is a question a little too prolix and intricate for us to engage in at present. Those who have a mind to have their curiosity in this respect satisfied, may see the arguments on both sides fairly stated in the learned ^t Connection, we have had so frequent occasion to quote.

What we have to observe farther is, that, in the several corrections, additions, and alterations, which Ezra made, he did not proceed according to his own humour and caprice, but was directed by the same spirit which at first assisted the writers of these sacred volumes. For besides that himself was a ^u prophet, or (as he is styled) ^x *a ready scribe in the law of Moses*, we can hardly suppose, but that in an affair of such consequence, he would not only use the best skill he had himself, but consult likewise with Haggai, Zechary, and Malachi, (the last of whom must needs have been alive in his time, and possibly the other two,) and do nothing without their advice; because, in matters of much less moment (*viz* where some who pretended to the priesthood could not prove their pedigree) we find him so very cautious, that he would determine nothing himself, but left the matter undecided, *until a priest should arise who* ^y *had Urim and Thummim*, whereby he might consult the divine will upon all occasions.

and that the same number of books has descended to us.

Thus was the canon of the Old Testament settled, in or about the times of Ezra: and, that it continued in the same manner or order until the publication of the gospel, (besides the authority of several Christian writers,) we have this remarkable testimony from ^z Josephus. "We have only two and twenty books," says he, " which comprehend the history of all ages, and merit " our belief: five belong to Moses, which contain what " relates to the origin of man, and the tradition of the
" several

---

^t Part 1. lib. 5. p. 497.   ^u The Jews look upon Ezra as another Moses; they call him the second founder of the law, and hold his person in so great esteem and veneration, that it is a common saying among their writers, If the law had not been given by Moses, Ezra was worthy to have been the publisher of it; *Lewis' antiq. Heb. lib.* 8.   ^x Ezra vii. 6.   ^y Chap. ii. 62, 63.   ^z Contra Apion.

"several successions and generations, down to his death.
"——From the death of Moses to the reign of Artaxerxes,
"(who was king of Persia after Xerxes,) the prophets
"who succeeded him have, in their books, written what
"happened in their time. The other books contain hymns
"to the praise of God, and precepts for the conduct of
"human life. What happened since the time of Artax-
"erxes down to our days, has likewise been recorded by
"the writers thereof; but they have not met with the like
"credit, because there has not been any certain succession
"of prophets during that time. And from hence, says he,
"it is manifest, what respect and estimation has been paid
"to the books which complete our canon; since, in so long
"a tract of time, no man has ventured either to add any
"thing to them, or diminish or alter any thing in them;
"since the Jews from their infancy are accustomed to call
"them *divine institutions*, to believe them stedfastly, and,
"upon occasion, to lay down their lives in defence of
"them."

That the same number of authentic books has been *Apocryphal books rejected.* transmitted to us, we may plainly perceive, if we will but return to the several catalogues which the fathers, in their writings, have left us of them, which the council of Laodicea enumerates, and sundry general councils afterwards confirm. And though, in process of time, several apocryphal books (as containing matters of Jewish history, and many moral precepts) were, by degrees, admitted into the service of the church, and publicly read for the instruction of the people; yet it would be no hard matter to shew, that some of the best and most learned writers of their times always denied their canonical authority. "The church
"indeed allowed them to be read, (as St Jerome tells us;)
"but she did not receive them into the canon of scripture?"
and in like manner our church declares concerning them, that she "doth read them for example of life, and instruc-
"tion of manners; but does not apply them to establish
"any doctrine." So that, though some of these be confessedly spurious, and accordingly have been rejected by the wisdom of the church; yet this can be made no argument against such as have been universally received, and handed down by unanimous, constant tradition.

"But though we have been careful to receive no *An objec-*
"more books than what are strictly canonical, yet how *tion.*
"shall we satisfy ourselves that we have received them all?
"In several parts of scripture we find books referred to,
"such

"such as *the book of the covenant, the book of the wars of the Lord, the book of Asher, the book of the acts of Solomon,* &c. none of which are now extant; and therefore, as we suppose them lost, we cannot but infer that our present canon of scripture is very lame and imperfect."

Answered, by shewing that none of the canonical books are lost.

What has given credit to this objection is the common notion that that the books here supposed to be lost were volumes of some size, and all indited by the Spirit of God; whereas we may observe, 1st, That the word *Sepher,* which we render *book,* signifies properly a bare *rehearsal* of any thing, or any kind of writing, be it ever so small; and that the custom of the Jews was to call every little *memorandum* by that name: for what we translate *a bill of divorcement,* is, [a] in the original, a *book of divorcement;* and the short account of our Saviour's genealogy is [b] *the book of the generation of Jesus Christ*. 2dly, That several of these tracts, which are not now extant, were written, not by persons pretending to any supernatural assistance, but by such [c] as were styled *recorders,* or *writers of chronicles,* as it is in the margin, an office of great honour and trust, but of a different kind from that of prophets. 3dly, That supposing they were indited by such as were properly prophets, yet they were not written by divine inspiration; "for prophets as [d] St. Austin observes) did not at times write under the guidance and direction of the Holy Ghost. In the fundamentals of religion, indeed, they were divinely assisted; but in other matters they only wrote as faithful historians." And, 4thly, That most of these pieces [e] are still remaining in the scriptures, though they go under other appellations; and that such as are not to be found there, were never designed for religious instruction, nor are they essential to man's salvation. And now to apply these observations to the books we imagine to be lost.

The *book of the covenant,* which is mentioned in Exod. xxiv. 7. and thought to be missing, is not any distinct book from the body of the Jewish laws. For whoever impartially examines that passage in Exodus, will find, that the book referred to is nothing else but a collection of such injunctions and exhortations as are expressly laid down in the four preceding chapters. The

[a] Deut xxiv. 1. [b] Mat. i. 1. [c] 2 Sam. viii. 16. 2 Kings xviii. 18. 2 Chron. xxix 8. [d] De civit. Dei, lib. 18. cap. 38. [e] Vid. Edward's Perfection of the Holy Scripture; and Jenkins's Reasonableness of the Christian Religion, vol. 2.

OR PREPARATORY DISCOURSE.

The *book of the wars of the Lord*, cited in Numb. xx. 14. and supposed to be wanting, is (in the opinion [f] of a very able judge) that very record, which, upon the defeat of the Amalekites, God commanded Moses to make, as a memorial of it, and *to rehearse it in the ears of Joshua*. So that it seems to be no more than a short account of that victory, together with some proper directions for Joshua's private use and conduct in the management of the subsequent war, but not all dictated by divine inspiration; and consequently no [g] canonical scripture.

The *book of Jasher*, mentioned in Josh. x. 13. is supposed by some to be the same with the book of Judges, because we find mention therein of the *sun's standing still*: but the conjecture of the Jewish historian [h] seems to be better founded, viz. that it was composed of certain records, (kept in a safe place at that time, and afterwards removed into the temple,) which gave an account of what happened to the Jews from year to year, and particularly of the *sun's standing still*; and (as it is in 2 Sam. i. 18.) directions for the *use of the bow*, i. e. for setting up of archery, and maintaining military exercises. So that this was not the work of an inspired person, but of some common historiographer, who wrote the annals of his own time, and might therefore deserve the name of *Jasher*, *The Upright*; because what he wrote was generally deemed a true and authentic account of all the events and occurrences which then happened.

Once more, the several *books of Solomon*, mentioned in 1 Kings iv. 32, 33. were no part of canonical scripture. His *three thousand proverbs* were perhaps only spoken, not written down. His *songs*, which were *a thousand and five*, and whereof we have but one, were very likely his juvenile compositions; and his *universal history of vegetables*, and that of *animals of all kinds*, as properly

---

[f] Dr. Lightfoot's Chronology of the times of the Old Testament. [g] Others are of opinion, that the book here under consideration is no other than the book of Judges, which may properly enough be called *the book of the wars of the Lord*; because it recounts the warlike enterprizes which those brave men who were stirred by God in an extraordinary manner, were so famous for, (or to express the remarkableness of the thing,) *The wars of the Lord* may signify as much as the great, wonderful, and renowned wars fought by the valiant Hebrews; Lewis's Antiq. Heb. lib. 8. [h] Joseph. Antiq. lib. 5. cap. 2.

perly belonged to philosophy. It was not necessary for every one to be acquainted with them: and though the loss of them (considering the matchless measure of wisdom wherewith God had endowed their author) is certainly very great; yet it is a loss which none but the busy searchers into nature have cause to bewail: nor have they so much cause either, if the conjectures of some learned men should prove true, *viz.* that these books of plants and animals were extant in the days of Alexander the Great; or that being perused and understood by Aristotle and Theophrastus, by the help of an interpreter, they were translated into their writings in the manner we now find them, and, in process of time, gained them great honour and renown. Upon the whole therefore we may conclude, that if any books seem to be wanting in our present catalogue, they are either such as lie secret and unobserved under other denominations, or such as had never the title of being canonical; as contained no points essential to man's salvation; and such, consequently, as we may live safely ignorant of here, and shall never be responsible for hereafter.

An objection.
" But suppose we have the whole number of our books,
" yet we are still at a loss for the true sense of them; because
" since the time of their first recording, they have been so
" chopped and changed by the management of those who
" had the custody of them; so foisted with errors, and load-
" ed with various readings, that they render the text purely
" precarious, and make every wise man doubtful and suspici-
" ous, whether any thing of certainty can be gathered from
" a book where the sense and phraseology is so very un-
" certain."

Answered, by shewing the occasion and benefit of various readings.
We readily grant indeed, that there is a great variety of different readings occurring in the books of the Old Testament; but, as in a multitude of copies this is a thing unavoidable, so it is one of the most effectual means, at this distance of time from all originals, to help us to the true sense and meaning of the text. For, put the case, that we had but one copy of the Bible by us, yet methinks it would be a desirable thing to have another; for [i] another, to join with the first, would give us more authority, as well as security. Now chuse that second where you will, there shall be numberless variations from the first, and yet half or more of the faults still remain in them both. A third therefore, and a fourth, and so on, are desirable, that, by a joint and mutual help, all the faults may be mended: and yet the more copies you call

to

[i] Phileleu. Lipf. Answer to a discourse of Free-thinking.

to your affiftance, the more do the various readings multiply upon you; becaufe every copy has its particular flips, though in a principal paffage or two it may do fingular fervice. Were the originals indeed ftill in being, they would fuperfede the ufe of all other copies; but fince that is impoffible from the nature of things, fince time and calamities muft confume all, the fubfidiary help muft be from the various tranfcripts conveyed down to us, when compared and examined together: and no one can be ignorant, how much a collation of this kind tends both to illuftrate the fenfe of any particular paffage, and to ftrengthen the authority of the whole.

Confider then, that before the ufe of printing, more manufcripts were made of the Holy Bible than of any Heathen author whatever: and that thefe manufcripts have been examined with more care, and collated with more exactnefs, and the various readings fet down, even to the moft minute difference; we are not to wonder if, with all this fcrupulous fearch and inquiry, the variations are fo many. The editors of profane authors do not ufe to trouble their reader with an ufelefs lift of every little flip committed by a lazy or ignorant fcribe. What is thought commendable in an edition of the fcriptures, and has the name of fairnefs and fidelity, would be deemed trifling and impertinent in them: but if the like fcrupuloufnefs were obferved in regiftring the fmalleft changes in profane, as is allowed, nay required in facred authors, the number of their variations would rife at leaft to a full equality.

We ought to account it therefore a fingular inftance of God's good providence, confidering the great antiquity of many books of the fcriptures, beyond that of any other books in the world; the multitude of copies that have been taken in all ages and nations; the difficulty to avoid miftakes in tranfcribing books in a language which has fo many of its letters, and of its words too, fo like one another; the defect of the Hebrew vowels, and the late invention (as moft are now agreed) of the points; the change of the Samaritan, or ancient Hebrew for the prefent Hebrew, or Chaldee character; the captivity of the whole nation of the Jews for feventy years; and the mixtures and changes which, during that time, were brought into their language: confidering, I fay, that all the accidents which have ever happened to create errors and miftakes in any book, have concurred to occafion them in the Old Teftament,

ment, we ought to esteem it a particular instance of God's provdence, that the different readings are fewer, and make much less alteration in the sense, than those of any book of the same bigness, and of any note, or antiquity, if all the copies should be as carefully examined, and every little variation as punctually set down, as those of Holy Scriptures have been. And much more are we to bless the divine providence, that whatever differences are to be found in the several copies of the Bible, they do not in the least prejudise the fundamental points of religion, nor weaken the authority of these sacred records. For this is the judgement of one [k] who had studied the subject much, and was sufficiently versed in scripture criticism, *viz.* " That the " things relating either to faith or practice, are plainly " contained in all copies whatever. Difference there is " indeed, in lesser things, as in matters of chronology, " which depend upon the alteration, or omission, or ad- " dition of a letter; or in the names of men, or of cities " or countries; but the principal doctrines of religion are " so dispersed throughout the scriptures, that they can re- " ceive no damage or alteration, unless the whole should " be changed, or very grossly corrupted."

And that the text was never altered, or corrupted.

For besides his providential care, (which we may well suppose to go along with writings of so divine a character), we find God making all proper and prudent provision for their preservation, by inserting a particular and strict prohibition in the law itself, [l] *That no one should presume to add unto, or diminish ought from it* : by enjoining the people to make it their constant study, [m] *to bind it*, as it were, *for a sign upon their hands, and as frontlets between their eyes, and to write it upon the gates and posts of their houses*; and by requiring them to read it diligently, both in private to their families, and after a more solemn manner in their public congregations. All which could not but make them competent judges of the law of Moses, and enable them to descry any change or material corruption which should at any time attempt to insinuate itself.

To secure the other inspired writings, a continued succession of prophets was of great service: and it seems next to impossible for any dangerous alteration to have been made, without detection and censure, so long as that order of men, whose office and zeal led them to correct any error

in

[k] Lud. Cappel. Crit. Sac. lib. 6. cap. 2. [l] Deut. iv 2. [m] Chap. vi. 8. 9.

in faith, as well as corruption in practice, was in being. Nor can we suppose it probable, that any person would attempt such alterations, where the copies were in so many hands, and so openly read and consulted, that there was scarce any private person who might not have known (if any such had happened) when and wherein they had been corrupted.

Nay, so far were the Jews from suffering corruptions to creep into the Holy Scriptures, that [n] if but *one word* happened to be altered in any copy, it was to be laid aside as utterly useless; unless it was sometimes given to a very poor man to read to his family, upon condition, that he brought it not with him to the synagogue, nor made any other use of it. The religious factions among the Jews were many times very violent; but we no where find any party accusing the other of corrupting, or falsifying scripture; nor does our Saviour himself, who so frequently reproves the Scribes and Pharisees for their traditions, and false glosses, ever once charge them with adulterating the text itself; which he certainly would not have failed to do, had they been culpable in that respect. On the contrary both he and the apostles appeal to it as true and authentic, and borrow their proofs from it, in confirmation of the Christian faith and doctrine. To conclude this argument then,

That from the time of Ezra, to the coming of our Saviour Christ, the Jews did not corrupt the text of the sacred writings, is plain from his not charging them with any such practice; which doubtless he would have done, (as well as reprove their false comments upon them), had they been equally guilty of both: and that, since the beginning of Christianity, neither they nor any other sect whatever, could possibly make any falsifications, and either add or diminish any thing material, without an immediate detection, is manifest from the multitude of true and authentic copies, which were every where dispersed as far as Christianity prevailed, and from that jealous and vigilant eye, which each party had upon the other: so that we may reasonably suppose, that all the little errors which may be remarked in them, proceeded not from any ill design, but merely from the ignorance or inattention of their transcribers. And indeed, [o] considering the many ages thro' which the books have passed, we have much more reason to wonder,

[n] Vid. Jenkins's Reasonableness, vol. 2. [o] Bishop Burnet on the Articles.

wonder, that they are brought down to us so entire, and so manifestly genuine, in all their main and fundamental points, than that we should see some instances of human frailty in those who copied and preserved them.

An objection.

"But be the books ever so genuine, and their tradition ever so certain, yet we cannot suppose them wrote by persons divinely inspired, so long as we see in them certain characters inconsistent with such a supposition. Surely the purest language, the most perfect style, the greatest clearness, the most exact method, the soundest reasoning, the most apparent consistency, and, in a word, all the exellencies of good writing, might be expected in a piece composed or dictated by the Spirit of God; but books wherein we find the reverse of all this, it is idle, if not impious, to ascribe to the Deity."

Answered, by shewing that translations are defective.

I. One great mistake which the generality of readers run into, is, to judge of the composition of the scripture, not from its original, but from its translations: for, [p], besides that in ancient writings, (such as the Bible is) there are allusions to many rites and customs that are now laid aside; and, for this reason, must needs seem flat or impertinent; which, when they were in use, had a great deal of spirit and propriety in them; and besides that the Hebrew, in particular, is a language of a peculiar cast, both in the contexture of its words, and the cadence of its periods, and contains certain expressions, whose emphasis can no more be translated into another language, than the water of a diamond can be painted, without detracting from the original: besides all this, I say, the translators themselves, sometimes by running into mistakes, and at all times by adhering too religiously to the letter of the text, have contributed not a little to make the style of the sacred writings appear less advantageous. For, whereas other translators have taken a liberty to accomodate the beauties of the language whereinto they translate, to the idiotisms of that wherein their author wrote; these have thought themselves restrained from using such freedom in a divine composition; and have therefore left several Hebraic, and other foreign phrases in their version, which seem a little uncouth, and give the reader (who can look no farther) a very odd notion of the original: though it is certainly manifest, that the most elegant piece of oratory that ever was framed, if we render it literally, and not give it true genius of the
language

[p] Vid. Boyle of the style of the Scripture; and Nicholl's Conference, vol.

language whereunto we are admitting it, will lose all its beauty, and appear with the same disadvantage.

II. Another mistake that we run into is, when we confine *eloquence to any nation, and account that the only proof of it, which is accommodated to the present taste. We indeed, in these European countries, whose languages, in a great measure, are derived from Greek and Latin, make them the patterns for our imitation, and account them the standard of perfection: but there is no reason why the eastern nations, whose languages have no affinity with them, should do the same; much less is it reasonable to expect it in writers who lived long before these Greek or Latin authors (we so much admire) were born. It is sufficient for them that they wrote according to the fashionable, and esteemed eloquence of their own times: but that the Holy Ghost should inspire them with certain schemes of speech, adapted to the modern taste, and such as were utterly unknown in the countries where they lived, is a thing that can never enter into any sober man's consideration. The truth is, since Moses was bred up in all the refined learning and wisdom of the Egyptians; since Solomon was excellent in all kind of knowledge, and in a manner idolized by the eastern world; and since Daniel's promising youth was improved by the learning of the Chaldean sages: we have all the reason imaginable to believe, that they wrote according to the perfection of style, which was then in use; that though their eloquence differs from ours, yet it is excellent in its kind; and that, if we have other notions of it, it is only because we are unacquainted with those bold allegories, and figurative ways of discourse; those dark sentences, surprising brevities, and inconnected transitions, wherein the nature of their true sublime did consist.

That eloquence is not peculiar to any country;

III. Another mistake we run into is, when we suppose that the critical rules of eloquence are any ways necessary in divine compositions. The design of God, in recording his laws, was to inform our understandings, to cure our passions, and rectify our wills; and if this end be but attained, it is no great matter in what form of diction the prescription be given. We never expect that a physician's receipt should be wrote in a Ciceronian style: and if a lawyer has made us a firm conveyance of an estate, we never enquire what elegancies there are in the writing. —When therefore,—God intends to do for us far greater things than these; when he is delivering the terms of our salvation,

nor necessary in a divine composition.

salvation, and prescribing the rules of our duty; why should we expect that he should insist on the niceties of style and expression, and not rather account it a diminution of his authority, to be elaborate in trifles, when he has the momentous issues of another life to command our attention, and affect our passions? In some of the greatest works of nature, God has not confined himself to any such order and exactness. ^q The stars, we see, are not cast into regular figures; lakes and rivers are not bounded by straight lines; nor are hills and mountains exact cones or pyramids. When a mighty prince declares his will by laws and edicts to his subjects, is he (do we think) careful at all about a pure style, or elegant composition? Is not the phrase thought proper enough, if it conveys as much as was intended? And would not the fine strains of some modern critics be thought pedantic and affected on such occasions? Why then should we expect in the oracles of God an exactness, that would be ^r unbecoming, and beneath the dignity of an earthly monarch, and which bears no proportion or resemblance to the magnificent works of the creation? A strict observation of the rules of grammar and rhetoric, in elegant expressions, harmonious periods, and technical definitions and partitions, may gratify indeed some readers; but then it must be granted, that these things have the air of human contrivance in them; whereas in the simple, unaffected, artless, unequal, bold, figurative style of the Holy Scriptures, there is a character singularly great and majestic, and what looks more like divine inspiration, than any other form of composition.

The style of scripture instructive, and affecting. These observations being premised, if we should now consider the nature of eloquence in general, as it is defined by ^s Aristotle, to be a *faculty of persuasion*, which Cicero makes to consist in three things, *instructing, delighting,* and *moving* our readers or hearers mind, we shall find, that the Holy Scriptures have a fair claim to these several properties.

For where can we meet with such a plain representation of things, in point of history, and such cogent arguments, in point of precept, as this one volume furnishes us

---

^q *Vid.* The Minute Philosopher, dialogue 4.

^r Cujusque orationem videris sollicitam et politam, scito animum quoque non minus esse pusillis occupatum: magnus remissius loquitur, et securius; quæcunque dicit plus habent fiduciæ quam curæ; Sen. epist. 115.

^s Rhet. l. 1. c. 2.

us with? Where is there an history written more simply and naturally, and at the same time more nobly and loftily, than that of the creation of the world? Where are the great lessons of morality taught with such force and perspecuity (except in the sermons Christ, and the writings of the apostles) as in the book of Deuteronomy? Where is the whole compass of devotion, in the several forms of confession, petition, supplication, thanksgiving, vows, and praises, so punctually taught us, as in the book of Psalms? Where are the rules of wisdom and prudence so convincingly laid down, as in the Proverbs of Solomon and the choice sentences of his Ecclesiastes? Where is vice and impiety of all kinds more justly displayed, and more fully confuted, than in the threats and admonitions of the prophets? And what do the little warmths, which may be raised in the fancy by an artificial composure and vehemence of style, signify in comparison of those strong impulses and movements which the Holy Scriptures make upon good men's souls, when they represent the frightful justice of an angry God to stubborn offenders, and the bowels of his compassion, and unspeakable kindness to all true penitents and faithful servants?

The Holy Scripture indeed has none of those flashy ornaments of speech, wherewith human compositions so plentifully abound; but then it has a sufficient stock of real and peculiar beauties to recommend it. To give one instance for all out of the history of Joseph and his family: the whole relation indeed is extremely natural; but the manner of his discovering himself to his brethren is inimitable. *' And Joseph could no longer refrain himself —— but, lifting up his voice with tears, said —— I am Joseph —— Doth my father yet live? —— And his brethren could not answer him; for they were troubled at his presence. And Joseph said to his brethren, Come near me, I pray you: and they came near, and he said I am Joseph —— your brother —— whom ye sold into Egypt.* Nothing certainly can be a more lively description of Joseph's tender respect for his father, and love for his brethren: And, in like manner, when his brethren returned, and told their father in what splendor and glory his son Joseph lived, it is said, that " *Jacob's heart fainted, for he believed them not; but when he saw the waggons which Joseph had sent for him, the spirit of Jacob, their father, revived: and Israel said, It is enough* —— *Joseph my son is yet alive —— I will go —— and see him before,*

        ᶠ Gen. xlv. 1. &c.   ᵍ Ver. 26. &c.

before I die. Here is such a contrast of different passions of utter despondency, dawning hope, confirmed faith, triumphant joy, and paternal affection, as no orator in the world could express more movingly, in a more easy manner or shorter compass of words.

Figurative and lofty sometimes.

Nay more, had I leisure to gratify the curious, I might easily shew, that those very figures and schemes of speech, which are so much admired in profane authors, as their great beauties and ornaments, are no where more conspicuous than in the sacred.

One figure, for instance, esteemed very florid among the masters of art, is when all the members of a period begin with the same word. The figure is called *anaphora*; and yet (if I mistake not) the 15th psalm affords us a very beautiful passage of this kind. *Lord who shall abide in thy tabernacle? Who shall dwell in thy holy hill? He that walketh uprightly; he that backbiteth not with his tongue; he that maketh much of them that fear the Lord; he that sweareth to his hurt, and changeth not; he that putteth not out his money to usury, nor taketh reward against the innocent. He that does these things shall never be moved.*

The ancient orators took a great deal of pride in ranging finely their *antitheta*. Cicero is full of this, and uses it many times to a degree of affectation; and yet I cannot find, any place where he has surpassed that passage of the prophet. [x] *He that killeth an ox, is as if he slew a man; he that sacrificeth a lamb, as if he cut off a dog's neck; he that offereth an oblation, as if he offered swine's blood.* But above all other figures, that, whereon poets and orators love chiefly to dwell, is the *hypotyposis*, or *lively description*; and yet we shall hardly find in the best classic authors, any thing comparable, in this regard, to the Egyptians destruction in the Red Sea, related [y] in the song of Moses and Miriam; to the description of the Leviathan [z] in Job; to the descent of God, and a storm at sea [a] in the Psalmist; to the intrigues of an adulterous woman [b] in the Proverbs to the pride of the Jewish ladies [c] in Isaiah; and to the plague of locusts [d] in Joel; which is represented like the ravaging of a country, and storming a city by an army; *A fire devoureth before them, and behind them a desolate wilderness,*

[x] Isa. lxvi. 3. [y] Exod. xv. [z] Ch. xli. [a] Psal. xviii. 17. [b] Ch. vii. [c] Ch. iv. [d] Ch. i.

wilderness, and nothing shall escape them.——Before their face people shall be pained; all faces shall gather blackness. They shall run like mighty men; they shall climb the wall like men of war; they shall march every one in his way, and they shall not break their ranks.——They shall run to and fro in the city; they shall run upon the wall; they shall climb up upon the houses; they shall enter into the windows as a thief.—— The description is more remarkable, becaufe the analogy is carried quite throughout without ftraining, and the whole proceffes of a conquering army in the manner of their march their deftroying the provifion, and burning the country, in their fcaling the walls, breaking into houfes, and running about the vanquifhed city, are fully delineated and fet before our eyes.

From thefe few examples (for it would be endlefs to proceed in inftances of this kind) it appears, that the Holy Bible is far from being defective in point of eloquence; and (what is a peculiar commendation of it) its ftyle is full of a grateful variety; fometimes majeftic, as becomes *that high and holy one who inhabiteth eternity;* fometimes fo low, as to anfwer the other part of his character, *who dwelleth with him that is of an humble fpirit*; and, at all times fo proper, and adapted fo well to the feveral fubjects it treats of, that ᶜ whoever confiders it attentively will perceive, in the narrative parts of it, a ftrain fo fimple and unaffected; in the prophetic and devotional, fomething fo animated and fublime; and in the doctrinal and perceptive, fuch an air of dignity and authority, as feems to fpeak its original divine.

at all times proper.

We allow indeed, that method is an excellent art, highly conducive to the clearnefs and perfpicuity of difcourfe; but then we affirm, that it is an art of modern invention in comparifon to the times when the facred penmen wrote, and incompatible with the manner of writing which was then in vogue. We indeed in Europe, who, in this matter, have taken our examples from Greece, can hardly read any thing with pleafure that is not digefted into order, and forted under proper heads; but the eaftern nations, who were ufed to a free way of difcourfe, and never cramped their notions by methodical limitations, would have defpifed a compofition of this kind as much as we do a fchool-boy's theme, with all the formalities of its *exordiums, ratios,* and *confirmatios.* And, if this was

Method, a modern invention;

ᶜ The Minute Philofopher, dial. 4.

was no precedent for other nations, much lefs can we think, that God Almighty's methods ought to be confined to human laws, which, being defigned for the narrownefs of our conceptions might be improper and injurious to his, whofe *thoughts are as far above ours, as the heavens are higher than the earth.*

<small>and not fo proper in divine compofitions.</small> The truth is, ᶠ infpiration is, in fome meafure, the language of another world, and carries in it the reafoning of fpirits, which, without controverfy, is vaftly different from ours. We, indeed, to make things lie plain before our underftandings, are forced to fort them out into diftinct partitions, and confider them by little and little, that fo at laft, by gradual advances, we may come to a tolerable conception of them; but this is no argument for us to think that pure fpirits do reafon after this manner. Their underftandings are quick and intuitive: they fee the whole compafs of rational inferences at once; and have no need of thofe little methodical diftinctions which oftentimes help the imperfection of our intellects. Now, though we do not affert, that the language of the Holy Scriptures is an exact copy of the reafoning of the fpiritual world; yet, fince *they came by the infpiration of the Holy Ghoft* it is but reafonable to expect that they fhould preferve fome fmall relifh of it; as books tranflated into another tongue always retain fome marks of their originals. And hence it comes to pafs, that though the Holy Ghoft does vouchfafe to fpeak in the language of men, yet, in his divine compofitions, there are fome traces to be found of that bold and unlimited ratiocination which is peculiar to the heavenly inhabitants, whofe noble and flaming thoughts are never clogged with the cold and jejune laws of human method. To which purpofe we may obferve, that, even among the Heathens, whenever their authors reprefent a perfon infpired, a Sibyl, a Caffandra, or a Tirefias, they never introduce him making a fet formal fpeech, but always faying fomething noble and fublime, which difdains all ordinary artificial fetters. And, if the greateft mafters of polite writing thought it proper to neglect all rules and reftraints in compofitions of pretended infpiration, why fhould that be accounted culpable in the Holy Scriptures which is held fo exquifite in Sophocles, or any other lofty tragedian?

But

ᶠ Nicholls's conference with a Theift, vol. 1.

But after all, the Holy Scriptures (as far as can be ex-*though, in* pected) are not destitute of method. They are not indeed *many ca-*wrote upon the plan of some Greek and Latin compositions; *fes, the scriptures* but they are delivered in such a manner as is easy to be un- *observe it:* derstood, not unpleasant to read, and, to those who are accustomed to oriental compositions, exceedingly beautiful. For, where can we find a more methodical history than that of Moses, beginning at the first creation of all things, and the formation of human kind; proceeding in the account of their increase, depravation, and almost total destruction by an universal deluge; after their second increase, relating their relapse into idolatry, and thereupon God's electing a peculiar people to serve him according to his own appointment; and so recording the first original and various adventures of their progenitors; the afflictions and wanderings of that chosen nation, and the polity which they should observe when once they were settled in the promised land? Nothing can be more clear and regular than this. And as for the other historians who wrote the transactions of the Jewish nation from the conquest of Canaan to the Babylonish captivity, they are so exact in observing the order and series of time, and in setting down the length of each prince's reign, that they afford a better foundation for historical truth, as well as chronological certainty, than is to be found in the best Heathen writers of this kind.

It cannot be expected indeed, that psalms and hymns wrote upon sundry occasions, or such proverbs and wise axioms as took their rise from different observations, and were noted down the instant they were conceived, should have any connection or mutual dependence. Prophecies too were to be loose, and unconfined to rule, as being the language of a spirit, which will admit of no restraint; but, as for the doctrinal and argumentative parts of the scripture, they are digested in such a manner as to make them plain and intelligible; and though the partitions and transitions of them are not so formally distinct as in some other books; yet they are perceivable enough to an attentive reader, and will receive great illustration from the analytical works of some expositors.

It must not be dissembled however, that the Hebrew *And why* tongue (wherein a great part of the Bible was written) has *sometimes* many words, consisting of the same syllables, and yet of *not.* very different significations; and that it is defective in several moods and tenses which our modern languages have:

so that, if the translator has mistaken the signification of the word, he spoils the connection; or, if he has not given the verb the right mood and tense, (which, in a great measure, he is obliged to guess at,) there will be a plain incoherence in the sense. Nor must it be forgot, that the present division of the scripture into chapters and verses (though of excellent use to the memory) has sometimes separated things which should have been united, and sometimes united matters that should have been seperated: and this disturbs the sense, and makes it look wild and incoherent to such as are not qualified to observe its propriety and connection in the original.

The causes of some obscurity in the scriptures;

These are some of the causes of the seeming irregularity, and the like may be said of the great obscurity which some have complained of in the Holy Scriptures; *viz.* that, where it is not occasioned by the subject-matter, which sometimes contains mysteries above all human comprehension, and sometimes alludes to customs and transactions which length of time has concealed from our knowledge, it usually happens, when the signification of words is ambiguous and uncertain in the original; when there occur some particular idioms in the Hebrew tongue not so familiar to us; when the construction is intricate, and the words make different senses, according as they are differently joined together; when the style itself is obscure by reason of metaphors and allegories, which are usual in the poetical books; when the writer passes from one subject to another somewhat abruptly, which frequently happens in the prophetical; or when he makes transpositions in the order of narration, as is sometimes perceivable in the historical. But, these cases excepted, (which with a little study and application of our own, as well as attention to those who undertake the exposition of these difficulties, may easily be remedied,) that the Holy Scriptures are, in all points necessary to salvation, and, to all persons of competent understanding, sufficiently plain and intelligible, the very design of God's having them wrote, is a sufficient demonstration. For, as the design of all writing is to convey our thoughts intelligibly to others, so would it be a great reflection upon the divine wisdom, if a book written by God's direction, and for the instruction of mankind, should fall short of that end, which even human compositions seldom fail of.

particularly in the prophets;

We cannot deny indeed but that there is a great obscurity generally spread over the writings of the prophets;

but

but then we affirm, that such obscurity is necessary for wise purposes and providential reasons. For, as the Creator of the world governs it by wisdom, and (where the free will of man is concerned) with great condescension; had the Holy Spirit revealed to the prophets future events so distinctly, as that they might have expressed the most minute circumstance of time, place, persons, &c. in proper terms; had the predictions, I say, been so plain and apparent, that every body, at first sight, might see the whole contrivance, and look through all the scenes of action, they could never have been accomplished, without offering violence (by some miraculous interposition) to men's voluntary determinations. Had God, for instance, foretold our Saviour's crucifixion, with all its particular circumstances, the manner how, the time when, the place where, and the persons by whom, it was to be effected; it is hardly supposable, that the chief priests, and so many principal men among the Jews, would have had an hand in it, without being perfectly carried on to it by an over-ruling power, against their own inclinations; which (besides its contrariety to the principles of human nature) must needs make God *the author of sin*. But since the prophecies concerning the Messias and his sufferings were delivered with such a mixture of obscurity, as never fully to be understood till after their accomplishment, they gave room for the Jews' malice to concur with God's providence in bringing this matter to pass: and so (as St. Paul tells us) [g] *because they knew him not, nor yet the voices of the prophets, they fulfilled them in condemning him*. So necessary it was that all the prophecies of future events should be couched under dark, and enigmatical phrases, lest, by being too plainly foretold, they might possibly chance to destroy themselves, and defeat their own intention.

We acknowledge still farther, that, besides the predictions of the prophets, there are several points contained in scripture quite remote from the common apprehension of mankind, and, in many respects, hard to be understood. But then we must observe withal, that, as these obscure passages are very few in comparison of the plain texts, and no more hinder us from understanding the plain, than the spots in the sun debar us from the light of it; so are they far from reflecting dishonour upon the dispensation itself. If we consider seriously with ourselves, we cannot

And the expediency of some mysteries.

[g] Acts xiii. 27.

cannot but say, that it is more reasonable to suppose, [h] that a revelation from God should contain something different in kind, and more excellent in degree, than what lay open to the common sense of men, or could be discovered even by the most sagacious philosophers. The councils of princes, we know, lie often beyond the ken of their subjects, who can only perceive so much as is revealed by those who sit at the helm, and are often unqualified to judge of the usefulness and tendency even of that, till in due time the scheme unfolds, and is accounted for by succeeding events. This makes the councils of princes revered, and preserves the dignity of the cabinet. And in like manner, why may we not suppose, that [i] as easiness of access is many times known to lay a man open to contempt; so, to protect his revelation from rude encroachments, by impressing an awe and reverential fear upon our minds, God has thought proper to surround it (as it were) with a sacred and majestic obscurity, and, in some parts of it, to exhibit such exalted truths as transcend the reach of human wisdom; thereby to humble the pride and haughtiness of our reason; and thereby to engage us in a closer and more diligent search into such subjects as will every moment furnish us with new matter to entertain the busiest contemplation, to the utmost period of human life.

Reasons for seeming contradictions in scripture. These are some reasons for the obscurity, and the like may be said for the seeming contradictions (especially in matters of chronology) which are said to occur in the sacred writings. For if we consider the different customs and ways of speaking which were in use in former days, but now are obsolete; and yet we might happily reconcile some repugnant expressions, if we were but acquainted with those usages, to which in all probability they allude: if we consider the narrow compass of the Hebrew tongue, wherein one word has sometimes a great many significations; and yet we might make several contradictory passages agree, if we knew but how to give the same word one signification in the first passage, and another in the second: and more especially, if we consider that chronology is a part of learning of all others the most difficult to be adjusted; that the least alteration of a word or letter may make an exceeding great difference; that the Jewish years do not exactly quadrate with those of other nations, either

as

[h] *Vid.* Minute Philosopher, dialogue 6. [i] South's sermons.

as to their length, or their beginning; and that the supernumerary months of kings' reigns do often puzzle the general computation; we cannot much wonder, that in the midst of so many difficulties, there should be found some seeming repugnancies in the sense of some texts, as well as in the accounts of time. But when we consider farther, that by shewing the different acceptation of the words and expressions in these seemingly interfering places; by settling the chronological accounts, and comparing them with other parts of scripture which have an analogy with them; and by using, in short, those several rules of interpretation and criticism which are wont to be employed in the explication of all other authors, all these incongruities are sufficiently cleared up by learned men; we shall be induced to think, that they are so far from invalidating the authority of the Holy Scriptures, that they do, in a great measure, confirm it. For if the scriptures had been written by a cabal of men designing to impose upon the world, undoubtedly these men would have used all circumspection and caution, that no sign of contradiction should have appeared in their writings, because nothing is so exact as a studied cheat; whereas it is no small argument of the veracity of these writers, that they agree with one another in all material points, and only neglect an exactness in some little punctilios, wherein nothing but a confederacy could have made them uniform.

But after all, we talk of contradictions, and other absurdities; of digressions, repetitions, false reasonings, impertinent, and sometimes rediculous relations in scripture, which, upon better examination, will be found reconcileable to good sense, and in some respect prove its very perfection and ornament. We may think it a little strange, for instance, that Cain, upon the murder of his brother, should be introduced, as saying [k] *every one that findeth me shall slay me;* and presently after, as [l] *going into the land of Nod,* and *there building him a city;* wheras, according to the common notion, there were but (besides himself) three persons, his father, mother, and his wife, upon the face of the whole earth: but now, if the word *Kol,* which we render *every one,* may as well be translated *every thing, every creature,* [m] every wild beast of the field,

though no real ones, when inquired into.

[k] Gen. iv. 14. [l] Ver. 17. [m] He was afraid (says Josephus) lest, while he wandered up and down in the earth (which was part of his punishment) he should fall among some beasts, and be slain by them; *Antiq. book* 1. *lib.* 3.

field, (the man's conscience foreboding that God might possibly let loose the brute-creation upon him,) and if, upon a moderate computation, the other descendents of Adam (for Moses takes notice only of the two lines of Cain and Seth) might be numerous enough to stock whole countries with inhabitants, (as some have calculated even to a demonstration) where will the absurdity be then?

Digressions in scripture. It may look perhaps like a careless ramble of thought, to see a prophet, (for it is only the prophetical works that this happens,) after he has begun a plain and methodical discourse upon an incidental word or expression, break out all at once into a long digression, which seems not so suitable to his main purpose; but if we attend to the matter of that digression, we shall generally find it a prediction of the glad tidings of the Gospel, the most important subject that inspired authors can employ their thoughts upon, and what the Holy Ghost took every occasion to suggest to their minds. Nor can we be ignorant, that in the best Heathen writers who pretended to inspiration (as most of their poets did) these very digressions (which were styled episodes) were thought their greatest beauties; and that in some of their loftiest compositions, (such as those of Pindar and Horace,[a] where he imitates Pindar,) these wild excursions were held essential to the poem, the only indications of the divine enthusiasm, and some of the daring flights of a bold aspiring muse, which despised all rules, and disdained to be controlled.

Repetitions in scripture whence occasioned. The repetitions in scripture we may perhaps take offence at, and think them more frequent in the Bible than in any other book. But when it is considered that the several tracts of the Bible were written by different persons, and at different times, it can be no more fault or blemish in it, that its different writers should sometimes happen to say the same things, than that the same history should be written by Appian and Curtius, or the same arguments made use of by Aristotle and Cicero.

This is a case, without a combination, unavoidable. But * when we consider withal, that the things which are said to be so often repeated, are generally such as relate to moral duties, which can never be sufficiently enforced, and that in inculcating these the sacred writers have used all the variety that can be expected; in some places exhorting men to goodness, from the reward; in others, from

---

[a] *Vid.* Carm. l. 3. ode 3. where the digression begins, line 18.
* Boyle of the style of the scriptures.

from the beauty of virtue; in some exhibiting the danger, in some the turpitude, and in others the folly of sin; here commending sobriety from its temporal, and there from its eternal recompence; here representing pride as contemptible to men, and there as hateful to God; and every where diversifying their arguments, to make them work upon the love, the hope, or the fear of their readers, from the consideration of the goodness, the promises, or the justice of God: when we observe the prophets denouncing judgements, sometimes against the people, sometimes against the priests, and at other times against the kings; some reprehending them for their pride, some for their idolatry, and others for their profanation of the Sabbath; one bringing them the joyful news of a restoration from their captivity, and another of their redemption by the Messias: one weeping over the Old Jerusalem, and another ravished with the thoughts of the New: when we consider, I say, this wonderful variety of **fresh matter** in the sacred writers, both moral and prophetical, we cannot but adore the goodness of God, in giving us *line upon line, and precept upon precept*; in condescending so graciously to our infirmities, that in almost every page of his Holy Word he has supplied us with fresh motives and exhortations to those great and momentous duties we are so apt to transgress; and must needs be very grossly prejudised, if we can suppose, that the writings either of Seneca, (who usually feeds his reader with nothing but whipt cream, or a very little sense frothed out into a multitude of words,) or even of the divine Plato himself, (who, stripped of his unintelligible rant, makes but a poor figure in point of solid sense,) any way comparable to the Holy Bible, wherein God seems to have provided for our entertainment, as well as our edification; and to have overspread it with a pleasing diversity of subjects and arguments, in the same manner that he has adorned the creation with a curious variety of plants and animals.

It must not be dissembled indeed, that, what with misrendering the connective particles, which have many different significations, and now and then ° misplacing a parenthesis in the Hebrew tongue, the thread of the discourse comes often to be interrupted; and those who overlook the figurative, and sometimes abrupt way of arguing usual among the eastern nations, (where the reader is often left to make the deduction for himself,) will meet with some perplexities: but where either this is not the case, *and its method of reasoning vindicated;*

° Parentheses were not originally in the Hebrew tongue.

or where these difficulties are surmounted, a man of a competent understanding may see the force and tendency of any scripture-argument as clearly as if it were drawn up in mood and figure. The art of logic is a novel invention, compared with the date of the authors we are now speaking of: and therefore they are not blameable for not being perfect in all the niceties of the Greek schools; especially considering, that even they had been masters of this art, since they were to address themselves to popular auditories, prudence would have directed them to make use of popular arguments, (as we find they did, which, in such a case, the greatest Heathen orators have always employed, and thence found, that they carried their point with better success than in the most irrefragable syllogisms.

[p] The Heathen moralists, we find, urge virtue from the rational topics of conveniency and inconveniency, by displaying the amiableness and advantages of good, and deformity and mischiefs of evil; and are not the arguments which Moses uses to engage the Jews to a compliance with the laws which God enjoined them, drawn from the obligation they owed him for his creating them; from his delivering them from bondage, and making them his chosen people; from the prosperity which their obedience would procure, and the certain calamities which their disobedience would bring upon them; are not the arguments which the prophets use, when they denounce such terrible judgements against them, and tax them with such vile ingratitude, such stupid idolatry, and such other awakening motives to repentance; are not these arguments, I say, as powerful to persuade a nation to abandon their sins, and adhere to the service of God, as the most pompous harangues concerning the wretchedness of vice, and the beatitudes of philosophic virtue? [q] especially, considering, that what these scriptural writers have left us comes backed with the authority of Almighty God, which is instead of a thousand arguments and reasonings.

and its relations neither impertinent, I mention but one objection more, and that is, the impertinence of some relations occurring in the historical, and the ridiculousness of some actions mentioned in the prophetical books of Scripture: but before we pass that censure, we should do well to consider, whether the sacred writers might not possibly have some farther prospect in recording these matters, than we, at this distance of time, are

[p] Young's Sermons. [q] Edwards on the Excellency of the Scripture.

are aware of. The book of Ruth, the history of Isaac and Rebecca, of Joseph and his brethren, &c. (which some are pleased to call little *family-stories*) deserve a better name, even though they were no more than short memoirs of the Jewish history, giving us an account of the lives of some considerable personages of that nation: but when we consider the whole scheme of God's providential dispensation, in sending the Messias into the world, and the method which he was pleased to take in preparing the way for it, by separating one man's family from whose loins the designed Saviour of the world was to descend) from his idolatrous relations and countrymen, and making his offspring the standard of true religious worship for many ages; it is but reasonable to suppose, that some particular account should be given of the origin of this extraordinary family, by which all the world has received such a wonderful benefit, and *all th. kingd ms of the earth have been blessed* in the birth of Jesus Christ. And when we consider farther, that many things relating to Abraham and Sarah, the sacrifice of Isaac, and the captivity and exaltation of Joseph, &c. are so particularly related, because God designed that these occurences should be types and shadows of some things remarkable under the gospel, viz. of the incarnation, passion, resurrection, and ascension of our Lord and Saviour; we cannot but perceive that, if the historian had omitted the relation of these ancient facts Christianity had wanted some considerable evidences of its truth, and the wise scheme of God's providence, in the salvation of the world, had not been so amply displayed.

There is more difficulty indeed, in accounting for some nor ridiculous; passages in the behaviour of the prophets, in whom any indiscretion may be held more inexcusable; because they are all along supposed to be guided by the Holy Ghost; and in those very actions which are thought liable to censure, had the immediate orders and injunctions of God: and yet when we read of Isaiah's [r] *walking naked, and barefoot three years*; of Jeremiah's taking *a long journey, only to carry a linen girdle, and hide it in the hole of the rock of the river Euphrates*; of Ezekiel's [t] *taking his household-stuff, and digging a hole through the wall of the city, to carry it out*, and of Hosea's [u] *going, and taking unto him a wife of whoredoms, and children of whoredoms*, &c. when we

[r] Isa. xx. 3. [s] Jer. xiii. 4. [t] Ezek. xii. 7. [u] Hos i. 2.

we read these extravagant actions, I say, if we were to understand them in a literal sense, we should be apt to account the doers of them distracted, rather than inspired; and under some temptation to think, that, by putting them upon such unaccountable offices, God was minded to make his servants ridiculous. The Scripture, however, has taken care to inform us, that [x] *the spirits of the prophets are subject to the prophets*, i. e. [y] they are not hurried on by a mad enthusiasm, but are always left in a composure of mind, fit to comport themselves, and to speak to the people, as the ministers of a rational and all-wise God.

Now there are three ways whereby learned men have undertaken to account for these seemingly strange and whimsical actions of the prophets. [z] Some suppose, that what, in these and several other places is told, was really and literally performed: others, that it was transacted in vision; and others again, that it is all no more than a parable, dictated by God to the prophet, and by the prophet recited to the people. However, to make these and such like actions of the several prophets, all of a piece and uniform, we are to observe, that whereas some of them are only parabolical, and others impossible to be transacted in reality, (for though Jeremiah, for instance, might take two long journies to Euphrates, about the affair of a girdle, without demurring to the authority of him that sent him; yet we can hardly think that he really sent *bonds and yokes* to the several princes that are mentioned. ch. xxvii. ver. 2. 3. much less that he took the wine cup *from the hand of God*, and made *the kings of all nations*, as is related, ch. xxv. ver. 15. &c. *drink thereof*); whereas, I say, the nature of the thing would not permit these and the like actions to be performed in reality, we have abundant reason to suppose, that they were performed in an imaginary sense only, *i. e.* that these actions of the prophets were, by a divine impulse, represented to them [a] in a dream or trance, which left in their minds a lively idea, and occasioned their publishing to the people, not only the representation themselves, but
what

---

[x] Vid. Lowth on Inspiration. [y] 1 Cor xiv. 32. [z] Waterland's Scripture vindication, part 3.

[a] That these actions of the prophets were not real, but merely imaginary, and such as were represented upon the stage of their fancies, when in a dream or a trance, must be plain to every one who considers the circumstances of them. Smith's select discourses.

what they were likewise designed to typify, with more force and energy. And accordingly we may observe, that, even in the Christian church, when the spirit of prophecy came to revive, these kind emblematical representations were likewise introduced, as is evident, not only from Agabus's taking *St. Paul's girdle,* [b] *and binding his own hands and feet,* to signify what should befal the owner thereof, as soon as he came to Jerusalem, but more particularly from St. Peter's vision [c] *of the sheet let down from heaven, wherein were all manner of four footed beasts of the earth, and wild beasts, and creeping things, and fowls of the air:* Which vision we find him, in his vindication [d] soon after, recounting to the Jews with all boldness, and explaining likewise the symbolical intent of it, *viz.* his commission, and delegation to preach to these Gentiles, in order to their conversion.

Thus we have taken a survey of the scriptures of the Old Testament; found out their authors, and the nature and degree of their inspiration; inquired into the number and order of their books, and by whose care and superintendency they were all digested into one code: traced down their descent, even to our own times, without any loss or considerable alteration; and (what we chiefly intended) endeavoured to satisfy the most popular objections that are usually made against them. And indeed the objections against them would be far from being so many, if we had a little more skill and knowledge in them; but the misfortune is, we live at a great distance from the apostolic age, and much more from the latest times of the inspired writers of the Old Testament, and so must needs be under some difficulties, from our unacquaintance with the style and way of writing, as well as the manners and customs of those ages. There will, of necessity, therefore, be some spots and dark places in them, as there are in the sun, not for want of light and elegance originally in them, (any more than for want of light in the sun), but by reason of some deficiency in ourselves, who are at a distance, and under such circumstances as intercept our sight, and hinder us from making true and exact observations. But if we could stand (as we are to judge of pictures) in the same light in which they were drawn, and had lived in the same ages in which these books were written, we should be able to make a much truer judgement, and penetrate much farther into the meaning of them, than we now can do. And even in our

but, taken all together, very beautiful and excellent.

[b] Acts xxi. 11.   [c] Acts x. 11.   [d] Ch. xi. 5.

our present situation, if we would make any tolerable judgement of them, we must not consider them separately, but as they all together make up a compleat system of religion: and therefore, (to conclude this argument in the words of a pious vindicator of the style of the Holy Scriptures), ᵉ "I conceive, says he, that, as in a lovely face, though the "eye, the nose, the lips, and the other parts, singly look- "ed on, may beget delight, and deserve praise; yet "the whole face must necessarily lose much, by not being "all seen together: so, though the several portions of "Scripture do, irrelatively, and in themseves sufficiently "evidence their heavenly extraction, yet he who shall at- "tentively survey that whole book of canonical writings, "which we now call the *Bible*, and shall judiciously, in "their system, compare and confer them together, may "discern, upon the whole matter, so admirable a con- "texture and disposition, as may manifest that book to "be the work of the same wisdom, which so accurately "composed the book of nature, and so divinely contrived "this vast fabric of the world." And therefore to proceed to other considerations.

The Bible the best and most ancient history in the word. The pretensions of the Egyptians and Chaldeans.

One commendation of that part of the Bible which is called the *Old Testament*, is, that it is the best, as well as most ancient history in the world. The Egyptians of old, we read, contended with the Babylonians and Chaldeans, for the glory of antiquity; and as the Babylonians divide the state of mankind into three governments, *viz*. the first under gods, which (according to them) contains ten generations, the second under demi-gods, or heroes, and the third under kings or men; and during the course of these three states, they reckon up above 30,000 years; so Manetho, the Egyptian historian, to display the antiquity of his nation, and throw the balance on their side, divides, in like manner, his chronological account into the same forms of government of gods, demi-gods, and kings; and from the pretended pillars of Hermes, (whence he compiled his history), makes the whole amount to upwards of 36,525 years. There is good reason, however, why we should despise such monstrous accounts as have only bare words for their foundation, and are plainly contrary to all observations on the progress of mankind, the improvement of husbandry, and the advancement of arts and sciences.

We acknowledge indeed, that the most ancient way of preserving any monuments of learning, in those elder times and

ᵉ Mr Boyle, p. 74.

and especially among the Egyptians, was by inscriptions on pillars; but besides the difficulties of conceiving how pillars of any kind should be able to withstand the violence of the deluge, without being defaced, besides, that no other historian, who has wrote of the affairs of Egypt, has once made mention of these pillars, and that Diodorus (who lived since the time of Manetho) never once quotes him as an author of any credit; there is, in truth, very little in his dynasties, besides names and numbers, except it be now and then a story of the Nile's overflowing with honey, of the moon's growing bigger, of a speaking lamb, and seven kings who successively reigned as many days, one king only a day; and such other strange and romantic accounts, as are enough to invalidate the authority of any writer.

The Chinese at present are very ambitious to be thought an ancient people, and would make us believe, that they can reckon up successions of kings and their reigns, for several thousand years before the beginning of the world assigned by Moses; but besides that, [f] the character which writers (who have lived among them do generally give that nation, *viz.* That they are men of a trifling and credulous curiosity, addicted to search after the philosopher's stone, and a medicine to make them immortal; and whatever advantage their situation and political maxims have given them, are far from being so learned, or so accurate in point of any science, as the Europeans: It is plain, from all accounts, that their antiquities reach no higher than the times of Fohi; for Fohi was their first king, and his age co-incides with that of Noah: So that upon the whole, we have good reason to question the authenticness of those annals which relate such fabulous things, as the sun's not setting for ten days, and the clouds raining gold for three days together. But of what antiquity soever their first writers might be, it is certain, that since the time of Hoan-ti, their XIth emperor, who, about 200 years before Christ, ordered (upon pain of death) all the monuments of antiquity, whether historical or philosophical, to be destroyed; there is little or no credit to be given to the books which they produce: and though they make mighty boasts of the date and perfection of such volumes as they pretend escaped the common wreck; yet if we may credit the testimony of persons who made it their particular business

(when

---

[f] Vid. Le Compte's memoirs, and Bianchini's hist. univers.

(when among them) to inquire, they have not any one copy, in an intelligible character, above 2000 years old.

<small>And Grecians refuted.</small> The Grecians of old were so very great pretenders to antiquity, that they scorned to have any father or founder of their nation assigned them; and therefore they affected to be called *Aborigines, et Genuini Terræ*, the eldest sons of the earth, if not coeval with it: and yet if we look into the date of their historians, we shall find, that none of them exceeded the times of Cyrus and Cambyses, [g] about 550 years before Christ; that several of their ancient writers have left nothing behind them, but barely their names; and that even from those whose works have descended to us, we have no account of any historical facts, older than the Persian war. Herodotus (who wrote a little more than 400 years before Christ) is called by Cicero the *Father of history*, as being the eldest Greek historian that we have extant; and yet when he pretends to relate the origin of any nation, or transactions of any considerable distance, he is forced to intersperse many fabulous reports which himself seems not to believe; and for this reason, some imagine it a point of modesty and ingenuity in him, that he calls the books of his history by the names of the *Muses*, on purpose to let his readers know, that they were not to look for mere history in them, but a mixture of such relations, as (though not strictly true) would nevertheless please and entertain them. However this be, it is certain, that Thucydides, in the very entrance of his history, not only confesses, but largely asserts the impossibility of giving any competent account of the times which preceded the Peloponnesian war; and therefore we find Plutarch, who ventured no farther back than the times of [h] Theseus, (a little before the ministry of Samuel,) justly observing, that, "as historians, in their geographical de-
"scriptions of countries, croud into the farthest parts of
"their maps, those places which they know nothing of,
"with some such remarks as those on the margin; *all
"beyond is nothing but dry desarts, impassable mountains,
"frozen seas, and the like*: So I may well say of the
"facts of history, that are farther off than the times of
"Theseus; *all beyond is nothing but monstrous, and tragical
"fictions*. There the poets, and there the inventors of
"fables dwell: nor is there any thing to be expected
                                                    "worthy

---

[g] Vid. Stillingfleet's Orig. Sac. chap. 4.   [h] Vid. the life of Theseus.

"worthy of credit, or what carries the least appearance of "certainty."

But now, whoever reads the Bible with care and impartiality, in the historical part of it, will find nothing fabulous or romantic; no computations of an immoderate size; no excursions into ages infinite and innumerable; no successions of monarchs, heroes, and demi-gods, for thousands of thousand generations. On the contrary, he will perceive, [1] that Moses, who was above a thousand years older than any historian we know of, (and upon that account deserves the greater credit,) has fixed the beginning of time at a proper period, about 2433 years before his own birth; has given us a fair and authentic history of the origin and formation of the world, of the creation and introduction of the parents of all mankind, of the peopling the earth with inhabitants, and of the first institution of civil government; that he has given the earliest account, not only of all useful callings and employments, such as gardening, husbandry, pasturage of cattle, &c. but of all the politer arts and sciences, such as poetry and music, history, geography, physic, anatomy, and philosophy of all kinds. In a word, he will perceive, that the sacred Bible is not only a record of all the most ancient learning, but a magazine of all learning whatever; and consequently, that he who desires to appear in the capacity of a scholar, either as a critic, a chronologer, an historian, an orator, a disputant, a lawyer, a statesman, a pleader, or a preacher, must not be unacquainted with this inexhaustible fund.

Another commendation of this most excellent book, is, that the language in which a great part of it is written, was the first original language in the world; but then the question is, Which is the original? The writers who have handled this subject, have produced the several claims of the Hebrew, the Chaldean, the Syrian, and the Arabian: but as the arguments for the Syrian and Arabian are but few and trifling, the chief competition seems to lie between the Hebrew and Chaldean.

The Bible wrote in the first and original language.

Now it is natural to suppose, that a primitive language should be plain and easy; should consist of simple and uncompounded sounds; of as few parts of speech, and as few terminations in those parts as possible. [k] Moods and

VOL. I. No. 1.   L   tenses,

---

[1] Edwards on the perfection of the Scriptures. [k] Shuckford's connection of sacred and profane history, vol. 1. lib. 2.

tenses, numbers, and persons in verbs, and the different cases in nouns, we may well imagine were the improvements of art and study, and not any first essay or original production; and in this respect we cannot but conceive, that the Hebrew tongue (I mean as it stands in our Bible, and not as the Rabbins have enlarged it) bids fair for the precedency. Its radical words (which are [1] not many) consist generally of three letters, or two syllables at the most. Its nouns are not declined by different cases, nor are its numbers distinguished by different terminations, as the Latin or Greek are, but by [m] the addition of a short syllable in the dual and plural, which at the same time denominates the gender. The gender is likewise included in the verb, which prevents the necessity of having many pronouns; and by varying its conjugations, (which are seldom irregular,) it has the less use for auxiliary verbs. Add to this, that the Hebrews use seldom any vowels in writing; have no compound nouns or verbs; few prepositions, few adjectives, no comparitives or superlatives; no great number of conjugations; but two moods, two tenses; no gerunds, no supines; and of particles of all kinds far from many; and then we can hardly conceive a language more simple and easy, more short and expressive than theirs.

The pretence of the Chinese and Chaldee.

Upon this account some of late have imagined, that the Chinese might possibly be the first original language of mankind: for besides that Noah very probably settled in these parts, its words are, even now, very few, not above twelve hundred; its nouns are but three hundred and twenty-six, and all its words confessedly monysyllables; so that, whatever the original of this tongue was, it seems very likely to have been the first that was planted in the country: for though it is natural to think, that mankind might begin to form single sounds at first, and afterwards come to enlarge their speech by doubling and redoubling them; yet it is not to be imagined, that if men had first known the copiousness of expression arising from words of more syllables than one, they would ever have reduced their language to its primitive monosyllables. But since we have not a sufficient knowledge of this language to make a competent judgement of it, we must wave its pretensions for the present.

The Chaldee, it must be owned, has a great many marks of this original simplicity in it: but then, what gives the

Hebrew

---

[1] About five hundred.   [m] *Im* is added to the plural in nouns masculine; and *oth* in such as are feminine.

OR PREPARATORY DISCOURSE.

Hebrew a farther claim to priority, are certain proper names of persons mentioned before the flood, such as [n] Adam, Eve, Cain, Abel, Seth, &c.; of ancient countries, such as [o] Lydia, Assyria, &c.; of ancient Heathen Gods, such as [p] Saturn, Jupiter, Belus, Vulcan, &c.; of several kinds of animals, and musical instruments; and in short of mountains, rivers, cities, and places, which derive their etymology, or right signification, from this tongue only; as Bochart, with an immense deal of oriental learning, has abundantly proved.

There are other learned men however, who being willing to compromise the matter between the two languages, (the Hebrew and Chaldee) are apt to fancy, [q] that if any one would be at the pains to examine them strictly, and to take from each what may reasonbly be supposed to be improvements made since their original, he will find the Chaldee and Hebrew tongues to have been at first the same. However that be, it is certain, that those who maintain the perpetuity of the same tongue from Adam to Moses, do assert, that before the confusion of Babel, there was but one universal language among all the nations upon the earth; that this very language (even after the confusion) was continued in its purity, in the family of Seth and Heber, from whom it had its name, and from whom Abraham, the *father of the faithful,* descended; that Abraham, notwithstanding his intercourse with other nations, still preserved this primitive tongue; and his descendents, notwithstanding their sojourning in the land of Egypt, were under no temptation to corrupt it, because they lived separately and by themselves in the land of Goshen, until the ministry of Moses. And if this be a true descent of the tongue, then we are sure, that the Pentateuch, and other books of the Old Testament, were all wrote (except some portions after the Babylonish captivity) in the same sacred primæval language, which God himself spake, which he taught our first parents, and wherein all the patriarchs, and worthies of old among his chosen people, were known to converse.

The Hebrew and Chaldee perhaps originally the same.

---

[n] Thus the word *Adam* comes from the Hebrew *Adamah,* which signifie *earth; Eve* or *Cheva* from *Chiah, life; Cain* from *Canah,* to *possess; Abel* signifies *vanity;* and *Seth* from *Shath,* to *substitute.*   [o] Thus *Lydia* from *Lud; Assyria* from *Assur.*   [p] Thus *Saturn* from *Satur, to hide one's self; Jupiter* from *Jehovah; Belus* from *Baal;* and *Vulcan* from *Tubal-Cain.*
[q] Vid. Shuckford's connection, vol. 1. lib. 2.

In a word, ⁷ the concifeness, fimplicity, energy, and fertility of the Hebrew tongue; the relation it has to the moft ancient oriental languages, which feem to derive their origin from it; the etymology of the names whereby the firft of mankind were called, and the names of animals, which are all fignificant in the Hebrew tongue, and defcribe the nature and property of thefe very animals; characters not to be found in any other language, and yet all meeting together in this, do raife a prejudice very much in favour of its primacy; and this certainly is no fmall commendation of the Bible, that it comprifes the compafs of a language which is the moft ancient, and (as fome think) the moft excellent in the world, and no where elfe to be found. If any critics or grammarians could fay the like concerning the Greek or Latin tongue, *viz.* that there is a certain book wherein either of thefe, in its firft purity, is wholly contained, they would be very lavifh in their encomiums of it, and the prelation of it to all other volumes whatever would not want a proper difplay.

The great refpect fhewn to the Bible,
And indeed, whatever the merry fcoffers of this age, or the graver lovers of fin and fingularity may think, it is certain, that in former days men of all orders and degrees, of the higheft ftation in life, as well as capacity in knowledge, of polite parts, as well as folid judgements, and converfant in all human, as well as divine literature, have all along held the Scriptures in fingular veneration; have employed their wit and eloquence in fetting forth their praife; and not only thought their pens, but poetry itfelf, ennobled by the dignity of fuch a fubject.

by perfons of the higheft rank,
David, in his time, was a confiderable prince, a mighty warrior, and fubduer of the nations that were round him; and yet his living in a military way made him no defpifer of the Scriptures; for obferve what a beautiful panegyric he has given us barely of that part which we call the Pentateuch: ⁸ *The law of the Lord is an undefiled law, converting the foul; the teftimony of the Lord is fure, and giveth wifdom unto the fimple; the ftatutes of the Lord are right, and rejoice the heart; the commandment of the Lord is pure, and giveth light unto the eyes; the judgements of the Lord are true, and righteous altogether: more to be defired are they than gold, yea, than much fine gold: fweeter alfo than the honey and the honey comb.* Moreover,

---

⁷ Calmet's dictionary.   ⁸ Pfal. xix. 7, &c.

ver, by them is thy servant taught, and in keeping of them there is great reward.

Ptolomy Philadelphus was one of the greatest monarchs in his age: he had large armies, fine fleets, vast magazines of warlike stores, and (what was peculiar in his character) he was a person of extensive learning himself, and the generous encourager of all liberal sciences, and so great a greatest collector of books, that in one library at Alexandria he had four hundred thousand volumes; and yet, as if he learning and wit. could not be at ease, nor think his collection complete, without the Bible, [t] he sent for an authentic copy from Jerusalem, and for a number of learned men to make a translation of it into the Greek tongue, for which he plentifully rewarded them: which puts me in mind of Mr. Selden, one of the greatest scholars and antiquaries of his age, and who, in like manner, made vast amassments of books and manuscripts from all parts of the world, (a library perhaps not to be equaled on all accounts, in the universe,) as he was holding a serious conference with Archbishop Usher, a little before he died, he professed to him, that [u] *notwithstanding he had possessed himself of such a vast treasure of books and manuscripts on all ancient subjects, yet he could rest his soul on none but the Scriptures.*

St. Paul was doubtless a good scholar, as well as a good Christian, and his knowledge in polite literature is distinguishable by the several citations which he makes of the ancient Heathen poets: and yet he is not ashamed to give us this character of the Bible: [x] *All scripture is given by the inspiration of God, and is profitable for doctrine, for reproof, for correction, for instruction in righteousness, that the man of God may be perfect, thoroughly furnished unto all good works.* Which calls to my remembrance what [y] another great man of our nation, in a letter to one of his sons, declares; " I have been acquainted somewhat (says he) with
" men and books: I have had long experience in learn-
" ing, and in the world: there is no book like the Bible
" for excellent learning, wisdom, and use; and it is want
" of understanding in them who think or speak other-
" wise.

Longinus, the world must own, was a competent judge of all kinds of eloquence. His little book on the subject, though impaired by the injury of time, has given us

specimen

[t] *Vid.* Prideaux's connection, part 2. l. 2. p. 110. [u] In his life, [x] 2 Tim. iii. 16. [y] Judge Hale.

specimen enough of his exquisite taste that way; and yet, though he was an Heathen, he *gives honour where honour is due*, and seems to praise and admire the true sublime of Moses more than that of any other author he quotes.

Tertullian (if we will think no worse of him for being one of the fathers of the church) was an excellent orator, a great philologist, and an acute reasoner; and yet we find him [z] *adoring the plenitude of the Scripture*. The noble Picus Mirandula was the best linguist and scholar of his age; and yet, after he had run through innumerable volumes, " he rested in the Bible, (as he tells us,) as the " only book wherein he had found out the true eloquence " and wisdom." And therefore it was no wild rant, but a sentence proceeding from mature judgement, that of Robert, king of Sicily, to Fran. Petrarcha: " I tell thee, my " Petrarcha, those holy letters are dearer to me than my " kingdom; and, were I under necessity of quitting one, it " should be my diadem."

We need less wonder then, that we find our profound logician Mr. Locke, declaring, that [a] " the little satisfac- " tion and consistency he found in most of the systems of " divinity, made him betake himself to the sole reading of " the Scripture, which he thought worthy of a diligent " and unbiassed search:" That we find our religious philosopher, Mr. Boyle, (as well as the learned Grotius) asserting the propriety and elegance of the sacred style; and our incomparable Newton [b] giving the preference to Scripture chronology, above that of the Egyptians, Greeks, Chaldeans, or any other nation whatever: That we find, I say, some persons of the most sparkling wit and fancy, descanting either on the sacred history of the Bible, or on some divine matters contained in it; a Milton taking the whole plan, and a great part of the very diction of his lofty poem thence; a Cowley, embellishing the story of King David; a Buchanan, rendering his psalms in Latin verse, and in English; a Prior, paraphrasing on the Ecclesiastes of his son. Which menifestly shews, that some of the greatest personages in the world, the most noble and refined wits, the most knowing and judicious heads, have born the greatest esteem for the Holy Scriptures, and not thought their learning or ingenuity misemployed in their service. And this will give us occasion to enquire a little into some of the principal versions and expositions that have been made of them.

Now

---

[z] Lib. adver. Hermogenem. [a] Jenkin's Preface to his Reasonableness of Christianity. [b] *Vid.* his Chronology of ancient kingdoms amended, *passim*.

Now the [c] first and principal version we have of the Holy Scriptures, is that which we call the *Septuagint* from the 70, or 72 interpreters, which Ptolomy Philadelpus (as we said before) employed in the work. For about the year of the world 3727, he being very intent on making a great liberary at Alexandria, committed the care of that matter to Demetrius Phalerius, a nobleman of Athens, and who at that time was his librarian. Demetrius, pursuant to the King's order, made diligent search every where; and being informed, that among the Jews there was a book of great note, called *The Law of Moses*, he acquainted the King with it; hereupon the King sent to Eleazar, the high priest, requesting him to send an authentic copy thereof, and (because he was ignorant of the Hebrew tongue) to send withal some men of sufficient capacity to translate it into Greek. The messengers who went upon this errand, and carried with them many rich presents for the temple, when they came to Jerusalem, were received with great honour and respect, both by the high-priest and all the people; and having received a copy of *The Law of Moses*, and six elders out of each tribe (*i. e.* seventy-two in all) to translate it, returned to Alexandria. Upon their arrival, the elders, by the King's appointment, betook themselves to the work, and first translated the Pentateuch, and (not long after) the rest of the old testament, into Greek. This is the substance of Aristeas's history; but herein he has intermixed so many strange and incredible things, that [d] many learned men have been inclined to think the whole

The Septuagint version.

of

---

[c] The other Greek translations by Aquila, Symachus, and Theodocian, are now lost, except only some fragments of them which still remain.

[d] *Vid.* Du Pin's history of the canon, *&c.* F. Simon's critical history of the Old Testament; Dr Hoddy *De Bibliorum textibus originalibus*; Dr Prideaux's connection of the Old and New Testament. *&c.* : and the reasons they give for their supposing the whole to be a fiction, are such as these. 1. That Aristeas, who pretends to be an Heathen Greek, speaks all along as a Jew, and (what is more) makes all the parties concerned speak in the same manner. 2. That by the seventy-two elders sent for from Alexandria to Jerusalem, it looks like a Jewish invention framed with respect to their Sandhedrim, which consisted of that number. 3. That the disuse of the Hebrew tongue, and the little acquaintance the Jews had with the Greek make it incredible that there should be found six men in each

tribe

of it a mere fiction, contrived by the Hellenistical Jews of Alexandria, on purpose to give the more sanction and authority to this translation, whose true original they relate to be thus.——Upon the building of Alexandria, and encouragement given to other nations (as well as Greeks and Macedonians) to come and inhabit it, great multitudes of Jews resorted thither. In process of time, they made a considerable part of the city; and by degrees so accustomed themselves to speak the Greek language, that they forgot their own; and were thereupon obliged to have the Scriptures translated into Greek, both for their private use and public service. It was the custom at that time to read the Pentateuch only in the synagogues; and therefore this was the first part of the Scriptures which they translated. In the days of Antiochus Epiphanes, the prophets were introduced, and then they were under a necessity of translating them likewise; [e] and in a short time after some private men might turn the rest of the books (which they call the *Hagiographa*) into the Greek language; and thus the whole version, which, from the fable of Aristeas, goes under the name of *the Septuagint*, came to be compleated. However this be, it is certain that this translation, as soon as it was finished, was held in esteem and veneration, almost equal to

tribe capable of this performance. 4. That the questions which Ptolemy put to the interpreters' and the answers which they returned him, carry with them an air of fiction. 5. That the letters of gold, in which the law was written, the island Pharos, and the cells appointed for the interpreters, their marvellous agreement in every point, and their wonderful dispatch in finishing the whole in seventy-two days, are much of the same cast. And 6. That the prodigious sum which Ptolemy is said to advance, in order to procure this version, in money, in plate, in precious stones, and presents, &c. to the amount of about two millions Sterling, together with many more absurdities and contradictions occurring in the history, is enough to prove it an idle story and romance, without any other foundation, except, that in the reign of Ptolemy Philadelphus, such a version of the law of Moses into the Greek language was made by the Jews of Alexandria; Prideaux's connection, part 2 l. 1.

[e] That this translation was made at different times, and by different persons, the various styles in which the several books are found written, the many ways in which the same Hebrew words, and the same Hebrew things are translated, in different places, and the greater accuracy to be observed in the translation of some books than of others, are a full demonstration; Prideaux, *ib.*

to the original, and was not only used by the Jews in their dispersion through the Grecian cities, but approved by the Grand Sanhedrim at Jerusalem, and always quoted and referred to by our Saviour and his apostles, whenever they made an appeal to the Holy Scriptures.

It is true indeed, (and what every common reader may observe), that there is frequently a manifest difference between this version and the Hebrew text: but the difference may well enough be accounted for, if we will but allow, that the vowels or points in the Hebrew tongue might possibly then not to be in use; that the same words in Hebrew are known to have different significations, which may give the translation a sense different from the original; that the translators themselves sometimes take a greater latitude, and render a passage not literally, but paraphrastically; that at other times they insert a word or two by way of explanation, which are not directly in the text, and perhaps now and then omit a word in the original, which they thought was sufficiently supplied by the emphasis of their Greek expression. These considerations, together with the known ignorance and negligence of transcribers, will account for the difference, if not for the errors and mistakes which occur in the translation. For that the translators themselves did wilfully misinterpret the Hebrew text, is a notion that cannot, with any justice, be admitted, considering that they had no manner of temptation so to do. I should rather think, that if there should be any dangerous corruptions in the Greek copies, [f] they were made after the coming of our Saviour, and when the Jews had utterly rejected him as an impostor; that the Jewish doctors, having got together a sufficient number of these copies, might make in them (what they could not so well do in the Hebrew text) such alterations as they thought proper, in order to justify their infidelity; and that in all probability they did then curtail some prophecies [g]

The reasons of its differing from the Hebrew text.

(as

---

[f] Mr. Whiston, in his Literal accomplishment of Scripture prophecy, and Collection of authentic records belonging to the Old and New Testament, has abundantly shewn, that several texts have been altered, and prophecies dislocated by the Jews in the Old Testament. [g] Thus Dr. Lightfoot observes, that in Isa. ix. 6. instead of these five names of Christ, *Wonderful, Counsellor, the Mighty God, the Everlasting Father, the Prince of Peace*, there is only inserted, *the Angel of the great Counsel*; in *Proem super Quæst in Gen.*

(as we find they are curtailed in the Greek version) relating to the divinity of the Messias; and, having changed the chronology of the LXX, by adding 1400 years to the account, cunningly dispersed them among the long lives of the antediluvian patriarchs, in order to make it believed, that Jesus of Nazareth, whom they crucified, was not the true Messias, but that the time of his appearence was passed and gone (as some of them still assert) a long tract of years before the Christian æra.

and how we ought to receive it.

The result then of all this is—that we ought to have that respect and esteem for the LXX's version which it deserves; not wholly reject it, because most of its errors and faults proceed from the mere mistaking of vowels; from the ambiguity of words; from the liberty which the translators took of paraphrasing; and from the neglect of transcribers: but on the other hand, not wholly embrace it, but rather read it with candour and caution; with caution, because it has fallen into ill hands, and has met with some designing men, who have done their utmost to corrupt it: and with candour, because it is the oldest Greek translation of the Bible; has been made use of by the sacred penman of the New Testament; is conducible to our better understanding the sense of the Hebrew; and as to its disagreement therewith, may, in a great measure, admit of a reconcilation.

The Chaldee paraphrases and why made.

Of all the translations which are in the oriental languages, [h] the Chaldee is of the greatest esteem and reputation among the learned. It is called, by way of eminence, the *Targum*: for as the word *targum* in Chaldee signifies in general *an interpretation*, or version of one language into another; so by the Jews it is appropriated to those paraphrases which go under the names of *Onkelos, Jonathan, Joseph, &c.* The use of these targums was to instruct the vulgar Jews, after their return from the Babylonish captivity: for [i] though many of the better sort retained the knowledge of the Hebrew tongue during that captivity, and taught it their children; and the Holy Scriptures, which were delivered after that time (excepting only some parts of Daniel and Ezra, and one verse in Jeremiah)

---

[h] Besides this, there are other oriental versions, *viz* the Syriac, which is looked upon as genuine and faithful; the Arabic which is neither of any great antiquity or authority; and several others. [i] *Vid* Prideaux's Connection, and Edwards on the Excellence of Scripture,

miah) were all written therein; yet the common people, by having so long conversed with the Babylonians, learned their language, and forgot their own: and therefore, that they might have the Bible in a language which they understood, there were several targums, at several times, made by different persons, and on different parts of Scripture.

The *targum* of *Onkelos*, because it comes up nearest to the standard of the Chaldee, (which is only perfect in the books of Daniel and Ezra,) is thought by some the most ancient; but others give the preference, in point of antiquity, to that of Jonathan, whom they place about thirty years before Christ, under the reign of Herod the Great. Its author is reputed to have lived much about our Saviour's time; and as he undertook to translate the Pentateuch only, so has he rendered it word for word, and, for the most part, very accurately and exactly. That of Onkelos.

That of *Jonathan*, son of Uzziel, which takes in the books of Joshua, Judges, Samuel, Kings, Isaiah, Jeremiah, Ezekiel and the minor prophets, has the like purity of style; but then it is quite different in the manner of its composure: for, instead of being a strict version, it is in many places very lax and paraphrastical, and, especially in the prophets, full of such comments, glosses, and allegories, as do not at all commend the work. Jonathan,

That which goes under the name of *Joseph*, surnamed *The Blind*, comprehends the other parts of Scripture called the *Hagiographa*; such as the book of Psalms, of Job, Esther, Proverbs, &c.; but this, and the rest of the targums, are so barbarous in their style, so full of mistakes, and so loaded with fables, that [k] they seem to be the compositions of some later Talmudists, rather than of any ancient paraphrast. To mention but one more, that of *Jerusalem* is only upon the Pentateuch, and [l] yet it is far from being perfect: for in it whole verses are frequently wanting; some are transposed, and others mutilated, which has made many of opinion, that it is no more than a fragment of some ancient paraphrase which is now lost. and Joseph;

The truth is, the only writings of this kind which the Jews have reason to value themselves upon, are those of Onkelos and Jonathan, and with these they are so infatuated, that they hold them to be of the same authority with the sacred text; and, for the support of this opinion, pretend and of what use they are

[k] *Vid.* Prideaux's Connect. part 2 lib. 8. p. 771.
[l] *Vid.* Calmet's Dictionary on the word *Targum*.

tend to derive them from the same fountain. For they say, "That when God delivered the written law to Moses upon Mount Sinai, he delivered with it, at the same time, the Chaldee paraphrase of Onkelos; and that, when by his Holy Spirit he dictated to the prophets the Scriptures of the prophetical books, he delivered severally to them the targum of Jonathan upon each book at the same time; and that both these targums were delivered down by tradition through such faithful hands as God, by his providence, had appointed; the first from Moses, and the other from the prophets themselves; till at last, through this chain of traditional descent, they came down to the hands of Onkelos and Jonathan, who did nothing more to them than only put them into writing."

How romantic soever this account may be, yet we are not to run into a contrary extreme, and think that these paraphrases are of no significance to us; since it is obvious, that they cannot fail of explaining many words and phrases in the Hebrew original, which will conduce to our better understanding of those scriptures on which they are wrote; and to hand down to us many of the customs and usages of the Jews in vogue in our Saviour's days, and thereby help us to illustrate many obscure passages which occur in the New Testament, as well as the Old.

Of the ancient Latin and vulgar translations; The Latin translations of the Bible, [m] even in St. Austin's time, were almost innumerable; but these were all made from the Septuagint, and not from the Hebrew, until St. Jerom (who was well versed in that language) observing the errors of the many Latin translations, and their frequent disagreement with the original, undertook a new one; and with great care and exactness translated from the Hebrew all the Old Testament, except the Psalms, which being sung in the church in the old Latin or Italian version, could not be changed without giving the people some offence. St. Jerom's translation, however, was not so universally received, but that some bishops (who were not so well acquainted with the Hebrew) absolutely rejected it; whilst others, who were better judges, and saw its conformity to the original, readily embraced it. During the time of this division, both translations were read in public, i. e. some books in St. Jerom's version, and some in

---

[m] Qui enim Scripturas ex Hebræa lingua in Græcam verterunt, numerari possunt; Latini autem interpretes nullo modo. *Aug. De doct. Christi, lib. 2. cap. 11.*

in the Italian, till at length another, which was composed of both, and is called by the Romanists, *Vetus et vulgata*, was thought more correct than either, and accordingly gained the ascendant.

The Romanists would make us believe, that this translation, which they so highly extol, is the very same with St. Jerom's; and that whatever variations may be perceived in it, they were occasioned by the force of time, and the negligence of transcribers. However this be, it cannot be denied, but that it has several considerable faults; that it leaves the original very often, and sometimes runs contrary to it; that it frequently follows the Septuagint, or the Chaldee paraphrase; that it abounds with barbarous words; with many places where its sense is corrupted, and in some quite lost: and yet [n] the Council of Trent thought fit to ordain and declare, "That the same ancient "and vulgar version, which has been approved of, and "used in the church for many ages past, shall be consi-"dered as the authentic version in all public lectures, dis-"putes, sermons, and expositions, which nobody shall pre-"sume to reject, under what pretence soever." A decree, which [o] the authors of that communion are forced to apologize for, by saying, that the Council did not intend thereby to restrain interpreters from consulting the Hebrew, and upon all occasions from rectifying that very translation by the original text; did not intend to compare that translation with the originals, either Hebrew or Greek, but only with the other translations that were then extant; did not intend to pronounce it absolutely perfect, and free from all errors, but only preferable to any other, and proper enough to be declared authentic, if it was but morally consonant to its original.

and the sentiments of the Romanists thereupon.

But whatever the merit or authority of this translation formerly was, not long after the year 1500, there arose several learned men, well skilled in languages, who seeing the corruptions that were in this, as well as other Latin versions, and comparing them with the originals, endeavoured to correct them from these fountains. In the Roman communion, those of the best note, were Ximenius, archbishop of Toledo, who gave us the first polyglot Bible; Sanct. Pagninus, a Dominican monk, who, in his translation, is a rigid observer of the original text, but somewhat

Of modern Latin translations;

---

[n] Sess. 4. [o] Du Pin on the canon, and Father Simon's Critical history.

what obscure; Malvenda, another Dominican, who is grammatical enough, but both obscure and barbarous; Cardinal Cajetan, who is literal without obscurity; the renowned Erasmus, whose version of the new Testament, in all respects, is justly commended; and of the Reformed religion, the most remarkable, are Sebastian Munster, a German, who renders the Hebrew text very closely and exactly; Leo Juda, a Zuinglian, who indulges a kind of paraphrase to make the sense more obvious; Castalio, who wrote in a neat and elegant, but as some think, too florid and affected a style; Theodore Beza, who has translated the New Testament with good success; and Junius and Tremellius, who, with a true and natural simplicity, did both of them jointly translate the Old Testament out of the Hebrew, and Tremellius alone, the New Testament out of the Syriac.

and their use. These are most of the later versions of the Bible which, more or less, have amended the faults of the vulgar Latin, and brought us nearer to the original. Upon the whole, therefore, we may conclude, that these several learned translators are all of them, in their kinds very useful; some, by keeping close to the original, and others, by using a latitude. In the main, they have presented us (tho' in a different style and manner) with the true and genuine meaning of the text: " But wheresoever the Latin transla-
" tors disagree," says a great man p of the Roman communion, and himself an able translator,) " or a reading is
" thought to be corrupted, we must repair to the original,
" in which the Scriptures were wrote: so that the truth
" and sincerity of the translators of the Old Testament
" must be examined by the Hebrew copies; and of the
" New, by the Greek ones."

The English translations. As soon as the Reformation began to appear in England, several editions of the Old and New Testament were published in our tongue. In the year 1527, Tindal translated the Pentateuch, and the New Testament, and afterwards, both he and Coverdale joined in the work, and finished the translation of the whole Bible: which being revised by Matthews, about ten years after, was reprinted. But it had not long been reprinted, before Henry VIII. forbade the sale of that, and every other English translation; and at the same time, ordered Tunstal, bishop of Durham, and Heath, bishop of Rochester, to make a new one, which was published in the year 1541: when, being displeased

p Cardinal Ximenius in his preface to Pope Leo.

sed with that likewise, he forbade all English translations whatever; so that, during this reign, no one was permitted to read the Scriptures in the vulgar tongue, without a proper license. In the reign of Edward VI. the editions of Tindal and Tunstal were revived: but as the life of that prince was but short, upon Queen Mary's succession to the throne, a violent persecution arose, and all English translations (as being done by Protestants, and thought injurious to the Roman cause) were utterly suppressed. During this reign, some Calvinists, who had fled for shelter to Geneva, made a new English translation of the Bible, according to the Geneva form, which was published in that city as soon as finished, but not in London until the year 1598. Many passages in this version were made to favour the Presbyterian cause; and therefore those of the Episcopal party, in the beginning of Queen Elisabeth's reign, endeavoured to get it suppressed; but not being able to accomplish their design, Archbishop Parker, in conjunction with several other bishops, made another translation in opposition to it. This is usually called the *Bishop's Bible*, or *translation*. It was made according to the Hebrew of the Old, and the Greek of the New Testament; but because, in many places, it receded from the Hebrew original, to come nearer to the Septuagint, it was not so well approved by King James I.; and therefore he ordered a new one to be made, which might be more conformable to the Hebrew text.

This is the translation which we read in our churches at this day: only the old version of the Psalms (as it is called; which was made by Bishop Tunstal, is still retained in our public liturgy: and though it cannot be denied, that this translation, especially taking along with it the marginal notes, (which are oftentimes of great service to explain difficult passages,) is one of the most perfect in its kind; yet I hope it will be no detraction to its merit, nor any diminution of the authority of the Holy Scriptures, to wish, that such as are invested with a proper authority, would appoint a regular revisal of it, that where it is faulty, it may be amended; where difficult, rendered more plain; where obscure, cleared up; and, in all points, made as obvious as possible to the apprehension of the meanest reader. *The translation in present use.*

The learned indeed may better dispense with a less perfect version. They know that there are faults in some copies, which must be rectified; sometimes a transposition *Rules for interpreting scripture.*

of terms, which must be replaced in their proper order; and many times various readings, some of which, for several reasons, are to be preferred before others. They know that there is a literal sense and a figurative, which must not be confounded; some propositions, which seem negative, and yet are to be taken interrogatively or affirmatively; and some parentheses, which darken the sense, unless they are more distinctly marked, than they commonly are in most translations. They know that the different pointing of the same Hebrew word gives them quite different senses; that the signification of the Hebrew verb changes according to its conjugation; that there are certain allusions to such customs and usages as explain many difficulties; and several ways of speaking among the Jews, and other eastern nations, which must be adjusted to our ideas. They know, that there are general expressions, which must be restrained to the particular subject in hand, and that the different circumstances of the subject, the connection with what goes before and after, and design of the author, must often determine the meaning.

The defects of our present translation. These, and many more rules of interpretation, are not unknown to the learned: but the common people, who are no less concerned to know the will of God, are entirely ignorant in this respect; and therefore, if a version be defective in several of these particulars, (as those who have examined ours with observation, are forced to acknowledge that it is,) if, when the original is figurative, our translators, in several places, have expressed it in a way not accommodated to our present notions of things, when they might have done it with the same propriety: if, when there is an ambiguity in any word or phrase, they have frequently taken it in a wrong sense; and for want of attending to the transposition or context, have run into some errors, and many times unintelligible diction; if they have committed palpable mistakes in the names of cities and countries, of weights and measures, of fruits and trees, and several of the animals which the Scripture mentions; and, lastly, if, by misapprehending the nature of a proposition, whether it be negative or affirmative, or the tense of a verb, whether past or future, they have fallen upon a sense, in a manner, quite opposite to the original; and, by not attending to some oriental customs, or forms of speech, have represented matters in a dress quite foreign to the English dialect: if in these, and such like instances, I say, our translators have made such mistakes, the people, who

who know not how to rectify them, must be misled; and therefore, to prevent the danger of this, we will instance a little in one or two of the most obvious of them.

Few or none, I hope, are so grossly ignorant, as to think that God has a body like unto ours, though the Suripture attributes *eyes*, *hands*, *mouth*, *bowels*, &c. to him; but yet, since people are ready to receive wrong notions by these, and such like figurative expressions, and since our language has words in abundance whereby to express them in a proper sense, it seems more reasonable, that when the original speaks of God's *hand* it should be traslated God's *power*; his *eyes*, his *care* and *providence*. his *mouth*, his *order and commandments*; his *bowels* his most *tender compassions*. &c.

The Scriptures, we may observe, frequently call cities, kingdoms, and their inhabitants, by the same names with their kings or founders: but certainly a version (if it is designed to be understood) should distinguish them exactly. Thus, the name of *Asher*, when it signifies the son of *Shem* should be kept in the translation; but when it signifies his country, it should be rendered *Assyria*; and when the *inhabitants* of the country, it should be translated *Assyrians*: but this rule of distinction our interpreters, to the great confusion of the reader, have not observed.

Prodigals divert themselves much with that quaint advice of Solomon, (as they call it), ꝗ *Cast thy bread upon the waters, and thou shalt find it after many days*: but would they only observe, that the Hebrew word *Lechem* not only signifies *bread* but likewise *wheat*, whereof it is made; and that the word *majim* not only denotes *waters*, but also *ground that is moist*, or lies near the waters; they might easily perceive, that the sense of the text is, —— *Throw thy grain into moist ground, and, in process of time, thou shalt find it again.*

The profane do likewise abuse another wholesome precept of Solomon, ʳ *Be not righteous over much, neither make thyself over wife*, as if a man can be too righteous, or too wise: whereas, would they but consider, that Solomon is here speaking of that justice which a man is to exercise towards others, (as the context plainly shews), they could not but perceive the propriety of this interpretation; — *Do not exercise justice too rigorously, neither set up for a man of too great wisdom.*

ꝗ Ecclef. xi. 1. ʳ Chap. vii. 16,

Some parents are so very severe and cruel to their children, as to observe no bounds in their correcting them; and they may possibly ground their severity upon this text, *Chasten thy son while there is hope and let not thy soul spare for his crying*, but had they any tolerable skill in the Hebrew tongue, they would soon see, that the latter part of the verse should be thus rendered; *But suffer not thyself to be transported so as to cause him to die.*

It is a strange kind of blessing that which God gives to the tribe of *Asher*, as our translators have ordered it; *Thy shoes shall be iron and brass and as thy days, so shall thy strength be;* but had they considered that the Hebrew word *mineal* never signifies a *shoe* in Scripture, but only a *bolt* or *bar*; and that the word which they render *strength* equally denotes *peace* or *rest*; they would have made better sense of the blessing thus :—— *Thy bolts shall be of iron and brass, and thou shalt have peace in thy days.*

It is a text of much obscurity, and hardly consistent with decency, to say, " *Moab is my wash pot, over Edom will I cast out my shoe, Philistia be thou glad of me*: but now, [x] considering that the word which is rendered *wash-pot*, is employed to express the lowest degree of servitude; and what is rendered a *shoe*, signifies often a *chain*, and so implies a state of *slavery* and bondage; there is a spirit and dignity in the words thus rendered,— *I will reduce the Moabites to the vilest servitude, I will also triumph over the Edomites, and make them my slaves and the Philistines shall add to my triumph.*

To name but one more, it would seem, at this day, not very decent, to see a man go naked; and especially if he pretended to a divine mission, most sober people would conclude him lunatic: and therefore when Isaiah is said to have [y] *walked three years naked and barefoot, for a sign and a wonder upon Egypt, and upon Ethiopia*, we must either suppose that this was [z] only acted in vision, (as several other things recorded of the prophets were), or that all the while he went only without his upper garment, (enough to denominate him *naked*) but wore his other clothes as usual; " For far be it from God (says [a] Mai-
" monides) to make his prophets ridiculous, or to prescribe
" their

---

[s] Prov. xix. 18.   [t] Deut. xxxiii. 25.   [u] Psal. lx. 8.
[x] Essay for a new translation.   [y] Isa. xx 3.   [z] Vid. Smith's select discourses.   [a] More Nev. part 2. chap. 46.

"them such actions, as must of course denote them fools
"and madmen."

These are some of the places wherein our translators
have been manifestly faulty; and I mention it again, that
I have produced these, not with any sinister design, but
purely to clear the sacred oracles from a censure which
the negligence of their interpreters may have possibly
brought upon them; and to shew the world, that the call
for a new, at least a more perfect translation, is neither
groundless nor unreasonable: but then, the question is,
how must this project be put in execution? or, who is the
person sufficient for such a work? My reply to those who
make this inquiry, must be in the sense of such, [b] as
have made it the subject of their most mature deliberation,
and have thereupon thought, that a new English version
might be composed out of our last edition, if improved
with such alterations and amendments, as might make the
style and sense, in many places, more accurate, and accommodate the whole to the taste of the most curious
reader: but then they assert, that the person who is to attempt this, or another translation perfectly new, must have
a competent knowledge of the Hebrew and Greek tongues,
and be daily conversant in reading the Scriptures, in order
to make their phrase and style, and manner of arguing,
familiar to him: must be sufficiently acquainted with the
Jewish, and other oriental rites and customs, their manners and schemes of diction, to which passages, almost
in every page, do allude: must be sufficiently skilled in
history, chronology, geography, &c.; in the proportion
of weights and measures; in the names of plants and animals; and indeed of all arts and sciences, either expressed
or referred to in the Scriptures; must be well versed in
critical learning, in the best commentators, both ancient
and modern; and especially in such writers as have given
us rules and directions preparatory to their right interpretation: that, being thus qualified, he must take abundant
care to have the text of the Bible (from whence he translates) duly established, by an exact collation of it with divers ancient copies, and ancient translations made from the
original language: that he must be a perfect master of the

How to make a new or better translation.

purity

[b] Vid. Father Simon's critical history, l. 3; Du Pin's history of the canon, l 1 c 10.; Dissert. S. Script. interpret.
per D. Whitby; An essay for a new translation of the Bible;
and Edward's excellency of the Holy Scripture.

purity and elegance, the strength and whole compass of the language, whereinto he translates, (because, in the course of the work, he will have frequent occasion to try it all:) that, in the main, he must keep close to the original text; but when the terms of the two languages are found incompatible, must consider the sense rather than the words of the original, if he would either do that or his own translation justice: that he must decline making use of Hebrew, or other exotic words, which, in a translation designed for common use, must needs be improper, as well as barbarous and unintelligible: must modernize a little (to make them more familiar) those words and forms of speech, which allude to ancient nations and customs; and (as some would have it) reduce the old geography, as well as weights and measures, and computations of all kinds, to the names and standards that are now in use: that when any equivocal word or phrase occurs, he must examine every sense, wherein it may be taken, and make choice of that which is most consonant to the author's design, and agrees best with the preceding and following discourse: that when any dark passage presents itself, he must consult those of the like import that are plainer; or (if none such there be) advise with the best commentators, and so determine; laying this down for a certain rule, that whenever a Scripture seems to express any thing contrary to right reason, it must admit of another meaning: and therefore, lastly, he must attend diligently to the different senses of Scripture, figurative and literal; watch narrowly when transpositions of words or phrases occur; when parentheses are wanting or redundant; and in what manner each chapter and verse is divided; because, upon a wrong disposition of these, much obscurity is known oftentimes to arise.

The division of the scriptures into sections, chapters, and verses.

The division of the Pentateuch into sections was of so early a date, that the ancient Jews accounted it one of those constitutions which Moses received from God on Mount Sinai. The whole was divided into 54 sections, according to the number of their Sabbaths in a year; and on each Sabbath day, a different section was read, until the whole number was concluded. After the Babylonish captivity, ᶜ the common people had almost forgot their mother-tongue, and were therefore forced to have the Scriptures, when read to them on the Sabbath day, interpreted in Chaldee: and that the reader and interpreter might keep their proper

ᶜ Vid. Prideaux's connect. part 1. l. 5.

proper periods, every pause was marked with two great points, which the Jews called *soph pasuck*, i. e. *the end of the verse*. In this manner the Jews divided their Scriptures into sections and verses; but the division of them into chapters and numerical verses (as we have them now) is of a much later date.

Hugo de Sancto Caro, (commonly called *Hugo Cardinalis*,) about the year 1240, being minded to write a commentary upon the Old Testament, found it necessary for his design, to invent a concordance; and to make the concordance more useful, he divided the books into shorter sections, than were in the Hebrew Bible; and these sections into subdivisions, the better to make his references. These sections are the chapters into which the Bible has ever since been divided; but the subdivisions were not marked by figures, (as are the verses with us,) but by the capital letters, A, B, C, D, E, F, G, placed on the margin, in equal distances from each other. In this state the Scriptures continued, till about the year 1438, Rabbi Nathan, being in like manner to make a concordance in Hebrew, imitated Hugo in the division of the Scriptural books into chapters; but instead of his capital letters, he took the old way of periods or verses, and distinguished them by numbers; a method which Vatabulus first followed in his edition of the Latin Bible, and Robert Stevens in his of the Greek New Testament; which has ever since been of common use in every edition of the Holy Scriptures, whether in the learned or vulgar languages.

Thus we have taken a sufficient view both of the internal and external parts of the Holy Scriptures, of those of the Old Testament more especially; and the proper result of all our inquiry is, the putting in practice that wholesome advice, which our blessed Saviour gives the Jews; *search the Scriptures, for in them you think* (and think with very great justice) that *you have eternal life*: and to facilitate that search, the design of the following sheets is,— by the help of analytic writers, to give the reader a plain and easy narrative of the historical parts of the Bible; by the assistance of the best critics and commentators, to explain difficult passages, and reconcile seeming contradictions; by the strength of reason and argument, to silence the cavils and objections which have given umbrage to profaneness and infidelity; and by these several means (if possible)

The design of the following work.

⁂ John v. 39.

fible) to retrieve the credit of the sacred writings; to reclaim the heart of the unbeliever, and stop the mouth of the noisy scoffer; to instruct the ignorant, confirm the weak and wavering, satisfy the curious and inquisitive, and, in short, **convince every** sober and impartial inquirer of the truth and justice of the Psalmist's prayer and sentiment, ^c *Teach us, O Lord, the way of thy statutes, and we shall keep it unto the end. Give us understanding, and we shall keep thy law; yea, we shall keep it with our whole heart; for great is the peace which they have, who love thy law and are not offended at it.* Amen.

^c Psal. cxix. 33, 34, 165.

THE

PREFACE.

AFTER so long an Apparatus, there will be less occasion to say much in the preface; and yet I thought it not improper to give the reader a little notice, from what motives it was that I have undertaken this work, and in what method I intend, with the blessing of God, to pursue it.

The Holy Bible itself, I readily grant, is, in a great measure, historical, and an history of an history may seem a solecism to those who do not sufficiently attend to the nature of these sacred writings, whose scope and method, and form of diction, are vastly different from any modern composition: wherein the idiom of the tongue in which it was penned, and the oriental customs to which it alludes, occasion much obscurity; the difference of time wherein it was wrote, and variety of authors concerned therein, a diversity of style, and frequent repetitions; the intermixture of other matters with what is properly historical, a seeming perplexity; the malice of foes, and negligence of scribes, frequent dislocations; and the defect of public records, (in the times of persecution,) a long interruption of about four hundred years; to say nothing that this history relates to one nation only, and concerns itself no farther with the rest of mankind, than as they had some dealings and intercourse with them. Whoever, I say, will give himself the liberty to consider a little the form and composition of the Holy Bible, and the weighty concerns which it contains, must needs be of opinion, that this, of all other books, requires to be explained where it is obscure; methodized where it seems confused; abridged where it seems prolix; supplied where it is defective; and analized when its historical matters lie blended and involved with other quite different subjects. This I call writing *an history of the Bible*: and hereupon I thought, with myself, that if I could but give the reader a plain and succinct narrative of what is purely historical in this sacred book, without the interposition of any other matter; if I could but settle the chronology, and restore the order of

things,

things, by reducing every passage and fact to its proper place and period of time; if I could but (by way of notes and without breaking in upon the series of the narrative part) explain difficult texts, rectify mis-translations, and reconcile seeming contradictions, as they occurred in my way; if I could but supply the defect of the Jewish story, by continuing the account of their affairs under the rule and conduct of the Maccabees; if I could but introduce profane history as I went along, and, at proper distances of time, sum up to my reader what was transacting in other parts of the then known world, while he was perusing the records of the Hebrew worthies; and, at the same time, if I could but answer such questions and objections as infidelity, in all ages, has been too ready to suggest against the truth and authority of the Scriptures; and with all, discuss such passages, and illustrate such facts and events as make the most considerable figure in Holy Writ: If I could but do this, I say, I thought I had undertaken a work which might possibly be of public use and benefit; seasonable at all times, but more especially in the age wherein we live, and (if I may be permitted to apply to myself the apostle's words such as might make me [a] *unto God a sweet savour in Christ in them that are saved, and in them that perish, to the one the savour of death unto death, and to the other the savour of life unto life.*

I am very well aware, that several have gone before me in works of the like denomination; but I may boldly venture to say, that none of them have taken in half that compass of view which I here promise to myself. Blome has given us a very pompous book; but besides that it is no more than a bare translation of *Sieur de Royamont's History of the Old and New Testament*, it omits many material facts, observes no exact series in its narration, but is frequently interrupted by insertions of the sentiments of the fathers, which prove not always very pertinent; and, in short, is remarkable for little or nothing else but the number of its sculptures, which are badly designed, and worse executed. Elwood, in some respects, has acquitted himself much better: he has made a pretty just collection of the Scripture-account of things; but then, when any difficulty occurs, he usually gives us the sacred text itself, without any explanatory note or comment upon it; and so not only leaves his reader's understanding as ignorant as he found it, but his mind in some danger of being tainted by

the

[a] 2 Cor. ii 15, 16.

PREFACE.

the unlawful parallels he makes between the acts of former and later times, and by a certain levity which he difcovers ^b upon feveral occafions, not fo becoming the facrednefs of his fubject. Howel has certainly exceeded all that went before him, both in his defign and execution of it. He has given us a continued relation of Scripture-tranfaction; has filled up the chafm between Malachi and Chrift; has annexed fome notes, which help to explain the difficulties that are chiefly occafioned by the miftakes of our tranflators: but in my opinion, he has been a little too fparing in his notes, and (as fome will have it) too pompous in his diction. He has omitted many things that might juftly deferve his notice, and taken notice of others that feem not fo confiderable. Some very remarkable events he has thought fit to pafs by without any comment; nor has he attempted to vindicate fuch paffages as the lovers of infidelity are apt to lay hold on, in order to entrench themfelves the fafer.

Whatever other men's fentiments might be, thefe things I thought in fome meafure effential, and at this time (more efpecially) extremely neceffary in an hiftory of the Bible; and to encourage my purfuit of this method, I have feveral helps and affiftances which thofe who went before me were not perhaps fo well accommodated with.

The foundation of a lecture by the Honurable Mr Boyle has given occafion for the principles of natural and revealed religion to be fairly ftated and the objections and cavils of infidelity of all kinds to be fully anfwered. The inftitution of another by the Lady Moyer has furnifhed us with feveral tracts, wherein the great articles of our Chriftian faith are ftrenuoufly vindicated, and, as far as the nature of myfteries will allow, accurately explained.

The uncommon licenfe which of late years has been taken to decry all prophecies and miracles, and to expofe feveral portions of Scripture as abfurd and ridiculous, has raifed up fome learned men (God grant that the number of them may every day increafe!) to contend earneftly for the faith, and, by the help of critical knowledge in ancient cuftoms and facred languages, to refcue from their hands fuch texts and paffages as the wicked and unftable were endeavouring to wreft, to the perverfion of other men's faith, as well as their own deftruction. The commentaries and annotations we have upon the Scriptures, both from

^b *Vid.* his account of the plague of lice of Pharaoh and his people; the ftory of Sampfon's foxes, and that of Efther.

PREFACE.

from our own countrymen, and from foreigners, have, of late years, been very folid and elaborate ; the diflertations, or particular treatifes on the moſt remarkable facts and events, extremely learned and judicious ; the harmoniſts, or writers, who endeavour to reconcile feeming contradictions, very accurate and inquifitive ; fuch as have wrote in an analytical way, clear and perfpicuous enough; and (to pafs by feveral others) facred geography has been fully handled by the great Bochart; facred chronology fufficiently afcertained by our renowned Uſher: and the chaſm in the facred ſtory abundantly fupplied by our learned Prideaux ; fo that there are no materials wanting to furnifh out a new and compleat hiſtory of the Bible, even according to the compafs and extent of my ſcheme. That therefore the reader may be apprifed of the method, I propofe to myſelf, and what he may reafonably expect from me, I muſt defire him to obferve, that, according to feveral periods of time, from the creation of the world to the full eſtabliſhment of Chriſtianity, my defign is, to divide the whole work into eight books. Whereof

The I. Will extend from the creation to the deluge.
The II. From the deluge to the call of Abraham.
The III. From the call of Abraham to the departure of the Ifraelites out of Egypt.
The IV. From the departure of the Ifraelites to their entrance into the land of Canaan.
The V. From their entrance into Canaan to the building of Solomon's temple.
The VI. From the building of the temple to the Babylonifh captivity.
The VII. From the captivity to the birth of Chriſt. And
The VIII. From the birth of Chriſt to the completion of the canon of the New Teſtament.

Each of thefe books I purpofe to divide into feveral chapters, and each chapter into three parts. The number of chapters will vary, according as the matter in each period arifes, but the parts in each chapter will be conſtantly the ſame, viz.

1ſt, *A Narrative Part*, which, in plain and eafy diction, will contain the fubſtance of the Scripture-hiſtory for fuch a determinate time.

2dly, *An Argumentative Part*, which will contain an anfwer to fuch objections as may poffibly be made againſt any paflage in the hiſtory comprifed in that time. And,

3dly,

PREFACE.

3dly, A Philological Part, which will contain the sentiments of the learned, both ancient and modern, concerning such remarkable events or transactions as shall happen in that time; or perhaps a summary account of what is most considerable in profane history, towards the conclusion of each period.

That the reader may perceive how I gradually advance in the Sacred History, and, by turning to his Bible, may compare the narrative with the text, and find a proper solution to any difficulty that shall occur in the course of his reading, I shall at the top of the page in each section, set down the book and chapter, or chapters, I have then under consideration, and the date of the year, both from the creation, and before and after the coming of Christ, wherein each remarkable event happened. And, that all things may be made as easy as possible to the reader, I shall take care not to trouble him with any exotic words in the text; but where there is occasion to insert any Hebrew expressions, for his sake, I shall chuse to do it in English characters, and to reduce every thing that I conceive may be above his capacity, to the notes and quotations at the bottom of the page.

The notes (besides the common references) will be only of four kinds.

1st, Additional when a passage is borrowed from any other author, whether foreign or domestic, to confirm or illustrate the matter we are then upon; marked thus *.

2dly, Explanatory when, by producing the right signification of the original, or inquiring into some ancient custom, and the like, we make the passage under consideration more intelligible; marked thus †.

3dly, Reconciliatory; when, by the help of a parallel place, or some logical distinction, we shew the consistency of two or more passages in Scripture, which, at first view, seem to be contradictory; marked ‖.

4thly, What we call *Emendatory* when, by considering the various senses of the original word, and selecting what is most proper, or, by having a due attention to the design of our author and the context, the mistakes in our translations are set right; marked ‡.

So that when the reader sees any of the characteristics, he may be assured what manner of note he is to expect. The chronological and other tables must be reserved to the conclusion of the work.

The Jewish account of Time, Money, and Weights.

An account of the Years, Months, and Kalander of the Jews; together with a reduction of the Money, Weights, and Measures, to the present standard, and manner of computation, to which the reader, in the course of the history, will have frequent occasion to refer.

THE JEWISH YEARS.

THE Hebrews did originally (even as the Syrians and Phœnicians) begin their year from the autumnal equinox: but, upon their coming up out of the land of Egypt, (which happened in the month Nisan,) they, in commemoration of that deliverence, made their year commence at the beginning of that month, which usually happened about the time of the vernal equinox. ^c This form they ever after made use of in the calculation of the times of their feasts, festivals, and all other ecclesiastical concerns; but in all civil matters, as contracts, obligations, and all other affairs that were of a secular nature, they still made use of the old form, and began their year as formerly, from the first of Tisri, which happened about the time of the autumnal equinox: so that the Jews had two ways of beginning their year; their sacred year (as they called it) with the month Nisan, and the civil year, with the month Tisri.

The form of the year which they anciently made use of, was wholly inartificial: for it was not settled by any astronomical rules or calculations, but was made of lunar months set out by the *phasis* or appearance of the moon. When they saw the new moon, they began their months, which sometimes consisted of 29, and sometimes of 30 days, according as the new moon did sooner or later appear. The reason of this was, because the synodical course of the moon, (*i. e.* from new moon to new moon) being 29 days and a half, the half day, (which a month of 29 days fell short of) was made up, by adding it to the next month, which made it consist of 30 days: so that their months were made up of 29 days, or 30 days, successively and alternately; with this certain rule, that the first or initial month (whether of their sacred or civil year) always consisted of 30 days, and the first day of each month was called

---

^c Prideaux's Connection, in the preface.

called the new moon. Of twelve of these months did their common year consist: but as twelve lunar months fell eleven days short of a solar year, so every one of these common years began eleven days sooner, which, in thirty years time, would carry back the beginning of the year through all the four seasons, to the same point again, and get a whole year from the solar reckoning. To remedy therefore the confusion that might from hence arise, their custom was, sometimes in the third year, and sometimes in the second, to cast in another month, (which they called *Veader*, or the second *Adar*,) and make their year then consist of thirteen months; so that by the help of this intercalation, they reduced their lunar year in some measure to that of the sun, and never suffered the one, for any more than a month at any time, to vary from the other.

This intercalation of a month, however, every second or third year, makes it impracticable to fix the beginnings of the Jewish months to any certain day in the Julian kalendar; but they therein always fell within the compass of 30 days, sooner or later, I have given the reader the best view I could of their co-incidence and correspondency, in the following scheme, wherein the first column gives the several names and order of the Jewish months, and the second of the Julian within the compass of which the said Jewish months have always, sooner or later their beginning and ending.

Jewish Months.

1 *Nisan*	takes in part of	March and April	7 *Tisri*	takes in part of	September and October
2 *Jyar*		April and May	8 *Machesvan*		October and November
3 *Sivan*		May and June	9 *Cisleu*		November and December
4 *Tamuz*		June and July	10 *Tebeth*		December and January
5 *Ab*		July and August	11 *Shebat*		January and February
6 *Elul*		August and September	12 *Adar*		February and March

The thirteenth month (*Veader*) is then only intercalated, or cast in, when the beginning of Nisan would otherwise be carried back into the end of February.

The Jewish account of Time, Money, and Weights.

The Jews of old had very exact kalendars, wherein were set down their several fasts and festivals, and all those days wherein they celebrated the memory of any great event that had happened in their nation; but these are no longer extant. All they have that favours of any antiquity, is their *Megillah Thaanith* or *Volume of affliction*, which contains the days of fasting and feasting that were heretofore in use among them, but are now laid aside; and therefore no longer to be found in their common kalendars. Out of this volume, however, as well as some of their other kalendars, I thought it not improper to set down some of their historical events, in order to let the reader see on what particular day of each month their memorial (whether by fasting or feasting) was observed.

THE JEWISH KALENDAR.

Months.	Days
2. NISAN or ABIB.	I. New moon. Beginning of the sacred or ecclesiastical year, a fast for the death of the children of Aaron, Lev. x. 1, 2.
	X. A fast for the death of Miriam, the sister of Moses, Numb. xx. 1.
	XIV. The Paschal Lamb slain on the evening of this day.
	XV. The great and solemn feast of the Passover.
	XVI. The oblation of the first fruits of the harvest.
	XXI. The conclusion of the Passover, or end of unleavened bread.
	XXIV. A fast for the death of Joshua.
2. JYAR or JIAR.	VII. The dedication of the temple, when the Asmoneans consecrated it again after the persecutions of the Greeks.
	X. A fast for the death of the high-priest Eli, and for the taking of the ark by the Philistines.
	XXIII. A feast for the taking of the city of Gaza by Simon Maccabeus, 1 Mac. xiii. 43, 44.
	XXVIII. A fast for the death of the prophet Samuel, 1 Sam. xxv. 1.

3. SIVAN.

Months.	Days
3. Sivan.	VI. *Pentecost*, or the fiftieth day after the passover, called likewise the *feast of weeks*, becaufe it happened feven weeks after the paffover.
	XV. A feaft for the victory of the Maccabees over the people of Bethfam, 1 Mac. v. 52.
	XVII. A feaft for the taking of Cæfarea by the Afmoneans.
	XXVII. A faft in remembrance of Jeroboam's forbidding his fubjects to carry their firft fruits to Jerufalem, 1 Kings xii. 27.
	XXX. A feaft in memory of the folemn judgement given by Alexander the Great, in favour of the Jews, againft the Ifhmaelites and Egyptians.
4. Tamuz or Thammuz.	IX. A faft for the taking of Jerufalem on that day, but whether by Nebuchadnezzar, Antiochus Epiphanes, or the Romans, it is not faid.
	XVII. A faft in memory of the tables of the law that were broken by Mofes, Exod. xxxii. 15.
5. Ab.	IX. A faft in memory of God's declaring to Mofes (as on this day) that none of the murmuring Ifraelites fhould enter into the land of Canaan, Numb. xiv. 29, 31.
	X. A faft, becaufe, on this fame day, the city and temple were taken and burnt, firft by the Chaldeans, and afterwards by the Romans.
	XVIII. A faft, becaufe that, in the time of Ahab, the evening lamp went out.
6. Elul.	VII. A feaft in memory of the dedication of the walls of Jerufalem by Nehemiah, Ezra, vi 16.
	XVII. A faft for the death of the fpies, who brought an ill report of the land of promife, Numb. xiv. 36, 37.

7. Tisri.

Months.	Days
7. TISRI.	I. The feast of trumpets, Lev. xxiii. 34. Numb. xxix. 1, 2.

III. A fast for the death of Gedaliah, whereupon the expulsion of the people, and the utter destruction of the land ensued, Jer. xli. 2.

VII. A fast for the Israelites worshipping the golden calf, and the sentence which God pronounced against them in consequence of that crime, Exod. xxxii. 6, &c.

X. The fast of expiation, as some think, in memory of man's fall, and expulsion out of paradise, Lev. xxiii. 19.

XV. The feast of tabernacles, in memory of their dwelling in tents, in their passage through the wilderness, Lev. xxiii. 34.

XXIII. The rejoicing for the law; or a feast instituted in memory of the law, which God gave them by the hand of Moses.

8 MARCHESVAN. VI. A fast upon the occasion of Nebuchadnezzar's putting out Zedekiah's eyes, after that he had slain his children in his fight, 2 Kings xxv. 7. Jer. lii. 11.

9. CISLEU. VI. A fast in memory of the book of Jeremiah torn and burnt by King Jehoiachim, Jer. xxxvi. 23.

VII. A feast in memory of the death of Herod the Great, a bitter enemy to the sages.

XXI. The feast of Mount Gerizim, upon their obtaining leave of Alexander the Great to destroy the temple of Samaria, which was situate there.

XXV. The feast of dedication, *viz.* of the temple, profaned by the order of Antiochus Epiphanes, and repaired and beautified by the care of Judas Maccabeus. This festival Christ honoured with his presence at Jerusalem. It is likewise called *the feast of lights*, because, during the time

The Jewish account of Time, Money, and Weights.

Months.	Days
	time of its celebration, the people were used to illuminate their houses, by setting up candles at every one's door. *Vid.* 1 Macc. iv. 52.; 2 Macc. ii. 16.; John x. 22.
10. TEBETH.	X. A fast in memory of the siege of Jerusalem, by Nebuchadnezzar, 2 Kings xxv. 1.
	XXVIII. A feast for the exclusion of the Sadducees out of the Sanhedrim, where they had once all the power.
11. SHEBETH.	IV. A fast in memory of the death of the elders who succeeded Joshua, Judg. ii. 10.
	XV. *The beginning of the years of trees*, when they were first allowed to eat the fruit thereof, after they were four years planted, Lev. xix. 23, *&c.*
	XXIII. A fast for the war of the ten tribes against that of Benjamin, for the outrage committed upon the body of the Levite's wife, Judg. xx.
	XXIX. A memorial of the death of Antiochus Epiphanes, a cruel enemy to the Jews, 1 Mac. vi.
12 ADAR.	VII. A fast in remembrance of the death of Moses, Deut. xxxiv. 5.
	XIII. Esther's fast, probably in memory of that which is mentioned in Esther iv. 16.
	XV. A feast in memory of the death of Nicanor, a bitter enemy to the Jews, 1 Mac. xv. 30.
	The feast of *Purim* or *Lots*; because, when Haman purposed to destroy all the Jews that were in Persia, according to the superstition of the country, he first drew lots, to know on what day of the year it would be best to put his design in execution, from whence the feast, in commemoration

Months.   Days
memoration of their escape, took its name.
XIII. The dedication of the temple of Zerubbabel, Ezra vi. 16.
XXVIII. A feast in commemoration of the repeal of the decree whereby the kings of Greece had forbidden the Jews to circumcise their children, to observe the Sabbath, and to reject foreign worship.

When the year consists of thirteen months, here is the place where the second month of *Adar*, or *Veader*, by way of intercalation, comes in.

JEWISH MONEY.

The custom of making money, of such a form, such an alloy, and such a determinate value, is not so ancient as some may imagine. [d] The original way of commerce was certainly by way of barter, or exchanging one kind of merchandise for another, as it is the custom, in some places, even to this day. In process of time, such metals as were generally esteemed to be most valuable, were received into traffic, but then the custom was to weigh them out to one another; till, finding the delays and other inconveniencies of this method, they agreed to give each metal a certain mark, a certain weight, and a certain degree of alloy, in order to fix its value; but it was a long while before men came into this agreement. The coinage of money among the Persians, Greeks, and Romans, was but of late date; among the Persians, no older than the times of Darius, son of Hystaspes; and among the Grecians, (from whom the Romans very probably took it,) of the same date with Alexander. We have no traces of this practice among the ancient Egyptians, before the time of the Ptolemies; nor had the Hebrews this custom among them, [e] until the government of Simon

---

[d] Calmet's dissertation, vol. 1.   [e] And yet the Jews have a tradition, that not only Joshua, David, and Mordecai, but even Abraham himself had found out the way of coining. It is said of Abraham indeed, that *he was very rich in silver and gold*, Gen. xiii. 2. But we no where read that this money

mon Maccabeus, to whom Antiochus Sidetes, King of Syria, granted the privilege of coining his own money in Judea.

Before that time, they made all their payments by weight: and therefore the reader need lefs wonder, that one and the fame word fhould denote both a certain weight of any commodity, and fuch a ᶠ determinate fum of money; what he has to remark is this —— ᵍ That among the ancients, the proportion of gold to filver was moft commonly as ten to one; fometimes it raifed to be as eleven to one, fometimes as twelve, and fometimes as thirteen: that though, in the time of King Edward I. it was here in England at fo low an eftimate as ten to one; yet it is now advanced to the value of fixteen to one, and in all the reductions of this kind that we make, is to be fo computed.

	l.	*s.*	*d.*	*q.*
The Gerah,	000	00	01	3
The Hebrew Drachm,	000	00	09	
Two Drachms made a Bekah,	000	01	06	
Two Bekahs made a Shekel,	000	03	00	
Sixty Shekels made a Mina,	009	00	00	
Fifty Minas made Talent,	450	00	00	
A Talent of gold, fixteen to one,	7200	00	00	

Jewish Weights.

	lb.	*oz.*	*gr. dec.*
The Gerah,	000	00	10 95
The Hebrew Drachm or Zuza,	000	00	54 75
Two Zuzas made a Bekath,	000	00	109½
Two Bekaths made a Shekel,	000	00	219
An hundred Shekels made a Mineth,	050	00	00
Thirty Mineths made a Talent,	1500	00	00

Measures money was ftamped with any impreffion; and yet the Jewifh tradition runs thus, *viz.* "That on Abraham's money were ftamped on one fide an old man and an old woman, on the other, a young man and a young maid; on Jofhua's money, on one fide an ox, on the other a monoceros: on David's money, on one fide a ftaff and a fcrip, on the other a tower; and on Mordecai's money, on one fide fackcloth and afhes, on the other a crown." But this feems to have the air of a Rabbinical fiction; *Lewis's Antiq Heb. lib. 6.* ᶠ For fo the word *fhakel* comes from *fhakal to weigh*; and may properly be interpreted *the weight; Lewis, ibid.* ᵍ Prideaux's connection, in the preface.

Measures of Length.

	Eng. feet. inch.	
The Hebrew Cubit, somewhat more than	0	21
The Zerith, or Span, a little more than	0	10
The Span of a Cubit, a little above	0	7
The Palm, or hand's breadth, somewhat above	0	3
The Fathom, which makes 4 Cubits, above	7	0
Ezekiel's Reed, which was 6 Cubits, above	10	0
The ancient Measuring-line, or Chain, which was 80 Cubits, above	145	0
A Sabbath day's journey, 2000 Cubits	3648	0

	Miles. Paces. Feet.		
An Eastern mile, 4000 Cubits,	1	10	0
A day's journey generally computed much about	33	0	0

Measures of Capacity.

Dry Measures.	*Liquid Measures.*
The Cab contained a quarter of a peck.	The Log came near to our pint.
The Omer, or Gnomer in the Hebrew, was the tenth part of an Ephah.	12 Logs made an Hin, which answered our gallon.
The Ephah is computed to be about our bushel; and	6 Hins made a Bath, which was about six gallons; and
The Homer is supposed to be ten.	10 Baths made an Homer, which was 60.

The reader will be pleased to observe, that in the valuation of money, I have chiefly followed Dean Prideaux, in his preface to the first part of his Connection of sacred and profane history, and in the reduction of weights and measures, our learned Cumberland: but whoever desires a fuller account of these matters, may consult the said Bishop Cumberland, Of the Jewish weights, measures, and monies; Mr. Brerewood, *De ponderibus et pretiis veterum nummorum;* Dr. Bernard, *De mensuris et ponderibus antiquis;* and others that have written on this argument, which is not a little difficult and perplexing.

THE
HISTORY
OF THE
BIBLE.

BOOK I.

CONTAINING AN ACCOUNT OF THINGS FROM THE CREA-
TION TO THE FLOOD; IN ALL, 1656 YEARS.

CHAP. I.

Of the Creation of the World.

THE INTRODUCTION.

THE chief design of the author of the Pentateuch is, to give a short account of the formation of the earth, and the origin of mankind; of the most remarkable events that attended them in the infancy of the world; and of the transactions of one particular nation more especially, from whence the Messias was to spring: and therefore it cannot well be expected, that he should extend his history to the creation of the supreme empyrean heaven, which God might make the place of his own residence, and the mansions of those celestial beings, whom he constituted the ministers of his court, and attendants on his throne *, an immense space of time, perhaps,

A. M. 1.
Ant. Chrif.
4004.
Gen. ch. 1.
and part of
ch. 2.

} The crea-
tion of the
supreme
heaven not
included in
Moses's ac-
count.

---

* This is no novel notion of our own, but what has been confirmed by many great authorities, as the learned and ingenious
Dr. Burnet testifies. For, speaking of some, who supposed that
the whole universe was created at one and the same time, and
the

A. M. 1.
Ant. Chrif.
4004.
Gen. ch. 1.
and part of ch. 2.

perhaps, before the Mosaic account of the origination of this planetary world begins.

In the introduction of the history indeed we are told, that *God created † the heaven and the earth:* but, when it is considered, that *heaven,* in Scripture-language, is very commonly set to signify no more than the upper region of the air; that we frequently read of [a] *the firmament of heaven,* [b] *the windows of heaven,* [c] *the bottles of heaven, and* [d] *the hoary frost of heaven,* &c. none of which extend beyond our atmosphere, we have no grounds to conclude, that at one and the same time God created every thing that is contained in the vast extra-mundane spaces of the universe. On the contrary, when we find him recounting to Job, that at the time [e] *when he laid the foundations of the earth, the morning stars sang together,* and

the highest heaven and angels included in the first day's work, " Hieronymi verba," says he, " libet hic opponere. *Sex mille* " *needum nostri orbis implentur anni, et quantas prius æternitates,* " *quanta tempora, quantas seculorum origines fuisse arbitrandum est,* " *in quibus angeli, throni, dominiones, cæteræque virtutes servierint* " *Deo.* In libro De Trinitate, (sive Novitiani, sive Tertulliani " fit,) tam mundus angelicus, quam super-firmamentarius, " conditus dicitur ante mundum Mosaicum, his verbis, *Quam* " *etiam superioribus. i. e. super ipsum quoque solidamentum partibus,* " *angelos prius instituerit Deus, spirituales virtutes digesserit, thro-* " *nos potestatesque præfecerit, et alia multa cælorum immensa spatia* " *condiderit,* &c. *ut hic mundus novissimum magis Dei opus esse ap-* " *pareat, quam solum & unicum.* Denique Catholicorum com- " munem hanc fuisse sententiam, notat Cassianus suo tempore, " nempe seculo quinto inuente: *ante illud Geneseos temporale* " *principium, omnes illas potestates cælestes Deum creasse, non* " *dubium est;*" Burnet's Archæolog. Phisoph. c. 8.

† By *heaven,* some understand in this place the highest super-firmamentary heaven, and by the *earth,* that pre-existent matter whereof the earth was originally made: and so the sense of the words will be—— " that God at first created the matter whereof the whole universe was composed, all at once, in an instant, and by a word's speaking; but it was the supreme heaven only which he then finished, and formed into a most excellent order, for the place of his own residence, and the habitation of his holy angels; the earth was left rude and indigested, in the manner that Moses has described it, until there should be a fit occasion for its being revised, and set in order likewise."

[a] Gen. i. 20.   [b] Gen vii. 11.   [c] Job. xxxviii. 37.
[d] *Ibid.* ver. 29.   [e] *Ibid.* ver. 4, 7.

Chap. I. *from the Creation to the Flood.* 3

and all the sons of God shouted for joy, we cannot but infer, that these *stars*, and these *sons of God*, were pre-existent; and consequently no part of the Mosaic creation.

A. M. 1.
Ant. Chrif. 4004.
Gen. ch. 1. and part of ch. 2.

By *the heaven* therefore we are to understand no more, than that part of the world which we behold above us: but then I imagine we have very good reason to extend our conceptions of this world above us so far, as to include in it the whole planetary system. † The truth is, the several planets that are contained within the *magnus orbis*,
(as

---

† The better to understand this, and some other matters, in our explication of the formation of celestical bodies, it is proper to observe, that there are three more remarkable systems of the world, the Ptolemaic, Copernican, and what is called the New System, which astronomers have devised.

1*st*. In the Ptolemaic, the earth and waters are supposed to be in the centre of the universe, next to which is the element of air, and next above that the element of fire; then the orb of Mercury, then that of Venus, and then that of the Sun; above the sun's orb those of Mars Jupiter, and Saturn; and above them all, the orbs of the fixed stars, then the chrystalline orbs, and lastly, the *cælum empyreum*, or *heaven of heavens*. All these massy orbs, and vast bodies borne by them, are in this system supposed to move round the terraqueous globe once in twenty four hours; and beside that, to perform other revolutions in certain periodical times, according to their distance from the supposed centre, and the different circumference they take.

2*dly*, In the Copernican system, the sun is supposed to be in the centre, and the heavens and earth to revolve round about it, according to their several periods; first Mercury, then Venus, then the Earth with its satellite the Moon; then Mars, then Jupiter with its four moons; lastly, Saturn with its five, or more moons revolving round it; and beyond, or above all these, is the firmament, or region of fixed stars, which are all supposed to be at equal distances from their centre the sun.

3*dly*, In the New System, the sun and planets have the same site and position as in the Copernican; but then, whereas the Copernican supposes the firmament of the fixed stars to be the bounds of the universe, and placed at equal distance from its centre the sun; this new hypothesis supposes, that there are many more systems of suns and planets, besides that in which we have our habitation; that every fixed star, in short, is a sun, encompassed with its complement of planets, both primary and secondary, as well as ours; and that these stars, with their planets are placed at regular distances from each other, and, according to their distances from us, seem to vary in their respective magnitudes; *Derham's Astra-theology*, in the preliminary discourse.

A. M. 1.
Ant. Chrif.
4004
Gen. ch 1.
and part of
ch 2.

(as it is called), or the circle which Saturn deſcribes about the ſun, have ſo near a ſimilitude and relation: the ſame form, the ſame centre, and the ſame common luminary with one another, that it can hardly be imagined but that they were the production of one and the ſame creation. And therefore, though the hiſtorian ſeems chiefly to regard the earth in his whole narration; yet there is reaſon to preſume, that the other parts of the planetary world went all along on in the ſame degrees of formation with it.

That this world was formed out of a pre exiſting chaos

2*dly*, It is to be obſerved farther, that this planetary world, or ſyſtem of things, was not immediately created out of nothing, (as very probably the ſupreme heavens were,) but out of ſome ſuch pre-exiſtent matter as the ancient Heathens were wont to call *chaos*. And accordingly we may obſerve, that in the hiſtory which Moſes gives us of the creation, he does not ſay, that God at once made all things in their full perfection, but that * *In the beginning he created the earth, i. e.* the matter whereof the chaos was compoſed, which *was without form,* without any ſhape or order, *and void*, without any thing living or growing in it; *and darkneſs was upon the face of the waters,* nothing was ſeen for want of light, which lay buried in the vaſt abyſs.

Accord-

---

* What our tranſlators render [*in the beginning*] ſome learned men have made [*in wiſdom*] *God created the heavens and the earth;* not only becauſe the Jeruſalem targum has it ſo, but becauſe the Pſalmiſt, paraphraſing upon the works of the creation, breaks forth into this admiration. *O Lord! how wonderful are thy works, in wiſdom haſt thou made them all.* Pſal. civ. 24. And again, exhorting us to give thanks unto the Lord for his manifold mercies, he adds *who by wiſdom made the heavens,* ibid. cxxxvi. 5. where, by *wiſdom,* as ſome imagine, he means the *ſon of God,* by whom (ſays the Evangeliſt, John i. 3.) *all things were made, or all things created* (ſays the apoſtle, Col. i. 16.) *that are in heaven, and that are in the earth;* and therefore the meaning of the phraſe muſt be, that God, in creating the world, made uſe of the agency of his ſon. *Fuit hæc apud antiquos* [ſays Petavius, *De officio ſex dierum, l. 1. c. 1.*] *pervagata, multumque communis opinio, principii nomine verbum ſignificari, ſeu filium.* And to this interpretation the word *Elohim* in the plural number, joined with *bara* a verb ſingular, ſeems to give ſome countenance; though others are of opinion, that a noun plural, governing a verb ſingular, is no more than the common idiom of the Hebrew tongue; and for this idiom a very conſiderable commentator

Chap. I. *from the Creation to the Flood.*

According to tradition then, and the representation which this inspired author seems to give us, * this chaos was a fluid mass, wherein were the materials and ingredients of all bodies, but mingled in confusion with one another, so that heavy and light, dense and rare, fluid and solid particles, were jumbled together, and the atoms or small constituent parts of fire, air, water, and earth, (which have since obtained the name of *elements*), were every one in every place, and all in a wild confusion and disorder. This seems to be a part of God's original creation; but why he suffered it to continue so long, before he transformed it into an habitable world, is a question only resolvable into the divine pleasure: since, according to the ideas we have of his moral perfections, there is nothing to fix the creation of any thing sooner or later, than his own arbitrary will determined. Only we may imagine, that, after the revolt of so many angels, God, intending to make a new race of creatures, in order to supply their place, and fill up (as it were) the vacancy in heaven; and withal, resolving to make trial of their obedience before he admitted them into his beatific presence, singled out one (as perhaps * there might be many chaotic bodies in the universe) placed at a proper distance from his own empyrean seat, to be the habitation

A. M. 1.
Ant. Chrif.
4004.
Gen. ch. 1.
and part of
ch. 2.

mentator assigns this reason— : That the Hebrew language was originally that of the Canaanites, a people strangely addicted to idolatry and polytheism; and who therefore made more use of the plural *Elohim*, than of the singular *Eloah*; which usage the Jews continued, though they were zealous asserters of the unity of the Godhead, and thereupon most commonly joined a verb of the singular number with it, pursuant to their notions of the divine unity; *Le Clerc's differt. De ling. Hebraica.*

* To mention one author out of the many which Grotius has cited, Ovid, in the beginning of his Metamorphoses has given us this description of it :

Ante mare, et terras, et quod tegit omnia, cœlum,
Unus erat toto naturæ vultus in orbe,
Quem dixere *chaos* : rudis, indigestaque moles,
Nec quicquam, nisi pondus iniris, congestaque eodem
Non bene junctarum discordia semina rerum, &c.

* Si materia chaus extitit ante mundi Mosaici principium, quid fuit, quem in finem extitit aut ubinam loci ante illud tempus? Respondeo, hæc non esse nimis sollicitè quærenda, cum magnâ ex parte notitiam nostriam fugiant. Sed vidimus quandoque novas stellas in cœlo oriri, quæ nunquam antea apparuerant ; quas tamen

¹ A. M. 1.
Ant. Chrif.
4004.
Gen. ch. 1.
and part of
ch. 2.

The wisdom of Moses's account of things.

bitation of the creatures he was about to form, and might delay the fitting it up for them until the time which his infinite wisdom had determined for their creation was fully come.

3*dly*, It is to be oferved farther, that though Moses might have in his view the whole planetary fyftem, and know very well, that every day each planet advanced in the fame proportion, as the earth did in its formation: yet what he principally chofe to infift on (as a fpecimen of all the reft) was this fublunary creation. He who was verfed in all *the learning of the Egyptians*, could not be unacquainted with the vulgar, or what is ufually called the *Ptolemaic hypothefis*, which came originally from Egypt into Greece; and yet, inftead of exprefsing his notions according to this, or any other fyftem, we find him giving us a plain narrative, how matters were tranfacted, without afferting or denying any philofophic truth. Had he indeed talked a great deal of globular and angular particles, of centrical motion, planetary vortices, atmofpheres of comets, the earth's rotation, and the fun's reft, he might pofsibly have pleafed the tafte of fome theorifts better; but theories we know are things of uncertain mode. They depend in a great meafure upon the humour and caprice of an age, which is fometimes in love with one, and fometimes with another. But this account of Mofes was to laft for ever, as being the ground-work which God defigned for all his future revelations; and therefore it was requifite to have it framed in fuch a manner, as that it might condefcend to the meaneft capacity, and yet not contradict any received notions of philofophy.

The Jews, it muft be owned, were a nation of no great genius for learning; and therefore, if Mofes had given them a falfe fyftem of the creation, fuch as a fimple people might be apt to fancy, he had both made himfelf an impoftor, and expofed his writings to the contempt and derifion of every man of underftanding: and yet, to have given them a particular explication of the true one, muft have

tamen præextitiffe, fub aliquâformâ, et alicubi locorum, æquum eft credamus. Præterea, cometas fæpe in cœlo advertimus, quarum origo, et primæ fedes nos latent. Denique, neutiquam fingendum eft, cœlos incorruptibiles : corpora cœleftia, proinde ac terreftria, fuas habent viciffitudines et tranfmutationes; atque ipfæ fixæ in planetas, mediante chao, converti poffunt, et viciffim planetæ excuffis fordibus, in fixas revivifcere, &c. ; *Burnet's Archæol. Philofoph. cap. 9.*

have made the illiterate look upon him as a wild romancer. By God's direction, therefore, he took the middle and wisest way, which was to speak exact truth, but cautiously, and in such general terms as might neither confound the minds of the ignorant Jews, nor expose him to the censure of philosophizing Christians: and we may well account it an evident token of a particular providence of God overruling this inspired penman, that he has drawn up the cosmogony in such a manner, as makes it of perpetual use and application; forasmuch as it contains no peculiar notions of his own, no principles borrowed from the ancient exploded philosophy, nor any repugnant to the various discoveries of the new.

4thly, It is to be observed farther, in relation to this account of Moses, that when God is said to give the word, and every thing thereupon proceeded to its formation, he did not leave matter and motion to do their best, whilst he stood by (according to Dr. Cudworth's expression) as an idle spectator of this *lusus atomorum*, and the various results of it; but himself interposed, and, conducting the whole process, gave not only life and being, but form and figure to every part of the creation.

The warmest abettors of mechanical principles do not deny, but that ª a divine energy at least must be admitted in this case, where a world was to be formed, and a wild chaos reduced to a fair, regular, and permanent system. The immediate hand of God (they cannot but acknowledge) is apparent in a miracle, which is an infraction upon the standing laws of nature; but certainly, of all miracles, the creation of the world is the greatest, not only as it signifies the production of matter and motion out of nothing, but as it was likewise the ranging and putting things into such order, as might make them capable of the laws of motion which were to be ordained for them. ᵇ For whatever notions we may have of the stated œconomy of things now, it is certain that the laws of motion (with which philosophers make such noise) could not take place before every part of the creation was ranged and settled in its proper order.

It may be allowed however, since, even in the Mosaic account, there are some passages, such as, *Let the earth bring forth grass, let the earth bring forth the living creature after his kind, and it was so,*) that whatever comes

*A. M. 1
Ant. Christ-
4004.
Gen. ch. 1.
and part of
ch. 2.*

The creation not left to matter and motion

ᵃ *Vid.* Whiston's Theory.
ᵇ *Vid.* Hale's Origin of mankind.

A. M. 1.
Ant. Chrif.
4004.
Gen. ch. 1.
and part of
ch. 2.

comes under the compaſs of mechanical cauſes, might poſsibly be effected by matter and motion, only ſet on work by infinite wiſdom, and ſuſtained in their being and operation by infinite power; but whatever is above the power of ſecond cauſes, ſuch as the production of matter out of nothing, the formation of the ſeeds of all animals and vegetables, the creation of our firſt parents, and inſpiring them with immortal ſouls, &c. theſe we affirm, and theſe we ought to believe, were the pure reſult of God's omnipotent power, and are aſcribed to him alone.

To this purpoſe we may obſerve, that before our author begins to acquaint us with what particular creatures were each day ſucceſſively brought into being, he takes care to inform us, (as a thing eſſential and preparatory to the work,) † *that the Spirit of God moved upon the face of the waters*. For, whether by *the Spirit of God*, we are to underſtand [a] his holy and eſſential Spirit, which is the third perſon in the ever-bleſſed Trinity, whether [b] that *plaſtic nature*, which (according to ſome) was made ſubſervient to him upon this occaſion, or any other emanation of the divine power and energy, it is reaſonable to ſuppoſe, that its moving, or incubation upon the chaotic maſs, derived into it a certain fermentation, impregnated it with ſeveral kinds of motive influence, and ſo ſeparated and digeſted its confuſed parts, as to make it capable of the diſpoſition and order it was going to receive.

The

† The word in the Hebrew, according to the opinion of ſome both ancient and modern interpreters, ſignifies literally *a brooding* upon the waters, even as a hen does upon her eggs; but, as there are only two places wherein the word occurs, [Deut xxxii. 11. and Jer. xxxiii. 9] Mr. Le Clerk contends, that in neither of theſe it will properly admit of this ſenſe; and therefore he rather thinks it (as our Ainſworth ſeems to do) to be a metaphor taken from the hovering and fluttering of an eagle, or any other bird, over its young, but not its ſitting over, or brooding upon them. A diſtinction of no great moment in my opinion.

[a] Cudworth's Intellectual ſyſtem.
[b] Gen. i. 2. It is obſerved by ſome later Jewiſh, as well as Chriſtian interpreters that the ſeveral names of God are often given as epithets to thoſe things which are the greateſt, the ſtrongeſt, and the beſt of their kind; and thereupon they think, that ſince the word *Ruach* ſignifies *the wind*, as well as *the Spirit*, *Ruach Elohim* ſhould be tranſlated *a moſt vehement wind*, inſtead

of

THE HISTORY.

IN this condition we may suppose the chaos to have been, when the † *fiat* for light was given; whereupon all the confused, stagnating particles of matter began to range into form and order. The dull, heavy, and terrene parts, which over-clouded the *expansum*, had their summons to retire to their respective centres. They presently obeyed the Almighty's orders, and part of them subsided to the centre of the earth, some to Jupiter, some to Saturn, some to Venus, &c. till the globes of these several planets were completed. And as the grosser parts subsided, the lighter, and more tenuous mounted up; and the lucid and fiery particles (being lighter than the rest) ascended higher, and, by the divine order, meeting together in a body, were put in a circular motion, and in the space of a natural day, made to visit the whole *expansum* of the chaos, which occasioned a separation of the light from darkness, and thereby a distribution of day and night †: and this was the work of the first day.

A. M. 1.
Ant. Chrif.
4004.
Gen. ch. 1.
and part of ch. 2.

The work of the first day.

The next thing which God Almighty commanded, was, that the waters, which as yet were universally dispersed over the face of the chaos, should retire to their respective

The second

of *the Spirit of God*; and that this signification agrees very well with Moses's account, which represents the earth so mixed with the waters, that it could not appear, and therefore stood in need of a wind to dry it. But besides that this sense seems to be a sad debasing of the text, it is certain, that the wind (which is nothing but the moving of the air) could not be spoken of now, because it was not created until the second day.

† The words are, *Let there be light*, which, as Longinus takes notice, is a truly lofty expression; and herein appears the wisdom of Moses that he represents God like himself, commanding things into being by his word, *i. e.* his will: for where-ever we read the words [*he said*] in the history of the creation, the meaning must be, that he willed so and so; *Patrick's comment*.

† If we rather approve the Copernican hypothesis, we must say, that the earth, having now received its diurnal and annual motion, and having turned round about its axis, for about the space of 12 hours, made this luminous body, now fixed in a proper place, appear in the east, which, in the space of 12 hours more, seemed to be in the west; and that this revolution made a distinction between day and night; *Bedford's chronology*.

A. M. 1.
Ant. Chrif.
4004.
Gen. ch. 1.
and part of
ch 2.

spective planets, and be restrained within their proper limits by several atmospheres. Hereupon all the aqueous parts immediately subsided towards the centres of the several planets, and were circumfused about their globes; by which means the great *expansum* was again cleared off, and the region of the air became more lucid and serene. And this is the operation which Moses calls *dividing the waters under † the firmament, from the waters which are above † the firmament*, for the waters under the firmament are the waters of the earth, the waters above the firmament are those of the moon, and other planets, which, in the second day's work, were dismissed to their several orbs, but were confusedly mixed, and overspread the whole face of the *expansum* before.

The third. Thus, on the second day, the delightful element of air was disintangled and extracted from the chaos: and one part of the business of the third, was to separate the other remaining elements, *water and earth*. For the watry particles, as we said, clearing the *expansum*, and falling upon the planetary orbs, must be supposed to cover the face of the earth, as well as other planets, when the great Creator gave the command for *the waters to be gathered into one place, and the dry land to appear*. Whereupon the mighty mountains instantly reared up their heads, and the waters, falling every way from their sides, ran into those large extended vallies, which this swelling of the earth, in some places, had made for their reception in others. The earth, being thus separated from the waters, and designed for the habitation of man and beast, (which were afterwards

to

† Gen. i 6. The LXX interpreters, in translating the word [*Rakiagh*] *the firm* or *solid*, seem to have followed the philosophy of the first ages: for the ancients fancied that the heavens were a solid body, and that the stars were fastened therein, which might likewise be the notion of Elihu, [Job xxxvii. 18.] since he represents the heaven to be strong or solid, *like a molten looking-glass*; whereas, the proper sense of the word is something *spread* or *stretched out*. And to this both the Psalmist and prophet allude, when they tell us, that *God spreadeth out the heaven like a curtain*, Psal. civ. 2. and *stretched them out by his discretion*, Jer. x 12.

† Several commentators suppose *the waters above the firmament* to be those which hang in the clouds; but the notion of their being planetary waters seems more reasonable, because at this time, there were no clouds, neither had it as yet rained on the earth, vid. Gen. ii. 6.

Chap. I.   *from the Creation to the Flood.*

to be created,) was first to be furnished with such things as were proper for their support; grass for cattle, and herbs and fruit-trees for the nourishment of man. Immediately therefore, upon the divine command, it was covered with a beautiful carpet of flowers and grass, trees and plants of all kinds, which were produced in their full proportion, laden with fruit, and not subjected to the ordinary course of maturation. For how great soever the fecundity of the primogenial earth might be, yet it is scarce to be imagined, how † trees and plants could be ripened, into their full growth and burthen of fruit, in the short period of a day, any other way than by virtue of a supernatural power of God, which first collected the parts of matter fit to produce them; then formed every one of them, and determined their kinds; and at last provided for their continuance, by a curious inclosure of their seed, in order to propagate their species, even unto the end of the world: And this was the work of the third day.

A. M. 1.
Ant. Chrif.
4004.
Gen. ch. 1.
and part of ch. 2.

When God had finished the lower world, and furnished it with all manner of store, that mass of fiery light, (which we suppose to have been extracted on the first day, and to have moved about the *expansum* for two days after,) was certainly of great use in the production of the æther, the separation of the waters, and the rarefaction of the land, which might possibly require a more violent operation at first, than was necessary in those lesser alterations, which were afterwards to be effected; and therefore, on the fourth day, God took and condensed it, and casting it into a proper orb, placed it at a convenient distance from the earth and other planets; insomuch, that it became a sun, and immediately shone out in the same glorious manner, in which it has done ever since.

The fourth

After this God took another part of the chaos, an opaque substance, which we call the *moon;* and having cast it into a proper figure, placed it in another orb, at a nearer

---

† There are two things wherein the production of plants, in the beginning, differed from their production ever since. 1st, That they have sprung ever since out of their seed either sown by us, or falling from the plants themselves; but in the beginning, were wrought out of the earth, with their seed in them, to propagate them ever after. 2dly, That they need now (as they have ever since the creation) the influence of the sun, to make them sprout; but then they came forth by the power of God, before there was any sun, which was not formed till the next day; *Patrick's comment. in loc.*

A. M. 1.
Ant. Chrif.
4004.
Gen. ch. 1 and part of ch. 2.

nearer diftance from the earth, that it might perpetually be moving round it, and that the fun, by darting its rays upon its folid furface, might reflect light to the terreftrial globe, for the benefit of its inhabitants: and, at the fame time, that God thus made the moon, he made, in like manner, † the other five planets of the folar fyftem, and their fatellites. Nor was it only for the difpenfation of light to this earth of ours, that God appointed the two great luminaries of the fun and moon to attend it, but for the meafure and computation of time likewife: that a fpeedy and fwift motion of the fun, (according to the Ptolemaic fyftem,) in twenty four hours round the earth, or of the earth (according to the Copernican) upon its own axis, might make a day; that the time from one change of the moon to another, or thereabouts, might make a month; and the apparent revolution of the fun, to the fame point of the ecliptic line, might not only make a year, but occafion likewife a grateful variety of feafons in the feveral parts of the earth, which are thus gradually and fucceffively vifited by the reviving heat of the fun-beams: And this was the work of the fourth day.

The fifth.

After the inanimate creation, God, on the fifth day, proceeded to form the animate; and becaufe fifh and fowl are not fo perfect in their kind, neither fo curious in their bodily texture, nor fo fagacious in their inftinct, as terreftrial creatures are known to be, he therefore began with them, and ‖ out of the waters, *i. e.* out of fuch matter

as

---

† I am very fenfible that the words in the text are, *He made the ftars alfo*, ver. 16.; but the whole fentence comes in fo very abruptly, that one would be apt to imagine, that after Mofes's time, it was clapped in by fome body who had a mind to be mending his hypothefis, or elfe was added, by way of marginal note, at firft; and at length crept into the text itfelf, (as F. Simon has evidenced in feveral other inftances) For the fixed ftars do not feem to be comprehended in the *fix day's work*, which relates only to this planetary world, that has the fun for its centre; Patrick's comment. and Nicholls's conference. vol 1 *Vid.* anfwer to the fubfequent objection.

‖ From the words in Gen. [ch i. ver. 20.] *Let the waters, bring forth abundantly the moving creature that hath life, and fowl, that may fly above the earth.* &c. fome have ftarted an opinion, that fowl derive their origin from the water; and others, from the words, *Out of the ground God formed every beaft of the field, and every fowl of the air*, raife another, viz.

that

Chap. I.   *from the Creation to the Flood.*   13

as was mixed and concocted with the water, he formed se‑   A. M. 1.
veral of different shapes and sizes; some vastly big, † to   Ant. Chrif.
shew the wonders of his creating power; and some ex‑   4004.
tremely small, to shew the goodness of his indulgent pro‑   Gen. ch. 1.
vidence. And (what is peculiar to this day's work (here   and part of ch 2.
we have the first mention made of God's blessing his crea‑
tures, and † *bidding them be fruitful and multiply,* i. e. giv‑
ing them, at their first creation, a prolific virtue, and a na‑
tural instinct for generation, whereby they might not only
preserve their species, but multiply their individuals: and
this was the work of the fifth day.

    Thus every thing being put in order; the earth co‑   The sixth.
vered with plants; the waters restored with fish; the air
replenished with fowl; and the sun placed at a proper di‑
stance, to give a convenient warmth and nourishment to
all;

that fowl took their beginning from the earth: but these two
texts are easily reconciled, because neither denies what the other
says, though they speak differently; as when Moses says, *Let the
waters bring forth fowl,* he does not by that say, that the earth
did not bring forth fowl. It is most reasonable therefore to think
that they had their original partly from the waters, and partly
from the earth; and this might render the flesh of fowl less gross
than that of beasts, and more firm than that of fishes. Hence
Philo calls fowl *the kindred of fish*; and that they are so, the great
congruity there is in their natures (they being both oviparous
which makes them more fruitful than other animals, and both
steering and directing their course by their tails) is a sufficient
indication.

   † Moses instances in the whale, because it is supposed to be the
principal and largest of all fishes; but the original word denotes
several kinds of great fish, as Bochart [in his Hierozoin. p, 1.
l. 1. c 7.] observes at large; and shews withal the prodigious
bigness of some of them; but he should have added, that the word
signifies *a crocodile* likewise, as well as *a whale*; *Patrick, and Le,
Clerc in loc.*

   † That fish and fowl should here have a blessing pronounced
upon them, rather than the beasts, which were made the sixth
day, some have supposed this to be the reason;—that the pro‑
duction of their young requires the particular care of divine
providence, because they do not bring them forth perfectly form‑
ed as the beasts do, but only lay their eggs, in which the young
are hatched and formed even when they are separate from their
bodies: and " what a wonderful thing is this," says one, " that
" when the womb (as we may call it) is separated from the
" genitor, a living creature like itself should be produced?"
Patrick's Comment.

A. M. 1.
Ant. Chrif.
4004.
Gen. ch. 1
and part of
ch 2.

all; in order to make this sublunary world a still more comfortable place of abode, in the beginning of the sixth, and last day, ‖ God made the terrestrial animals, which the sacred historian distributes into three kinds : 1*st*, *Beasts*, by which we understand all wild and savage creatures, such as lions, bears, wolves, &c. 2*dly*, *Cattle*, all tame and domestic creatures, designed for the benefit and use of men, such as oxen, sheep, horses, &c. And, 3*dly*, *Creeping things*, such as serpents, worms and other kinds of insects.

Thus, when all things which could be subservient to man's felicity were perfected; when the light had, for some time, been penetrating into, and clarifying the dark and thick atmosphere; when the air was freed from its noisome vapours, and become pure and clear, and fit for his respiration; when the waters were so disposed, as to minister to his necessities by mists and dews from heaven,

‖ In the 24th verse of this chapter. it is said. that God commanded the earth to produce such and such animals : *Let the earth bring forth the living creature after his kind;* and yet. in the very next verse, it follows that *God made the beast of the earth, and every thing that moveth, after his kind:* but this seeming contradiction is easily reconciled, by putting together the proper meaning of both these passages, which must certainly be this ——that God himself effectually formed these terrestrial animals, and made use of the earth only as to the matter whereof he constituted their parts. Some indeed have made it a question, whether these several creatures were at first produced in their full state and perfection, or God only created the seeds of all animals, (*i e.* the animals themselves in miniature,) and dispersed them over the face of the earth, giving power to that element, assisted by the genial heat of the sun, to hatch and bring them forth; but for this there is no manner of occasion, since it is much more rational to suppose that God did not commit the formation of things to any intermediate causes, but himself created the first set of animals in the full proportion and perfection of their specific natures, and gave to each species a power afterwards, by generation, to propagate their kind ; for that even now, and in the present situation of things any perfect species cannot, either naturally or accidentally, be produced by any preparation of matter, or by any influence of the heavens, without the interposition of an almighty power, physical experiments do demonstrate.) *Patrick's Commentary; and Bentley's Sermons at Boyle's Lecture.*

ven, and by springs and rivers from the earth; when the surface of the earth was become dry and solid for his support, and covered over with grass and flowers, with plants and herbs, and trees of all kinds, for his pleasure and sustenance; when the glorious firmament of heaven, and the beautiful system of the sun, moon, and stars, were laid open for his contemplation, and, by their powerful influences, appointed to distinguish the seasons, and make the world a fruitful and delicious habitation for him; when, lastly, all sorts of animals in the sea, in the air, and on the earth, were so ordered and disposed, as to contribute, in their several capacities, to his benefit and delight: when all these things, I say, were, by the care and providence of God, prepared for the entertainment of this principal guest, it was then that man was created, and introduced into the world in a manner and solemnity not unbecoming the lord and governor of it. To this purpose we may observe, that God makes a manifest distinction between him and other creatures, and seems to undertake the creation, even of his body, with a kind of mature deliberation, if not consultation with the other persons of the ever-blessed Trinity; † *Let us make man.*

However

---

† Gen. i. 26. The Jewish doctors are of opinion, that the consultation was real, and held with such angelical beings as God might employ in the work of man's creation; and they tell a story upon this occasion which seems a little fictitious, *viz.* that as Moses was writing his book by God's appointment, and these words came to be dictated, he refused to set them down, crying out, *O Lord! wouldst thou then plunge men in error, and make them doubt of the doctrine of the unity?* Whereupon it was answered by God, *I command thee to write, and if any will err, let them err.* Several modern expositors account it only a majestic form of speech, as nothing is more common than for kings and sovereign princes to speak in the plural number, especially when they are giving out any important order or command. It has been observed however, that as there were no men, and consequently no great men, when this was spoken; so there was no such manner of speech in use among men of that rank for many ages after Moses. Their common custom was, in all their public instruments and letters (the better to enhance the notion of sovereignty) to speak in the first person, as it was in our nation not long ago, and is in the kingdom of Spain to this very day; and therefore, upon the authority of almost all the fathers of the church. " Nam hæc verba Deum
" Patrem ad Filium, et Spiritum Sanctum, aut saltem ad Fili-
" um

A. M. 1.
Ant. Chrif.
4004.
Gen. ch. 1.
and part of
ch 2.

However this be, it is certain that the force and energy of the expreſſion denotes thus much——that the production of mankind at firſt was ſo immediately the work of Almighty God, that the power of no ſubordinate intelligence could be capable of it: that the curious ſtructure of man's body, the accommodation of it to faculties, and the furniſhing it with faculties that are accommodated to it, (even as to its animal life,) imports a wiſdom and efficacy far above the power of any created nature to effect. And this may poſſibly ſuggeſt the reaſon, why, in the formation of his body, God made choice of *the duſt of the ground, viz.* that from the incongruity of the matter we might judge of the difficulty, and learn to attribute the glory of the performance to him alone. And if the creation of the body of our great progenitor was a work of ſo much divine wiſdom and power, we cannot but expect, that the ſpiritual and immaterial nature, the immortal condition, active powers, and free and rational operations, which, in reſemblance of the Divine Being, the ſoul of man was to participate, ſhould require ſome peculiar and extraordinary conduct in its production at firſt, and union with matter afterward; all which is expreſſed by God's *breathing into the man's* † *noſtrils the breath of life,* i. e. doing ſomething analagous to breathing, (for God has no body to breathe with,) whereby he infuſed a rational and immortal ſpirit (for we muſt not ſuppoſe that God gave any part of his own eſſence) into the man's head, as the principal ſeat thereof; *and* ∥ *man became a living ſoul.*

As ſoon as Adam found himſelf alive, and begun to caſt his eyes about him, he could not but perceive that he was

in

" um dixiſſe, omnes fere patres, ab ipſis apoſtolorum tempori-
" bus, fidenter pronunciant;" *Whitby ſtructuræ patrum.* Others have thought, that this language of Moſes repreſents God ſpeaking, as he is, *i. e.* in a plurality of perſons.

‡ The original word, which our tranſlators render *noſtrils,* ſignifies more properly *the face or head.*

∥ It is not to be doubted, but that Eve, *the mother of all living,* was created by Almighty God, and inſpired with a rational and immortal ſoul, the ſame day with her huſband: for ſo it is ſaid, that in the ſixth day, *male and female created he them,* ver. 27.; and therefore the hiſtorian only reaſſumes the argument in the ſecond chapter, to give us a more full and particular account of the woman's origin, which was but briefly delivered, or rather indeed but hinted at in the firſt.

Chap. I. *from the Creation to the Flood.*

in no small danger as being surrounded with a multitude of savage creatures, all gazing on him, and (for any thing he knew) ready and disposed to fall upon and devour him. And therefore, to satisfy his mind in this particular, God took care to inform him, that all the creatures upon earth were submitted to his authority; that on them he had impressed an awe and dread of him; had invested him with an absolute power and dominion over them; and, to convince him of the full possession of that power, he immediately appointed every creature to appear before him, which they accordingly did, and * by their lowly carriage, and gestures of respect suitable to their several species, evidenced their submission; and as they passed along, such knowledge had Adam then of their several properties and destinations, that he assigned them their names, which a small skill in the Hebrew tongue will convince us, were very proper, and significant of their natures.

This survey of the several creatures might possibly occasion some uneasy reflections in Adam, to see every one provided with its mate, but himself left destitute of any companion of a similar nature ; and therefore, to answer his desires in this particular likewise, ᶜ *God caused a deep sleep to fall upon him*, which was intended, not only as an expedient for the performance of the wonderful operation upon him without sense of pain, * but as a trance, or extasy

A. M. 1.
Ant. Chris. 4004
Gen. ch. 1. and part of ch. 2.

---

* Milton has expressed himself, upon this occasion, in the following manner :

<pre>
As thus he spake, each bird, and beast, behold
Approaching, two and two; these cow'ring low
With blandishment; each bird stoop'd on his wing.
I nam'd them, as they pass'd, and understood
Their nature; with such knowledge God endu'd
My sudden apprehension.   Book 8.
</pre>

ᶜ Gen ii. 21.

* In like manner, he makes this sleep which fell upon Adam to have been a kind of trance or extasy, (for so the LXX translate it.) and thus he relates the occasion and nature of it.

<pre>
He ended, and I heard no more; for now
My earthly by his heavenly over-power'd,
Which it had long stood under, strain'd to th' height
In that celestial colloquy sublime,
(As with an object that excels the sense,)
Dazzled and spent,) sunk down, and sought relief
Of sleep, which instantly fell on me, call'd
By nature as in aid, and clos'd my eyes.
Mine eyes he clos'd, but open left the cell
</pre>

Of

A. M. 1.
Ant. Chrif.
4004.
Gen ch. 1.
and part of ch. 2

extasy likewise, wherein was represented to his imagination, both what was done to him, and what was the mystical meaning of it, and whereby he was prepared for the reception of that divine oracle ^d concerning the sacred institution of marriage, which presently, upon his awaking, he uttered.

While Adam continued in this sleep, God, who, with the same facility wherewith he made him, could have formed the woman out of the *dust of the earth*, (being willing to signify that equality and partnership, that love and union, and tenderness of endearment, which ought to interfere between husband and wife,) took part of the substance of the man's body, ‡ near his side, and closing up the orifice again, out of that substance he † formed the body of Eve, and then *breathing into her the breath of life*, made her, in like manner, *become a living soul*.

This was the * conclusive act of the whole creation: and upon a general survey of such harmony risen from principles

> Of fancy, my internal sight; by which
> (Abstract as in a trance) methought I saw,
> Though sleeping, where I lay, and saw the shape
> Still glorious, before whom awake I stood——
> Under his forming hands a creature grew
> Man-like, but different sex; so lovely fair,
> That what seem'd fair in all the world, seem'd now
> Mean, or in her summ'd up, in her contain'd,
> And in her looks, which from that time infus'd
> Sweetness into my heart, unfelt before;
> And into all things from her air inspir'd
> The spirit of love, and amorous delight. Book 8.

^d Gen. ii. 23.

‡ As the original word does not strictly signify *a rib*, and is all along rendered by the LXX *pleura*, so I thought it not improper to give it that construction, thereby to cut off from infidels an occasion for raillery, and to spare them all their wit about the redundant or defective rib of Adam.

† The original word signifies *building* or *framing* any thing with a singular care, contrivance and proportion; and hence our bodies are in Scripture frequently called *houses*, Job iv. 19. 2 Cor. v. 1.; and sometimes *temples*, John ii. 15.; 1 Cor. iii. 16.

* It is not very necessary to determine at what season of the year the world was made; yet it seems most probable, that it was about the autumnal equinox, and that not only because the trees were laden then with fruit, as the history tells us our first parents did eat of them; but because the Jews did then begin their

Chap. I.   *from the Creation to the Flood.*   19

principles so jarring and repugnant, and so beautiful a va- | A. M. 1.
riety and composition of things from a mere mass of con- | Ant. Chrif.
fusion and disorder, God was pleased with the work of | 4004.
his hands; and having pronounced it good, or properly a- | Gen. ch. 1.
dapted to the uses for which it was intended, *he rested from* | and part of
all his work, i. e. he ceased to produce any more creatures, | ch 2.
as having accomplished his design, and answered his original idea; and thereupon he * sanctified, and set apart the
next

their civil year (*viz* in the month *Tisri*, which answers to part
of our September and October) from whence their sabbatical
and jubilee years did likewise commence, Exod. xxiii 16.
xxxiv. 22.; Lev. xxv. 9   The month *Abib* (which answers to
part of our March and April) had indeed the honour afterwards to be reckoned among the Jews the beginning of their
year in ecclesiastical matters, because the children of Israel, on
that month, came out of the land of Egypt; but from the very
creation, the month *Tisri* was always counted the first of their
civil year, because it was the general opinion of the ancients,
that the world was created at the time of the autumnal equinox; and for this reason, the Jews do still, in the æra of the
creation, as well as in that of contracts, and other instruments,
compute the beginning of their year from the first day of
Tisri. Herein, however the Jews differ from us; that whereas they make the world only 3760, most of the Christian chronologers will have it to be much about 4000 years older than
Christ; so that by them 5732 years, or thereabouts, are thought
a moderate computation of the world's antiquity *Vid* Usher's
annals; Bedford's chronology; and Shuckford's connection.

* Whether the institution of the Sabbath was from the beginning of the world, and one day in seven always observed by
the patriarchs, before the promulgation of the law; or whether the sanctification of the seventh day is related only by way
of anticipation, as an ordinance not to take place until the introduction of the Jewish œconomy, is a matter of some debate
among the learned; but I think with little or no reason, for
when we consider, that as soon as the sacred penman had said,
God ended his work, and rested, he adds immediately, in the words
of the same tense, *he blessed the seventh day, and sanctified it;* when
we compare this passage in Genesis with the twentieth chapter
of Exodus, wherein Moses speaks of God's *blessing and sanctifying the Sabbath,* not as an act then first done, but as what he had
formerly done upon the creation of the world; when we remember, that all the patriarchs from Adam to Moses had set
times for their solemn assemblies, and that these times were weekly, and of divine institution; that upon the return of these
weekly

A. M. 1. next ensuing day, (which was the seventh from the begin-
Ant. Chrif. ning of the creation, and the first of Adam's life,) as a time
4004. of solemn rest and rejoicing for ever after, to be observed
Gen. ch. 1, and expended in acts of praise and religious worship, and
and part of in commemoration of the infinite wisdom, power, and
ch. 2. goodness of God, in the world's creation.

THE OBJECTION.

against Mo- "BUT how great soever the display of the divine at-
ses's ac- " tributes may seem in the glorious works of the
count of the
creation; " creation, yet Moses, one would think, is far from endea-
" vouring to give us the most advantageous representa-
" tion of them. To speak the world into being at once,
" and in an instant, had been more agreeable to the no-
" tions we have of an almighty power, than the spinning
" it out into so many days labour. But allowing this suc-
" cession of time to have been real, what a sad blunder
" does the historian make, even at his first setting out, when
" he talks of *light*, before there was any such thing as the
" sun, and of the moon's being *a great light*, when eve-
" ry body knows it to be an opaque body; when he dis-
" tributes the whole work into such unequal proportions,
" and accounts for some parts of it, in a manner inconsis-
" tent with the wisdom of its maker. For on the first
" day, to have no more to do than what might be dis-
" patched in the twinkling of an eye, but on the third,
" to have all the waters of the abyss drained off, and broad
" channels dug for the reception of the sea; to have the
" sun, moon, and other planets, together with the stars,
" (a vast number of immense bodies!) all made on the
" fourth; and when one piece of clay would have done
" for both, to have two distinct creations for our first pa-
" rents; and (what is worst of all) in the hurry of the
" work

weekly Sabbaths, very probably it was that Cain and Abel offered their respective sacrifices to God; and that Noah, the
only righteous person among the Antediluvians, Abraham,
the most faithful servant of God after the flood, and Job, that
perfect and upright man, who feared God, and eschewed evil, are all
supposed to have observed it; we cannot but think, that the
day whereon the work of the creation was concluded, from the
very beginning of time, was every week (until men had corrupted their ways) kept *holy* as being the *birth day of the world*,
(as Philo *De mundi opificio* styles it,) and the *universal festival of
mankind;* Bedford's Scripture-chronology, and Patrick's commentary.

Chap. I.   *from the Creation to the Flood.*   21

" work (for the sixth day, being the winding up of all, A. M 1.
" was a day of great hurry,) to forget the creation of the An. Christ.
" poor woman's soul, to say nothing of the strange *sub-* Gen. ch. 1.
" *stratum* of her body: These, and several other particu- and part of
" lars, are enough to make us suspect the physical truth ch. 2.
" of our author's cosmogony, and to pronounce it not
" much better than what we meet with in the theology, or
" histories of other ancient nations."

  ᵉ *Where wast thou, when I laid the foundations of the earth?* ᵃⁿˢʷᵉʳᵉᵈ,
Declare if thou hast understanding. Whereupon are the foun- that a gra-
dations thereof fastened, and who laid the corner stone thereof? dual and
is a question very proper to be put to those who demand successive
a reason for the actions of God: for if they cannot com- comported
prehend the works themselves, they are certainly very best with
culpable in inquiring too busily into the time and manner the glory of
of his doing them. But (to gratify the inquisitive for God.
once) though we do not deny, that all things are equally
easy to almighty power, yet it pleased the divine Architect
to employ the space of six days in the gradual formation
of the world, because he foresaw, that such procedure
would be a means conducive to the better instruction both
of men and angels. Angels (as we hinted before) were
very probably created, when the supreme heavens were
made, at least some considerable time before the production of this visible world. Now, though they be great and
glorious beings, yet still they are of a finite nature, and
unable to comprehend the wonderful works of God. There
are some things (as ᶠ the apostle tells us) that these celestial creatures *desire to look into;* and the more they are
let into the knowledge and wisdom of God, the more they
are incited to praise him. ᵍ That therefore they might
not want sufficient matter for this heavenly exercise, the
whole scene of the creation, according to the several degrees and nature of things, seems to have been laid open
in order before them, that thereby they might have a more
full and comprehensive view of the divine attributes therein exhibited, than they could have had, in case the world
had started forth in an instant, or jumped (as it were) into
this beautiful frame and order all at once; just as he who
sees the whole texture and contrivance of any curious piece
of art, values and admires the artist more, than he who
beholds it in the gross only.

Vol. I. No. 2.   S   God

  ᵉ Job. xxxviii. 4, 6.   ᶠ 1 Pet. i. 12.   ᵍ Jenkins's reasonableness of the Christian religion.

A. M. 1.
Ant. Chrif
4004
Gen. ch. 1.
and part of
ch 2.

God was therefore pleased to display his glory before the angels, and by several steps and degrees, excite their praise, and love, and admiration, which moved them to songs and shouts of joy. By this means, his glory, and their happiness were advanced, far beyond what it would have been, had all things been created, and ranged in their proper order in a moment. By this means they had time to look into their first principles and seeds of all creatures, both animate and inanimate, and every day presented them with a glorious spectacle of new wonders; so that the more they saw, the more they knew, and the more they know of the works of God, the more they for ever love and adore him. But this is not all.

By this successive and gradual creation of things, in the space of six days, the glory of God is likewise more manifest to man, than it would have been, had they been made by a sudden and instantaneous production. The heavens, and *all the host of them*, we may suppose, were made in an instant, because there were then perhaps no other creatures to whom God might display the glory of his works; but as they were made in an instant, we have little or no perception of the manner wherein they were made: but now, in this leisurely procedure of the earth's formation, we see, as it were, every thing arising out of the primordial mass, first the simple elements, and then the compounded and more curious creatures, and are led, step by step, full of wonder and admiration, until we see the whole completed. So that, in condescension to our capacity, it was, that God divided the creation into stated periods, and prolonged the succession of what he could have done in six moments, to the term of six days, that we might have clearer notions of his eternal power and godhead, and every particular day of the week, new and particular works, for which we are to praise him. And this, by the by, suggests another argument, founded on the institution of the Sabbath-day: For if, *in six days, the Lord made heaven and earth, and, resting on the seventh day, did bless and sanctify it*, this seems to imply, that God obliged himself to continue the work of the creation for six days, that shewing himself (if I may so say) a divine example of weekly labour, and sabbatical rest, he might more effectually signify to mankind, what tribute of duty he would require of them, *viz.* that one day in seven, abstaining from business and worldly labour, they
should

should devote and consecrate it to his honour, and religi- | A M. 1.
ous worship. | Ant. Chrif.
| 4004.
There is therefore no necessity of departing from the | Gen. ch. 1.
literal sense of the Scripture in this particular. The reite- | and part of
rated acts, and the different operations mentioned by Mo- | ch. 2.
ses, ought indeed to be explained in such a manner, as is
consistent with the infinite power, and perfect simplicity
of the acts of God, and in such a manner, as may exclude
all notions of weakness, weariness, or imperfection in him;
but all this may be done without receding from a successive creation, which redounds so much to the glory of
God, and affords the whole intelligent creation so fair a
field for contemplation.

Some of the Jewish doctors are of opinion, that in the | Why light
first day, when God created light, at the same time, he | before the
formed and compacted it into a sun; and that the sun is | sun.
mentioned again on the fourth day, merely by way of repetition; while others maintain, that this light was a certain luminous body (not unlike that which conducted the
children of Israel in the wilderness) that moved round the
world, until the day wherein the sun was created. But
there is no occasion for such conjectures as these: every
one knows, that *darkness* has, in all ages, been the chief
idea which men have had of a *chaos*. [h] Both poets
and philosophers have made *Nox*, and *Erebus*, and *Tar-
tarus*, the principal parts and ingredients of its description;
and therefore it seems very agreeable to the reason of mankind, that the first remove from the chaos should be a
tendency to light. But then by light (as it was produced
the first day,) we must not understand the darting of rays
from a luminous body, such as do now proceed from the
sun, [i] but those particles of matter only, which we call
fire, (whose properties we know are *light* and *heat*,) which
the Almighty produced, as a proper instrument for the preparation, and digestion of all other matter. For fire, being naturally a strong and restless element, when once it
was disentangled and set free, would not cease to move,
and agitate, from top to bottom, the whole heavy and confused mass, until the purer and more shining parts of it
being separated from the grosser, and so uniting together,
(as things of the same species naturally do,) did constitute
that light, which, on the fourth day, was more compressed
and consolidated, and so became the body of the sun.

S 2 The

[h] Patrick's comment. in locum.   [i] Nicholl's conference, vol. 1.

A.M. 1.
Ant. Chrif.
4004.
Gen. ch. 1.
and part of
ch. 2.

No difproportion in
the work of
each day.

The author of the Book of Wisdom tells us indeed, that [k] *God ordered all things in measure, and number, and weight;* but we cannot from hence infer, that in the *hexemeron*, he was so nice and curious, as to weigh out to himself in gold scales (as it were) his daily work by grains and scruples. We indeed, who are finite creatures, may talk of the *heat and burthen of the day*, and, in a weekly task, are forced to proportion the labour of each day to the present condition of our strength; but this is the case of human infirmity, and no way compatible to God. To omnipotence nothing can be laborious, nor can there be more or less of pains, where all things are equally easy. But, in the mean time, how does it appear, that even, in human conception, the work of the third day, which consisted in draining the earth, and stocking it with plants; or even of the fourth day, wherein the sun and moon, and other planets were made, was more difficult, than that of the first, which is accounted the simple production of light?

The compass of the chaos (as we supposed) took up the whole solar system, or that space, which Saturn circumscribes in his circulation round the sun: and if so, what a prodigious thing was it, to give motion to this vast unweildly mass, and to direct that motion in some sort of regularity; in the general struggle and cumbustion, to unite things that were no ways akin, and to sort the promiscuous elements into their proper species; to give the properties of rest and gravitation to one kind, and of ascension and elasticity to another: to make some parts subside and settle themselves, not in one continued solid, but in several different centres, at proper distances from each other, and so lay the foundation for the planets; to make others aspire and mount on high, and having obtained their liberty by hard conflict, join together, as it were, by compact, and make up one body, which, by the tenuity of its parts, and rapidity of its motion, might produce light and heat, and so lay the foundation for the sun; to place this luminous body in a situation proper to influence the upper parts of the chaos, and to be the instrument of rarefaction, separation, and all the rest of the operations to ensue; to cause it, when thus placed, either to circulate round the whole planetary system, or to make the planetary globes to turn round it, in order to produce the vicissitudes of day and night, to do all this, and more than this, I say,

[k] Wis. xi. 20.

Chap. I. *from the Creation to the Flood.* 25

say, as it is included in the single article of creating light, is enough to make the first day, wherein nature was utterly impotent, (as having motion then first impressed upon her,) a day of more labour and curious contrivance than any subsequent one could be, when nature was become more awake and active, and some assistance might possibly be expected from the instrumentality of second causes.

<small>A. M. 1.
Ant. Chrif.
4004
Gen. ch. 1.
and part of
ch 2.</small>

To excavate some parts of the earth, and raise others, in order to make the waters subside into proper channels, is thought a work not so comporting with the dignity and majesty of God; and therefore * some have thought that it possibly might have been effected by the same causes that occasion earthquakes, *i. e.* by subterraneous fires and flatuses. What incredible effects the ascension of gunpowder has, we may see every day: how it rends rocks, and blows up the most ponderous and solid walls, towers, and edifices, so that its force is almost irresistible. And why then might not such a proportionable quantity of the like materials, set on fire together, raise up the mountains, (how great and weighty soever,) and the whole superficies of the earth above the waters, and so make receptacles for them to run into. ¹ Thus we have a channel for the sea, even by the intervention of second causes: nor are we destitute of good authority to patronize this notion; for, after that the Psalmist had said, *the waters stand above the mountains,* immediately he subjoins, *at thy rebuke they fled, at the voice of thy thunder* (an earthquake, we know, is but a subterraneous thunder) *they hasted away, and went down to the valley beneath, even unto the place which thou hadst appointed to them.*

<small>How channels for the sea might easily be made.</small>

However this be, it is probable, and (if our hypothesis ᵐ be right) it is certain, that on the fourth day, the sun, moon, and planets, were pretty well advanced in their formation. The luminous matter extracted from the chaos on the first day, being a little more condensed, and put into a proper orb, became the sun, and the planets had all along been working off, in the same degrees of progression with

<small>The work of the fourth day not disproportionably great.</small>

---

* This we may conceive to have been effected by some particles of fire still left in the bowels of the earth, whereby such nitrosulphureous vapours were kindled, as made an earthquake, which both lifted up the earth, and also made receptacles for the waters to run into; *Patrick's Comment.*

¹ Psal. civ. 6, 7, 8.   ᵐ Ray's Wisdom of God in the creation.

A. M. 1.
Ant. Chrif.
4004.
Gen. ch. 1.
and part of
ch. 2.

with the earth; so that the labour of this day could not be so disproportionably great as is imagined. It is true indeed, the Scripture tells us, that God on this day, *not only made the sun and the moon, but that he made the stars also;* and, considering the almost infinite number of these heavenly bodies, (which we may discern with our eyes, and much more with glasses,) we cannot but say, that a computation of this kind would swell the work of the fourth day to a prodigious disproportion: but then we are to observe, that our English translation has interpolated the words [*he made,*] which are not in the original; for the simple version of the Hebrew is this——and ⁿ *God made two great lights, the greater light to rule the day, and the lesser light to rule the night and the stars;* which last words [*and the stars*] are not to be referred to the word [*made*] in the beginning of the verse, but to the word [*rule,*] which immediately goes before them; and so this sentence, *the lesser light to rule the night, and the stars:* will only denote the peculiar usefulness and predominancy of the moon above all other stars or planets, in respect of this earth of ours; in which sense it may not improperly be styled (as * some of the most polite authors are known to call it) the *ruler of the night*, and *a queen*, or *goddess*, as it were, *among the stars*. With regard to us therefore, who are the inhabitants of the earth, the moon, though certainly an opaque body, may not be improperly called *a great light;* since, by reason of its proximity, it communicates more light, (not of its own indeed, but what it borrows from the sun,) and is of more use and benefit to us than all the other planets put together. Nor must we forget (what indeed deserves a peculiar observation) that the moon, ° by its constant deviations towards the poles, affords a stronger and more lasting light to the inhabitants of those forlorn regions, whose long and tedious nights are of some days, nay, of some months continuance, than if its motion were truly circular, and the rays it reflects consequently more oblique. A mighty comfort and refreshment this to them, and a singular instance

Why the moon may be called great light

ⁿ Gen. i. 16.

* Lucidum cœli decus—syderum regina bicornis; *Hor.* Astrorum decus; *Virg. Æn*—Obscuri dea clara mundi; *Seneca Hip.* Arcanæ moderatrix Cinthia noctis; *Statius Theb.*
—Phœben imitantem lumina fratris
Semper, et in proprio regnantem tempore noctis; *Manil.*
° Derham's Astro-theology, ch. 4.

stance of the great Creator's wisdom in contriving, and mercy in preserving all his works!

A. M. 1. Ant. Chrif. 4004. Gen. ch. 1.

St. Paul, in his epistle to the Romans, makes all mankind (as certainly our first parent literally was) clay in the hands of the potter, and thereupon he asks this question; *and part of ch. 2.* ᵖ *Nay but, O man, who art thou, that repliest against God? Shall the thing formed say to him that formed it, why hast thou formed me thus? Hath not the potter power over the clay, of the same lump to make one vessel unto honour, and another unto dishonour?* It but badly becomes us therefore to inquire into the reason that might induce God to make the man and the women at different times, and of different materials; and it is an impertinent, as well as impious banter, to pretend to be so frugal of his pains. What if God, willing to shew a pleasing variety in his works, condescended to have the matter, whereof the woman was formed, pass twice through his hands, in order to * soften the temper, and meliorate the composition? Some peculiar qualities, remarkable in the female sex, might perhaps justify this supposition: but the true reason, as I take it, is couched in these words of Adam ᑫ, *This is now bone of my bone, and flesh of my flesh; she*

Why the woman was made of a rib.

ᵖ Rom. ix. 20. 21.
* Milton has given us a very curious description of Eve's qualifications, both in body and mind.

>Though well I understand, in the prime end
>Of nature, her th' inferior in the mind,
>And inward faculties, which most excel:
>In outward also her resembling less
>His image, who made both, and less expressing
>The character of that dominion giv'n
>O'er other creatures; yet when I approach
>Her loveliness, so absolute she seems,
>So in herself complete, so well to know
>Her own, that what she wills to do, or say,
>Seems wisest, virtuousest, discreetest, best.
>All higher knowledge in her presence falls
>Degraded, wisdom in discourse with her
>Loses discountenanc'd, and like folly shews.
>Authority and reason on her wait,
>As one intended first, but after made
>Occasionally; and, to consummate all,
>Greatness of mind, and nobleness their seat
>Build in her loveliest, and create an awe
>About her, as a guard angelic plac'd. Book 8.

ᑫ Gen. ii. 23. 24.

A. M. 1. *she shall be called † woman, because she was taken out of man:*
Ant. Chrif. *therefore shall a man leave his father and his mother, and cleave*
4004.
Gen. ch 1. *to his wife, and they shall be one flesh.*
and part of   Since God was determined then to form the woman out
ch. 2.   of some part of the man's body, and might probably have a
mystical meaning in so doing; to have taken her (like the
poet's Minerva) out of the head, might have intitled her to
a superiority which he never intended for her; to have
made her of any inferior, or more dishonourable part,
would not have agreed with that equality to which she was
appointed; and therefore he took her out of the man's side,
to denote the obligations to the strictest friendship and society: to beget the strongest love and sympathy between
him and her, as parts of the same whole; and to recommend marriage to all mankind, as founded in nature, and
Why the as the re-union of man and woman.
woman's
soul is not   It is an easy matter to be sceptical; but small reason, I
mentioned think, there is to wonder, why no mention is made in this
in the works place of the inspiration of the woman's soul. What the
of creation. historian means here, is only to represent a peculiar circumstance in the woman's composition, *viz.* her assump-
tion from the man's side: and therefore what relates to the
creation of her soul must be presumed to go before, and is
indeed signified in the preface God makes before he begins
the work; [r] *It is not good that man should be alone, I will
make him an help-meet for him,* i. e. of the same [s] essential
qualities with himself.   For we cannot conceive of what
great comfort this woman would have been to Adam, had
she not been endowed with a rational part, capable of conversing with him; had she not had, I say, the same understanding, will, and affections, though perhaps in a lower degree, and with some accommodation to the weakness
of her sex, in order to recommend her beauty, and to en-
dear that softness wherein (as I hinted before) she had
The ridi- certainly the pre-eminence.
culous ac-
counts   Such is the history which Moses gives us of the origin
which other of the world, and the production of mankind: and if we
nations give should now compare it with what we meet with in other
us of the nations recorded of these great events, we shall soon per-
creation.   ceive, that it is the only rational and philosophical account
extant; which, considering the low ebb that learning was
at

† Arjus Montanus, renders the Hebrew word *virago*, in the
margin *virissa*, i. e. *she-man*.

[r] Gen. ii. 18   [s] So the original word means, and so
the vulgar Latin has translated it.

at in the Jewish nation, is no small argument of its divine revelation. What a wretched account was that of the Egyptians, (from whence the Epicureans borrowed their hypothesis,) that the world was made by chance, and mankind grew out of the earth like pumkins? What strange stories does the Grecian theology tell us of *Ouranos* and *Pe*, *Jupiter* and *Saturn*; and what sad work do their ancient writers make, when they come to form men and women out of projected stones? How unaccountably does the Phœnician historian ᶜ make a dark and windy air the principle of the universe; all intelligent creatures to be formed alike in the shape of an egg, and both male and female awakened into life by a great thunder-clap? The Chinese are accounted a wise people, and yet the articles of their creed are such as these——That one Tayn, who lived in heaven, and was famous for his wisdom, disposed the parts of the world into the order we find them; that he created out of nothing the first man Panson, and his wife Pansone; that this Panson, by a power from Tayn, created another man called *Tanhom*, who was a great naturalist, and thirteen men more, by whom the world was peopled, till, after a while, the sky fell upon the earth, and destroyed them all; but that the wise Tayn afterwards created another man, called *Lotziram*, who had two horns, and an odoriferous body, and from whom proceeded several men and women, who stocked the world with the present inhabitants. But, of all others, the Mahometan account is the most ridiculous; for it tells us, that the first things which were created, were *the Throne of God,* * *Adam, Paradise,* and a great *pen,* wherewith God wrote his decrees: that this throne

A. M. 1.
Ant. Chrif.
4004.
Gen. ch. 1.
and part of
ch. 2.

was

ᶜ *Vid.* Cumberland's Sanchoniatho.

* As to the formation of Adam's body, Mahometans tell us many strange circumstances, *viz.* That after God, by long continued rains, had prepared the slime of the earth, out of which he was to form it, he sent the angel Gabriel, and commanded him, of seven lays of earth, to take out of each an handful: that upon Gabriel's coming to the Earth, he told her, that God had determined to extract that out of her bowels, whereof he proposed to make man, who was to be sovereign over all, and his vicegerent: that, surprised at this news, the Earth desired Gabriel to represent her fears to God, that this creature, whom he was going to make in this manner, would one day rebel against him, and draw down his curse upon her: that Gabriel returned, and made report to God of the Earth's remonstrances; but God resolving to execute his design, dispatched Michael,

and

A M. 1.
Ant. Chrif.
4004.
Gen ch 1
and part of
ch. 2

was carried about upon angels' necks, whose heads were so big, that birds could not fly in a thousand years from one ear to another; that the heavens were propped up by the mountain Koff; that the stars were fire-brands, thrown against the devils when they invaded heaven, and that the earth stands upon the top of a great cow's horn; that this cow stands upon a white stone, this stone upon a mountain, and this mountain upon God knows what; with many more absurdities of the like nature.

And the justness of that of Moses.

These are some accounts of the world's creation, which nations of great sagacity in other respects have at least pretended to believe. But alas! how sordid and trifling are they, in comparison of what we read in the book of Genesis, where every thing is easy and natural, comporting with God's majesty, and not repugnant to the principles of philosophy? Nay, where every thing, agrees with the positions of the greatest men in the Heathen world, * the sentiments of their wisest philosophers, and the descriptions of their

and afterwards Asraphel, with the same commission: that these two angels returned in like manner to report the Earth's excuses and absolute refusal to contribute to this work; whereupon he deputed Azrael, who, without saying any thing to the Earth took an handful out of each of the seven different lays or beds, and carried it to a place in Arabia, between Mecca and Taief: that after the angels had mixed and kneaded the earth which Azrael brought, God, with his own hand formed out of it an human statue, and having left it in the same place for some time to dry, not long after communicating his spirit, or enlivening breath, infused life and understanding into it, and clothing it in a wonderful dress, suitable to its dignity, commanded the angels to fall prostrate before it, which Eblis (by whom they mean Lucifer) refusing to do, was immediatly driven out of paradise. *N.B.* The difference of the earth employed in the formation of Adam, is of great service to the Mahometans in explaining the different colours and qualities of mankind who are derived from it, some of whom are white, others black, others tawny. yellow, olive-coleured, and red; some of one humour, inclination, and complexion, and others of a quite different; *Calmet's Dictionary* on the word *Adam*.

* *Thales*, quem primum Græci putant rerum naturalium causas esse rimatum, mundum opus esse Dei, Deumque antiquissimum esse rerum omnium, utpote ortûs expertem, asserti. *Pythagoras*, cùm mundi hujus fabricam et ornatum contemplaret videri sibi, aiebat, audire vocem illam Dei, quâ existere jussus est. *Plato*,

non

their most renowned poets. So that were we to judge of Moses at the bar of reason, merely as an historian; had we none of those supernatural proofs of the divinity of his writings, which set them above the sphere of all human composition; had his works none of that manifest advantage of antiquity above all others we ever yet saw; and were we not allowed to presume, that his living near the time which he makes the æra of the world's creation, gave him great assistances in point of tradition; were we, I say, to wave all this that might be alledged in his behalf; yet the very manner of his treating the subject gives him a preference above all others. Nor can we, without admiration, see a person who had none of the systems before him which we now so much value, giving us a clearer idea of things, in the way of an easy narrative, than any philosopher, with all his hard words and new-invented terms, has yet been able to do; and, in the compass of two short chapters, comprising all that has been advanced with reason, even from his own time to this very day. *A. M. 1. Ant. Chrif. 4004. Gen. ch. 1. and part of ch. 2.*

DISSERTATION I.

The wisdom of God in the works of the Creation.

THOUGH the author of the Pentateuch [a] never once attempts to prove the being of a God, as taking it all along for a thing undeniable; yet it may not be improper for us, in this place, to take a cursory view of the works of the creation, (as far at least as they come under the Mosaic account,) in order to shew the existence, the wisdom, the greatness, and the goodness of their almighty Maker.

Let us then cast our eyes up to the firmament, where the rich handy-work of God presents itself to our sight, and ask *The being and wisdom of God proved from the make and motion of heavenly bodies.*

non ex æterna materia, suique coæquali, Deum mundum compegisse ratus est, sed eduxisse ex nihilo, solâque suâ voluntate ad id eguisse, neque solum à Deo, sed ad Dei similitudinem factum esse hominem, et animos nostros Deo esse cognatos et similes, eidem Platoni notum fuit. Vocandi quoque ad partes poetæ: inter Latinos *Virgilius*, cum canentem inducit Silenum, ut coactis rerum seminibus mundi tener orbis concreverit; præcipue *Ovidius*, cum cœli terræque narrat ortum, hominisque ad Dei effigiem conficti; et, inter Græcos, imprimis *Hesiodus*. qui rerum omnium machinationem, suavissimis carminibus, Mosaicæ doctrinæ consonis, in Theogoniá, celebravit; *Huetii Alnetanæ Quæstiones*.

[a] Vid. Stillingfleet's Orig. Sacr. l. 3. c. 1.

A. M. 1.
Ant. Chrif.
4004.
Gen. cn. 1.
and part of
ch 2.

ask ourselves some such questions as these. What power built, over our heads, this vast and magnificent arch, and *spread out the heavens like a curtain?* Who garnished these heavens with such a variety of shining objects, a thousand, and ten thousand times ten thousand different stars, new suns, new moons, new worlds, in comparison of which this earth of ours is but a point, all regular in their motions, and swimming in their liquid æther? Who painted the clouds with such a variety of colours, and in such diversity of shades and figures, as is not in the power of the finest pencil to emulate? Who formed the sun of such a determinate size, and placed it at such a convenient distance, as not to annoy, but only refresh us, and nourish the ground with its kindly warmth? If it were larger, it would set the earth on fire; if less, it would leave it frozen: if it were nearer us, we should be scorched to death; if farther from us, we should not be able to live for want of heat: who then hath made it so commodious ᵇ *a tabernacle* (I speak with the Scriptures, and according to the common notion) *out of which it cometh forth,* every morning, *like a bride-groom out of his chamber, and rejoiceth, as a giant, to run his course?* For so many ages past, it never failed rising at its appointed time, nor once missed sending out the dawn to proclaim its approach: but at whose voice does it arise, and by whose hand is it directed in its diurnal and annual course, to give us the blessed vicissitudes of the day and night, and the regular succession of different seasons? That it should always proceed in the same strait path, and never once be known to step aside; that it should turn at a certain determinate point, and not go forward in a space where there is nothing to obstruct it; that it should traverse the same path back again in the same constant and regular pace, to bring on the seasons by gradual advances: that the moon should supply the office of the sun, and appear at set times, to illuminate the air, and give a vicarious light, when its brother is gone to carry the day to the other hemisphere; ᶜ that it should procure, or at least regulate the fluxes and refluxes of the sea, whereby the water is kept in constant motion, and so preserved from putrefaction, and accommodated to man's manifold conveniencies, besides the business of fishing, and the use of navigation: in a word, that the rest of the planets, and all the innumerable host of
heavenly

ᵇ Psal. xix. 4, 5.   ᶜ Ray's Wisdom of God in the creation.

heavenly bodies should perform their courses and revolutions, with so much certainty and exactness, as never once to fail, but, for almost this 6000 years, come constantly about in the same period, to the hundredth part of a minute; this is such a clear and incontestable proof of a divine architect, and of that counsel and wisdom wherewith he rules and directs the universe, as made the Roman philosopher, with good reason, conclude, "That [d] whoever "imagines, that the wonderful order, and incredible "constancy of the heavenly bodies, and their motions "(whereupon the preservation and welfare of all things "do depend) is not governed by an intelligent being, him- "self is destitute of understanding. For shall we, when "we see an artificial engine, a sphere, a dial, for instance, "acknowledge, at first sight, that it is the work of art and "understanding; and yet, when we behold the heavens, "moved and whirled about with an incredible velocity, "most constantly finishing their anniversary vicissitudes, "make any doubt, that these are the performances, not "only of reason, but of a certain excellent and divine "reason?"

A. M. 1.
Ant. Chrif.
4004.
Gen. ch. 1.
and part of
ch. 2.

And if Tully, from the very imperfect knowledge of astronomy, which his time afforded, could be so confident, that the heavenly bodies were framed, and moved by a wise and understanding mind, as to declare, that, in his opinion, whoever asserted the contrary, was himself destitute of understanding; [e] what would he have said, had he been acquainted with the modern discoveries of astronomy; the immense greatness of the world, that part of it (I mean) which falls under our observation; the exquisite regularity of the motions of all the planets, without any deviation or confusion; the inexpressible nicety of adjustment in the primary velocity of the earth's annual motion; the wonderful proportion of its diurnal motion about its own centre, for the distinction of light and darkness; the exact accommodation of the densities of the planets to their distances from the sun: the admirable order, number, and usefulness of the several satellites, which move about the respective planets; the motion of the comets, which are now found to be as regular and periodical, as that of other planetary bodies; and, lastly, the preservation of the several systems, and of the several planets and comets in the same system,

[d] Tully De nat. deorum. [e] Clarke's Demonstration of a God.

A. M. 1.
Ant. Chrif.
4004.
Gen. ch. 1.
and part of
ch. 2

system, from falling upon each other: what, I say, would Tully, that great master of reason, have thought and said, if these, and other newly discovered instances of the inexpressible accuracy and wisdom of the works of God, had been observed and considered in his days? Certainly Atheism, which even then was unable to withstand the arguments drawn from this topic, must now, upon the additional strength of these later observations, be utterly ashamed to show its head, and forced to acknowledge, that it was an eternal and almighty Being, God alone, who gave these celestial bodies their proper mensuration and temperature of heat, their dueness of distance, and regularity of motion, or, in the phrase of the prophet, *who established the world by his wisdom, and stretched out the heavens by his understanding*.

The air and its meteors.

If, from the firmament, we descend to the orb whereon we live, what a glorious proof of the divine wisdom do we meet with in this intermediate expansion of the air, which is so wonderfully contrived, as, at one and the same time, to support clouds for rain, and to afford winds for health and traffic; to be proper for the breath of animals by its spring, for causing sounds by its motion, and for conveying light by its transparency? But whose power was it, that made so thin and fluid an element, the safe repository of thunder and lightning, of winds and tempests? By whose command, and out of whose treasuries, are these meteors sent forth to purify the air, which would otherwise stagnate, and consume the vapours, which would otherwise annoy us? And by what skilful hand is the ᵍ water, which is drawn from the sea, by a natural distillation made fresh, and bottled up, as it were, in the clouds, to be sent upon the *wings of the wind* into different countries, and, in a manner, equally dispersed, and distributed over the face of the earth, in gentle showers?

From the earth, and its animals.

Whose power and wisdom was it, that *hanged the earth upon nothing*, and gave it a spherical figure, the most commodious that could be devised, both for the consistency of its parts, and the velocity of its motion? that *weighed the mountains in scales*, and *the hills in a balance*, and disposed of them in their most proper places for fruitfulness and health? That diversified the climates of the earth into such an agreeable variety, that, at the farthest distance, each one has its proper seasons, day and night,

ᶠ Jer. li. 15. ᵍ Ray's Wisdom of God in the creation.

night, winter and summer? that clothed the face of it
with plants and flowers, so exquisitely adorned with various
and inimitable beauties, that even *Solomon, in all his glory,*
was not arrayed like one of them? That placed the plant in
the seed (as the young is in the womb of animals) in such
elegant complications, as afford at once both a pleasing and
astonishing spectacle? that painted and perfumed the flowers, gave them the sweet odours which they diffuse in the
air for our delight, and, with one and the same water, dyed
them into different colours, the scarlet, the purple, the
carnation, surpassing the imitation, as well as comprehension of mankind? that has replenished it with such an infinite variety of living creatures, [h] so like, and at the
same time so unlike to each other, that of the innumerable particulars wherein each creature differs from all others, every one is known to have its peculiar beauty, and
singular use? Some walk, some creep, some fly, some
swim; but every one has members and organs [i] fitted
to its peculiar motions. In a word, the pride of the horse,
and the feathers of the peacock, the largness of the
camel, and the smallness of the insect, are equal demonstrations of an infinite wisdom and power: Nay, * the
smaller

A. M. 1.
Ant. Christ.
4004.
Gen. ch. 1.
d part of
ch. 1.

[h] Dr Sam. Clarke's serm. vol, 2. [i] Ray's Wisdom of God
in the creation.

* *Where has nature disposed so many senses, as in a gnat?*
(says Pliny in his Natural history, when considering the body
of that insect,) "Ubi visum prætendit? ubi gustatum applicavit?
"ubi odoratum inseruit? ubi vero truculentam illam, et portione
"maximam vocem, ingeneravit? qua subtilitate pennas adnex-
"uit? prælongavit pedum crura, disposuit jejunam caveam, uti
"alvum, avidam sanguinis, et potissimum humani, accendit?
"telum vero, perfodiendi tergori quo spiculavit ingenio? atque,
"ut in capaci, cum cerni non possit exilitas, ita reciproca ge-
"minavit arte, ut fodiendo acuminatum, pariter forbendoque
"fistulosum esset?" And if Pliny made so many queries concerning the body of a gnat, (which, by his own confession, is none
of the least of insects,) what would he, in all likelihood, have
done, had he seen the bodies of these animalcula, which are discernable by glasses, to the number of 10, 20, or 30 thousand in
a drop of pepper-water, not larger than a grain of millet? And
if these creatures be so very small, what must we think of their
muscles, and other parts? Certain it is, that the mechanism, by
which nature performs the muscular motion, is exceedingly
minute and curious, and to the performance of every muscular
motion,

A. M. 1.
Ant. Chrif
4004.
Gen. ch. 1.
and part of
ch. 2.

smaller the creature is, the more amazing is the workmanship; and when in a little mite, we do (by the help of glasses) see limbs perfectly well organized, an head, a body, legs, and feet, all distinct, and as well proportioned for their size, as those of the vastest elephants; and consider withal, that, in every part of this living atom, there are muscles, nerves, veins, arteries, and blood; and in that blood ramous particles and humours; and in those humours, some drops that are composed of other minute particles: when we consider all this, I say, can we help being lost in wonder and astonishment, or refrain crying out, with the blessed apostle, [k] *O the depth of the riches both of the wisdom, and knowledge of God! how unsearchable are his works, and his ways of creation and providence past finding out!*

But there is another thing in animals, both terrestrial and aqueous, no less wonderful than their frame; and that is their natural instinct. In compliance with the common forms of speech I call it so, but in reality, it is the providential direction of them, by an all-wise, and all-powerful mind. For what else has infused into birds the art of building their nests, either hard or soft, according to the constitution of their young? What else makes them keep so constantly in their nests, while they are hatching their young, as if they knew the philosophy of their own warmth, and its aptness for animation? what else moves the swallow, upon the approach of winter, to fly to a more temperate climate, as if it understood the celestial signs, the influence of the stars, and the change of seasons? What else [l] causes the salmon, every year, to ascend from the sea up a river, some four or five hundred miles perhaps, only to cast its spawn, and secure it in banks of sand, until the young be hatched, or excluded, and then return to the sea again? How these creatures, when they have been wandering, a long time, in the wide ocean, should again find out, and repair to the mouth of the same rivers, seems to me very strange, and hardly accountable, without having recourse ether to some impression given at their first creation, or the immediate and continual direction, of a superior cause.

motion, in greater animals at least, there are not fewer distinct parts concerned, than many millions of millions, and these visible through a microscope; *Ray's Wisdom of God in the creation.*

[k] Rom. xi. 33.   [l] Ray's Wisdom of God.

Chap. I. *from the Creation to the Flood.*

cause. In a word, ᵐ can we behold the spider's net, the silk worms' webs, the bees' cells, or the ants' granaries, without being lost in the contemplation, and forced to acknowledge that infinite wisdom of their Creator, who either directs their unerring steps himself, or has given them a genius (if I may so call it) fit to be an emblem, and to shew mankind the pattern of art, industry, and frugality?

A. M. 1. Ant. Chrif. 4004. Gen. ch. 1. and part of ch. 2.

If from the earth, and the creatures which live upon it, we cast our eye upon the water, we soon perceive, that it is a liquid and transparent body, and that, had it been more or less rarified, it had not been so proper for the use of man: but who gave it that just configuration of parts, and exact degree of motion, as to make it both so fluent, and at the same time so strong, as to carry and waft away the most unwieldy burthens? Who hath taught the rivers to run, in winding streams, through vast tracts of land, in order to water them more plentifully; then throw themselves into the ocean, to make it the common centre of commerce; and so, by secret and imperceptible channels, return to their fountain-head, in one perpetual circulation? Who stored and replenished these rivers with fish of all kinds, which glide, and sport themselves in the limpid streams, and run heedlessly into the fisher's net, or come greedily to the angler's hook, in order to be caught (as it were) for the use and entertainment of man? *The great and wide sea* is a very awful and stupendous work of God, and the flux and reflux of its waters are not the easiest phenomena in nature. ⁿ All that we know of certainty is this, that the tide carries and brings us back to certain places, at precise hours: but whose hand is it that makes it stop, and then return with such regularity? A little more or less motion in this fluid mass would disorder all nature, and a small incitement upon a tide ruin whole kingdoms: who then was so wise, as to take such exact measures in immense bodies, and who so strong, as to rule the rage of that proud element at discretion? Even he, ᵒ *who hath placed the sand for the bound thereof, by a perpetual decree, that it cannot pass;* and placed the Leviathan (among other animals of all kinds) *therein to take his pastime, out of whose nostrils goeth a smoke, and whose breath kindleth coals;* so that *he maketh the deep to boil like a pot, and maketh the sea like a pot*

From the water, and its animals.

Vol. I. No. 2.   U   of

ᵐ Charnock's existence of a God.   ⁿ Fenelon's demonstration of a God.   ᵒ Jer. v. 22.

of ointment, as the author of the book of [p] Job elegantly describes that most important creature.

If now, from the world itself, we turn our eyes more particularly upon man, the principal inhabitant that God has placed therein, no understanding certainly can be so low and mean, no heart so stupid and insensible, as not plainly to see, that nothing but infinite wisdom could, in so wonderful a manner, have fashioned his body, and inspired into it a being of superior faculties, whereby he [q] *teacheth us more than the beasts of the field, and maketh us wiser than the fowls of heaven.*

Should any of us see a lump of clay rise immediately from the ground into the complete figure of a man, full of beauty and symmetry, and endowed with all the parts and faculties we perceive in ourselves, and possibly far more exquisite and beautiful: should we presently, after his formation, observe him perform all the operations of life, sense, and reason; move as gracefully, talk as eloquently, reason as justly, and do every thing as dexterously, as the most accomplished man breathing; the same was the case, and the same the moment of time, in God's formation of our first parent. But (to give the thing a stronger impression upon the mind) we will suppose, [r] that this figure rises by degrees, and is finished part by part, in some succession of time; and that, when the whole is completed, the veins and arteries bored, the sinews and tendons laid, the joints fitted, and the liquor (transmutable into blood and juices) lodged in the ventricles of the heart, God infuses into it a vital principle; whereupon the liquor in the heart begins to descend, and thrill along the veins, and an heavenly blush arises in the countenance, such as scorns the help of art, and is above the power of imitation. The image moves, it walks, it speaks: it moves with such a majesty, as proclaims it the lord of the creation, and talks with such an accent, and sublimity of sentiment, as makes every ear attentive, and even its great Creator enter into converse with it: were we to see all this transacted before our eyes, I say, we could not but stand astonished at the thing; and yet this is an exact emblem of every man's formation, and a contemplation it is, that made holy David break out into this rapturous acknowledgement [s] *Lord! I will give thee thanks, for I am fearfully and wonderfully made;*

[p] Job. xli. 31.   [q] Job. xxxv. 11.   [r] Hale's origination of mankind.   [s] Psal. cxxxix. 14, 16.

Chap. I.   *from the Creation to the Flood.*   39.

made; marvellous are thy works, and that my soul knoweth right well: thine eyes did see my substance, yet being imperfect, and in thy book were all my members written.

A. M. 1.
Ant. Chrif. 4004.
Gen. ch. 1. and part of ch. 2.

Nay, so curious is the texture of the human body, and in every part so full of wonder, that even Galen himself, (who was otherwise backward enough to believe a God,) after he had carefully surveyed the frame of it, and viewed the fitness and usefulness of every part, the many * several intentions of every little vein, bone, and muscle, and the beautiful composition of the whole, fell into a pang of devotion, and wrote an hymn to his Creator's praise. ᵗ And, if in the make of the body, how much more does the divine wisdom appear in the creation of the soul of man, a substance immaterial, but united to the body by a copula imperceptible, and yet so strong, as to make them mutually operate, and sympathize with each other, in all their pleasures and their pains; a substance endued with those wonderful faculties of thinking, understanding, judging, reasoning, chusing, acting, and (which is the end and excellency of all) the power of knowing, obeying, imitating, and praising its Creator; though certainly neither it, nor any superior rank of beings, angels, and archangels, or the *whole host of heaven* can worthily and sufficiently do it; ᵘ *for who can express the mighty acts of the Lord, or shew forth all his praise?*

Thus, which way soever we turn our eyes, whether we look upwards or downwards, without us, or within us, upon the animate or inanimate parts of the creation; we shall find abundant reason to take up the words of the Psalmist, and say, ˣ *O Lord, how wonderful are thy works! in wisdom hast thou made them all; the earth is full of thy riches.* ʸ *O, that men would therefore praise the Lord for his*

U 2   *goodness,*

* Galen, in his book *De formatione fœtus*, takes notice, that there are, in a human body, above 600 muscles, in each of which there are, at least, ten several intentions, or due qualifications, to be observed; so that, about the muscles alone, no less than 6000 several ends and aims are to be attended to. The bones are reckoned to be 284, and the distinct scopes, or intentions of each of these, are above 40; in all, about 12,000; and thus it is in some proportion with all the other parts, the skin, ligaments, vessels, and humours; but more especially with the several vessels of the body, which do, in regard of the great variety and multitude of those several intentions required to them, very much exceed the *homogeneous* parts; *Wilkin's nat. rel.*

ᵗ Clarke's serm, vol 1.   ᵘ Psal. cvi. 2.   ˣ Ibid. civ. 24.   ʸ Ibid. cvii. 21, 22.

A. M. 1.
Ant. Chrif.
4004.
Gen. ch. 1.
and part of
ch. 2

goodnefs, and declare the wonders that he doth for the children of men! that they would offer him the facrifice of thankfgiving, and tell out all his works with gladnefs!

CHAP. II.

Of the ftate of man's innocence.

THE HISTORY.

Gen ch. 2.
from ver. 8.

God's conducting Eve to Adam, marrying, and blefsing them.

AS foon as the feventh day from the creation (the firft day, as we faid, of Adam's life, and confequently the firft day of the week) was begun, Adam, awaking out of his fleep, and mufing, very probably, on his vifion the preceding night, beheld the fair figure of a woman approaching him, † conducted by the hand of her almighty Maker; and as fhe advanced, the several innocent beauties that adorned her perfon, the comelinefs of her fhape, and gracefulnefs of her gefture, the luftre of her eye, and fweetnefs of her looks, difcovered themfelves in every ftep more and more.

It is not to be expreffed, nor now conceived, * what a full tide of joy entered in at the foul of our firft parent,
when

† It is the general opinion of interpreters, both Jewifh and Chriftian, that God himfelf, or, more particularly, the fecond perfon in the ever-bleffed Trinity, God the Son (who is therefore ftyled in Scripture [Ifa. lxiii. 9.] *the Angel of God's prefence*) appeared to Adam, on this and fundry other occafions, in a vifible glorious majefty, fuch as the Jews call the *Schechinah*, which feems to have been *a very fhining flame*, or *amazing fplendor of light*, breaking out of a thick cloud, of which we afterward read very frequently, under the name of *the glory of the Lord*, and to which we cannot fuppofe our firft parents to have been ftrangers. We therefore look upon it as highly probable, that this divine Majefty firft conducted Eve to the place where Adam was, and not long after their marriage, conveyed them both, from the place where they were formed, into the garden of Eden; *Patrick's Commentary*.

* Milton has expreffed the joy and tranfport of Adam, upon his firft fight of Eve, in the following manner:

When out of hope, behold her! not far off;
Such as I faw her in my dream, adorn'd
With what all earth, or heaven could beftow,
To make her amiable. On fhe came,

Led

Chap. II.   *from the Creation to the Flood.*   41

when he surveyed this lovely creature, who was destined to be the partner and companion of his life; when, by a secret sympathy, he felt that she was of his own likeness, and complexion, *bone of his bone, and flesh of his flesh,* his very self, diversified only into another sex; and could easily foresee, that the love and union which was now to commence between them was to be perpetual, and for ever inseparable. ᵃ For the same divine hand which conducted the woman to the place where Adam was, presented her to him in the capacity of a matrimonial father; and, * having joined them together in the nuptial state, pronounced

A. M. 1.
Ant. Chrif.
4004.
Cen. ch. 2.
his from ver. 8.

    Led by her heav'nly Maker (though unseen)
    And guided by his voice; not uninform'd
    Of nuptial sanctity, and marriage rites.
    Grace was in all her steps, heav'n in her eye,
    In ev'ry gesture dignity and love.
    I overjoy'd, could not forbear aloud.
    " This turn hath made amends, thou hast fulfill'd
    " Thy words. Creator bounteous, and benign!
    " Giver of all things fair! but fairest this
    " Of all thy gifts."   Book 8.

ᵃ *Vid.* Patrick's Commentary.

* The words of Milton upon this occasion are extremely fine.

    ————————— all heav'n
    And happy constellations, on that hour
    Shed their selectest influence; the earth
    Gave sign of gratulation, and each hill:
    Joyous the birds; fresh gales, and gentle airs
    Whisper'd it to the woods, and from their wings
    Flung rose, flung odours, from the spicy shrub,
    Disporting.   Book 8.

Nor can we pass by his episode upon marriage, which, for its grave and majestic beauty, is inimitable.

    Hail wedded love! mysterious law! true source
    Of human offspring! sole propriety
    In paradise, of all things common else!
    By thee adult'rous lust was driv'n from men,
    Among the bestial herds to range; by thee
    (Founded in reason, loyal, just, and pure)
    Relations dear, and all the charities
    Of father, son, and brother, first were known.
    Perpetual fountain of domestic sweets!
    Whose bed is undefil'd, and chaste pronounc'd——
    Here love his golden shafts employs; here lights
    His constant lamp, and waves his purple wings;
    Reigns here and revels——   Book 4.

A. M. 1.
Ant. Chrif.
4004.
Gen. c. 1
from v. 1. 8.

The Situa-
tion of
Paradise.

pronounced his benediction over them, to the intent that [b] they might enjoy unmolested the dominion he had given them over the other parts of the creation, and, being themselves † fruitful in the procreation of children, might live to see the earth replenished with a numerous progeny, descended from their loins.

In the mean time God had taken care to provide our first parents * with a pleasant and delightful habitation in the

---

[b] *Vid.* Gen. i. 28, 29, 30.

† The words of the text are, *Be fruitful, and multiply, and replenish the earth:* whereupon some have made it a question, whether his is not a command, obliging all men to marriage and procreation, as most of the Jewish doctors are of opinion? But to this it may be replied 1*st*, That it is indeed a command obliging all men so far, as not to suffer the extinction of mankind, in which sense it did absolutely bind Adam and Eve, as also Noah, and his sons, and their wives after the flood: but, 2dly, that it does not oblige every particular man to marry, appears from the example of our Lord Jesus, who lived and died in an unmarried state; from his commendation of those who made themselves *eunuchs for the kingdom of God* Matth. xix. 12. and from St. Paul's frequent approbation of virginity, 1 Cor. vii. 1, &c. And therefore, 3*dly*, it is here rather a permission than a command, though it be expressed in the form of a command as other permissions frequently are. *Vid.* Gen. ii. 16. Deut. xiv. 4; *Pool's Annotations*.

* The description which Milton gives us of the garden of paradise, is very agreeable in several places, but in one more especially, where he represents the pleasing variety of it.

—— Thus was this place
A happy rural seat of various view.
Groves, whose rich trees wept od'rous gums, and balm;
Others, whose fruit burnish'd with golden rind,
Hung amiable; (Hesperian fables true,
If true, here only) and of delicious taste.
Betwixt them lawns, or level downs, and flocks,
Grazing the tender herb, were interpos'd;
Or palmy hillock, or the flow'ry lap
Of some irriguous valley spread her store.
Flow'rs of all hue, and without thorn the rose.
Another side umbrageous grots, and caves
Of cool recess, o'er which the mantling vine
Lays forth her purple grape, and gently creeps
Luxuriant. Mean while murm'ring waters fall
Down the slope hills, dispers'd, or in a lake

(That

Chap. II.   *from the Creation to the Flood.*   43

the country of Eden, ᶜ which was watered by four ri- | A. M. 1.
vers; by the *Tigris*, in Scripture called *Hiddekel*, on one | Ant. Chrif.
fide, and by *Euphrates* on the other, which, joining their | 4004
ftreams together in a place where (not long after the flood) | Gen. ch. 2.
the famous city of Babylon was fituate, pafs through a large | from ver. 8.
country, and then dividing again, form the two rivers,
which the facred hiftorian calls *Pifon*, and *Gihon*, and fo
water part of the garden of paradife, wherein were all kinds
of trees, herbs, and flowers, which could any way delight
the fight, the tafte, or the fmell.

Among other trees however, there were two of very | The tree of
remarkable names and properties planted *in the midft*, | life, and
or moft eminent part of the garden, to be always within | that of
the view and obfervation of our firft parents, *the tree of* | knowledge,
life, fo called, ᵈ becaufe it had a virtue in it, not only | why fo cal-
to repair the animal fpirits, as other nourifhment does, | led.
but likewife to preferve and * maintain them in the fame
equal temper and ftate wherein they were created, without pain, difeafes, or decay; and *the tree of knowledge of
good and evil*, fo called, ᵉ not becaufe it had a virtue
to confer any fuch knowledge, but * becaufe the devil, in
his

(That to the fringed bank, with myrtle crown'd,
Her chryftal mirror holds) unite their ftreams.
The birds their choir apply. Airs, vernal airs,
Breathing the fmell of fields, and groves, attune
The trembling leaves, while univerfal PAN
Knit with the GRACES, and the HOURS, in dance
Lead on the eternal fpring.—Book 4.

ᶜ Hiftoire de la Bible, par M. Martin.   ᵈ Patrick's
Comment.; *et vid*. ch 3. ver. 20.

* Others think, that the *tree of life* was fo called, in a fymbo-
lical fenfe, as it was a fign and token of that life which man had
received from God, and of his continual enjoyment of it, without
diminution, had he perfifted in his obedience, and as this garden,
fay they, was confeffedly a type of heaven, fo God might intend
by this tree to reprefent that immortal life which he meant to
beftow upon mankind himfelf, Rev. xxii, 2. according to which
is that famous faying of St. Auftin, *Erat ei in cæteris lignis ali-
mentum, in iftis vero facramentum*; Patrick's Commentary.

ᵉ Nicholl's Conference, vol. 1.

* Others think the *tree of knowledge* was fo called, either in
refpect to God, who was minded by this tree to prove our
firft parents, whether they would be good or bad, which was to
be

A. M. 1.
Ant. Chrif.
4004.
Gen. ch. 2.
from ver. 8.

his temptation of the woman, pretended that it had; pretended, that ᶠ as God knew all things, and was himself subject to no one's controul, so the eating of this tree would confer on them the same degree of knowledge, and put them in the same state of independency: and from this unfortunate deception (whereof God might speak by way of anticipation) it did not improperly derive its name.

The prohibition given our first parents.

Into this † paradise of much pleasure, but some danger, wherein was one tree of a pernicious quality, though all the rest were good in their kind, and extremely salutary, the Lord God conducted our first parents, who, at this time, were naked, and yet not ashamed, because their innocence was their protection. They had no sinful inclinations in their bodies, no evil concupiscence in their minds, to make them blush; and withal, the temperature of the climate was such, as needed no clothing to defend them from the weather, God having given them (as we may imagine) a survey of their new habitation, shewn them the various beauties

be known by their abstaining from the fruit, or eating it; or in respect to them, who, in the event, found by sad experience, the difference between good and evil, which they knew not before; but they found the difference to be this, that good is that which gives the mind pleasure and assurance; but evil that which is always attended with sorrow and regret; *Pool's Annotations*, and *Young's Sermons*, vol. 1.

ᶠ Estius in difficiliora loca.

† The word *paradise*, which the Septuagint make use of (whether it be of Hebrew, Chaldee, or Persian original) signifies *a place enclosed for pleasure and delight*: either a park where beasts do range, or a spot of ground stocked with choice plants, which is properly a garden; or curiously set with trees, yielding all manner of fruit, which is an orchard. There are three places in the Hebrew text of the Old Testament, wherein this word is found. 1. Nehemiah, ii. 8. where that prophet requests of Artaxerxes' letters to Asaph, *the keeper of the king's forest*, or paradise; 2dly, in the Song of Solomon, [iv. 13.] where he says, that the plants of the spouse *are an orchard of pomegranates*; and 3dly, in Ecclesiastes [ii. 5.] where he says, *he made himself gardens*, or paradises. In all which senses the word may very fitly be applied to the place where our first parents were to live: since it was not only a pleasant garden and fruitful orchard, but a spacious park and forest likewise, whereinto the several beasts of the field were permitted to come; *Edward's Survey of religion*, vol. 1. *and Calmet's Dictionary on the word* Paradise.

Chap. I. *from the Creation to the Flood.* 45

ties of the place, the work wherein they were to employ themselves by day, and * the bower wherein they were to repose themselves by night, granted them to eat of the fruit of every tree in the garden, except that one, *the tree of knowledge of good and evil*, which (how lovely soever it might appear to the eye) he strictly charged them not so much as to touch, upon the penalty of incurring his displeasure, forfeiting their right and title to eternal life, and entailing upon themselves, and their posterity, ‖ mortality, diseases, and death.

Ant. Chrif. 4004. Gen. ch. 1. from ver 8.

With

* The description which Milton gives us of this blissful bower, is extremely fine.
——It was a place,
Chos'n by the sov'reign Planter, when he fram'd
All things to man's delightful use: the roof
Of thickest covert, was inwoven shade,
Laurel and myrtle, and what higher grew
Of firm and fragrant leaf. On either side
Acanthus and each od'rous bushy shrub,
Fenc'd up the verdant wall. Each beauteous flow'r
Iris, all hues, roses, and jessamin,
Rear'd high their flourish'd heads between, and wrought
Mosaic: under foot the violet,
Crocus, and hyacinth, with rich inlay,
Broider'd the ground, more colour'd than with stone
Of costliest emblem. Other creatures here,
Beast, bird, insect, or worm, durst enter none;
Such was their awe of man !   Book 4.

‖ The words in our version are, *In the day thou eatest thereof, thou shalt surely die;* which seem to imply, that on the day that Adam should eat of the tree of knowledge, he should die; which eventually proved not so, because he lived many years after; and therefore (as some observe very well) it should be rendered, *Thou shalt deserve to die without remission;* for the Scripture frequently expresses by the future not only what will come to pass, but also what ought to come to pass; to which purpose there is a very apposite text in 1 Kings, ii. 37. where Solomon says to Shimei, —— *Go not forth hence* (viz. from Jerusalem) *any whither; for in the day thou goest out, and passest over the brook Kidron, thou shalt surely die,* i. e. *thou shalt, deserve death without remission.* For Solomon reserved to himself the power of punishing him when he should think fit; and, in effect, he did not put him to death the same day that he disobeyed, any more than God did put Adam to death the same day that he transgressed

A. M. 1.
Ant. Chrif.
4004
Gen. ch. 2
from ver. 8.

Their employment in paradise

With this small restraint which the divine wisdom thought proper to lay upon Adam, as a token of his subjection, and a test of his obedience, God left him to the enjoyment of this paradise, where every thing was pleasant to the sight, and accommodated to his liking. Not thinking it convenient however for him, even in his state of innocence, to be idle or unemployed, here he appointed him to dress and keep the new plantation, which, by reason of its luxuriancy, would in time, he knew, require his care. Here he was to employ his mind, as well as exercise his body; to contemplate and study the works of God; to submit himself wholly to the divine conduct; to conform all his actions to the divine will; and to live in a constant dependence upon the divine goodness. Here he was to spend his days in the continual exercises of prayer and thanksgiving; and, it may be, the natural dictates of gratitude would prompt him to offer some of the fruits of the ground, and some living creatures, by way of sacrifice to God. Here were thousands of objects to exercise his intellective faculties, to call forth his reason, and employ it; but that wherein the ultimate perfection of his life was doubtless to consist, was the union of his soul with the supreme good, that infinite and eternal Being, which alone can constitute the happiness of man.

Their happiness.

[g] O! Adam, beyond all imagination happy: with uninterrupted health, and untainted innocence, to delight thee; no perverseness of will, or perturbation of appetite, to discompose thee; a heart upright, a conscience clear, and an head unclouded, to entertain thee; a delightful earth for thee to enjoy; a glorious universe for thee to contemplate; an everlasting heaven, a crown of never-fading glory for thee to look for and expect; and, in the mean time, the author of that universe, the King of that heaven, and giver of that glory, thy God, thy Creator, thy benefactor, to see, to converse with, to bless, to glorify, to adore, to obey!

This gressed in eating the forbidden fruit. This seems to be a good solution; though some interpreters understand the prohibition, as if God intended thereby to intimate to Adam the deadly quality of the forbidden fruit, whose poison was so very exquisite, that, on the very day he eat thereof, it would certainly have destroyed him, had not God's goodness interposed, and restrained its violence; *Vid. Essay for a new Translation; and Le Clerc's Comment.*

[g] Revelation examined, part 1.

Chap. II.   *from the Creation to the Flood.*

This was the designed felicity of our first parents. Neither they, nor their posterity were to be liable to sorrow or misery of any kind, but to be possessed of a constant and never-failing happiness; and, after innumerable ages and successions, were, in their courses, to be taken up into an heavenly paradise. For [h] that the terrestrial paradise was to Adam a type of heaven and that the never-ending life of happiness promised to our first parents (if they had continued obedient, and grown up to perfection under that œconomy wherein they were placed) should not have been continued in this earthly, but only have commenced here, and been perpetuated in an higher state, *i. e.* after such a trial of their obedience as the divine wisdom should think convenient, they should have been translated from earth to heaven, is the joint opinion * of the best ancient, both Jewish and Christian writers.

A. M. 1.
Ant. Chrif.
4004.
Gen. ch. 2.
from ver. 8.
and designed translation;

The Objection,

"BUT how delightful soever the garden of Eden might
" be, a type of heaven, and an entrance into the re-
" gions

against the reality of a terrestrial paradise.

[h] Bull's State of man before the fall.

* This same learned writer, (*viz.* Bishop Bull) has compiled a great many authorities from the fathers of the first centuries, all full and significant to the purpose, and to which I refer the reader, only mentioning one or two of more remarkable force and antiquity, for his present satisfaction. Justin Martyr, speaking of the creation of the world, delivers not his own private opinion only, but the common sense of Christians in his days; " We have been taught," says he, " that God, being
" good, did, in the beginning, make all things out of an un-
" informed matter for the sake of men, who, if by their works
" they had rendered themselves worthy of his acceptance, we
" presume, should have been favoured with his friendship, and
" reigned together with him, being made incorruptible, and
" impassable;" *Apol.* 2   Athanasius, among other things worthy our observation, concerning the primordial state of our first parents, has these remarkable words· " He brought them
" therefore into paradise, and gave them a law, that if they
" should preserve the grace then given, and continue obedient,
" they might enjoy in paradise a life without grief, sorrow,
" or care; besides that they had a promise also of an immorta-
" lity in the heavens;" *De incarnatione verbi.* And therefore we need less wonder, that we find it an article inserted in the common offices of the primitive church; and that in the most ancient liturgy now extant [that of Clemens] we read these
words

A. M. 1.
Ant. Chrif.
4004
Gen. ch. 2.
from ver. 8.

"regions of eternal blifs; yet all this feems to be but
"an imaginary and romantic defcription of what never
"had any exiftence in nature. In the whole habitable
"world we can meet with no fuch place, as had the four
"great rivers of Euphrates, Tigris, Ganges, and the Nile,
"(which two latter, according to fome men's opinions,
"are the Pifon and Gihon of Mofes) all concurring to
"water it: and therefore the oddnefs of this geography
"has led feveral learned men to place this paradife in the
"third heaven, in the orb of the moon, in the moon it-
"felf, in the middle region of the air, &c. and of thofe who
"allow it a fituation in this fublunary world, fome have
"carried it into a far diftant country, quite concealed from
"the knowledge of men; whilft others had rather have it
"lie in Tartary, in China, in Armenia, in Mefopotamia, in
"Syria, in Perfia, in Babylonia, in Arabia, in Paleftine,
"in Ethiopia, &c. In fhort, there is fcarce any corner of
"the known world, wherein this wonderful garden has
"not been feated; and therefore others have more wifely
"concluded, that there was never any fuch determinate
"place; that [k] the whole earth, before its devaftation,
"was entirely paradifiacal; that Mofes, in his account,
"only puts a part for the whole, the better to accommo-
"date it to his reader's conception; or that, if ever there
"was a local paradife, the violent concuffions which hap-
"pened at the flood did unfettle the bounds of countries,
"and courfes of rivers, and fo totally change the face of
"nature, that it is next to impoffible now to find it out."

Difference of opinion no argument a- gainft it.

That learned men fhould differ in their opinion about a queftion, which, it muft be confeffed, has its difficulties attending it, is no wonderful thing at all; but that Mofes, who wrote about 850 years after the flood, fhould give us fo particular a defcription of this garden, and that other facred writers, long after him, fhould make fuch frequent mention of it, if there was never any fuch place, nay, if there were not then remaining fome marks and characters of its fituation, is pretty ftrange and unaccountable. The very words concerning Adam: "When thou broughteft him into
"the paradife of pleafure, thou gaveft him free leave to eat of
"all other trees, and forbadeft him to tafte of one only, for the
"hope of better things: that if he kept the commandment, he
"might receive immortality as the reward of his obedience;"
Apoft. Conft. lib. 8. *cap.* 12.

[i] Burnet's Theory.   [k] Burnet's Theory; and Archæol philofoph

very nature of his description shews, that Moses had no imaginary paradise in his view, but a portion of this habitable earth, bounded with such countries and rivers as were very well known by the names he gave them in his time, and (as it appears from other passages in Scripture) for many ages after. [l] Eden is as evidently a real country, as Ararat, where the ark rested, or Shinaar, where the sons of Noah removed after the flood. We find it mentioned as such in Scripture, as often as the other two; and there is the more reason to believe it, because, in the Mosaic account, the scene of these three memorable events is all laid in the neighbourhood of one another.

Moses, we must allow, is far from being pompous or romantic in his manner of writing; and yet it cannot be denied, but that he gives a manifest preference to this spot of ground above all others; which why he should do, we cannot imagine, unless there was really such a place as he describes: nor can we conceive, [m] what other foundation, both the ancient poets and philosophers could have had, for their fortunate islands, their elysian fields, their garden of Adonis, their garden of the Hesperides, their Ortygia and Toprobane, (as described by Diodorus Siculus,) which are but borrowed sketches from what our inspired penman tells us of the first terrestrial paradise.

It is not be questioned then, but that, in the antediluvian world, there really was such a place as this garden of Eden, a place of distinguished beauty, and more remarkably pleasant in its situation; otherwise we cannot perceive, [*] why the expulsion of our first parents from that abode should

---

[l] Univers. hist. book 1. chap. 1.   [m] Huet. Quæst. Aletan.

[*] Eve's lamentation upon the order which Michael brought for their departure out of paradise, is very beautiful and affecting in Milton.

O unexpected shock, worse far than death!
Must I thus leave thee, Paradise, thus leave
Thee, native soil? Those happy walks and shades,
Fit haunt of gods! where I had hope to spend
Quiet, though sad, the respite of that day
Which must be mortal to us both! O flow'rs,
That never will in other climate grow,
My early visitation, and my last
At ev'n, which I had bred with tender hand

should be thought any part of their punishment; nor can we see, what occasion there was for placing a *flaming sword* about the *tree of life*; or for appointing an host of the cherubims to guard the entrance against their return. The face of nature, and the course of rivers, might possibly be altered by the violence of the flood; but this is no valid exception to the case in hand: [a] because Moses does not describe the situation of paradise in antediluvian names. The names of the rivers, and the countries adjacent, *Cush*, *Havilah*, &c. are names of later date than the flood; nor can we suppose, but that Moses (according to the known geography of the world, when he wrote) intended to give us some hints of the place, near which Eden, in the former world, and the garden of paradise, were seated.

Now the description which Moses gives us of it, is delivered in these words.——— [o] *And the Lord God planted a garden eastward in Eden, and a river went out of Eden to water the garden, and from thence it was parted, and became into four heads. The name of the first is Pison, that is it which compasseth the whole land of Havilah, where there is gold, and the gold of that land is good: there is the Bdellium, and the Onyx stone. And the name of the second river is Gihon; the same is it that compasseth the whole land of Cush. And the name of the third river is Hiddekel; that is it which goes before Assyria: and the fourth is Euphrates.* So that to discover the place of paradise, we must find out the true situation of the land of Eden, whereof it was probably a part, and then trace the courses of the rivers, and inquire into the nature of the countries which Moses here specified.

The word *Eden*, which in the Hebrew tongue (according to its primary acceptation) signifies, *pleasure* and *delight*; in a secondary sense, is frequently made the proper name of several places, which are either more remarkably fruitful in their soil, or pleasant in their situation. Now, of

> From the first op'ning bud, and gave ye names!
> Who now will rear you to the sun, and rank
> Your tribes, or water from the ambrosial fount?
> Thee, lastly, nuptial bow'r, by me adorn'd,
> With what to sight, or smell, was sweet! from thee
> How shall I part, and whether wander down
> Into a lower world?——— Book 11.

---

[a] Shuckford's Connect. l. 1. [o] Gen. ii. 8, &c.

of all the places which go under this denomination, the learned have generally looked upon these three, as the properest countries wherein to enquire for the terrestrial paradise:

1. The first is that province which the prophet ᵖ Amos seems to take notice of, when he divides Syria into three parts, *viz.* Damascus, the plain of Aven, and the house of Eden, called *Cœlo-Syria*, or the *hollow Syria*, because the mountains of Libanus and Antilibanus inclose it on both sides, and make it look like a valley. But ᑫ (how great soever the names be that seem to patronize it) this, by no means, can be the Eden which Moses means; not only because it lies not to the east, but to the north of the place where he is supposed to have wrote his book, but more especially, because it is destitute of all the marks in the Mosaical description, which ought always to be the principal test in this inquiry.

2. The second place, wherein ʳ several learned men have sought for the country of Eden, in Armenia, between the sources of the Tigris, the Euphrates, the Araxis, and the Phasis, which they suppose to be the four rivers specified by Moses. But this supposition is far from being well founded, because, according to modern discoveries, the Phasis does not rise in the mountains of Armenia, (as the ancient geographers have misinformed us,) but at a great distance from them, in mount Caucasus: nor does it run from south to north, but directly contrary, from north to south, as some ˢ late travellers have discovered: So that, according to this scheme, we want a whole river, and can no ways account for that which (according to Moses's description of it) *went out of the country of Eden, to water the garden of paradise.*

3. The third place, and that wherein the country of Eden, as mentioned by Moses, seems most likely to be seated, is Chaldea, not far from the banks of the river Euphrates. To this purpose, when we find Rabshekah vaunting out his master's actions, ᵗ *Have the gods of the na-*

tions

ᵖ Ch. i. 5. ᑫ Its chief abettors are Heideggar in his *Historia Patriarch*; *Le Clerc in Gen.* ii. 8.; P. Abram in his *Pharus Vet Test*; and P. Hardouin in his edition of *Pliny.*

ʳ The chief patrons of this scheme are Santon in his *Atlas*; Reland in his *Dissertat. de situ paradisi*; and Calmet, both in his Dictionary and Commentary on Gen. ii. 8. ˢ *Vid.* Thavenot. and Sir John Chardin's travels, ᵗ 2 Kings xix. 12. and Isa. xxxvii. 12.

A. M. 1.
Ant. Chrif.
4004.
Gen. ch. 1.
from ver. 8

tions delivered them which my fathers have destroyed, as Gazan, and Haran, and Rezeph, and the children of Eden, which were in Telassar? As *Telassar*, in general, signifies any garrison or fortification; so here, more particularly, it denotes ᵘ that strong fort which the children of Eden held in an island of the Euphrates, towards the west of Babylon, as a barrier against the incursions of the Assyrians on that side. And therefore, in all probability, ˣ the country of Eden lay on the west side, or rather on both sides of the river Euphrates, after its conjunction with the Tigris, a little below the place where, in process of time, the famous city of Babylon came to be built.

Thus we have found out a country called *Eden*, which, for its pleasure and fruitfulness, * (as all authors agree,) answers the character which Moses gives of it; and are now to consider the description of the four rivers, in order to ascertain the place where the garden (we are in quest of) was very probably situate.

The river Pison.

The first river is Pison, or *Phison*, (as the son of Sirach calls it,) that which compasseth the land of Havilah. Now, for the better understanding of this, we must observe, that ʸ when Moses wrote his history, he was, in all probability, in Arabia Petræa, on the east of which lies Arabia Deserta; but the sterility of the country will not admit of the situation of the garden of Eden in that place; and therefore we must go on eastward (as our author directs us) until we come to some place, through which Euphrates and Tigris are known to shape their course. Now Euphrates and Tigris, though they both rise out of the mountains of Armenia, take almost quite contrary courses. Euphrates runs to the west, and passing through Mesopotamia, waters the country where Babylon once stood; whereas

---

ᵘ *Vid.* Bedford's Scripture-chronology.   ˣ Calvin [on Gen ii. 8.] was the first starter of this opinion, and is, with some little variation, followed by Marinus, Bochart, Huetius, Bishop of Auranches, and divers others.

* Herodotus, who was an eye-witness of it, tells us, that where Euphrates runs out into Tigris, not far from the place where Ninus is seated, that region is, of all that he ever saw, the most excellent; so fruitful in bringing forth corn, that it yieldeth two hundred fold; and so plenteous in grass, that the people are forced to drive their cattle from pasture, lest they should surfeit themselves by too much plenty; *Vid. Hered. Clio. lib.* ; and *Quint. Curt. l.* 5.

ʸ *Vid.* Wells's Geography; and Patrick's Commentary.

as Tigris takes towards the east, and passing along Assyria, waters the country where the once famed city of Nineveh stood. After a long progress, they meet a little below Babylon, and, running a considerable way together in one large stream, with Babylonia and Chaldea on the west, and the country of Susiana on the east side, they separate again not far from Bassora, and so fall, in two channels, into the Persian gulf, inclosing the island Teredon, now called Balsara.

A. M, 1.
Ant. Chrif.
4004.
Gen, ch. 2.
from ver 8.

Now, taking this along with us, we may observe farther, that there are two places in Scripture which make mention of the land of Havilah. In the one we are told, that ² *the Israelites dwelt from Havilah unto Shur, that is before Egypt;* and in the other, that ᵃ *Saul smote the Amalekites from Havilah, until thou goest to Shur, that is before Egypt;* where, by the expression, *from Havilah unto Shur,* is probably meant the whole extent of that part of Arabia which lies between Egypt to the west, and a certain stream or river which empties itself into the Persian gulf, on the east. That Havilah is the same with this part of Arabia, is farther evinced from its abounding with very good gold. For all authors, both sacred and profane, highly commend the gold of Arabia; tell us, that it is there dug in great plenty; is of so lively a colour, as to come near to the brightness of fire; and of so fine a kind, so pure and unmixed, as to need no refinement. *Bdellium* (which by some interpreters is taken for *pearl,* and by others for an *aromatic gum*) is, in both these senses, applicable to this country: for the * bdellium, or gum of Arabia, was always held in great esteem; nor is there any place in the world which produces finer * pearls, or in greater quantities, than the sea about Baharen

The land of Havilah,

---

² Gen, xxv. 18,   ᵃ 1 Sam. xv. 7.

* Galen comparing the gum of Arabia with that of Syria, gives some advantage to the former, which he denies to the other; *De simp. medic. lib.* 6. And Pliny prefers the bdellium of Arabia before that of any other nation, except that of Bactriana; *Plin. lib.* 12. *cap.* 9.

* Nearchus, one of Alexander's captains, who conducted his fleet from the Indies, as far as the Persian gulf, speaks of an island there abounding in pearls of great value; *Strabo, lib.* 16. And Pliny, having commended the pearls of the Indian seas, adds, that such as are fished towards Arabia, in the Persian gulf, deserve the greatest praise; *lib* 6. *cap.* 28.

haren, an island situated in the Persian gulf; and as for * the onyx-stone in particular, (if we will believe what Pliny tells us,) the ancients were of opinion, that it was no where to be found but in the mountains of Arabia. It seems reasonable therefore to conclude, (according to all the characters which Moses has given us of it,) that that tract of Arabia which lies upon the Persian gulf, was, in his days called *the land of Havilah*, and that the channel which, after Euphrates and Tigris part, runs westward into the said gulf, was originally called *Pison*; and this the rather, because † some remains of its ancient name continued a long while after this account of it.

The river Gihon.

The second river is Gihon, that which compasseth, or runneth along, *the whole land of* ‡ *Cush*. Where we may observe

---

* Strabo tells us, that the riches of Arabia, which consisted in precious stones and excellent perfumes, (the trade of which brought them a great deal of gold and silver, besides the gold of the country itself,) made Augustus send Ælius Gallus thither, either to make these nations his friends, and to draw to himself their riches, or else to subdue them; *lib.* 16. Diodorus Siculus describes at large the advantages of Arabia, and especially its precious stones, which are very valuable, both for their variety and brightness of colour; *lib.* 2. And (to name no more) Pliny who is very curious in remarking the countries of precious stones, assures us, that those of the greatest value came out of Arabia; *lib. ult.*

† It is a great while since both this river and the river Gihon have lost their names. The Greek and Roman writers call them still, after their parting, by the names they had before they met, *Euphrates* and *Tigris*; but there was some remainder of the name of *Pison* preserved in the river *Pisotigris*, which is *Pison* mixed with *Tigris* (as Mr Carver observes.) By Xenophon it is called simply *Physcus*, in which the name of *Phison* is plainly enough retained, and went under that name until the time of Alexander the Great. For Q. Curtius commonly calls *Tigris* itself by the name of *Phisis* and says it was so called by the inhabitants thereabout, which in all probability, was the name of this other river *Phison* but, in process of time, lost by the many alterations which were made in its course, as Pliny tells us; *Patrick's Commentary*.

‡ The LXX translation renders the Hebrew word *Cush*, by the name of *Ethiopia* and in this mistake is all along followed by our English version, (whereas by the land of Cush is always meant some part of Arabia,) which has led Josephus, and several others, into a notion, that the river Gihon was the Nile in Egypt;

observe, that Moses has not affixed so many marks on the Gihon, as he does on the Pison, and that probably for this reason; [b] because, having once found out the Pison, we might easily discover the situation of the Gihon. For Pison being known to be the first river, in respect to the place where Moses was then writing, it is but natural to suppose, that Gihon (as the second) should be the river next to it; and, consequently, that other stream, which, after the Euphrates and Tigris are parted, hold its course eastward, and empties itself in the Persian gulf. For all travellers agree, that the country lying upon the eastern stream, which other nations call *Susiana*, is by the inhabitants to this day, [*] called *Chuzestan*, which carries in it plain footsteps of the original word *Cush*, or (as some write it) *Chuz*.

Though therefore no remains of this river Gihon are to be met with in the country itself; yet, since it lies exactly the second in order, according to the method that Moses has taken in mentioning the four rivers; and, since the province it runs along and washes was formerly called *the land of Cush*, and has at this time a name not a little analagous to it; there is no doubt to be made, but that the said easterly channel, coming from the united stream of the Euphrates and Tigris, is the very Gihon described by Moses.

The third river is Hiddekel, that which goeth towards the east of, or, (as it is better translated) *that which goeth along the side of Assyria*. It is allowed by all interpreters, as well as the LXX, that this river is the same with Tigris, which or (as Pliny says) was called *Diglito*, in those parts where its course was slow, but where it began to be rapid, it took the other name. And, though it may be difficult to shew any just analogy between the name of *Hiddekel*

The river Hiddekel

and supposing withal, that the country of Havilah was some part of the East-Indies, they have run into another error, and taken Pison for the Ganges, whereby they make the garden of Eden contain the greatest part of Asia, and some part of Africa likewise, which is a supposition quite incredible; *Patrick*, ibid.; *Bedford's Scripture-chronology*; and *Shuckford's Connection*.

[b] Wells's Historical geography, vol. 1.

[*] Benjamin of Navarre tells us, that the province of Elam, whereof Susa is the metropolis, and which extends itself as far as the Persian gulf, at the east of the mouth of the river Euphrates, or Tigris, (as you please to term it,) is called by that name; *Wells*, ibid.

A. M. 1.
Ant. Chrif.
4004.
Gen. ch. 2.
from ver 8.

dekel and *Tigris*; yet, if we either obferve Mofes's method of reckoning up the four rivers, or confider the true geography of the country, we fhall eafily perceive, that the river Hiddekel could properly be no other. [c] For as, in refpect to the place where Mofes wrote, Pifon lay neareft to him, and fo, in a natural order, was named firft, and the Gihon, lying near to that, was accordingly reckoned fecond; fo, having paffed over that ftream, and turning to the left, in order to come back again to Arabia Petræa, (where Mofes was,) we meet, in our paffage, with Tigris in the third place; and fo, proceeding weftward through the lower part of Mefopotamia, come to Pherath, or Euphrates, at laft. For Tigris (we muft remember) parts Affyria from Mefopotamia, and meeting with Euphrates a little below Babylon, runs along with it in one common channel, until they feparate again, and make the two ftreams of Pifon and Gihon, which, as we faid before, empty themfelves into the Perfian gulf.

Euphrates, and the four heads of the rivers.

The fourth river was † *Euphrates*; but this lay fo near the country of Judea, and was fo well known to the inhabitants thereof, that there was no occafion for Mofes particularly to defcribe it. From the courfe of thefe four rivers, however, which he manifeftly makes the bounds and limits of it, we may perceive, that the land of Eden muft neceffarily lie upon the great channel which the Tigris and Euphrates make, while they run together, and where they part again, muft there terminate: for fo the facred text informs us, viz. that *a river went out of Eden to water the garden, and from thence it was parted, and became into four heads*; which words manifeftly imply, that in Eden the river was but one, *i. e.* one fingle channel; but *from thence, i. e.* when it was gone out of Eden, it

---

[c] Wells's Geography.

† *Euphrates* is of the fame fignification with the *Hebrew Pherath*, and is probably fo called, by reafon of the pleafantnefs, at leaft the great fruitfulnefs, of the adjacent country. It muft not be diffembled however, that it is one of thofe corrupt names which our tranflations have borrowed from the Septuagint verfion, and which probably the Greeks, as Reland [De fitu paradifi] judicioufly obferved, took from the Perfians, who often fet the word *ab* or *au*, which fignifies *water*, before the names of rivers, of which word, and *Frat*, (as it is ftill called by the neighbouring people) the name *Euphrates* is apparently compounded; *Univerf. Hift. book* 1. *chap.* 3.

it was parted, and became four streams or openings, (for so the Hebrew word may be translated,) two upwards, and two below. For, supposing this channel to be our common centre, we may, if we look one way, *i. e.* up towards Babylon, see the Tigris and Euphrates coming into it; and, if we look another way, *i. e.* down towards the Persian gulf, see the Pison and the Gihon running out of it.

It seems reasonable then to suppose, that this country of Eden lay on each side of this great channel, partly in Chaldea, and partly in Susiana: and, what may confirm us in this opinion, is, the extraordinary goodness and fertility of the soil. For, as it is incongruous to suppose, that God would make choice of a barren land wherein to plant the garden of paradise; so all ancient historians and geographers inform us, that not only Mesopotamia, Chaldea, a good part of Syria, and other neighbouring countries, were the most pleasant and fruitful places in the world; but modern travellers likewise particularly assure us, that in all the dominions which the Grand Seignior has, there is not a finer country, (though, for want of hands, it lies in some places uncultivated) than that which lies between Bagdat and Bassora, the very tract of ground, which, according to our computation, was formerly called *the land of Eden.*

In what precise part of the land of Eden the garden of paradise was planted, the sacred historian seems to intimate, by informing us, that it ᵈ *lay eastward in Eden:* for he does not mean, that it lay eastward from the place where he was then writing, (that every body might easily know,) but his design was to point out, as near as possible, the very spot of ground where it was anciently seated. If then the garden of paradise lay in the easterly part of the country of Eden, and ᵉ *the river which watered it* ran through that province (as the Scripture tells us it did) before it entered into the garden, then must it necessarily follow, that paradise was situated on the the east side of one of the turnings of that river, which the conjunction of the Tigris and Euphrates makes, (now called *the river of the Arabs,*) and very probably at the lowest great turning, which Ptolemy takes notice of, and not far from the place where *Aracca* (in Scripture called *Erec*) at present is known to stand.

A. M. 1.
Ant. Chrif. 4004.
Gen. ch. 2.
from ver. 8.

In what part of E. den the garden of paradise was

Thus

ᵈ Gen. ii. 8.   ᵉ Chap. ii. 10.

A. M. 1.
Ant. Chrif.
4004.
Gen. ch. 2.
from ver. 8

The alterations in the present country accounted for.

Thus we have followed the path which * the learned and judicious Huetius, bishop of Auranches, has pointed out to us, and have happily found a place wherein to fix this garden of pleasure. And, though it must be owned, that there is no draught of the country which makes the rivers exactly answer the description that Moses has given us of them; yet, it is reasonable to suppose, † that he wrote according to the then known geography of the country; that if the site, or number of rivers about Babylon, have been greatly altered since, this, in all probability, has been occasioned by the cuts and canals which the monarchs of that great empire were remarkable for making; and that all modern observators find greater variations in the situation of places, and make greater corrections in all their charts and maps, than need to be made in the description of Moses, to bring it to an agreement even with our latest accounts of the present country, and rivers near Chaldea. But I espouse this opinion, without any formal opposition to the sentiments of other learned men, who doubtless,

---

* Upon this occasion, it may not be improper to set down a brief exposition of his opinion in his own words. "Je dis "donc, que la paradis terrestre estoit situé sur le canal que for- "ment le Tigre et l'Euphrate joints ensemble, entre le lieu de "leur jonction, et celuy de la separation qu'ils font de leurs "eaux, avant que de tomber dans le golphe Persique. Et "comme ce canal faisoit quelques detours, et quelques cour- "bures je dis, (pour entrer dans une plus grande precision.) "que le paradis estoit situé sur une de ces courbures, et appa- "remment sur le bras meridional de la plus grande, (qui a "esté marquée par Agathodæmon dans les Tables geogra- "phiques de Ptolemée; lorsque ce fleuve revient vers l'orient, "apres avoir fait un long retours vers l'occident environ a "trente deux degrez trente-neuf minutes de latitude septentri- "onale, et a quatre vingt degrez diz minutes de longitude, "(selon le deliniation de Agathodæmon.) a peu pres la ou il "place l'Aracca, qui est l'Erec de l'Ecriture. L'ajoute en- "core que les quatre testes de ce fleuve sont le Tigre et l'Eu- "phrate avant leur junction et les deux canaux, par ou il "tombe dans la mer, apres sa division; que le plus occiden- "tal de ce deux canaux est le Phison; que le pais de Chavilah, "qu'il traverse, est une partie de l'Arabie Heureuse, et une "partie de l'Arabie Deserte; que le Gehon est le canal orien- "tal des deux, dont j'ay parle; et que le pais de Chus est la Su- "siana." Vid. *Traité de la situation du paradis, p. 16.*

† Shuckford's Connection, book 1.

doubtless, in this case, are left to their own choice; since the situation of paradise, (as the learned Bishop concludes,) whether it be in one part of the world, or in another, can never be esteemed as an article of our Christian faith.

A. M. 1. Ant. Chrif. 4004. Gen. ch. 2. from ver. 8.

DISSERTATION II.

Of the image of God in man.

WHOEVER looks into the history of the creation, as it is recorded by Moses, will soon perceive, that there was something so peculiar in the formation of man, as to deserve a divine consultation, and that this peculiarity chiefly consists in that † divine image and similitude wherein it pleased God to make him. This pre-eminence the holy penman has taken care, ᵍ in two several places, to remind us of, in order to imprint upon us a deeper sense of the dignity of human nature; and therefore it may be no improper subject for our meditation in this place, to consider a little, wherein this divine image or likeness did consist; how far it is now impaired in us; and in what measure it may be recovered again.

What the image of God impressed upon man in the state of his integrity was, it is as difficult a matter for us, who date our ignorance from our first being, and were all along bred up with the same infirmities about us wherein we were born, to form any adequate perception of, ʰ as it is for a peasant bred up in the obscurities of a cottage, to fancy in his mind the unseen splendors of a court; and therefore we have the less reason to wonder, that we find such a variety of opinions concerning it.

A difficulty to conceive what the image of God was.

ⁱ Some of the Jewish doctors were fond enough to imagine, that Adam at first had his head surrounded with a it.

Different opinions concerning

† The words in the text are, *in our image, after our likeness*, which seem to be much of the same import; only a learned Jewish interpreter has observed, that the last words, *after our likeness*, give us to understand, that man was not created properly and perfectly in *the image of God*, but only in a kind of resemblance of him; for he does not say, *in our likeness*, as he does, *in our image*; but, *after* our likeness; where the *caph* of similitude (as they call it) abates something of the sense of what follows, and makes it signify only an approach to the divine likeness, in understanding, freedom of choice, spirituality, immortality, &c; *Patrick's Commentary.*

ᵍ Gen. i 26, 27. ʰ South's sermons, vol. 1. ⁱ Calmet's Dictionary on the word *Adam*.

A. M. 1.
Ant. Chrif.
4004.
Gen. ch. 2
from ver. 8.

a visible radiant glory which accompanied him where-ever he went, and struck awe and reverence into the other parts of the animal creation; and that his person was so completely perfect and handsome, that even God, before he formed him, assumed an human body of the most perfect beauty, and so, in a literal sense, made him after his own image and resemblance. But there needs no pains to refute this groundless fancy.

[k] Philo is of opinion, that this *image of God*, was only the idea of human nature in the divine understanding, by looking on which he formed man, just as an architect about to build an house, first delineates the scheme in his mind, and then proceeds to erect the fabric. But this opinion, how true soever, does not come up to the point in hand; because it makes no distinction between man and other creatures, (for they were likewise made according to the ideal image in the divine intellect) though it may be manifestly the intent of the Scripture-account to give him a particular preference.

[l] Origen, among ancient Christian authors, will have it to be the *Son of God*, who is called [m] *the express image of the Father*: but there is no such restriction in the words of Moses. They are delivered [n] in the plural number; and therefore cannot, without violence, be applied to one single person in the Godhead; and, among the moderns, some have placed it in holiness alone; whilst others have thought it more properly seated in dominion. But these are only single lines, and far from coming to the whole portraiture.

Its division and explication,

The divine similitude, in short, is a complex thing, and made up of many ingredients; and therefore (to give our thoughts a track in so spacious a field) we may distinguish it into *natural* and *supernatural*; and accordingly, shall, 1st, consider the supernatural gifts and ornaments; and then, 2dly, those natural perfections and accomplishments wherein this image of God, impressed on our first parents, may be said to consist.

[o] An eloquent father of the church has set this whole matter before us in a very apt similitude, comparing this animal and living effigies of the *King of Kings*, with the image of

---

[k] De mundi opificio. [l] *Vid.* Edward's Survey of religion, vol. 1. [m] Heb. i. 3. [n] Gen. i. 26. *Let us make man.* [o] Greg. Nyssen. Le hominis opificio, cap 4.

Chap. II.   *from the Creation to the Flood.*

of an emperor, so expressed by the hand of an artificer, either in sculpture or painting, as to represent the very dress and ensigns of royal majesty, such as the purple robe, the sceptre, and the diadem, &c. But as the emperor's image does represent, not only his countenance and the figure of his body, but even his dress likewise, his ornaments and royal ensigns; so man does then properly represent in himself the image and similitude of God, when to the accomplishments of nature (which cannot totally be extinguished) the ornaments of grace and virtue are likewise added; when " man's nature (as he expresses it) is not clothed in purple " nor vaunts its dignity by a sceptre or diadem, (for the " archetype consists not in such things as these,) but in-" stead of purple, is clothed with virtue, which of all o-" thers, is the most royal vestment; instead of a sceptre, " is supported by a blessed immortality; and, instead of a " diadem, is adorned with a crown of righteousness."

A. M. 1.
Ant. Chrif. 4004.
Gen. ch. 2. from ver. 8.

That our first parents, besides the seeds of natural virtue and religion sown in their minds, and besides the natural innocence and rectitude wherein they were created, were endued with certain gifts and powers supernatural, infused into them by the Spirit of God, is manifest, not only from the authority of ᵖ Christian writers, but from the testimony of Philo the Jew likewise, who is very full of sublime notions concerning the divine image, and, in one place more especially, expresses himself to this purpose. ᑫ " The " Creator made our soul," says he, " while inclosed in a " body able of itself to see and know its maker; but, con-" sidering how vastly advantageous such knowledge would " be to man, (for this is the utmost bound of its felicity,) " he inspired into him from above something of his own " divinity, which, being invisible, impressed upon the in-" visible soul its own character; that so even this earthly " region might not be without some creature made after " the image of God:" and this * he asserts to be the recondite sense of Moses's words in the history of man's creation.

The supernatural part of it as to the soul.

And

ᵖ *Vid.* Bull's State of man before the fall.   ᑫ Lib. Quod det potiori infid. foleat, p. 171.

* " The great Moses," says he, " makes not the species of the " rational soul to be like to any of the creatures, but pronounceth " it to be the image of the invisible God, as judging it then to " become the true and genuine coin of God, when it is formed " and impressed by the divine seal, the character whereof is

" the

A. M. 1.
Ant. Chrif
4004.
Gen. ch. 2.
from ver. 8

Inſtances
thereof.

And indeed we need go no farther than this hiſtory of Moſes, to prove the very point we are now upon. For, whereas it acquaints us, that the firſt man, in his ſtate of integrity, was able to ſuſtain the approaches of the divine preſence, and converſe with his maker in the ſame language, it is reaſonable to ſuppoſe, that it was a particular vouchſafement to him, to confirm his mind, and enlighten his underſtanding in this manner; becauſe no creature is fit to converſe with God without divine illumination, nor is any creature able to bear his majeſtic appearance, that is not fortified and prepared for it by a divine power.

Whereas it tells us, that *God brought every living creature unto Adam, to ſee what he would call them, and whatever, he called them, that was the name thereof;* it can hardly be ſuppoſed (conſidering the circumſtances of the thing) but that this was the effect of ſomething more than human ſagacity. That, in an infinite variety of creatures, never before ſeen by Adam, he ſhould be able on a ſudden, without labour or premeditation, to give names to each of them, ſo adapt and fitted to their reſpective natures, as that God himſelf ſhould approve the nomenclature, is a thing ſo aſtoniſhing, that we may venture to ſay, [*] no ſingle man, among all the philoſophers ſince the fall, no Plato, no Ariſtotle, among the ancients, no Des Cartes, no Gaſſendus,

no

" the eternal word. For God," ſaith he, "breathed into his face
" the breath of life; ſo that he who receives the inſpiration muſt
" of neceſſity repreſent the image of him that gives it, and for
" this reaſon it is ſaid that man was made after the image of
" God;" *lib. De plantatione Noe.*

r Gen. ii. 19.

* The knowledge of Adam is highly extolled by the Jewiſh doctors. Some of them have maintained, that he compoſed two books, one concerning the creation, and another about the nature of God. They generally believe, that he compoſed the xci. pſalm; but ſome of them go farther, and tell us, that Adam's knowledge was not only equal to that of Solomon and Moſes, but exceeded even that of angels; and, for the proof of this, they produce this ſtory—That the angels having ſpoke contemptuouſly of man, God made this anſwer,——That the creature whom they deſpiſed was their-ſuperior in knowledge; and, to convince them of this, that he brought all the animals to them, and bid them name them, which they being not able to do, he propoſed the thing to Adam, and he did it immediately: with many more fancies of the ſame ridiculous nature; *Saurin's Diſſertations*,

no Newton, among the moderns; nay, no academy **or roy-** A M. 1.
al fociety whatever durſt have once attempted it. Ant. Chriſt.
4004.
Whereas it informs us, that Adam no ſooner ſaw his Gen. ch. 2.
wife brought unto him, but ˢ he told exactly her origi- from ver. 8.
nal, and gave her a name accordingly, though he lay in the
profoundeſt ſleep and inſenſibility all the while that God
was performing the wonderful operation of taking her out
of his ſide; this can be imputed to nothing, but either an
immediate inſpiration, or ſome prophetic viſion (as we ſaid
before) that was ſent unto him while he ſlept. ᵗ From the
conformity of parts which he beheld in that goodly crea-
ture, and her near ſimilitude to himſelf, he might have
conjectured indeed, that God had now provided him with
a meet help, which before he wanted; but it **is** ſcarce imaginable, how he could ſo punctually deſcribe **her riſe** and
manner of formation, and ſo ſurely propheſy, **that** the general event to his poſterity would be, for the **ſake of** her
ſex, *to leave father and mother, and cleave to their wives,* other-
wiſe than by divine illumination; " which enabled him ᵘ
(as one excellently expreſſes it) " to view eſſences in them-
" ſelves, and read forms without the comment of their
" reſpective properties; which enabled him **to ſee** conſe-
" quences yet dormant in their principles, and effects yet
" unborn, and in the womb of their cauſes; which ena-
" bled him, in ſhort, to pierce almoſt into future contin-
" gencies, and improved his conjectures and ſentiments e-
" ven to a prophecy, and **the** certainties of a prediction."
Theſe ſeem to be ſome of the ſupernatural gifts, **and** As to the
what we may call the chief lines, wherein the image **of body.**
God was ſo conſpicuous upon Adam's ſoul; and there was
this ſupernatural in his body likewiſe, that ˣ whereas it
was made *of the duſt of the earth,* and in its compoſition
conſequently corruptible, either **by a power** continually
proceeding from God, whereof ʸ *the tree of life* was the
divine ſign and ſacrament, or **by the inherent virtue of** the
tree itſelf, perpetually repairing the decays of nature, it
was to enjoy the privilege of immortality. ᶻ Not ſuch an
immortality as the glorified bodies **of** ſaints ſhall hereafter
poſſeſs (for they ſhall be made wholly impaſſable, and ſet
free from the reach of any outward impreſſions and ele-
mental

ˢ Gen. ii. 23. ᵗ Bull's Sermons and diſcourſes.
ᵘ South's ſermons, vol. 1. ˣ Hopkin's Doctrine of the
two covenants. ʸ Gen. ii. 9. ᶻ Edward's Survey
of religion, vol. 1.

<small>A. M. 1.
Ant. Chrif.
4004.
Gen. ch. 2.
from ver. 8.</small> mental diforders, which may impair their vigour, or endanger their diffolution,) but an immortality by donation, and the privilege of an efpecial providence, which engaged itfelf to fway and over-rule the natural tendency which was in man's body to corruption; and, notwithftanding the contrarieties and diffentions of a terreftrial conftitution, to continue him in life as long as he fhould continue himfelf in his obedience.

<small>The natural part as to the foul.</small> 2. Another chief part of the divine image and fimilitude in our firft parents, was an univerfal rectitude in all the faculties belonging to the foul. Now the two great faculties, or rather effential acts of the foul, are the *underftanding* and *will*; which, though (for the clearer conception of them) we may feparate, are in their operation fo blended and united together, that we cannot properly think them diftinct faculties. It is the fame individual mind which fees and perceives, as well as chufes or rejects the feveral objects that are prefented to it. When it does the former, we call it the *underftanding*, and when the latter, the *will*; fo that they are both radically and infeparably the fame, and differ only in the manner of our conceiving them. Nay, the cleareft and only diftinct apprehenfion we are able to form of them, (even when we come to confider them feparately,) is only this, that the underftanding is chiefly converfant about intelligible, the will about eligible objects; fo that the one has truth, and the other goodnefs in its view and purfuit. There are, befides thefe, belonging to the foul of man, certain paffions and affections, which (according to the common notion and manner of fpeaking) have chiefly their refidence in the fenfitive appetite; and however, in this lapfed condition of our nature, they may many times mutiny and rebel, yet, when kept in due temper and fubordination, are excellent hand-maids to the [a] foul. Though the Stoics look upon them all as finful defects, and deviations from right reafon; yet it is fufficient for us, that our bleffed Saviour (who took upon him all our natural, but none of our finful infirmities) was known to have them, and that our firft progenitor, in the ftate of his greateft perfection, was not devoid of them. Let us then fee how far we may fuppofe that the image of God might be impreffed upon each of thefe.

[b] His foul itfelf was a rational fubftance, immaterial, and immortal; and therefore a proper reprefentation of that

---

[a] South's Sermons, vol. 1.   [b] Edward's Survey.

that supreme Spirit, whose wisdom was infinite, and essence eternal.

[c] His understanding was, as it were, the upper region of his soul, lofty and serene; seated above all sordid affections, and free from the vapours and disturbances of inferior passions. Its perceptions were quick and lively; its reasonings true, and its determinations just. A deluded fancy was not then capable of imposing upon it, nor a fawning appetite of deluding it to pronounce a false and dishonest sentence. In its direction of the inferior faculties, it conveyed its suggestions with clearness, and enjoined them with power; and though its command over them was but suasive, yet it had the same force and efficacy as if it had been despotical.

His will was then very ductile and pliant to the motions of right reason. It pursued the directions that were given it, and attended upon the understanding, as a favourite does upon his prince, where the service is both privilege and preferment: and, while it obeyed the understanding, it commanded the other faculties that were beneath it; gave laws to the affections, and restrained the passions from licentious sallies.

His passions were then indeed all subordinate to his will and intellect, and acted within the compass of their proper objects. His love was centered upon God, and flamed up to heaven in direct fervours of devotion. His hatred (if hatred may be supposed in a state of innocence) was fixed only upon that which his posterity only love, *sin*. His joy was then the result of a real good, suitably applied, and filled his soul (as God does the universe) silently and without noise. His sorrow (if any supposed disaster could have occasioned sorrow) must have moved according to the severe allowances of prudence; been as silent as thought, and all confined within the closet of the breast. His hope was fed with the expectation of a better paradise, and a nearer admission to the divine presence; and (to name no more) his fear, which was then a guard, and not a torment to the mind, was fixed upon him, who is only to be feared, God, but in such a filial manner, as to become an awe without amazement, and a dread without distraction.

It must be acknowledged indeed, that the Scriptures do not expressly attribute all these perfections to Adam in his first estate; but, since the opposite weaknesses now infest

the

[c] South's sermons, vol. 1.

the nature of man fallen, we must conclude (if we will be true to the rule of contraries) that these, and such like excellencies, were the endowments of man innocent. And if so, then is there another perfection arising from this harmony, and due composure of the faculties, which we may call *the crown and consummation of all*, and that is a good conscience. For, as in the body, when the vital and principal parts do their office, and all the smaller vessels act orderly, there arises a sweet enjoyment upon the whole, which we call *health;* so in the soul, when the supreme faculties of the understanding and will move regularly, and the inferior passions and affections listen to their dictates, and follow their injunctions, there arises a serenity and complacency upon the whole soul, infinitely beyond all the pleasures of sensuality, and which, like a spicy field, refreshes it upon every reflection, and fills it with a joyful *confidence towards God.*

These are some of the natural lines (as we may distinguish them) which the finger of God pourtrayed upon the soul of man: and (so far as a spiritual being may be resembled by a corporeal) [d] the contrivance of man's bodily parts was with such proportion and exactness, as most conduced to its comeliness and service. His stature was erect and raised, becoming him who was to be the lord of this globe, and the observer of the heavens. A divine beauty and majesty was shed upon it, such as could neither be eclipsed by sickness, nor extinguished by death; [e] for Adam knew no disease, so long as he refrained from the forbidden tree. Nature was his physician, and innocence and abstinence would have kept him healthful to immortality. And from this perfection of man's body, especially that port and majesty which appeared in his looks and aspect, there arose, in some measure, another lineament of the divine image, *viz.* [f] that dominion and sovereignty wherewith God invested him over all other creatures. For there is even still remaining in man a certain terrific character, (as [g] one calls it,) which, assisted by that instinct of dread that he hath equally implanted in their natures, commands their homage and obeisance; insomuch, that it must be hunger or compulsion, or some violent exasperation or other,

---

[d] Bate's Harmony of the divine attributes. [e] South's sermons, vol. 1. [f] Gen. i. 26. [g] Cornelius Agrippa, De occult. philos.

ther, that makes them at any time rebel against their maker's vicegerent here below.

This is the best copy of the divine image that we can draw: only it may not be amiss to add, [h] that the holiness of man was a resemblance of the divine purity, and his happiness a representation of the divine felicity. And now, to look over it again, and recount the several lines of it. What was supernatural in it, was a mind fortified to bear the divine presence, qualified for the divine converse, fully illuminated by the divine Spirit; and a body that (contrary to the natural principles of its composition) was indulged the privilege of immortality. What was natural to it, was an universal harmony in all its faculties; an understanding fraught with all manner of knowledge; a will submitted to the divine pleasure; affections placed upon their proper objects; passions calm and easy; a conscience quiet and serene: resplendent holiness, perfect felicity, and a body adorned with such comeliness and majesty, as might justly challenge the rule and jurisdiction of this inferior world.

If it be demanded, how much of this image is defaced, lost, or impaired; the answer is, that [i] whatever was supernatural and adventitious to man by the benignity of Almighty God, (as it depended upon the condition of his obedience to the divine command,) upon the breach of that command, was entirely lost: What was perfective of his nature, such as the excellency of his knowledge, the subordination of his faculties, the tranquility of his mind, and full dominion over other creatures, was sadly impaired: but what was essential to his nature, the immortality of his soul, the faculties of intellection and will, and the natural beauty and usefulness of his body, does still remain, notwithstanding the concussions they sustained in the fall.

If it be asked, what we must do in order to repair this defaced image of God in us? the only answer we can have in this case, is, from the sacred oracles of Scripture. We must [k] *be renewed in the spirit of our mind, and put on the new man, which after God is created in righteousness and true holiness:* We must [l] *be followers of God as dear children grow in grace,* [m] *be renewed in knowledge,* and [n] *conformed to the image of his Son:* We must [o] *give all diligence to add to our faith virtue;*

---

[h] Bate's Harmony.   [i] Hale's Origination of mankind.
[k] Eph. iv. 23, 24.   [l] Eph. v. 1.   [m] Col. iii. 10.   [n] Rom. viii. 29.   [o] 2 Pet. i. 5, &c.

A. M. 1.
Ant. Chrif.
4004.
Gen. ch. 2.
from ver. 8.

virtue; and to virtue, knowledge; and to knowledge, temperance; and to temperance, patience; and to patience, godliness; and to godliness, brotherly kindness; and to brotherly kindness, charity: that we may [p] *be complete in him, who is the head of all principality and power:* and that [q] *as we have borne the image of the earthly, we may also bear the image of the heavenly* Adam.

[p] Col. ii. 10.   [q] 1 Cor. xv. 49.

CHAP. III.

Of the fall of man.

THE HISTORY.

THE sacred historian indeed gives us no account of Satan, the chief of the fallen angels, and grand adversary of God and man; but, from several other places in Scripture, we may learn, that he at first was made like other celestial spirits, perfect in his kind, and happy in his condition, but that, through pride or ambition, as we may suppose, falling into a crime, (whose circumstances to us are unknown,) he thence fell into misery, and, together * with his accomplices, was banished from the regions of bliss; that, * in his state of exile, having lost all hopes, and despairing

* That profane, as well as sacred writers, had the same notion of the fall of wicked angels, is manifest from a tradition they had (though mixed with fable) of the Titans and Giants invading heaven, fighting against Jupiter, and attempting to depose him from his throne, for which reason he threw them down headlong into hell, where they are tormented with incessant fire; and therefore Empedocles, in the verses recited by Plutarch, makes mention of the fate of some dæmons, who, for their rebellion, were, from the summit of heaven, plunged into the bottom of the great deep, there to be punished as they deserved. To which the story of Ate, who once inhabited the air, but being always hurtful to man, and therefore, hateful to God, was cast down from thence, with a solemn oath and decree, that she should never return again, seems not a little to allude; *Huetius, in Alnetan. Quæst. lib.* 2.

* Our excellent Milton represents Satan within prospect of Eden, and near the place where he was to attempt his desperate enterprize

Chap. III.   *from the Creation to the Flood.*   69

spairing of reconciliation with the Almighty, he abandoned himself to all kinds of wickedness, and, upon the creation of man, out of pure envy to the happiness which God had designed for him, resolved upon a project to draw him into disobedience, and thence into ruin and perdition; but how to put his scheme in execution was the question. The woman he perceived (as by nature more ductile and tender) was the properer subject for his temptations; but some form he was to assume, to enable him to enter into conference with her. ʳ The figure of a man was the fittest upon this occasion; but then it would have discovered the imposture, because Eve knew very well, that her husband was the only one of that species upon the face of the earth. And therefore considering, that the serpent, which before the fall was a bright and glorious creature, and (next to man) † endued with the greatest talents of sagacity and understanding,

A. M. 1.
Ant. Chrif. 4004
Gen. ch. 3.

enterprise against God and man, falling into doubts, and sundry passions, and then, at last, confirming himself in his wicked design.

> But say I could repent, and could obtain,
> By act of grace, my former state; how soon
> Wou'd height recal high thoughts! how soon unsay
> What feign'd submission swore! Ease wou'd recant
> Vows made in pain, as violent and void——
> All hope excluded thus, behold, instead
> Of us, outcast, exil'd, his new delight,
> Mankind, created; and for him this world,
> So farewell Hope! and, with Hope, farewell fear!
> Farewell Remorse! all good to me is lost
> Evil be thou my good! by thee at least
> Divided empire with heaven's King I hold;
> By thee, and more than half perhaps, will reign:
> As man, e'er long, and this new world shall know.
>   Book 4.

ʳ L'histoire du Vieux et Nouveau Testament, par M. Martin.

† Milton, who is an excellent commentator upon the whole history of the fall, brings in the devil, after a long search to find out a beast proper for his purpose, concluding at last to make use of the serpent.

> Him, after long debate (irresolute
> Of thought revolv'd) his final sentence chose
> Fit vessel, fittest imp of fraud in whom
> To enter, and his dark suggestions hide
> From sharpest sight: for in the wily snake
> Whatever sleights, none wou'd suspicions mark,

A. M. 1.
Ant. Chrif.
4004.
Gen. ch. 3.

understanding, would be no improper instrument for his purpose, he usurped the organs of one of these, and through them, he addressed himself to the woman, the first opportunity when he found her alone.

After * some previous compliments (as we may imagine) and congratulations of her happy state, the tempter put on an air of great concern, and seemed to interest himself not a little in her behalf, by wondering why God, who had lately been so very bountiful to them, should deny them the

> As from his wit, and native subtilty
> Proceeding; which in other beast observ'd,
> Doubt might beget of diabolic pow'r
> Active within, beyond the sense of brute. Book 9.

The wisdom and subtilty of the serpent are frequently mentioned in Scripture, as qualities which distinguish it from other animals; and several are the instances, wherein it is said to discover its cunning. 1st When it is old, by squeezing itself between two rocks, it can strip off its old skin, and so grows young again. 2dly, As it grows blind, it has a secret to recover its sight by the juice of fennel. 3dly, When it is assaulted, its chief care is to secure its head, because its heart lies under its throat, and very near its head. And, 4thly, When it goes to drink at a fountain, it first vomits up all its poison, for fear of poisoning itself as it is drinking; with some other qualities of the like nature: *Calmet's Dictionary*

But a modern author of our own has given us this further reason for the devil's making use of the serpent in this affair, viz.——That as no infinite being can actuate any creature, beyond what the fitness and capacity of its organs will admit; so, the natural subtilty of the serpent, and perhaps the pliableness, and forkiness of its tongue (which we know enables other creatures to pronounce articulate sounds,) added to the advantages of its form, made it the fittest instrument of delusion that can be imagined; *Revelation examined*.

* Milton has very curiously described the artful and insinuating carriage of the serpent, upon his first approach to speak to Eve.
> He, bolder now, uncall'd, before her stood,
> But, as in great admiring; oft he bow'd
> His turret crest, and sleek enamell'd neck,
> Fawning; and lick'd the ground whereon she trod.
> His gentle dumb expressions turn'd at length
> The eye of Eve, to mark his play: he, glad
> Of her attention gain'd, with serpent tongue
> Organic, or impulse of vocal air,
> His fraudulent temptation thus began. Book 9.

the use of a tree *, whose fruit was so tempting to the eye, so grateful to the palate, and of such sovereign quality to make them wise: and when Eve replied, that such was the divine prohibition, even under the penalty of death itself *, he immediately subjoins, that such a penalty was an empty threat, and what would never be executed upon them; that God would never destroy the *work of his own hands*, creatures so accomplished as they were, for so slight a transgression; and that the sole intent of this prohibition was, to continue them in their present state of dependence and ignorance, and not admit them to that extent of knowledge, and plenitude of happiness, which their eating of this fruit would confer upon them: for God himself

A. M. 1.
Ant. Chrif.
4004.
Gen. ch. 3.

---

* The first words in his address are, *Yea, hath God said, ye shall not eat*, &c. which do not look so much like the beginning, as the conclusion of a discourse, as the Jews themselves have observed: and therefore it is not improbable, that the tempter, before he spake these words, represented himself as one of the heavenly court, who was come, or rather sent, to congratulate the happiness which God had bestowed on them in paradise; an happiness so great, that he could not easily believe he had denied them any of the fruit of the garden; *Patrick's Commentary*.

* Burnet, in his *Archæologiæ philosophicæ*, has given us the whole dialogue (as he has framed it at least) between the serpent and Eve; which, though a little too light and ludicrous for so solemn an occasion, yet, because the book is not in every one's hands, I have thought fit to set down in his own words. " *Serp*. Salve
" pulcherrima, quid rerum agis sub hac umbra? *Ev*. Ego hujus
" arboris pulcritudinem contemplor. *Serp*. Jucundum quidem
" spectaculum, sed multo jucunditores fructus gustastia', men domina? *Ev*. Minime vero: Deus nobis interdixit esu hujus arboris, *Serp*. Quid audio! Quis iste Deus qui suis invidet innocuas
" naturæ delicias? nihil suavius nihil salubrius hoc fructu. Quam-
" obrem interdiceret, nisi per legem ludicram? *Ev*. Quinimo sub
" pœna mortis interdixit. *Serp*. Rem male capis procul dubio:
" nihil habet mortiferi hæc arbor, sed potius divini aliquid, et
" supra vires communis naturæ. *Ev*. Ego non habeo quid tibi
" respondeam, sed adibo virum. *Serp*. Quid virum interpellas de
" retantilla? *Ev*. Utarne? Quid pulchrius hoc pomo? Quam suave redolet? Sed forsan male sapit. *Serp*. Est esca, crede mihi,
" angelis non indigna. Fac perculum, et, si male sapit, rejicito,
" et me insuper habeto pro mendacissimo. *Ev*. Experiar; est
" quidem gratissimi saporis: non me fefellisti. Porrige huc alterum, ut viro afferam. *Serp*. Commodum meministi. En tibi
" alterum: adi virum. Vale, beatula.—Ego interea elabar, illa curet cætera;" *lib*. 2. *cap* 7.

A. M. 1.
Ant. Chrif.
4004
Gen. ch. 3.

self knew, that † that the proper use of this tree was, to illuminate the understanding, and advance all the other faculties of the soul to such a sublimity, that the brightest angels in heaven should not surpass them; nay, that they should approximate the Deity itself, in the extent of their intellect, and independence of their being. In short, he acquainted Eve, that the jealousy of the Creator was the sole motive of his prohibition; that the fruit had a virtue to impart † an universal knowledge to the person, who tasted it; and that therefore God, who would admit of no competitor, had reserved this privilege to himself. Above all, he engaged her to fix her eyes upon the forbidden fruit; he remarked to her its pleasantness to the sight, and left her to guess at its deliciousness. Eve, in the very midst of the temptation had a freedom of choice; but the fond conceit of *knowing good and evil*, of becoming like God, and of changing her felicity (great indeed, but subordinate) for an independent state of happiness, and especially the deceitful bait of present sensual pleasure, blinded her reason by degrees; and as she stood gazing on the tree, filled all her thoughts,

† It is very well worth our observation, how ambiguous and deceitful the promise, which the tempter makes our first parents, was: for by *opening the eyes*, she understood a further degree of wisdom, as the same phrase imports, Acts xxvi 18.; and Eph. i. 18: but he meant their perceiving their own misery, and confusion of conscience, as fell out immediately: by *being like gods*, she understood the happiness of God the Father, Son, and Holy Ghost, as appears by the words of God himself, ver. 22 ; but he meant it of angels, (frequently styled *Elohim*. i. e. *gods*,) and of such fallen angels as himself, who are called *principalities and powers*, Col ii. 15. And *by knowing good and evil*, she understood a kind of divine omniscience, or knowing all manner of things, (as the phrase frequently signifies;) but he meant it, that thereby she should experience the difference between *good and evil*, between happiness and misery, which she did to her cost. A method this of cunning and reserve, which he has practised in his oracular responses ever since; *Ainsworth's annotations*.

† The words *good and evil*, when applied to knowledge, comprehend every thing that is possible for man to know; for so the woman of Tekoa, in her address to King David, tells him 2 Sam.xiv. 17. *as an angel of God is my Lord the King, to discern good and bad*; and that by the terms *good and bad*, we are to understand *all things*, the 20th verse of that chapter will inform us, where she continues her compliment, and says *My Lord is wise, according to the wisdom of an angel, to know all things that are on the earth*; Le Clerc's Commentary.

thoughts, and the whole capacity of her soul. The sight of the fruit provoked her desire; the suggestions of the tempter urged it on; her natural curiosity raised her longing: and the very prohibition itself did something to inflame it; so that, at all adventures, she put forth her hand, and plucked, and eat.

A. M. 1.
Ant. Chrif.
4004.
Gen. ch. 3.

> Earth felt the wound, and nature, from her seat,
> Sighing, through all her works, gave signs of woe,
> That all was lost. ˢ

She however had no such sense of her condition; but, fancying herself already in the possession of that chimerical happiness, wherewith the devil had deluded her, she invited her husband (who not unlikely came upon her while she was eating) to partake with her. ' The most absurd arguments appear reasonable, and the most unjust desires equitable, when the person, who proposes them, is beloved; the devil therefore knew very well what he did, when he made his first application to the woman. Her charms and endearments, which gave her the ascendency over her husband's affection, would be of more efficacy (he knew) than all the subtile motives which he could suggest; and therefore he made use of her to engage him in the like defection: and after some small reluctancy, (as we may suppose,) he, ᵘ like an uxorious man, was by her entreaties prevailed on, (contrary to the sense of his duty, and convictions of his own breast,) to violate the command, merely because she had done it, and to share whatever fate God's indignation for that transgression should bring upon her. Thus the solicitations of the woman ruined the man, as the inchantments of the tempter ruined the woman. She held forth the fair enticing fruit to him; and he, rather than see her perish alone, chose to be involved in the same common guilt. ˣ

> Earth trembled from her entrails, as again
> In pangs, and nature gave a second groan;
> Sky lowr'd, and, murmuring thunder, some sad drops
> Wept, at completing of the mortal sin. ʸ

ˢ Milton, Book 9.   ᵗ Saurin's Dissertations.   ᵘ Mede's Discourses.   ˣ Edward's Survey of religion.   ʸ Milton, Book 9.

A. M. 1.
Ant. Chrif.
4004
Gen. ch. 3.

For as soon as they had eaten of the forbidden fruit, † *their eyes were opened*, but in a sense quite different from what the tempter had promised them, *viz.* to see their own folly, and the impendent miseries, and make sad reflections upon what they had done. They had acquired knowledge, indeed, but it was a knowledge arising from sorrowful experience, that the serpent had beguiled them both, and drawn them from the good of happiness and innocence, which they knew before, into the evil of sin and misery, which (until that fatal moment) they had no conception of. ˣ They saw a living God provoked; his grace and favour forfeited; his likeness and image defaced; and their dominion over other creatures withdrawn from them. They saw, very probably, the heavens grow angry and stormy; the angel of the Lord standing with his sword, threatening them with vengeance; and the devil himself, who before had seduced them, throwing off the disguise, and now openly insulting over them. They saw that † *they were*

---

† Le Clerc observes, that it is reputed an elegancy in the sacred writing to make use of the figure, which rhetoricians call *antanaclasis* whereby they continue the same word or phrase that went before, though in a quite different sense; as the learned Grotius upon John i. 16. and Hammond on Matth. viii. 22 have abundantly shewn; and for this reason he supposes, that Moses repeats *their eyes were opened*, which the devil had used before, though he means it in a sense quite different from the former.

ˣ Miller's History of the church.

† Those who take the word *naked* in a literal sense, suppose, that upon the fall, the air, and other elements, immediately became intemperate, and disorderly; so that our first parents soon knew, or felt, that they were naked, because the sun scorched them, the rain wet them, and the cold pierced them. *Vid.* Patrick's Commentary; and King on the origin of evil. But others take the expression rather in a figurative sense, *viz.* to denote the commission of such sins as man in his senses may well be ashamed of; and to this purpose they have observed, that when Moses returned from the mount, and found that the people had made and consecrated a golden image, the expression in Scripture is, *That the people were naked*, i. e. were become vile and reprobate sinners, (for so the word *gumnos* signifies in the New Testament, Rev. xvi. 15.; *for Aaron had made them naked, unto their shame, among their enemies*, Ex. xxxii. 25.; *Vid.* Le Clerc's Commentary. Now those who take it in this sense, have observed farther, that by the word *nakedness* (according to

the

Chap. III. *from the Creation to the Flood.* 75

were naked; were stripped of all their intellectual and moral A. M. 1.
ornaments; were subjected to irregular appetites and in- Ant. Chrif.
ordinate lusts; and blushed to see their external glory so 4004.
much debased, that ‡ they took and platted together fig- Gen. ch. 3.
leaves, (which in eastern countries are very large,) in
order to make themselves ‡ such coverings as might both
protect

the usual modesty of the Hebrew tongue) are meant all the irregular appetites to venereal pleasures, which Adam and Eve
were strangers to in their state of innocence, but began now first
to experience, and which the intoxicating juice of the forbidden tree might very probably excite; *Nichells's Conference, vol.* 1.

<pre>
      As with new wine intoxicated both,
      They swim in mirth, and fancy that they feel
      Divinity within them, breeding wings,
      Wherewith to scorn the earth: but that false fruit
      Far other operation first display'd,
      Carnal desire inflaming: he on Eve
      Began to cast lascivious eyes, she him
      As wantonly repay'd, in lust they burn.   *Milton*, book 9.
</pre>

‡ Our translation indeed tells us, that our first parents *sowed fig-leaves together*, which gives occasion to the usual sneer. *What they could do for needles and thread?* But the original word *tapar* signifies no more than to *put together, apply*, or *fit*, as is plain from Job xvi. 15. and Ezek. xiii. 28.; and the word *gneleh*, which we render *leaves*, signifies also *branches of trees*, such as were to make booths or bowers, Neh. xviii. 15. So that, *to adapt or fit branches* (which is translated *sowing leaves together*) is only to twist and plat the flexible branches of the fig-tree round about their waists, in the manner of a Roman crown, for which purpose the fig-tree, of all others, was the most serviceable, because, as Pliny tells us, [l. 16. c. 24] it had *folium maximum er umbrosissimum*; Patrick's Commentary.

‡ The word, in the translation is *aprons*; but since in the original it may signify any thing that covers or surrounds us, it may every whit as properly here be rendered a *bower*, or *arbor*, covered with the branches of the fig tree wherein the fallen pair thought to have hid themselves from the sight of God; to which interpretation the subsequent verse seems to give some countenance; *Le Clerc's Commentary*. Nor is Milton's description of the fig-tree uninclinable to this sense:

<pre>
      ——— Such as at this day spreads her arms,
      Branching so broad and long, that in the ground
      The bended twigs take root, and daughters grow
                                                      About
</pre>

A. M. 1.
Ant. Chrif.
4004
Gen. ch. 3.

protect them from the injuries of the weather, and conceal their fhame. Nor was their guilt attended with fhame only, but with fear likewife, and many difmal apprehenfions. † Before they finned, they no fooner heard *the voice of the Lord* coming towards them, but they ran out to meet him, and, with an humble joy, welcomed his gracious vifits; but now * God was become a terror to them, and they a terror to themfelves. Their confciences fet their fin before them in its blackeft afpect; and, as they had then no hopes of a future mediator, fo there *remained nothing for them but a certain fearful looking for of judgement, and fiery indignation, ready to devour them.* And accordingly, no fooner did they hear the found of God's majeftic prefence drawing nearer and nearer to the place where they were, (which happened towards the cool of the evening, but they immediately betook themfelves to the thickeft and clofeft places they could find in the garden, in order to hide themfelves from his infpection; for fo far were they fallen in their underftanding, as never to reflect, that *all* places and things are *naked and open to the eyes of him, with whom they had to do.*

Out

About the mother tree; a pillar'd fhade
High over-arch'd, and echoing walks between.
There oft the Indian herdfman fhunning heat,
Shelters in cool and tends his pafturing herds
In loop-holes, cut through thickeft fhade.   Book 9.

† The word *voice* may be equally rendered *noife:* and fince God's ufual way of notifying his prefence afterwards was either by *a fmall ftill voice or noife*, 1 Kings. xix. 12 or by a noife like *that of great waters*, Ezek. i. 24. or like *the ruftling of wind in the trees.* 2 Sam v. 24. we may reafonably fuppofe, that it was either a foft gentle noife like a breeze of wind among the trees of paradife, or a louder one, like the murmuring of fome large river, which gave Adam notice of God's approaching; *Le Clerc's Commentary.*

* Milton makes Adam, upon this occafion, exprefs himfelf in this manner:

—— How fhall I behold the face
Henceforth of God or angel, erft with joy
And raptures oft beheld?——O! might I here
In folitude live favage, in fome glade
Obfcur'd, where higheft woods (impenetrable
To ftar or fun-light) fpread their umbrage broad,
And brown as evening! Cover me ye pines,
Ye cedars, with innumerable boughs
Hide me, where I may never fee them more. Book 9.

Chap. III. *from the Creation to the Flood.*

A. M. 1.
Ant. Chrif. 4004.
Gen. ch. 3.

Out of their dark retreat, however, God calls the two criminals, who, after a short examination, acknowledge their guilt indeed, but lay the blame of it, the man upon the woman, and the woman upon the serpent: whereupon God proceeds to pronounce sentence upon them, but first of all, upon the devil, as being the prime offender. The devil had made the serpent the instrument of his deception; and therefore † God first degrades it from the noble creature it was before this fact, to a foul creeping animal, which, instead of going erect, or flying in the air, was sentenced to creep upon its belly, and thereupon become incapable of eating any food but what was mingled with dust. And to the devil, who lay hid under the covert of the serpent, (and therefore is not expresly named,) he declares, that how much soever he might glory in his present conquest, a time should come, when a child, descended from the seed of that very sex he had now defeated, *i. e.* the MESSIAS, should ruin all his new-erected empire of sin and death; and, ^a *having spoiled principalities and powers, should make a shew of them openly, triumphing over them in his cross.* This could not fail of being matter of great comfort and consolation to Adam and Eve, to hear of the conquest of their malicious enemy, before their own sentences were pronounced; * which, to

the

---

† Josephus, in the beginning of his Antiquities, pretends, that all creatures using the same language, and consequently being endued with reason and understanding, the serpent, excited by envy, tempted Eve to sin, and, among other things, received this signal punishment, *viz.* that it should be deprived of its feet, and ever after crawl upon the ground which Aben Ezra, and several other Rabbins, confi m : but what is certain in the serpent's punishment, is this——that it actually eats the dry and dusty earth, (as Bochart and Pliny tell us, otherwise we can hardly conceive how it could subsist in dry and sandy deserts, to which God, in a good measure, has condemned it; *Revel. examined.*

^a Col. ii. 15.

* It is remarkable, that a woman is the only creature we know of, who has any sorrow in conception. This Aristotle expresly affirms, and only excepts the instance of a mare conceiving by an ass, and, in general, where there is any thing monstrous in the fœtus. Other creatures, we find, are in more perfect health, and strength, and vigour, at that time than before; but Aristotle reckons up ten different maladies, to

Vol. I. No. 3.   B b   which

A. M. 1.
Ant. Chrif.
4004.
Gen. ch. 3.

the woman, was forrow in conception, pain in child-birth, and conftant fubjection to her hufband's will; to the man, * a life of perpetual toil and flavery; and to them both, as well as all their pofterity, a temporal death, at the time appointed.

Nor was it mankind only which felt the fad effects of the induction of fin, but * even the inanimate part of the creation

which the woman is then naturally fubject. And, as fhe is fubject to ficknefs in the time of her conception, fo it is farther remarkable, that fhe brings forth her offspring with more pain and agony than any other creature upon earth, even though fhe has fome advantages in her make above other creatures, that might promife her, in this cafe, an alleviation: and therefore we may fuppofe, that, upon God's faying to the woman, *In forrow thou fhalt bring forth children*, a real effect did immediately accompany the word fpoken, and caufe fuch a change in the woman's body, as, in the courfe of nature, muft have occafioned the extraordinary pain here fpoken of; for fo we find, that in the fentence pronounced againft the ferpent, againft the earth, and againft man, the word of God was not only declarative, but executive likewife, as producing a real change by a new modification of matter, or conformation of parts; *Revelation examined; and Bibliotheca Biblica vol.* 1.

* The words in the text are, *In the fweat of thy face, fhalt thou eat bread*, ver. 19. From whence fome conclude, that the earth, before the fall, brought forth fpontaneoufly, (as feveral of the ancient poets have defcribed the golden age,) and without any pains to cultivate it; as indeed there needed none, fince all things at firft were, by the divine power, created in their full perfection. What labour would have been neceffary in time, if man had continued innocent, we do not know; only we may obferve from the words, that lefs pains would then have been required, than men are now forced to take for their fuftenance. The wifdom, goodnefs, and juftice of God, however, is very confpicuous, in decreeing, that toil and drudgery fhould be the confequence of departing from an eafy and rational obedience; in making the earth lefs defirable to man, when his guilt had reduced him to the neceffity of leaving it; and in keeping in order thofe paffions and appetites which had now broke loofe from the reftraint of reafon, by fubduing their impetuofity with hard labour; *Patrick's Commentary; and Revelation examined*.

* Milton brings in God, foon after the fall, appointing his holy angels to make an alteration in the courfe of the celeftial bodies, and to poffefs them with noxious qualities, in order to deftroy

creation suffered by it. The fertility of the earth, and se- A. M. 1.
renity of the air, were changed; the elements began to Ant. Chrif.
jar; the seasons were intemperate, and the weather grew Gen. ch. 3.
uncertain: so that to defend themselves against the immoderate heat, or cold, or wind, or rain, which now began
to infest the earth, our first parents were instructed by God
* how to make themselves vestments of the skins of those
beasts, which, very probably, they were appointed to sacrifice,

stroy the fertility of the earth, and thereby punish man for his
transgression.

—————————— The sun
Had its first precept so to move, so shine,
As might affect the earth with cold and heat
Scarce tolerable; and from the north to call
Decrepid winter; from the south to bring
Solstitial summer's heat. To the blank moon
Her office they prescrib'd, to th' *other five*
Their planetary motions and aspects
Of noxious efficacy, and when to join
In synod unbenign; and taught the *fix'd*
Their influence malignant when to shower:
Which of them, rising with the sun, or falling,
Should prove tempestuous. To the winds they set
Their corners, when with bluster to confound
Sea, air, and shore: the thunder then to roll
With terror through the dark aerial hall——
These changes in the heavens, though slow, **produce**
Like change on sea, and land; siderial blast,
Vapour, and mist, and exhalation hot,
Corrupt and pestilent. Book 10.

* It cannot be denied, but that the skins of beasts were a very ancient sort of clothing. Diodorus Siculus [lib. 1.] where
he introduces Hercules in a lion's skin, tells us no less; and the
author to the Hebrews makes mention of this kind of habit:
but the Jewish doctors have carried the matter so far, as to
maintain, that as Adam was a priest, this coat of his was his
priestly garment which he left to his posterity: so that Abel,
Noah, Abraham, and the rest of the patriarchs, sacrificed in it,
until the time that Aaron was made high priest, and had peculiar vestments appointed him by God. But all this fine fiction of theirs falls to the ground, if we can but suppose with
some, that by the word which we render *coats*, we may not improperly understand *tents*, or *arbors*, to defend our first parents
from the violence of the heats, and such hasty showers as were
common

A. M. 1.
Ant. Chrif.
4004.
Gen. ch. 3.

fice, either in confirmation of the covenant of grace, couched in the fentence pronounced againft the ferpent, or as a reprefentation of that great expiatory facrifice, which, in the fulnefs of time, God might inform them, was to be offered as a propitiation for the fins of all mankind: and, upon this account, it very likely was, that Adam changed his wife's name (who, as fome think, was called *Iſſcha* before) into that of *Eve*, as believing that God would make her the mother of all mankind, and of the promifed feed in particular, by whom he hoped for a reftoration both to himfelf and his pofterity, and to be raifed from death to a ftate of happinefs and immortal life.

Confidering then † what a fad cataftrophe this tranfgreffion of theirs had brought upon human nature, and that

common in the countries adjacent to paradife, and where the winter was not fo cold as to require coats made of fkins, which would certainly be too warm. That they could not be the fkins of flain animals is very manifeft, becaufe as yet there were no more than two of each fpecies, male and female, nor had they propagated. And therefore others have imagined, that if the original word muft mean *coats*, they were more probably made of the bark of trees, which are called *depkata*, *the fkins of them*, as well as the hides of animals. Vid, *Le Clerc*, and *Patrick's Commentary*; and *Bibliotheca Bib. vol.* 1.

† The words in the text are thefe, *Behold the man is become as one of us, to know good and evil; and now, left he put forth his hand, and tafte of the tree of life, and live for ever*, Gen. iii. 22. The former of thefe fentences is held by moft interpreters to be an irony, fpoken in allufion to the devil's manner of tempting Eve, ver. 5.; but, from the latter part of the words, this queftion feems to arife, "Whether Adam and Eve, if they had "tafted of the tree of life, after their tranfgreffion, fhould have "lived for ever?" Now it is very manifeft, that by the violation of God's command, they had juftly incurred the penalty, *In the day thou eateſt thereof thou ſhalt ſurely die*, i. e. fhalt furely become mortal: from whence it follows, that whether they had, or had not eaten, of the tree of life, they were, the moment they fell, fubject to the neceffity of dying, nor could the virtue of the tree be it what it would, preferve them from the execution of the fentence; and therefore thefe latter words, *And now, left he put forth his hand and tafte of the tree of life, and live for ever* are, in like manner, fpoken farcaftically, and as if God had faid, "Left the man fhould vainly fancy in himfelf, "that by eating of the tree of life, he fhall be enabled to "live for ever, let us remove this conceit from him, by remov-

ing

Chap. III. *from the Creation to the Flood.*

that such a scene of complicated misery might not be perpetuated by means of the tree of life, God, in his great mercy, found it convenient to remove them from the garden of paradise into that part of the country lying towards the east, where at first he created them; and that he might prevent their meditating a return, he secured every passage leading to it with a guard of angels, (some of which flying to and fro in the air, in bright refulgent bodies, seemed to flash out fire on every side, or to resemble the † vibrations of a flaming sword) that thereby he might deter them from

A. M. 1.
Ant Chrif.
4004.
Gen ch. 3.

"ing him from this place, and for ever debarring him from any hopes of coming at that tree again;" *Estius in diff. loca.*

Examples of God's speaking by way of sarcasm, or upbraiding, are not uncommon in Scripture: but considering that, *in the midst of judgement, he here thinketh upon mercy;* that before the the sentence against our first parents, he promises them a restoration, and after sentence past, does nevertheless provide them with clothing, some have thought, that the words, by taking the original verb (*vid.* Gell's essay) to signify *the time past* (as it may well enough do), are rather an expression of pity and compassion, and of the same import as if God had said, "The man was once, like one of us, to know good and to pursue it; to know evil, and to avoid it; (for that is the perfection of moral knowledge;) but behold how he is now degenerated! And therefore, left this degeneracy should continue upon him, and he become obdurate, the best way will be to seclude him from the tree of life, by expelling him from paradise." But this opinion seems to ascribe too much to the power of the tree, and is not supported with authority equal to the former.

† What is meant by the flaming sword represented to be in the hands of the cherubim at the entrance of the garden of paradise, is variously conjectured by learned men: but, of all essays of this kind, that of Tertullian, who thought it was the Torrid Zone, is the most unhappy; *Tertul. Apol. cap.* 47 The words of Lactantius are [Justit. Divin. l 2. c. 12.] *Ipsam paradisum igne circumvallavit,* He *encompassed paradise with a wall of fire:* from whence a learned man of our nation, pretending that the original word signifies *a dividing flame,* as well as a flaming sword, supposes, that this flame was an ascension of some combustible matter round about the garden, which excluded all comers to it, till such time as the beauty of the place was defaced; *Nicholls's Conference vol.* 1. Some Rabbins are of opinion, that this flaming sword was an angel, founding their sentiments on that passage in the Psalms, where it is said, that

A. M. 1.
Ant. Chrif. 4004.
Gen. ch. 3.

from any thoughts of ever attempting a re-entrance, until he fhould think fit to deftroy, and utterly lay wafte the beauty of the place. Thus fell our firft parents, and, from the happieft condition that can be imagined, plunged themfelves and their pofterity into a ftate of wretchednefs and corruption: for, as from one common root, [b] *fin entered into the world, and death by fin; fo* **death** *paffed upon all men, forafmuch as all have finned,* and **been** defiled by this original pollution.

THE OBJECTION.

The objection againft Mofes's account of the fall.

" BUT, upon fuppofition that the ftate of perfection
" wherein our firft parents were created, was really
" as complete as is pretended; we cannot well conceive
" how it was poffible for them to fall from it at all, or at
" leaft in fo fhort a fpace as the Scripture-account repre-
" fents it, after their creation. Some great and enormous
" offence, one would fuppofe, they had committed; but
" who could dream, that the bare eating of a little forbid-
" den fruit could be fo provoking, as to bring upon them
" that wretched depravity of nature, which ever fince we
" have been complaining of? The *counfels of God are a great*
" *deep;* but what reafon can be given, why he fhould put
" their virtue upon the trial, when he could not but fore-
" fee, that they certainly would be foiled by the wiles of the
" tempter? Or, if a probation was thought neceffary, why
" was their abftinence from the fruit of a certain tree made
" the teft of their obedience, when fo many more mo-
" mentous precepts might have befitted their condition as
" well? We may account the ferpent as fubtle as we pleafe,
" but how he could over-reach mankind in the perfection
" of their knowledge; or, if the devil lay concealed in the
" ferpent's body, what inducement he could have to af-
" fume the form of fo deteftable a creature; and what
" fhould hinder Eve from not being frightened when fhe
" heard

that *God maketh his angels fpirits, and his minifters a flaming fire,* Pfal. civ. 4. And hereupon another learned man of our nation has imagined, that this flaming fword (which was accounted by the Jews a fecond angel) was of a different kind from the cherubim, *viz.* a feraph, or flaming angel, in the form of a flying fiery ferpent, whofe body vibrated in the air with luftre, and may fitly be defcribed by the image of fuch a fword; *Tennifon of Idolatry.*

[b] Rom. v. 12.

Chap. III.   *from the Creation to the Flood.*   83

"heard him begin to speak, and instead of staying to talk
"with him, flee immediately to her husband, we cannot
"conceive. If the devil, in this disguise, was like to be
"an over-match for her, why did God admit of such an
"unequal conflict? Or, if the conflict was to be, why did
"not he send her succours from above? When so great a
"price, as the lives of all mankind, was set upon her
"head, why did not he enable her to overcome the wiles
"of the tempter? Why did not he order a guard of an-
"gels, or some more powerful influxes of his holy Spirit,
"to assist and secure her standing? But if the thing was
"so, that God decreed her fall, it is hard measure, one
"would think, to condemn her and her posterity for it;
"and looks as if he was angry beyond bounds, when he
"cursed the earth, and the serpent, which were both in-
"capable of sin, and consequently no ways culpable; when
"he drives the unhappy pair out of paradise with such pre-
"cipitancy, and leaves them to shift for themselves in a
"naked barren land; and (what is worst of all) when he
"entails their sin, and consequent depravation, upon their
"innocent posterity, until the end of the world; and all
"this for no greater crime than eating an apple or two,
"when robbing an orchard, now-a-days, is accounted a
"crime not worth a whipping: to say nothing of the odd-
"ness of that part of the sentence, wherein serpents were
"appointed to bite men by the heel, and men to bruise
"them on the head. This certainly can never be right in
"the letter; and therefore our safest way will be, to take
"this whole account of Moses in a figurative and allegori-
"cal sense; and to suppose, (with several, both Jewish
"and Christian writers,) that the history of the fall exhi-
"bits the defection of the soul; the serpent represents
"concupiscence; the man, to whom he durst not apply
"himself, is the picture of reason; and the woman, whom
"he so easily seduced and overcame, the emblem of sense,
"and so on."

How long our first parents continued in their state of innocence, and in the possession of the garden of Eden, is not so well agreed. The account of their fall, in the series of history, follows immediately their introduction into their blissful abode; whereupon ᵉ most of the Jewish doctors, and some of the Christian fathers, were of o- pinion, that they preserved their integrity but a very short while;

ᵉ Edward's Survey, vol. 1.

A.M. 1.
Ant. Chrif. 4004.
Gen. ch. 3

while; that in the close of the same day wherein they were made, they transgressed the covenant, and were the very same day cast out of paradise. But we are to consider, that many circumstances are omitted in the Scriptures concerning the state of our first parents, and the manner of their transgression; that Moses makes mention of nothing but what is conducive to his main design, which is to give a brief account of the most remarkable transactions that had happened from the beginning of the world to his time; and that there are sundry good reasons which may induce us to believe, that the state of man's innocence was of a longer duration than those, who are for precipitating matters, are pleased to think it.

Longer than is usually imagined.

God indeed can do what he pleases in an instant; but man necessarily requires a succession of time to transact his affairs in; and therefore when we read of Adam, in the same day that he was created, (and that was not until God had made every beast of the field,) [d] inquiring into the nature of every living creature, and imposing on them proper names; falling into a deep sleep, and, with some formality, (without doubt,) receiving his wife from the hand of God; removing into the garden of paradise, and (as we may well suppose) walking about, and taking some survey of it; receiving from God both a promise and prohibition, and thereupon (as we may suppose again) [e] ratifying the first great covenant with him: when we read of all these things, I say, we cannot but think, that some time must be required for the doing of them; and therefore to suppose, after this, [f] that in the close of the same day, the woman wandered from her husband, met with the serpent, entered into a parley with him, was overcome by his insinuations, did eat of the forbidden fruit, did prevail with her husband to do the same, and thereupon perceiving themselves naked, did instantly fall to work, and make themselves aprons: to suppose, that in the same evening God comes down, summons' the criminals before him, hears their excuses, decrees their punishments, drives them out of paradise, and places two cherubim to guard all avenues against their return; this is crowding too long a series of business into too short a compass of time, and thereby giving an handle to infidelity, when there is no manner of occasion for it.

We

---

[d] Burnet's Archæologiæ philosophicæ.   [e] Bull's State of man before the fall.   [f] Nicholls's Conference, vol. 1.

We, who are not ignorant of Satan's devices, and how ready he is to wait for a favourable occasion to address his temptations to every man's humour and complexion, can hardly suppose, [g] that he would have set upon the woman immediately after the prohibition was given; and not rather have waited, until it was in some measure forgot, and the happy opportunity of finding her alone should chance to present itself: but such an opportunity could not well instantly have happened, because the love and endearments between this couple, at first, we may well imagine, was so tender and affecting, as not to admit of the least absence or separation: nor must we forget (what the history itself tells us) that they were so much accustomed to [h] *the voice of God walking in the garden in the cool of the day*, as not to account it any new thing; and so well acquainted with the nature and plantation of the garden, as to run directly to the darkest thickets and umbrages, in order to hide themselves from his sight; which must have been the result of more than an hour or two's experience. And therefore, (if we may be allowed to follow others in their conjectures) [i] it was either on the tenth day of the world's age, that our first parents fell, and were expelled paradise, in memory of which calamity, [k] *the great day of expiation*, (which was the tenth day of the year,) wherein *all were required to afflict their souls*, was, in after ages, instituted; or (as others would rather have it) on the eighth day from their creation: [l] that as the first week in the world ended with the formation of man and woman, the second was probably concluded with their fatal seduction.

When man is said to have been made according to the likeness and image of God, it cannot be supposed, but that he was created in the full perfection of his nature; and yet [m] it must be remembered, that * no created being can,

A. M. 1
Ant. Chrif. 4004.
Gen ch. 3.

How he came to fall

in

---

[g] Patrick's Commentary. [h] Gen. iii. 10. [i] Usher's Annals. [k] Lev. xvi. 29. [l] Edward's Survey, vol. 1. [m] Clarke's Inquiry into the original of moral evil.

* God, though he be omnipotent, cannot make any created being *absolutely perfect*; for whatever is absolutely perfect must necessarily be self-existent: but it is included in the very notion of a creature, as such, not to exist of itself, but of God. An absolutely perfect creature therefore implies a contradiction; for it would be of itself, and not of itself, at the same time. Absolute perfection therefore is peculiar to God; and should he communicate his own peculiar perfection to another, that other

Vol. I. No. 3.   C c   would in its own nature, be incapable of sin and default. Its perfections, be they what they will, are finite, and whatever has bounds set to its perfections, is, in this respect, imperfect, *i. e.* it wants those perfections which a being of infinite perfections only can have; and whatever wants any perfection, is certainly capable of miscarrying. And as every finite creature is capable of default, so every rational being must necessarily have a liberty of choice, *i. e.* it must have a will to chuse, as well as an understanding to reason; because a faculty of understanding, without a will to determine it, if left to itself, must always think of the same subject, or proceed in a series and connection of thoughts, without any end or design, which will be a perpetual labour in vain, or a thoughtfulness to no purpose. And as every rational being has a liberty of choice, so, to direct that choice, it must of necessity have a prescribed rule of its actions.

God indeed, who is infinite in perfection, is a rule to himself, and acts according to his own essence, from whence it is impossible for him to vary; but the most perfect creatures must act by a rule, which is not essential to them, but prescribed them by God, and is not so intrinsic in their natures, but that they may decline from it; for a free agent may follow, or not follow, the rule prescribed him, or else he would not be free.

Now, in order to know how it comes to pass, that we so frequently abuse our natural freedom, and transgress the rules which God hath set us, we must remember, that " the soul of man is seated in the midst, as it were, between those more excellent beings, which live perpetually above, and with whom it partakes in the sublimity of its nature and understanding, and those inferior terrestrial beings,

would be God. Imperfection must therefore be tolerated in creatures, notwithstanding the divine omnipotence and goodness; for contradictions are no objects of power. God indeed might have refrained from acting, and continued alone self-sufficient, and perfect to all eternity; but infinite goodness would by no means allow of this; and therefore since it obliged him to produce external things, which things could not possibly be perfect, it preferred these imperfect things to none at all; from whence it follows, that imperfection arose from the infinity of divine goodness; *King's Essay on the origin of evil.*

ⁿ Stillingfleet's Orig. facr.

Chap. III. *from the Creation to the Flood.* 87

with which it communicates, through the vital union it has
with the body; and that, by reason of its natural freedom,
it is sometimes assimilated to the one, and sometimes to the
other of these extremes. We must observe further, that,
° in this compound nature of ours, there are several powers
and faculties, several inclinations and dispositions, several
passions and affections, differing in their nature and ten-
dency, according as they result from the soul or body;
that each of these has its proper object, in a due applica-
tion of which it is easy and satisfied; that they are none of
them sinful in themselves, but may be instruments of much
good, when rightly applied, as well as occasion great mis-
chief by a misapplication; and therefore a considerable part
of virtue will consist in regulating them, and in keeping our
sensitive part subject to the rational. This is the original
constitution of our nature: and since our first parents
were endued with the same powers and faculties of mind,
and had the same dispositions and inclinations of body, it
cannot be, but that they must have been liable to the same
sort of temptations; and consequently liable to comply
with the dictates of sense and appetite, contrary to the di-
rection of reason, or the precepts of Almighty God. And
to this cause the Scripture seems to ascribe the commission
of the first sin, when it tells us, that *the woman saw the tree,
that it was good for food, and pleasant to the eye, and desirable to
make one wise,* i. e. it had several qualities which were a-
dapted to her natural appetites; was beautiful to the sight,
and delightful to the taste, and improving to the under-
standing; which both answered the desire of knowledge
implanted in her spiritual, and the love of sensual pleasure
resulting from her animal part; and these, heightened by
the suggestions of the tempter, abated the horror of God's
prohibition, and induced her to act contrary to his express
command.

God indeed all along foreknew that she would fall in
this inglorious manner; but his foreknowledge did not
necessitate her falling, neither did his wisdom ever conceive,
that a fallen creature was worse than none at all. ᵖ The
divine nature, as it is in itself, is incomprehensible by hu-
man understanding: and not only his nature, but likewise
his powers and faculties, and the ways and methods in
which he exercises them, are so far beyond our reach, that
we are utterly incapable of framing just and adequate no-

A. M. 1.
Ant. Chrif.
4004
Gen. ch. 3.

God's pre-
science no
occasion of
her sin.

C c 2 tions

° Clarke of the original of moral evil. ᵖ Bishop King's
Sermon of predestination.

A. M. 1.
Ant. Chrif
4004.
Gen. ch. 3.

tions of them. We attribute to him the faculties of wisdom, understanding, and foreknowledge; but at the same time, we cannot but be senfible, that they are of a nature quite different from ours, and that we have no direct and proper conceptions of them. When we indeed forefee or determine any thing, wherein there is no poffible matter of obftruction, we fuppofe the event certain and infallible; and, were the foreknowledge and predetermination of God of the fame nature with ours, we might be allowed to make the fame conclufion: but why may not it be of fuch a perfection in God, as is confiftent both with the freedom of man's will, and contingency of events? *As the heavens are higher than the earth, fo are his ways far above our ways:* and therefore, though it be certain that he who made Eve, and confequently knew all the fprings and weights, wherewith fhe was moved, could not but forefee, how every poffible object, that prefented itfelf, would determine her choice; yet this he might do, without himfelf giving any bias or determination to it at all: q juft as the man, who fees the fetting of the chimes, can tell, feveral hours before, what tune they will play, without any pofitive influence, either upon their fetting, or their playing. So that Eve, when fhe was tempted, could not fay, *I was tempted by God*, for God tempteth none; neither had the divine prefcience any influence over her choice, but r *by her own luft was fhe drawn away, and enticed; and when luft had conceived, it brought forth fin, and fin, when it was finifhed, brought forth death.*

The reafon ablenefs of God's giving man a law.

That fome command was proper to be laid upon man in his ftate of innocence, is hardly to be denied. s Dependence is included in the very notion of a creature; and as it is man's greateft happinefs to depend on God, whofe infinite wifdom can contrive, and infinite power can effect whatever he knows to be moft expedient for him; fo was it Adam's advantage to have a conftant fenfe of that dependence kept upon his mind, and (for that reafon) a fure and permanent memorial of it, placed before his eyes, in fuch a manner, as might make it impoffible for him to forget it.

And as this dependence on God was Adam's greateft happinefs, fo it feems neceffary on God's part, and highly comporting with his character of a creator, that he fhould require

q Young's Serm. vol. 1.   r James i. 14, &c.   s Revelation examined.

Chap. III.   *from the Creation to the Flood.*   89

require of his creatures, in some acts of homage and obedience, (which homage and obedience must necessarily imply some kind of restraint upon their natural liberty) an acknowledgement and declaration of it.   And if some restraint of natural liberty was necessary in Adam's case, what restraint could be more easy, than the coercion of his appetite from the use of one tree, amidst an infinite variety of others, no less delicious; and at the same time, what restraint more worthy the wisdom and goodness of God, than the prohibition of a fruit, which he knew would be pernicious to his creature?

A. M. 1.
Ant. Chrif.
4004.
Gen. ch. 3.

The prohibition of some enormous sin, or the injunction of some great rule of moral virtue, we perhaps may account a properer test of man's obedience; but if we consider the nature of things, as they then stood, we may find reason perhaps to alter our sentiments.[t] The Mosaic tables are acknowledged by all to be a tolerable good system, and to comprize all the general heads of moral virtue; and yet, if we run over them, we shall find, that they contain nothing suitable to man in the condition wherein we are now considering him.

The fitness of that which he gave Adam

Had God, for instance, forbidden the worship of false gods, or the worship of graven images; can we suppose, that Adam and Eve, just come out of the hand of their maker, and visited every day with the light of his glorious presence, could have even been guilty of these? Besides that, the worship of false gods and images was a thing which came into the world several hundreds of years afterwards, either to flatter living princes, or supply the place of dead ones, who, the silly people fancied, were become gods.   Had he prohibited perjury and vain swearing; what possible place could these have had in the infant and innocent state of mankind?   Perjury was never heard of, till the world was better peopled, when commerce and trade came in use, when courts of judicature were settled, and men began to cheat one another, and then deny it, and so forswear it: and oaths and imprecations could never have a being in a state of innocence: they borrow their original manifestly from the sinfulness of human nature.

The like may be said of all the rest.   How could Adam and Eve have *honoured their father and their mother*, when they

[t] Nicholls's Conference, vol. 1. and Jenkins's Reasonableness, vol. 2.

they never had any? What poſſible temptation could they have to be guilty of murther, when they muſt have acted it upon their own fleſh? How could they commit adultery, when they were the only two upon the face of the earth? How be guilty of theft, when they were the ſole proprietors of all? How bear falſe witneſs againſt their neighbour, or covet his goods, when there was never a neighbour in the world for them to be ſo unjuſt to? And ſo (if we proceed to Chriſtian precepts) how could they love enemies, how could they forgive treſpaſſes, when they had no one in the world to offend againſt them? And the duties of mortification and ſelf-denial, &c. how could they poſſibly exerciſe theſe, when they had no luſt to conquer, no paſſion to overcome, but were all ſerene and calm within?

Since, therefore, all the moral precepts, that we are acquainted with, were improper for the trial of man's obedience in his ſtate of innocence; it remains, that his probation was moſt properly to be effected, by his doing or forbearing ſome indifferent action, neither good or evil in itſelf, but only ſo far good or evil, as it was commanded or forbidden. And if ſuch a command was to be choſen, what can we imagine ſo natural and agreeable to the ſtate of our firſt parents, (conſidering they were to live all their lives in a garden) as the forbidding them to eat of the fruit of a certain tree in that garden, a tree hard at hand, and might every moment be eaten of, and would therefore every moment give them an opportunity of teſtifying their obedience to God by their forbearing it? A wiſe appointment this, had not the great enemy of mankind come in, and defeated it.

Who the ſerpent was

Who this great enemy of mankind was, and by what method of inſinuation he drew our firſt parents into their defection, Moſes, who contents himſelf with relating facts as they happened outwardly, without any comment, or expoſition of them, or who, by a metonymy in the Hebrew tongue, uſes the inſtrumental for the efficient cauſe, tells us expreſsly, that it was the ſerpent; and for this reaſon, ſome of the ancient Jews ran into a fond conceit, that ᵘ this whole paſſage is to be underſtood of a real ſerpent; which creature, ˣ they ſuppoſe, before the fall, to have had the faculty of ſpeech and reaſon both. But this is too groſs a conception to have many abettors; and therefore

---

ᵘ Le Clerc's Commentary and eſſays.   ˣ Joſephus, and ſeveral others.

fore the common, and indeed the only probable opinion is, A. M. 1.
that it was the devil; some wicked and malicious spirit Ant. Chrif.
(probably one of the chief of that order) who envied the Gen. ch 3.
good of mankind, the favours God had bestowed on them,
and the future happiness he had ordained for them, and
was thereupon resolved to tempt them to disobedience,
thereby to bring them to the same forlorn condition with
himself, and his other apostate brethren; and that, to effect his purpose, he made use of a serpent's body, wherein
to transact his fraud and imposture.

Why the devil chose to assume the form of a serpent, Why the
rather than that of any other creature, we may, in some devil assum-
measure, learn from the character which the Scripture of a serpent.
gives us of it, viz. that *it was more subtle than any beast of the
field, that the Lord God had made*: where the word *subtle*
may not so much denote the craft and insidiousness, as the
gentle, familiar, and insinuating nature of this creature.
⁷ That the serpent, before the fall, was mild and gentle,
and more familiar with man, than any other animal: that
* it did not creep on the ground, but went with its head
and breast reared up, and advanced; that by frequently
approaching our first parents, and playing and sporting
before them, it had gained their good liking and esteem,
is not only the sentiment both ᶻ of Jews and ᵃ Christians,
but what seems likewise to have some foundation in Scripture: for when God says, *That he will put enmity between
the serpent and the woman, and between his seed and her seed*,
the implication must be, that there was some sort of kindness and intimacy between them before.

There

---

⁷ Mede's Discourses.
* The beauty of the serpent, which the devil made choice
of, is thus described by Milton:
    So spake the enemy of mankind, inclos'd
    In serpent, inmate bad! and toward Eve
    Address'd his way: not with indented wave,
    Prone on the ground, as since, but on his rear,
    Circular base of rising folds, that tower'd,
    Fold above fold, a surging maze? his head
    Crested aloft, and carbuncle his eyes;
    With burnish'd neck of verdant gold, erect
    Amidst his circling spires, that on the grass
    Floated redundant: pleasing was his shape,
    And lovely.——   Book 9.
ᶻ Josephus's Antiq. l. 1.   ᵃ Basil. Hom. De paradiso.

There is no absurdity then in supposing, that this creature was beloved both by Adam and Eve. She especially might be highly delighted, and used to play and divert herself with it. [b] She laid it perhaps in her bosom, adorned her neck with its windings, and made it a bracelet for her arms. So that its being thus intimate with the woman, made it the properer instrument for the devil's purpose, who sliding himself into it, might wantonly play before her, until he insensibly brought her to the forbidden tree: and then, twisting about its branches, might take of the fruit and eat, to shew her, by experience, that there was no deadly quality in it, before he began his address; and his speech might be the less frightful or surprising to her, who, in the state of her innocence, not knowing what fear was, might probably think (as he might positively affirm) [a] that this new-acquired faculty proceeded from the virtue of the tree.

But there is another conjecture still more probable, if we will not allow, that the serpent was not of a common ordinary species, but one very probably something like that flying fiery sort, which, we are told, are bred in Arabia and Egypt. [c] They are of a shining yellowish colour like brass, and by the motion of their wings, and vibration of their tails,
reverberating

[b] Mede's Discourses.
[a] Eve, upon hearing the serpent speak, inquires by what means it was, that it came by that faculty; and is told, that it was by eating of a certain tree in the garden.
 I was at first, as other beasts that graze
 The trodden herb, of abject thoughts and low——
 Till on a day roving the field, I chanced
 A goodly tree far distant to behold,
 Laden with fruit of various colours, mixt
 Ruddy and gold——
 To satisfy the sharp desire I had
 Of tasting these fair apples, I resolv'd
 Not to defer——
 Sated at length, e'er long, I might perceive
 Strange alteration in me, to degree
 Of reason in my inward powers, and speech
 Wanted not long, though to this shape retain'd,
 Thenceforth to speculation high or deep
 I turn'd my thoughts, and with capacious mind
 Consider'd all things visible in heaven,
 Or earth, or middle.   Book 9.
[c] Tennison of Idolatry; Patrick's Commentary; and Nicholls's Conference, vol. 1.

reverberating the sun-beams, make a glorious appearance. Now, if the serpent, whose body the devil abused, was of this kind, (though perhaps of a species far more glorious,) it was a very proper creature for him to make use of. For these serpents we find called in Scripture *seraphs*, or *seraphim*, which gave the name to those bright lofty angels who were frequently employed by God to deliver his will to mankind, and, coming upon that errand, were wont to put on certain splendid forms, some the form of *cherubim*, i. e. *beautiful flying oxen*, and others the shape of *seraphim*, i. e. *winged and shining serpents*. Upon this hypothesis we may imagine farther, that the devil, observing that good angels attended the divine presence, and sometimes ministered to Adam and Eve in this bright appearance, usurped the organs of one of these shining serpents, which, by his art and skill in natural causes, he might improve into such a wonderful brightness, as to represent to Eve the usual *shechinah*, or angelical appearance, she was accustomed to; and, under this disguise, she might see him approach her without fear, and hear him talk to her without surprise, and comply with his seduction with less reluctancy; as supposing him to be an angel of God's retinue, and now dispatched from heaven to instruct her in some momentous point, as she had often perhaps experienced before during her stay in paradise.

A [d] learned Jew has expounded this transaction in a new and uncommon way. He supposes that the serpent did not speak at all, nor did Eve say any thing to it; but that, being a very nimble and active creature, it got upon the tree of knowledge, took of the fruit, and eat it; and that Eve, having seen it several times do so, and not die, concluded with herself, that the tree was not of such a destructive quality as was pretended; that as it gave speech and reason to the serpent, it would much more improve and advance her nature; and was thereupon emboldened to eat.

This opinion is very plausible, and, in some degree, founded on Scripture: for though the woman might perceive by her senses, that the fruit was pleasant to the eye, yet it was impossible she could know, either that it was good for food, or desirable to make one wise, any other way than by the example and experiment of the serpent, which, merely by eating of that fruit, (as she thought,) was

A. M. 1.
Ant. Christ
4003.
Gen. ch. 3.

How Eve came to be deluded.

---

[d] Isaac Aberbenel.

A. M. 1.
Ant. Chrif
4004
Gen. ch. 3.

changed from a brute into a rational and vocal creature. This, I say, is a pretty plausible solution; and yet it cannot be denied, but that the text seems to express something more, and that there was a real dialogue between the woman and the serpent, wherein the serpent had the advantage. And therefore (to persist in our former exposition) it is not improbable, that the tempter, before ever he accosted Eve, transformed himself into the likeness of an angel of light, and prefacing his speech with some short congratulations of her happiness, might proceed to ensnare her with some such cunning harangue as this.

A paraphrase upon the tempter's speech;

"And can it possibly be, that so good a God, who has so lately been so bountiful to you, as to give you such an excellent being, and invest you with power and dominion over all the rest of his creatures, should now envy you any of the innocent pleasures of nature? Has he indeed denied you the use of the tree of knowledge? But why did he plant it at all? Why did he adorn it with such beautiful fruit? Why did he place it on an eminence in the garden, for you to behold daily, unless he is minded to mock and tantalize you? The true design, both of the prohibition and penalty which you relate, is to keep you in ignorance, and thereby oblige you to live in perpetual dependence on him. He knows full well, that the virtue of this tree is to illuminate the understanding, and thereby to enable you to judge for yourselves, without having recourse to him upon every occasion. ᵉ To judge for himself is the very privilege that makes him God; and for that reason he keeps it to himself: but eat but of this tree, and ye shall be like him; your beings shall be in your own hands, and your happiness vast and inconceivable, and independent on any other. What effect it has had on me, you cannot but see and hear, since it has enabled me to reason and discourse in this wise; and, instead of death, has given a new kind of life to my whole frame. And, if it has done this to a brute animal, what may not creatures of your refined make, and excellent perfections expect from it? Why should you shrink back, or be afraid to do it then? You have here an opportunity of making yourselves for ever; and the trespass is nothing. What harm in eating an apple? Why this tree of
"knowledge

ᵉ Bishop King's Discourse on the fall, at the end of his Origin of evil.

Chap. III.   *from the Creation to the Flood.*

"knowlege more sacred than all the rest? Can so great
"a punishment as death be proportionate to so small a
"fault? I come to assure you, that it is not; that God has
"reversed his decree, and eat you what you will, ye surely
"shall not die."

A. M. 1.
Ant. Christ.
4004.
Gen. ch. 3

[f] Thus the serpent suggested to Eve, that God had imposed upon her, and she was willing to discover whether he had or not. Curiosity, and a desire of independency, to know more, and to be entire master of herself, were the affections which the tempter promised to gratify; and an argument like this has seldom failed ever since to corrupt the generality of mankind: insomuch that few, very few, have been able to resist the force of this temptation, especially when it comes (as it did to Eve) clothed with all the outward advantage of allurement. For whoever knows the humour of youth, and how he himself was affected at that time, cannot but be sensible, that as the fairness of the fruit, its seeming fitness for food, the desire of being independent, and under her own management and government, were inducements that prevailed with our first parents to throw off the conduct of God; so this curiosity of trying the pleasures of sense, this itch of being our own masters, and chusing for ourselves, together with the charming face of sin, and our ignorance and inexperience of the consequences of it, are generally the first means of our being corrupted against the good maxims and principles we received from our parents and teachers.

And the probability of its success.

It is in the essential constitution of man, (as we said before,) that he should be a free agent; and, if we consider him now as in a state of probation, we shall soon perceive, that God could not lay any restraint upon him, nor communicate any assistance to him, but what was consistent with the nature he had given him, and the state he had placed him in. God created man a free agent, [g] that he might make the system of the universe perfect, and supply that vast *hiatus* which must otherwise have happened between heaven and earth, had he not interposed some other creature (endued with rationality, master of his own elections, and consequently capable of serving him voluntarily and freely) between angels and brutes. In the very act of creating him, therefore, God intended that he should be

That man's liberty of choice was natural, and not to be restrained.

D d 2   rational,

[f] Bishop King's Sermon on the fall.   [g] Bishop King's Essay on the origin of evil.

A. M. 1.
Ant. Chrif.
4004.
Gen. ch. 3

rational, and determined, as it were by a law, that he should be free; and, having ingrafted this in his make, it would have been a violation of his own laws, and infraction on his own work, to have interposed, and hindered the use of that faculty, which, by the law of nature, he had established. We do not expect, that the situation of the earth, or the course of the sun should be altered on our account, because these seem to be things of great importance; and we apprehend it unreasonable, that, for our private advantage, the order and harmony of things should be changed, to the detriment of so many other beings. But, to alter the will, to stop the election, is no less a violation of the laws of nature, than to interrupt the course of the sun, because a free agent is a more noble being than the sun. The laws of its nature are to be esteemed more sacred, and cannot be changed without a great miracle; there would then be a kind of shock and violence done to nature, if God should interfere, and hinder the actions of free-will; and perhaps it would prove no less pernicious to the intellectual system, than the sun's standing still would be to the natural.

To apply these reflections to the matter now before us. Had God, to prevent man's sin, taken away the liberty of his will, he had thereby destroyed the foundation of all virtue, and the very nature of man himself. For virtue would not have been such, had there been no possibility of acting contrary, and man's nature would have been divine, had it been made impeccable. Had God given our first parents then such powerful influences of his holy Spirit, as to have made it impossible for them to sin, or had he sent a guard of angels, to watch and attend them so as to hinder the devil from proposing any temptation, or them from hearkening to any; had he, I say, supernaturally over-ruled the organs of their bodies, or the inward inclinations of their minds, upon the least tendency to evil; in this case he had governed them, not as free, but as necessary agents, and put it out of his own power to have made any trial of them at all. All therefore that he could do, and all that in reason might be expected from him to do, was to give them such a sufficient measure of power and assistance, as might enable them to be a match for the strongest temptation; and this, there is no question to be made, but that he did do.

We

ʰ We, indeed, in this degenerate state of ours, find a great deal of difficulty to encounter with temptations. We find a great blindness in our understandings, and a crookedness in our wills. We have passions, on some occasions, strong and ungovernable; and oftentimes experience an inclination to do evil, even before the temptation comes: but our first parents, in their primitive rectitude, stood possessed of every thing as advantageous the other way. They had an understanding large and capacious, and fully illuminated by the divine Spirit. Their will was naturally inclined to the supreme good, and could not, without violence to its nature, make choice of any other. Their passions were sedate, and subordinate to their reason; and, when any difficulties did arise, they had God at all times to have recourse to: by which means it came to pass, that it was as hard for them to sin, as it is difficult for us to abstain from sinning; as easy for them to elude temptations then, as it is natural for us to be led away by temptations now. And therefore, if, notwithstanding all these mighty advantages towards a state of impeccancy, they made it their option to transgress, their perverseness only is to be blamed, and not any want of sufficient assistance from their bounteous Creator.

A M. 1.
Ant. Chris. 4004
Gen. ch. 3.

That God gave him sufficient abilities to stand:

Great indeed is the disorder which their transgression has brought upon human nature; but there will be no reason to impeach the goodness of God for it, if we take but in this one consideration, That what he thought not fit to prevent by his almighty power, he has, nevertheless, thought fit to repair by the covenant of mercy in his son Jesus Christ. By him he has propounded the same reward, everlasting life after death, which we should have had, without death, before; and has given us a better establishment for our virtue now, than we could have had, had we not been sufferers by this first transgression.

And that, upon his fall, he has provided him with an adequate remedy.

ᶦ For let us suppose, ⁱ that, notwithstanding our first parents had sinned, yet God had been willing that original righteousness should have equally descended upon their posterity; yet we must allow, that any one of their posterity might have been foiled by the wiles of the tempter, and fallen, as well as they did. Now had they so fallen, (the covenant of grace being not yet founded,) how could they ever have recovered themselves to any degree of acceptance with God? Their case must have been the same,

ᵏ Nicholls's Conference, vol. 1. ⁱ Young's Sermons.

as desperate, as forlorn, as that of fallen angels was before: whereas, in the present state of things, our condition is much safer. Sin indeed, by reason of our present infirmity, may more easily make its breaches upon us, either through ignorance or surprise; but it cannot get dominion over us, without our own deliberate option, because it is an express gospel-promise against the power of sin, that [k] *it shall not have dominion over us;* against the power of the devil, that [l] *greater is he that is in you, than he that is in the world;* against the power of temptations, that [m] *God is faithful, who will not suffer us to be tempted above what we are able;* against discouragement from the pretence of our infirmities, that [n] *we may do all through Christ that strengthens us;* and, in case of failing, that [o] *we have an Advocate with the Father, and a propitiation for our sins.* Thus plentifully did God provide for man's stability in that state of integrity, thus graciously for his restoration, in this state of infirmity. In both cases, his goodness has been conspicuous, and has never failed!

Why God cursed the serpent.

In like manner, (to absolve the divine nature from any imputation of passion or peevishness, of injustice or hard usage, in cursing the serpent and the earth; in driving our lapsed parents out of paradise, and in entailing their guilt and punishment upon the latest posterity,) we should do well to remember, that the serpent, against which the first sentence is denounced, is to be considered here in a double capacity; both as an animal, whose organs the devil employed in the seduction of the woman; and as the devil himself, lying hid and concealed under the figure of the serpent: for the sentence, we may observe, is plainly directed to an intelligent being and free agent, who had committed a crime which a brute could not be capable of.

Now if we consider what a glorious creature the serpent was before the fall, we cannot but suppose that God intended this debasement of it, [p] not so much to express his indignation against it, (for it had no bad intention, neither was it conscious of what the devil did with its body,) as to make it a monument of man's apostacy, a testimony of his displeasure against sin, and an instructive emblem to deter all future ages from the commission of that

which

---

[k] Rom. vi. 14.   [l] 1 John iv. 4.   [m] 1 Cor. x. 13.
[n] Phil. iv. 13.   [o] 1 John ii. 1.   [p] Patrick's Commentary; and Mede's Discourses.

which brought such vengeance along with it. In the Levitical law we find, that if a man committed any abomination with a beast, [q] the beast was to be slain as well as the man; and, by parity of reason, the serpent is here punished, if not to humble the pride, and allay the triumph of the devil, by seeing the instrument of his success so shamefully degraded, at least to remind the delinquents themselves of the foulness of their crime, and the necessity of their repentance, whenever they chanced to behold so noble a creature as the serpent was, reduced to so vile and abject a condition, merely for being the means of their transgression.

But God might have a farther design in this degradation of the serpent: he foresaw, that, in future ages, Satan would take pride in abusing this very creature to the like pernicious purposes, and, under the semblance of serpents of all kinds, would endeavour to establish the vilest idolatry, even the idolatry of his own hellish worship. That therefore the beauty of the creature might be no provocation to such idolatry, it was a kind and beneficent act in God to deface the excellence of the serpent's shape, and, at the same time, inspire mankind with the strongest horror and aversion to it. Nor can it be denied, but that, [r] if we suppose the devil possessed the serpent, and was, as it were, incarnate in it, the power of God could unite them as closely as our souls and bodies are united, and thereby cause the punishment inflicted on the literal serpent to affect Satan as sensibly as the injuries done our bodies do reach our souls; at least, while that very serpent was in being.

To consider Satan then under the form of a serpent, we shall see the propriety of the other part of the sentence denounced against him, and what comfort and consolation our criminal parents might reasonably collect from thence. That this part of the sentence, *I will put enmity between thee and the woman, and between thy seed and her seed; it shall bruise thy head, and thou shalt bruise his heel,* is not to be understood in a literal sense, (because such sense is absurd and ridiculous,) every reader of competent understanding must own: and therefore its meaning must be such as will best agree with the circumstances of the transaction. Now the transaction was thus:——Adam, tempted by his wife, and she by the serpent, had fallen from

A. M. 1.
Ant. Chrif.
4004.
Gen. ch. 3.

The latter part of the sentence against the serpent explained.

[q] Lev. xx. 15. [r] Bishop King's Sermon on the fall.

A. M. 1.
Ant. Chrif. 4004.
Gen. ch. 3.

from their obedience, and were now in the presence of God expecting judgement. ˢ They knew full well, at that juncture, that their fall was the victory of the serpent, whom, by experience, they found to be an enemy to God and man: to man, whom he had ruined by seducing him to sin; and to God the noble work of whose creation he had defaced. It could not therefore but be some comfort to them, to hear the serpent first condemned, and to see that, however he had prevailed against them, he had gained no victory over their maker, who was able to affert his own honour, and to punish this great author of iniquity. Nor was it less a consolation to them to hear from the mouth of God likewise, that the serpent's victory was not a complete victory over even themselves; that they and their posterity should be able to contest his empire; and though they were to suffer much in the struggle, yet finally they should prevail, bruise the serpent's head, and deliver themselves from his power and dominion over them.

This certainly is the lowest sense wherein our first parents could have understood this part of the sentence denounced against the serpent; and yet this very sense was enough to revive in them comfortable hopes of a speedy restoration. For when Adam heard that the seed of the woman was to destroy the evil spirit, he undoubtedly understood Eve to be that woman, and some issue of his by her to be that seed; and accordingly we may observe, that when Eve was delivered of Cain, the form of her exultation is, ᵗ *I have gotten a man from the Lord,* i. e. I have gotten a man through the signal favour and mercy of God. ᵘ Now this extraordinary exultation cannot be supposed to arise from the bare privilege of bearing issue, for that privilege (as she could but not know before this time) she had in common with the meanest brutes; and therefore her transport must arise from the prospect of some extraordinary advantage from this issue, and that could be no other than the destruction of her enemy.

Cain indeed proved a wicked man; but when she had conceived better expectations from Abel, and Cain had slain him, she, nevertheless, recovered her hopes upon the birth of Seth; because ˣ God, saith she, *hath appointed me another seed,* or one who will destroy the power of Satan, instead

---

ˢ Bishop Sherlock's Use and intent of prophecy. ᵗ Gen. iv. 1. ᵘ Revelation examined, vol. 1. ˣ Gen. iv. 25.

Chap. III. *from the Creation to the Flood.*

instead of Abel, whom Cain slew. Thus we see, that the obscurity in which it pleased God to foretell the destruction of the evil spirit, gave rise to a succession of happy hopes in the breast of Adam and Eve; who (if they had known that this happiness was to be postponed for four thousand years) would, in all probability, have inevitably fallen into an extremity of despair.

<small>A. M. 1.
Ant. Christ.
4004.
Gen. ch. 3.</small>

But how necessary soever God might think it, to give our first parents, some general hopes and expectations of a restoration; yet, being now fallen into a state of sin and corruption, which must of course infect their latest posterity, he found it expedient to deprive them of that privilege of immortality, wherewith he had invested them, and (as an act of justice and mercy both) to turn them out of paradise, and debar them from the tree of life: of justice, in that they had forfeited their right to immortality, by transgressing a command, which nothing but a vain, criminal curiosity could make them disobey; and of mercy, in that, when sin had entailed all kinds of calamity upon human nature, in such circumstances, to have perpetuated life, would have been to perpetuate misery.

<small>Why God turned our first parents out of paradise,</small>

This, I think, can hardly be accounted the effect of passion or peevishness: and, in like manner, God's cursing the ground, or (what is all one) his depriving it of its original fruitfulness, by a different turn given to the air, elements, and seasons, was not the effect of anger, or any hasty passion, (which God is not capable of,) but of calm and equitable justice; since it was man (who had done enough to incur the divine displeasure) that was to suffer by the curse, and not the ground itself: for the ground felt no harm by *bringing forth thorns and thistles*, but Adam, who for some time had experienced the spontaneous fertility of paradise, was a sufficent sufferer by the change, when he found himself reduced to hard labour, and forced *to eat his bread by the sweat of his brows.*

<small>and cursed the ground.</small>

It must be acknowleged therefore, ʸ that there was good reason, why the penalty of the first transgression should be greater than any subsequent one; because it was designed to deter posterity, and to let them see, by this example, that whatever commination God denounces against guilt will most infallibly be executed. We mistake, however, the nature of God's laws, and, do in effect, renounce his

<small>The nature of the divine prohibition.</small>

ʸ Revelation examined.

A.M. 1
Ant. Chrif.
4004
Gen. ch. 3

his authority, when we suppose, that good and evil are in the nature of things only, and not in the commandments and prohibitions of God. ² Whatever God is pleased to command or forbid, how indifferent soever it be in itself, is for that very reason, so far as it is commanded or forbidden by him, as truly good or evil, as if it were absolutely and morally so, being enacted by the same divine authority, which makes all moral precepts obligatory. God, in short, is our law-giver, and whatever he commands, whether it be a moral precept or positive injunction, so far as he enacts it, is of the same necessary and indispensable obligation. Upon this it follows, that all sin is a transgression of the law, and a contempt of God's authority: but then the aggravations of a sin do arise from the measure of its guilt, and the parties advantages to have avoided it; under which consideration, nothing can be more heinous than the sin of our first parents. It was not only a bare disobedience to God's command, by a perfect infidelity to his promises and threats; it was a sort of idolatry in believing the devil, and putting a greater trust in him, than in God. It was an horrible pride in them to desire to be like God, and such a diabolical pride, as made the evil angels fall from heaven. Covetousness, and a greedy theft it was, to desire and purloin, what was none of his own; and one of the most cruel and unparalleled murthers that ever was committed, to kill and destroy so many thousands of their offspring. ᵃ Add to this, that it was a disobedience against God, an infinite being, and of infinite dignity; a God, who had given them existence, and that so very lately, that the impresses of it could not be worn out of their memory; that had bestowed so much happiness upon them, more than on all the creation besides; that had made them lords over all, and restrained nothing from them, but only the fruit of this one tree. Add again, that they committed this sin, against the clearest conviction of conscience, with minds fully illuminated by the divine Spirit, with all possible assistance of grace to keep them from it, and no untoward bent of nature, or unruly passion to provoke them to it: and, putting all this together, it will appear, that this was a sin of the deepest dye, and that no man, now-a-days, can possibly commit a crime of such a complicated nature, and attended with such horrid aggravations.

The heinousness of transgressing it.

It

² Jenkins's Reasonableness, vol. 2.   ᵃ Nicholls's Conference, vol. 1.

Chap. III.   *from the Creation to the Flood.*   103

It is the opinion of some, [b] that the fruit of the forbidden tree might be impregnated with some fermenting juice, which put the blood and spirits into a great disorder, and thereby divested the soul of that power and dominion it had before over the body; which, by its operation, clouded the intellect, and depraved the will, and reduced every faculty of the mind to a miserable depravity, which, along with human nature, has been propagated down to posterity: [c] as some poisons (we know) will strangely affect the nerves and spirits, without causing immediate death; and [d] as the Indians (we are told) are acquainted with a juice which will immediately turn the person who drinks it into an idiot, and yet leave him, at the same time, the enjoyment of his health and all the powers and faculties of his body. But whatever the effect of the fruit might be, and whether the corruption of our nature and death, (with all the train of evils, which have descended to us,) lay in the tree, or in the will of God, there is no question to be made, but that our wise Creator might very justly decree, that human nature in general should be affected with it, and our happiness or unhappiness depend upon the obedience or disobedience of our first parents. We daily see, that children very often inherit the diseases of their parents, and that a vicious and extravagant father leaves commonly his son heir to nothing else but the name and shadow of a great family, with an infirm and sickly constitution. And if men generally now partake of the bad habits and dispositions of their immediate parents, why might not the corruption of human nature, in the first, have equally descended upon all the rest of mankind? [e] The rebellion of a parent, in all civil governments, reduces his children to poverty and disgrace, who had a title before to riches and honours; and for the same reason, why might not Adam forfeit for himself, and all his descendents, the gift of immortality, and the promise of eternal life? God might certainly bestow his own favours upon his own terms: and therefore, since the condition was obedience, he might justly inflict death, *i. e.* withhold immortality from us; and he might justly deny us heaven (for the promise of heaven was an act of his free bounty) upon the transgression and disobedience of our

A. M. 1.
Ant. Chrif. 4004.
Gen. ch. 3

And the justice of imputing it to Adam's posterity.

E e 2   first

---

[b] Jenkins's Reasonableness, vol. 2.   [c] Jenkins's Reasonableness, vol. 2.   [d] Revelation examined, vol. 1.
[e] Jenkins's Reasonableness, vol. 2.

A.M. 1.
Ant. Chrif.
4004.
Gen. ch. 3.

first parents. We were in their loins, and from thence our infection came: they were our representatives, and in them we fell: but then, amidst all this scene of calamity, we have one comfortable, one saving prospect to revive us, viz. that [f] *Adam was the figure of him that was to come; and therefore, as by the offence of one, judgement came upon all mankind to condemnation, even so by the righteousness of one, the free gift came upon all men unto justification of life.*

This is the account we have of the fall: and though we pretend not to deny, that in some places there are figurative expressions in it, as best comporting with the nature of ancient prophecy, and the oriental manner of writing; yet this can be no argument, why we should immediately run to an allegorical interpretation of the whole.

Moses no allegorical writer.

That not only the poets, but some of the greatest philosophers likewise, had a strange affectation for such figurative documents, in order to conceal their true notions from the vulgar, and to keep their learning within the bounds of their own schools, we pretend not to deny: and yet, since it is apparent, that Moses could have no such design; [g] since he had no reason to fear any other philosophers setting up against him, or, running away with his notions; since he affects no other character, but that of a plain historian, and pretends to relate matters just as they happened, without any disguise or embellishment of art; since he orders his books (which he endeavours to suit to the vulgar capacity) to be *read in the ears of all the people,* and commands *parents to teach them to their children;* it cannot be supposed, but that the history of the fall, as well as the rest of the book of Genesis, is to be taken in a literal sense. All the rest of the book is allowed to be literal, and why should this part of it only be a piece of Egyptian hieroglyphic? Fable and allegory, we know, are directly opposite to history: the one pretends to deliver truth undisguised; the other to deliver truth indeed, but under the veil and cover of fiction; so that, if this book of Moses be allowed to be historical, we may as well say, that what Thucydides relates of the plague of Athens, or Livy of the battle of Cannæ, is to be understood allegorically, as that what Moses tells us of the prohibition of the fruit of the tree of knowledge, or of Adam and Eve's expulsion from

[f] Rom. v. 14, 18.   [g] Nicholls's Conference, vol. 1.

Chap. III.   *from the Creation to the Flood.*   105

from the garden of paradise for breaking it, is to be inter- A. M. 1.
preted in a mystical sense.   Ant. Christ.
                                                              4004.
Nay, we will put the case, that it were consistent with Gen. ch. 3.
the character of Moses to have amused the people with fables and allegories; [h] yet we can hardly believe, but that
the people retained some tradition among them concerning
the formation of our first parents, and the manner of their
defection. This they might easily have had from their illustrious ancestor Abraham, who might have deduced it
from Noah, and thence, in a few successions, from Adam
himself: and if there was any such tradition preserved a-
mong them, Moses must necessarily have lost all his credit
and authority, had he pretended to foist in a tale of his
own invention, instead of a true narration. For the short
question is, —— [i] Did the children of Israel know the historical truth of the fall, or did they not? If they did
know it, why should Moses disguise it under an allegory,
rather than any of the rest of the book of Genesis? If they
did not know it, how came it to be forgotten in so few generations of men, supposing it had ever been known to A-
dam's posterity? If Adam's posterity never rightly knew
it, but had the relation thereof always conveyed down in
metaphor and allegory, then must Adam, in the first place,
impose upon his sons, and they upon succeeding generations; but for what reason we cannot conceive, unless that
the most remarkable event that ever befel mankind
(except the redemption of the world by Christ) so came
to pass, that it was impossible to tell it to posterity any o-
ther way than in allegory.

It can scarce be imagined, but that some of the ancient The history
writers of the Jewish church, as well as the inspired wri- of the fall,
ters of the New Testament, had as true a knowlege of these proved to
                                                              be literal
distant traditions, as any modern espouser of allegories can from the
pretend to; and therefore, [k] when we read in the book Scripture.
of Wisdom, that [l] *God created man to be immortal, and
made him to be the image of his own eternity; but that, through
the envy of the devil, death came into the world:* when the son
of Sirach tells us, that [m] *God, at the first, filled man with
the knowlege of understanding, and shewed him good and evil,*
but [n] that *error and darkness had their beginning together with
                                                            sinners;*

---

[h] Moses Vindicatus.   [i] Jenkins's Reasonableness,
vol. 2.   [k] *Vid.* Bishop Sherlock's Dissert. 2. annexed
to his Use and intent of prophecy.   [l] Wisd. ii. 23, 24.
[m] Ecclus. xvii. 7.   [n] Ibid. xi. 16.

sinners; that º death is the sentence of the Lord over all flesh; ᵖ *that the covenant, from the beginning, was, Thou shalt die the death; and that* ᑫ *of woman came the beginning of sin, and through her we all die:* when we read, and compare all these passages together, I say, can there be any reasonable foundation to doubt in what sense the ancient Jewish church understood the history of the fall?

Nay more: When not only we find the wicked, and the enemies of God represented under the image ʳ of a *serpent,* of a *dragon,* of a *leviathan, the crooked serpent,* &c.; and the prophet telling us expressly, that ˢ *dust shall be the serpent's meat;* but our blessed Saviour likewise declaring, that ᵗ *the devil was a murtherer from the beginning, a liar, and a father of lies;* St Paul asserting, that ᵘ *the woman being deceived, was first in the transgression,* and that ˣ *the serpent beguiled her through his subtilty;* and St John, in his Revelation, ʸ calling that wicked and malicious spirit, the *devil,* or the *dragon, Satan,* or the *old serpent,* indifferently; we cannot but perceive, that these passages are not only plain references to the first deception of mankind under the form of that creature, but that they virtually comprise the sum and substance of the Mosaic account. ᶻ So that, if we have any regard either to the tradition of the Jewish church, or the testimony of Christ and his apostles, we cannot but believe, that the history of man's fall, and the consequences thereupon, were really such as Moses has represented them.

And to confirm us in this belief, we may observe farther, that the tradition of almost every nation is conformable to his relation of things: ᵃ That not only the state of man's innocence, in all probability, gave rise to the poet's fiction of the golden age; but that the story of Adam and Eve, of the tree, and of the serpent, was extant among the Indians long ago, and (as travellers tells us) is still preserved among the Brachmans, and the inhabitants of Peru: ᵇ That, in the old Greek mysteries, the people used to carry about a serpent, and were instructed to cry *Eva,* whereby the devil seemed to exult, as it were, over the

º Eccluf. xli 3.   ᵖ Ibid. xiv. 17.   ᑫ Ibid. xxv. 24.
ʳ Isa. xiv. 29. xxvii. 1.   Micah vii. 17.   ˢ Isa lxv. 25.
ᵗ John viii. 44.   ᵘ 1 Tim. ii. 14   ˣ 2 Cor. xi. 3.
ʸ Rev. xii. 9. xx 2.   ᶻ Moses Vindicatus.   ᵃ Grotius De veritate.   ᵇ Nicholls's Conference, vol. 1.

the unhappy fall of our first mother; and that ᶜ in his worship in adolatrous nations, even now, * there are frequent instances of his displaying this his conquest under the figure of a serpent: strong evidences of the truth of the Mosaic account! to say nothing of the *rationale* which it gives us of our innate *pudor circa res venereas*, of the pains of child-birth, of the present sterility of the earth, of the slowness of children's education, of their imbecility above all other creatures, of the woman's subjection to her husband, of our natural antipathy to viperous animals, and (what hath puzzled the wisest of the heathen sages to discover) of the depravation of our wills, and our strong propensity to what is evil.

This origin of evil is a question which none of them could resolve. They saw the effect, but were ignorant of the cause; and therefore their conjectures were absurd. ᵈ Some of them laid the whole blame on matter, as if its union with the mind gave it a pernicious tincture. Others imagined a pre-existent state, and that the bad inclinations which exerted themselves in this world were first of all contracted in another. ᵉ Several established two principles, the one the author of all the good, and the other the author of all the evil (whether natural or moral) that is found in human nature: and, in prejudice to this absurdity, many betook themselves to Atheism, and denied any first principle at all; accounting it better to have no God in the world, than such an unaccountable mixture of good and evil. But now, had but these wise men had the advantage of reading the Mosaic account, they would never have taken up with such wild hypotheses, but immediately concluded with our Saviour's argument, that ᶠ *a corrupt tree cannot bring forth good fruit;* because the explication of the rise of sin, by an original lapse,

---

ᶜ *Vid.* Heideggeri Historia patriarchum, vol. 1.

* Phlip Melancthon tells us a story to this purpose, of some priests (somewhere in Asia) who carry about a serpent in a brazen vessel, and, as they attend it with a great deal of music and charms in verse, the serpent lifts up itself, opens its mouth, and thrusts out the head of a beautiful virgin; the devil in this manner, glorying in his miscarriage of Eve among these poor idolaters. And an account of much the like nature is given us in books of travels into the West-Indies; *Nicholls's Conference,* vol. 1.

ᵈ Nicholls's Conference, vol. 1.   ᵉ Bishop King on the origin of evil.   ᶠ Matth. vii. 18.

A. M. 1.
Ant. Chrif.
4004.
Gen. ch. 3.

lapfe, is not only freed from thefe abfurdities wherewith other explications abound, but, according to the fenfe which the author of the Book of Wifdom has of it, fets the goodnefs of God in the creation of the world in its proper light; viz. [g] *that God made not death, neither hath he pleafure in the deftruction of the living. He created all things, that they might have their being, and the generations of the world were healthful. There was no poifon of deftruction in them, nor the kingdom of death upon the earth, until that ungodly men called it to them;* [h] *and fo error and darknefs had their beginning together with finners.*

DISSERTATION III.

Of original fin.

ORIGINAL fin indeed is a phrafe which does not occur in the whole compafs of the Bible; but the nature of the thing itfelf, and in what manner it came to be committed, are fufficiently related: fo that thofe who admit of the authority of the Scriptures, make no queftion of the fact. The great matter in difpute is, what the effect of this tranfgreffion was; what guilt it contained; what punifhment it merited; and in what degree its guilt and punifhment both may be faid to effect us.

Different opinions concerning it.

Some have not ftuck to affirm, [i] that in the beginning of the world, there was no fuch thing as any exprefs covenant between God and man; that the prohibition of the tree of knowledge was given to our firft parents only, and they alone confequently were culpable by its tranfgreffion; that Adam, in fhort, was mortal, like one of us; he was no reprefentative for his pofterity; his fin purely perfonal; and that the imputation of guilt, down to this time, for an offence fo many thoufand years ago committed, is a fad reflection upon the goodnefs and juftice of God.

In oppofition to this, others think proper to affirm, that at the firft creation of things, there was a covenant made with all mankind in Adam, their common head, and proxy, who ftipulated for them all; that by a tranfgreffion of this covenant, our firft parents fell from their original

[g] Wifd i. 13 &c [h] Ecclus. xi. 16. [i] Burnet on the articles; and Taylor's polemical difcourfes.

ginal righteousness, and thence became dead in sin, and actually defiled in all their faculties of soul and body; and that this corruption is not only the parent of all actual transgressions, but (even in its own nature) brings guilt upon every one that is born into the world, whereby he is bound over to the wrath of God, and the curse of the law, and so made subject to death, with all the miseries that attend it, spiritual, temporal, and eternal.

There is another opinion which concerns itself not with the imputation of the guilt, but only with the punishment of this transgression, and thereupon supposes, that though Adam, as to the composition of his body, was naturally mortal, yet, by the supernatural gift of God, (whereof the tree of life was a symbol or sacrament,) he was to be preserved immortal: from whence it is inferred, [k] That the denunciation of the sentence, *(In the day thou eatest thereof, thou shalt surely die,)* is to be understood literally indeed, but then extended no farther than natural death; which, considering the fears, and terrors, and sundry kinds of misery which it occasions, may be reputed punishment severe enough, though fairly consistent with our notions of God's goodness and justice, because it is but a temporal punishment, and abundantly recompenced by that eternal redemption which all mankind shall have in Christ Jesus.

Others again do so far approve of this, as to think it in part the punishment of original sin; but then they suppose, that besides this natural mortality, there is a certain weakness and corruption spread through the whole race of mankind, which discovers itself in their inclination to evil, and insufficiency to what is good. This say they, [†] the very

---

[k] Locke's. Reasonableness of Christianity: and *Tractus De Imputatione divina peccati Adami per Dan. Whitby.*

[†] St. Austin, in his fourth book against Julian, brings in Cicero [De repub. l. 3] complaining, "Non a matre, sed a noverca "natura editum esse hominem in vitam; corpore nudo, fragili, "et infirmo; animo anxio ad molestias, humili ad timores, molli "ad labores; in quo tamen velut obrutus inest ignis quidam divi- "nus mentis." Whereupon the holy father makes this remark, "Rem vidit author iste, causam nescivit: latebat enim eum, cur "esset grave jugum super, filios Adam; quia, sacris literis non "eruditus, ignorabat originale peccatum."

A. M. 1.
Ant. Chrif
4004.
Gen. ch. 3

very Heathens complain of; this † the Scriptures every where testify; and therefore they conclude, that since man was not originally made in this condition, (for God created him after his own image,) he must have contracted all this from his fall; and that therefore the threatening of death had an higher signification than the dissolution of the soul and body, *viz.* the loss of the divine favour, of all supernatural gifts and graces, and a total defection of the mind from God, which immediately ensued upon the transgression.

A proper state of the question.

These are some of the principal opinions, (for the little singularities are innumerable,) and, in the midst of so many intricacies, to find out a proper path for us to pursue, we may resolve the whole controversy into this one question:——" Whether human nature be so far corrupted, " and the guilt of our first parents transgression so far " imputed to their posterity, that every person, from the " mother's womb, must necessarily go astray, and must " certainly fall into everlasting perdition, without the " means appointed in the new covenant for his preserva- " tion?" And in searching into this, the sentiments of the fathers, much more the alterations of the schoolmen, will help us very little. † The former are so divided in their opinions,

---

† The Scriptures state the corruption of human nature in such terms as these, *viz.* that *by one man sin entred into the world by whose disobedience many were made sinners*, Rom. x. 19. that *by nature therefore we are the children of wrath*, Eph. ii. 3. and *unable to receive the things of the Spirit, or to know them because they are spiritually discerned*, 1 Cor. ii. 14. for *what is born of flesh, is flesh*, John iii. 6.: and *who can bring a clean thing out of an unclean?* Job xiv. 4. The royal Psalmist therefore makes, in his own person, this confession of our natural depravity; *Behold I was shapen in wickedness, and in sin did my mother conceive me*, Psal. li. 5. and St. Paul makes this public declaration of our inability to do good; *I know that in me (*i. e. *in my flesh) dwelleth no good thing: for to will is present with me, but to perform that which is good, I find not; for though I delight in the law of God after the inward man, yet I see another law in my members, warring against the law in my mind, and bringing me into captivity to the law of sin which is in my members. O wretched man that I am! who shall deliver me from the body of this death?* Rom. vii. 18. *&c.*

† Vossius, in his history of Pelagianism, assures us, that the whole Catholic-church was always of opinion, that the guilt of Adam's

opinions, and the latter so abstruse in their arguments upon this subject, that an honest inquirer will find himself bewildered, rather than instructed; and therefore our safest recourse will be to the declarations of God's will, explained in a manner comporting with his attributes.

<small>A. M. 1. Ant. Chrif. 4004. &c. ch. 3</small>

That God, who is the fountain of our being, is infinitely pure and holy, and can therefore be neither the author nor promoter of any sin in us, is obvious to our first conceptions of him; and therefore, if the corruption of our nature be supposed to be such as necessarily and unavoidably determines us to wickedness, without the least tendency to good, to give it a counterpoise, those who maintain the negative of the question, are in the right so far as they stand in defence of God's immaculate purity, and are known to be asserters of the freedom of human choice, without which the common distinctions of virtue and vice, and the certain prospects of rewards and punishments, are entirely lost. But when they carry the point so far as to deny any alteration in human nature now, from what it was at its first creation; as to deny, that Adam, in his state of uprightness, had any gifts and graces supernatural, any clearness in his understanding, any strength in his will, any regularity in his affections, more than every man of maturity and competent faculties has at this day; when they adventure to affirm, that there is no necessity of grace in our present condition, to assist our hereditary weakness, to enlighten our minds, and incline our wills, and conduct our affections to the purposes of holiness, but that every man may do what is good and

<small>And the most probable explication of it.</small>

Adam's sin was imputed to his posterity to their condemnation; so that children dying therein were consigned to everlasting punishment, at least to an everlasting separation from God: and, to confirm this assertion, he quotes a multitude of passages out of almost all the doctors of the Greek church. Taylor and Whitby, and some other writers upon this argument, produce the testimony of the same fathers to evince the very contrary position; so that there is no depending upon any thing where authors are so inconsistent with themselves, and so repugnant to one another. The truth is, before Pelagius appeared in the world most of the ancient writers of the church were very inaccurate, both in what they thought and wrote concerning original sin and free-will; and it seems as if the providence of God permitted that Heretic to arise, that thereby he might engage the maintainers of orthodoxy to study those points more maturely; *Whitaker De peccato orig. l. 2.*

A. M. 1.
Ant. Chrif.
4004.
Gen. ch. 3.

and acceptable to God by the power of his own natural abilities, they then run counter to the common experience of human infirmity; they overlook the declarations of God's word concerning his gracious assistance; and seem to despise the kind overture of that blessed agent, whereby we are *renewed and sanctified in the spirit of our minds*.

In like manner, when the maintainers of absolute depravation contend, that man, in his present condition, is far departed from original righteousness, and, of his own accord, very much inclined to evil; that the order of his faculties is destroyed, and those graces which constituted the image of God, departed from him; that in this state he is now unable to raise himself from the level of common impotence, but requires the intervention of some superior principle to aid and assist him in his progress towards heaven; they say no more than what experience teaches us, and what the sacred records, which acquaint us with the dispensation of grace, are known to authorise. But when they carry their positions to a greater extent than they will justly bear; when they affirm, that ever since the first defection, the mind of man is not only much impaired, but grievously vitiated in all its faculties, having a strong aversion to every thing that is good, and an invincible propensity to what is evil; not one thought, word, or wish, that tends towards God, but the seeds and principles of every vice that bears the image and lineaments of the devil, inherent in it: when they advance such doctrines as these, I say, they debase human nature too low, and seem to impute such iniquity to its maker as can hardly be wiped off, if every human soul be naturally inclined to all kind of wickedness when it comes from the hand of his creating power.

There is certainly therefore another way of accounting for these difficulties, without any prejudice to the divine attributes, and that is this:——Not by ascribing any positive malignity to human nature, but only the loss of the image of God; because a mere privation of rectitude, in an active subject, will sufficiently answer all the purposes for which a positive corruption is pleaded. [1] The soul of man, we know, is a busy creature: by the force of its own nature it must be in action; but then, without grace, and the image of God assisting and adorning it, it cannot act

---

[1] Hopkins on the two covenants.

act regularly and well. So that the difference between Adam and us, is not that we have violent inclinations to all manner of wickedness implanted in our nature, any more than he, in his innocence, had in his; but that we, in our present condition, want sundry advantages which he, in the height of his perfection, was not without. He had the free power of obedience; he had the perfect image of his maker in all the divine qualities of knowledge and holiness, which we have not; and therefore, when we say, that he communicated to his posterity a corrupted nature, it must not be understood, as if that nature, which we receive, was infected with any vicious inclinations or habits, to sway and determine our mind to what is evil; but the meaning is, that he communicated to us a nature, which has indeed a power to incline, and act variously, but that he did not, withal, communicate to us the image of God, nor that fulness of knowledge and power of obedience, which were requisite to make all its actions and inclinations holy and regular: and our nature is therefore said to be corrupted, because it is comparatively bad; because it is reduced to its mere natural state, which at the best is a state of imperfection, and deprived of that grace which should have restrained it from sin, and of those other high endowments wherewith at first it was invested.

_{A. M. 1.}
_{Ant. Chrif.}
_{4004.}
_{Gen. ch. 3.}

This is a fair account of our original corruption: it stands clear of the difficulties that attend the other opinions, and is not inconsistent with the notions we have of the divine attributes. For barely to withdraw those extraordinary gifts, which were not essential to man's nature, but such as God additionally had bestowed upon him; and he, by his transgression, unworthily forfeited, is what agrees very well with the wisdom and justice, and holiness of God to do; though to infuse a positive malignity, or such a strong inclination to wickedness in us, as induces a necessity of sinning, most certainly does not.

That *the judge of all the world cannot but do right* and he, *who keepeth mercy from generation to generation,* can have no hand in any cruel action, is a certain truth, and what our first reflections on the divine nature teach us. Those therefore who maintain, that Adam's sin is not imputed to us to our damnation, or, that children unbaptised, are not the objects of divine vengeance, nor shall be condemned to hell, or an eternal expulsion from God's presence, for what was done many thousand years before they were born, are so far in the right, as they oppose

A. M. 1.
Ant. Chrif.
4004.
Gen. ch. 3.

pose an opinion which clouds the amiable attributes of God, and represents him in a dress of horror, and engaged in acts of extreme severity at least, if not unrelenting cruelty. Hell certainly is not so easy a pain, nor are the souls of children of so cheap and so contemptible a price, as that God should snatch them from their mother's womb, and throw them into perdition without any manner of concern; and therefore, when men argue against such positions as these, they are certainly to be commended, because therein they vindicate the sacred attributes of God: but when they carry their opposition to a greater length than it will justly go, so as to affirm —— that there was no such thing as a covenant between God and Adam, or if there was, that Adam contracted for himself only; that his guilt consequently was personal, and cannot in justice, be imputed to us; that since we had no share in the transgression, there is no reason why we should bear any part in the punishment; that we are all born, in short, in the same state of innocence, and are under the same favour and acceptance with Almighty God, that Adam, before the first transgression, was: when they advance such positions as these, in maintainance of their opposition, they sadly forget, that while they would seem advocates for the mercy and goodness of God, they are taking away the foundation of the second covenant; destroying the necessity of a divine mediator; and overlooking those declarations in Scripture, which affirm, that ᵐ *all the world is become guilty before God; that all men, both Jews and Gentiles, are under sin; have come short of the glory of God,* ⁿ *and are by nature the children of wrath.*

To make an agreement then between the word of God, and his attributes in this particular, we may fairly allow, that there really was a covenant between God and Adam at the first creation; that in making that covenant, Adam, as their head and common representative, stipulated for all mankind, as well as for himself; and that, in his transgression of it, the guilt and the punishment due thereupon, was imputed to all his posterity. This we may allow was the state and condition wherein Adam left us; but then we must remember, that ᵒ the whole scheme of man's salvation was laid in the divine counsel and decree from all eternity; that God, foreseeing man would fall, determined

ᵐ Rom. iii. 9, 19, 23.   ⁿ Eph. ii. 3.   ᵒ Jenkins's Reasonableness, vol. 2.

Chap. III.   *from the Creation to the Flood.*

determined to send his Son to redeem him, and determined to do this long before the transgression happened: so that the wisdom and goodness of God had effectually provided before-hand against all the ill consequences of the fall, and made it impossible, that Adam's posterity should become eternally miserable, and be condemned to the flames and pains of hell, any other way than through their own personal guilt and transgressions. The redemption of the world was decreed, I say, from eternity, and was actually promised before any child of Adam was born, even before the sentence was pronounced upon our first parents; and as soon as it was pronounced, its benefits, without all controversy did commence. So that, upon this hypothesis, every infant that comes into the world, as it brings along with it the guilt of Adam's sin, brings along with it likewise the benefits of Christ's meritorious death, *which God hath set forth, as a* standing *propitiation for the sins of the whole world.* Nor can the want of baptism be any obstruction to this remedy, since the remedy was exhibited long before the rite was instituted; and since that rite, when instituted, (according to the sense of some learned fathers, was more a pledge of good things to come, * a type of our future resurrection, a form of adoption into the heavenly family, and of admission to those *rich promises of God, which are hid in Jesus Christ,* than any ordinance appointed for the *mystical washing away of sin.*

In short, as long as St Paul's epistles are read, the original compact between God and man, the depravation of human nature, and the imputation of Adam's guilt, must be received as standing doctrines of the church of Christ: but then we are to take great care, in our manner of explaining them, to preserve the divine attributes sacred and inviolate: and this may happily be effected, if we will but suppose, that our hereditary corruption is occasioned, not by the infusion of any positive malignity into us, but by the subduction of supernatural gifts from us; that the covenant of grace commenced immediately after the covenant of works was broken, and has included all mankind

A. M. 1.
Ant. Chrif.
4004
Gen. ch. 3.

The whole summed up

---

* Baptizantur infantes (juxta Chrysostomum et Theodoretum) ut baptismus ipsis sit arca futurorum bonorum, typus futuræ resurrectionis, Dominicæ passionis communicatio, atque ut superne regenerati, sanctificati in adoptionis jus adducti et unigeniti cohæredes, per sacrorum mysteriorum participationem, sint; *Whitby De imputatione peccati Adami.*

A. M. 1.
Ant. Chrif.
4004.
Gen. ch. 3.

kind ever since; that the blood of Christ shields his children from the wrath of God; and that the imputation of Adam's guilt, and obnoxiousness to punishment, is effectually taken away, by the meritorious oblation of that *Lamb of God which was slain from the foundation of the world.*

CHAP. IV.

Of the murther of Abel, and the banishment of Cain.

THE HISTORY.

A. M. 128.
Ant. Chrif.
3876.
Gen. ch. 4.
to ver. 25.

Cain and Abel's birth

OUR first parents, we may suppose, * after a course of penance and humiliation for their transgression, obtained the pardon and forgiveness of God; and yet the corruption, which their sin introduced, remained upon human nature, and began to discover itself in that impious fact which Cain committed on his brother Abel. Cain was the first child that was ever born into the world; and his mother Eve was so fully persuaded, that the promised

---

* The oriental writers are very full of Adam's sorrows and lamentations upon this occasion. They have recorded the several forms of prayer wherein he addressed God for pardon and forgiveness; and some of the Jewish doctors are of opinion, that the thirty-second psalm, wherein we meet with these expressions, *I acknowledge my sin unto thee, and mine iniquity have I not hid; I said I will confess my transgression unto the Lord, and thou forgavest the iniquity of my sin,* was of his composing.

Our excellent Milton, to the same purpose, introduces Adam, after a melancholy soliloquy with himself, and some hasty altercations with Eve, proposing at length this wholesome advice to her:

What better can we do, than to the place
Repairing where he judg'd us, prostrate fall
Before him reverent; and there confess
Humbly our faults, and pardon beg; with tears
Wat'ring the ground, and with our sighs the air
Frequenting, sent from hearts contrite, in sign
Of sorrow unfeign'd, and humiliation meek?
Undoubtedly he will relent, and turn
From his displeasure: in whose looks serene,
When angry most he seem'd, and most severe,
What else but favour, grace, and mercy shone? Book 10.

mised seed would imediately descend from her, that she supposed him to be the person who was to subdue the power of the great enemy of mankind; and therefore, upon her delivery, she cried out, in a transport of joy, † *I have gotten a man from the Lord*, and accordingly gave him the name of Cain, which signifies *possession* or *acquisition*: never suspecting, that as soon as he grew up, he would occasion her no small sorrow and disconsolation.

A. M. 128.
Ant. Christ. 3876.
Gen. ch. 4. ver. 25.

The next son that she bore, (which was the year following,) was called ‡ *Abel*, denoting *sorrow* and *mourning*; but very probably he might not receive that name, until his tragical end, which caused great grief to his parents, verifying the meaning of it. Other children, we may presume, were all along born to our first parents; but these are the two who, for some time, made the principal figure; and as they had the whole world before them, there was small reason (one would think) for those feuds and contentions, which, in after ages, embroiled mankind. But the misfortune was, they were persons of quite different tempers; and accordingly, when they grew up, betook themselves to different employments; Cain, who was of a surly, sordid, and avaricious temper, to the tilling of the ground; and Abel, who was more gentle and ingenuous in his disposition, to the keeping of sheep. It

† *Ish eth Jehovah*, which our translation makes *a man from the Lord*, should rather be rendered *the man, the Lord*, Helvicus has shewn, in so many instances in Scripture, that *eth* is an article of the accusative case, that it seems indeed to be the Hebrew idiom; besides, that it is a demonstrative, or emphatic particle which points at something or person, in a particular manner; and therefore several, both Jewish and Christian doctors, have taken the words in this sense: ——That our grandmother Eve, when delivered of Cain, thought she had brought forth the Messias, the God-man, who was to *bruise the serpent's head*, or destroy Satan's power and dominion according to the promise, which God had made her; *Edward's Survey of religion*, vol. 1.

‡ Others derive the name from a word which signifies *vanity*, and are of opinion, that Eve intended thereby, either to declare the little esteem she had of him, in comparison of her first born; or to shew the vanity of her hopes, in taking Cain for the Messiah; or to denote, that all things in the world, into which he was now come, were mere *vanity and vexation of spirit*; Patrick's Commentary, and Saurin's Dissertation.

A. M. 128.
Ant. Chrif.
3876
Gen. ch. 4
to ver. 25.

Their ob-
jections.

It was a cuſtomary thing, even in the infancy of the world, to make acknowledgments to God, by way of oblation, for the bountiful ſupply of all his creatures; and accordingly ‖ theſe two brothers were wont to bring offerings, ſuitable to their reſpective callings: Cain, as an huſbandman, the fruits of the ground; and Abel, as a ſhepherd, the **firſtlings, or** (as ſome will have it) the ‡ milk of

‖ In the laſt verſe of this chapter we read, that it was in the days of Enos, when *men firſt began to call on the name of the Lord;* and yet, in the third and fourth verſes thereof, we find that Cain and Abel brought their reſpective offerings to the place (as we may ſuppoſe) of divine worſhip. Now if the beginning of divine worſhip was in the days of Enos, what worſhip was this in the days of Cain and Abel? To have two beginnings for the ſame worſhip, is a thing incongruous, unleſs we can ſuppoſe, that the two brothers, when they came with their oblations, did not worſhip at all; neither opening their lips in the divine benefactor's praiſe, nor invocating a bleſſing upon what his bounty had ſent them, which is highly inconſiſtent with the character of worſhippers. But in anſwer to this, we muſt obſerve that the worſhip of God is of two kinds, public and private; that the worſhip wherein theſe brothers were concerned, was of the latter ſort; for Cain is mentioned by himſelf, and Abel by himſelf. They came to the place of worſhip ſeverally; their ſacrifices were not the ſame: neither were the offerers of the ſame mind. But the worſhip which was inſtituted in the time of Enos, was of a public nature, when ſeveral families, under their reſpective heads, met together in the ſame place and joined in one common ſervice, whether of prayers, praiſes, or ſacrifices. Though the phraſe of *men's beginning to call upon the name of the Lord,* may poſſibly bear another conſtruction, as we ſhall ſhew when we come to examine the place itſelf; *Street's Dividing of the hoof.*

‡ It is a pretty common opinion, that the eating of fleſh was not permitted before the flood; and it is the poſition of Grotius, that no carnal ſacrifices were at that time, offered; becauſe nothing, but what was of uſe to man was to be conſecrated to God. The ſcarcity of cattle might very well excuſe their being ſlain in the worſhip of God; and therefore ſince the ſame word in Hebrew, [*Hhalab,* or *Hheleb,*] according to its different punctuation, ſignifies both *fat* and *milk,* and accordingly is rendered both ways by the LXX, many learned men ſeem rather to favour the latter, as finding it a cuſtom among the ancient Egyptians, to ſacrifice milk to their deities, as a token and acknowledgment of the fecundity of their cattle; *Le Clerc's*

Commentary

of his flock. Upon some set and solemn occasion then, [p] (and not improbably at the end of harvest,) as they were presenting their respective offerings, God, who estimates the sincerity of the heart more than the value of the oblation, † gave a visible token of his acceptance of Abel's sacrifice, preferable to that of Cain, which so enraged, and transported him with envy against his brother, that he could not help shewing it in his countenance.

A. M. 128. Ant. Chris. 3876. Gen. ch. 4. to ver. 25.

God's expostulation with Cain.

God, however, in great kindness, condescended to expostulate the matter with him, telling him, [q] "That "his respect to true goodness was impartial, where-ever "he found it, and that ‡ therefore it was purely his own "fault, that his offering was not equally accepted; that "piety

Commentary, and *Saurin's Dissertation*. But the learned Heidegger is of an opinion quite the contrary; *Vid. Exercit.* 15. *De cibo antediluviano*.

[p] Heidegger's Historia patriarchum.

† The Jews are generally of opinion, that this visible token of God's accepting Abel's sacrifice, was a fire, or lightning, which came from heaven, and consumed it. The footsteps of this we meet with in a short time after, Gen. xv. 17. and the examples of it were many in future ages, *viz.* when Moses offered the first burnt-offering according to the law, Lev. ix. 24.; when Gideon offered upon the rock, Jud. vi. 21.; when David stayed the plague, 1 Chron. xxi. 26.; when Solomon consecrated the temple, 2 Chron. vii. 1; and when Elijah contended with the Baalites, 1 Kings xviii. 38 *&c.* And accordingly, we find the Israelites, (when they wish all prosperity to their king,) praying, that God would be pleased *to accept* (in the Hebrew, *turn into ashes*) *his burnt sacrifice*, Psal. xx. 3.; *Patrick* and *Le Clerc's Commentary*.

[q] Patrick's Commentary.

‡ The words in our translation are, *If thou doest well, shalt thou not be accepted?* ver. 7. which some render, *shalt thou not receive*, viz. a reward? others *shalt thou not be pardoned?* and others again, *thou shalt be elevated to dignity*. But if we consider, what God says to Cain in the two foregoing verses, *that his countenance was fallen*. we cannot but perceive, that in this he promises him, that if he did well, he should have his face *lifted up*, and that he should have no more reason to be sad; for so the Scripture frequently expresses a fearless and chearful state: *If iniquity be in thine hand*, says one of Job's friends, *put it away from thee, and let not wickedness dwell in thy tabernacles; for then thou shalt lift up thy face without spot*, Job. xi. 15.; *Essay for a new translation*.

A. M. 128.
Ant. Chrif.
3876.
Gen. ch. 4.
to ver. 15.

"piety was the proper difpofition for a facrificer; and
"that, if herein he would emulate his brother, the fame
"tokens of divine approbation fhould attend his obla-
"tions; ʳ that it was folly and madnefs in him to har-
"bour any revengeful thoughts againſt his brother; be-
"cauſe, if he proceeded to put them in execution, ‡ a
"dreadful puniſhment would immediately overtake him;
"and that leaſt of all he had reaſon to be angry with him
"whoſe preference was only a token of his ſuperior vir-
"tue, and not intended to ſupplant him of his birthright,
"ˢ which fhould always be inviolate, and his brother
"be obliged to † pay him the refpect and homage that
                                                    "was

ʳ Poole's Annotations.

‡ The words in our tranſlation are, *Sin lieth at thy door:* where, by *ſin*, the generality of interpreters mean, the puniſhment of ſin, which is hard at hand, and ready to overtake the wicked. But our learned Lightfoot obſerves, that God does not here preſent himſelf to Cain, in order to threaten, but to encourage him, as the firſt words of his ſpeech to him do import; and that therefore the bare deſcription of *lying at the door*, does plainly enough infinuate, that the text does not ſpeak either of errors or puniſhment, but of a *ſacrifice for ſin*, which the Scripture often calls by the Hebrew word here, and which was commonly placed before the door of the ſanctuary, as may be ſeen in ſeveral paſſages in Scripture. So that, according to this ſenſe, God is here comforting Cain, even though he did amiſs in maligning his brother, and referring him to the propitiation of Chriſt, which, even then, was of ſtanding force for the remiſſion of ſin; *I ſay for a new tranſlation.* But this ſenſe of the word ſeems a little too far fetched.

ˢ Le Clerc's Commentary.

† The words in the text are *unto thee ſhall be his defire*, Gen. iii. 16. which (however ſome expofitors have clouded them) will appear to be plain and eafy enough, if we do but confider, that there are two expreſſions, in the Hebrew tongue, to fignify the readineſs of one perſon to ſerve and refpect another. The one is [*aine el yad*] or *our eyes are to his hand*; the other [*teſhukah el*] or *our defire is to him.* The former expreſſes our outward attendance, and the latter the inward temper and readineſs of our mind to pay refpect. Of the former we have an inſtance in Pſal. cxxxiii. *The eyes of ſervants are to the hand of their maſters, and the eyes of a maiden are to the hand of her miſtreſs, i. e.* they ſtand ready with a vigilant obſervance to execute their orders. We meet the other expreſſion in the place before us, and it imports an inward temper and
                                                       difpofition

" was due to his primogeniture; which, if he was minded A. M. 128.
" to preserve, his wisest way would be to be quiet, and Ant. Chrif.
" not proceed one step farther in any wicked design." 3876.
                     Gen. ch. 4.
This was a kind admonition from God; but so little ef- to ver. 15.
fect had it upon Cain, that instead of being sensible of his
fault, and endeavouring to amend, he grew more and more
incensed against his brother; insomuch that at last he took
a resolution to kill him; but dissembled his design, until
he should find a proper opportunity.

And, to this purpose, coming to his brother one day,
and pretending great kindness to him, he asked him very
friendly to take a walk with him in the fields, where,
having got him alone, * upon some pretence or other, he
picked a quarrel with him, and so fell upon him, and slew
him,

disposition of mind to pay respect and honour. *His desire will be unto thee* i. e. he will be heartily devoted (as we say in English) to honour and respect you. And *thou shalt* [or mayest] *rule over him*, i. e. you may have any service from him you can desire; *Shuckford's Connection. vol.* 1.

* According to the English translation, Moses tells us, ver. 8. that *Cain talked with Abel his brother*. The words strictly signify, *Cain said unto Abel his brother*; after which there is a blank space left in the Hebrew copies, as if something was wanting. The Samaritan Pentateuch, and the LXX version supply this, by adding the words,——*Let us go into the fields*; but the Jerusalem Targum, and that of Jonathan, have supplied us with their whole conversation——As they went along, " I
" know, says Cain, that the world was created by the mercy of
" God, but it is not governed according to the fruit of our
" good works, and there is respect of persons in judgement.
" Why was thy oblation favourably accepted, when mine was
" rejected? Abel answered and said unto Cain, The world was
" created in mercy, and is governed according to the fruits
" of our good works. There is no respect of persons in judge-
" ment; for my oblation was more favourably received, be-
" cause the fruit of my works was better, and more precious,
" than thine. Hereupon Cain in a fury breaks out, There is
" no judgement, nor judge, nor any other world; neither shall
" good men receive any reward, nor wicked men be punished.
" To which Abel replied, There is a judgement and a judge,
" and another world, in which good men shall receive a re-
" ward, and wicked men be punished." Upon which there ensued a quarrel, which ended in Abel's death. So that, according to this account, Abel suffered for the vindication of the truth, and was, in reality, the first martyr; *Esthius in difficiliora loca*.

A. M. 128
Ant. Chrif.
3876.
Gen. ch. 4.
to ver. 15.

and fentence againſt him.

him, and afterward ᵗ buried him in the ground; to prevent all diſcovery: but it was not long before he was called to an account for this horrid fact. God appeared to him, and having queſtioned him about his brother, and received ſome ſullen and evaſive anſwers from him, directly charged him with his murther; and then repreſenting it, in its proper aggravations, as a crime unpardonable, and what cried aloud to heaven for vengeance, he proceeded immediately to paſs ſentence upon him.

Cain's chief ᵘ deſign and ambition was, to make himſelf great and powerful, in favour with God, and in credit with men, without any one to ſtand in competition with him; but in every thing he intended, he found himſelf diſappointed, for attempting to accompliſh his ends in ſo wicked a manner. Inſtead of growing great and opulent, the ground was ſentenced *not to yield him her ſtrength*, *i. e.* he was to be unproſperous in his huſbandry and tillage: inſtead of enjoying God's favour without a rival, he was baniſhed from his preſence, and for ever excluded from that happy converſe with the Deity, which, in theſe firſt ages of the world, it was cuſtomary for good men to enjoy: and inſtead of being a man of renown among his family, he became *a fugitive and vagabond:* was baniſhed from his native country, and compelled to withdraw into ſome diſtant and deſolate part of the earth, as an abominable perſon, not worthy to live, nor fit to be endured in any civil community.

The ſame principle, which leads wicked men to the commiſſion of crimes, in hopes of impunity, throws them into deſpair, upon the denunciation of puniſhment. This ſentence of Cain, though infinitely ſhort of the heinouſneſs of his guilt, made him believe, † that he was to undergo
much

ᵗ Joſephus's antiq. l. 1. c. 3.   ᵘ Shuckford's Introduction, vol. 1.

† The words in our tranſlation are, *My puniſhment is greater than I can bear;* but as the Hebrew word *Aven*] ſignifies *iniquity*, rather than puniſhment, and the verb [*Naſha*] ſignifies *to be forgiven*, as well as to *bear*, it ſeems to agree better with the context, if the verſe be rendered either poſitively, *My iniquity is too great to be forgiven*, or (as the Hebrew expoſitors take it) by way of interrogation, *Is my iniquity too great to be forgiven?* which ſeems to be the better of the two; *Shuckford's Connection vol.* 1. A learned annotator has obſerved, that as there are ſeven abominations in the heart of him that loveth not
his

Chap. IV.   *from the Creation to the Flood.*   123

much greater evils than it really imported; and that not A M. 128.
only the miseries of banishment, but the danger likewise of Ant. Chrif.
being slain by every one that came near him, was ensuant 3876.
upon it. But, to satisfy him in this respect, God was plea- Gen. ch. 4.
sed to declare, that his providence should protect him from to ver. 25.
all outward violence: and, to remove the uneasy apprehension from his mind, vouchsafed to give him a sign (very
ˣ probably by some sensible miracle) that no creature
whatever should be permitted to take away his life; but,
that whoever attempted it should incur a very severe punishment; because God ʸ was minded to prolong his days
in this wretched estate, as a monument of his vengeance,
to deter future ages from commiting the like murther.

Thus, by the force of the divine sentence, Cain left Cain's ba-
his parents and relations, and went into a strange country. nishment,
He was banished from that sacred place where God vouchsafed † frequent manifestations of his glorious presence; and
though by the divine decree no person was permitted to
hurt

his brother, Prov. xxvi. 25. there were the like number of transgressions in Cain's whole conduct; for, 1st, he sacrificed without faith; 2dly, was displeased that God respected him not;
3dly, hearkened not to God's admonition; 4thly, spake dis-
semblingly to his brother; 5thly, killed him in the field; 6thly,
denied that he knew where he was; and, 7thly, neither asked,
nor hoped for mercy from God, but despaired and so fell into
the condemnation of the devil; *Ainsworth's Annotations.*

ˣ Universal History, numb. 2.   ʸ Patrick's Commentary.

† Both Lightfoot, Heidegger, and Le Clerc, seem to be of
opinion, that what we render the *presence of the Lord,* was the
proper name of that particular place where Adam, after his expulsion from paradise, dwelt; and accordingly we find that
part of the country which lies contiguous to the supposed situation of paradise, called by Strabo [lib. 16 *prosopora*] However this be, it is agreed by all interpreters, that there was *a
divine glory,* called by the Jews SCHECHINAH, which appeared
from the beginning. (as we said before, page 40. in the notes)
and from which Cain being now banished, never enjoyed the
sight of it again. If, after this, Cain turned a downright ido-
later, (as many think,) it is very probable that he introduced
the worship of the sun (which was the most ancient idolatry)
as the best resemblance he could find of the glory of the Lord
which was wont to appear in a flaming light; *Patrick's Commentary.*

A. M. 118
Ant. Chrif.
3786
Gen. ch. 4
to verſe 25

hurt him, yet, being conſcious of his own guilt, he was fearful of every thing he ſaw or heard: till having wandered about a long while in many different countries, he ſettled at length with his wife and family in the land of Nod; where, in ſome tract of time, and after his deſcendants were ſufficiently multiplied, he built a city, that they might live together, and be united, the better to defend themſelves againſt incurſions, and * to ſecure their unjuſt poſſeſſions; and this place he called after the name of his ſon *Enoch*, which, in the Hebrew tongue, ſignifies *a dedication*.

His deſcendants.

This Enoch begat Jarad; Jarad begat Mehujael; Mehujael begat Methuſael; and Methuſael begat Lamech, who was † the firſt introducer of polygamy. For he married two wives, Adah and Zillah, by the former of which he had two

* The words of Joſephus are theſe. " So far was Cain
" from mending his life after his afflictions, that he rather
" grew worſe and worſe, abandoning himſelf to his luſts, and
" all manner of outrage, without any regard to common juſ-
" tice. He enriched himſelf by rapine and violence, and made
" choice of the moſt profligate of monſters for his companions,
" inſtructing them in the very myſtery of their own profeſſion.
" He corrupted the ſimplicity and plain dealing of former
" times, with a novel invention of weights and meaſures, and
" exchanged the innocency of that primitive generoſity and
" candour for the new tricks of policy and craft. He was
" the firſt who invaded the common rights of mankind by
" bounds and incloſures, and the firſt who built a city, for-
" tified, and peopled it;" *Antiq. l.* 1. c 3; *and Le Clerc's Commentary.*

† Le Clerc, ſuppoſing that the increaſe of females at the beginning of the world was much greater than that of males, is of opinion that there might poſſibly want a man to eſpouſe one of the women which Lamech married; nor can he think that Moſes intended to blame him for what was the conſtant practice of ſome of the moſt eminent of the poſt-diluvian patriarchs. Biſhop Patrick likewiſe makes this apology for him. " His
" earneſt deſire of ſeeing that bleſſed ſeed," ſays he, " which
" was promiſed to Eve, might perhaps induce him to take more
" wives than one, hoping, that by multiplying his poſterity,
" ſome or other of them might prove ſo happy as to produce
" that ſeed. And thus he might poſſibly perſuade himſelf to be
" more likely, becauſe the right which was in Cain, the firſt-born,
" he might now conclude, was revived in himſelf; and that
" the curſe laid upon Cain was by this time expired, and his
" poſterity reſtored to the right of fulfilling the promiſe." Both
Selden

Chap. IV. *from the Creation to the Flood.*

two children; Jabal, † who made great improvements in the management of cattle, and found out the use of tents, ᶻ or moveable houses, to be carried about to places of fresh pasturage; and Jubal, who was the first inventor of all musical instruments, and himself a great master and performer. By the latter he had Tubal-Cain, the first who discovered ᵃ the art of forging and polishing metals, and thereupon devised the making all sorts of armour, both defensive and offensive; and whose sister Naamah (a name denoting *fair* and *beautiful*,) is supposed to have first found out the art of spinning and weaving.

A. M. 128. Ant. Chrif. 3876. Gen. ch. 4. to ver. 25.

ᵇ This is the register of Cain's posterity for seven generations: and Moses, perhaps, might the rather enumerate them, to shew who were the real authors and inventors of certain arts and handicrafts, ᶜ which the Egyptians too vainly assumed to themselves: but then he barely enumerates them, without ever remarking how long any of them lived, (a practice contrary to what he observes in the genealogy of the Sethites,) as if he esteemed them a generation so reprobate as ᵈ not to deserve a place in the book of the living.

The murther of Abel had, for a long time, occasioned a great animosity between the family of Seth and the descendents of Cain, who, though at some distance, lived in perpetual apprehensions that the other family might come upon

Lamech's discourse to his wives.

Selden and Grotius plead for the lawfulness of polygamy before the Levitical dispensation; but the learned Heidegger (who has a whole dissertation upon the subject) has sufficiently answered them, and proved at large, that this custom of multiplying wives is contrary both to the law of God and the law of nature; *Historia patriar. exercit.* 7.

† The words in the text are,——*He was the father of such as dwell in tents;* for the Hebrews call him the father of any thing who was the first inventor of it, or a most excellent master of that art: and from the affinity of their names, as well as the similitude of their inventions, learned men have supposed, that Jabal was the Pales; and Jubal the Apollo; *Tubal-Cain* (which in the Arabic tongue, still signifies a *plate of iron* or *brass*) the Vulcan, and his sister Naamah the Venus, or (as some will have it) the Minerva of the Gentiles; *Heidegger's Hist. patriar.;* and *Stillingfleet's Origines, l. 3. c. 5.*

ᶻ Le Clerc's Commentary. ᵃ Heidegger's Historia patriar.
ᵇ Howell's History of the Bible. ᶜ Le Clerc's Commentary.
ᵈ Patrick's Commentary.

A. M. 128.
Ant. Chri∫.
3876.
Gen. ch. 4.
to ver. 15.

upon them unawares, and revenge Abel's untimely death: but Lamech, when he came to be head of a people, endeavoured to reason them out of this fear. For ᵉ calling his family together, † he argued with them to this purpose. "Why should we make our lives uneasy with these "groundless suspicions? What have we done, that we
"should

ᵉ Shuckford's Connection, vol. 1.

† This speech of Lamech, as it stands unconnected with any thing before it, is supposed by many to be a fragment of some old record which Moses was willing to preserve; and, because it seems to fall into a kind of metre, some have thought it a short sketch of Lamech's poetry, which he was desirous to add to his son's invention of music, and other arts. Many suppose, that Lamech, being plagued with the daily contentions of his two wives, here blusters and boasts of what he had done and what he would do, if they gave him any farther molestation. Others imagine, that as the use of weapons was found out by one of his sons, and now become common, his wives were fearful, lest somebody or other might make use of them to slay him; but that, in this regard, he desires them to be easy, because, as he was not guilty of slaying any body himself, there was no reason to fear any body would hurt him. The Targum of Onkelos, which reads the words interrogatively, favours this interpretation much; *Have I slain a man to my wounding or a young man to my hurt?* i. e. I have done no violence or offence to any one, either great or small, and have therefore no cause to be apprehensive of any to myself. But the Rabbins tell us a traditional story, which, if true, would explain the passage at once. The tradition is,—' That Lamech, when he ' was blind, took his son Tubal Cain to hunt with him in the ' woods, where they happened on Cain, who being afraid of ' the society and converse of men, was wont to lie lurking up ' and down in the woods; that the lad mistook him for some ' beast stirring in the bushes, and directed his father, how, ' with a dart, or an arrow, he might kill him: and this (they ' say) was the man whom he killed by his wounding him; ' and that afterwards, when he came to perceive what he had ' done, he beat Tubal Cain to death for misinforming him: ' and this was the young man whom he killed by hurting ' or beating him.' But besides the incongruity of a blind man's going a hunting, this story is directly contrary to the promise of God, which assured Cain, that no person should kill him, and seems indeed to be devised for no other purpose, but merely to solve the difficulty of the passage. Among the many interpretations which have been made of it, that which I have offered seems to be the most natural and easy,

" should be afraid? We have not killed any man, nor of- A. M. 128.
" fered any violence to our brethren of the other family; Ant. Christ.
" and surely reason must teach them, that they can have Gen. ch. 4.
" no right to hurt or invade us. Cain indeed, our an- to ver. 15.
" cestor, killed Abel; but God was pleased so far to for-
" give his sin, as to threaten to take the severest vengeance
" on any one that should kill him; and if so, surely they
" must expect a much greater punishment, who shall pre-
" sume to kill any of us. For *if Cain shall be avenged seven
" fold, surely Lamech,* or any of his innocent family, *seventy
" seven fold.*" And it is not improbable, that by frequent
discourses of this kind, as well as by his own example,
he overcame the fears and shyness of the people, and (as
we shall find it hereafter) encouraged them to commence
an acquaintance with their brethren, the children of Seth.
This is the sum of what the Scripture teaches us of the
deeds of Cain, and his wicked offspring, who were all
swept away in the general deluge.

THE OBJECTION.

" BUT how little soever the Scripture teaches us of that there
" Cain and his adventures, yet it certainly teaches us were other
" too much, ever to believe that Adam and Eve were the Adam.
" primogenial parents of mankind. f According to the
" Mosaic account, Cain and Abel were at this time the
" only two persons (excepting their parents) upon the face
" of the earth; and yet, when we read that Abel was a
" keeper of sheep, we cannot but suppose, that he kept
" them for this reason,——that none of his neighbours
" might come and steal them away; and that Cain was a
" tiller of the ground, we cannot but infer, that there were
" at that time all such artificers as were requisite to carry
" on such an occupation, smiths and carpenters, millers
" and bakers, &c.

" When

fy, and is not a little countenanced by the authority of Josephus. " As for Lamech," says he, " who saw as far as any
" man into the course and methods of divine justice, he could
" not but find himself concerned in the prospect of that dread-
" ful judgement which threatened his whole family, for the
" murther of Abel, and, under this apprehension, he breaks
" the matter to his two wives;" *Antiq. lib.* 1. 3.

f *Vid.* La Peirere's Systeme theolog. p. 1. l. 3.; and Blount's
Oracles of reason.

A. M. 128.
Ant. Chrif.
3876.
Gen. ch. 4
to verse 25.

"When Cain intended to murther his brother, he en-
"ticed him to go with him into the field: now the field,
"we know, is ufually oppofed to a town, and therefore he
"decoyed him thither, that he might avoid the eyes of his
"fellow-citizens, who would otherwife have feen him, and
"immediately dragged him away to punifhment. With
"fome weapon or other Cain muft have killed his brother,
"becaufe we read of ᵍ a large effufion of blood; and yet,
"who was the cutler that made him the fword? Or, from
"what band of robbers was it that he had it?

"After fentence was denounced againft him, *Every one
"that findeth me fhall flay me*, fays he: but if his father
"and mother were the only perfons befides himfelf, what
"reafon had he for fuch an apprehenfion? Or for what
"purpofe fhould God fet a mark upon this murderer, for
"fear that any one fhould flay him, if there were not mul-
"titudes of men in the world that either defignedly or ac-
"cidentally might do it?

"But allowing that Adam and Eve had fome few chil-
"dren befides in the province of Eden, yet how came
"Cain, when banifhed from his native country, to find
"the land of Nod (a land which by the bye, no one can
"tell where it lies) fo well peopled in thofe early days, as
"there to meet with women enough, out of whom to chufe
"a wife, and men in abundance to build him a city;
"which, to diftinguifh it from other cities, (as then there
"might be many,) he called by the name of his fon E-
"noch? Thefe things are inconfiftent, and can never be
"reconciled, unlefs we fuppofe, that there was really a
"race of mankind before Adam, and that Mofes never in-
"tended to write of the primitive parents of all the world,
"(fince, within the compafs of a few lines, he lets fall fo
"many expreffions denoting the contrary,) but only to
"give us an account of the origin of the Jewifh nation,
"which we fondly imagine to be the hiftory of the univer-
"fal creation."

Anfwered,
by fhewing
that Mofes
intended to
treat of the
firft man.

Now, though it cannot be denied but that Mofes might
principally defign to give us a hiftory of the Jewifh nation;
yet, in the beginning of his account, and till they came to
be diftinguifhed from other nations in the patriarch Abraham, he could not have that under his peculiar confideration. He acquaints us, we find, with the origination of
the firft of other animals, whence they arofe, and in what
manner

ᵍ Ver. 10, 11.

manner they were perfected; and when he came to treat of the formation of human creatures, it is but reasonable to imagine, that he intended likewise to be understood of the first of their kind. Now, that Adam and Eve were the first of their kind, the words of our Saviour, [h] *from the beginning of the creation God made them male and female*, are a full confirmation; because he produces the very same precept that was applied to Adam and Eve at their creation, *therefore shall a man leave his father and his mother, and cleave to his wife:* and that there could be none before them, the reason why [i] *Adam called his wife's name Eve, because she was the mother of all living*, i. e. the person who was to be the root and source of all mankind that were to be upon the earth, is a plain demonstration: for if she was the mother of all living, there certainly was no race of men or women before her.

A.M. 118.
Ant. Chrif. 3875.
Gen. ch. 4. to verse 25.

St. Paul, while he was at Athens, endeavoured to convince the people of the vanity of that idolatry into which he perceived them fallen, by this argument, among others, ———that [k] *God had made of one blood all nations of men, for to dwell on all the face of the earth.* [l] Some Greek copies read it ἐξ ἑνὸς, *of one man*, leaving out αἵματος, wherein they are followed by the vulgar Latin: but allowing the common reading to be just, yet still the word αἷμα, or *blood*, must be taken in the † sense wherein it occurs in the best Greek authors, namely, for the stock or root out of which mankind came; and so the Apostle's reasoning will be———"That however men are now dispersed in their habitations, and differ much in language "and customs from each other, yet they all were original- "ly the same stock, and derived their succession from the "first man that God created." Neither can it be conceived, on what account [m] *Adam* is called in Scripture *the first man*, and that *he was made a living soul of the earth, earthly*,

[h] Mark x. 6.   [i] Gen. iii. 20.   [k] Acts xvii. 26.
[l] Stillingfleet's Orig. sacr. l. 3. c. 4.
† Homer employs it in this acceptation:

Εἰ ἐτεόν γ' ἐμὸς ἐσσι, καὶ αἵματος ἡμετέροιο.

Thence those that are near relations are called by Sophocles, οἱ πρὸς αἵματος and accordingly Virgil uses *sanguis* in the same sense:
† *Trojano a sanguine duci;* Stillingfleet's Orig. sacr. l. 3. c. 4.
[m] 1 Cor. xv. 45.

A. M. 128.
Ant. Chrif
3876.
Gen. ch. 4.
to ver. 25.

earthly, unless it were to denote, that he was absolutely the first of his kind, and so was to be the standard and measure of all that followed.

How Cain might till his ground, and why Abel might keep his cattle.

The design of Moses is not to give us a particular account of the whole race of mankind descended from Adam, ⁿ but only of those persons who were most remarkable, and whose story was necessary to be known, for the understanding of the succession down to his time. Besides those that are particularly mentioned in Scripture, we are told in general, that *Adam* º *begat sons and daughters;* and if we will give credit to an ancient eastern tradition, he had in all thirty-three sons, and twenty-seven daughters, which, considering the primitive fecundity, would in a short time be sufficient to stock that part of the world at least where Adam dwelt, and produce a race of mechanics able enough to supply others with such instruments of husbandry as might then be requisite for the cultivation of the ground. ᵖ For in the infancy of the world, the art of tillage was not come to such a perfection but that Cain might make use of wooden ploughs and spades, and instead of knives and hatchets, form his tools with sharp flints or shells, which were certainly the first instruments of cutting. And though in those early days there was no great danger of Abel's losing his cattle by theft; yet, to provide them with cool shades in hot climates, to remove them from place to place as their pasture decayed, to take care of their young, and guard them from the incursions of beasts of prey, (with many more incidental offices,) was then the shepherd's province, as well as now.

That there might be vast numbers of people then in the world.

According to the computation of most chronologers, it was in the hundred and twenty-ninth year of Adam's age, that Abel was slain; for the Scripture says expressly, that *Seth* ᑫ (who was given in the lieu of Abel) was *born in the hundred and thirtieth year,* (very likely the year after the murther was committed,) to be a comfort to his disconsolate parents. So that Cain must be an hundred and twenty-nine years old when he abdicated his own country; at which time there might be a sufficient quantity of mankind upon the face of the earth, to the number, it may be, of an hundred thousand souls. For if the children of Israel, from seventy persons, in the space of a hundred and ten years, became six hundred thousand fighting men, (though

ⁿ Patrick's Commentary.   º Gen. v. 4.   ᵖ Nicholls's Conference, vol. I.   ᑫ Gen. v. 3.

(though great numbers of them were dead during this increase,) we may very well suppose, that the children of Adam, whose lives were so very long, might amount at least to a hundred thousand in a hundred and thirty years, which are almost five generations.

A. M. 128.
Ant. Chrif. 3876
Gen. ch. 4. to verse 15.

Upon this supposition, it will be no hard matter to find Cain a wife in another country; † though it is much more probable that he was married before his banishment, because we may well think that all the world would abhor the thoughts of marriage with such an impious vagabond and murtherer. Upon this supposition we may likewise find him men enough to build and inhabit a city; especially ʳ considering that the word [*Hir*] which we render *city*, may denote no more than a certain number of cottages, with some little hedge or ditch about them: and this cluster of cottages (as was afterwards customary) he might call by his son's name rather than his own, which he was conscious was now become odious every where. Upon this supposition, lastly, we may account for Cain's fear, lest every one that lighted on him would kill him; for by this time mankind was greatly multiplied, and ˢ though no mention is made of Abel's marriage, (as, in so short a compendium, many things must necessarily be omitted,) yet he perhaps might have sons who were ready to pursue the fugitive, in order to revenge their father's death; or some of his own sisters, enraged against him for the loss of their brother, might possibly come upon him unawares,

What the wife; the city;

---

† There is an oriental tradition, that Eve, at her two first births brought twins, a son and a daughter; Cain, with his sister Azron, and Abel, with his sister Awin; that when they came to years of maturity, Adam proposed to Eve, that Cain should marry Abel's twin-sister, and Abel Cain's, because that was some small remove from the nearest degree of consanguinity, which even in those days, was not esteemed entirely lawful; that Cain refused to agree to this, insisting to have his own sister, who was the handsomer of the two; whereupon Adam ordered them both to make their offerings, before they took their wives, and so referred the dispute to the determination of God; that while they went up to the mountain for that purpose, the devil put it into Cain's head to murder his brother, for which wicked intent his sacrifice was not accepted: and that they were no sooner come down from the mountain, than he fell upon Abel, and killed him with a stone; *Patrick's Commentary; and Universal History*, No. 2.

ʳ Le Clerc's Commentary.   ˢ Patrick's Commentary.

A. M. 118.
Ant. Chrif.
3876.

unawares, or when they found him afleep, and fo difpatch him.

Gen. ch 4. to verfe 15.

Various are the conjectures of learned men ‡ concerning the mark which God fet upon Cain, to prevent his being killed. Some think that God ftigmatized him on his forehead with a letter of his own name, or rather fet fuch a brand upon him, as fignified him to be accurfed. Others fancy that God made him a peculiar garment, to diftinguifh him from the reft of mankind, who were clothed with fkins. Some imagine, that his head continually fhaked; others, that his face was blafted with lightning; others, that his body trembled all over; and others again, that the ground fhook under him, and made every one fly from him: whereas the plain fenfe of the words is nothing more, than that God gave Cain a fign, or wrought a miracle before his face, thereby to convince him, that though he was banifhed into a ftrange land, yet no one fhould be permitted to hurt him; and to find out the land into which he was banifhed, is not fo hard a matter as fome may imagine.

and mark fet upon Cain,

The land of Nod, where, or what it was

The defcription which Mofes gives us of it is this.—— *And Cain went out from the prefence of the Lord, and dwelt in the land of Nod, on the eaft fide of Eden; and there he built a city, and called the name of it after the name of his fon Enoch.* Hereupon " the learned Huetius obferves,

---

‡ Almoft all the verfions have committed a miftake in tranflating ver. 15 that *God had put a mark upon Cain, left any finding him fhould kill him.* The original fays no fuch thing, and the LXX have very well rendered it thus—*God fet a fign before Cain, to perfuade him, that whoever fhould find him fhould not kill him.* This is almoft the fame with what is faid in Ex. x. 1. that *God did figns before the Egyptians*; and Ifa. lxvi. 19. that *he would fet a fign before the Heathen*; where it is evident, that God did not mean any particular mark which fhould be fet on their bodies, but only thofe figns and wonders which he wrought in Egypt, to oblige Pharaoh to let his people go; and the miraculous manner wherein he delivered them from the Babylonifh captivity. This expofition is natural, and agreeable to the methods of divine providence, which is wont to convince the incredulous by figns and wonders; nor could any thing elfe affure Cain, in the fear he was under, that the firft who met him fhould not kill him, after what God had faid to him in the exprobation of his crime; *Patrick's Commentary; and Saurin's Differtation.*

t Gen. iv. 16, 17.   u De la fitu. du paradis.

serves that Ptolemy, in his discription of Susiana, places there a city called *Anuchtha*; and that the syllable *tha*, which ends the word, is, in the Chaldee language, a termination pretty common to nouns feminine, and consequently no part of the name itself: from whence he infers, that this Anuchtha, mentioned by Ptolemy, is the same with the city Enoch mentioned by Moses; especially since Ptolemy places it on the east side of Eden, which agrees very well with what Moses says of the land of Nod. [x] But though it be allowed, that Anuchtha and Enoch be the same name, yet it will not therefore follow, that there was no other city so called but that which was built by Cain. It is certain, that there was another Enoch, the son of Jared, and father of Methuselah, a person of remarkable piety, in the antediluvian age; and why might not the city, mentioned by Ptolemy, be called after him, in respect to his illustrious character, and miraculous exemption from death? or rather, why might it not take its name from some other Enoch, different from both the former, and living some generations after the flood? For it is scarce imaginable, how the city of Enoch, built before the flood, should either stand or retain its ancient name, after so violent a concussion, and total alteration of the face of nature.

Nor should it be forgot, that the province of Susiana, where Huetius places the land of Nod, is one of the most fruitful and pleasant countries in the world; whereas, considering that Cain's banishment was intended by God to be part of his punishment, it seems more reasonable to think, that he should, upon this account, be sent into some barren and desolate country, remote from the place of his nativity, and separated by mountains, and other natural obstructions, from the commerce of his relations. For which reason the learned Grotius is clearly of opinion, that the country into which Cain was sentenced to withdraw, was Arabia deserta: to the barrenness of which, the curse that God pronounces against him, seems not improperly to belong. [y] *And now thou art cursed from the earth, and when thou tillest the ground, it shall not, henceforth, yield unto thee her strength.* But after all, their opinion is not to be found fault with, who suppose, that the word *Nod*, which signifies an *exile*, or *fugitive*, is not a proper, but only an appellative name; and that therefore,

[x] Well's Geography.   [y] Gen. iv. 11.

A. M. 128
Ant. Chrif.
3876.
Gen. ch. 4.
10 ver. 15

A recapitulation of the anſwer.

fore, where-ever the country was where Cain took up his abode, that, in after ages, was called *the land of Nod*, or the land of *the baniſhed man*.

Thus the account, which Moſes gives us of the murther of Abel, ſtands clear of the imputation of all abſurdity or contradiction, wherewith the lovers of infidelity would gladly charge it. The time when his brother murthered him, was in the 129th year of the world's creation, when, † according to a moderate computation, their and their parent's deſcendants could not but be very numerous. The manner in which he murthered him might not be with a ſword or ſpear (which perhaps then were not in uſe,) * ſince a club, or ſtone, or any rural inſtrument, in the hand of rage and revenge, was ſufficient to do

† Though we ſhould ſuppoſe, that Adam and Eve had no other children than Cain and Abel in the year of the world 128, which (as the beſt chronologers agree) was the time of Abel's murther; yet, as it muſt be allowed, that they had daughters married with theſe two ſons, we require no more than the deſcendants of theſe two children, to make a conſiderable number of men upon the earth in the ſaid year 128. For, ſuppoſing them to have been married in the 19th year of the world, they might eaſily have had each of them eight children, ſome males, ſome females, in the 25th year. In the 50th year there might proceed from them, in a direct line, 64 perſons; in the 74th year, there would be 572; in the 98th, 4096; and in the 122d year, they would amount to 32,768. If to theſe we add the other children, deſcended from Cain and Abel, their children, and the children of their children we ſhall have in the aforeſaid 122d year, 421.164 men, capable of generation, without ever reckoning the women, both old and young, or ſuch children, as are under the age of 17 years. *Vid. Deſſert chronol. geogr. critique ſur la Bible diſſert.* 1. in the Journal of Paris, Jan. 1712, vol. LI. p. 6.

* There is an oriental tradition, that when Cain was confirmed in the deſign of deſtroying his brother, and knew not how to go about it, the devil appeared to him in the ſhape of a man, holding a bird in his hand; and that, placing the bird upon a rock, he took up a ſtone, and with it ſqueezed its head in pieces. Cain, inſtructed by this example, reſolved to ſerve his brother in the ſame way: and therefore, waiting till Abel was aſleep, he lifted up a large ſtone, and let it fall, with all its weight, upon his head, and ſo killed him; whereupon God cauſed him to hear a voice from heaven, to this purpoſe, *The reſt of thy days ſhalt thou paſs in perpetual fear;* Calmet's Dictionary on the word *Abel*.

do the work. The place where he murthered him, is said to be in the field, [x] not in contradistinction to any large and populous city then in being, but rather to the tents, or cottages, where their parents and offspring might then live. The cause of his murthering him, was [a] a spirit of emulation, which, not duly managed, and made a spur to virtue, took an unhappy turn, and degenerated into malice: and the true reason of all (as the Apostle has stated it) was, that [b] *Cain was of that wicked one, and slew his brother, because his own works were wicked, and his brother's righteous.*

A. M. 128 Ant. Chrif. 3876, Gen. ch. 4. to ver. 15.

DISSERTATION IV.

Of the institution of sacrifices.

THE first plain account that we meet with of sacrifices, is here in the examples of Cain and Abel. Mention is made indeed of the skins of some beasts, wherewith God directed our first parents to be clothed; but expositors are not agreed, whether what we render skins might not denote some other sort of covering, or shelter from the weather; or, if they were the real skins of beasts, whether these beasts were offered unto God in sacrifice or no; whereas, in the Scripture before us, we have oblations of both kinds, *bloody* and *unbloody sacrifices*, (as they are commonly distinguished;) the fruits of the field, offered by Cain, and the firstlings of the flock, by Abel. So that from hence we may very properly take an occasion, to inquire a little into the original of sacrifices; for what ends and purposes they were at first appointed; and by what means they became an acceptable service unto God.

Sacrifices, when they first began.

The Scriptures indeed make no mention of the first institution of sacrifices; and from their silence, in this respect, some have imagined, that they proceeded originally from a dictate of nature, or a grateful inclination to return unto God some of his own blessings. But in so short an account of so large a compass of time, (as we have said before,) it may well be expected, that several things should be omitted. To this purpose, therefore, others have observed, that Moses says nothing [c] of Enoch's prophecy; nothing [d] of Noah's preaching; nothing [e] of the peopling of

Of divine institution at first.

---

[a] Le Clerc's Commentary.   [a] Shuckford's Connection.
[b] 1 John iii. 12.   [c] Jude 14.   [d] 2 Pet. ii. 15.   [e] Vid. Gen. x.

A. M. 128.
Ant. Chrif.
3876.
Gen. ch. 4
to ver. 25.

of the world; though thefe be referred to in other parts of Scripture: ᶠ nor does he here introduce the facrifices of Cain and Abel, with an intent to inform us of the origin of that rite, but merely to let us know what was the unhappy occafion of the firft murther that ever was committed in the world.

The ᵍ Jews indeed, to whom he primarily wrote, knew very well, that their own facrifices were of divine inftitution, and that God had manifefted his acceptance of them, at the very firft folemn oblation after that inftitution, by a miraculous fire from the divine prefence; nor had they any reafon to doubt, but that they were fo inftituted, and fo accepted from the beginning: and therefore there was lefs reafon for Mofes to expatiate upon a matter, which had doubtlefs defcended to them in a clear and uninterrupted tradition.

A grateful fenfe of God's bleffings will, at any time, engage us to offer him the *calves of our lips*, (as the Scripture terms them,) or the warmeft expreffions of our praife and thankfgiving; but what dictate of nature, or deduction of reafon, could ever have taught us, that, to deftroy the beft of our fruits, or the beft of our cattle, would have been a fervice acceptable to God? Goodnefs, and mercy, and lenity, and compaffion, are the ideas we have of that infinite being; and who would then have thought, that putting an innocent and inoffenfive creature to torture, fpilling its blood upon the earth, and burning its flefh upon an altar, would have been either a grateful fight, or *an offering of a fweet fmelling favour* to the Moft High?

No ʰ being, we know, can have a right to the lives of other creatures, but their Creator only, and thofe on whom he fhall think proper to confer it: but it is evident, that God, at this time, had not given man a right to the creatures, even for neceffary food, much lefs for unneceffary cruelty; and therefore to have taken away their lives, without God's pofitive injunction, would have been an abominable act, and enough to diffecrate all their oblations. When therefore we read, that his acceptance of facrifices of old was ufually teftified by way of inflammation, or fetting them on fire, by a ray of light which iffued from his glorious prefence, we muft allow, that this was a proof of

ᶠ Outram De facrificiis.   ᵍ Revelation examined.
ʰ Revelation examined.

of his previous inftitution of them; otherwife we cannot possibly think, why he should so far concern himself about them, as even to be at the expence of a miracle, to denote his approbation of them. [i] *Who hath known the mind of the Lord,* is the Apoftle's way of arguing, *or who hath been his counfellor?* And, in like manner, without a divine revelation, it would have been the height of vanity and presumption, to have pretended to determine the way of reconciliation with him, and (without his order and appointment) to have entered upon a form of worfhip, entirely new and ftrange, by killing of beafts, and burning their fat. [k] *No man* (fays another Apoftle) *taketh this honour to himfelf, but he that is called of God, as was Aaron;* nor can any one lay hold on the promife of forgivenefs of fins (which is the great defign of all facrificing) any other way than by fymbols of God's own inftitution.

In [l] moft nations indeed, the cuftom of facrificing did prevail: but that it did not arife from any principle of nature or reafon, is manifeft from hence —— [m] that the graveft and wifeft of the Heathen philofophers always * condemned bloody facrifices as impious, and unacceptable to their Gods; but this they would not have done, had they looked upon them as any branch of natural religion, which none were more warm in extolling than they. It is no improbable conjecture, therefore, that other nations might

A. M. 128.
Ant. Chrif. 3876.
Gen. ch. 4. to ver. 25.

---

[i] Rom. xi. 34. [k] Heb v. 4. [l] Heidegger's Hiftor. patriar. exercit. 1. [m] Edward's Survey of religion, vol. 1.

* It is the opinion of Tertullian, [Apol. ch. 46.] that none of the ancient philofophers ever compelled the people to facrifice living creatures. Theophraftus is quoted by Porphyry in Eufebius, [Prep. Evan. l. 1. c. 9.] as afferting that the firft men offered handfuls of grafs; that, in time, they came to facrifice the fruits of the trees: and, in after ages, to kill and offer cattle upon altars. Many other authors are cited for this opinion. Paufanias [De Cerere Phrygialenfi] seems to intimate, that the ancient facrifice was only fruits of trees (of the vine efpecially,) and of honey combs and wool. Empedocles [De antiquiffimis temporibus] affirms, that the firft altars were not ftained with the blood of creatures; and Plato [De legibus l. 6.] was of opinion, that living creatures were not anciently offered in facrifice, but cakes of bread, and fruits, and honey, poured upon them; for

Nen bove mactato cœleftia numina gaudent,

was an old pofition of more writers than Ovid. *Vid.* Shuckford's Connection, vol. 1. l. 2.

A. M. 128
Ant. Chrif.
3876.
Gen ch. 4.
to ver. 15.

might take the rite of sacrificing from the Jews, to [n] which the devil, in Heathen countries, might instigate his votaries, purely to ape God, and imitate his ordinances: or, if this commencement of sacrificing among them is thought to be too late, why may not we suppose, that they received it by tradition from their fore-fathers, who had it originally from Adam, as he had it from God by a particular revelation? Now that there was some warrant and precept of God for it, seems to be intimated by the author to the Hebrews, when he tells us, that [o] *by faith Abel offered unto God a more acceptable sacrifice, than Cain:* for [p] *it faith cometh by hearing, and hearing by the word of God,* faith is founded on some word, and relieth on divine command or promise; and therefore, when Abel offered the best of his flock in sacrifice, he did what was enjoined him by God, and his practice was founded upon a divine command, which was given to Adam, and his sons, though Moses, in his short account of things, makes no mention of it.

In fine, if it appears from history, that sacrifices have been used all over the world, have spread as far, as universally among men, as the very notions of a Deity; if we find them almost as early in the world as mankind upon the earth, and, at the same time, cannot perceive that mankind ever could, by the light of reason, invent such notions of a Deity, as might induce them to think, that this way of worship would be an acceptable service to him; if mankind indeed could have no right to the lives of the brute-creation, without the concession of God; and yet it is evident, that they exercised such right, and God approved of their proceeding, by visible indications of his accepting the sacrifices; then must we necessarily suppose, that sacrifices were of his own institution at first; and that they were instituted for purposes well becoming his infinite wisdom and goodness.

The ends and designs of God's instituting them.

For we must remember, that Adam and Eve were, at this time, become sinners, and though received into mercy, in constant danger of relapsing; that, by their transgression, they had forfeited their lives, but as yet could have no adequate sense, either of the nature of the punishment, or the heinousness of the sin which procured it; and that now they were to beget children, who were sure to inherit

[n] Heidegger's Histor. patriar. exercit. 8. [o] Heb. xi. 4.
[p] Rom. x. 17.

rit their parents, corruption and infirmity. Since man, therefore, had forfeited his life by his transgressions, and God, notwithstanding, decreed to receive him into mercy, nothing certainly could better become the divine wisdom and goodness, than the establishment of some institution, which might at once be a monition both of the mercy of God, and the punishment due to sin. And because God foresaw that man would often sin, and should often receive mercy, it was necessary, that the institution should be such as might frequently be repeated; and in such repetition, frequently remind man of his own endless demerit, and of God's infinite goodness to him; to which purpose the institution of sacrifices for sin was of excellent use and service.

A. M. 128.
Ant. Chrif. 2876.
Gen. ch. 4. to ver. 15.

Both from the commandment which at first was given to Adam, and the sentence which was afterwards denounced against him, we learn, that death was the penalty of his disobedience; and since it was so, certainly it was highly proper, that he should know what he was to suffer; and consequently, that he should see death in all its horror and deformity, in order to judge rightly of the evil of disobedience. And what could exhibit this evil more strongly, than the groans and struggles of innocent creatures, bleeding to death for his guilt, before his eyes, and by his own hands? Sights of this kind are shocking to human nature even yet, though custom hath long made them familiar: with what horror then, may we imagine that they pierced the hearts of our first parents, and how was that horror aggravated, when they considered themselves as the guilty authors of so much cruelty to the creatures which were about them? Nay, when the groans of these dying animals were over, what a sad, a ghastly spectacle must their cold carcasses yield? and even after their oblation, how dismal a meditation must it be, to consider the beauty and excellency of these animate beings reduced to an handful of dust; especially, when they could not see them in that condition, but under sad conviction, that they themselves must follow the same odious steps to destruction?

We can hardly conceive, how God could strike the human soul with a deeper sense of misery from guilt, or with more abhorrence of the sad cause of that misery, than by this method of appointing sacrifices: nor can we imagine how our first parents could have ever sustained themselves under such afflicting thoughts, had not God, in his infinite goodness,

A. M. 128
Ant. Chrif.
3876.
Gen. ch. 4.
t. ver. 25.

goodness, caused some ray of hope to shine through this scene of mortality and misery, and made sacrifices (at the same time that they were such lively emblems of the horror of guilt) the means of its expiation, and the seals of his covenant of grace.

ᵠ That God entered into a covenant of mercy with man, immediately after the fall, is evident from the sentence passed upon the serpent, wherein that covenant is comprised: and therefore, as we find that, in after ages, his usual way of ratifying covenants of this kind was by sacrifices; so we cannot imagine that he failed to do so at this time, when such mercy was more wanted than ever it was since the foundation of the world. Sacrifices indeed have no natural aptitude to expiate guilt, in which sense, the apostle affirms it ʳ *to be impossible for the blood of bulls, and of goats, to take away sins.* The death of a beast is far from being equivalent to the death of a man, but infinitely short of that eternal death to which the man's sinfulness does consign him: but still, as sacrifices are federal rites, and one of those external means which God had instituted, under the antediluvian dispensation, for man's recovery from sin, we cannot but suppose, but that, when piously and devoutly offered, they were accepted by him, for the expiation of transgressions; though it must be owned, that they did not, of themselves, or by their own worthiness, atone for any thing, but only in virtue of the expiatory sacrifice of the Messias to come, whereof they were no more than types and shadows. To speak strictly and properly, therefore, these sacrifices did not really and formally, but typically and mystically expiate, *i. e.* they did not pacify God's anger, and satisfy his justice, and take away sin, by their own force and efficacy, but as they were figures and representations of that universal sacrifice, which (in the divine intention) *was slain from the foundation of the world,* and, *in the fulness of time,* was to come down from heaven, in order to fulfil the great undertaking of *making atonement for the sins of all mankind.*

The means of making them acceptable to God.

Thus to represent the horrid nature of sin, and to seal the eternal covenant of mercy; to be types of the great expiatory sacrifice of Christ's death, and a standing means of obtaining pardon and reconciliation with God, seems to be some of the principal ends of God's instituting sacrifices at first: and what was of use to gain them a favourable acceptance in his sight, we may, in some measure, learn from the

ᵠ Revelation examined.   ʳ Heb. x. 4.

the reasons, that are usually alledged, for his rejection of Cain's, and approbation of Abel's sacrifice.

A. M. 128.
Ant. Christ. 3876.
Gen. ch 4. ver. 15.

Most of the Jewish interpreters have placed the different events of these two sacrifices in the external quantity or quality of them. They tell us, that *Cain brought of the fruits of the ground* indeed, but not of the *first fruits* (as he should have done,) nor the fullest ears of corn, (which he kept for himself,) but the lankest and latest; and, even what he brought, 'twas with a niggardly hand and grudging mind; so that he raised God's aversion [s] *by offering to him of that which cost him nothing:* Whereas Abel found a kind acceptance, because [t] *he honoured the Lord with his substance:* He brought of the *firstlings of his flock*, and the very best and fattest of them, as thinking nothing too good to be offered in devotion and gratitude to him from whom he received all.

" Allowing the maxim of the Jewish church, *viz. that without blood there is no remission*, to have been good, from the first institution of sacrifice, a very learned writer supposes, that Abel came, as a petitioner for grace and pardon, and brought the atonement appointed for sin; but Cain appeared before God as a just person, wanting no repentance and brought an offering in acknowlegement of God's goodness and bounty, but no atonement in acknowlegement of his own wretchedness; and that upon this account his oblation was rejected, as God's expostulation with him seems to imply: *If thou dost well, shalt thou not be accepted? And if thou dost not well, sin lieth at thy door*, i. e. if thou art righteous, thy righteousness shall save thee; but if thou art not, by what expiation is thy sin purged? it lieth still at thy door.

The author to the [x] Hebrews has given us, I think, a key to this difficulty, when he tells us, that *by faith Abel offered unto God a more excellent sacrifice than Cain.* [y] The *faith* (of which the apostle gives us several instances in this chapter) is the belief of something declared, and, in consequence of such belief, the performance of some action enjoined by God: *By faith Noah, being warned by God, prepared an ark*, i. e. he believed the warning which God gave him and obediently made the ark which he had appointed him to make: *By faith Abraham, when called* to go into a strange land

VOL. I. No. 3. K k

[s] 2 Sam. xxiv. 24. [t] Prov. iii 9. [u] Bishop Sherlock's Use of Prophecy, dis. 3. [x] Chap. xi, ver. 4. [y] Shuckford's Connect. vol. 1. l. 2.

A. M. 128.
Ant. Chrif.
3876.
Gen. ch. 4.
to ver 25.

land, *which God promised to give him for an inheritance, obeyed*, i. e. he believed that God would give him what he had promised, and, in consequence of such belief, did what God commanded him: And thus it was, that *Abel, by faith, offered a better sacrifice than Cain*, because he believed what God had promised, that *the seed of the woman should bruise the serpent's head*, and, in consequence of such belief, offered such a sacrifice for his sins, as God had appointed to be offered, until the seed should come.

² In order to offer a sacrifice by faith then, there are three things requisite. 1st, That the person who offers should do it upon the previous appointment and direction of God. 2dly, That he should consider it as a sign and token of the promise of God made in Christ, and of remission of sins through his blood; and 3dly, That, while he is offering, he should be mindful withal (in the phrase of St Paul) *to present himself a living sacrifice, holy, and acceptable unto God.* In the first of these qualifications Cain was right enough, because he had learned from his father, that, as God had appointed sacrifices, it was his duty to offer them: But herein was his great defect, that while he was offering, he gave no attention to what he was about; nor once reflected on the promise of God, made in paradise, nor placed any confidence in the merits of a Saviour, to recommend his services; but, vainly imagining that his bare oblation was all that was required to his justification, he took no care to preserve his soul pure and unpolluted, or to constitute his members as *instruments of righteousness unto God.* In short, his oblation was the service of an hypocrite, lying unto God, and using the external symbols of grace *for a cloak of maliciousness*; whereas Abel's sacrifice was attended with awful meditations on that *seed of the woman* which was to become the world's redeemer, with warm applications to him for mercy and forgiveness and with holy resolutions of better obedience, of abandoning all sin, *and always abounding in the work of the Lord;* and therefore there is no wonder, that their services met with so different a reception. For, however sacrificing was an external rite, yet the *opus operatum* would by no means do, unless the attention of the mind, and the integrity of the heart went along with it, ᵇ *he that killed an ox was as if he slew a man; and he that sacrificed a lamb as if he cut off a dog's neck;* so detestable in the sight of God

---

ᵃ Heideggar's Hist. patriar. exercit. 5.   ᵇ Isa. lxvi. 3.

God was * the richest oblation, when the sacrificer was not a good man; nay, so ready was he to pass by all observances of this kind, if the worshipper came but, in other respects, qualified: ᵇ *For he that keepeth the law bringeth offerings enough; he that taketh heed to the law offereth a peace-offering; he that requiteth a good turn offereth fine flour; and he that giveth alms sacrificeth praise. To depart from wickedness is a thing pleasing to the Lord; and to forsake unrighteousness is a propitiation.*

A. M. 128.
Ant. Chrif. 3876.
Gen. ch. 4. to ver. 25.

* That it is not the quality of the sacrifice, but the mind and disposition of the sacrificer, which God regards, was the general sentiment of the wisest Heathens, as appears by that excellent passage in **Persius**:

Compositum jus, fasque animo, sanctosque recessus
Mentis, et incoctum generoso pectus honesto,
Hæc cedo, ut admoveam templis, et farre litabo.

SAT. 2.

And that other in Seneca:
Non in victimis, licet optimæ sint, auroque præfulgent, deorum est honos, sed pia et recta voluntate venerandum; *De senect. l. 1. c. 6.*

ᵇ Eccluf. xxxv. 1, &c.

CHAP. V.

Of the general Corruption of Mankind.

THE HISTORY.

GREAT * was the grief, no doubt, which our first parents felt upon the loss of the righteous Abel, and the expulsion of their wicked son Cain; but, to alleviate, in some measure, this heavy load of sorrow, God was pleased to promise them another son, whose fate should

A. M. 130.
Ant. Chrif. 3874.
Gen. ch. 5. and 6 to ver 13.

K k 2
be
the birth of Seth.

* The Jewish, and some Christian doctors, say, that Adam and Eve mourned for Abel one hundred years, during which time they lived separate, Adam particularly, in a valley near Hebron thence named *the valley of tears*. And the inhabitants of Ceylon pretend, that the salt lake on the mountain of Columbo, was formed by the tears which Eve shed on this occasion. All fiction; *Calmet's Dictionary.*

A. M. 130. be different, and himself a lasting comfort and consolation
Ant. Chrif. to them: And therefore, as soon as Eve was delivered of
3874.
Gen. ch. 5. the child, she called his name *Seth*, which signifies *substi-*
and 6 to *tute*, because God had been so good as to send him in the
ver. 13. room of his brother Abel, whom Cain slew. Adam, when
          he had Seth, was 130 years old: He lived after that 800
A catalogue years, and begat several other children (though Moses
of Adam's
posterity in makes no mention of them.) So that the ‖ whole of his
the line of life was 930 years.
Seth.
A. M. 235.   Seth, when he was 105 years old, had a son named *Enos*:
          After which time he lived 807 years; so that the whole
          of his life was 912.

A M 315   Enos, when 90, had a son named *Cainan*: After which
          he lived 815 years; in the whole 905.

A M 325   Cainan, when 70, had a son named *Mahalaleel*: After
          which he lived 840 years; in all 910.

A M 460   Mahalaleel, when 65, had a son named *Jared*: After
          which he lived 830 years; in all 895.

A M 622   Jared, when 162, had a son named *Enoch*: After which
          he lived 800 years; in all 962.

A M 687   Enoch, when 65, had a son named *Methuselah*: After
          which he lived 300; in all 365.

‖ If it be asked, how it came to pass, that Adam, who was
immediately created by God, and, consequently, more perfect
than any of his kind, did not outlive Methuselah, who was the
eighth from him? the answer which some have given, *viz.* That
his grief and affliction of mind for the loss of paradise, and the
misery which, by his transgression, he had entailed upon his
offspring, might affect his constitution, and, by degrees, impair
his strength, is not much amiss: but there is another reason
which seems to me better founded, *viz.* That, whereas Adam
was created in the full perfection of his nature, and all his descendants, being born infants, did gradually proceed to maturity; subducting the time from their infancy to their manhood,
we shall find, that Adam out-lived them all: For we must not
compute, as we do now, (when the extent of man's life is usually no more than 70) that his complete manhood was at 30,
or thereabouts. In the very catalogue now before us, we read
of none (except Enoch, and two others who begat children before they were 90 or upwards; and therefore, subtracting those
years (which we may suppose interfered between his birth and
his manhood) from the age of Methuselah, we may perceive,
that Adam surpassed him to the number of almost sixty; *Estius
in diffic. loca.*

Chap. V.   *from the Creation to the Flood.*   145

Methuselah, when 187, had a son named Lamech: A. M. 130.
After which he lived 782; in all 969.   Ant. Chrif.
                                            3874,
Lamech, when 182, had a son named *Noah*: After Gen. ch. 5.
which he lived 595; in all 777: And   and 6 to
                                       ver. 13.
Noah, when he was 500 years old, had three sons,
Shem, Ham, and Japhet, † from whom the world, after A. M. 874.
the deluge, was replenished.   A. M. 1056.
                                A. M. 1556.
† This is the genealogy which Moses gives us of the
posterity of Adam, in the line of Seth, until the time of But far
                                                the from being
                                                    all.

† Of these three sons, the eldest was Japhet, as appears from Gen. x. 21. the second was Shem, from Gen. x. 21. and the youngest Ham, from Gen ix. 24. Nevertheless, both here, and a little lower, Shem is named first; whether it was; that the rights of primogeniture were transferred to him (though the sacred historian says nothing of it;) or God was minded, thus early to shew, that he would not be confined to the order of nature, in the disposal of his favours, which he frequently bestowed upon the younger children; or (what I think the most likely) because the nation of the Jews were to descend from him, and he, and his posterity, were to be the principal subject of this whole history : *Patrick and Le Clerc's Comment, and Poel's Annota.*

† From this catalogue we may farther observe, that the custom in those times was, to give children their names according to the occurrences in life; or expectations of their parents. Thus Seth, being a good man, was grieved to see the great degeneracy in other parts, though he endeavoured to preserve his own family from the contagion; and therefore called his son *Enos*, which signifies *sorrowful*. *Enos*, perceiving the posterity of Cain to grow every day worse and worse, was concerned for their iniquity, and began to dread the consequences of it; and therefore called his son *Cainan*, which denotes *lamentation*. Though Cainan had his name from the wickedness of Cain's family, yet he himself was resolved to maintain the true worship of God in his own; and therefore called his son *Mahalaleel*, i. e, *a praiser and worshipper of God*. In the days of Mahalaleel (as the tradition tells us) a defection happened among the sons of Seth, who went down from the mountains where they inhabited, and adjoined themselves to the daughters of Cain : and therefore he called his son's name *Jared*, which signifies *descending*. Jared, to guard against the general corruption, devoted himself and his descendants, more zealously to the service of God, and, accordingly, called his son *Enoch*, which means *a dedication*. Enoch, by the spirit of prophecy, foreseeing the destruction which would come upon the earth, immediately after the death of his son, called his name *Methuselah*, which imports as much;
                                            for

A. M. 130. the deluge; but we must observe, that these are far from
Ant. Chris. being all his progeny. In the case of our great progenitor
3874.
Gen. ch. 5. Adam, he informs us, that after the birth of Seth, ᵃ *he*
and 6. to *had several sons and daughters*, though he does not so much
ver. 13.   as record their names; and the like we may suppose of the
           rest of the antediluvian patriarchs. For it is incongruous
to think, that Lamech was 181, and Methuselah, 187, before they ever had a child, when it, so plainly appers, that
his father Enoch had one at 65. The true reason then of
this omission is ———— that the historian never intended to
give us a catologue of the collateral branches (which doubtless were many) but only of the principal persons by whom,
in a right line, the the succession was continued down to
Noah, and thence to Abraham, the founder of the Jewish
nation.

The divisi-   Not long after the departure of Cain, the whole world
on of the was divided into two families, or opposite nations: The
world into family of Seth, which adhered to the service of God, † be-
the families
of Cain and   came
Seth.

for the first part of the word [*Methu*] signifies *he dies*, and [*Selah*]
the *sending forth of water*. Methuselah, perceiving the wickedness of the world, in the family of Seth, as well as that of Cain,
to grow every day worse and worse, called his son *Lamech*,
which intimates *a poor man, humbled*, and *afflicted with grief*,
for the present corruption and fear of future punishment: And
Lamech conceiving better hopes of his son (as some imagine)
that he should be the promised seed, the restorer of mankind after the deluge, or a notable improver of the art of agriculture
called his name *Noah*, which denotes *a comforter*; *Bedford's
Scripture chronology*. We may observe, from this catalogue,
however, that the patriarchs, in those days, were not so superstitious, as to think any thing ominous in names and therefore we
find, that Jared feared not to call his son *Enoch*, by the very
name of Cain's eldest son, Gen. iv. 17. even a Methuselah called his son *Lamech*, by the name of one of Cain's grand-children
ch. iv. ver. 18.; *Patrick's Commentary*.

ᵃ Gen. v. 4.

† The words in our translation are,—*then i. e.* in the days of
Enos, *began men to call upon the name of the Lord*, ch. iv. 26.;
but, it being very probable, that public assemblies for religous
offices, were held long before this time, and that even when
Cain and Abel offered their sacrifices, their families joined with
them in the worship of God; some men of great note, such as,
Bertram, Hackspan, and Heidegger take them in the same sense
with our marginal translation; *then began men,* ; i. e. the chil-
                                                              dren

came more frequent in religious offices; and, as their number increased, met in larger assemblies, and in communion, to perform the divine worship by way of public liturgy; and, [b] for this their piety and zeal, were styled the *sons* or *servants, of God*, in distinction to the family of Cain, which now became profligate and profane, renouncing the service of God, and addicting themselves to all manner

A. M. 130.
Ant. Chrif.
3874.
Gen. ch. 5.
and 6. to
ver. 13.

dren of Seth) *to call themselves by the name of the Lord*, i. e. the servants and worshippers of the Lord, in contradistinction to the Cainites, and such profane persons as had forsaken him. It must not be dissembled however, that the word *Hochal*, which we translate *began*, in several places of Scripture signifies *to profane*; and upon this presumption many of the Jewish writers, and some of no obscure fame among us, have taken the words so, as if Moses intended to intimate to us, that men began now to apostatize from the worship of God, to fall into idolatry, and to apply the most holy name, which alone belongs to the great Creator of heaven and earth, to created beings, and especially to the sun. But, considering that Moses is here speaking of the pious family of Seth, and not of that of Cain; that when the Hebrew word signifies *to profane*, it has always a noun following it; but when an affirmative mood follows, (as in the passage before us,) it always signifies *to begin*; and withal, that the eastern writers represent this Enos as an excellent governor, who, while he lived, preserved his family in good order, and, when he died, called them all together, and gave them a charge to keep all God's commandments, and not to associate themselves with the children of Cain: considering all this, I say, we can hardly suppose that Moses is here pointing out the origin of idolatry, but rather the invention of some religious rites and ceremonies in the external worship of God at this time, or the distinction which good men began to put between themselves and such as were openly wicked and profane. For that the true meaning of the expression *Karabeshem*, according to our marginal translation, is to *call* or *nominate by*, or *after* the name of any one, is manifest from several instances in Scripture. Thus, Gen. iv. 17, *Jikra, he called* the name of the city *Beshem, by,* or *after* the name of his son. Numb. xxxii. 42 *Jikra, he called it Nobahbeshem, by,* or *after* his own name; and in Psal. xlix. 11. *Kareau, they call* their lands *Bishmotham, by,* or *after their* own *names*: and the name here intimated is afterwards expressly given them by Moses himself, Gen. vi. when he tells us, that *the sons of God saw the daughters of men*: Patrick's Commentary, and Calmet's Dictionary on the word *Enos*; and Shuckford's Connection, vol. 1. l. 1.

[b] Heidegger's Histor. patriarch.

A. M. 130
Ant. Chrif.
3874
Gen. ch. 5.
and 6.
to verfe 13.

ner of impiety and lafciviousness; from whence they had the name of the *sons* and *daughters of men*.

In this period of time, Enoch, one of the family of Seth, and the seventh in a direct line from Adam, a person of singular piety and sanctity of life, not only took care of his own conduct, * as considering himself always under the eye and observation of a righteous God, but, by his good advices and admonitions, endeavoured likewise to put a stop to the torrent of impiety, and reform the vices of the age; for which reason God was pleased to shew a signal token of his kindness to him; for he exempted him from the common fate of mankind, and, without suffering death to pass upon him, translated him into the regions of bliss.

Adam's death,

In this period of time, Adam, who (according to the sentence denounced against him at the fall) was to return to his native dust, * departed this life, and (as the tradition

* This seems to be the natural sense of the expression of *walking with God*; and excellent to this purpose is this passage of Seneca, if we take what he tells us of the presence of God in a Christian sense: " Sic certe vivendum, *says he*, tanquam in " conspectu vivamus; sic cogitandum, tanquam aliquis in pec-" tus intimum infpicere possit, et potest. Quid enim prodest " ab homine aliquid esse secretum? nihil Deo clausum est. " Inest animis nostris, et cogitationibus mediis intervenit;" lib. 1. ep 83; *Le Clerc's Commentary*. But, considering how usual a thing it was, in these early ages of the world, for angels to be conversant with good men, it may not improperly be said of Enoch, and of Noah both, that they walked with God in this sense, *viz.* that they had oftentimes familiar converse with these messengers, who might be sent with instructions from him how they were to behave upon several occasions: for this answers the traditions of the Heathens, *viz.* that in the golden age, their gods had frequent intercourse with men:

Ille Deum vitam accipiet, divisque videbit
Permistos heroas, et ipse videbitur illis, *Virg. ecl.* 4.

And to the same purpose,

Sæpius et sese mortali oftendere cœtu
Cœlicolæ, nondum spreta pietate, solebant. *Catul. in Nup.
Thet. et Pelei*,

* Where Adam was buried cannot be collected from Scripture, St. Jerom [in Matt. xxvii.] seems to approve of the opinion of those who imagine that he was buried at Hebron, in the cave of Machpelah, or the double cave, which Abraham, many ages after,

dition is) having called his son Seth, and the other branches of his numerous family about him, he gave them strict charge, that they should always live separate, and have no manner of intercourse with the impious family of the murtherer Cain.

A. M. 130.
Ant Chrif.
3874.
Gen. ch. 5,
and 6, to
ver. 13.

In this period of time, Noah, the great-grandson of Enoch, and a person of equal virtue and piety, was born: and as it was discovered to Enoch at the birth of Methuselah, that soon after that child's death, the whole race of mankind should be destroyed for their wickedness; so was it revealed to Lamech, at the birth of his son, ^c that he and his family should be preserved from the common destruction, and so become the father of the new world; and for this reason † he called him *Noah*, which signifies *a comforter:*

Noah's birth and name.

ter, bought for a burying place for himself and family, Gen. xxiii. 3. &c. The oriental Christians say, that when Adam saw death approaching, he called his son Seth, and the rest of his family to him, and ordered them to embalm his body with myrrh, frankincense, and cassia, and deposit it in a certain cave, on the top of a mountain, which he had chosen for the repository of his remains, and which was thence called *the cave of Al-Konuz*, a word derived from the Arabian *Kanaza*, which signifies *to lay up privately*. And this precaution (as the Jews will have it) was ordered by Adam to be taken, lest his posterity should make his relicts the object of idolatry. Several of the primitive fathers believe, that he died in the place where Jerusalem was afterwards built, and that he was interred on mount Calvary, in the very spot where Christ was crucified; but others are of opinion, that (though he did not die at Jerusalem) yet Noah, at the time of the deluge, put his body into the ark, and took care to have it buried there by Melchisedec, the son of Shem, his grandson. The Mahometans will have his sepulchre to have been on a mountain near Mecca, and the ancient Persians, in Serendil, or Ceylon: so ambitious is every nation to have the father of all mankind reposited with them. When Eve, the mother of all living, died is no where expressed in Scripture; but there are some who venture to tell us, that she outlived her husband ten years; *vide the Universal History: and Calmet's Dictionary on the word* Adam.

^c Bedford's Scripture-chronology.

† The substance of Lamech's prophecy, according to our translation, is this; ―――― *He called his son Noah, saying, This same shall comfort us, concerning the work and toil of our hands, because of the ground which the Lord hath cursed;* and the sense of learned men upon it hath been very different. Some

A. M. 130.
A. t. Chrſt 3874.
Gen ch 5 an 6, to ver. 13

forter: though others imagine, that the name was therefore given him, becauſe his father, by the ſpirit of prophecy, foreknew, that God, in his days, would remove the curſe of barrenneſs from off the face of the earth, and, after the time of the deluge, reſtore it to its original fertility.

After are of opinion, that there is nothing prophetical in this declaration of Lamech's, and that the only cauſe of his rejoicing was, to ſee a ſon born, who might in time be aſſiſting to him in the toil of cultivating the ground. But in this there is nothing particular: in this ſenſe Lamech's words may be applied by every father at the birth of every ſon; nor can we conceive why a peculiar name ſhould be given Noah, if there was no particular reaſon for it. The Jewiſh interpreters generally expound it thus, *He ſhall make our labour in tilling the ground more eaſy to us,* in that he ſhall be the inventor of ſeveral proper tools and inſtruments of huſbandry, to abate the toil and labour of tillage: and ſome will tell us, that he therefore received his name, becauſe he firſt invented the art of making wine, a liquor that chears the heart and makes man forget ſorrow and trouble. But the invention of fit tools for tillage, after that Tubal-Cain had become ſo great an artificer in braſs and ſilver, ſeems to belong to one of his deſcendants, rather than Noah; and as Noah was not the firſt huſbandman in the world, ſo neither can it be concluded, from his having planted a vineyard, that he was the firſt vine-dreſſer. Another opinion, not altogether unlike this is,——that Lamech, being probably informed by God, that his ſon Noah ſhould obtain a grant of the creatures for food, Gen ix 5. and knowing the labour and inconveniencies they were under, rejoiced in foreſeeing what eaſe and comfort they ſhould have, when they obtained a large ſupply of food from the creatures, beſides what they could produce from the ground by tillage. The reſtoration of mankind by Noah, and his ſons ſurviving the flood, is thought by many to anſwer the comfort which Lamech promiſed himſelf and his poſterity; but the learned Heidegger, after an examination of all theſe, and ſome other opinions, ſuppoſeth that Lamech, having in mind the promiſe of God, expected that his ſon ſhould prove the bleſſed ſeed, the Saviour of the world, who was to bruiſe the ſerpent's head, and, by his atonement, expiate our ſins, which are the works of our own hands, and remove the curſe which lay upon ſinners. But this, in my opinion, is too forced an expoſition. Lamech, it is certain, in virtue of God's promiſe, expected a deliverance from the curſe of the earth, and foreſaw that that deliverance would come through his ſon: but how came it through his ſon, unleſs it came in his ſon's days? And in what inſtance

After the death of Adam, the family of Seth (to fulfil their father's will) removed from the plain where they had lived, to the mountains over against paradise, where Adam is said to have been buried; and for some time lived there in the fear of God, and in the strictest rules of piety and virtue. But as the family of Cain daily increased, they came at length to spread themselves over all the plain which Seth had left, even to the confines of the hill-country, where he had fixed his abode, and there they * lived in all kind of riot, luxury, and licentiousness.

*A. M. 930.
Ant. Chrif. 3074.
Gen. ch. 5.
& 6.
ver. 13.*

The wickedness of the Cainites.

The noise of their revellings might possibly reach the holy mountain where the Sethites dwelt; whereupon some of them might be tempted to go down, merely to gratify their

*A. M. 1042.
Ant. Ch. rif. 1962.*

The defection of the Sethites.

instance could it appear, unless it were something subsequent to the flood? And what could that possibly be, unless the removal of the sterility of the earth, and restoring it to its original fruitfulness? For which reason we find God, after the flood, declaring, that he *he will not curse the earth for man's sake;* and solemnly promising, that *while the earth remaineth, seed-time and harvest shall not cease,* Gen. viii. 22. Vid. Heidegger's Hist. patriar.; Patrick and Le Clerc's Commentary; Pool's Annotations; Shuckford's Connection; and Bishop Sherlock's Use and intent of prophecy, dissertation 4.

* Some of the oriental writers have given us a large account of their manner of living. " As to the posterity of Cain," say " they, the men did violently burn in lust towards the women, " and, in like manner, the women, without any shame, com-" mitted fornication with the men; so that they were guilty " of all manner of filthy crimes with one another, and meeting " together in public places for this purpose. two or three men " were concerned with the same woman, the ancient women, " if possible, being more lustful and brutish than the young. ' Nay, fathers lived promiscuously with their daughters, and " the young men with their mothers; so that neither the chil-" dren could distinguish their own parents, nor the parents " know their own children. So detestable were the deeds of " the Cainites, who spent their days in lust and wantonness, in " singing and dancing, and all kinds of music, until some of " the sons of Seth, hearing the noise of their music and riotous " mirth, agreed to go down to them from the holy mountain, " and, upon their arrival, were so captivated with the beauty " of their women, (who were naked) that they immediately " defiled themselves with them, and so were undone. For when " they offered to return again to their former abodes, the " stones of the mountain became like fire, and permitted them " to pass no farther;" *Eutych. Annals, p. 27.*

<small>A.M. 1042
Ant. Chrif.
2961.
Gen. ch. 5.
and 6 to
ver. 13.</small> their curiosity perhaps at first, but being taken with their deluding pleasures, and * intoxicated with the charms of their women, (who were extremely beautiful,) they forgot the charge which their forefathers had given them, and so took to themselves wives of the daughters of Cain; from which criminal mixture were born men of vast gigantic stature, who for some time infested the earth: and, in a few generations after, the whole family of Seth (very probably after the death of their pious ancestor) followed the like example, and, forgetting their obligations to the contrary, entered into society with the Cainites, and made intermarriages with them; from whence arose another race of men, no less remarkable for their daring wickedness then for their bold undertakings and adventurous actions.

<small>The general corruption of the world.</small> Evil communications naturally corrupt good manners: and so the example of the wicked family prevailed, and, by degrees, eat out all remains of religion in the posterity of Seth. Noah indeed, who was a good and pious man, endeavoured what he could, ^e both by his counsel and authority, to bring them to a reformation of their manners, and to restore the true religion among them; * but all he could do was to no purpose. The bent of their thoughts had taken another turn; and all their study and contrivance was, how to gratify their lusts and inordinate passions.

---

* Our excellent Milton describes the manner of their being captivated with the daughters of Cain in these words:

————————— They on the plain
Long had not walk'd, when from their tents, behold,
A bevy of fair women, richly gay,
In gems, and wanton dress: to th' harp they sung
Soft amorous ditties, and in dance came on.
The men, though grave, ey'd them; and let their eyes
Rove without rein; 'till in the amorous net
First caught, they lik'd, and each his liking chose. Book. 11.

^e Josephus's Antiq. l. 1. c. 4.

* Josephus tells us, that Noah, for a long while, opposed the growing impiety of the age; but that at last, finding himself and family in manifest danger of some mortal violence for his good-will, he departed out of the land himself, and all his people; *Antiq. l. 1. c. 4.*; and (as the tradition is) he settled in a country called *Cyparisson*, which had its name from the great quantity of cypress-trees which grew there, and whereof (as we shall observe hereafter) in all probability he built the ark.

passions. In one word, the whole race of mankind was become so very wicked, that one would have really thought they had been confederated together against heaven, to violate God's law, to profane his worship, and spurn at his authority; so that his patience and long suffering came at length to be wearied out: and though he is not a man, that he should repent, or the son of man, that he should grieve at any thing, yet his concern for the general corruption is represented under that notion, the better to accommodate it to our capacity, and to express his fixed resolution of destroying all mankind for their iniquity, and with them all other creatures made for their use, ‖ as if he had repented that ever he made them.

A.M. 1042.
Ant. Chrif.
2962.
Gen. ch. 5.
and 6 to
verse 13.

Before

‖ As languages were at first invented by such persons as were neither philosophers nor divines, we cannot at all wonder, that we meet with many improprieties in speech, and such actions imputed to God, as no ways comport with the dignity of his nature. Thus, when the Holy Scriptures speak of God, they ascribe hands, and eyes, and feet to him; not that he has any of these members, according to the literal signification; but the meaning is, that he has a power to execute all those acts, to the effecting of which, these parts in us are instrumental, *i. e.* he can converse with men, as well as if he had a tongue or mouth; can discern all that we do or say, as perfectly as if he had eyes and ears; and can reach us, as well as if he had hands or feet, &c. In like manner, the Scripture frequently represents him, as affected with such passions as we perceive in ourselves, viz. as angry and pleased, loving and hating, repenting and grieving, &c.; and yet, upon reflection, we cannot suppose, that any of these passions can literally affect the divine nature; and therefore the meaning is, that he will as certainly punish the wicked, as if he were inflamed with the passion of anger against them; as infallibly reward the good, as we will those for whom we have a particular affection; and that when he finds any alteration in his creatures, either for the better or the worse, he will as surely change his dispensations towards them, as if he really repented, or changed his mind. It is by way of analogy and comparison, therefore, that the nature and passions of men are ascribed to God: so that when he is said to repent or grieve, the meaning must be, not that he perceived any thing that he was ignorant of before, to give him any uneasiness, (for *known unto him are all his ways from the beginning,*) but only that he altered his conduct with regard to men, as they varied in their behaviour towards him, just as we are wont to do when we are moved by any of those passions

and

154   *The History of the BIBLE,*   Book I.

A.M. 1536.
Ant. Chrit. 2468.
Gen. ch. 5. and 6. to ver. 13.

Before he resolved upon their destruction, however, we find him in great struggle and conflict with himself; his justice calling for vengeance, and his mercy pleading for forbearance; till at length his justice prevailed, and denounced the sentence of condemnation upon the wicked world: but still with this reserve—— That if, ‖ within the space of 120 years, (which was the term limited for their repriveal,) they should forsake their evil ways, repent, and reform, his mercy should be at liberty to interpose, and reverse their doom. All which he communicated to his servant Noah, who, for his justice and singular piety in that corrupt and degenerate age, had found favour in his sight; and for whose sake his family, which consisted of eight persons in all, was to be exempted from the general destruction.

And God's resolution to destroy it.

The Objection.

The objection.

" BUT how great soever the wickedness of the ante-
" diluvian world might be, yet it comports but bad-
" ly with the goodness, and wisdom, and foreknowledge of
" God, to have created the race of mankind, and provid-
" ed such a delightful place for their habitation, and then,
" in

and changes of affections, we, *who dwell in houses of clay, and whose foundations are in the dust*: for the very Heathens can tell us, that *majestatis diminutio est, et confessio erroris, mutanda facere; necesse est enim ei eadem placere, cui, nisi optima placere non possunt;* Seneca in Præf. nat. quæst. *Vid.* Le Clerc's Commentary: Bishop King on Predestination: and Ainsworth's Annotations.

‖ This was the term allowed mankind for their repentance, and prevention of their ruin: and yet, if we compare ch. v. 32. with ch. vii. 11. we shall find, that between this time and the flood, there were but 100 years. How then did God perform his promise: Now, in answer to this, it may be said, that the increasing wickedness of mankind might justly hasten their ruin, and forfeit the benefit of this indulgence: but what I take to be the true solution is this: ———— This promise (though mentioned after what we read in ch. v. 32.) seems nevertheless to have been made 20 years before it: for that verse is added there out of its proper place, only to complete the genealogy: and therefore, after this narrative of the wickedness of the world, it is repeated here in its due order, in the 10th verse: nor are such transpositions uncommon in Scripture, without any diminution to its authority; *Pool's Annotations.*

"in so short a compass of time, to cancel the work of
"his own hands, by destroying the beauty of the one, and
"the lives of the other. For seven generations together
"(if ᶠ Josephus tells truth) men lived in the exercise of
"virtue, and in the love and fear of God. The family
"of Seth were very famous for their holiness, justice, and
"purity; and (as † eastern writers say) were continually
"employing themselves in the worship and praises of God.
"One of them, in particular, was so remarkable for his
"virtue and piety, that he had a privilege granted him,
"which the Son of God himself (when on earth) could
"not obtain, *viz.* a translation into immortality, without
"undergoing the pains of death; and yet, in a genera-
"tion or two following, we read, that ᵍ *All flesh had
"corrupted his way upon the earth, and that every imagina-
"tion of his heart was evil continually,* insomuch that *it re-
"pented and grieved the Lord that he had made man.* Now if
"God foresaw that man would so soon become so very
"wicked, why did he make him at all? Or, if foreseeing
"this, he nevertheless thought proper to make him, why
"was he so concerned at finding him to be just what he
"foresaw he would prove? To destroy the wicked race
"of Cain indeed, in some particular branch of it, for tes-
"timony of his displeasure against the rest, this might have
"been consistent with his wisdom and justice, and other
"sacred attributes: but to lay waste the whole earth all

A.M. 1536.
Ant. Chrif.
2468.
Gen. ch. 5.
and 6. to
ver. 13.

at

ᶠ Antiq. l. 1. c. 4.
† Immediately after the death of Adam, (say several of these writers,) Seth being wearied with the wickedness of the family of Cain, his neighbours, and fearing that now they would become more profligate, retired from the plain where he lived before, and taking with him his eldest son Enos, and Cainan the son of Enos, and Mahalaleel the son of Cainan, and their wives, brought them up unto the top of that mountain where Adam was buried; that these inhabitants of the mountains became very famous for their holiness, justice, and purity; that they continually employed themselves in the praises of God, and in cultivating their minds in sublime speculations; and that when they were removed to a greater distance from the earth, they were so very near the celestial paradise, that they heard the voices of angels celebrating the praises of God, and joined with them in their sacred hymns and heavenly benedictions. *Bedford's Scripture chronology.*

A.M. 1536.
Ant. Chrif.
2468.
Gen. ch. 5.
and 6. to
ver. 13.

"at once, and even the brute creation, which was not capable of offending? to pull down what he had for the space of 1656 years been establishing, and to put himself to the trouble of beginning again, and re-peopling the shattered and defaced earth from the loins of four progenitors only, argues too much levity and caprice, ever to be imputed to a wise and unchangeable God.

"The whole history of this period of time indeed (according to the account of Moses) is so glaringly romantic, and so repugnant to other parts of Scripture, that a man who ventures to think for himself, will hardly be induced to credit it. The Apostle to the Corinthians tells us, that [h] *flesh and blood cannot inherit the kingdom of God, neither doth corruption inherit incorruption:* and yet [i] here we have a man, who (according to the Christian interpretation) was immediately taken up into heaven (but in what vehicle? there is the question) without any change or alteration, that we read of. Christ, in his gospel, has told us expressly, that [k] *the angels of God neither marry, nor are given in marriage,* and the * simplicity of their nature must induce us to think, that they are not capable of generation; and yet [l] here again we are told, that the *sons of God took themselves wives of the daughters of men.* But, allowing the *sons of God* to signify the descendants of Seth, yet where was the great damage in their marrying the daughters of Cain? We read of no law to prohibit such marriages, *and where no law is, there can be no transgression;* and yet the destruction of the world is represented as proceeding from this one cause. The poets indeed do frequently entertain us with many pleasant stories of their gods turning gallants to ladies, of their assuming human shape, living in obscurity for some time, and submitting to employs far beneath their quality, and all for the love of the fair sex; but, in a

"book

[h] 1 Cor. xv. 50.   [i] Gen. v. 24.   [k] Matth. xxii. 30.

* The learned Heidegger, in his Dissertation *De Nephilim, seu gigantibus antediluvianis*, has abundantly shewn from Scripture, from reason, and from the nature of angels, that neither simply by themselves, nor incorporate in any human body, are they capable of begetting children; nor could it have been consistent with the attributes of God, for him to have permitted any such abomination.

[l] Gen vi. 2.

Chap. V.   *from the Creation to the Flood.*   157

" book of divine extract and sacred truth, we little expec- A M 1536.
" ted to be told of amorous intrigues. The giants of old, Ant. Crist.
" of what monstrous size and strength they were, how Gen ch. 5.
" they fought against the gods, and piled † mountain up- and 6. to
" on mountain, in order to scale heaven, and dethrone ver. 13.
" them, is a popular subject among the sons of Parnassus;
" but who ever thought to have met ᵐ with the foun-
" dation of all these fictions in so grave an author as Mo-
" ses? In short, his whole account of the translation of
" Enoch, and the deluge of Noah; of the sons of God,
" and the daughters of men; of giants and *incubuses*,
" and other such monstrous absurdities, favour very strong
" of the fabulous age, and seem to be calculated for no
" other purpose than merely to banter the easy faith of the
" vulgar, and to gratify such as delight in fiction."

That God of his infinite wisdom might, for very good Answered,
reasons, think proper to create man at first, and in all the by shewing
full perfection of his nature, notwithstanding he could not how the
                                                          antediluvi-
                                                    but   an world
                                                          came to be
† The poets have described the attempt of the ancient giants so wicked.
in such strains as these:

 Neve foret terris securior arduus æther.
 Affectasse ferunt regnum cœleste gigantes,
 Altaque congestos struxisse ad sydera montes *Ovid, Met. l. 1.*
 —————Immania vidi
 Corpora qui manibus magnum rescindere cœlum
 Agressi, superisque Jovem detrudere regnis.
 Ter sunt conati imponere Pelio Ossam
 Scilicet; atque Ossæ frondosum involvere Olympum;
 Ter pater extructos disjecit fulmine montes. *Virg. Æn. 6.*
  et Geor 1.

 Magnum illa terrorem intulerat Jovi
 Fidens juventus horrida brachiis,
  Fratreique tendentes opaco
  Pelion imposuisse Olympo.
 Sed quid Typhœus, quid validus Mimas,
 Aut quid minaci Porphyrion statu,
  Quid Rhœcus, evulsisque truncis
  Enceladus jaculator audax,
 Contra sonantem Palladis Ægida
 Possent ruentes? *Hor. Car. l. 3. ode* 4.

 ᵐ Gen. vi. 4.

A M.1536
Ant. Chril
2468.
Gen. ch. 5.
and 6. to
ver 13.

but foresee, that he would sadly degenerate, and turn rebel to his will, is a question we have already endeavoured to resolve, ⁿ when we treated of the fall of Adam; and by what means his posterity, in the succession of so few generations, as passed from the creation to the flood, became so very corrupt, as to lay God under a necessity to destroy them, may in a great measure be imputed to the length of their lives, and the strength and vigour of their constitutions. For, supposing all mankind, since the original defection, to be born in a state of depraved nature, with their understandings impaired, their wills perverted, and their passions inflamed; ° we can scarce imagine any restraint consistent with human freedom, sufficient to check their unruly appetites in that height of vigour, and confidence of long life. For if we, who rarely, and with no small difficulty, stretch out the span of seventy years, are hardly with-held from violence and villainy by all the dictates of reason and terrors of religion, what can we conceive sufficient to have kept them back, in their strength and security in sin from a continued series of 8 or 9 hundred years? No interposition of Providence can be supposed available to the reformation of mankind under these circumstances, unless it were such as would either change their nature, or destroy their freedom; and therefore we have reason to believe, that in the space of about 1800 years from the creation, God found them degenerated to such a degree, as if they had lost all sense of their humanity; for this some have made the import of the text, *my spirit shall not always strive with man, for that he also is flesh,* i. e. it is in vain to use any farther methods of mercy, or monitions of providence with man, who is now entirely given up to fleshly appetites, and by that means sunk down into the lowest condition of brutality.

By what gradations man arrived at his height of corruption, is not so evident from Scripture: but there are two passages, ᵖ *the earth was corrupt before God, and the earth was filled with violence;* which seem to point out some particular vices: for by *violence* is plainly meant cruelty, and outrage, and injustice of every kind; and by *corruption,* the Jews always understand, either idolatry, or unlawful mixtures and pollutions; the latter of which seems to be denoted here because of the subsequent explication

ⁿ *Vid.* pag. 87, 88. ° Revelation examined, vol. 1.
ᵖ Gen. vi. 11.

Chap. V.   *from the Creation to the Flood.*   159

cation of the words, *for all flesh had corrupted his way upon the earth.*

   Now, if we look into the history, we shall find, that the first act of violence was committed by Cain upon his brother Abel; the first act of incontinence by Lamech, in the matter of his polygamy; and that as one of his sons invented the instruments of luxury, so the other invented the instruments of violence and war. As luxury therefore naturally begets a disposition to injure others in their property, and such a disposition, armed with offensive weapons, in the hands of men of a gigantic stature and strength, (as many of the antediluvians very probably were, tends to beget all manner of insolence and outrage to our fellow-creatures; so these two cardinal vices might naturally enough introduce that train of corruption which drew God's judgements upon the inhabitants of the earth.

   Had God indeed given them no intimations of this his design, no calls to repentance, no means and opportunities of becoming better, before he determined their destruction, something might then be said in opposition to the righteousness of this procedure; but ᑫ since, from the very beginning, he was pleased, in the sentence he passed upon the serpent, to give them a remarkable promise, that the seed of the woman should destroy the power of that evil spirit which brought sin into the world, and consequently, ʳ that all parents were obliged to train up their children in the ways of virtue and religion, without which it was impossible for any of them to be the promised seed, which was to restore mankind to their original perfections; since he himself instituted sacrifices, as a means admirably well fitted to inspire mankind with an horror of guilt, and be, at the same time, a perpetual memorial of the divine mercy from generation to generation; since, in his expulsion of Cain from his presence, and exaltation of Enoch into heaven, he made an open declaration to all future ages, that his vengeance should at all times pursue sin, but his bounty had always in store an ample reward for the righteous; since at this time he exhibited himself to mankind in a more sensible manner than he does now, causing them to hear voices, and to dream dreams, and, by sundry extraordinary means, convincing them of

A. M. 1536.
Ant. Chrif.
2468
Gen. ch. 5.
and 6. to
ver. 13.

God's justice vindicated in destroying all mankind.

M m 2   their

ᑫ Shuckford's Connect. vol. 1. l. 1.   ʳ Revelation examined, vol. 1.

<small>A. M. 1536.
Ant. Chr. f
2468.
Gen. ch. 5.
and 6 to
ver. 13</small>

their duty, and giving them directions for the conduct of their lives; since, at this time, they had the principles of religion (which were but very few) conveyed to them by an easy tradition, which, by Methuselah's living 248 years with Adam, and dying but a little before the flood, in the compass of 1600 years and more, had but two hands to pass through: and, lastly, since God appointed Noah in particular to be *a preacher of righteousness*,[s] as the Apostle styles him, to exhort that wicked race to forsake their sins, and return unto him; to warn them of their impending doom, if they persisted in their provocations; to give them notice, that 120 years was the stated time of their reprieve, and that, at the end of that period, his fixed determination was to destroy them utterly, unless their amendment averted the judgement: Since these and many more methods of mercy were all along employed by God (and especially in the days that his long-suffering waited, while the ark was preparing) for the recovery of mankind, before the deluge came upon them, they are sufficient to vindicate the ways of God with man, and to justify his severity in bringing in the flood upon the world of the ungodly, which neither his restraints nor rewards, nor all the monitions and exhortations of his prophets, added to his own declarations, institutions, inflictions, and denunciations of vengeance, could reclaim, in the course of so many centuries.

<small>and other living creatures.</small>

Other living creatures, it is true, were not culpable in this manner: They all answered the ends of their production, and man was the only rebel against his maker. But as, in an universal deluge, it was impossible to preserve them alive without a miracle; so, having, in some measure, been made instrumental to man's wickedness, innocent though they were, they were all to be destroyed, in order to evince the malignity of sin, and God's abhorrence of it. For the great end of his providence, in sending the deluge was not so much to ease himself of his adversaries, as to leave a perpetual monument of his unrelenting severity, that thereby he might deter future ages from the like provocations. And this is the inference which the Apostle draws from all his judgements of old: "*If God spared not the angels*, says he, *that sinned, but cast them down to Hell; if he spared not the old world, but brought in a flood*
upon

<small>[s] 2 Pet. ii. 5.   [t] Le Clerc's Commentary.   [u] 2 Pet. ii. 4. &c.</small>

Chap. V.   *from the Creation to the Flood.*   161

upon the ungodly; if he turned the cities if Sodom and Gomor- A M. 1536.
rha into ashes, and condemned them with an overthrow; these are ant Chrif.
an ensample unto those, that after shall live ungodly; for ;how- Gen. ch. 5.
ever they may escape in this life, he hath reserved the unjust d 6 to
unto the day of judgement to be punished. ver. 13.

The Scripture indeed seems to impute all this iniquity
to the marriages between the sons of God and the daugh- The sons of
ters of men; but the misfortune is, that several interpre- evil angels;
ters, being led away by the authority of the LXX. who
(according to Philo) did anciently render what we style the
sons of God, by ἄγγελοι τοῦ Θεοῦ have supposed, that wicked
and apostate angels assumed, at this time, human bodies,
and, having had carnal communication with women, begat of them a race of giants; and from this original, the
notion of *incubi,* or devils conversing with women in the
like manner, has ever since been derived. St. Austin,
† among many others, is very positive in this opinion.
"³ Several people have had the trial," says he, "and se-
"veral have heard it from those who knew it to be true,
"that the *silvani* and *fauni,* commonly called *incubi,* have
"been often fatal to women, and have defiled their bed.
"It is likewise affirmed with so much confidence, that
"certain demons (called *durii* among the Gauls, have not
"only attempted, but likewise perpetrated these kinds of
"impure actions, that it would be foolish to make any
"question of it." But besides the incompatibleness of
the notion of a spirit, and the nature of an *incubus, the
sons of God* are here represented under circumstances quite
different to what we may suppose of any demons assuming
human shape.

ᵞ An *incubus* (if any such there be) can desire commerce with a woman, for no other reason, but only to
draw

† Dr Whitby, in his Scripturæ patrum. p. 5. has instanced
in almost all the fathers of the four first centuries, who were of
this opinion; such as Justin Martyr, Irenæus, Athenagoras,
Clemens Alexandrinus, Tertullian, St Cyprian, Lactantius,
Eusebius, &c and supposes that this notion took its rise from
the vain traditions of the Jews; because we find not only Philo reading the word ἄγγελοι in the Septuagint version,
but Josephus likewise asserting, "that the angels of God mix-
"ing with women, begat an insolent race (not much unlike
"that of the giants in the Greek fables) overbearing right with
"power;" Antiq. l. 1. c. 4.

³ De civitate Dei, l. 15. c. 23.   ᵞ Heidegger's Hist.
patriar.

A.M. 1536. Ant. Chrif 2468. Gen. ch. 5. and 6 to ver. 13

draw her into the gulf of perdition. Any carnal gratification of his own cannot be his motive, becaufe pleafure, in an affumed body, if it is pretended to, muft be fictitious: But here *the fons of God* are faid to be enamoured with the daughters of men, and (to fatisfy their lufts) *to take to themfelves wives of all that they chufe*, which denoting a fettled marriage and cohabitation with them, can hardly be imagined in the cafe before us. From thofe marriages we may farther obferve, that a generation of living men, called in Scripture *men of renown*, did enfue; but it is impious to think, that God would ever concur with the devil, violating the laws of generation which he had eftablifhed, and proftituting the dignity of human nature, by ftamping his own image upon, or infufing an human foul into whatever matter a fiend fhould think fit to engenerate.

not great men and magiftrates

In prejudice taken to this opinion, therefore, feveral interpreters have made choice of another, which, though fomewhat more reafonable, is neverthelefs fubject to exceptions. It fuppofes, that, by the *fons of God* in this place, are meant the princes, great men, and magiftrates in thofe times, who, inftead of ufing their authority to punifh and difcountenance vice, were themfelves the greateft examples and promoters of lewdnefs and debauchery; taking *the daughters of men*, or of the inferior and meaner fort of the people, and debauching them by force. But ᵃ befides the harfhnefs of the conftruction, which (contrary to Scripture-phrafe) makes all great and powerful fons to be called *the fons of God*, and all mean and plebeian women *the daughters of men*, there is this error in the fuppofition, that the great men we are now fpeaking of, did not offer any force or violence to thefe inferior women; *they faw that they were fair, and made choice of them for wives*. They did not take them merely to lie with them, and fo difmifs them; but voluntarily entered into a ftate of matrimony and cohabitation with them. And this being all the matter wherein is the heinoufnefs of the offence, if men of a fuperior rank marry with their inferiors, efpecially when an excefs of beauty apologizes for their choice? Or, why fhould a few unequal matches be reckoned among fome of the chief caufes which brought upon the world an univerfal deftruction?

But the defcendants f Seth.

The moft common, therefore, and indeed the only probable opinion is, that the *fons of God* were the defcendants

ᵃ Ibid.

dants of Seth, who, for the great piety wherein they continued for some time, were so called, and that *the daughters of men* were the progeny of wicked Cain: And why the intermarriages of these two families (even though there was no express prohibition from God) came to be so provoking to him, and in the end so destructive to themselves, is the next point of our inquiry.

<small>A.M. 1536. Ant. Chris. 2468 Gen. ch. 5. and 6. to verse 13</small>

It has been a question among the learned, whether or no, in the ages before the flood, idolatry was practised? but there seems to be no great foundation for our doubting it, though some have endeavoured to establish it upon incompetent texts. The only expression in Scripture that bears a proper aspect this way is in Gen. vi. 5. where we are told, *That God saw, that the wickedness of man was great in the earth, and that every imagination of the thoughts of his heart was only evil continually.* The words seem parallel to that passage of the Apostle, [a] *they became vain in their imaginations, and their foolish heart was darkened;* —— whereupon it follows, *that they changed the glory of the incorruptible God into an image, made like to corruptible man, and to birds, and four-footed beasts, and creeping things.* Since therefore Moses makes use of [b] the like expression concerning the age soon after the flood, men fell into idolatry, until the true worship of God was again established in Abraham's family, it seems very probable that he intended us an intimation hereof in the manner of his expressing himself: Nor can we imagine but that, when St. Peter compares the false teachers of his age with the people of the antediluvian world, in the nature of their punishment, he means to inform us, that they resembled them likewise in the nature of their crime, in their [c] *bringing in damnable heresies,* and abetting such doctrines, as *even denied the Lord that bought them;* or that, when St. Jude [d] expresses his indignation against certain *ungodly men* in his days, *who denied the only Lord God, and our Lord Jesus Christ,* in such words as these, *Woe unto them, for they are gone in the way of Cain;* he leaves us to infer, that Cain and his posterity were the first that threw off the sense of a God, and, instead of the Creator, began to worship the creature.

<small>The idolatry of the Cainites.</small>

Now if the Cainites were, at this time, not only profligate in their manners, but abettors of infidelity, and promoters

---

[a] Rom. i. 21, 23.   [b] Gen. viii. 21.   [c] 2 Pet. ii. 1, 5.
[d] Ver. 4, 11.

A. M. 1516.
Ant. Chrif
2468.
Gen. ch. 5
and 6 to
ver. 13

promoters of idolatry; for the family of Seth, who professed the true worship of God, to enter into communion, or any matrimonial compacts with them, could not but prove of fatal consequence. 'Tis a solemn injunction which God gives the Israelites, against all idolatrous nations, *Thou shalt not make marriages with them; thy daughter thou shalt not give unto his son, nor his daughter shalt thou take unto thy son:* And, that this is no special but a general prohibition, extensive to all nations that profess the true worship of God, is evident from the reason that is annexed to it; *for they will turn away thy son from following me, that they may serve other gods.* This was what Balaam knew full well, and therefore, perceiving that he could injure the children of Israel no other way, he advised the Moabites to commence a familiarity with them; whereupon it soon came to pass, that *The people began to commit whoredom with the daughters of Moab, and they called the people unto the sacrifices of their gods, and the people did eat, and bowed down to their gods.*

'Twas the danger of seduction into a state of idolatry that made Abraham, before the law, so very anxious and uneasy, lest his son Isaac should marry a Canaanitish woman; and though we, under the gospel, ᵍ *know very well, that an idol is nothing in the world, and that there is none other God but one,* yet we are admonished by the same Apostle, who teaches us this, *Not to be unequally yoked together with unbelievers; for what fellowship,* says he, *has righteousness with unrighteousness, what communion hath light with darkness, or what part hath he that believeth with an infidel?* ʰ From all which it seems to follow, that the sin was very heinous in the family of Seth, to mix with the wicked seed of Cain, when they could not but foresee, that the consequence would be their seduction from the true worship of God; and that the heinousness of their sin seems still to be enhanced, if, what some oriental writers tell us be true, viz. that God gave them this prohibition by the mouth of their great forefather Adam, and that their custom was, at certain times, to swear by *the blood of Abel* (which was their solemn oath) that they would never leave the mountainous country where they inhabited, nor have any communion with the descendants of Cain.

How

ᵉ Deut. vii 3. 4.   ᶠ Num. xxv. 1, 2.   ᵍ 1 Cor. viii. 4.
ʰ 2 Cor. vi. 14, &c.

Chap. V.   *from the Creation to the Flood.*

How the commixture of the two different families came to produce a set of giants is not so easy a matter to determine. Those who pretend to reduce it to natural causes, or the eager lust and *impetus* of their parents, are vastly mistaken, ¹ because giants there were among the Cainites, before this conjunction, and we read of several in other nations many ages after the flood. The more probable opinion therefore is, ᵏ that God permitted it in vengeance to their parent's crimes, and that the children begotten by such unlawful mixtures might, (some of them at least,) be accounted monstrous in their kind, (for thus the word *Nephilim* certainly signifies,) and so become the abhorrence of all future generations.

A. M. 1536.
ant. Christ.
2468.
Gen. ch. 5.
and 6 to ver. 13

The giants whence they sprung

It must be acknowleged, indeed, that translators have not agreed in their notions of this word. Aquila, instead of *gigantes*, renders it ˡ *men who attack*, or fall with impetuosity upon their enimies; and Symmachus will have it mean ᵐ *violent and cruel men*, the only rule of whose actions is their strength and force of arms: And from hence some have imagined, that the giants spoken of in Scripture were famous for the crimes and violences they committed rather than the height or largeness of their stature. But to hinder this from passing for a truth, we have the histories of all ages, both sacred and profane, and several other remains and monuments, to evince † the being of such prodigious creatures in almost every country.

ⁿ That there were multitudes of giants in the land of promise, before the Israelites took possession of it, such as Og king of Basan, and the Anakims, whom ᵒ the Moabites called *Enims*, i. e. *terrible men*, and ᵖ the Ammonites, *Zamzummims*, i. e. *the inventors of all wickedness*, whose posterity were in being in the days of David, and whose bones were to be seen at Hebron, the chief place of

The real existence of them.

ˡ Gen vi 4.   ᵏ Vid. Heidegger's Vit. patriar. and Patrick's Commentary.   ˡ Ἐπιπίπτοντες   ᵐ Βίαιοι

† Mr Whiston, in his original records, has a supplement concerning the old giants, wherein, according to the Apocryphal book of Enoch, he divides the giants into three kinds, and in this division thinks himself countenanced by the works of Moses, Gen. vi. 2, &c.; the first and lowest kind of which are called *Eliudim*, and are of stature from 4 cubits to 15; the second are *Nephilim* from 15 to 40 cubits; and the third, or great giants, 40 cubits at least, and many times above.

ⁿ Huetii Aletan. Quest.   ᵒ Deut. ii. 11.   ᵖ Ver. 21.

A.M.1536
Ant Chrif
2468.
Gen ch. 5.
and 6. to
ver. 13.

ענק

of their abode, is manifest from the sacred records. ^q *All the people* (say the spies who were sent to take a survey of the land) *are men of stature; and there we saw the giants, the sons of Anak, which came of the giants,* so unmeasurably large, that *we were but like grasshoppers* in comparison of them. And therefore we need less wonder, that we find ^r Josephus, upon the same occasion, telling us, "That " the race of giants was not then extinct, who, on ac- " count of their largeness and shapes (not at all to be " likened to those of other men) were amazing to see, and " terrible to hear of." Homer ^s speaks of the giants Otus and Ephialtes, who, at the age of nine years, were nine cubits about, and six and thirty in height; he likewise describes ^t the bigness of the Cyclops Polyphemus, who was of such prodigious strength, that he could, with the greatest facility, take up a stone which two and twenty fourwheeled chariots would scarce be able to move. This we allow to be, in some measure, romantic, but still it confirms the tradition, that several persons of old were of a gigantic stature.

" That the Cyclopes and Læstrigones," ^u says Bochart, " were once in Sicily, we have the account, not only in " the poets, Homer, Hesiod, and Euripides, Virgil, Ovid, " and Silius, but in the historians and geographers (I " mean Thucydides and Strabo) who were Grecians, and " in Trogus, Mela, Pliny and others, who were Romans; " And that there was something of truth in the fables con- " cerning them, we are assured by those bones of giants, " which were dug out of the earth in the memory of our " fathers." ^x

But

^q Numb. xiii. 33.   ^r Antiq. l. 5. c. 2.   ^s Odyss l. 11.
^t Ibid. l. 9.   ^u Cannan i. 30.

^x Fazellus relates, and out of him Cluverius, that, A. D. 1547, near Panormum in Sicily, the body of a giant was dug up, about 18 cubits or 27 feet tall. The same authors relate, that, A D 1516, was dug up, near Mazarene in Sicily, the body of a giant. 20 cubits or 30 feet tall. The same authors relate, that, A. D 1548, near Syracuse, was dug up another body of the same dimension. They inform us, that A. D. 1550, near Enteila in Sicily was dug up a body of about 22 cubits or 33 feet high, whose skull was about 10 feet in circumference; and they describe the corps of a giant of portentous magnitude, found standing in a vast cave, near Drepanum in Sicily, A. D. 1342, whose staff was like the mast of a ship,

and

But I forbear more instances of this kind, and, * referring the reader, for his farther conviction, to such authors as have professedly handled this subject, shall only crave leave to make this remark —— ʸ that, in all probability, no small part of the eldest cities, towers, temples, obelisks, pyramids, and pillars, some of which are still remaining, and deservedly esteemed the wonders of the world, † were the structure of these ancient giants; and, as they surpass the abilities of all later ages, so they seem to me to be the visible and undeniable remains, monuments, and demonstrations, not only of their existence, but of their prodigious stature and strength likewise; since in an age, ignorant of mechanical powers and engines, such vast piles of building could no otherwise have been erected.

Without concerning ourselves then with the fictions and fables of the poets, or ᶻ whether the giants of old rebelling against heaven, were able to heap mountains upon

A.M. 1536.
Ant. Chrif.
2468.
Gen. ch. 5.
and 6 to
ver 13.

mountains

and the forepart of whose skull would contain some Sicilian bushels, which are about a third part of our English bushel. *Vide* Whiston's Supplement concerning the old giants, in his Authentic Records, part 2.

* They that desire to see more instances of this kind may find them cited by Huetius, in his Quest. Aletan. l. 2.; Aug De civit. Dei l. 15.; Joseph. Antiq. l. 1. c. 5 18.; Pliny, l. 1.; Heidegger's Hist. patr. exercit. 11.; Grotius De veritate. l. 1.; Hackwell's Apolog. l. 3 ; Whiston's Original Records, part 2.; and our Philosophical Transactions, N. 234. 272 274. 346. and 370.

ʸ Whiston's Supplement part 2.

† The works of this kind which our author reckons up, are, 1 The *Giants Dance* upon Salisbury Plain in England, now called *Stone-henge*. 2 The *Giants Causeway* in the north of Ireland. 3. The *Circular Gigantic Stone* at Ravenna   4. The *Tower of Babel* 5. The Two *Obelisks* mentioned by Herodotus. 6. The *Temple of Diana* in Egypt. 7. The *Labyrinth* in Egypt. 8. The Lake *Mœris*, 480 miles long, and dug by human labour, all by the same Herodotus. 9. The *Sphinx* of Egypt. 10. The *most ancient Temple* in Egypt.   11. The *Agrigentine Temple*. 11. The *Pyramidal Obelisk*, all mentioned by Diodorus Siculus. 13. The *Temple of Solomon*. 14. The *Palace of Solomon* at Jerusalem. 15 That at Balbeck. 16. That at Tadmor 17 The *Palace* and *Buildings* at Persepolis. 18. The *Temple of Belus* at Babylon. 19. The *Temple* at Chillembrum. And 20 The *first Temple of Diana* at Ephesus ; Whiston's Sup.

ᶻ Calmet's Dissertation sur les geans, vol. 2.

A.M. 1136.
Ant. Chrif.
2468.
Gen. ch 5.
and 6.
to verse 13

mountains, in order to scale it, or to hurl rocks, and islands, and huge flaming trees against it, in order to shake, or set it on fire; all that we pretend to say is, that in ancient days, there were giants, in great numbers, who (excepting the largeness of their stature) were formed and fashioned like other men, and waged no other war with heaven, than what all wicked persons are known to do, when they provoke the Divine Majesty by their crimes and enormous impieties. This is the whole of what the Scriptures assert, and I know no occasion we have to defend the wild hyperboles of the poets.

The reality of Enoch's translation, and what it means.

Amidst the antediluvian corruption, and even while these abominable and gigantic men were in being, Moses makes particular mention of one person of eminent sanctity, and who found a favour extraordinary, for having preserved his innocence, and persisted in his duty, notwithstanding the wickedness of the age wherein he lived. Enoch was certainly, in other respects, an extraordinary person. [a] St Jude distinguishes him as a prophet: [b] the Arabians represent him as a great scholar; the Babylonians look upon him as the author of their astrology; the Greeks call him their *Atlas*, and affirm, that he was the first who taught men the knowlege of the stars; but it was not for these rare qualities, so much as for his singular piety and virtue, that God exempted him from the common fate of mankind.

The Jewish doctors indeed will have the words of Moses concerning him to import no more, than his sudden and untimely death, because he lived not near so long as the other patriarchs. But the paraphrase which St Paul gives us of them, [c] *By faith Enoch was translated, that he should not see death, and was not found, because God had translated him; for, before his translation, he had this testimony, that he pleased God;* this paraphrase, I say, will not suffer us to doubt of the truth of the Christian interpretation. And indeed, [d] unless the Christian interpretation be true, the whole emphasis of Moses's words is lost, and they become a crude tautology. For, if we say, that *Enoch was not*, i. e. was no longer living, because *God took him*, i. e. God caused him to die; it is the same, as if we should say, *God caused him to die, because he took him away by death,* which is flat and insipid, a proof of the same thing by the same

---

[a] Ver. 14, &c. [b] Calmet's Dictionary on the word *Enoch*.
[c] Heb. xi 5. [d] Heidegger's Hist. patriar. exercit. 9.

Chap. V.   *from the Creation to the Flood.*   169

same thing, and hardly confiftent with common fenfe; A.M. 1536.
whereas, if we interpret the words in this manner ant Chrif.
Enoch was not, i. e. was no where to be found, was feen Gen. ch. 5.
neither among the living nor the dead here on earth, *for* and 6. to
God took him, i. e. becaufe God tranflated to another place, ver. 13.
foul and body together, without undergoing the pains of
death; here is a grace and energy in the expreffion, not
unbecoming the ftyle of an infpired penman.

The reafon which Mofes affigns for God's taking him,
in this wife, is, that *he walked with God:* But if God's taking him means no more than his hafty death, it was far
from being a divine atteftation of his piety, (becaufe length
of days are the promifed reward of that;) and therefore we
may be allowed to infer, that his walking with God was
not the caufe of his ablation by death, but of his affumption into glory. The truth is, ᵉ about 57 years before
this event, Adam, the father of all living, had fubmitted
to the fentence denounced againft him, and refigned his
breath; and whatever notions his pofterity might have of
a life immortal in reverfion, yet it feemed expedient to the
divine wifdom, at this time, in the perfon of Enoch, to
give them, as it were, anticipation of it, and to fupport and
comfort them under the fenfe of their mortality, with the
profpect, and affured hope, that after the dark entry of
death was paffed, they were to be admitted into the man-
fions of blifs.

Our Saviour, indeed, when he came upon earth, though Why Chrift
declared from heaven to be the Son of God, who was was not ex-
not exempted from the common condition of our morta- empted
lity. ᶠ *Forafmuch as the children are partakers of flefh and blood* from death.
he alfo himfelf likewife took part of the fame, that through death,
he might deftroy him who had the power of death, i. e. the devil. His errand was to propitiate for our fins; but fince,
ᵍ *without fhedding of blood there is no remiffion*, the decree was,
that he fhould die, which when he had fatisfied he rofe a-
gain; and after forty days converfe with his difciples *even*
ʰ *while they beheld him*, we are told, *he was taken up into*
heaven, and a cloud received him out of their fight. And, in
like manner, if the end of Enoch's affumption was for the
conviction of mankind in that great article of faith, the
reality of another world, it feems reafonable to believe,
that the thing was done publicly and vifibly; that either
fome bright and radiant cloud, guided by the miniftry of
angels,

ᵉ Patrick's Commentary.   ᶠ Heb. ii. 14.   ᵍ Ch. ix. 22.
ʰ Acts xix. and Luke xxiv. 51.

A.M. 15:6
Art. Chr.
2468.
Gen. ch. 5
and 6 to
ver. 11.

angels, gently raised him from the earth, and mounted with him upon high, (which seems to be our Saviour's case,) or that a *strong gust of wind*, governed by the same angelic powers, in some vehicle or other, resembling a bright *chariot and horses*, transported him into heaven, (which seems to be the case of Elijah,) and that, in his passage thither, his body was transformed, his corruptible into incorruption, his mortal into immortality *in a moment, in the twinkling of an eye*, [k] as we are told it will happen to those who are alive, when the *last trumpet shall sound*.

The place to which Enoch was translated;

It is an idle conceit therefore of some of the Jewish, as well as Christian doctors, that Enoch was not translated into the celestial, but only into the old terrestrial paradise, wherein Adam, before his transgression lived. Whether the beauty of that place went to ruin, or no, as soon as our first parents were ejected, and no hand left to dress it, it is certain, it could never withstand the violence of the flood; and consequently Enoch must have perished in it, unless we can suppose, * that he was preserved by some such miracle as the Israelites were, when they passed through the Red-sea, and that the waves, towering up on all sides, surrounded it like a wall, and kept that particular spot dry; which is by too much bold a supposition, especially when it contradicts that authority, which tells us, that [l] *the waters prevailed exceedingly upon the earth, and that all the high hills, which were under the whole heavens, were covered.*

and some Heathen evidences thereof:

Whatever therefore some may fancy to themselves, we acknowledge now no other paradise, than what is represented in the Scriptures, as a place in which God gives the brightest evidence of his presence, and communicates his glory with the utmost majesty: a place which St. Paul calls [m] *the third heaven*, whereunto Elijah was translated,

---

[l] 2 Kings ii. 11.   [k] 1 Cor. xv. 52.

* Bonferius ait, Verisimile esse paradisum ab imbribus servatum immunem, undique ad latera sese attollentibus aquis, et quasi in murum solidatis, quemadmodum soliæ aquæ Maris Rubri Israelitis in medio aquarum transeuntibus Verum non hic quid verisimile sit quæritur, sed quid pro certo affirmari possit. Ubi miraculi nullum vestigium apparet, non licet propria opinione verisimilitudinis illud astruere; *Heidegger, Vit. patriar De raptu Enochi, exercit.*

[l] Gen. vi. 19.   [m] 2 Cor. xii. 2.

lated, and wherin our blessed Saviour is now *preparing mansions for us, that where he is, we may be also*. Into this happy place we suppose Enoch to have been conveyed, and it is no mean confirmation of the truth of the Mosaic account, that we find, among the Heathen world, notions of the like translation: that we find Bacchus assuring Cadmus, that by the help of Mars, he should live for ever in the *isles of the blessed:* that we find Aganympha made immortal by the favour of Jupiter; and, after the death of her husband, Herculus, Alcmena, translated by Mercury, and married to Rhadamantus; with many more allusions of the like nature [o].

A.M.|1536.
Ant. Chri[st]
1408.
Gen. ch 5.
and 6. to
ver 13

And in like manner, it is far from being a bad argument for the truth and reality of the flood [p], that we find, almost every where in the Latin and Greek historians, horrid descriptions of the lives of the giants, which occasioned that heavy judgement: that we find Berosus the Chaldean, as he is quoted by [q] Josephus, relating the same things which Moses does, concerning the great deluge, the destruction of mankind by it, and the ark, in which Nochus (the same with Noah) was preserved, and which rested on the tops of the Armenian mountains: that we find Abydenus, the Assyrian (as he is cited [r] by Eusebius) taking notice of the wood of the vessel, wherein Xisuthrus († for so he calls Noah) was saved, and telling us, that the people of Armenia made use of it for amulets to drive away diseases, that we find Alexander Polyhistor, in a passage produced [s] by Cyril, informing us of an Egyptian priest who related to Solon, out of the sacred books of the Egyptians, (as he supposes) that, before the particular deluges known and celebrated by the Grecians, there was of old an exceeding great inundation of waters, and devastation of the earth: and (to mention no more) that we find [t] Lucian giving us a long account of an ancient tradition, which

As likewise of the flood:

---

[o] John xiv. 2, 3. [o] Huetii Quæst. Aletanæ, l. 2. c. 10. [p] Grotius De verit.l. 1§. 16. [q] Cont. App. l. 1. [r] Prepar. Evange. l 9.

† M. Le Clerc in his notes upon Grot. De verit [l. 1. §. 16] seems to intimate, that *Xisuthrus, Ogyges,* and *Deucalion,* are all names signifying the same thing in other languages, as *Noah* does in Hebrew, wherein Moses wrote; and that the deluges which are said to have happened in their times, and are thought to be different, were in reality one and the same.

[s] Contra Julianum.
[t] De Dea Syria.

A. M. 1536.
Art. Chri.
2468.
Gen. ch. 5
and 6, &
ver. 13.

which the people of Hierapolis had of the deluge, * varying very little from what our sacred historian relates: when we find all this, I say, we cannot but acknowledge, that these, and the many more historians who are usually produced upon this head, are a strong testimony of the truth and authority of Moses; and therefore, to conclude this reply, or vindication of him, with the reflection of the learned ᵘ Scaliger upon the agreement he perceived between Moses and Abydenus, in the account they both give of the dove and the raven which Noah is said to have sent out; "Though the Greek historians (says he) do not " always agree in particulars with the sacred one, yet they
" are

* The account though somewhat long, is not unpleasant, and deserves our observation. This race of men (says he) which now is, was not the first: these are of a second generation, and from their first progenitor Deucalion, who increased to so great a multitude as we now see. Now of these former men they tell us this story —They were contentious, and did many unrighteous things: they neither kept their oaths, nor were hospitable to strangers: for which reason this great misfortune came upon them: All on a sudden the earth disembowelled itself of a great quantity of water, great showers fell, the rivers overflowed, and the sea swelled to a prodigious height; so that all things became water, and all men perished. Only Deucalion was left unto the second generation upon the account of his prudence and piety; and the manner in which he was saved was this——He had a great ark or chest, into which he came with his children and the women of his house, and then entered hogs, and horses, and lions, and serpents, and all other animals which live upon the earth, together with their mates. He received them all, and they did him no harm; for by the assistance of heaven there was a great amity between them, so that all failed in one chest as long as the water did predominate. This is the account which all the Greek historians give of Deucalion. But what happened afterwards (as it is told by the people of Hierapolis) is worthy our observation, viz. That in their country there was a chasm into which all this water sunk, whereupon Deucalion built an altar, and erected a temple over it, which he consecrated to Juno: and to verify this story, not only the priests but the other inhabitants likewise of Syria and Arabia, twice every year, bring abundance of water, which they pour into the temple, and though the chasm be but small, yet it receives a prodigious quantity of it; and when they do this, they relate how Deucalion first instituted this custom in memory of that calamity, and his deliverance from it.

ᵘ Not. in Fragm. in append. ad emend. temp.

"are rather to be pitied for not having had the advantage
"of true and authentic antiquities and records to set them
"right, than to forfeit their value and authority, from
"such slips and deviations from the truth of the story as
"render their testimony and confirmation of the truth of
"the sacred history much stronger, because much less to
"be suspected than if they agreed with it in every circum-
"stance."

A M 1536.
Ant. Chri.
2468.
Gen. ch. 5.
and 6 to
ver. 13.

DISSERTATION. V.

*Of the Heathen history, the chronology, religion, learning, longe-
vity, &c. of the antediluvians.*

WE are now arrived at a period, where it may be convenient to take some notice of such Heathen writers
as have given us an account of the times before the flood,
through which we have hitherto been tracing Moses: and
those that are esteemed of the best credit and repute, are
only three; Berosus, who wrote the history of the Chaldeans; Sanchoniatho, who compiled that of the Phœnicians; and Manetho who collected the antiquities of Egypt.

The Heathen historians from the creation to the flood.

The Chaldeans were certainly a nation of great and
undoubted antiquity. [x] In all probability they were the
first formed into a national government after the flood, and
therefore were more capable of having such arts and sciences flourish among them as might preserve the memory of
eldest times, to the latest posterity: and yet, even among
these people, who enjoyed all the advantages of ease,
quiet, and a flourishing empire, we find no credible and
undoubted records preserved. Berosus, their historian,
was, (as [y] Josephus assures us) a priest of Belus, and a Babylonian born, but afterwards flourished in the isle of Cos,
and was the first who brought the Chaldean astrology into
request among the Greeks; in honour of whose name and
memory, the Athenians (who were great encouragers of
novelties) erected a statue for him with a golden tongue,
a good emblem of his history, [z] says one, which made
a fair and specious shew, but was not within what it pretended to be, especially when it attempts to treat of ancient
times. It cannot be denied, however, but that some
fragments

The history of Berosus.

Vol. I. No. 4.   O o

---

[x] Stillingfleet's Orig. sacr. l. 1. c. 5.   [y] Cont. App. l. 1.
[z] Vid. Universf. hist.; and Shuckford's Connect. l. 1.

A.M. 1536
Ant. Chrif.
2468
Gen. ch. 5.
and 6 to
ver. 13.

fragments of it which have been preferved from ruin by the care and induftry of Jofephus, Tatianus, Eufebius, and others, have been very ufeful, not only for proving the truth of Scripture-hiftory to the Heathens, but for confirming likewife fome paffages relating to the Babylonifh empire.

After a defcription of Babylonia, and a ftrange ftory concerning a certain creature, which, in the firft year of the world, came out of the Red-fea, and, converfing familiarly with men, taught them the knowledge of letters, and feveral arts and fciences, he proceeds to give us a fhort account of ten kings which reigned in Chaldea before the flood, and thefe correfponding with the number which Mofes mentions, Alorus, the firft, is fuppofed to be Adam; and Xifuthrus, the laft, Noah; and of this Xifuthrus he purfues the ftory in this manner.

[a] Cronus, or Saturn, appearing to him in a dream, gave him warning, that on the 15th day of the month Dæfius, mankind fhould be deftroyed by a flood, and therefore commanded him to build a fhip; and, having firft furnifhed it with provifions, and taken into it fowls and four-footed beafts, to go into it himfelf, with his friends and neareft relations. Xifuthrus did as he was ordered, built a veffel, whofe length was five furlongs, and breadth two furlongs; and having put on board all that he was directed, went into it, with his wife, children, and friends. When the flood was come, and began to abate, he let out fome birds, which finding no food, nor place to reft on, returned to the fhip again. After fome days, he let out the birds again, but they came back with their feet daubed with mud; and when, after fome days more, he let them go the third time, they never came back again, whereby he underftood that the earth appeared again above the water, and fo, taking down fome of the planks of the fhip, he faw it refted upon a mountain. This is the fubftance of what we have in Berofus, who varies very little from our facred hiftorian during this period.

of Sanchoniatho,

Sanchoniatho is highly commended both by Porphyry, the great adverfary of Chriftianity, and by his tranflator into Greek, Philo Biblius. Theodoret is of opinion, that his name, in the Phœnician tongue, fignifies Φιλαλήθης, *a lover of truth;* which name, as Bochart imagines, was given him when he firft fet himfelf to write

hiftory:

[a] *Ibid.*   [b] Stillingfleet's Orig. facr. l. 1. c. 2.

Chap. V. *from the Creation to the Flood.* 175

history: but how faithful he has been in transcribing his A.M. 1536
account of things from his records, we cannot determine, Ant. Christ.
unless we had the books of Taautus, and the sacred inscrip- 2468.
tions and records of cities, from whence he pretends to have Gen. ch. 5.
extracted his history, to compare them together. If we and 6. to
may judge by what remains of his writings, which is only ver. 13.
his first book concerning the Phœnician theology extant in
Eusebius, we shall hardly think him deserving so large a
commendation: but be that as it will, the method wherein he proceeds is this.——After having delivered his cosmogony, or generation of the other parts of the world, he tells us, that the first pair of human creatures were Protogonus and Æon, (as Philo, his translator, calls them,) the latter of whom found out the food which is gathered from trees: that their issue were called *Genus* and *Genea*, who were the first that practised idolatry; for, upon the occasion of great droughts, they made their adorations to the sun, calling him *Beelsamen*, which, in Phœnician, is *the Lord of heaven;* that the children of these were *Phos*, *Pur*, and *Phlox*, i. e. light, fire, and flame, who first found out the way of generating fire, by rubbing peices of wood against one another: that these begat sons of vast bulk and stature, whose names were given to mount Cassius Libanus, Antilibanus, and Brathys, whereon they seized: that of these were begotten Memrumus, and Hypsuranius, the latter of whom was the inventor of huts made of reeds and rushes, and had a brother called *Usous*, the first worshipper of fire and wind, in whose time women became very abandoned and debauched: that many years after this generation, came Agreus and Halieus, the inventors of the arts of hunting and fishing: that of these were begotten two brothers, the first forgers and workers in iron; the the name of one is lost, but Chrysor (who is the same with Vulcan) found out all fishing tackle, and, in a small boat, was the first that ventured to sea, for which he was afterwards deified: that from this generation came two brothers, Technites and Autochthon, who invented the art of making tiles; from these Agrus, and Agrotes, who first made courts about houses, fences, and cellars; and from these Amynus, and Magus, who shewed men how to constitute villages, and regulate their flocks. This is the substance of what Sanchoniatho relates during this period; and how far it agrees with the account of Moses, especially in the idolatrous line of Cain, our learned bishop Cumberland has all along made his observations.

A. M. 1536.
Ant. Chrif.
.2468.
Gen. ch. 5,
and 6, to
ver. 23.
‾‾‾
and of Manetho.

Manetho Sebennita was high-prieft of Heliopolis in the time of Ptolemy Philadelphus, by whofe order he wrote his hiftory; but that which deftroys the credit of it, (though it gave him an opportunity of invention,) is, that [c] he profeffes to tranfcribe his Dynafties from infcriptions on the pillars of Hermes (whom the Egyptians, out of veneration, call *Trifmegiftus*) in the land of Seriad, which land no one knows any thing of, and which pillars being engraven before the flood, can hardly be fuppofed to efcape undefaced.

The plain truth is, the LXX tranflation was, not long before this time, finifhed; and when the Jewifh antiquities came to appear in the world, the Egyptians (who are mighty pretenders this way) grew jealous of the honour of their nation, and were willing to fhew, that they could trace up their memoirs much higher than Mofes had carried thofe of the Ifraelites [d] This was the chief defign of Manetho's making his collections. He was refolved to make the Egyptian antiquities reach as far backwards as he could; and therefore, as many feveral names as he found in their records, fo many fucceffive monarchs he determined them to have had; never confidering that Egypt was at firft divided into three, and afterwards into four fovereignties for fome time, fo that three or four of his kings were many times reigning together: which, if duly confidered, will be a means to reduce the Egyptian account to a more reafonable compafs.

* The fubftance of the account however (as it ftands unexplained in Manetho) is this:——That there were in Egypt thirty dynafties of gods, confifting of 113 generations,

---

[c] *Vid.* Stillingfleet's Orig. facr. l. 1. c. 2. N°. 11. [d] Shuckford's Conneft part 1. l. 1.

* The accounts of Manetho feem at firft fight fo extravagant that many great writers look upon them as mere fictions, and omit attempting to fay any thing concerning them; though other learned men (and more efpecially our countryman Sir John Marfham, in his Can. chron. p 1) not well fatisfied with this proceeding, have undertaken an examination of them and with fome fuccefs. The misfortune is, we have none of the original works from whence they were collected, nor any one author that properly gives us any light or knowledge of them. The hiftorians Diodorus Siculus, and Herodotus, did not examine thefe matters to the bottom; and we have no remains of the old Egyptian Chronicon, or of the works of Manetho, except fome quotations in the works of other writers. The Chronographia

Chap. V.   *from the Creation to the Flood.*   177

tions, and which took up the space of 36,525 years; that   A.M. 1536.
when this period was out, then there reigned eight demi-   Ant Chrif.
gods in the space of 217 years; that after them succeeded   2468.
a race of heroes, to the number of 15, and their reign took   Gen. ch. 5.
up 443 years; that all this was before the flood, and then   and 6 to
began the reign of their kings, the first of whom was   ver 13.
Menes.

Now, in order to explain what is meant by this prodigious number of years, we must observe, ᵉ that it was a very usual and customary thing for ancient writers to begin their histories with some account of the origin of things, and the creation of the world. Moses did so in his book of Genesis; Sanchoniatho did so in his Phœnician history; and it appears from Diodorus, that the Egyptian antiquities did so too. Their accounts began about the origin of things, and the nature of the gods; then follows an account of their demi-gods, and terrestrial deities; after them came their heroes, or first rank of men; and last of all, their kings. Now, if their kings began from the flood; if their heroes and demi-gods reached up to the beginning of the world: then the account which they give of the reigns of their gods, before these, can be only their theological speculations put into such order as they thought most philosophical.

To make this more plain, we must observe farther, that the first and most ancient gods of the Egyptians, and of all other nations, (after they had departed from the worship of the true God, were the luminaries of heaven; and it is very probable, that what they took to be the period of time in which any of these deities finished their course, that they might call *the time of his reign.* Thus a perfect and complete revolution of any star which they worshipped,

of Syncellus, wrote by one George, an abbot of the monastery of St. Simeon, and called *St Syncellus*, as being suffragan of Tarasius, patriarch of Constantinople, is the only work we can have recourse to. From these antiquities Syncellus collected the quotations of the old Chronicons of Manetho, and of Eratosthenes, as he found them in the works of Africanus and Eusebius; and the works of Africanus and Eusebius being now lost, (for it is known that the work which goes under the name of *Eusebius's Chronicon* is a composition of Scaliger's) we have nothing to be depended upon but what we find in Syncellus above mentioned; *Shuckford's Connect.*

ᵉ Shuckford's Connect l. 1.

178   *The History of the* BIBLE,   Book I.

A.M 1536.   shipped, was the reign of that star; and as a period of
Ant. Chrif 36,525 years is what they call an entire mundane revolu-
2468.
Gen. ch. 5. tion, *i. e.* when the several heavenly bodies come round to
and 6 to   the same point, from which all their courses began; so is
verse 13.   it very remarkable, that they made the sum total of the
reigns of all their several Gods, to amount to the self-same
space of time. This I take to be a true state of the Egyptian dynasties: and if so, it makes their history not near so extravagant as has been imagined, and sinks their account of time some hundred years short of the Jewish computation.

The differ- The Jewish computation indeed is not a little ambi-
ence be-   guous, by reason of the different methods, which men find
tween the
Hebrew   themselves inclined to pursue. The three common ways of
and Sama-   computing the time from the creation to the flood, are,
ritan com- that which arises from the Hebrew text, from the Sama-
putations: ritan copies, and from the LXX interpretation.

The computation of Moses.

1. According to the Hebrew text.	Began his life in the year of the world	Had his son in the year of his life	Lived after his son's birth, years	Lived in all, years	Died in the year of the world
Adam - -	1	130	800	930	930
Seth - -	130	105	807	912	1042
Enos - -	235	90	815	905	1140
Cainan - -	325	70	840	910	1235
Mahalaleel -	395	65	830	895	1290
Jared - -	460	162	800	962	1422
Enoch - -	622	65	300	365	987
Methuselah -	687	187	782	969	1656
Lamech - -	874	182	595	777	1651
Noah - -	1056	500			

2. Accordingly

1. According to the Samaritan.	Began his life in the year of the world	Had his son in the year of his life	Lived after his son's birth, years	Lived in all years	Died in the year of the world
Adam -	1	130	800	930	930
Seth -	130	105	807	912	1042
Enos -	235	90	815	905	1140
Cainan -	325	70	840	910	1235
Mahalaleel	395	65	830	895	1290
Jared -	460	62	785	847	1307
Enoch -	522	65	300	365	887
Methuselah	587	67	653	720	1307
Lamech -	654	53	600	653	1307
Noah -	707	500			

3. According to the Septuagint.	Began his life in the year of the world	Had his son in the year of his life	Lived after his son's birth, years	Lived in all years	Died in the year of the world
Adam -	1	230	700	930	930
Seth -	230	205	707	912	1042
Enos -	435	190	715	905	1340
Cainan -	625	170	740	910	1535
Mahalaleel	795	165	720	895	1690
Jared -	960	162	800	962	1922
Enoch -	1122	165	200	365	1487
Methuselah	1287	187	782	969	2256
Lamech -	1474	188	565	753	2227
Noah -	1662	500			

The difference between the Hebrew and Samaritan computation is easily perceived, by comparing the two former tables together; nor will it be any hard matter to reconcile them, if we consider what *f* St Jerom informs us of

---

f In quæst, in Genes.

A.M. 1536.
Ant. Chrif.
2468.
Gen. ch 5.
and 6, to
ver 13

of *viz.* that there were Samaritan copies which made Methuſelah 187 years old at the birth of Lamech; and Lamech 182 at the birth of Noah. Now, if this be true, it is eaſy to ſuppoſe 62 (the age of Jared at the birth of Enoch) to be a miſtake of the transcriber, who might drop a letter, and write 62 instead of 162; and thus all the difference between the Hebrew and Samaritan copies will entirely vaniſh.

And between the Hebrew and Septuagint,

But it is not ſo between the Hebrew and the Septuagint. The Hebrew, according to the higheſt calculation, makes no more than 1656 years before the flood, but the Septuagint raiſe it to no leſs than 2262; ſo that in this one period (without ſaying any thing of the wide difference between them in ſubſequent times) there is an addition of above 600 years, which can † hardly be accounted for by any miſtake of tranſcribers, becauſe all the ancient and authentic copies, both of the Hebrew and Septuagint, agree exactly in their computation. And therefore the generality of learned men, deſpairing of a reconciliation, have fairly entered the liſts, and taken the ſide which they thought moſt tenible.

Arguments for the Septuagint.

Thoſe who eſpouſe the cauſe of the Greek verſion, draw up their arguments in this rank and order. They tell

† Lud. Capellus [in his *Chron. ſacr. in apparatu Waltoni ad Bibl. Polyglot.*] attempts to reconcile this difference, by telling us from St Auſtin [De Civitate Dei cap. 13] that this edition was not made by the LXX themſelves, but by ſome early transcriber from them, and probably for one or other of theſe two reaſons; 1ſt Perhaps, thinking the years of the antediluvians to be but lunar, and computing, that at this rate the ſix fathers (whoſe lives are thus altered) muſt have had their children at 5, 6, 7, or 8 years old (which could not but look incredible;) the tranſcriber, I ſay, finding this, might be induced to add 100 years to each, in order to make them of a more probable age of manhood at the birth of their reſpective children: or, 2dly, If he thought the years of their lives to be ſolar, yet ſtill he might imagine, that infancy and childhood were proportionably longer in men who were to live 7, 8, or 9 hundred years, than they are in us; and that it was too early in their lives for them to be fathers at 60, 70, or 90 years of age; and for this reaſon, might add 100 years, to make their advance to manhood (which is commonly not till one fourth part of life is over) proportionable to what was to be the term of their duration; *Shuckford's Connection*, l. 1,

tell us, that the alteration in the Septuagint computation must have been purposely made; because, where letters must necessarily have been added, and where sometimes both parts of a verse, and sometimes two verses together are altered, and so altered, as still to keep them consistent with one another; this, whenever done, must be done designedly, and for no other reason that they can imagine, but rarely a detection of errors in the Hebrew copies.

A.M. 1536.
Ant. Chrisf.
2468.
Gen. ch. 5.
and 6. to
ver. 13.

They tell us, that, though they have no positive proof of such errors in the present Hebrew copies, yet they have good grounds to suspect there are such, because that, before the time of Antiochus, the Jews, while in peace, were so very careless about their sacred writings, that they suffered several variations to creep into their copies; that when Antiochus fell upon them, he seized and burnt all the copies he could come at, so that none, but such as were in private hands, escaped his fury; that, as soon as that calamity was over, those copies which were left, in private hands, the Jews got together, in order to transcribe others from them; and that, from these transcriptions, came all the copies now in use. Now suppose, say they, that these private copies which escaped the fury of Antiochus, but were made in an age confessedly inaccurate, had any of them dropt some numerical letters, this might occasion the present Hebrew text's falling short in its computations: And, to confirm this,

They tell us, that Josephus, [g] who expressly declares, that he wrote his history from the sacred pages, [h] in his account of the lives of the antediluvian patriarchs, agrees with the Septuagint; and that the Greek historians before Josephus, such as Demetrius Phalerius, Philo the elder, Eupolemus, &c. very accurate writers, and highly commended by Clemens Alexandrinus, and Eusebius, in their calculation, differ very much from the common Hebrew: So that not only Josephus, but these elder historians likewise must have either seen, or been informed of certain Hebrew copies which agreed with the Septuagint, and differed from what have descended to us. In short,

They tell us, [i] that the whole Christian church, Eastern and Western, and all the celebrated writers of the church, are on their side; that all the ancient manuscripts have exactly the same computations with the common Septuagint,

Vol. I. No. 4.   P p

[g] Contra App. l. 1.   [h] Antiq. l. 1. c. 3.   [i] Shuckford's Connection; and Heidegger's Hist. patriar.

A.M. 1536
Ant. Chrif.
2458.
Gen. ch. 5
and 6 to
verfe 13.

tuagint, except here and there a variation or two, not worth regarding; and therefore they conclude, that, as there is a manifeft difagreement between the Greek and Hebrew copies in this refpect, the miftake fhould rather be charged upon the Hebrew, than the Septuagint; becaufe, as the Hebrew is thought by fome to fall fhort, and the Septuagint to exceed, in its account of the lives of the patriarchs, 'tis obvious to conceive, that a fault of this kind may be incurred by way of omiffion rather than addition.

For the Hebrew computation.

Thofe who maintain the authority of the Hebrew text, as the ftandard and rule of reckoning the years of the patriarchs, oppofe their adverfaries in this manner.

They tell us [k] that the Hebrew text is the original, in which the Spirit of God indicted the Scriptures of the Old Teftament, and being, confequently, authentic, is better to be trufted than any tranflation made by men liable to error, as the LXX interpreters were; and that the Jews, to whom [l] were committed thefe oracles of God, ufed the greateft diligence to preferve them pure and entire, infomuch, that in the courfe of fo many years (as [m] Jofephus teftifies in his time) no perfon durft add, take away, or mifplace any thing therein.

They tell us, that no reafon can be affigned, why the Hebrew text fhould be corrupted, but many very probable ones, why the Septuagint might; fince, either to exalt the antiquity of their own nation, or to conform to the dynafties of the Egyptians, the Jewifh interpreters at Alexandria might falfify their chronology; fince, in this very point, there are fo many different readings in the Septuagint, and fo many errors and mif-tranflations in it, that [n] the learned Dr Lightfoot (to whom, as yet, no fufficient reply has been made) has proved it a very corrupt and imperfect verfion.

They tell us that the Hebrew computations are fupported by a perfect concurrence and agreement of all Hebrew copies now in being; that there have been no various readings in thefe places, fince the Talmuds were compofed; that, even in our Saviour's time, this was the current way of caculation, fince the paraphrafe of *Onkelos*
(which

[k] Millar's Church hiftory.   [l] Rom. iii. 2.   [m] Contra Appl. l 1.   [n] *Vid.* Ejus opera, tom, 2. p, 932, edit. Ultraject. 1699.

Chap. V.   *from the Creation to the Flood.*   183

(which is on all hands agreed to be about that age) is the $\begin{smallmatrix}\text{A.M. 1536.}\\\text{Ant. Chrif.}\\\text{2468.}\\\text{Gen. ch. 5,}\\\text{and 6, to}\\\text{ver. 13.}\end{smallmatrix}$ same exactly with the Hebrew in this matter; that St Jerom and St Auftin (who were the beft fkilled in the Hebrew tongue of any fathers in their age) followed it in their writings, and the vulgar Latin, which has been in ufe in the church above a 100 years, entirely agrees with it.

They tell us, that Demetrius, the real hiftorian, (for † Phalerius was none,) lived not before the reign of Ptolemy Philopater, the grandfon of Philadelphus, near feventy years after the LXX tranflation was made: that Philo was contemporary with our Saviour, wrote almoft 300 years after the faid tranflation, and, living conftantly at Alexandria, might very well be fuppofed to copy from it; that Jofephus, though a Jew, and perfectly fkilled in the Hebrew language, in many inftances, (which learned º men have pointed out,) adheres to the Greek in oppofition to the Hebrew; and that the fathers, of the firft ages of the church, though they were very good men, had no great extent of learning; underftood the Greek tongue better than the Hebrew; and for that reafon gave the preference to the Septuagint computation.

In this manner do the advocates for the Hebrew text defend its authority: And, fince it is confeffed, there has been a tranfmutation fomewhere, if that tranfmutation was defignedly and on purpofe done, (as the adverfe party agrees,) 'tis indifferent ᵖ whether it was done by way of addition or fubtraction: Only as it is evident, that the Greeks

† Demetrius Phalerius was the firft prefident of the college of Alexandria, to which the library belonged, where the original manufcripts of the Septuagint were repofited. He was a great fcholar as well as an able ftatefman and politician; but I doubt Bifhop Walton is miftaken, when (in his 9th Prolegom. ad Bib. Polyglot.) he quotes him as one of thofe Greek hiftorians whofe works might prove the Septuagint computation to be more probable than the Hebrew. The Phalerian Demetrius lived a bufy, active life, was a great officer of ftate, both at home and abroad, and I do not find that ever he wrote any hiftory. 'Twas Demetrius the hiftorian therefore, that the Bifhop fhould have quoted; but he, living in the time that I mentioned, does not make much to this purpofe; *Shuckford's Connect* l. 1.

º *Vid.* Cave's Hift.; Litt. p 2 in Jofeph; and Well's Differtation upon the Chronicles of Jofephus, p. 19, —— 21.

ᵖ Heidegger's Hift. patriar.

A.M. 1536.
Ant. Chri. 2468.
Gen. ch. 5. and 6. to ver. 13.

Greeks did compute by numerical letters, whereas it is much questioned, that the Hebrews ever did, the mistake or falsification rather seems to lie on the side of the Greek translators, the very form of whose letters was more susceptible of it.

This is a true state of the controversy, wherein the arguments for the Hebrew computation do certainly preponderate; though the names, the venerable † names, on the contrary side, have hitherto been more numerous.

The religion.

It might be some entertainment to the reader, could we but give him any tolerable view of the religion, polity, and learning, of the antediluvian people: But the Sacred history, in this respect, is so very short, and the hints suggested therein, so very few, and so very obscure withal, that, during this period, we are left, in a great measure, in the dark. However, we cannot but observe, that it is a mistaken notion of some authors, who affirm, that at the beginning of the world, for almost 2000 years together, mankind lived without any law, without any precepts, without any promises from God; and that the religion from Adam to Abraham was purely natural, and such as had nothing but right reason to be its rule and measure. The antediluvian dispensation indeed was, in the main, founded upon the law of nature; but still it must be acknowledged, that there was (as we shewed before) a divine precept concerning sacrifices; that there was a divine promise concerning the blessed seed; and that there were several other precepts and injunctions given the patriarchs, besides those that were built upon mere reason.

The law of sacrifices (which confessedly at this time obtained) was partly natural, and partly divine. As sacrifices were tokens of thankfulness and acknowledgements, that the fruits of the earth, and all other creatures, for the

† The names for the Septuagint computation, which the learned Heidegger, in his hist. patriar (as he takes them from Baronius,) has reckoned up, are such as these: Theophilus Bishop of Antioch, St Cyprian, Clemens Alexandrinus, Hippolytus, Origin, Lactantius, Epiphanius, Philastrius Orosius, Cyril, the two Anastasii, Nicephorus, and Suada; to whom he might add several more, as Heidegger suggests, while those among the ancients who contended for the Hebrew calculation, were only St Austin and St Jerom, but men of great skill and proficiency in the Hebrew language; *De ætate patriarcharum, exer,* 10.

the use and benefit of man were derived from God; they were a service dictated by natural reason, and so were natural acts of worship: But, as they carried with them the notion of expiation and atonement for the souls of mankind especially as they referred to the Messias, and signified the future sacrifice of Christ, they were certainly instituted by God, and the practice of them was founded upon a divine command.

A.M. 1536.
Ant. Chrif.
2468.
Gen. ch. 5.
and 6. to
ver 13.

It is not to be doubted, ⁿ but that Adam instructed his children to worship and adore God, to commemorate his goodness, and deprecate his displeasure; nor can we suppose, but that they, in their respective families, put his instructions in execution; And yet we find, that in the days of Enos, (besides all private devotion) a public form of worship was set up; that the people had the rites of their religion, which God had appointed, fixed, and established; and that, very probably, as Cain built cities for his descendants to live in, so Enos might build temples, and places of divine worship, for his to resort to.

The distinction of clean and unclean animals was another divine injunction under this dispensation. God refers Noah to it, as a thing well known, when he commands him ʳ to put into the ark seven pairs of clean, and two of unclean creatures: And ˢ though, in respect of man's food, this distinction was not before the law of Moses, yet some beasts were accounted fit and others unfit for sacrifices from the beginning. The former were esteemed clean, and the latter unclean: And it seems safer to make a positive law of God the foundation of this distinction, than to imagine that men, in such matters as these, were left to their own discretion.

The prohibition of marrying with infidels or idolaters, was another article of this dispensation, as appears from God's angry resentment when the children of Seth entered into wedlock with the wicked posterity of Cain. And, to mention no more, under this period were given those six *great precepts of Adam* (as they are generally called) whereof the Jewish doctors make such boast; ᵗ and of these the

1st

ⁿ Edward's Survey of religion, l. 1.   ʳ Gen. vii. 2.
ˢ Patrick's Commentary.

ᵗ The commandments given to the sons of Noah are the same with these. They are an abridgement of the whole law of nature; but have one positive precept annexed to them; and are

generally

186　　　*The History of the BIBLE,*

A.M. 1536.
Ant. Chrif.
2468.
Gen. ch. 5.
and 6. to
ver. 13.

1st was of strange worship, or idolatry; t
the most holy name, or blasphemy; the
the nakedness, or unlawful copulation; t
shed, or homicide; the 5th of theft and
6th of judgement, or the administration
public courts of judicature. So that, fro
God did not leave himself without a witness
terms it) but, in one degree or other, mad
festations of his will to mankind.

Polity

That government of one kind or ot
to the well-being of mankind, seems to
founded in the nature of things, the relatic
at first, stood towards one another, and th
cations in them, which, in a short time, cc
pear. The first form of government, wit
versy, was patriarchal; But this form was
when men of superior parts came to disting
when the head of any family either out-
witted his neighbour, and so brought hir
dominion, either by compulsion or re
vernment, however, at this time, seems
placed in fewer hands, than it is now: No
ber of people was less, but their con
larger, and their kingdoms more extensive.

generally placed in this order. " 1. Thou sh
" gods, but the maker only of heaven and
" shalt remember to serve the true God, the L
" by sanctifying his name in the midst of thee
" not shed the blood of man created after th
" 4. Thou shalt not defile thy body, that thou
" ful and multiply, and, with a blessing rep
" 5. Thou shalt be content with that which t
" thou wouldst not have done to thyself, th
" do to another. 6. Thou shalt do right jud
" one, without respect to persons. 7. Thou
" flesh in the blood, nor any thing that hath l
" thereof." This is the heptalogue of Noah,
which, as the Jews tell us, were delivered to h
constantly observed by all the uncircumcised w
true God; *Bibliotheca Bib. occaf. annot.* 15. *vol.*

* To this purpose Cicero [*De legibus*, l. 3. c
" Sine imperio, nec domus ulla, nec gens, nec
" sum genus stare, nec rerum, natura omnis,
" potest." Seneca asserts, that " Istud [impe
" lum, per quod respublica cohæret: Ille spiri
" hæc tot millia trahunt: nihil ipsa per se futi
" præda, si mens illa imperii subtrahatur."

flood; ᵗ insomuch, that it may well be questioned, whether, after the union of the two great families of Seth and Cain, there was any distinction of civil societies, or diversity of regal governments at all. It seems more likely, that all mankind then made but one great nation, living in a kind of anarchy, and divided into several disorderly associations; which, as it was almost the natural consequence of their having, in all probability, but one language; so it was a circumstance which greatly contributed to that general corruption which otherwise perhaps could not so universally have prevailed. And for this reason we may suppose, that no sooner was the posterity of Noah sufficiently increased, but a plurality of tongues was miraculously introduced, in order to divide them into distinct societies, and thereby prevent any such total depravation for the future.

<small>A.M.1536. Ant. Chrif. 2468. Gen ch. 5. and 6. to ver. 13.</small>

The enterprising genius of man began to exert itself very early in music, brass-work, iron-work and every science, useful and entertaining, and the undertakers were not limited by a short life. They had time enough before them to carry things to perfection: but whatever their skill, learning, or industry performed, all remains and monuments of it have long since perished.

<small>and the learning of the antediluvians.</small>

ᵘ Josephus indeed gives us this account of Seth's great knowledge in astronomy, and how industrious he was to have it conveyed to the new world. " Seth, and his de-
" scendants;" says he, " were persons of happy tempers,
" and lived in peace, employing themselves in the study of
" astronomy, and in other searches after useful knowledge;
" but, being informed by Adam, that the world should
" be twice destroyed, first by water, and afterwards by fire,
" they made two pillars, the one of stone, and the other
" of brick, and inscribed their knowledge upon them, sup-
" posing that the one or other of them might remain for
" the use of posterity." ˣ But how strangely improbable is it, that they, who foreknew that the destruction of the world should be by a flood, should busy themselves to write astronomical observations on pillars, for the benefit of those who should live after it? Could they think, that their pillars would have some peculiar exemption, above other structures, from the violence and outrage of the waters? If they believed that the flood would prove universal, for whose instruction did they write their observations? If they did not, to what end did they write them at all, since the

<small>Seth's pillars.</small>

persons

<small>ᵗ Universf. hist. l. 1. n. 2. ᵘ Antiq. l, 1. c. 2. ˣ Stillingfleet's Orig. sac, l, 1. c. 2,</small>

A.M. 1536.
Ant. Chrif.
2468.
Gen. ch. 5.
and 6 to
ver. 13

persons who survived, might communicate their inventions to whom they pleased? The plain truth is, [y] Josephus, who frequently quotes Heathen authors, and Manetho in particular, to this story of Seth's pillars from the pillars of Hermes mentioned in that historian: for as the Jews had an ancient tradition concerning Seth's pillars, Josephus, in reading Manetho, might possibly think his account misapplied, and thereupon imagine, that he should probably hit on the truth, if he put the account of the one and the tradition of the other together; and this very likely might occasion his mistake.

and Enoch's prophecy.

[z] The Eastern people have preserved several traditions of very little certainty concerning Enoch. They believe, that he received from God the gift of wisdom and knowledge to an eminent degree, and that God sent him thirty volumes from heaven, filled with all the secrets of the most mysterious science. St Jude, it is certain, seems to cite a passage from a prophecy of his; nor can it be denied, but that in the first ages of Christianity, [†] there was a book, well known to the Jews, that went under his name: but besides

[y] Shuckford's Connection, l. i. [z] Calmet's Dictionary on the word *Enoch*.

[†] Joseph Scaliger, in his annotations upon Eusebius's Chronicon, has given us some considerable fragments of it, which Heidegger in his hist. Patriarch, has translated into Latin, which the curious, if they think proper, may consult: but the whole seems to be nothing but a fabulous collection of some Jew or other, most unworthy the holy patriarch. Tertullian, however, has defended it with great warmth, and laments much, that all the world is not as zealous as himself, in the maintenance of its authenticalness. He pretends, that it had been saved by Noah in the ark, from thence transmitted down to the church and that the Jews, in his days, rejected it, only because they thought it was favourable to Christianity; *Miller's history of the church, and Saurin's Differtations*. The great objections against this book are, that neither Philo, nor Josephus (those diligent searchers into antiquity,) make any mention of it; and that it contains such fabulous stories as are monstrous and absurd. But to this some have answered, that such a book there certainly was, notwithstanding the silence of these Jewish antiquaries: and that, after the apostle's time, it might be corrupted, and many things added to it by succeeding heretics, who might take occasion from the antiquity thereof, and from the passage of Michael's contending with the devil about the body of Moses, to interpolate many fables and inventions of their own; *Raleigh's History of the world*.

besides that this piece is now generally given up for spurious, there is no need for us to suppose, that St Jude ever quoted any passage out of this, or any other book of Enoch.

^a Enoch was a prophet, we are told, and as such was invested with authority, *to cry aloud, and spare not*, to reprove the wicked, and denounce God's judgements against them; and as he was a good man, it was easy for St Jude to imagine, that he would not sit still, and see the impieties of the people grow so very exorbitant, without endeavouring to repress them, by setting before them *the terrors of the Lord*. He could not discharge the office of a good man, and a prophet without forewarning them of the ^b *Lord's coming, with ten thousand of his saints, to execute judgement upon all, and to convince all that were ungodly among them*: and because this was his office and duty, the Apostle infers, (as by the Spirit of God he might certainly know,) that he did so, though he might not make that inference from any passage in his prophecy; because it is a known observation, that † many things are alluded to it in the New Testament, which were never perhaps in any book at all.

Of all the strange matters that occur in this period of time, there is nothing which looks so like a prodigy as the longevity of those men who at first inhabited the earth; nor is any event so apt to affect us with wonder, as the disproportion between their lives and ours. We think it a great thing, if we chance to arrive at fourscore, or an hundred years; whereas they lived to the term of 7, 8, 9 hundred, and upwards, as appears * by the joint testimony

^a Heideggar's Hist. patriar.   ^b Jude ver. 14 15.

† There are many instances in the New Testament of facts alluded to, which we do not find in any ancient books. Thus the contest between Michael and the devil is mentioned, as if the Jews had, some where or other, a full account of it. The names of the Egyptians, Jannes, and Jambres, are set down, though they are no where found in Moses's history. St Paul tells us, that Moses exceedingly quaked and feared on mount Sinai; but we do not find it so recorded any where in the Old Testament. In all these cases, the apostles and holy writers hinted at things, commonly received as true, by tradition among the Jews, without transcribing them from any real book; *Shuckford's Connect. l. 1.*

* Manetho, who wrote the story of the Egyptians; Berosius, who wrote the Chaldean history; those authors, who give us an account of the Phoenician antiquities; and among the Greeks,

A.M.1536. Ant. Chrif. 2468. Gen. ch. 5. and 6. to ver. 13. ny both of sacred and profane history. The only suspicion that can arise in our minds upon this occasion, is, that the computation might possibly be made, not according to solar, but lunar years; but this, instead of solving the difficulty, runs us into several gross absurdities.

The space of time, between the creation and the flood, is usually computed to be 1656 years, which, if we suppose to be lunar, and converted into common years, will amount to little more than 127; too short an interval, by much, to stock the world with a sufficient number of inhabitants. From one couple we can scarce imagine, that there could arise 500 persons in so short a time; but suppose them a thousand, they would not be so many as we sometimes have in a good country village. And were the flood gates of heaven opened, and the great abyss broken up, to destroy such an handful of people? were the waters raised fifteen cubits above the highest mountains, throughout the face of the whole earth, to drown a parish or two? This certainly is more incredible than the longest age which the Scriptures ascribe to the patriarchs; besides that, this short interval leaves **no room** for ten generations, which we find from Adam to the flood; nor does it allow the patriarchs age enough, (some of them, upon this supposition, must not be above five years old,) when they are said to beget children.

It is generally allowed, and may indeed be proved by the testimony of Scripture, that our first fathers lived considerably longer, than any of their posterity have done since; but, according to this hypothesis, (which depresses the lives of the antediluvians, not only below those who lived next the flood, but even below all following generations to this day,) Methuselah, who was always accounted the oldest man since the creation, did but reach to the age of 75, and Abraham, who is said to have died in a good old age, was not completely 15.

The patrons of this opinion therefore would do well to tell us, when we are to break off this account of lunar years in the sacred history. If they will have it extended no farther than the flood, they make the postdiluvian fathers longer-lived than the antediluvian, but will be puzzled to assign a reason, why the deluge should occasion longevity. If

---

Hesiodus, Hecateus, Hellanicus, Ephorus, &c. do unanimously agree, that in the first ages of the world, men lived a thousand years; *Burnet's Theory, l. 2, c. 4.*

If they will extend it to the postdiluvians likewise, they will then be entangled in worse difficulties; for they will make their lives miserably short, and their age of getting children altogether incongruous and impossible.

From the whole therefore we may conclude that the years whereby Moses reckons the lives of the antediluvians, were solar years, much of the same length with what we now use; and that therefore there must be a reason, either in their manner of life, their bodily constitution, the temperament of the world wherein they lived, or (what is most likely, the particular vouchsafement of God, to give them this mighty singular advantage above us.

Some have imputed this extraordinary length of life in the antediluvians to the sobriety of their living, and simplicity of their diet; that they eat no flesh, and had no provocations to gluttony, which wit and vice have since invented. This indeed might have some effect, but not possibly to the degree we now speak of; since there have been many moderate and abstemious people in all ages, who have not surpassed the common period of life.

Others have ascribed it to the excellency of the fruits, and some unknown quality in the herbs and plants of those days: but the earth, we know, was cursed immediately after the fall, and its fruits, we may suppose, gradually decreased in their virtue and goodness, until the time of the flood; and yet we do not see, that the length of men's lives decreased at all during that interval.

Others therefore have thought, that the long lives of the men of the old world proceeded from the strength of their stamina, or first principles of their bodily constitution; which, if they were equally strong in us, would maintain us, as they think, in being, as long: but though it be granted, that both the strength and stature of their bodies were greater than ours, and that a race of strong men, living long in health, will have children of a proportionably strong constitution; yet, that this was not the sole and adequate cause of their longevity, we have one plain instance to convince us, *viz.* that Shem, who was born before the deluge, and had in his body all the virtue of an antediluvian constitution, fell 300 years short of the age of his forefathers, because the greatest part of his life was passed after the flood.

---

^c Burnet's Theory of the earth, l. 2. c. 4.

The ingenious theorist whom I have quoted, for this reason, imagines, that before the flood, the situation of the earth to the sun was direct and perpendicular, and not, as it is now, inclined and oblique. From this position he infers, that there was a perpetual equinox all the earth over, and one continued spring; and thence concludes, that the equality of the air, and stability of the seasons were the true causes of the then longevity; whereas the change, and obliquity of the earth's posture, occasioned by the deluge, altered the form of the year, and brought in an equality of seasons, which caused a sensible decay in nature, and a gradual contraction in human life.

His reasoning, upon this point, is very elegant. " There " is no question," says he, " but every thing upon earth, " and especially the animate world, would be much more " permanent, if the general course of nature was more " steady, and more uniform. A stability in the heavens " makes a stability in all things below; and that change, " and contrariety of qualities which we have in these re-" gions, is the fountain of corruption — the æther in " their little pores, the air in their greater, and the va-" pours and atmosphere that surround them, shake, and " unsettle their texture and continuity; whereas, in a fixed " state of nature, where these principles have always the " same constant and uniform motion, a long and lasting " peace ensues, without any violence, either within, or " without, to discompose them. We see, by daily expe-" rience," continues he, " that bodies are kept better in " the same medium, (as we call it,) than when they are " sometimes in the air, and sometimes in the water, moist " **and dry**, hot and cold, by turns; because these different " states weaken the contexture of their parts. But our " bodies, in the present state of nature, are put in an hun-" dred different mediums, in the course of a year; the " winds are of a different nature, and the air of a different " weight and pressure, according as the weather and sea-" sons affect them. All these things are enough to wear out " our bodies soon, very soon, in comparison of what they " would last, if they were always incompassed with one " and the same medium, and that medium were always of " one and the same temper."

This is all **very pretty**: but the author's grand mistake is, that it was **not** so in the primitive earth. He has no authority to show, that how high soever the waters

might

might swell at the deluge, the centre of the earth gave way *or the foundations of the round world were shaken.* The earth, no doubt, had, before, as well as after the flood, an annual as well as diurnal motion. ᵈ It stood to the sun in the same oblique posture and situation, and was consequently subject to the same seasons and vicissitudes that the present earth is; and if the air was more mild, and the elements more favourable at that time, this we may account the peculiar blessing of God, and not the result of the earth's position to the sun, or any fancied stability in the weather. The truth is, whatever we may attribute to second causes, why bodies that are naturally mortal and corruptible should subsist so long in the primitive ages of the world; yet the true cause of all is to be ascribed to the will of God, who impregnated our first parents with such vigour, and gave their posterity for some time such robust constitutions, as depended not upon the nature of their diet, the stability of the seasons, or the temperature of the air. After the flood, God soon made a sensible change in the length of man's days. For, perceiving the general iniquity to increase again, and thereupon designing to make an alteration in the world's continuance, he hastened the period of human life, that the number of souls he intended to send into the world before the consummation of all things, might have a speedier probation. Man's age accordingly went on sinking by degrees, until a little before David's time, it came to be fixed at what has been the common standard ever since. ᵉ *The days of our age are threescore years and ten: and though some men be so strong, that they come to fourscore years, yet is their strength then but labour and sorrow, so soon passeth it away,* **and we are gone.** This is our stated period; and therefore for us, who live in this postdiluvian world, and have the term of our trial so much shortened, the subsequent prayer of the devout Psalmist will always be necessary, always seasonable; *So teach us to number our days, that we may apply our hearts unto wisdom.*

ᵈ *Vid.* Keill's Examination of Burnet's theory.   ᵉ Psal. xc. 10.

A. M. 1656, &c.
An: Chrif.
2348, &c.
from Gen.
vi. 12. to
ix. 20.

CHAP. VI.

Of the deluge.

THE HISTORY.

GOD (as we faid before) had given mankind a reprieval for an hundred and twenty years; but when he faw that all his lenity and forbearance tended to no purpofe, except it was to make them more bold and licentious in their fins, he declared to his fervant Noah, that within a fhort time his refolution was to deftroy them, and with them all other creatures upon the face of the earth, by a flood of waters; but ‡ affured him, at the fame time, that fince he had comported himfelf better, and approved his fidelity to his maker, he would take care to preferve him and his family, and whatever other creatures were neceffary

‡ The words in our tranflation are, *With thee will I eftablifh my covenant:* but 1ft, by the word *covenant,* we are not here to underftand a mutual compact or agreement, but only a fimple and gracious promife, as it is likewife ufed, Numb. xviii. 19, xxv. 12 and in feveral other places; which promife, though only mentioned here, was doubtlefs made before, as may eafily be gathered from thefe words, and fome foregoing paffages, and from the neceffity that Noah fhould have fome fuch fupport and encouragement during all the time of his miniftry. 2dly, This covenant of God might relate to his fending the promifed feed, and redemption of mankind by the Meffias; and in this fenfe will import, that as the Meffias was to come out of Noah's loins fo the divine providence would take care to preferve him alive. But, 3dly, A learned and Right Reverend author is of opinion, that this covenant of God relates to his reinftating the earth in its primitive fertility in Noah's lifetime. To which purpofe he obferves, that as foon as the flood was over, God declares, *I will not again curfe the ground for man's fake:* from which declaration it appears, (fays he) 1ft, That the flood was the effect of that curfe which was denounced againft the earth for man's fake; and 2dly That the old curfe was fully executed and accomplifhed in the flood; in confequence of which, a new bleffing is immediately pronounced upon the earth, Gen. xiii. 22. *While the earth remaineth, feed-time, and harveft, and cold, and heat, and fummer and winter, and day and night, fhall not ceafe;* Pool's Annot. and Bifhop Sherlock's Ufe and intent of prophecy.

necessary for the restoration of their species from the general calamity.

To this purpose he gave him orders to build a kind of vessel, not in the form of ships now in use, but rather inclining to the fashion of a ‡ large chest or ark, and himself prescribed the plan whereby he was to proceed.——— That to make the vessel firm and strong, and able to endure the pressure of the waves, the wood most proper for that purpose ‡ should be cypress; and that to prevent the waves from penetrating, or the sun from cracking it, as well

A. M. 1656, &c. Ant. Christ. 2349, &c. from Gen. vi. 11, to ix. 20.

The make and fashion of the ark.

---

‡ The word *thebath*, which we render *ark*, is only read here, and in another place, where Moses, when an infant, is said to have been put into one made of bulrushes, Exod. ii. 3. It is supposed to come from a root which signifies *to dwell* or *inhabit*; and may therefore here denote a *house*, or *place of abode*. And indeed, if we consider the use and design, as well as the form and figure of this building, we can hardly suppose it to be like an ark or chest, wherein we usually store lumber, and put things out of the way; but rather like a farm-house, such as are in several countries where the cattle and people live all under one roof. As soon as men began to hew down timber, and to join it together, for the purpose of making houses nothing can be supposed a more simple kind of edifice than what was made rectangular, with a bottom or floor, to prevent the dampness of the ground; a sloping cover or roof to carry off the rain that should fall; stalls and cabins for the lodgement of man and beast; and, to keep out wind and weather effectually, a coat of bitumen or pitch. Of this kind was this building of Noah's, and may therefore rather be termed a place of abode, than an ark or chest, properly so called; *Le Clerc's Comment in locum*.

‡ The timber whereof the ark was framed Moses calls *gopher-wood*; but what tree this gopher was, is not a little controverted. Some will have it to be cedar, others the pine, others the box, and others (particularly the Mahometans) the Indian plane-tree; but our learned Fuller in his Miscellanies, has observed, that it was nothing else but that which the Greeks call Κυπάρισσος, or the *cypress-tree*; for, taking away the termination, *cupar*, and *gopher* differ very little in the sound. This observation the great Bochart has confirmed, and shewn very plainly, that no country abounds so much with this wood as that part of Assyria which lies about Babylon. And to this we may add the observation of Theophrastus, who, speaking of trees that are least subject to decay, makes the cypress-tree the most durable of all; for which Vitruvius gives us this reason, *viz.* that the

A. M. 1656, &c. Ant. Chrif. 2349, &c. from Gen vi 12, to ix. 20.

well as to secure it from worms, and make it glide more easy upon the water, his business would be, as soon as it was finished, † to pitch it, or rather smear it all over with bitumen, (whereof there was plenty in the country), both within and without; that, to make its proportion regular, its length should be six times more than its breadth, and ten times more than its height; and, to give it capacity enough, the first of these should be † 300 cubits, that is, in our measure, 450 feet; the second 50 cubits, or 75 feet; and the third 30 cubits, or 45 feet; that to make it commodious for the reception of every thing, it was to consist of three stories or decks, of equal height each, and each divided into stalls and apartments proper for the things that were to be put into it; that for turning off the rain, the roof was to be made sloping; that for letting in of light, * there were windows to be so and so disposed,

or

the sap, which is in every part of the wood, has a peculiar bitter taste, and is so very offensive, that no worm or other corroding animal will touch it; so that such works as are made of this wood will in a maner last for ever. *Vid. Univers. hist; Patrick's Comment; Bochart's Phaleg. l. 1. c. 4.; and Bedford's Scrip. chronol. l. 1 c. 9.*

† The Arabic translation says expressly, *pitch it with pitch*, but the bitumen (which was plentiful in that country, and as others think intended here) was of the same nature, and served to the same use as pitch, being glutinous and tenacious, and proper to keep things together; *Patrick's Comment.*

† A cubit is the measure from the elbow to the finger's end, containing six hands breadths or a foot and a half: so that 300 cubits make exactly 450 feet. There are some however who take these for geometrical cubits, every one of which contin six, of the common; but there is no need for any such computation since, taking them for common cubits, it is demonstrable (as will appear hereafter that there might be room enough in the ark for all sorts of beasts and birds, together with Noah's family and their necessary provision; *Ainsworth's Annot.; and Patrick's Comment.*

* There are various translations of the word *zohar* which occurs but once in the whole bible in this sense. It seems to be derived from a root in the Chaldee, which signifies to *shine*, or *give light:* and therefore our version renders it *a window*; but if so, it must be collective, and mean several windows, because it is not likely that there should be but one in so vast a building and from the following words; *in a cubit shalt thou finish it above,* some have supposed, that the window was to

be

Chap. VI.   *from the Creation to the Flood.*   197

† or some other conveniency answerable to them; and that, for the more easy induction of the many things it was to contain, a door or entry-port was to be made in its side.

A. M. 1656, &c. Ant. Chrif. 2349 &c. from Gen. vi 11. to ix 10.

These were the instructions which God gave Noah, who accordingly went to work, and being assisted with the hands of his family, (for †the rest of the world doubtless derided him,) in the time that was appointed him, and seven days before the rain began to fall, * he had completed the whole.

The things to be taken into it.

---

be a cubit square, or but a cubit high, which would have been much too small. But the relative *it* being, in the Hebrew, of the feminine gender, and *zohar* of the masculine these two words cannot agree; and therefore the proper antecedent seems to be the *ark*, which was covered with a roof raised a cubit high in the middle. This however, in the original, may signify no more than an injunction to build the ark by the cubit, as the common measure, by which the work was to be marked out and directed. *Vid. Universe. hist.; Saurin's Dissert.; and Lamy's Introduction.*

† What that other conveniency was, we shall have occasion to shew when we come to treat of the word *zohar*, (which we here render *window*) in answer to the subsequent objection.

† The Apostle to the Hebrews (xi. 7.) mentions Noah's building the ark as an heroic act of faith ; *By faith Noah,* says he, *being warned of God of things not seen as yet, moved with fear, prepared an ark, to the saving of his house, by which he condemned the world, and became heir of the righteousness which is by faith :* for we may well imagine, that this work of his was not only costly and laborious, but esteemed by the generality very foolish and ridiculous; especially when they saw all things continue in the same posture and safety for so many scores of years together; whereby Noah, without doubt, became all that while the song of drunkards, and the sport of the wits of the age ; *Pool's Annot.* The Mahometans have a tradition, that when he began to work upon this famous vessel, all that saw him derided him, and said, " You are building a ship; if you can bring water to it, you will " be a prophet, as well as a carpenter;" but he made answer to these insults. "You laugh at me now, but I shall have my turn to " laugh at you; for at your own cost you will learn, that there " is a God in heaven who punishes the wicked;" *Calmet's Dict. on the word* Noah.

* It is somewhat strange, that the torrent of interpreters should suppose, that Noah was 120 years about this work, when he gives no intimation to that purpose, but sufficient reasons to

Vol. I. N°. 4   R r   believe,

A. M.
1656, &c.
Ant. Chrif.
2349, &c.
from Gen.
vi. 12. to
ix. 20.

whole. Whereupon God gave him inftructions, that he fhould take into the ark every living thing of all flefh, both cattle, and beafts of the field, birds, and fowls of the air, and reptiles of all kinds; † of the unclean, one pair

believe that he was not near fo long as is imagined. It is plain from fcripture, that *he was 500 years old when he begat Shem, Ham and Japhet*; (Gen. v. 32.) and that when he received the command for building the ark, the fame fons were married; for the text fays expressly, *Thou fhalt come into the ark, thou, and thy fons, and thy wife, and thy fons wives with thee.* (Gen. vi. 18. So that all the time between the birth and marriage of the faid fons muft at leaft be fuppofed to intervene before the command to build the ark was given; and between the command and the execution of it muft not be fo long as is imagined, without a concurrence of miracles, to prevent that part of it which was firft built from being rotten and decayed before the laft part of it was finifhed; *Saurin's Differt.* In what place Noah built and finifhed his ark, is no lefs made a matter of difputation. One fuppofes that he built it in Paleftine, and planted the cedars whereof he made it in the plains of Sodom: another takes it to have been built near mount Caucafus, on the confines of India: and a third in China, where he imagines Noah dwelt before the flood. But the moft probable opinion is, that it was built in Chaldea, in the territories of Babylon, where there was fo great a quantity of cyprefs in the groves and gardens, in Alexander's time, that that prince built a whole fleet out of it for want of other timber. And this conjecture is confirmed by the Chaldean tradition, which makes Xifuthrus (another name for Noah) fet fail from that country. *Vid Univerf. hift. l.* 1. c. 1.

† The diftinction between beafts that were clean and unclean, being made by the law, has given fome a colour to imagine, that Mofes wrote this book, after his coming out of Egypt, and receiving the law; but to this it may be anfwered, that though, with refpect to man's food, the diftinction of clean and unclean was not before the law, yet fome were accounted fit for facrifices, and others unfit, from the very firft beginning; and then unclean beafts, in this place, muft denote fuch as are rapacious which were not to be offered to God. In fhort, fince the rite of facrificing was before the flood, we may very well be allowed to fuppofe that this diftinction was alfo before it; and to fuppofe farther, that as the rite was undoubtedly of God's inftitution, fo the difference of clean and unclean creatures to be facrificed was of his appointment likewife. But there is a farther doubt arifing from this paffage, and that is——whether there

Chap. VI. *from the Creation to the Flood.* 199

pair only, but of the clean seven pair; that when the general desolation was over, they might increase again, and replenish the earth; and that when every thing was thus settled and disposed of, himself and his family should likewise go into the ark, and take up their apartments.

Pursuant to these directions, Noah and his family went into the ark, (leaving the rest of the world in their security and sensuality,) in the 600th year of his age, much ᵃ about the middle of September; when, in a few days after, ᵃ the whole face of nature began to put on a dismal aspect, as if the earth were to suffer a final dissolution, and all things return to their primitive chaos. ⁂ The cataracts of heaven were opened, the abyss of waters,

A. M.
1656, &c.
Ant. Chrif.
2349, &c.
from Gen.
vi. 12. to
ix. 20.

A short description of the flood.

there went into the ark but seven of every clean, and two of every unclean species or fourteen of the first and two of the last. Some adhere to the former exposition, but others to the latter, which seems to be the natural sense of the Hebrew words, *seven and seven* and *two and two*. Besides, if there were but seven of the clean beasts, one must have been without a mate and if it be suggested, that the odd one was for sacrifice, it is more than Moses tells us, who, on the contrary, repeats it, that the animals all went in by pairs; *Patrick's Commentary; Pool's Annotations; and Univerf. History, c.* 1.

ᵃ The words in the text are, *In the second month*; but, for the better understanding of this, we must remember, that the year among the Hebrews was of two kinds; the one ecclesiastical, which began in March, and chiefly regarded the observation of their fasts and festivals, of which we read Exod xii. 2. and the other civil for the better regulating of men's political affairs, which began in September. Accordingly the second month is thought by some to be part of April, and part of May, the most pleasant part of the year, and when the flood was least expected, and least feared; but by others, part of October, and part of November, a little after that Noah had gathered in the fruits of the earth, and laid them up in the ark: so that the flood came in with the winter, and was by degrees dried up in the following summer. And this opinion seems to be more probable, because the most ancient, and first beginning of the year, was in September; and the other beginning of the year in March was but a later institution among the Jews; with respect to their festivals and other sacred affairs, which are not at all concerned here; *Pool's Annotations*.

ᵃ. Howell's Complete history

⁂ Ovid, who is supposed to have extracted most of the beginning of his Metamorphoses out of the sacred records, has

R r 2 described

waters in the centre of the earth poured out, and the sea, forgetting its bounds, overspread the earth with a dreadful inundation.

Too late does wretched man perceive the approach of his deserved fate; and in vain does he find out means for his preservation. The tops of the hills, the tallest trees, the strongest towers, and the loftiest mountains, can give him no relief; it is but a small reprieve at most that they can yield him; for as the waters swell, and the waves come rushing on, hills, trees, towers, mountains, and every little refuge, must disappear with him. Noah himself cannot help him. Though he might now remember his predictions, and so flee to him for succour, yet God has shut the door of the ark, and it cannot be opened: [b] and so it shall be to every one, at the last great day, who shall not be found in Christ, the only ark of our salvation.

Its rise.

For forty days and nights together, without the least intermission, did the clouds continue raining; when at length the ark began to flaot, and to move from place to place as the waves drove it. And though there might be some short cessations afterwards, yet, at certain intervals the rain continued falling, and the waters swelling, till in process of time, the flood began to cover the mountains, and,

described both the induction and retreat of the waters in a manner very conformable to the original, from whence he had them. Their induction thus:

———Madidis Notus evolat alis,
Terribilem piceâ tectus caligine vultum———
Utque manu latâ pendentia nubila pressit:
Fit fragor: hinc densi funduntur ab æthere nimbi.———
Ipse tridente suo terram percussit: at illa
Intremuit, motuque sinus patefecit aquarum.
Expatiata ruunt per apertos flumina campos,
Cumque satis arbusta simul, pecudesque, virosque,
Tectaque, cumque suis rapiunt penetralia sacris, &c.

Their retreat thus:

Nubila disjecit, nimbisque Aquilone remotis,
Et cœlo terras ostendit, et æthera terris———
Jam mare littus habet: plenos capit alveus amnes:
Flumina subsidunt: colles exire videntur:
Surgit humus: crescunt loca decrescentibus undis.
Postque diem longum nudata cacumina sylvæ
Ostendunt, limumque tenent in fronde relictum. *Lib.* 1.

[b] Miller's History of the church; Patrick's Commentary; and Pool's Annotations.

and, by a gradual increase, came at last to raise its surface fifteen cubits (above twenty-two feet of our measure) higher than the tops of the highest of them.

In this elevation the flood continued until the latter end of March: when, as one one friend is apt to remember another in distress, (the Scripture here speaks in the style of men,) so God, reflecting upon Noah, and the poor remains of his creation, floating in the ark, caused a drying north wind to arise, the flood-gates of heaven to be stopped, and the irruption of the waters out of the womb of the earth to cease; by which means the deluge began to abate, and the waters subside, so that in a short time, the ark, which must have drawn great depth of water, stuck on a mountain, named *Ararat*, and there rested; and not long after, the tops of other mountains began to appear.

This happened in the beginning of May, when the summer was coming on apace: but Noah, wisely considering, that although the mountains were bare, the valleys might still be overflowed, waited forty days longer before he attempted any farther discovery; and then † opening the window,

A. M.
1656. &c.
Ant. Chrif.
2349 &c.
from Gen.
vi. 12. to
ix. 20.

and decrease.

The raven and dove sent out.

---

† It is very observable, that the words which we render *window* in ch. 6. ver. 16 and ch. 8. ver. 6 of Genesis, are far from being the same: in the former place, the word is *zohar*, (the nature of which we shall have a proper occasion to explain) in the latter, it is *hhalon*, which signifies indeed *an oval hole or window* in any building, but here is a window of a peculiar denomination. That it was customary among the Jews to have a room in the upper part of their houses set apart for divine worship, in Hebrew called *Beth-alijah*, or simply *alijah*, in Greek ὑπερῷον, and in Latin *oratorium*; and that, in this place of prayer, there was always an *hhalon*, an hole or window, which pointed to the *kibla* or place whereunto they directed their worship, is evident from several passages in Scripture. Among the Jewish constitutions, in the code, called *Beracoth*, there is a certain canon grounded upon this custom, *viz. That no man shall pray, but in a room where there is an* hhalon *opening towards the holy city:* and of Daniel it is particularly related, that when he knew that the decree for his destruction was signed, *he went into the house, and his* hhalon, *his window, being open in his chamber towards Jerusalem, he kneeled upon his knees three times a day, as he did aforetime*, Dan. vi. 10. for that this was not a common window, but one dedicated to religious worship, is plain from the people's discerning, by its being open that he
was

A. M.
1656, &c.
Ant. Chrif.
2349, &c.
from Gen.
vi. 12, to
ix. 20.

window, he let go a raven, as suppoſing that the ſmell of dead bodies would allure him to fly a good diſtance from the veſſel; but the experiment did not do; the raven, after ſeveral unſucceſsful flights, finding nothing but water, returned to the ark again. Seven days after this, he let fly a dove, a bird of a ſtrong pinion, and, from the remoteſt places always accuſtomed to come home, and therefore proper to make farther diſcoveries. But ſhe finding nothing but water likewiſe, immediately returned to the ark, and was taken in. After this he waited ſeven days more, and then ſent her forth again; and ſhe, in the evening, brought in her mouth an olive-branch, the emblem of peace, and a token to Noah that the waters were abated much. Whereupon he waited ſeven days more, and then let her fly the third time; but ſhe finding the waters gone, and the earth dry, returned no more; ſo that he was now thinking of uncovering the roof, and going out of the ark himſelf; but having a pious regard to the divine providence and direction in all things, he waited five and fifty days longer, and then received orders from God for him and his family to quit the veſſel, but to take care at the ſame time that every other creature ſhould be brought forth with him.

Thus ended * Noah's long and melancholy confinement; which, by a due computation from the time of his

was at prayers. Nor is it improbable that this window might have ſome viſible ſign, either of the name of God or of the holy city, or of the ſanctuary, or the like, inſcribed on it; becauſe it is a conſtant tradition, that theſe oratories or rooms for prayer were always ſo made as to have their angles anſwer to ſuch certain points of the heaven, and to have the mark of adoration ſo evidently diſtinguiſhed, that none might miſtake it, if they caſt but their eye upon the wall. Now, as the practice among the Jews of worſhipping in upper rooms, with their faces towards a hole or window in the wall, was never introduced by any poſitive law, and yet univerſally prevailed, it is reaſonable to believe, that at firſt it was derived from Noah, and that the windows in their oratories were made in imitation of this *hhalon*, or point of adoration in the ark; *Bibliotheca Biblica, vol. 2.; Occaſ. Annot. in the appendix.*

* Mr Baſnage [in his Antiq. Judaiq. tom. 2 p. 299.] has given us the kalendar of this melancholy year of Noah's confinement.

The

his going into the ark, to that of his coming out, was exactly the space of a solar year.

A. M. 1656 &c.
Ant. Chrif. 2319. &c.
from Gen. vi 11. to ix. 20.

THE OBJECTION.

"BUT, granting [c] that a vessel fashioned according
"to the description which Moses gives us of the
"structure of the ark, could *live* (as the seamen phrase it)
"in

The year of the world's creation, 1656.

Month.
 I. September. Methuselah died at the age of 969 years.
 II. October. Noah and his family entered the ark.
 III. November the 17th, *The fountains of the great deep were broken open.*
 IV. December the 26th. The rain began, and continued forty days and forty nights.
 V. January. All the men and beasts that were upon the earth were buried under the waters.
 VI. February. The rain continued.
 VII. March. The waters remained in their elevation till the 27th, when they began to abate.
 VIII. April the 17th. The ark rested on Mount Ararat.
 IX. May. They did nothing while the waters were retreating.
 X. June the 1st. The tops of the mountains appeared.
 XI. July the 11th. Noah let go a raven, which (as Besnage thinks) returned to him no more.
 The 18th. He let go a dove, which returned.
 The 25th. He let go the dove again, which returned with an olive branch.
 XII. August the 2d. The dove went out the third time, and returned no more.
 I. September the 1st. The dry land appeared.
 II. October the 27th. Noah went out of the ark with his family. During this long continuance in the ark, the form of prayer, which some oriental writers make Noah to have offered unto God, runs in this manner: "O Lord, thou art truly
" great, and there is nothing so great as that it can be compar-
" ed to thee; look upon us with an eye of mercy, and deliver
" us from the deluge of waters. I intreat this of thee for the
" love of Adam, thy first man; for the love of Abel, thy saint;
" for the righteousness of Seth, whom thou hast loved. Let
" us not be reckoned in the number of those, who have dis-
" obeyed thy commandments; but still extend thy merciful
" care to us, because thou hast hitherto been our deliverer, and
" all thy creatures shall declare thy praise. Amen;" *Calmet's Dictionary on the words* Deluge *and* Noah.

 [c] Parker's Bibliotheca Biblica, vol. 1. part 1. Occasional Annotat. 12.

A. M. 1656, &c. Ant. Chrif. 2349, &c. from Gen. vi. 12. to ix. 10.

"in such a tempest of waters so long together; yet what can we think would become of Noah and his family, with all the several kinds of birds, beasts, and reptiles, ᵈ stowed up, all this while, in a close hutch, without the least breath of fresh air? How could they see to go about their business (and certainly they had business enough, to attend such a multitude of creatures) when they must have lived all this while, without the least light either of sun, moon, or the stars? And in this state of darkness, wherein day and night to them were both alike, how could they possibly measure time, or tell the precise number of the months and days, that they had continued in the ark?

"The ark indeed, according to the description of Moses, was a large building: But had it been ten times larger, it could never have contained the several couples of all kinds, which were ordered to be brought into it. Had they been huddled together, the wild and the tame, the strong and the weak promiscuously, they would have soon dispatched one another, without troubling the deluge. Had proper cells and partitions been made for them, 'tis hardly conceivable, what a prodigious space, such a number as was merely necessary, would have taken up. For, if we compute only the creatures of the old world, the room allowed them in the ark will hardly contain so many different species together, with their respective food and provender; but then, if we take in all the beasts of the new world, and such as are found under the southern hemisphere, we shall scarce find room for the animals themselves, much less for the great store of provisions that will be necessary to keep them alive so long. But the greatest wonder is, ᵉ how the many animals, which are peculiar to several parts of America, could get into Chaldea, or wherever the ark was built; and, after the deluge was over, could return to their native country. Nay, even allowing this to be practicable, it will still puzzle our imagination to conceive, how either man or beast, could possibly live, by reason of the sharpness of the air, when once the ark came to be raised above the middle region, above the tops of the highest mountains.

"It is a much more reasonable scheme, therefore, and what rids us of all these difficulties, to suppose, that the "flood

ᵈ *Ibid.* Occasional Annot. 11.   ᵉ If. Vossius De ætate mundi, p. 283.

"flood was not universal, but confined to some particular
"countries; that, as its primary design was to destroy
"mankind only, (who could hardly be thought, in so
"short a time, to have overspread the whole face of the
"earth,) there was no necessity to carry the waters be-
"yond the bounds of what was inhabited; and that the
"waters required to raise the deluge some fifteen cubits
"above the highest mountains, are more than what the
"clouds, the rivers, the sea, and all the supposed cavities
"of the earth, were able to produce. For, to come to
"an estimate of this, ᶠ we must first suppose water enough
"to cover the plain surface of the earth, the fields, and
"lower grounds; then we must heap up so much more up-
"on this, as will reach above the tops of the highest moun-
"tains; so that, drawing a circle over the tops of the
"highest mountains, quite round the earth, (suppose from
"pole to pole) and another to meet round the middle of
"the earth, all that space or capacity, contained within
"these circles, is to be filled up with water; and what a
"prodigious mass must this needs make?

"In a word, we allow the flood to have been so far uni-
"versal, that it overwhelmed all the parts of the then in-
"habited world, and that all the race of mankind, except
"Noah's family, was destroyed in it; but that it should
"extend itself over the whole globe, we see no manner of
"reason, because the whole globe was not then inhabited:
"Nor can we find out, in the whole storehouse of nature,
"a sufficient quantity of water to overflow it to the height
"which Moses talks of, even though the whole of it had
"been inhabited. And therefore we may well be allowed
"to conclude, that the deluge was local, and might pro-
"bably happen in that tract of ground, which lies between
"the four seas, the Persian, the Caspian, the Euxine, and
"the Syrian, in which compass are the Tygris, the Eu-
"phrates, and several other large rivers, that might be
"contributory to the inundation."

A. M. 1656, &c. Ant. Chri. 1319, &c. from Gen. vi. 11. to ix. 10.

How many wise ends the providence of God might have in bringing this destruction upon the earth, it is impossible for us to find out: but even supposing that he had but this one, viz. to rid himself of a generation that was become profligate, and past all hopes of amendment; yet the number

Answered, by shewing the deluge to be universal, from the number of the world's inhabitants.

ᶠ Burnet's Theory, l. 1. c. 2.

A. M. 1656, &c. Ant. Chrif. 2349, &c. from Gen. iv. 12. to ix. 20.

number of mankind, which, before the flood, was vaftly fuperior to what the prefent earth perhaps is capable of fuftaining, caufed every place to be inhabited, and that none might efcape the avenging hand, caufed every place to be overflowed. And indeed, if we confider the longevity of the firft inhabitants of the earth, and the pretty near equality of their ages (which feem to have been providentially defigned for the quick propagation of mankind) we fhall foon perceive, that, in the fpace of 1600 years, mankind would become fo numerous, that the chief difficulty would be where we fhould find countries to receive them. For if, in the fpace of about 266 years (as the facred hiftory acquaints us) the pofterity of Jacob, by his fons only, (without the confideration of Dinah his daughter) amounted to fix hundred thoufand males above the age of twenty, all able to bear arms, what increafe may not be expected from a race of patriarchs, living 6, 7, 8, or 9 hundred years apiece, and fome to the five hundredth year of their lives begetting fons and daughters. For, ᵍ if we fuppofe the increafe of the children of Ifrael to have been gradual, and proportionate through the whole 266 years, it will appear, that they doubled themfelves every fourteen years at leaft; and if we fhould continue the like proportion through the entire hundred and fourteen periods (which the fpace from the creation to the deluge admits) the product, or number of people on the face of the earth at the deluge, would at leaft be the hundredth in a geometric double proportion, or feries of numbers, 2, 4, 8, 16, &c. where every fucceeding one is double to that before it: And to how an immenfe fum this proportion would arife, * thofe who know any thing

---

ᵍ Whifton's Theory of the earth, l. 3. c. 3.

* The ingenious Dr Burnet [in his Theory of the earth l. 1.] has computed the multiplication of mankind in this method. "If we allow the firft couple, *fays he*, at the end of 100 "years, or of the firft century, to have left ten pair of breed- "ers (which is no hard fuppofition) there would arife from "thefe, in 1500 years, a greater number than the earth was "capable of, allowing every pair to multiply in the fame decu- "ble proportion, that the firft pair did. But, becaufe this would "rife far beyond the capacity of the earth, let us fuppofe them "to increafe, in the following centuries, in a quintuple propor- "tion only, or, if you will, only in a quadruple, and then the "table of the multiplication of mankind, from the creation to "the flood, would ftand thus:

Century

Chap. VI.   *from the Creation to the Flood*   207

thing of the nature of geometric progressions, will soon perceive. So that had the antediluvians only multiplied as fast before, as it is certain the Israelites did since the flood, the number of mankind actually alive and existing at the deluge must have been not only more than what the present earth does contain, but prodigiously more than what the whole number of mankind can be justly supposed, ever since the deluge; nay indeed, with any degree of likelihood, ever since the first creation of the world. Upon which account, though this calculation must not at all be esteemed real, or to exhibit in any measure the just number of the posterity of Adam alive at the time of the deluge, yet it certainly shews us how vastly numerous (according to the regular method of human propagation) the offspring of one single person may be; how plentifully each quarter of the world must then have been stocked with inhabitants; and that consequently, to destroy its inhabitants, the inundation must have fallen upon every quarter, and encompassed the whole globe.

{A. M. 1656, &c. Ant. Chrif. 2349. &c. from Gen. vi. 11. to ix. 20.}

And accordingly, if we take the circuit of the globe, and inquire of the inhabitants of every climate, we shall find, [h] that the fame of this deluge is gone through the earth, and that in every part of the known world there are certain records or traditions of it; that the Americans acknowledge, and speak of it in their continent; that the Chinese (who are the most distant people in Asia) have the tradition

{From tradition.}

Century		Century	
1	10	9	655360
2	40	10	2621440
3	160	11	10485760
4	640	12	41943040
5	2560	13	167772160
6	10240	14	671088640
7	40960	15	2684354560
8	163840	16	10737418240

This product is too excessive high, if compared with the present number of men upon the face of the earth, which I think is commonly estimated to between three and four hundred millions; and yet this proportion of their increase seems to be low enough, if we take one proportion for all the centuries. For though in reality the same measure cannot run equally through all the ages, yet we have taken this as moderate and reasonable between the highest and the lowest; but if we had only taken a triple proportion, it would have been sufficient (all things considered) for our purpose.

[h] Burnet's Theory, *Ibid.*

tradition of it; that the several nations of Africa tell various stories concerning it; and that in the European parts, the flood of Deucalion is the same with that of Noah, only related with some disguise. So that we may trace the deluge quite round the globe, and (what is more remarkable still) every one of these people have a tale to tell, some one way, some another, concerning the restoration of mankind, which is a full proof that they thought all mankind were once destroyed in that deluge.

Nay, instead of the surrounding globe, we need only turn aside the surface a little, and look into the bowels of the earth, and we shall find arguments enough for our conviction. For * the beds of shells which are often found on the tops of the highest mountains, and the petrified bones and teeth of fishes which are dug up some hundreds of miles from the sea, are the clearest evidences in the world, that the waters have, some time or other, overflowed the highest parts of the earth; nor can it, with any colour of reason, be asserted, that these subterraneous bodies are only the mimickry or mock-productions of nature, for that they are real shells, the nicest examination

---

* A learned author, who has lately undertaken an examination of revelation, has enforced this argument with a good deal of life and spirit. "Whereas Moses assures us, (says he,) that *the waters prevailed fifteen cubits above the highest mountains,* let the mountains themselves be appealed to for the truth of this assertion. Examine the highest eminences of the earth, and they all, with one accord, produce the spoils of the ocean, deposited upon them on that occasion, the shells and skeletons of sea-fish and sea-monsters of all kinds. The Alps, the Appenine, the Pyrenees, the Andes, and Atlas, and Ararat, every mountain of every region under heaven, from Japan to Mexico, all conspire, in one uniform, universal proof, that they all had the sea spread over their highest summits. Search the earth, and you will find the mouse-deer, natives of America, buried in Ireland; elephants, natives of Asia and Africa, buried in the midst of England: crocodiles, natives of the Nile, in the heart of Germany; shell fish, never known in any but the American seas, together with entire skeletons of whales, in divers countries; and what is more, trees and plants of various kinds, which are not known to grow in any region under heaven. All which are a perfect demonstration that Moses's account of the deluge is incontestibly true;" *part* 1. *dissertation* 2.

Chap. VI.   *from the Creation to the Flood.*

examination both of the eye and microscope does evince, and that they are true bones, may be proved by burning them, which (as it does other bones) turns them first into a coal, and afterwards into a calx.

A. M. 1656, &c. Ant. Chrif. 2349, &c. from Gen. vi. 12. to ix. 29

These considerations bid fair for the universality of the deluge; but then, if we take in the testimony of Scripture, this puts the matter past all doubt. For when we read, that, by reason of the deluge, ⁱ *every living substance was destroyed, which was upon the face of the ground, both man and cattle, and the creeping things, and the fowl of the heaven;* that during the deluge, ᵏ *the waters exceedingly prevailed, and all the high hills that were under the whole heavens were covered;* and that, when the deluge was over, God made a covenant with Noah, that ˡ *there should be no more a flood to destroy the earth, and to cut off all flesh;* we cannot but conclude, that every creature under heaven, except what was preserved in the ark, was swept away in the general devastation.

from Scripture,

And, indeed, unless this devastation was general, we can hardly conceive what necessity there was for any ark at all. ᵐ Noah, and his family, might have retired into some neighbouring country, as Lot and his family saved themselves by withdrawing from Sodom, when that city was to be destroyed. This had been a much better expedient, and might have been done with much more ease, than the great preparations he was ordered to make, of a large vessel, with stalls and apartments for the reception of beasts and birds. Beasts might have possibly saved themselves by flight; but if they did not, Noah might, after the deluge, have furnished himself from other places, which this desolation had not reached; and as for the birds, they, without much difficulty, might have flown to the next dry country, perching upon trees, or the tops of mountains, by the way, to rest themselves if they were tired, because the waters did not prevail upon the earth all on a sudden, but swelled by degrees to their determinate height.

and from reason.

Now, if the swelling of these waters to a height, superior to that of the loftiest mountains, was only topical, we cannot but allow, that unless there was a miracle to keep them up on heaps, they would certainly flow all over the earth; because these mountains are certainly high enough to have made them fall every way, and join with the seas,

ⁱ Gen. vii. 23.   ᵏ Ch. vii. 19.   ˡ Ch. ix. 11.   ᵐ Burnet's Theory, l. 1.

which environ the earth. All liquid bodies, we know, are diffusive: their parts being in motion, have no tie or connection one with another, but glide, and fall off any way, as gravity and the air press them; and therefore, when the waters began to arise at first, long before they could swell to the height of the hills, they would diffuse themselves every way, and thereupon all the valleys and plains, and the lower parts of the earth, would be filled all the globe over, before they could rise to the tops of the mountains in any part of it. So vain and unphilosophical is the opinion of those, who, to evade the difficulty of the question, would fain limit or restrain the deluge to a particular country, or countries. For if we admit it to be universal, say they, where shall we find a sufficient quantity of water to cover the face of the earth, to the height that Moses mentions?

Some indeed have thought it the best, and most compendious way, to call in the arm of omnipotence at once, and to affirm, That God created waters on purpose to make the deluge, and then annihilated them again, when the deluge was to cease. But our business is not here to inquire what God could work by his almighty power; but to account for this event, in the best manner we can, from natural causes. " Moses, it is plain, has ascribed it to natural causes, the continued rains for forty days, and the disruption of the great abyss; and the manner of its gradual increase and decrease, wherein he has represented it, is far from agreeing with the instantaneous actions of creation and annihilation.

Others, instead of a creation, have supposed a transmutation of element, viz. either a condensation of the air, ° or a rarefaction of the waters; but neither of these expedients will do: for, besides that air is a body of a different species, and (as far as we know) cannot, by any compression or condensation, be changed into water, even upon the supposition that all the air in the atmosphere were in this manner condensed, it would not produce a bed of water over all the earth, above two and thirty feet deep; because it appears, by undoubted experiment, that a column of air from the earth to the top of the atmosphere, does not weigh more than two and thirty feet of water:

much

ⁿ Burnet's Theory, l. 1. c. 3.   ° Kircher De Arca Noe, l. 2. c. 4.

Chap. VI.   *from the Creation to the Flood.*

A. M. 1656, &c. Ant. Chrif. 2349, &c. from Gen. vi. 12, to ix. 20.

much lefs would the fpirit of rarefaction anfwer the purpofe, [p] becaufe, if we fuppofe the waters but fifteen times rarer than they naturally are, as we moft certainly do, to make them reach the tops of the higheft mountains,) it will be difficult to conceive, how they could either drown man or beaft, keep alive the fifh, or fupport the heavy bulk of the ark. The truth is, Mofes, in his account of the deluge, fays not one word of the tranfmutation of elements: the forty days rain, and the difruption of the abyfs, are the only caufes which he affigns; and thefe, very likely, will fupply us with a fufficient quantity of water when other devices fail.

[q] A very fagacious naturalift, obferving, that at certain times, there are extraordinary preffures on the furface of the fea, whch force the waters outwards upon the fhores to a great height, does very reafonably fuppofe, that the divine power might, at this time, by the inftrumentality of fome natural agent, to us at prefent unknown, fo deprefs the furface of the ocean, as to force up the water of the abyfs through certain channels and apertures, and fo make them a partial and concurrent caufe of the deluge. It cannot be denied indeed, but that the divine providence might, at the time of the deluge, fo order and difpofe fecond caufes, as to make them raife and impel the water to an height fufficient to overflow the earth; but then, becaufe there muft be another miracle required to fufpend the waters upon the land, and to hinder them from running off again into the fea, our author feems to give the preference to another hypothefis, which, at the time of the deluge, fuppofes the centre of the earth to have been changed, and fet nearer to the centre or middle of our continent, whereupon the Atlantic and Pacific oceans muft needs prefs upon the fubterraneous abyfs, and fo compel the water to run out at thofe wide mouths, and apertures, which the divine power had made in breaking up the fountains of the great deep. Thus the waters being poured out upon the face of the earth, and its declivity changed by the removal of the centre, they could not run down to the fea again, but muft neceffarily ftagnate upon the earth, and overflow it, till upon its return to its old centre, they in like manner would retreat to their former receptacles. But the misfortune of this hypothefis is, that

befides

[p] Burnet's Theory, and Le Clerc's Commentary. [q] Ray in his Physico-theological difcourfe concerning the deluge.

besides the multitude of miracles required in it, it makes the deluge topical, and confined to our continent only, whereas, according to the testimony of the spirit of God in the Holy Scriptures, it was certainly universal.

A very ingenious theorist seems to be of opinion himself, and labours to persuade others, that the * deluge was occasioned by the dissolution of the primæval earth; the dissolution of the earth by the fermentation of the inclosed

---

r Dr Burnet.

* To have a more perfect idea of the author's scheme, we must remember, that he conceives the first earth, from the manner of its formation, to have been externally regular and uniform, of a smooth and even surface, without mountains, and without a sea; and that all the waters, belonging to it were inclosed within an upper crust, which formed a stupenduous vault around them. This vast collection of waters he takes to have been the great deep, or abyss of Moses, and that the disruption it was the chief cause of the deluge. For he supposes, that the earth being for some hundreds of years, exposed to the continual heat of the sun, which, by reason of the perpendicular position, which, as he imagines, the earth's axis then had to the plane of the ecliptic, was very intense, and not allayed by the diversity of seasons, which now keep our earth in an equality of temper; its exterior crust was, at length, very much dried, and when the heat had pierced the shell, and reached the waters beneath it, they began to be rarefied, and raised into vapours; which rarefaction made them require more space than they needed before, and finding themselves pent in by an exterior earth, they pressed with violence against the arch to make it yield to their dilatation: and as the repeated action of the sun gave force to these inclosed vapours more and more, so, on the other hand, it weakened more and more the arch of the earth, that was to resist them, sucking out the moisture that was the cement of its parts, and parching and chapping it in sundry places; so that, there being then no winter to close up its parts, it every day grew more and more disposed to a dissolution, till at length, when God's appointed time was come, the whole fabrick broke; the frame of earth was torn in pieces, as by an earthquake; and those great portions or fragments, into which it was parted, fell down into the abyss, some in one posture, some in another.

Thus the earth put on a new form, and became divided into sea, and land; the greatest part of the abyss constituting our present ocean, and the rest filling up the cavities of the earth. Mountains and hills appeared on the land, islands in the sea,

closed waters; the fermentation of the waters, by the continued intense heat of the sun; and the great heat of the sun, by the perpendicular position of the axis of the earth to the plane of the ecliptic. But allowing the position of the earth to be what he imagines, ⁵ yet it seems difficult to conceive, how the heat of the sun should be so intense, as to cause great cracks in it, and so raise the waters in it into vapours; or how the waters, thus rarefied, should be of force sufficient to break through an arch of solid matter, lying upon them some hundred miles thick. It is much more probable, that if the action of the sun was so strong, the abyss (which the theorist makes the only store house of waters in the first earth) would have been almost quite exhausted, before the time of the deluge: nor can we believe that this account of things is any way consonant to the Mosaic history, which describes a gradual rise and abatement, along continuance of the flood, and not such a sudden shock and convulsion of nature, as the theorist intends, in which, without the divine intervention, it was impossible for the ark to be saved.

A. M. 1656, &c. Ant. Chrif. 2349, &c. from Gen. vi. 12. to ix. 11.

ᵗ Another learned theorist endeavours to solve the whole matter, and supply a sufficiency of water from the trajection of a comet. For he supposes, "That, in its "descent towards the sun, it pressed very violently upon "the earth and by that means, both raised a great tide "in the sea, and forced up a vast quantity of subterraneous "waters; that as it passed by, it involved the earth, in its "atmosphere for a considerable time; and as it went off, "left a vast tract of its tail behind, which (together with "the waters, pressed from the sea, and from the great a- "byss) was enough to cover the face of the whole earth, "for the perpendicular height of three miles." But (to pass by smaller objections) that which seems to destroy his whole hypothesis is this———ᵘ That it is far from being clear, whether the atmosphere of a comet be a watery substance or not. The observations of the most curious inquirers make it very probable, that the circle about the body

and rocks upon the shore, so that, at one shock, providence dissolved the old world, and made a new one out of its ruin. *Vide* the Universal history, l. 1. c. 1. where this extract out of Burnet's theory is made.

⁵ Keil's Examination of Burnet's theory.   ᵗ Mr Whiston.
ᵘ Keil's Answer to Whiston's Theory; and Nicholl's Conference, vol. 1.

A. M.
1656. &c.
Ant. Chrif.
2349, &c.
from Gen.
vi. 12. to
ix. 20.

dy of a comet is nothing, but the curling or winding round of the smoak, rising at first to a determinate height, from all parts of the comet, and then making off to that part of it which is opposite to the sun; and if this opinion be true, the earth, by passing through the atmosphere of a comet, ran a greater risque of a conflagration, than a deluge.

These are the several expedients which the wit of men hath devised, to furnish a sufficient quantity of water, in order to effect a deluge, but all incompetent for the work. Let us now turn to the sacred records, and see what the two general causes assigned therein, *the opening of the windows of heaven*, and *the breaking up of the fountains of the great deep*, are able to supply us with, upon this occasion.

The two reasons which the Scripture assigns:
1. Continued rains;

1. By *the opening of the windows of heaven*, must be understood the causing the waters which were suspended in the clouds, to fall upon the earth, not in ordinary showers, but in floods, or (as the Septuagint translate it) in cataracts, [x] which travellers may have the truest notion of, who have seen those prodigious falls of water, so frequent in the Indies, and where the clouds many times do not break into drops, but fall, with a terrible violence, in a torrent.

How far these treasures of waters in the air might contribute to the general inundation, we may, in some measure, compute from what we have observed in a thundercloud, [y] which in the space of less than two hours, has sometimes poured down such a vast quantity of water, as besides what sunk into the dry and thirsty ground and filled all the ditches and ponds, has caused a considerable flood in the rivers, and set all the meadows on float.

Now, had this cloud (which for ought we know moved forty miles forward in its falling) stood still, and emptied all its water upon the same spot of ground, what a sudden and incredible deluge would it have made made in the place? What then must we suppose the event to have been, when the flood-gates of heaven were all opened, and on every part of the globe, the clouds were incessantly pouring out water with such violence, and in such abundance, for forty days together?

It

---

[x] Patrick's Commentary.   [y] Ray on the deluge.

It is impossible for us indeed to have any adequate conception of the thing, [z] though the vast inundations which are made every year in Egypt, only by the rains which fall in Ethiopia, and the like annual overflowings of the great river Oroonoque in America, whereby many islands and plains, at other times inhabited, are laid twenty feet under water, between May and September, may give us a faint emblem, and be of some use to cure our infidelity in this respect.

A. M. 1656, &c.
Ant. Chr. f. 2349, &c.
from Gen. vi 12, to ix. 20

2 The other cause which the Scripture makes mention of, is the *breaking up of the fountains of the great deep*, whereby those waters, which were contained in vast quantities in the bowels of the earth, were forced out, and thrown upon the surface of it. [a] That there is a mighty collection of waters inclosed in the bowels of the earth, which constitutes a large globe, in the interior or central part of it; and that the waters of this globe communicate with that of the ocean, by means of certain hiatus, or apertures, passing between it and the ocean, [*] is evident from the Caspian and other seas, which receive into themselves many great rivers, and having no visible outlets, must be supposed to discharge the water they receive, by subterraneous passages into this receptacle, and by its intervention, into the ocean again. The [b] Mediterranean in particular, besides the many rivers that run into it, has two great currents of the sea, one at the straits of Gibraltar, and the other

[a] the breaking up of the abyss;

---

[z] Patrick's Commentary. [a] Woodward's Natural history.

[*] The Caspian sea is reckoned in length to be above an hundred and twenty German leagues, and in breadth, from east to west, about ninety of the same leagues. There is no visible way for the water to run out: and yet it receives into its bosom near an hundred large rivers, and particularly the great river Wolga, which of itself is like a sea for largeness, and supposed to empty so much water into it in a year's time, as might suffice to cover the whole earth; and yet it is never increased nor diminished, nor is observed to ebb or flow, which makes it evident, that it must necessarily have a subterraneous communication with other parts of the world. And accordingly, Father Avril, a modern traveller, tells us, that near the coast of Xylam there is in this sea a mighty whirlpool, which sucks in every thing that comes near it, and consequently has a cavity in the earth into which it descends. *Vid.* Moll's Geography at the end of Persia in Asia, p. 67.; Stillingfleet's Orig. sac. l. 3. c. 4.; and Bedford's Scripture-chronology, c. 12.

[b] Nicholl's Conference, vol. 1.

A. M.
1656, &c.
Ant. Chrif.
2349, &c.
from Gen.
vi. 11, &c.
ix. 10.

other at the Propontis, which bring in such vast tides of water, that, many ages ago, it must have endangered the whole world, had it not emptied itself, by certain secret passages, into some great cavity underneath. And for this reason, some have imagined, ^c that the earth altogether is one great animal, whose abyss supplies the place of the heart in the body of the earth, to furnish all its aqueducts with a sufficiency of water, and whose subterraneous passages are like the veins of the body, which receive water out of the sea, as the veins do blood out of the liver, and in a continued circulation, return it to the heart again.

However this be, it is certainly more than probable, (because a matter of divine revelation,) that there is an immense body of water inclosed in the centre of the earth, to which the Psalmist plainly alludes, when he tells us, that ^d *God founded the earth upon the seas, and established it upon the floods;* that ^e *he stretched out the earth above the waters;* that ^f *he gathered up the waters as in a bag,* (so the best translations have it,) *and laid up the deep as in a store-house.* Nay, there is a passage or two in the Proverbs of Solomon, (where wisdom declares her antiquity, and pre-existence to all the works of the earth,) which sets before our eyes, as it were, the very form and figure of this abyss: ^g *When he prepared the heavens, I was there, when he set a compass upon the face of the deep, and strengthened the fountains of the abyss.* Here is mention made of the abyss, and the fountains of the abyss; nor is there any question to be made, but that the fountains of the abyss here are the same with those which Moses mentions, and which, as he tells us, were broken up at the deluge. And what is more observable in this text, the word which we render *compass,* properly signifies *a circle,* or circumference, or an orb, or sphere: so that, according to the testimony of Wisdom, who was then present, there was in the beginning a sphere, orb, or arch, set round the abyss, by the means of which, the fountains thereof were strengthened; for we cannot conceive, how they could have been strengthened any other way, than by having a strong cover or arch made over them.

If

^c Stillingfleet's Orig. sacr. cxxxvi. 6. ^f Psal. xxxiii. 7. Sir Walter Raleigh's History.
^d Psal. xxiv. 2. ^e Psal. ^g Prov. viii. 27. 28.

If such then be the form of this abyss, that it seems to be a vast mass or body of water lying together in the womb of the earth, it will be no hard matter to compute what a plentiful supply might have been expected from thence, in order to effect an universal deluge. [h] For if the circumference of the earth (even according to the lowest computation) be 21,000 miles, the diameter of it (according to that circumference) 7000 miles; and consequently from the superficies to the centre, 3500 miles; and if (according to the best account) * the highest mountain in the world (taking its altitude from the plain it stands upon) does not exceed four perpendicular miles in height; then we cannot but conclude, that in this abyss there would be infinitely more water than enough, when drawn out upon the surface of the earth, to drown the earth to a far greater height than Moses relates. In a word, since it is agreed on all hands, that in the time of the chaos, the waters did cover the earth, insomuch that nothing of it could be seen, till God was pleased to make a separation: why should it be thought so strange a thing, that, upon a proper occasion, they should be able to cover the earth again; [i] especially when the waters above the firmament came down to join those below, as they did at the beginning?

[k] Seneca, treating of that fatal day (as he calls it) when the deluge shall come, (for he supposed that the world

A. M. 1656, &c.
Ant. Chrif. 2349, &c.
from Gen. vi. 12. to ix. 20.

Its sufficiency to drown the world.

[h] Patrick's Commentary.

* It is very probable, that men are exceedingly mistaken as to the height of mountains, since, upon examination, it appears that the highest in the world is not four miles perpendicular. Olympus, whose height is so extolled by the poets, does not much exceed a mile and a half. The mount Athos which is said to cast its shadow into the isle of Lemnos, (according to Pliny 87 miles) is but two miles in height; nay, the very Pike of Teneriff, which is reputed the highest mountain in the world, may be ascended in three days, which (according to the proportion of eight furlong's to a day's journey) make it much about the height of a German mile perpendicular, as Varenius confesses. And as for those mountains in Peru, in comparison of which (as the Spaniards tell us) the Alps are no more than cottages, they themselves allow, that they may be ascended in four days, which still reduces them much within the compass of four miles, and thereby makes the account of the flood, and its overtoping the highest mountains, not so improbable as some imagine; *Stillingfleet's Orig. sacr. lib. 3. cap. 4.*

[i] *Vid.* l. 1. c. 1. p. 6. [k] *Nat. Quæst.* 3. c. 27.

A. M.
1656, &c.
Ant. Chrif.
2249. &c.
from Gen.
vi. 12. to
ix. 20.

world was to be destroyed alternately, first by water, and after that by fire,) and questioning how it might be effected, whether by the force of the ocean overflowing the earth, by perpetual rains without intermission, by the swelling of rivers, and opening of new fountains, or (what he rather supposes) by a general concourse and combination of all these causes, concludes his inquiry at last with these remarkable words, " There are vast lakes (says he) " which we do not see, much of the sea which lies hidden " and concealed, and many rivers which glide in secret; " so that there may be causes of a deluge on all sides, " when some waters flow under the earth, others flow " round about it, and being long pent up, may overwhelm " it. And as our bodies sometimes dissolve into sweat, " so the earth shall melt, and, without the help of other " causes, shall find in itself what shall drown it.——There " being in all places, both openly and secretly, both from " above and from beneath, an eruption of waters ready to " overflow and destroy it."

But whatever solutions we may gather, either from sacred or profane authors, it seems necessary, after all, to call in the divine power to our assistance. ¹ For though the waters which covered the earth at the creation might be sufficient to cover it again; yet how this could be effected by mere natural means, cannot be conceived. Tho' the waters, suspended in the clouds, might fall in great torrents for some time, yet, when once their store was exhausted, (as at this rate it could not last long,) nothing but an almighty voice could have commanded a fresh supply of forty days continuance from those other planetary spaces where he had settled their abode; and though the subterraneous stores did certainly contain a fund sufficient to complete the deluge, yet there wanted on this occasion an almighty hand, either to break down the arch which enclosed the abyss, or by some secret passages to force the waters out of it upon the surface of the earth; and so stopping the reflux, suspend them for such a determinate time, at such an elevation. There needed some almighty hand, I say, to do this: and accordingly we may observe, that though Moses makes mention of two natural causes that might be conducive to the work, yet he introduces God as superintending their causes, and assuming indeed the whole performance to himself: for *behold I, even I, do*
bring

¹ Univerf. History, l. 1. c. 1.

bring a flood of waters upon the earth, to destroy all flesh wherein is the breath of life, from under heaven, and every thing that is on the earth shall die.

<small>A. M. 1656, &c. Ant. Chrif. 2349, &c. from Gen. vi. 12. to ix. 20.</small>

Thus, with the help and concurrence of God, we have found a sufficient quantity of water for the destruction of the old world: let us now consider the make and capacity of the vessel wherein the several animals that were to replenish the new were to be preserved.

<small>Moses's manner of describing the ark.</small>

ᵐ Could we but imagine, that by some strange revolution the whole art of shipping should come to be lost in this part of the world, and that there happened to remain such a short account of one of our largest ships (the Royal Anne, for instance) as that it was so many foot long, broad, and deep; could contain in it some hundreds of men, with other living creatures, and provisions for them all during several months; and that the strength of it was such, that it was not broken in pieces all the time that the great storm endured; would it not be very pleasant for any one to conclude from hence, that this ship, according to the description of it, was nothing but an oblong square, without any more contrivance than a common chest made by the most ignorant joiner? And yet such are some men's inferences when they talk of this noble structure.

<small>Its design to float in calm weather.</small>

Moses indeed makes mention of little else but the dimensions of the ark, its stories, and capacity to hold the things to be placed in it; but it does not therefore follow, but that it might have the convexity of a keel, (as many large flat bottomed vessels have,) as well as a prow, to make it cut the waters more easily. The design of the vessel however was not to make way, (as they call it at sea,) but to preserve its inhabitants; and this it was more capable of doing (as † may be proved to a demonstration) than if it had

---

ᵐ Biblioth. Biblica; Occas. annot. 13.

† For let us suppose, that without any addition of art, it was nothing more than an oblong square, whose length was sextuple to the breadth, and decuple to the height; it is demonstrable, that a piece of wood of that proportion being lighter than the water, will be always supported by it. For instance, take a plank of oak exactly square, let it be one foot broad, six foot long, and seven or eight inches thick, answering the proportion of the ark; there is nobody, I believe, will say, that any waves or winds will be strong enough to break this piece of timber, notwithstanding its right angles. Now, let any solid of this fashion be multiplied in a decuple, centuple, or millecuple

A. M. 1656, &c.
Ant. Chrif. 2349 &c. from Gen vi. 13. to ix. 20.

had been built according to the moſt modern model, even ſuppoſing the waters, from the firſt to the laſt, to have been never ſo boiſterous. But this they were not: whatever ſtorms and convulſions there might be in particular places, when the flood gates of heaven were at firſt opened, and the fountains of the great deep broken up, (and then the ark was not afloat,) the ſacred text takes no notice of any rough weather till after the 150 days of the flood's gradual increaſe, when, upon the ceaſing of the rains from above, and the waters from beneath, God ſent forth a ſtrong driving wind, but then the ark was at reſt. So that all the time that the ark was afloat, or (as the Scripture expreſſes it) while it *went on the face of the waters*, the winds were aſleep, and the weather, though rainy, was free from all ſtorms and angry commotions. Upon the whole, therefore, we may conclude, that, be the ſtructure of the ark what it will, it was certainly ſuited both to the burthen it was to carry, and the weather it was to live in; and on this, and ſundry other accounts, * upon experiment, perhaps it may be found to be the moſt complete and perfect model that ever was deviſed.

Its capacity to hold every thing that was to be put in it

Had we never ſeen a ſhip, and ſhould be told what a number of men, and what a quantity of proviſion and merchandiſe one of the largeſt rates will carry, it would ſeem no leſs incredible to us than what Moſes tells us of the things which were contained in the ark. The ark, according

millecuple proportion, and let the force of the waves, and the invaſive power of the wind, be multiplied alſo with it in the ſame proportion, the reſiſtance of a rectangular ſolid (which is perfectly impenetrable, and exactly the caſe of the ark) will be proof againſt any given force whatever; *Bibliotheca Biblica vol.* 1.; *Occaſ. annot.* 13.

* About the beginning of the laſt century, Peter Janſon, a Dutch merchant, cauſed a ſhip to be built for him, anſwering in its reſpective proportions, to thoſe of Noah's ark, the length of it being a 120 foot, the breadth of it 20, and the depth of it 12. At firſt this ark was looked upon no better than as a fanatical viſion of this Janſon, (who was by profeſſion a Menoniſt,) and, whilſt it was building, he and his ſhip were made the ſport of the ſeamen, as much as Noah and his ark could be. But afterwards it was found that ſhips built in this faſhion were, in the time of peace, beyond all others moſt commodious for commerce; becauſe they would hold a third part more, without requiring any more hands, and were found far better runners than any made before; *Bibliotheca Biblia,* ibid.

according to his account, was 300 cubits in length, 50 in breadth, and 30 in height; and if we suppose the cubit, here mentioned, at the lowest computation, to be but a foot and an half long, yet was the length of it according to that proportion) 450 feet, the breadth 75, and the height 45; and consequently the whole capacity 1,580,750 cubical feet, which was space enough, in all conscience to receive every thing, and much more than every thing that was to be contained in it. For it appears from the sacred text, that the form of the ark was rectangular; ⁿ and being intended only for a kind of float to swim above the water, the flatness of its bottom did render it much more capacious. It appears from the same text, that this ark consisted of three stories, and the whole height of it being 45 feet; it may well be supposed that this height was equally divided among the three stories, and so each story was 15 foot high, only deducting a foot and an half, or one cubit, for the slope of the roof, or the cover of the upper story. ᵒ It is likewise pretty well agreed by interpreters, that the lowest story was appointed for four-footed animals, as most commodious for them; the middle story for their provender, and what they were to live upon; and the upper story partly for the birds, and what they were to eat, and partly for Noah and his family, together with their utensils: and that each of these stories was spacious enough to receive what was to be put therein, will appear to any one who will give himself the trouble ᵖ of making a geometrical calculation.

A. M. 6 6 &c.
Ant. Chrisſt. 2349, &c.
from Gen. vi. 12. to ix. 20.

He

ⁿ Wilkins's Essay towards a real character.   ᵒ Wells' Geography, vol. 1. cap 2.; Lamy's Introduction.

ᵖ Buteo has plainly demonstrated, that all the animals contained in the ark could not be equal to 500 horses; (the learned Heidegger, from Temporarius, makes them 400 oxen;) and yet it is not to be questioned, but that a building very near as long as St Paul's Church, and as broad as the middle isle of that church is high within, is capable of offording stabling for such a number of horses, *Vid.* Dr Bundy's translation of Lamy's introduction. Kircher (in his *Arca Noe*, c. 8.) has given us large calculations of the dimensions of the ark, and from thence concludes, that this vessel was capacious enough to receive, not only Noah and his family, all other creatures and their food but even an entire province likewise. Wilkins, (in his Essay towards a real character), and from him Wells (in his Geography

A. M.
1656, &c.
Ant. Chrif.
2349, &c.
from Gen.
vi. 12. to
ix. 20.

The number of animals;

He who looks upon the ſtars, as they are confuſedly ſcattered up and down in the firmament, will think them to be (what they are ſometimes called) innumerable, and above the power of all arithmetic to count; and yet, when they are diſtinctly reduced to their particular conſtellations, and deſcribed by their ſeveral places, magnitudes, and names, it appears, that of thoſe which are viſible to the naked eye, there are not many more than a thouſand in the whole firmament, and few more than half ſo many (even taking in the minuter kinds of them) to be ſeen at once in any hemiſphere. And in like manner, he who ſhould put the queſtion, How many kinds of beaſts or birds there are in the world? would be anſwered, even by ſuch as in other reſpects are knowing and learned enough, that there are ſo many hundreds of them as cannot be enumerated; whereas, upon a diſtinct inquiry into all ſuch as are yet known, or have been deſcribed by credible authors, it will appear, that they are much fewer than is commonly imagined, [p] not an hundred ſorts of beaſts, and not two hundred of birds.

And why fewer than is imagined.

And yet, out of this number, as ſmall as it is, we muſt except all animals that are of equivocal generation, as inſects; all that are accuſtomed to live in water, as fiſh and water-fowl; all that proceed from a mixture of different ſpecies, as mules; and all that, by changing their climate, change their colour and ſize, and ſo paſs for different creatures, when in reality they are the ſame. We muſt obſerve farther, that all creatures of the ſerpentine kind, the

phy of the Old Teſtament) have both entered into a large detail of things, and given us an exact and complete idea of the capacity of the ark, and of its proportion together, with what it might contain. Le Peletier (in his *Differ. ſur l'arch de Noe*) follows another Engliſh author, Biſhop Cumberland, who, in his Diſcovery of the weights and meaſures of the Jews, has, proved, that the ancient cubit of the Jews was the old derah of Memphis; whereupon Peletier allows 1,781,377 cubical feet of Paris for the whole contents of the ark, ſo that it might hold (as he pretends) 42,413 tons of lading. But a certain anonymous author has publiſhed a diſſertation upon the ſame principles, wherein he compares the ark to our modern ſhips, and computes its meaſure according to the tons it might contain, and thereupon makes it larger than 40 ſhips of 1000 tons each. Vid *Differt. hiſt. circun- geograph. &c.* d. 2.; *Journal de Paris ſur Janvier* 1712, *tom.* 51. *p.* 9.

[p] Wilkins's Eſſay

Chap. VI.   *from the Creation to the Flood.*   223

the viper, snake, flow-worm, lizard, frog, toad, &c. might have sufficient space for their reception, and for their nourishment in the hold or bottom of the ark, which was probably three or four foot under the floor, whereon the beasts are supposed to stand: and that the smaller creatures, such as the mouse, rat, mole, &c. might find sufficient room in several parts of the ark, without having any particular places or cells appointed for them: so that the number of the several species of animals to be placed in the first or lowest story, upon the foot of this deduction, stands thus.

A. M. 1656, &c. Ant. Chrisf. 2349, &c. from Gen. vi. 12. to ix. 10.

Beasts which live on hay.		On fruits and roots.		On flesh.	
The Horse	Stone-buck	The Hog	The Lion	Stoat
Ass	Shamois	Baboon	Bear	Weesle
Camel	Antelope	Ape	Tyger	Castor
Elephant	Elke	Monkey	Pard	Otter
Bull	Hart	Sloth	Ounce	Dog
Urus	Buck	Porcupine	Cat	Wolf
Bison	Rein-deer	Hedge-hog	Civet-cat	Fox
Bonasus	Roe	Squirrel	Finet	Badger
Buffalo	Rhinoceros	Guinea pig	Polecat	Jackall
Sheep	Camelopard	Ant-bear	Martin	Caraguya.
Stepciseros	Hare	Armadilla		
Broad-tail	Rabbit	Tortoise.		
Goat	Marmotte.			

Now, concerning these creatures God gives Noah this injunction: *ᵃ Of every clean beast, thou shalt take to thee by sevens, the male and the female; and of beasts that are not clean, by two, the male and the female.* Taking the words then in their highest acceptation, *viz.* that Noah was to receive into the ark one pair of every species of unclean animals, and seven pair of every species of clean; yet, considering that the species of unclean animals, which were admitted by pairs only, are many in comparison of the clean, and the species of large animals few in comparison of the smaller; we cannot but perceive (as by a short calculation it will appear) that this lower story, which was ten cubits high, three hundred long, and fifty broad, *i. e.* 225,000 solid feet in the whole, would be capable of receiving, with all manner of conveniency, not only all the sorts of beasts that we are acquainted with, but probably all those other kinds which are any where to be found under the copes of heaven.

The lowest story large enough for their reception, and why

It is a pretty general opinion, and what seems to be founded on Scripture, that before the flood, both men, beasts,

The middle story sufficient to contain their provender, and why

U u 2

ᵃ Gen. viii. 2.

A. M.
1656, &c.
Ant. Chrif
2349, &c.
from Gen.
vi. 12. to
ix. 20.

beafts, and birds fed only upon fruits and vegetables. ʳ *Behold I have given you every herb,* says God, *bearing feed, which is upon the face of all the earth, and every tree in which is the fruit of a tree yielding feed, to you it shall be for meat ; and to every beaft of the earth, and to every fowl of the air, and to every thing that creepeth upon the earth, wherein there is life; I have given every green herb for meat:* * Nor do there want inftances in hiftory of fome very ravenous creatures that have been brought to live upon other kind of food than flefh. So that

---

ʳ Chap. i. 29, 30.

* It is not to be denied, but that feveral learned men have taken great pains to provide flefh for the carnivorous animals fhut up in the ark, when it is beyond all controverfy that the ftomachs of fuch animals are fitted for the digeftion of fruits and vegetables; that fuch food would be more falutary both for them and their keepers, and would create a lefs demand of drink throughout the courfe of fo long a confinement; and yet there is not the leaft foundation from the text to fuppofe, that any fuch provifion was made for creatures of fuch an appetite, but feveral inftances in hiftory do fhew, that even the moft rapacious of them all may be brought to live upon other diet than flefh. Thus Philoftratus, in his Apollonius, l. 5. tells us of a lion in Egypt, which, though it went into the temple conftantly, would neither lick the blood of facrifices, nor eat any of the flefh when it was cut in pieces, but fed altogether on bread and fweat-meats: and Sulpitius Severus [Dial. 1. c. 7.] gives us this account of a Monk of Thebais. " When we came to
" the tree, whither our courteous hoft led us we there perceiv-
" ed a lion, at the fight of which I and my guide began to
" tremble; but as the holy man went directly up to it, we,
" though in no fmall fright, followed after. The beaft, at our
" approach, modeftly retired, and ftood very quiet and ftill,
" while the good man gathered it fome branches of apples, and
" as he held them out, the lion came up and eat them, and fo
" went off." The like ftory is told by Phocas, in his defcription of the Holy Land, cap. 13. of fome lions beyond the river Jordan, whom an Anchorite, named *Iberus* fed with pulfe and crufts of bread: and to the animals in the ark, feeding in this manner, the prophet Ifaiah, fpeaking of the times of the Meffiah, [ch. 11. 6, 7] is fuppofed by our author to allude *The wolf fhall dwell with the lamb and the leopard lie down with the kid, and the calf, and the young lion, and the fatling together, and a little child fhall lead them; and the cow and the bear fhall feed, their young ones fhall lie down together and the lion fhall eat ftraw with the ox:* Heidegger's Hift. patr. exer. 17.

that there was no necessity for Noah's providing so many supernumerary sheep (as some would have it) to feed the carnivorous animals for a whole year. ˢ The same divine providence which directed all the animals, of whatever country, to make towards the ark, which took from them their fierceness, and made them tame and gentle upon this occasion, might likewise beget in them a loathing of flesh, (supposing they eat it before,) and an appetite for hay, corn, fruits, or any other eatables that were most obvious in this time of distress. And as they were shut up, and could not spend themselves by motion, but might have their stomachs palled with the continued agitation of the vessel, they may well be supposed to stand in need of less provision than at other times.

A. M. 1656, &c. Ant. Christ. 2349, &c. from Gen. vi. 12. to ix. 20.

If then (to make our computation) we should say, that ᵗ all the beasts in the lower story of the ark were equal, in their consumption of food, to 300 oxen, (which is more by a great deal than some calculations have allowed,) that 30 or 40 pounds of hay are ordinarily sufficient for an ox for one day; and that a solid cubit of hay, well compressed, will weigh about 40 pounds; then will this second story, being of the same dimensions with the other, i. e. 225,000 solid feet, not only allow a space for a sufficient quantity of hay, but for other repositories of such fruits, roots, and grain, as might be proper for the nourishment of those animals that live not upon hay; and for such passages and apertures in the floor as might be necessary for the putting down hay and other provender to the beasts in the lower story.

Upon the whole therefore it appears, that the middle story of the ark was likewise large enough to hold all that was requisite to be put therein: and as for the third and upper story, there can no manner of doubt be made, but that it was sufficient to hold all the species of birds, even though they were many more than they are generally computed. The accurate bishop **Wilkins** * has divided them into

The upper story sufficient for its purpose.

ˢ Heidegger's Hist. patriar. *ibid.*   ᵗ Wilkin's Essay, part 2. c. 5.

* The manner of his reckoning them up is this:

1. Carnivorous birds — — — 66
2. Phytivorous birds of short wings — — 17
3. Phytivorous birds of long wings — — 18
4. Phytivorous birds of short thick bills — 16
5. Insectivorous

A. M. 1656, &c.
Ant. Chrif. 2349, &c.
from Gen. vi. 12. to ix. 20.

into nine forts, and reckon them to be an hundred and ninety-five in the whole; but then the greateſt part of them are ſo very ſmall, that they might well enough be kept in partitions or cages piled one upon another. The food neceſſary for their ſuſtenance would not take up any great proportion of room, and the remainder of the ſtory would make a commodious enough habitation for Noah and his family, together with little cloſets and offices, wherein to diſpoſe of their ſeveral domeſtic matters and utenſils.

Bifhop Wilkins's reflection upon the whole.

Upon the whole inquiry then, ſays the ſame learned prelate, it does, of the two, appear more difficult to aſſign a ſufficient number and bulk of neceſſary things to anſwer the capacity of the ark, than to find ſufficient room in it for the convenient reception of them; and thereupon he truly, as well as piouſly, concludes, "That had the
" moſt ſkilful mathematicians and philoſophers been ſet to
" conſult what proportions a veſſel deſigned for ſuch an
" uſe as the ark was, ſhould have in the ſeveral parts of
" it, they could not have pitched upon any other more
" ſuitable to the purpoſe than theſe mentioned by Moſes
" are; inſomuch, that the proportion of the ark (from
" which ſome weak and Atheiſtical perſons have made
" ſome poor efforts to overthrow the authority of the ſacred
" Scriptures) does very much tend to confirm and eſtabliſh
" the truth and divine authority of them. Eſpecially,
" if we only conſider, that in theſe days men were leſs
" verſed in arts and ſciences; at leaſt, that the ark was,
" in all probability, the firſt veſſel of any bulk that was
" made to go upon the water: whence the juſtneſs of
" the proportion obſerved in its ſeveral parts, and the ex-
" actneſs of its capacity to the uſe it was deſigned for, are
" reaſonably

5. Infectivorous birds the greater — — 15
6. Infectivorous birds the leſs — — 12
7. Aquatic birds near wet places — — 17
8. Aquatic fiſſipedes — — 16
9. Aquatic plenipedes — — 18

In all—195

To theſe perhaps may he added ſome exotic birds; but as the number of theſe is but ſmall, ſo we may obſerve the carnivorous, which is the largeſt ſpecies, that they were reputed unclean, and conſequently, but two of each ſort admitted into the ark; *Bedford's Scrip. chron.* 2. 12.

ⁿ Wilkins, *ibid.*

"reasonably to be aſcribed, not to bare human invention and contrivance, but to the divine direction, expreſsly given to Noah by God himſelf, as the ſacred hiſtorian acquaints us."

<small>A. M. 1656, &c. Ant. Chriſ. 2349 &c. from Gen. vi. 12 to ix. 20.</small>

Thus we have placed the ſeveral kinds of creatures in the ark, and furniſhed them with a competent ſtock of proviſion.

And now, if it ſhould be aſked, **How** came they all thither? the reply in that caſe will be this —— ˣ That the country of Eden is very reaſonably ſuppoſed by learned men to be next adjacent to the garden of that name, from whence Adam was expelled; and that, as all early accounts of that country paint it out to us, as one of the moſt fruitful and delicious regions in the earth, (though now greatly changed,) there is no reaſon to imagine, that Adam ſought for any habitation beyond it. There, according to many concurring circumſtances, was this famous ark built: there is gopher-wood (very reaſonably ſuppoſed to be cypreſs) found in great abundance; there is aſphaltus, wherewith the ark, to defend it from the impreſſion of the waters, was daubed and ſmeared both within and without; and not far from thence is mount Ararat, where the ark, as the waters began to abate, is known to have reſted: and in this ſituation, there is not any reaſon to imagine, that any one ſpecies of animals could be out of Noah's reach. ʸ There they were all natives of the ſame country, and he perhaps, ſome time before the flood, might have tamed ſome of every kind, ſo that, when the deluge came on, they might eaſily be brought to the ark, and every one ranged in its proper place, before that Noah ſhut it up.

<small>How the ſeveral creatures were brought to the ark.</small>

But now, that they are all ſhut up, what ſhall we do for air to keep them alive, or for light, to direct them in what they are to do? Mention indeed is made of a window, left in the upper part of the ark; but this is ſaid to be no more than a cubit ſquare, and what is this in proportion to ſo vaſt a fabric? Either therefore we muſt deviſe ſome relief for them in this exigence, or we ſhall ſoon find the poor remains of the creation in utter darkneſs, and in the ſhadow of death.

<small>How they lived for want of air and light</small>

ᶻ As the word *Zohar*, which we render *window*, is never mentioned in the ſingular number through the whole compaſs

---

ˣ Revelation Examined, part 1.   ʸ Howell's Hiſtory, vol. 1. l, 1.   ᶻ Vid. Bibliotheca Biblica, vol. 1.; Occaſional annot.

A. M. 1656, &c. Ant. Chrif. 2349, &c. from Gen. vi. 12 to ix. 20.

compafs of the Bible, but only this once, it perhaps may be no very eafy thing to find out its true fignification. Whether the LXX interpreters underftood the meaning of it; whether they knew, in the Greek language, any word capable of expreffing it; or whether they might think it of fo facred a nature, as not proper to be publifhed at all; but fo it is, that they prudently have omitted it in their tranflation, and will have the precept, or direction, which God gives Noah, to mean no more, than that he fhould finifh the ark, by clofing it on the top, and compacting it well together.

The word has its original from a verb which fignifies *to burn*, or *or fhine like oil*; and indeed where-ever it occurs (as it fometimes occurs in the dual number,) it always fignifies fome bright and luminous body: and accordingly, fome of the Jewifh doctors were of opinion, that this muft have been a kind of precious ftone, or carbuncle, which was hung up in the midft of the ark, to give light all around: and to this purpofe, R. Levi tells us, that, " during the whole 12 months that Noah was fhut up in the " ark, he needed neither the light of the fun by day, nor " the light of the moon by night; for there was a jewel " belonging to him which he hung up in the ark; and as " it waxed dim, he knew that it was day, but as its luftre " was more intenfe, he knew that it was night." But this opinion is not well founded: becaufe fuch authors as have written beft upon the qualities of precious ftones, do all agree, that (whatever the ancients may fay,) there is no fuch thing as a night-fhining carbuncle to be found in nature.

That it is poffible to make a felf-fhining fubftance, either liquid or folid, the hermetical phofphor of Balduinus, the aerial and glacial noctilucas of Mr Boyle, and feveral other preparations of the like fort, together with the obfervations of the moft accurate philofophers upon the production and propagation of light, and the prodigious ejaculation of infenfible effluviums, are fufficient demonftration. The moft furprifing fubftance of this kind was the pantarba of Jarchus, " which fhone in the day as fire, or as the " fun, and at night, did difcover a flame, or light, as bright " as day, though not altogether fo ftrong; which was, in " fhort, of that fiery and radiant nature, that if any one " looked on it in the day-time, it would dazzle the eyes " with innumerable gleams and corufcations:" nor can we well doubt, but that Noah, who (as oriental traditions fay) was a profound philofopher; who was certainly a perfon son of much longer experience, than any later liver can pretend to; (and what is more) was under the peculiar favour and direction of God, perceiving the necessity of the thing, should be equally able to prepare some perpetual light, which should centrally send forth its rays to all parts of the ark, and by its kind effluviums, cherish every thing that had life in it. Now, if this be allowed, (and this is more consonant to the letter of the text † than any other interpretation that has hitherto been advanced,) then will all the difficulties, which either are, or can be raised about the manner of subsistence, in a close vessel, by creatures of so many different species, vanish immediately. But, if it be not allowed, then it is impossible, without admitting a whole train of miracles, to give the least account, how respiration, nutrition, motion, or any other animal function whatever, could be performed in a vessel so closely shut up: and therefore it is the safest to conclude that, according to the divine direction, there must have been something placed in the ark, which, by its continual emanation

A. M. 1656, &c. Ant. Chris. 2349. &c. from Gen. vi. 12, to ix. 10.

---

† P. Lamy, to evade some difficulties that he could not so well solve, tells us, That the form of the ark, is so little ascertained by Moses, that every one is left to his own conjectures concerning it: and therefore he supposes, that as the ark was divided into three stories, or floors, and the word *Zohar*, which we translate *window*, signifies, *splendor, light, noon*, &c. the whole second story (in which he places the animals) was quite open all round, except some parts, which were grated to hinder the birds from flying in and out: otherwise, he cannot conceive how they could have had sufficient light, and air, and a free passage for it, to prevent stagnations, and many other inconveniencies which, upon this supposition, would have been removed. The lower story indeed was included within wooden walls, and well guarded with pitch, as being all under water; but the two upper stories, being above water, were either entirely open, or secured with lattices and grates; and the top, or open parts, covered with goat skins, and sheep-skins, sewed together, (as the tabernacle afterwards was,) which Noah could easily let down, or, roll up, according as rain, or storm, or a want of air made it necessary. And then, as for keeping the beasts clean, he supposes, that the stalls were so open and shelving at the bottom, that water might have been let in high enough to have washed the feet of the cattle, and to have cleansed the stalls of itself. *Vid.* his Introduction to the Holy Scriptures. lib. 1. cap. 3.; and Bedford's Scripture-chronology, cap. 11. But all this is pure imagination, and inconsistent with the notion which the sacred history give us of it.

A. M. 1656, &c. Ant. Chrif. 2349, &c. from Gen. iv. 21. to ix. 20.

emanation, might both purify and invigorate the included air) might correct and fweeten all noxious vapours and exhalations; and, like the fun, fend fuch a vivifying light, that nothing fhould die that was within the ark, *i. e.* fo far as the beams thereof did reach.

How in the middle region of the air.

Thus we have refcued Noah and his family from the danger of fuffocation in their confinement, by the fupply of a vicarious light, to purify the air, and difpel all vapours, as well as enable them to go about their work: but now, that the waves fwell, and the veffel mounts on high, even above the top of the higheft hills under heaven, they run into another quite different danger, *viz.* that of being ftarved to death, amidft the colds, and extreme fubtility of the air, in the middle region, wherein no creature can live. [a] But the middle region of the air, we ought to remember, is not to be looked upon as a fixed point, which never either rifes or falls. It is, with refpect to us, more or lefs elevated, according to the greater or lefs heat of the fun. In the cold of winter, it is much nearer to the earth, than in the warmth of fummer; or (to fpeak more properly) the cold which reigns in the middle region of the air during the fummer, reigns likewife in the lower region during the winter. Suppofing the deluge then to out-top the higheft mountains, it is evident, that the middle region of the air muft have rifen higher, and removed to a greater diftance from the earth, and waters; and, on the contrary, that the lower region muft have approached nearer to both, in proportion as the waters of the deluge increafed or decreafed: fo that, upon the whole, the ark was all along in the lower region of the air, even when it was carried fifteen cubits above the higheft mountains; and the men and beafts which were inclofed in it, breathed the fame air, as they would have done on earth, a thoufand, or twelve hundred paces lower, had not the deluge happened.

How Noah could meafure time.

But during this whole courfe of the ark, fince Noah was fhut up in fo clofe a place, where he was not capable of making any obfervations, where indeed he could fee neither fun, moon, nor ftars, for many months, it may very well be wondered, how he could poffibly have any juft menfuration of time, had we not reafon to fuppofe, that he certainly had within the ark a chronometer of one kind or other, which did exactly anfwer to the motion of the heavens without. The invention of our prefent horological machines

---

[a] *Vide* Calmet's Dictionary on the word *Deluge.*

machines indeed, and particularly of the pendulum watch, (which is the moſt exact corrector of time,) is but of modern date; but it does not therefore follow, but that the ſame, or other equivalent pieces of art might, in former ages, have been perfectly known to ſome great men. Suppoſe that Mr Hughens, or ſome other, was the inventor of pendulums in theſe parts of the world, yet it is more than probable, that there was a pendulum-clock made many years before at Florence, by the direction of the great Galileo; and that, long before that, there was another at Prague, which the famous Tycho Brahe made uſe of, in his aſtronomical obſervations. And therefore, unleſs we fondly imagine, that we poſtdiluvians have all the wit and ingenuity that ever was, we cannot but think, that Noah, who not only had long experience himſelf, but ſucceeded to the inventions of above 1600 years, (which, conſidering the longevity of people then, were much better preſerved than they can be now,) was provided with horological pieces of various kinds, before he entered the ark. Or, if we can ſuppoſe him deſtitute of theſe, yet what we have ſaid of the *zohar*, is enough to evince, that by the obſervation of that alone, there could be no difficulty in diſtinguiſhing the nights from the days, and keeping a journal accordingly.

But now, that the flood ſubſides, and the ark is landed, and all its inhabitants are to diſembark, how can we ſuppoſe, that ſeveral of the animals ſhall be able to find their way from the mountains of Armenia, into the diſtant parts of the Weſt Indies, which (as far as we can find) are joined to no other part of the known world, and yet have creatures peculiar, and ſuch as cannot live in any other climate? This is a queſtion that we muſt own ourſelves ignorant of, [b] in the ſame manner, as we pretend not to ſay, by what means that vaſt continent was at firſt peopled. But by what method ſoever it was that its firſt inhabitants came thither, whether by ſtreſs of weather, or deſigned adventure, by long voyages by ſea, or (ſuppoſing a paſſage between one continent and another) by long journeyings by land, it is plain, that by the ſame means, ſome creatures at firſt might have been conveyed thither: and as their number, at that time, could be but ſmall, we may ſuppoſe that, by a promiſcuous copulation with one another, they might beget a ſecond ſort, which in proceſs of time, the

A. M. 1656. &c. Ant Chriſt. 2349, &c. from Gen. vi 12. to ix. 20.

How the creatures, which left the ark might get into the Weſt Indies

natu

[b] *Vid.* Univerſal Hiſtory. Of this however we ſhall give the conjectures of the learned, when we come to treat of the diſperſion of nations in our next book.

<small>A. M. 1656, &c.
Ant. Chrif 2349, &c. from Gen. vi. 12, to ix. 20.</small>

nature and temperature of the climate might so far alter, as to make them pass for a quite different species, and so affect their constitution, as to make them live not so commodiously in any other climate. To convey either men or beasts, all on a sudden, from the warmest parts of Africa, to the coldest places in the north, would be a probable means to make them both perish; but the case would not be so, if they were to be removed by insensible degrees, nearer to these places: nor can we say, that there never were such creatures in those parts of Asia, where Noah is thought to have lived, as are now to be found in America; because it is very well known, that formerly there have been many beasts of a particular species in some countries, such as the hippopotami in Egypt, wolves in England, and beavers in France, where at present there are few or none of them to be found.

<small>Why God made use of this method</small> If, after all, it should be asked, why God made use of this, rather than any other method, to destroy the wicked, and preserve the righteous? the proper answer is, that whatever pleaseth him, that hath he done, both in heaven and in earth; for as his will is not to be controlled, so neither is it to be disputed. For argument's sake, however, let us suppose, for once, that instead of drowning the world, God had been pleased to destroy by plague, famine, or some other sore judgement, all mankind, except Noah and his sons, who were to be eye-witnesses of this terrible execution: to live to see the earth covered with dead bodies, and none left to bury them, the fields uncultivated, and the cities lie waste and desolate without inhabitants, who can conceive what the horror of such a sight would have been? And who would have been content to live in such a world, to converse only with the images of death, and with noisome carcases? But God, in mercy, shut up Noah in the ark, that he should not see the terrors and consternations of sinners when the flood came; and he washed away all the dead bodies into the caverns of the earth, with all the remains of their old habitations. So that when Noah came out of the ark, he saw nothing to disturb his imagination, nor any tokens of that terrible vengeance which had over-run the world, to offend his sight: only, when he looked about him, and saw every thing gone, he could not but fall into this contemplation, that God, when he enters into judgement with the wicked, *will not pity, nor spare, nor have mercy, but destroy.* He will

<small>*dash*</small>

<small>e Jer. xiii. 14.</small>

Chap. VI. *from the Creation to the Flood.* 233

dash them one against another, even father and son together, and ᵉ *cause his fury to rest upon them, until his anger be accomplished.*

A. M. 1656, &c.
Ant. Chrif. 2349, &c.
from Gen. vi. 12. to ix. 10.

DISSERTATION VI.

Of Mount Ararat.

BEFORE we conclude this chapter, and this book together, it may not be improper to give the reader some account of the mountains of Ararat in general; in what part of the world that particular one which is here intended is said to be situate; and, according to the relations both of ancient geographers and modern travellers, of what form and magnitude this mountain is. But in this inquiry some difficulties will arise, by reason of the different traditions concerning it.

The author of the verses * which go under the name of the *Sibylline Oracles*, places the mountains of Ararat in the borders of Phrygia, not far from Celænæ, at the head of the two rivers Marsyas and Meander: but it appears from good authorities, that there is in reality no mountain at all in that place, or at most, but a small hill, an eminence made by art, and not by nature; and therefore the learned Bochart has happily found out the ground of this mistake, when he tells us, that not far from this city Celænæ, there is another town called *Apamea*, and firnamed Κιβωτὸς or *the ark;* not from any tradition that Noah's ark ever rested there, but purely on account of its situation, because it is encompassed with three rivers, Marsyas, Obrimas,

Different opinions concerning it.

ᵈ Ezek. v 13.

* The verses, as they are set down by *Gallæus de Sibyllis*, p. 589. are these:

Ἐϛὶ δὲ τις Φρυγίης ἐπ' ἠπείροιο κελαινῆς
Ἠλίβατον τανύμηκες ὄρος, Ἀραρατ δὲ καλεῖται——
Μαρσύην ἔνθα φλίβες μεγάλου ποταμοῖο πέφυκαν,
Τῇ δὲ Κιβωτὸς ἔμεινεν ἐν ὑψηλοῖο καρήνῳ.

But that which shews the spuriousness of these verses, is this:
——That the Sibyl, speaking of herself as contemporary with Noah, takes notice of the river Marsyas, which, whatever name it had at first, was certainly after the death of Midas, called *the fountain of Midas*, and retained that name until the time of Marsyas, by whom it was altered; and this must be long after the death of this Sybil; *Bedford's Scripture-chronology. l. 2. c. 2.*

A. M.
2655, &c.
Ant. Chrif.
2349, &c.
from Gen.
vi. 11. to
ix. 20.

mas, and Orgas, which give it the resemblance of a chest or ark, in the same manner that the port of Alexandria was so called, by reason of the bay which enclosed the ships.

Sir Walter Raleigh, [e] and from him some later writers [f] are of opinion, that the mountains of Ararat were those of Caucasus, towards Bactria and Saga Scythia. This, as they imagine, agrees with the general notion, that the Scythians might contend for the antiquity of their original with any other nation; with the Chaldean tradition, concerning the actions of the great man Xisuthrus, who is commonly supposed to be the same with Noah; with the language, learning, and history of the Chinese, who are thought to be Noah's immediate descendents; and with the journey which some of his other descendents are said to have taken, *viz.* [g] *from the east to the land of Shinar*. A modern chronologer has endeavoured to prove, that the place where Noah built the ark was called *Cyparisson*, not far from the river Tygris, and on the north-east side of the city of Babylon; that while the flood continued, it sailed from thence to the north-east, as far as the Caspian sea, and when the flood abated, the north-wind brought it back by a southern course, and landed it upon Mount Caucasus, east of Babylon, and about nine degrees distant from it in longitude; and that this opinion, as he imagines, is more agreeable to the course which the ark, by meeting with contrary currents, would be forced to make; to the sense of Scripture, in bringing the sons of Noah from the east, and in settling the children of Shem (who went not to Shinar) in this place, and to the great conveniency of Noah's landing not too far from the country where he lived before the flood, that thereby he might be capable of giving better directions to his family how to disperse themselves, and to replenish the new world as occasion did require. But besides that there appears little or no authority for all this, the observation of travellers into those countries may make it be questioned, whether such a vessel as the ark is represented, drawing much water, and very unfit for sailing, could be able to reach mount Caucasus from the province of Eden (where it is generally thought to have been built) in the space of the flood's increase, which was no more than an hundred and fifty days. The most

---

[e] His History of the world. [f] Heylin's Cosmography; and Shuckford's Connection, l. 2. [g] Gen. xi. 2.

most probable opinion therefore is, that by the word *Ararat*, the Holy Scriptures denote that country which the Greeks, and from them other western nations, do call *Armenia*. In this sense it is taken by the Septuagint, by the Chaldee paraphrase, by the Vulgate, by Theodoret, and by divers others. The learned Bochart has brought together a multitude of arguments, all tending to the same conclusion: but then the question is, on what particular mountain it was that the ark landed?

A. M. 1656. &c. Ant. Chrif. 1349. &c. from Gen. vi. 12. to ix. 20.

1. The most prevailing opinion for some time was, that one of the mountains which divide Armenia on the south from Mesopotamia, and that part of Assyria which is inhabited by the Curds, (from whence the mountains took the name *Curdu*,) which the Greeks changed into *Cordiæi*,* and several other names, was the place where the ark landed: and what makes for this opinion, is, that whereas the deluge was in a great measure occasioned by the overflowing of the ocean, as the Scriptures tell us, that flux of waters which came from the Persian sea, running from the south, and meeting the ark, would of course carry it northward upon the Gordiæan mountains, which seems to be voyage enough for a vessel of its bulk and structure to make in the stated time of the flood's increase.

The most considerable.

The tradition which affirms the ark to have rested on these mountains, must have been very ancient, since it is the tradition of the Chaldeans themselves, and in former ages was very little questioned, till men came to inquire into the particular part of those mountains whereon it settled, and then the authors seemed to place it out of Armenia; Epiphanius on the mount Lubar, between the country of the Armenians and Gordiæans; and all the eastern authors both Christian and Mahometan, on mount Themanin, or Al-Judi, which overlooks the country of Diarrhabia, or Mousal, in Mesopotamia.

To confirm this tradition however, we are told, that the remainders of the ark were to be seen upon these mountains. Berosus and Abydenus both declare, that there was such a report in their time; the former observes farther, that several of the inhabitants thereabouts scraped the pitch

---

* The Greek and Latin writers name them *Carduchi, Cardici, Cordiæi, Cordueni, Cordi, Cordæi, Curdi*, &c. The orientals call them likewise *Gardon, Cordyn, Curue*, &c. Bochart supposes that they are the same which are called by mistake in Josephus, *Caron, Vid*. Univers. hist.; and Phaleg. lib. 1. cap. 3.

pitch off the planks as a rarity, and carried it about them for an amulet; and the latter says, that they used the wood of the vessel against several diseases with wonderful success; as the relicks of this ark were likewise to be seen in the time of Epiphanius, if we may believe him. The town of Themanin, which signifies *eight*, situate at the foot of the mountain Al-Judi, was built, we are told, in memory of the eight persons who came out of the ark; and formerly there was a monastery, called *the monastery of the ark*, upon the Curdu mountains, where the Nestorians used to celebrate a festival, on the very spot where they supposed the ark stopped; but in the year of Christ 776, that monastery was destroyed by lightning, together with the church, and a numerous congregation in it; and since that time, the credit of this tradition has in some measure declined, and given place to another, which at present prevails.

2. This opinion places mount **Ararat** towards the middle of Armenia, near the river Araxes, or Aras, above 280 miles distant from Al-Judi, to the north-east. [h] St. Jerom seems to have been the first who hath given us an account of this tradition. "Ararat (says he) is a champain "country, incredibly fertile, through which the Araxes "flows at the foot of the mount Taurus, which extends so "far; so that by the mountains of Ararat, whereon the ark "rested, we are not to understand the mountains of Ar- "menia in general, but the highest mountains of Taurus, "which overlook the plains of Ararat." Since his time, its situation in this place has been remarked by several other writers, and all the travellers into these places now make mention of no other mount Ararat than what the Armenians call *Masis*, (from Amasia, the third successor of Haikh, the founder of their nation,) and what the Mahometans do sometime name *Agri-dagh*, i. e. *the heavy or great mountain*, and sometimes *Parmak-dagh*, the *finger-mountain*, alluding to its appearance; for as it is strait, very steep, and stands by itself, it seems to resemble a finger, when held up.

The mount Ararat, which the Armenians, as we said, call *Masis*, and sometimes *Mesesoussar*, (because the ark was stopped there when the waters of the flood began to abate, stands about twelve leagues to the east (or rather south-east) of Erivan, (a small city seated in the upper Armenia,)

Armenia) four leagues from Aras, or Araxes, and ten to the north-west of Nakschivan; which, because *nak*, in Armenian, signifies *a ship*, and *schivan, stopped* or *settled*, is supposed to have its name from the same occasion. This mountain is encompassed by several little hills, and on the top of them are found many ruins, which are thought to have been the buildings of the first men, who might fear, for some time, to go down into the plains. It stands by itself, in the form of a sugar-loaf, in the midst of one of the greatest plains that is to be seen, and separated from the other mountains of Armenia, which make a long chain. It consists of two hills, whereof the less is more sharp and pointed; but the larger (which is that of the ark) lies north-east of it, and rears its head far above the neighbouring mountains. It seems so high and big indeed, that when the air is clear, it does not appear to be above two leagues from Erivan, and yet may be seen some four or five days journey off; but from the middle to the top, it is always covered with snow, and for the space of three or four months in the year, has its upper part commonly hid in the clouds.

A. M. 1656, &c. Ant Chrif. 2319, &c. from Gen. vi. 12. to ix 20.

The Armenians have a tradition, that on the summit of this mountain there is still a considerable part of the ark remaining, but that it is impossible to get up to the top of it. ⁱ For they tell us of one traveller, a person of singular piety, who endeavoured to do it, and had advanced as far as the middle of the mountain; when, being thirsty, and wanting water, he put up a prayer to God, who caused a fountain to spring out of the ground for him, and so saved his life; but at the same time, he heard a voice, saying, *Let none be so bold as to go up to the top of this mountain.*

How difficult the ascent of this mountain is (without any particular revelation) we may inform ourselves from the following account which Mr Tournefort gives us of it.

" About two o'clock in the afternoon, ᵏ (says he),
" we began to ascend the mountain Ararat, but not without difficulty. We were forced to climb up in loose
" sand, where we saw nothing but some juniper and
" goats-thorn. The mountain, which lies south and
" south-south-east from *Eimiadzim*, or *the three churches*,

Tournefort's account of it.

ⁱ La Boulaye's Voyages. ᵏ *Vide* his Voyages into the Levant, letter 7.

A. M.
1656, &c
Ant. Chrif.
2349. &c.
from Gen.
vi. 12. to
ix. 20.

"is one of the moſt ſad and diſagreeable ſights upon earth; "for there are neither trees nor ſhrubs upon it, nor any "convents of religious, either Armenians or Franks. "All the monaſteries are in the plain, nor can I think the "place inhabitable, in any part, becauſe the ſoil of the "mountain is looſe, and moſt of it covered with ſnow.

"From the top of a great abyſs, (as dreadful an hole "as ever was ſeen,) oppoſite to the village of Akurlu, "(from whence we came,) there continually fall down "rocks of a blackiſh hard ſtone, which make a terrible "reſound. This, and the noiſe of the crows that are con- "tinually flying from one ſide to the other, has ſomething "in it very frightful; and to form any notion of the place, "you muſt imagine one of the higheſt mountains in the "world opening its boſom, only to ſhew one of the moſt "horrid ſpectacles that can be thought of. No living a- "nimals are to be ſeen but at the bottom, and towards "the middle of the mountain. They who occupy the "loweſt region, are poor ſhepherds and ſcabby flocks. "The ſecond region is poſſeſſed by crows and tygers, "which we paſſed by, not without giving us ſome dread "and uneaſineſs. All the reſt of it, i. e. half of it, has "been covered with ſnow ever ſince the ark reſted there, "and theſe ſnows are covered half the year with very thick "clouds.

"Notwithſtanding the amazement which this fright- "ful ſolitude caſt us into, we endeavoured to find out "the monaſtery we were told of, and enquired whether "there were any religious in caverns. The notion they "have in the country, that the ark reſted here, and the "veneration which all the Armenians have for this moun- "tain, (for they kiſs the earth as ſoon as they ſee it, and "repeat certain prayers after they have made the ſign of "the croſs), have made many imagine, that it muſt be filled "with religious. However, they aſſured us that there was "only one forſaken convent at the foot of the gulf; that "there was no fountain throughout the whole mount; "and that we could not go in a whole day to the ſnow, "and down again to the bottom of the abyſs; that the "ſhepherds often loſt their way; and that we might judge "what a miſerable place it was, from the neceſſity they "were under to dig the earth from time to time, to find "a ſpring of water for themſelves and their flocks; and "in ſhort, that it would be folly to proceed on our way, "becauſe they were ſatisfied our legs would fail us; nor
would

Chap. VI. *from the Creation to the Flood.* 239

"would they be obliged to accompany us for all the trea-
"fures of the King of Persia.

"When we considered what the shepherds had told us,
"we advised with our guides; and they, good men, un-
"willing to expose themselves to the danger of dying for
"thirst, and having no curiosity, at the expence of their
"legs, to measure the height of the mountain, were at
"first of the same sentiments with the shepherds; but af-
"terwards concluded, that we might go to certain rocks,
"which were more prominent and visible than the rest,
"and so return by night to the place where we were; and
"with that resolution we went to rest. In the morning,
"after that we had eat and drank very plentifully, we be-
"gan to travel towards the first ridge of rocks, with one
"bottle of water, which, to ease ourselves, we carried
"by turns; but notwithstanding we had made pitchers
"of our bellies, in two hours time they were quite dried
"up; and as water shook in a bottle is no very plea-
"sant liquor, our hopes were, that when we came
"to the snow, we should eat some of it to quench our
"thirst.

A. M. 1656, &c.
Ant. Christ 2349, &c.
from Gen. vi. 12. to ix. 20.

"It must be acknowledged, that the sight is very much
"deceived when we stand at the bottom, and guess at the
"height of a mountain; and especially, when it must be
"ascended through sands as troublesome as the Syrtes of
"Africa. It is impossible to take one firm step upon the
"sands of mount Ararat; in many places, instead of
"ascending, we were obliged to go back again to the mid-
"dle of the mountain; and, in order to continue our
"course, to wind sometimes to the right, and sometimes
"to the left.

"To avoid these sands, which fatigued us most into-
"lerably, we made our way to the great rocks, which
"were heaped one upon another. We passed under
"them, as through caverns, and were sheltered from all
"the injuries of the weather, except cold, which was
"here so keen and intense, that we were forced to leave
"the place, and came into a very troublesome way, full
"of large stones, such as masons make use of in building,
"and were forced to leap from stone to stone, till I,
"for my part, was heartily weary, and began to sit down,
"and repose myself a little, as the rest of the company
"did.

"After

A. M. 1656, &c.
Ant. Chrif 2349, &c.
from Gen. vi. 12, to ix, 10.

"After we had rested ourselves, we came about noon to a place which afforded us a more pleasing prospect. We imagined ourselves so near, that we could have even touched the snow (we thought) with our teeth; but our joy lasted not long; for what we had taken for snow, proved only a chalk-rock, which hid from our sight a tract of land above two hours journey distant from the snow, and which seemed to have a new kind of pavement, made of small pieces of stones broke off by the frost, and whose edges were as sharp as flints. Our guides told us, that their feet were quite bare, and that ours in a short time would be so too; that it grew late, and we should certainly lose ourselves in the night, or break our necks in the dark, unless we would chuse to sit down, and so become a prey to the tygers. All this seemed very feasible; and therefore we assured them, that we would go no farther than the heap of snow, which we shewed them, and which, at that distance, appeared hardly bigger than a cake; but when we came to it, we found it more than we had occasion for; the heap was above thirty paces in diameter. We every one eat as much as we had a mind for, and so, by consent, resolved to advance no farther. It cannot be imagined how much the eating of snow revives and invigorates: we therefore began to descend the mountain with a great deal of alacrity; but we had not gone far, before we came to sands, which lay behind the abyss, and were full as troublesome as the former; so that about six in the afternoon we found ourselves quite tired out and spent. At length, observing a place covered with mouse-ear, whose declivity seemed to favour our descent, we made to it with all speed, and (what pleased us mighty well) from whence it was that our guides shewed us (though at a considerable distance) the monastery, whither we were to go to quench our thirst. I leave it to be guessed what method Noah made use of to descend from this place, who might have rid upon so many sorts of animals, which were all at his command: but as for us, we laid ourselves upon our backs, and slid down for an hour together upon this green plat, and so passed on very agreeably, and much faster than we could have gone upon our legs. The night and our thirst were a kind of spurs to us, and made us make the greater speed. We continued therefore sliding in this manner,

"as

"as long as the way would permit; and when we met "with small flints which hurt our shoulders, we turned "and slid on our bellies, or went backwards on all four. "Thus by degrees we gained the monastery; but so dis-"ordered and fatigued by our manner of travelling, that "we were not able to move hand or foot."

A. M. 1656, &c. Ant. Chris. 2349, &c. from Gen. vi. 12, to ix. 20.

I have made my quotation from this learned botanist and most accurate traveller the longer, not only because it gives us a full idea of the mountain, so far as he ascended, but some distrust likewise of the veracity [l] of a certain Dutch voyager, who seems to assure us, that he went five days journey up mount Ararat to see a Romish hermit; that he passed through three regions of the clouds, the first dark and thick, the next cold and full of snow, and the third colder still; that he advanced five miles every day, and when he came to the place where the hermit had his cell, he breathed a very serene and temperate air; that the hermit told him, he had perceived neither wind nor rain all the five and twenty years that he had dwelt there; and that on the top of the mountain there still reigned a greater tranquility, which was a means to preserve the ark without decay or putrefaction.

An objection stated and answered.

There is one objection which may be made to all that we have said concerning the situation of this famous mountain, and that is —— Whereas the sons of Noah, when they quitted the country where the ark rested, are said to [m] *journey from the east into the land of Shinar*, it is plain, that if they removed from any part in Armenia, they must have gone from the north or north-west; but this we shall take occasion to examine when we come to treat of their migration. In the mean time, it is worthy our observation, and some argument of our being in the right, [n] that the situation of Ararat, as we have supposed it, whether it be mount Masis, or the mountain of Cardu, was very convenient for the journey of the sons of Noah, because the distance is not very great, and the descent easy, especially from the latter, into the plains of Mesopotamia, whereof Shinar is a part. Nor should we forget, that the neighbourhood, which the sacred history, by this means, preserves between the land of Eden, where man was created, that of Ararat, where the remains of mankind were saved;

[l] Struy's Voyages, chap. 17. [m] Gen. xi. 2.
[n] Unverf. Hist. l. 1. c. 1. p. 110.

A. M. 1656, &c.
Ant. Chrif. 2349, &c. from Gen. vi. 12. to ix. 2.

saved; and that of Shinar, where they fixed the centre of their plantations, is much more natural, and seems to have a better face and appearance of truth, than to place these scenes at so vast a distance, as some commentators have done.

That there were mountains before the deluge.

One inquiry more, not concerning mount Ararat only, but every other mountain that is dispersed over the whole earth, is this——Whether they were in being before the induction of the flood? The ingenious author of the Theory, so often quoted, is clearly of opinion, that º the face of the earth, before the deluge, was smooth, regular, and uniform, without mountains, and without a sea; and that the rocks and mountains which every where now appear, were made by the violent concussions which then happened, and are indeed nothing else but the ruins and fragments of the old world. But all this is confuted by the testimony of divine wisdom, who declaring her own pre-existence, ᵖ *I was set up from everlasting*, says she, *from the beginning, or ever the earth was; when there was no depth, I was brought forth; when there was no fountains abounding with water, before the mountains were settled, before the hills was I brought forth; while as yet God had not made the earth, nor the fields, nor the highest part of the dust of the world.* So that, according to this declaration, not only the fountains of waters which we see upon the face of the earth, but even mountains which some have accounted its greatest deformities) and all hills were part of the original creation, and cotemporary with the first foundations of the earth; and tho' a deluge can scarce be supposed to overspread the globe, without making some transmutation in it, yet that it could not shock the pillars of the round world, or cause a total dissolution in nature, we have the same divine testimony assuring us, that at the time of the first creation, ᵠ *God laid the foundation of the earth so sure, that it should not be removed for ever.*

Their use and pleasantness.

It is a groundless imagination then to ascribe the origin of mountains and other lofty eminences to a certain disruption of the earth in the time of the deluge; when God, from the very first beginning, designed them for such excellent purposes. For, besides, that several of these rocks and

---

º Burnet's Theory, l. 1. c. 5.   ᵖ Prov. viii. 23, &c.
ᵠ Psal. civ. 5.

and mountains (as well as the broad sea) are really an awful sight, and fill the mind with just notions of God's tremendous Majesty, which a small river or a smooth surface does not do so well; and besides, that they yield food for several animals formed by nature to live upon them, and supply us from without, with many wholesome plants, and from within with many useful metals; by condensing the vapours, and so producing rain, fountains, and rivers, they give the very plains and valleys themselves the fertility which they boast of. For this seems to be the design of hills, (says ʳ a learned inquirer into the original of springs and fountains,) "That the ridges, being placed through "the midst of the continent, might serve, as it were, for "alembicks, to distil fresh water for the use of man and "beast; and their heights to give a descent to those "streams which run gently, like so many veins of the mi- "crocosm, to be more beneficial to the creation."

ˢ Nay, we may appeal to the sense of mankind, whether a land of hills and dales has not more pleasure and beauty both, than any uniform flat, which then only affords delight when it is viewed from the top of an hill. For what were the Tempe of Thessaly, so celebrated in ancient story for their unparalleled pleasantness, but a vale divided by a river, and terminated with hills? are not all the descriptions of poets embellished with such ideas, when they would represent any places of superlative delight, any blissful seats of the muses and nymphs, any sacred habitations of gods and goddesses? They will never admit that a wild flat can be pleasant, no not in the * Elysian fields: they too must be diversified. Swelling descents and declining vallies are their chief beauties; nor can they imagine * even paradise a place of pleasure, or heaven itself * to be heaven without them. So that such a place as our present earth is, distinguished into mountains, rivers, vales, and hills,

ʳ Dr. Halley. ˢ Bentley's Sermons at Boyle's lectures.

* At pater Anchises penitus convalle virenti,
Hoc superate jugum—et tumulum capit. *Vir. Æn.* 6

* Flowers worthy of paradise, which not wise art,
In beds and curious knots, but nature boon,
Pour'd forth profuse, on hills, and dale, and plain.

* For earth hath this variety from heav'n
Of pleasure, situate on hill or dale. *Milton's Paradise lost, book* 4.

A. M. 1656. &c. Ant. Chrif. 2349, &c. from Gen. vi. 1. to ix. 20.

and hills, muſt, even in point of pleaſure, claim a pre-eminence before any other, that preſenting us with no more than a ſingle ſcene, and, in one continued plain ſuperficies, muſt of neceſſity pall the proſpect. But then, if we conſider farther the riches that are repoſited in theſe mountains, the gold and precious ſtones, the coal, the lead, the tin, and other valuble minerals that are dug out of their bowels, all uſeful in their kinds, and fitted for the accommodation of human life, we ſhall be apt to overlook the fantaſtical pleaſantneſs of a ſmooth outſide, and to think with Moſes, the man of God, that *Bleſſed of the Lord is any land for the chief things of the ancient mountains, and for the precious things of the laſting hills.*

Deut. xxxiii. 13, 15.

The end the firſt Book.

THE
HISTORY
OF THE
BIBLE.

BOOK II.

CONTAINING AN ACCOUNT OF THINGS FROM THE FLOOD TO THE CALL OF ABRAHAM; IN ALL, 426 YEARS, AND SIX MONTHS.

CHAP. I.

The remainder of what is recorded of Noah, to his death.

THE HISTORY.

AS soon as Noah and his family were landed, and all the creatures committed to his charge were come safe out of the ark, he selected some of every kind, both beasts and birds, but such only as were clean, and, by God's appointment, proper for sacrifice; and, having built the first altar that we read of, restored the ancient rite of divine worship, and † offered burnt-sacrifices thereon. And this

A. M. 1657, &c. Ant. Chrif. 2347, &c. from Gen. viii 20 to the end of ch. 9.

Noah's sacrifice, and the promises and grants which God gives him.

† Josephus tells us, that Noah, in a persuasion that God had doomed mankind to destruction, lay under a mortal dread for fear of the same judgement over again, and that it would end in an anniversary inundation; so that he presented himself before the Lord with sacrifices and prayers, " humbly beseech-
" ing him, in mercy, to preserve the order of the world in its
Vol. I. N° 4,　　　　　Z z　　　　　frame;

A. M. 1657, &c.
Ant. Chrif. 2347, &c.
from Gen. viii. 12. to the end of ch. ix.

this he did with so grateful a sense of the divine goodness, and so reverential a fear of the divine majesty, as procured him a gracious acceptance, and in testimony of that acceptance, several grants and promises.

God's promises were, that ‡ though mankind were naturally wicked, and apt to go astray from the very womb, yet, be their iniquities ever so great, he would not any more destroy the earth † by a general deluge, or disturb the order of nature, and ‡ the several seasons of the year, and

"frame; to punish the guilty, and spare the lives of the innocent: and not to proceed with rigour, for the wickedness of some particulars, to the destruction of the whole; otherwise the survivers of this calamity would be more wretched than those that were washed away in the common ruin, if, after having suffered horror of thought, and the terror of so dismal a spectacle, they should only be delivered from one calamity, to be consumed by another;" *Antiq.* l. 1 c. 4. But that this should be the purport of his prayer is not very likely, because we find no such indications of terror in Noah, who knew the great and criminal causes of the deluge to be such, as could not happen every year, and who having found favour in the eyes of God, and a miraculous preservation from a general destruction, can hardly be supposed to have cast away his confidence in him so soon, and instead thereof, to be possessed with an abject and servile fear: and therefore we may conclude, that the nature of this prayer and sacrifice was eucharistical, and not deprecatory; *Heidegger's Hist. patriar. exercit* 19.

‡ The words in our translation are *I will not again curse the ground any more for man's sake, for the imagination of man's heart is evil;* which is certainly very injuriously rendered, because it makes the sacred author speak quite contrary to what he designed, and is an affront to the justice, goodness, and wisdom of God, who, by this translation of *for* instead of *though*, might seem to bless man for his evil imaginations; *Essay for a new translation.*

† For particular inundations there have been at several times, in divers places, whereby towns and countries have been overwhelmed, with all their inhabitants; *Pool. Annot.*

‡ All the versions do manifestly in this place confound the four seasons of the year, which Moses exactly distinguishes. For the Hebrew word *kor*, which they render *cold*, signifies the *winter*, because of the cold that then reigns. The word *chom*, which they render *heat*, signifies the *spring*, because of the heat which abounds in Judea about the end of the spring, in the months

Chap. I.   *from the Flood to the Call of Abraham.*   247

and their regular vicissitudes: and in confirmation of this, he appointed the rainbow for a token, which (whether it used to appear before the flood or no) was now to be the ratification of the truth of his promise, and his faithful witness in heaven.

A. M. 1657, &c. Ant. Chrif. 2347, &c. from Gen. viii. 20. to the end of ch. ix.

The grants which God gave Noah and his sons were not only * the same dominion which our first parents before

months of May and June, which are the harvest-time in that country. The word *kajts*, which they render *summer*, does indeed signify so; but then the word *cheroph*, which they term the *winter*, should be rendered *autumn*, which is the time of plowing and cultivating the ground, as may be seen Prov. xx. 4. So that the whole sentence, which contains the promise of God. Gen. viii. 22. if rendered justly, should run thus.—*While the earth remaineth, seed-time and harvest, winter and spring, summer and autumn, day and night, shall not cease;* an Essay for a new translation. We cannot but observe however, that this vicissitude of times and seasons, which is here promised as a blessing to mankind is a full confutation of the dreams of such writers as are apt to fancy " That in the primordial earth there was " every where a perpetual spring and equinox; that all the parts " of the year had one and the same tenor, face, and temper; and " that there was no winter nor summer, seed-time nor harvest, " but a continual temperature of the air, and verdure of the " earth;" which, if it were true, would make this promise of God a punishment, rather than a blessing to mankind. *Vid. Burnet's Theory, l. 2 c 3.; and Heidegger's Hist. patriar. exercit. 19.*

* A learned and Right Reverend author, to shew the renovation of the earth after the deluge, and its deliverance from the curse inflicted upon it by reason of Adam's transgression, runs the parallel between the blessings and privileges granted to Adam soon after his creation, and those restored to Noah and his posterity soon after the flood. To our first parents it is said, *Have dominion over the fish of the sea, and over the fowl of the air and over every living thing that moveth on the earth,* Gen. i. 28. To Noah and his sons it is said, *The fear of you, and the dread of you, shall be upon every beast of the earth, and upon every fowl of the air, and upon all that moveth upon the earth, and upon all the fishes of the sea, into your hand are they delivered,* Gen. ix. 2. To Adam and Eve are granted for food, *Every herb bearing seed —— and every tree, in the which is the fruit of the tree, yielding seed,* Gen. i. 29. But Noah and his sons have a larger charter,—*Every moving thing that liveth shall be meat to you, even as the green herb, have I*

given

A. M. 1657, &c. Ant. Chrif. 2347, &c. from Gen. viii. 20. to the end of ch. ix.

fore the fall had over the animal creation, and a full power to keep them in fubmiffion and fubjection; but a privilege likewife to kill any of thefe creatures for food; only with this reftriction, that they were not to † put them to unneceffary torture, or to eat any part of their blood, which might be a means to introduce the fhedding of human blood. The human kind, notwithftanding their apoftacy,

given you all things, **Gen.** ix. 3. The bleffing upon the earth, at the creation was,——*Let the earth bring forth grafs, and herb yielding feed, and the fruit tree yielding fruit after his kind,* Gen. i. 11.——The bleffing after the flood is,——*While the earth remaineth, feed-time and harveft fhall not ceafe,* Gen. viii. 22 In the beginning, *the lights in the firmament were appointed to divide the day from the night, and to be for feafons, and for days, and years,* Gen. i 14 After the flood, the new bleffing is,——*That fpring and autumn, fummer and winter, and day and night, fhall not ceafe,* Gen viii. 22. Whereupon our author afks, What is beftowed in the firft bleffings that is wanted in the fecond ? What more did Adam enjoy in his happieft days ? What more did he forfeit in his worft, with refpect to this life, than that which is contained in thefe bleffings ! If he neither had more, nor loft more, all thefe bleffings you fee exprefsly reftored to Noah and his pofterity: and from all this laid together, he concludes, that the old curfe upon the ground was, after the deluge, finifhed and completed; *Ufe and intent of prophecy p.* 91.

† The words in the text are,——*But flefh with the life thereof, which is the blood thereof, fhall you not eat.* This the Hebrew doctors generally underftand to be a prohibition to cut off any limb of a living creature, and to eat it, while the life. *i. e.* the blood, was in it : *dum adhuc vivit, et palpitat, feu tremit,* as a modern interpreter has truly explained their fenfe. And in this they are followed by feveral Chriftians, who think (as Maimonides did) that there were fome people in the old world fo favage and barbarous, that they did eat raw flefh, while it was yet warm from the beaft, out of whofe body it was cut piece-meal. Plutarch tells us, that it was cuftomary in his time to run red hot fpits through the bellies of live fwine, to make their flefh more delicious; and I believe fome among us, have heard of whipping pigs, and torturing other creatures to death for the fame purpofe. Now thefe things could not be committed, if fuch men thought themfelves bound in confcience to abftain from all unneceffary cruelties to the creatures, and to bleed them to death with all the difpatch they could, before they touched them for food. *Vid. Patrick's Commentary; and Revelation examined, vol.* 2. *p.* 20.

stacy, did still retain some lineaments of the divine similitude; and therefore, whosoever murthered any of them, did thereby deface the image of God; and whether it were man † or beast, stranger or near relation, was appointed by the magistrate to be put to death: and with these grants and promises, he gave them encouragement (as he did our first progenitors) to *be fruitful and multiply, and replenish the earth*, which was now left almost destitute of inhabitants.

A. M. 1657. &c. Ant. Chrif. 2347, &c. from Gen. viii. 20. to the end of ch. ix.

But how much soever the deluge might deprive the earth of its inhabitants, it had not so totally destroyed the trees, and plants, and other vegetables, but that, in a short time, they began to appear again; and being encouraged by the kindly warmth of the sun, discovered their several species by the several fruits they bore. Noah before the flood † had applied himself to husbandry, and now, upon the recovery of the earth again, betook himself to the same occupation. Among his other improvements of the ground, he had planted a vineyard, and perhaps was the first man who invented a press to squeeze the juice out of the grape, and so make wine. Natural curiosity might tempt him to taste the fruit of his own labour; but being either unacquainted with the strength of this liquor, or, through age and infirmity, unable to bear it, so it was, that drinking a little too freely, he became quite intoxicated with it; and so falling asleep in his tent, lay

† If it here should be asked, How any beast that is neither capable of virtue or vice can be deemed culpable in case it should chance to kill any man? The answer is, That this law was ordained for the benefit of men, for whose use all beasts were created. For, 1st, Such owners as were not careful to prevent such mischiefs, were hereby punished; 2dly, Others were admonished by their example to be cautious; 3dly, God thereby instructed them, that murder was a most grievous crime, whose punishment extended even to beasts; and, 4thly, The lives of men were hereby much secured, when such beasts as might do the like mischief another time, were immediately dispatched, and taken out of the way; *Patrick's Commentary.*

† Anciently the greatest men esteemed nothing more honourable, and worthy their study, than the art of agriculture. *Nihil homine libero dignius*, nothing more becoming a gentleman, was the saying of the Roman orator; and for the truth of this, the Fabii, the Cato's, the Varro's, the Virgil's, the Pliny's, and other great names, are sufficient witnesses; *Bibliotheca Biblica*, vol. 1. p. 251.

lay with his body uncovered, and in a very indecent posture, was exposed to the eyes of his children.

A. M. 2657, &c. Ant. Chrif 2347. &c. from Gen. viii. 20. to the end of ch. ix.

Ham, who espied his father in this condition, instead of concealing his weakness, proclaimed it aloud, and to his other two brothers Shem and Japhet made him the subject of his scorn and derision : but so far were they from being pleased with his behaviour in this respect, that taking a garment, and laying it upon both their shoulders, they went backward, till, coming to their father, they dropt the garment upon him, and so covered the nakedness which their pious modesty would not permit them to behold. Nor is it improbable, that, to prevent the like indecency, they watched him during the remaining time of his sleep, and might possibly, upon his awaking, acquaint him with what had happened : whereupon, perceiving how unworthily his son Ham had served him, † he cursed his race in the person of Canaan his grandson, and reflecting how respectfully his other two sons had behaved, he rewarded their pious care with each one a blessing, which, in process of time, was fulfilled in their posterity.

Ham's immodesty to his father Noah.

This is all that the Scripture informs us of concerning Noah, only we are given to understand, that he lived 350 years after the deluge, in all 950; and if we will believe the tradition of the orientals, he was buried in Mesopotamia where, not far from a monastery, called *Dair-Abunah*, i. e. *the monastery of our father*, they shew us, in a castle, a large sepulchre, which they say belonged to him : but as for the common opinion of his dividing the world among his three sons before his death, giving to Shem Asia, to Ham Africa, and to Japhet Europe, there is no

And Noah's death.

---

† It is a tradition among the Eastern writers, that Noah, having cursed Ham and Canaan, the effect of his curse was, that not only their posterity were made subject to their brethren, and born, as we may say, in slavery, but that likewise, all on a sudden, the colour of their skin became black : (for they maintain, that all the blacks descended from Ham and Canaan); that Noah, seeing so surprising a change, was deeply affected with it, and begged of God, that he would be pleased to inspire Canaan's masters with a tender and compassionate love for him ; and that his prayer was heard. For notwithstanding we may still at this day observe the effect of Noah's curse in the servitude of Ham's posterity, yet we may remark likewise the effect of his prayer, in that this sort of black slaves is sought for, and made much of in most places ; *Calmet's Dictionary on the word,* Ham.

Chap. I. *from the Flood to the Call of Abraham.* 251

no manner of foundation for it, either in Scripture or tradition.

A. M. 1657, &c.
Ant. Chrif. 2347, &c.
from Gen. viii. 20, to the end of ch. 9.

The Objection.

"BUT how short soever this post-diluvian part of
" Noah's history may be thought, it is long enough,
" we find, to contain many more absurdities and misrepre-
" sentations of things than can easily be digested. It might
" be the opinion of the Heathen world, perhaps, that their
" gods were pleased with the smell of incense, and (as one
" [b] expresses it) would leave their ordinary diet of nectar
" and ambrosia, to snuff up the smoak and fat of sacrifices;
" yet surely it gives us too gross and carnal a notion of the
" great God of heaven and earth, that he should be so far
" delighted with the sweet favour of any oblation, as to
" have his heart attendered, his relentings kindled, and
" himself drawn into a hasty resolution never to destroy
" the earth any more, when it is apparent, that since that
" time he has brought upon it several inundations, and at
" the end is resolved to consume it with a general confla-
" gration.

" The rainbow indeed may be accounted a very beauti-
" ful sight in the heavens; but as it proceeds from a natu-
" ral cause, [c] from the reflection and refraction of the
" rays of the sun from innumerable drops of rain in a
" cloud, it can be no proper token of a covenant com-
" mencing at that time. As there was a sun and clouds
" before the flood, the same phænomenon must have fre-
" quently appeared and consequently lost its validity; nor
" can we suppose, that God should ever be so unmindful
" of his covenant, as to stand in need of so slight, so com-
" mon a remembrancer.

" The permission of the animal food to Noah and his po-
" sterity may be thought perhaps a peculiar privilege; but
" [d] when we read of the same dominion over all crea-
" tures, and the same distinction of clean and unclean
" beasts in the times before the flood that we find in
" the times of Noah, either we must suppose the distinc-
" tion to be frivolous, and the dominion given to man
" more extensive, after he had sinned, than it was before;
" or we must allow, that this is a privilege no more than
" " what

[b] Lucin. De Sacrif. vol. 1. p. 309.   [c] Saurin's Differ-sation.   [d] Heidegger's Hist. patriar. exer. 15,

A. M. 1657, &c.
Ant. Chrif. 2347, &c.
from Gen. viii. 20. to the end of ch. 9.

"what all antediluvians had; and consequently, that it is a misrepresentation to call it *a new grant*.

"Man, in his state of innocence, and while the image of God shone radiantly about him, held all other creatures under a voluntary subjection: but the many sad accidents which we read of continually, are too sure a testimony, that this part of the grant is in a manner quite withdrawn, and that *the fear of us and the dread of us*, is so little impressed upon several kinds of beasts, that on sundry occasions they turn upon their masters, and rebel.

"The Lord and Sovereign of the post-diluvian world was the Patriarch Noah, who must consequently be a man of business, as having the chief government of affairs devolved upon him; and yet, after this period of time, we hear no manner of tidings of him, except it be in one scurvy story of his planting a vineyard, getting scandalously drunk, and exposing himself to the scorn and derision of all about him. It is somewhat strange, that, in all the antediluvian ages, the use of the vine should not be found out, or that Noah, who was now above 600 years old, should not be acquainted with its intoxicating quality; but if he was not, the more he was to be pitied; and Moses (one would think) should have imitated his two dutiful sons, and, in compassion to his infirmity, cast the kind veil upon his nakedness. But instead of that, to represent this favourite of God, and grave sire of mankind, lying in his tent in the shameful manner that he does, and then, as soon as he awakes from his wine, to give him the spirit of prophecy, and set him a venting his curses and his blessings at random, looks as if he were acting the part of Ham, and exposing a weak man's failings to the public. For, according to this representation, what other reason can we assign for the several notorious blunders that he makes; [c] for his mistaking the name of *Canaan* (who seems to be innocent in the whole affair) instead of that of his guilty son *Ham*, in the curse; for preferring his younger son Shem before the first-born Japhet, in the blessing; and for the many unaccountable reveries of enlarging Japhet, making him dwell in the tents of Shem, and Ham to become the servant of servants? What account can we give for these extravagancies, I say, but "that

---

[c] *Vid.* Gen. ix. 25, 26, 27.

Chap. I.   *from the Flood to the Call of Abraham.*   253

"that of suppofing that the good old patriarch was not
yet got out of his cups, and returned to his fenfes?"

It is a fad perverfion of the ufe of human underftanding, and no fmall token of a fecret inclination to infidelity, when men make the condefcenfions of Scripture an argument againft its divine authority; and from the figures and allufions which it employs, in accommodation to their capacities, draw conclufions unworthy of its facred penmen, and unbecoming the nature of God.

In relation to facrifices, we find God declaring himfelf very fully in thefe words: *Hear, O my people, and I will fpeak; I myfelf will teftify againft thee, O Ifrael, for I am God, even thy God. I will not reprove thee, becaufe of thy facrifices, or for thy burnt-offerings, becaufe they were not always before me. I will take no bullock out of thine houfe, or he-goat out of thy folds;——for thinkeft thou that I will eat bull's flefh, or drink the blood of goats? Offer unto God thankfgiving, and pay thy vows unto the Moft High, and call upon me in the time of trouble, fo will I hear thee, and thou fhalt praife me.* So that it is not the oblation itfelf, but the grateful fenfe and affections of the offerer, that are acceptable to God, and which, by an eafy metaphor, may be faid to be as grateful to him ᵍ as perfumes or fweet odours are to us.

And indeed, if either the fenfe of gratitude or fear, if either the apprehenfion of God's peculiar kindnefs, or of his wrathful indignation againft fin, did ever produce a fincere homage, ʰ it muft have been upon this occafion when the Patriarch called to remembrance the many vows he had made to God in the bitternefs of his foul, and in the midft of his diftrefs; when, coming out of the ark, he had before his eyes the ruins of the old world, fo many dreadful objects of the divine vengeance; and at the fame time faw himfelf fafe amidft his little family, which muft have all likewife perifhed, had they not been preferved by a miraculous interpofition. And with fuch affections of mind as this fcene could not but excite, it would be injurious not to think that his prayers and oblations were anfwerably fervent, and his joy and thankfgiving fuch as became fo fignal a deliverance.

But it was not upon account of thefe only that his fervice found fo favourable a reception. Sacrifices ⁱ (as we fhewed before) were of divine inftitution, and prefigurative of

A. M. 1657, &c. Ant. Chrif. 2347, &c. from Gen. viii. 20. to the end of ch. ix.

Anfwered, by fhewing why Noah's facrifice was accepted.

Vol. I. No. 4.   3 A

ᶠ Pfal. l. 7. &c.   ᵍ Patrick's Commentary.   ʰ Saurin's Differtations.   ⁱ *Vid.* p. 135, &c.

A. M. 1657, &c. Ant. Chri. 2347, &c. from Gen. viii. 20, to the end of ch. ix.

of that great propitiation which God, in due time, would exhibit in the death of his son. Whatever merit they have, they derive from Christ, [k] *who gave himself for us, an offering, and a sacrifice to God for a sweet-smelling savour.* It was in the sense of this, therefore, that Noah approached the altar which he had erected; and while he was offering his appointed sacrifices, failed not to commemorate *this Lamb of God, which was slain from the foundation of the world,* and so found his acceptance in the beloved; for he is the [l] *angel which comes and stands at the altar, having a golden censer, and to whom is given much incense, that he may offer it with the prayers of the saints, upon the golden altar, which is before the throne.*

That the covenant hereupon restrained God neither from particular inundations;

We mistake the matter however very much, if we imagine, that the merit of Noah's sacrifice (even when purified with the blood of Christ) was the procuring cause of the covenant here mentioned. The covenant was in the divine counsel from everlasting, and God only here takes an occasion to acquaint Noah with it; but then we may observe, that he expresses himself in such terms as lay no restraint upon him from sending a judgment of waters, or from bringing a general conflagration upon the world at the last day. He binds himself only *never to smite any more every living thing in the manner he had done,* i. e. with an universal deluge; but if any nation deserves such a punishment, and the situation of their country well admits of it, he may, if he pleases, without breach of this covenant, bring a local inundation upon them; though it must be acknowledged, that whenever we find him threatening any people with his [m] *sore judgments,* he never makes mention of this.

nor the general conflagration.

It was a general tradition among the Heathens, that the world was to undergo a double destruction, one by water, and the other by fire. The destruction by fire St Peter has given us a very lively description of. [n] *The heavens and the earth, which are now,* says he, *are kept in store, reserved unto fire, against the day of judgment;* for then *shall the heavens pass away with a great noise, and the elements melt with fervent heat, and the earth also, and the works that are therein, shall be burnt up.* But all this is no infraction upon the covenant made with Noah, which relates to the judgement of a flood: And though this catastrophe will certainly be more terrible than the other, yet it has this great difference

[k] Eph. v. 2.   [l] Revel. viii. 3.   [m] Vid. Ezek. xiv. 21.
[n] 2 Pet. iii. 7. 10.

difference in it, º that it is not sent as a curse, but as a blessing upon the earth: not as a means to deface and destroy, but to renew and refine it; and therefore the same Apostle adds, ᵖ *Nevertheless we, according to his promise, look for new heavens and a new earth, wherein dwelleth righteousness.*

Thus the covenant of God standeth sure: but then, in relation to the sign or sacrament of it, whether it was previous or subsequent to the deluge, this has been a matter much debated among the learned. It cannot be denied indeed, but that * this curious mixture of light and shade discernible

A. M. 1657 &c. Ant Chrif. 2347, &c. from Gen. viii. 20. to ch ix.

That the rainbow, the sign of the covenant, did not exist before the flood.

º Heidegger's Hist. patriar. vol. 1. exer. 19. ᵖ 2 Pet. iii. 13.

* The learned Heidegger has given us an account of the nature and colours of the rainbow, and by what different causes they are produced, in words so very expressive, that I chuse to give them in the original, rather than run the hazard of injuring their emphasis by a bad translation. " Efficit iridem potissi-
" mum sol, seu radius solaris in vaporem receptus, inque eo
" refractus propter diversa receptacula; unum rarius, aera;
" alterum densius vaporem; qui et solarem recipit radium, et
" in oculum reflectit: ita ut in iride sit partim ἀνακλασις, sive
" *radii luminosi* in profunditate vaporis, refractio; parum
" δικλασις, seu *radii ejus ad oculum reflectio*, quæ non possunt
" sociari nisi in nube rorida, et in pluvias jam resolvenda;
" quippe in tantum rara ut eum aliquantum radius solaris
" penetret, et in tantum etiam densa, et ubi radius sese paulu-
" lum insinuarit, eundem repercutiat. Circularis et arcuata
" est ejus figura, ob figuram solis ipsius; quia semper iris ap-
" paret ex adverso solis, repercussis ejus radiis ab opposita nube.
" Colores iridis, ex varia lucis et umbrarum mixura, sunt tres
" potissimum; φοινικεος, *puniceus* et *rubicundus*; πρασιος *porraceus*,
" sive *viridis*, et ἀλιηγος, *cæruleus*. Cum enim solares radii pri-
" mum subeunt nubem, quia minus transitur opaci, color est
" rubicundus, seu puniceus; ubi paulo magis penetrarit, im-
" peditur aliquantum coloris ardor, atque sic fit viridis; at in
" profundum vaporis admissus, usque ad infimam arcus curva-
" turam, ob opacitatem remittit color, estque cæruleus;" *Exercit* 19. This description is pretty lively, and gives us some idea of this strange phænomenon; and yet we must own, that the nature of refraction, on which the colours of the rainbow do depend, is one of the abstrusest things that we meet with in the philosophy of nature. Our renowned Boyle, who wrote a treatise on the subject of colours, after a long and indefatigable search into their natures and properties, was not able so much as to satisfy himself what light is, or (if it be a body) what kind of corpuscles, for size and shape, it consists of, or how

A 2 these

A. M.
657 &c.
Ant. Chrif
2347. &c
from Gen
viii. 20. to
the end of
ch. ix.

discernible in the rainbow, arises naturally from the superficies of those parts which constitute a cloud, when the rays of the sun, from the adverse part of the hemisphere, are darted upon it; and for this reason, ^q whenever there is the like disposition of the sun to the cloud, it may be imagined that the same phænomenon may be seen, and consequently, at certain times, has been seen, not from the deluge only, but from the first foundation of the world. ^r But as this opinion has nothing in Scripture to enforce it, so there are no grounds in nature to give it any sanction, unless we will assert this manifest untruth,---That every disposition of the air, and every density of a cloud, is fitly qualified to produce a rainbow.

This meteor (as the Scripture informs us) * was appointed

these insensible corpuscles could be so differently, and yet withal so regularly, refracted: and he freely acknowledges, that however some colours might be plausibly enough explained in the general, from experiments he had made, yet whensoever he would descend to the minute and accurate explication of particulars, he found himself very sensible of the great obscurity of things. Dr Halley, the great ornament of his profession, makes the same acknowledgement; and after having, from the given proportion of refraction, accounted both for the colours and diameter of the rainbow, with its several appearances, he could hence discern (as he tells us) farther difficulties lying before him: particularly, from whence arose the refractive force of fluids: which is a problem of no small moment, and yet deservedly to be placed among the mysteries of nature, *nondum sensibus, aut ratiociniis nostris objecta:* and the noble Theorist of light himself, after his many surprising discoveries, built even upon vulgar experiments, found it too hard for him to resolve himself in some particulars about it; and notwithstanding all his prodigious skill in mathematics, and his dexterous management of the most obvious experiments, he concludes it at last to be a work too arduous for human understanding, absolutely to determine what light is, after what manner refracted, and by what modes and actions it produceth in our minds the phantasies of colours. *Biblioth. Biblica, vol.* 2. *occaf annot.* 2 *in the appendix.*

^q *Vid.* Brown's Pseudodoxia epidemica. ^r Dr Jackson upon the Creed. l. 4. c. 16.

* That this rainbow was thought to be of somewhat more than mere natural extraction the physical theology of the ancient Heathens seems to testify, and it is not improbable, that from the tenor of God's covenant here made with Noah, which might be communicated to them by tradition, Homer, the great

father

pointed by God to be a witness of his covenant with the new world, and a messenger to secure mankind from destruction by deluges; so that had it appeared before the flood, the sight of it afterwards would have been but a poor comfort to Noah and his posterity, whose fear of an inundation was too violent, ever to be taken away by a common and ordinary sign.

A. M. 2657, &c. Ant. Chrif. 1347, &c. from Gen. viii. 20, to the end of ch. ix.

For suppose that God Almighty had said to Noah, ᵇ "I make a promise to you, and to all living creatures, "that the world shall never be destroyed by water again; "and for confirmation of this, behold, I set the sun in "the firmament:" would this have been any strengthening of Noah's faith, or any satisfaction to his mind? "Why, "(says Noah) the sun was in the firmament when the "deluge came, and was a spectator of that sad tragedy; "and as it may be so again, † what sign or assurance "in

father of Epic poetry, does, by an easy and lively fiction, bring in Jupiter, the king of heaven, sending Iris, his messenger, with a peremptory command to Neptune, the prince of waters, to desist from any farther assisting the Grecians, and annoying the Trojans, and at the same time that Iris is sent with this message to the watery deity, the poet has so contrived the matter, that Apollo, or the sun, which is the parent and efficient cause of the rainbow, is sent with another message to Hector, and the Trojans, in order to encourage them to take the field again, and renew their attack. The meaning of all which fine machinery is no more than this,——That after a great deal of rain which had caused an inundation, and thereby made the Trojan horse useless, the sun began to appear again, and the rainbow in a cloud opposite to the sun, which was a sure prognostic of fair weather; *Bibliotheca Biblica, vol. 1. occaf. annot. 2. in the appendix.*

ᵇ Burnet's Theory.

† When God gives a sign in the heavens, or on the earth, of any prophecy or promise to be fulfilled, it must be something new, or by some change wrought in nature, whereby he testifies to us, that he is able and willing to stand to his promise. Thus God puts the matter to Ahaz, *Ask a sign of the Lord, ask it either in the depth, or in the height above;* and when Ahaz would ask no sign, God gives him one unasked: *Behold a virgin shall conceive, and bear a son.* Thus when Abraham asked a sign, whereby he might be assured of God's promise, that his seed should inherit the land of Canaan, it is said, that *when the sun went down, and it was dark, behold a smoaking furnace, and a burning lamp passed between the pieces of the beasts* which he had cut asunder, Gen.

A. M. 1657, &c. Ant. Chrif. 2347, &c from Gen. viii. 20, to the end of ch. ix.

" in this againſt a ſecond deluge?" But now if we ſuppoſe, on the other hand, that the rainbow firſt appeared to the inhabitants of the earth after the deluge, nothing could be a more proper and appoſite ſign for providence to pitch upon, in order to confirm the promiſe made to Noah and his poſterity, that the world ſhould no more be deſtroyed by water. The rainbow had a ſecret connection with the effect itſelf, and ſo far was * a natural ſign; and as it appeared firſt after the deluge, and was formed in a thin, watery cloud, there is, methinks, a great eaſineſs and propriety of its application for ſuch a purpoſe. For if we ſuppoſe, that while God Almighty was declaring his promiſe to Noah, and what he intended for the ſign of it, there appeared, at the ſame time, in the clouds, *

a Gen. xv. 17. And in like manner, in the ſign given to Hezekiah for his recovery, and to Gideon for his victory; in the former caſe, *the ſhadow went back ten degrees in Ahaz's dial*, Iſa. xxxviii. 8.; and in the latter, *the fleece was wet, and all the ground about it dry*; and then (to change the trial) *it was dry, and all the ground about it wet*, Judg. vi. 38, 39. Theſe were all ſigns, proper, ſignificant, and ſatisfactory, having ſomething new ſurpriſing, and extraordinary in them, denoting the hand and interpoſition of God: but where every thing continues to be as it was before, and the face of nature, in all its parts, the very ſame, it cannot ſignify any thing new, nor any new intention of the author of nature; and, conſequently, cannot be a ſign or pledge, a token or aſſurance of the accompliſhment of any new covenant or promiſe made by him; *Burnet's Theory*, l. 2. c. 5.

* Common philoſophy teaches us, that the rainbow is a natural ſign that there will not be much rain after it appears, but that the clouds begin to diſperſe. For as it never appears in a thick cloud, but only in a thin, whenever it appears after ſhowers which come from thick clouds, it is a token that they now grow thin, and therefore the God of nature made choice of this ſign, rather than any other, to ſatiſfy us, that he would never ſuffer the clouds to thicken again to ſuch a degree, as to bring another deluge upon the earth; *Patrick's Commentary*. " Fit " iris ab adverſo ſole, mittente radios in nubem non denſum; " ſignificat ergo naturaliter, quod et juſſu Dei imbrem nunquam " obruturum mundum: qui enim poſſit, cum neque cœlum to- " tum obductum nubibus ſit, neque, quæ adſunt, ſunt valde " denſæ?" *Valeſius, De S. Philoſ. c. 9.*

* The ingenious Marcus Marci is of opinion, that the rainbow, which firſt appeared to Noah after the flood, and was ſo particularly dignified by God, as to be conſecrated for a divine ſign,

a fair rainbow, that marvellous and beautiful meteor, which Noah had never seen before, it could not but make a most lively impression upon him, quickening his faith, and giving him comfort and assurance, that God would be stedfast to his purpose.

A. M. 1657, &c. An: Christ. 2347, &c. from Gen. vii. 10 to ch. ix

For God did not *set this bow in the clouds for his own sake,* to engage his attention, and revive his memory, whenever he looked on it, (though that be the expression which the Holy Spirit, speaking after the manner of men, has thought fit to make use of), but for our sakes was it placed there, as an illustrious symbol of the divine mercy and goodness, and to confirm our belief and confidence in God: and therefore, whenever ᵗ *we look upon the rainbow,* we should do well to *praise him who made it; for very beautiful is it in the brightness thereof. It compasseth the heaven with a glorious circle, and the hands of the Most High have bended it.*

And for whose sake it was appointed.

And as the goodness of God was very conspicuous to Noah and his posterity, in giving them a new sign for the confirmation of his promises; so it was no less remarkable in the new charter which he granted them, for the enlargement of their diet. That our first parents *, in their state

That flesh was not eaten before the flood.

sign, was not the common one, but a great and universal iris, inimitable by art, which he has defined by a segment of a circle, dissected into several gyrations (or rounds) by the diversity of the colours, differing from one another, begotten by the sun-beams refracted in the atmosphere, and terminated with an opaque superficies. But whether this serves to explain the matter any better, or whether the common rainbow be not an appearance illustrious enough to answer the purposes for which it was intended, we leave the curious to enquire; and shall only observe farther, that whether it was an ordinary or an extraordinary bow which appeared to Noah, it is the opinion of some, that the time of its first appearing was not immediately after he had sacrificed, (as is generally supposed), but on the 150th day of the flood, when God remembered Noah, upon which very day of the year they likewise calculate the birth of Christ (as pre-typified thereby) to have exactly fallen out, and that even the glory of the Lord, which shone round about the shepherds, was a gracious phenomenon, corresponding with this sign of the covenant; *Bibliotheca Biblica. ibid.*

ᵗ Ecclesiasticus, xliii. 11. 12.

* This notion the Pagan poets and philosophers had received: for Ovid, in his description of these times, gives us to understand,

A. M. 1657, &c. Ant Chrif. 2347, &c from Gen viii. 20 to the end of ch. ix.

state of integrity, had not the liberty of eating flesh, is very evident, because they were limited by that injunction which appoints herbs and fruits for their food: ^u *Behold I have given you every herb bearing seed which is upon the face of the earth, and every tree in the which is the fruit of the tree yielding seed: to you it shall be for meat.* Nay, so far was mankind from being indulged the liberty of eating flesh at that time, that we find the beasts of the field, creatures that in their nature are voracious, and the fowl of the air, and every thing that creepeth upon the earth, under the same restraint, as having nothing allowed them for their food but the herbage of the ground; because it was the Almighty's will, that in the state of innocence no violence should be committed, nor any life maintained at the loss and forfeiture of another's.

This was the original order and appointment, and so it continued after the fall; for we can hardly suppose, that God would allow a greater privilege to man after his transgression than he did before. On the contrary, we find him ^x *cursing the ground* for man's sake, and telling him expresly, that *in sorrow he should eat of it all the days of his life;* and though it should bring forth thorns and thistles to him, yet here the restriction is still continued, *Of the herbs of the field thou shalt eat,* which is far from implying

stand, that they fed on no flesh, but lived altogether on herbs and fruits, when he introduces Pythagoras, a great inquirer into the ancient and primitive practices of the world, expressing himself in this manner:

  At vetus illa ætas, cui fecimus aurea nomen,
  Fœtibus arboreis, et quas humus educit, herbis
  Fortunata fuit; nec polluit ora cruore.
  Tunc et aves tutæ movere per aera pennas,
  Et lepus impavidus mediis erravit in arvis;
  Nec sua credulitas piscem suspenderat hamo.
  Cuncta sine insidiis, nullamque timentia fraudem,
  Plenæque pacis erant.   *Met l* 15.

Porphyry, in his book, *De abstinentia,* asserts the same thing, viz. That in the golden age no flesh of beasts was eaten, and he is to be pardoned in what he adds afterwards, viz. That war and famine introduced this practice. He was not acquainted with Genesis; he knew not that God's order to Noah after the flood was, that *every living creature should be meat for him;* Edwards's Survey of religion, vol. 1, p. 117.

  ^u Gen. i. 29, 30.   ^x Ch. iii. 17, 18.

plying a permission to make use of living creatures for that purpose.

Nay, farther, we may observe, that such a permission had been inconsistent with God's intention of punishing him by impoverishing the earth; since, had God indulged him the liberty of making use of what creatures he pleased for his food, he might easily have made himself an amends for the unfruitfulness of the earth, by the many good things which nature had provided for him. The dominion therefore which God at first gave mankind over brute-animals, could not extend to their slaying them for food, since another kind of diet was enjoined them; nor could the distinction of clean and unclean respect them as things to be eaten, but as things to be sacrificed. The first permission to eat them was given to Noah and his sons, and is plainly a distinct branch of power, from what God grants, when he tells them, *y The fear of you, and the dread of you shall be upon every beast of the earth*, &c.

If it be asked, for what reason God should indulge Noah and his posterity in the eating of flesh after the flood, which he had never permitted before it? the most probable answer is —— That he therefore did it because the earth was corrupted by the deluge, and the virtue of its herbs, and plants, and other vegetables, sadly impaired by the saltness, and long continuance of the waters, so that they could not yield that wholesome and solid nutriment which they did before: though others rather think, that God indulged them in this, *z because of the hardness of their hearts*; and that, perceiving the eagerness of their appetites towards carnal food, and designing withal to abbreviate the term of human life, he gave them a free licence to eat it; but knowing, at the same time, that it was less salutary than the natural products of the earth, he thence took occasion to accomplish his will and determination, of having the period of human life made much shorter. Nor is the reason, which *a* Theodorat assigns, for God's changing the diet of men from the fruits of the earth, to the flesh of animals, much amiss, viz. "That, foreknowing, in future
"ages, they would idolize his creatures, he might aggra-
"vate the absurdity, and make it more ridiculous so to do,
"by their consuming at their tables what they sacrificed at
"their altars; since nothing is more absurd, than to wor-
"ship what we eat."

A. M.
1657, &c.
Ant. Chrisi.
2347, &c.
from Gen.
viii. 20. to
the end of
ch. ix.

Why it was granted to Noah and his posterity.

y Gen. ix. 2.   *z* Matth. xix. 8.   *a* In Gen. quæst. 55. p. 44.

A. M. 1657, &c.
Ant. Chrif. 2347, &c.
from Gen. viii. 20. to ch. ix.

That man's dominion over brute creatures still continues.

It cannot be denied indeed, but that the grant of dominion which God gave Adam, in his state of innocence, is now much impaired; and that the creatures, which to him were submissive through love, by us must be used with severity, and subjected by fear: but still it is no small happiness to us, that we know how to subdue them; that the horse and the ox patiently submit to the bridle and the yoke; and such creatures as are immorigerous, we have found out expedients to reclaim. For though man's strength be comparatively small, yet there is no creature in the earth, sea, or air, but what, * by some stratagem or other, he can put in subjection under him.

But *b canst thou draw out Leviathan with an hook? or his tongue with a cord, which thou lettest down? Canst thou put an hook into his nose? or bore his jaw through with a spear? Will he make many supplications unto thee? Will he speak soft words unto thee? Wilt thou take him for a servant for ever?* All these questions, how expressive soever of the several qualities of this portentous creature, may, nevertheless, be answered in the affirmative, viz. That how large soever in bulk, and how tremendous soever in strength this animal may be, yet the Greenland fishermen, who every year return with its spoils, do literally perform what our author seems to account impossible; they *c fill his skin with barbed irons, and his head with fish spears:* and so they *play with him as with a bird; they bind him for their maidens, and part him among their merchants.*

* This superiority of man over all other creatures, his holding them in subjection, and making them subservient to his uses, we find elegantly described by Oppianus, in the following verses:

———ἢ γάρ τι πέλει Καθυπέρτερον ἀνδρῶν.
Νόσφι Θεῶν μούνοισι δ᾽ ὑπείξομεν ἀθανάτοισιν.
Ὅσσους μὲν κατ᾽ ἔρισον ἰδεῖν ἀτρέκεον ἔχοντας
Θῆρας ὑπερφιάλους βροτὸς ἐσβέσσεν: ὅσσα δὲ φῦλα
Οἰωνῶν νεφέλησι καὶ ἠέρι δινεύοντα
Εἷλε, χαμαίζηλον περ ἔχων δέμας ὑδὲ λέοντα;
Ῥυσαὶ ἀγηνορίη δμηθήμεναι ὧδ᾽ ἰσάωσιν
Αἰτόν ἀνεμόεις πτερυγων ῥόθος ἀλλὰ καὶ Ἰνδόν
Θῆρα κελαινοβρινον ὑπείρεον ἄχθος ἀνάγκῃ
Κλίναν ἐπιξρίσαντες, ὑπὸ ζεύγλησι δ᾽ ἔδεκαν
Οὐρήων ταλαεργὸν ἔχειν πόνον ἑλκυσῆρα.

Lib. 5. Halieuticwn. ver. 10. &c.

b Job. xli. 1. &c.   *c* ver. 5, &c.

Chap. I.   *from the Flood to the Call of Abraham.*   263

In short, God has implanted in all creatures, a fear and dread of man. ᵈ This is the thing which keeps wolves out of our towns, and lions out of our streets: and though the sharpness of hunger, or violence of rage, may at certain times make them forget their natural instinct, (as the like causes have sometimes divested man of his reason,) yet, no sooner are these causes removed, but they return to their ordinary temper again, without pursuing their advantage, or combining with their fellow-brutes to rise up in rebellion against man, their lord and master.

A. M. 1657, &c. Ant. Chrif. 2347, &c. from Gen. viii. 10. to the end of ch. ix.

ᵉ Some modern writers of no small note are clearly of opinion, that the Ararat where the ark rested, was mount Caucasus, not far from China, where Noah and some part of his family settled, without travelling to Shinar, or having any hand in the building of Babel; and the arguments they alledge for the support of this opinion, are such as these,——That the Mosaic history is altogether silent, as to the peopling of China at the dispersion, and wholly confines itself within the bounds of the then known world; that the Chinese language and writing are so entirely different from those among us, (introduced by the confusion at Babel,) that it cannot well be supposed they were ever derived from them; and that (taking their first king Fohi and Noah to be the same person) there are several ᶠ traditions relating to them, wherein they seem to agree, that the reign of Fohi coincides with the times of Noah, and the lives of his successors correspond with the men of the same ages recorded in Scripture; and from hence they infer, that the true reason why Moses makes so little mention of Noah, in the times subsequent to the flood, is

Why Moses makes so little mention of Noah after the flood.

3 B 2   this,

ᵈ Miller's History of the church, l. 1. c. 1.   ᵉ Dr Alix, in his Reflections on the books of the Holy Scriptures; Mr Whiston in his Chronology of the old Testament; Shuckford, in his Connection; and Bedford, in his Scripture chronology.

ᶠ Thus, in the Chinese history, Fohi is said to have had no father which agrees well enough with Noah, because the memory of his father might be lost in the deluge; that Fohi's mother conceived him, as she was encompassed with a rainbow; which seems to allude to the rainbow's first appearing to Noah after the flood; and that Fohi carefully bred up seven sorts of creatures, which he used to sacrifice to the supreme Spirit of heaven and earth, which is an imperfect tradition of Noah's taking into the ark, of every *clean beast by sevens*, and of his making use of none but these in all his burnt-offerings; *Shuckford's Connection. lib.* 2.

<small>A. M. 1657, &c. Ant. Chrif. 2347, &c. from Gen. viii. 10. to the end of ch. ix.</small>

this——That he lived at too great a distance, and had no share in the transactions of the nations round about Shinar, to whom alone, after the dispersion of mankind, he is known to confine history. This indeed is solving the difficulty at once: but then, as this opinion is only conjectural, the histories and records of China are of a very uncertain and precarious authority, and such as are reputed genuine, of no older date than some few centuries before the birth of Christ, the major part of the learned world has supposed, either that Noah, settling in the country of Armenia, did not remove from thence, nor had any concern in the work of Babel, and so fall's not under the historian's consideration; or that, if he did remove with the rest into the plains of Shinar, being now superannuated, and unfit for action, the administration of things was committed to other hands, which made his name and authority the less taken notice of.

<small>Why he records the account of his drunkenness.</small>

It must be acknowledged, however, that the design of the sacred penman is, to be very succinct in his account of the affairs of this period, because he is hastening to the history of Abraham the great founder of the Jewish nation, and whose life and adventures he thinks himself concerned, upon that account, to relate more at large. However this be, it is certain, from the tenor of his writing, that he is far from leading us into any suspicion of his having a private malignity to Noah's character. He informs us, that, amidst the corruption of the antediluvian world, he preserved himself immaculate, and did therefore find favour in the sight of God, and was admitted to the honour of his immediate converse: that, to preserve him from the general destruction, God instructed him how to build a vessel of security, undertook the care and conduct of it himself, and, amidst the ruins of a sinking world, landed it safe on one of the mountains of Armenia; that, as soon as the deluge was over, God accepted of his homage and sacrifice, and not only renewed to him the same charter which he had originally granted to our first progenitor, but over and above that, gave him an enlargement of his diet which he had not granted to any before; and with him made an everlasting covenant, never to destroy the world by water any more, whereof he constituted his bow in the clouds to be a glorious symbol. In this point of light it is that Moses has, all along, placed the patriarch's character; and therefore, if, in the conclusion of it, he was forced to shade it with one act of intemperance, this, we may reasonably

ably conclude, proceeded from no other passion but his love of truth; and to every impartial reader must be * a strong argument of his veracity, in that he has interspersed the faults with the commendations of his worthies, and, through his whole history, drawn no one character so very fair, as not to leave some blemishes, some instances of human frailty still abiding on it. And indeed, if we consider the thing rightly, we shall find it an act of singular kindness and benefit to us, that God has ordered the faults and miscarriages of his saints so constantly to be recorded in Scripture; since they are written for our instruction, to remind us of our frailty, and to alarm our caution and fear.

A. M. 1657, &c. Ant. Chrif. 2347, &c. from Gen. viii. 20, to the end of ch. xi.

Noah, we read, had escaped the pollutions of the old world, and approved his fidelity to God in every trying juncture; and yet we see him here falling, of his own accord, and shamefully overcome in a time of security and peace; when he had no temptations to beset him, nor any boon companions to allure him to excess; and therefore his example calls perpetually upon *g him that thinketh he standeth, to take heed lest he fall*. More especially, it informs us, that *h wine is a mocker, strong drink is raging, and whosoever it deceived thereby, is not wise*; and therefore it exhorts, in the words of the wise man, *i Look not thou upon wine when it is red, when it giveth its colour in the cup, when it moveth itself aright. At the last it will bite like a serpent, and sting like an adder. Thine eyes shall behold strange women, and thine heart shall*

---

* To confirm, in some measure, the truth of this account of Moses, we have an Heathen story, which seems to have sprung from some tradition concerning it; for it tells us, that, on a certain day, Myrrha, wife, or (as others say) nurse to Hammon, and mother of Adonis, having her son in her company, found Cyniftas sleeping in his tent, all uncovered, and in an indecent posture. She ran immediately, and informed Hammon of it; he gave notice of it to his brothers, who, to prevent the confusion which Cyniftas might be in to find himself naked, covered him with something. Cyniftas, understanding what had passed, cursed Adonis, and pursued Myrrha into Arabia; where, after having wandered nine months, she was changed into a tree which bears myrrh. Hammon and Ham are the same person, and so are Adonis and Canaan; *Calmet's Dictionary on the word* Ham.

g 1 Cor. x. 12. &c. h Prov. xx. 1. i Ch. xxiii. 31, &c.

shall utter perverse things; yea, thou shalt be as he that lieth down in the midst of the sea, and as he that lieth upon the top of a mast.

There is not however all the reason that is imagined, to suppose that Noah was drunk to any such excessive degree. The same word which is here used occurs [k] in another place in the book of Genesis, where we read, that *Joseph's brethren drank, and were merry with him;* and yet the circumstances of the entertainment will not suffer us to think, that they indulged themselves in any excess, in the presence of him whom as yet they knew to be no other than the governor of Egypt. And in like manner, if we may be allowed to take the word here in an innocent sense, its import will only be, that Noah drank of the wine plentifully, perhaps, but not to a debauch, and so fell asleep. For we must observe, that Moses's design is, not to accuse Noah of intemperance, but only to shew upon what occasion it was the Canaanites, whom the people under his command were now going to engage, were accursed, and reprobated by God, even from the days of Noah; and consequently, in more likelihood to fall into their hands.

Without perplexing ourselves therefore to find out such excuses as several interpreters have devised, as that Noah was unacquainted with the nature of the vine in general, * or with the effects of this in particular, or that the age and infirmity of his body, or the deep concern and melancholy of his mind, made him liable to be overcome with a very little; we may adventure to say, that he drank plentifully, without impeaching his sobriety; and that while he was asleep, he chanced to be uncovered, without any stain upon his modesty. There is a great deal of difference between satiety and intemperance, between refreshing nature, and debauching it; and considering withal, that the fashion of men's habits was at that time

loose,

---

[k] Ch. xliii. 34.

* It is a Jewish tradition or allegory, that the vine which Noah planted was not of an ordinary terrestrial growth, but was carried down the river out of paradise, or at least out of Eden, and found by him; and as some have imagined that *the tree of knowledge of good and evil* was a vine, so, by the description given thereof, and the fatal consequences attending it, there seems to be a plain allusion to it, and some reason to believe that it was one and the same tree by which the nakedness both of Adam and Noah was exposed to derision; *Targ. Jonath.*

Chap. I.   *from the Flood to the Call of Abraham.*   267

loose, (as they were likewise in subsequent ages before the use of breeches was found out,) such an accident might have easily happened, without the imputation of any harm.

¹ The Jewish doctors are generally of opoinion, that Canaan, * having first discovered his grandfather's nakedness, made himself merry therewith, and afterwards exposed it to the scorn of his father. Whoever the person was, it is certain that he is called ᵐ *the younger,* or *little son of Noah,* which cannot well agree with Ham, because he was neither little, nor his younger son, but the second, or middlemost, as he is always placed; ⁿ nor does it seem so pertinent to the matter in hand, to mention the order of his birth, but very fit (if he speaks of his grandson) to distinguish him from the rest. So that if it was Canaan who treated his grandsire in this unworthy manner, the application of the curse to him, who was first in the offence, is

A. M. Ant. Chrif. 1657, &c. from Gen. viii 10 to o the end ch. ix.

Why Noah cursed Canaan, and not Ham.

---

¹ Calmet's Dictionary on the word *Canaan*.

* Interpreters have invented several other reasons, why the curse which properly belonged to Ham was inflicted on his son Canaan; as 1st, When Canaan is mentioned, Ham is not exempted from the malediction, but rather more deeply plunged into it because parents are apt to be more affected with their children's misfortunes than their own; especially, if themselves brought the evil upon them by their own fault or folly. 2dly, God having blessed the three sons of Noah at their going out of the ark, it was not proper that Noah's curse should interfere with the divine blessing, but very proper that it should be transferred to Canaan, in regard to the future extirpation of the people which were to descend from him. But, 3dly, Some imagine that there is here an *ellipsis,* or defect of the word *father,* since such relative words are frequently omitted, or understood in Scripture. Thus Mat. iv. 21. *James of Zebedee* for *the son of Zebedee* ; John xix. 25. *Mary of Cleopas* for *the wife of Cleopas*; and Acts vii. 16. *Emmor of Sychem* for *the father of Sychem,* which our translation rightly supplies; and in like manner, *Canaan* may be put for *the father of Canaan* as the Arabic translation has it, *i. e. Ham,* as the Septuagint here render it. And though Ham had more sons, yet he may here be described by his relation to Canaan, because in him the curse was more fixed and dreadful, reaching to his utter extirpation, whilst the rest of Ham's posterity in after ages were blessed with the saving knowledge of the gospel; *Pool's Annotations.*

ᵐ Gen. ix. 24.   * Patrick's Commentary.

A. M.
1657, &c.
Ant. Chrif.
2347, &c.
from Gen
viii. 20, to
the end of
ch. ix.

is far from being a miftake in Noah. It is no random anathema which he let fly at all adventures, but a cool, deliberate denunciation, which proceeded not from a fpirit of indignation, but of prophecy. The hiftory indeed takes notice of this malediction immediately upon Noah's awaking out of his fleep, and being informed of what had happened; but this is occafioned by its known brevity, which (as we have often remarked) relates things as inftantly fucceffive, when a confiderable fpace of time ought to interfere. In all probability, thefe predictions of Noah, which point out the different fates of his pofterity, were fuch as [o] we find † Jacob pronouncing over his fons a little before his death: and it is not unlikely that the common opinion of Noah's dividing the earth among his, might take its original from thefe laft words that we read of him, which were certainly accomplifhed in their event.

The curfe verified.

The curfe, upon Canaan is, that he fhould be a fervant to Shem: and [p] about 800 years after this did not the Ifraelites, defcendants of Shem, take poffeffion of the land of Canaan, fubdue thirty of its kings, deftroy moft of its inhabitants, lay heavy tributes upon the remainder, and, by oppreffions of one kind or other, oblige fome to fly into Egypt, [*] others into Africa, and others into Greece? He

was

[o] Gen. xlix.

† That which may confirm us in this opinion is,—That Jacob, when he calleth his children together, acquaints them that his purpofe is *to tell them that which fhall befal them in the laft days;* and that he does not always prefage bleffings, but fometimes illluck to their pofterity, and (in the fame manner that Noah does now and then drops a note of his difpleafure, according as their behaviour has been: For thus he fays of Simeon and Levi, in regard to the flaughter the Shechemites, *Curfed be their anger, for it was fierce; and their wrath, for it was cruel,* Gen. xlix. 7.

[p] Patrick's Commentary, in locum

[*] Procopius [De bello Vandal. l. 2. c. 10] tells us, that in the province of Tingitana, and in the very ancient city of Tingis, which was founded by them, there are two great pillars to be feen, of white ftone, erected near a large fountain, with an infcription in Phœnician characters to this purpofe, *We are people preferved by flight from that robber Jefus, the fon of Nave who purfued us.* And what makes it very probable that they went their flight this way, is the great agreement, and almoft identity of Punic, with the Canaanitifh or Hebrew language; *Calmet's Dictionary on the word* Canaan.

was doomed likewise to be a servent to Japhet; and did not the Greeks and Romans, descended from Japhet, utterly destroy the relicks of Canaan, who fled to Tyre, built by the Sidonians; to Thebes, built by Cadmus, and to Carthage, built by Dido? For who has not heard of the conquests of the Romans over the Africans?

A. M. 1657. &c. ant. Christ. 2347. &c. from Gen. viii. 10. to the end of ch. ix.

The blessing upon Japhet is, that his territories should be enlarged: [q] and can we think otherwise, when (as we shall shew anon) not only all Europe, and the Lesser Asia, but Media likewise, and part of Armenia, Iberia, Albania, and the vast regions towards the north, which anciently the Scythians, but now the Tartars, inhabit, fell to the share of his posterity? It was likewise declared, that he should dwell in the tents of Shem; and is it not notorious, that the Greks and Romans invaded, and conquered that part of Asia where the posterity of Shem had planted themselves? that both Alexander and Cæsar were masters of Jerusalem, and made all the countries thereabout tributary? " You (says [r] Justin Martyr, speaking to " Trypho the Jew concerning his nation) who are de" scended from Shem, according as God has appointed, " came into the land of the children of Canaan, and " made it your own; and in like manner, according to " the divine decree, the sons of Japhet (the Romans) have " broke in upon you, seized upon your whole country, " and still keep possession of it. Thus the sons of Shem " (says he) have overpowered and reduced the Canaanite; " and the sons of Japhet have subdued the sons of Shem, and " made them their vassals; so that the posterity of Canaan " are become, in a literal sense, *servants of servants*."

The blessing upon Japhet.

There is something peculiar in the blessing which Noah gives Shem; for [s] *blessed* (says he) *be the Lord God of Shem*: but why the God of Shem, and not the God of Japhet? As to the behaviour of these two sons towards their father, it was the same. They joined in the pious office done to him; so that in this respect they were equal, and equally deserving of a blessing. Nay, if any preference was due to either from the father, it was to Japhet, his first-born; for, so he was, though commonly last named, when the sons of Noah are mentioned together. Now this being the case, how comes Shem to be preferred? And what is the blessing

And upon Shem, verified.

[q] Patrick's Commentary, 288.   [r] Dial. contra Tryp. Jud. p.   [s] Gen. ix. 26.

A. M. 1657. &c.
Ant. Chrif. 2347, &c.
from Gen viii. 20. to the end of ch. ix.

bleffing conferred on him? A temporal bleffing it could not be; for that was before confirmed with all the fons of Noah. Day and night, fummer and winter, feed-time and harveft, were a common gift to the world, and beftowed (as our Saviour obferves) *on the evil, as well as on the good*. We may therefore prefume, that the bleffing here given to Shem was of a different kind, founded upon [t] *a better covenant, and eftablifhed upon better promifes*, than any temporal grant can be. And accordingly we may obferve, that the fame promife which was given to Adam after the fall, *viz.* that the feed of the woman fhould finally prevail, was renewed to Noah before the flood; for [u] *with thee will I eftablifh my covenant*, fays God; and therefore, as the Apoftle to the Hebrews tells us of this patriarch, [x] *that he was heir of the righteoufnefs, which is by faith;* he certainly forefaw that in Seth's family God would fettle his church; that of this feed Chrift fhould be born according to the flefh; and that the covenant which fhould reftore man to himfelf and to his maker, fhould be conveyed through his pofterity. And this accounts for the preference given to Shem; for Noah fpake not of his own choice, but declared the counfel of God, who had now, as he frequently did afterwards, *chofen the younger before the elder.*

Thus it appears upon inquiry, that thefe prophecies of Noah were not the fumes of indigefted liquor, but [y] *the words of truth and fobernefs:* and though their fenfe was not fo apparent at the time of their being pronounced, yet their accomplifhment has now explaind their meaning, and verified that obfervation of the Apoftle, (which very probably alludes to the very predictions now before us,) *No prophecy is of any private interpretation; for the prophecy came not of old time by the will of men, but holy men of God fpake as they were moved by the Holy Ghoft.*

DISSERTATION I.

Of the prohibition of blood.

The meaning of the prohibition

THE grant which God was pleafed to give Noah and his pofterity, to eat the flefh of all living creatures, has this remarkable reftriction in it, [a] *But flefh, with the life*

[t] Heb. viii. 6. [u] Gen. vi. 18. [x] Heb. xi. 7. [y] Acts xxvi. 25. [a] Gen. ix. 4.

life thereof, which is the blood thereof, shall you not eat. Whether this prohibition related to the eating of things strangled, and such as died of themselves, in which the blood was settled, (as [a] some will have it,) or to the eating of the flesh of creatures reeking in **blood**, and their limbs cut off while they themselves were yet alive, (as others [h] imagine,) is not so material here to inquire; since the former was prohibited by subsequent laws, both [c] in the Jewish and Christian church, and the latter was a practice too abhorrent to human nature, one would think, to need any prohibition at all. Whether therefore it be blood congealed, or blood mingled in the flesh, that is here primarily intended, the injunction must at least equally extend to blood simple and unmixed; nor can any interpretation imaginable be more natural and obvious than this:———
" Though I give you the flesh of every creature that you
" shall think proper to make use of for food, yet I do not
" at the same time give you the blood with it. The blood
" is the life, or vehicle, or chief instrument of life, in eve-
" ry creature; it must therefore be reserved for another
" use, and not be eaten."

This is the true sense of the prohibition, compared with these parts of the Levitical law wherein we find it re-enjoined: but then the question is, whether this injunction be obligatory upon us now, under the dispensation of the gospel? or, whether the gospel, which is the law of liberty, has set us free from any such observance? and a question it is that ought the rather to be determined, because some have made it a matter of no small scruple to themselves, whilst others have passed it by with neglect, as a law of temporary duration only, and now quite abrogated.

That therefore the reader may, in this matter, chiefly judge for himself, I shall fairly state the arguments on both sides; and when I have done this, by a short examination into the merits of each evidence, endeavour to convince myself, and others, on which side of the question it is that truth preponderates; and consequently, what ought to be the practice of every good Christian in relation to this law.

Those who maintain the lawfulness of eating blood, do not deny but this prohibition obliged Noah and his posterity

A. M. 1657, &c. Art. Chrif. 2347, &c. from Gen. viii. 20. to the end of ch. x.

The question thereupon.

The arguments for the eating of blood.

[a] St. Chrysostom, and Ludovicus De Dieu. [b] Maimonides, and our Selden De jure gentium. [c] *Vid.* Lev. xvii. 12.; and Acts xv. 20.

sterity, *i. e.* all mankind, to the time of the promulgation of the law, do not deny, but that, at the giving of the law, this prohibition was renewed, and more explicit reasons were given for the observation of it; nay, do not deny, but that under the gospel it was enjoined, by a very competent authority, to some particular Christians at least, for some determinate time. But then they contend, that during these several periods, there could be no moral obligation in the injunction, but that, (setting aside the divine authority,) [d] *neither if they did eat, were they the worse neither if they did not eat, were they the better.*

For if there was any moral turpitude in the act of eating blood, or things commixed with blood, how comes it to pass (say they) that though God prohibited his own people the Jews, yet he suffered other nations to eat [e] *any thing that died of itself,* and consequently had the blood settled in it? *If* [f] *meat condemneth us to God,* the same providence which took care to restrain the Jews [g] *(for is he the God of the Jews only; is he not also of the Gentiles?)* from what was detestable to him, as well as abhorrent to human nature, would have laid the same inhibition upon all mankind; at least he would not have enjoined his own people to give to a proselyte of the gate, or to sell to an alien or Heathen such meat as would necessarily ensnare them in sin.

The law therefore which enjoined Noah and his children to abstain from blood, must necessarily have been a law peculiar to that time only. [h] Cain, in the first age of the world, had slain Abel, while there were but few persons in it: God had now destroyed all mankind, except eight persons; and to prevent the fate of Abel from befalling any of them, he forbids murder under a capital punishment; and to this purpose, forbids the use of blood, as a proper guard upon human life in the infancy of the world.

Under the Mosaic covenant he renews this law indeed, but then he establishes it upon another foundation, and makes blood therefore prohibited, because he had appointed it [i] 'to be offered upon the altar, and to make an atonement for men's souls: for it is the blood *(saith he)* that maketh an atonement for the soul;' and was reserved for

---

[d] 1 Cor. viii. 8. [e] Deut. xiv. 21. [f] 1 Cor. viii. 8. [g] Rom. iii. 29. [h] Miscellanea sacra, vol. 2. [i] Lev. xvii. 11.

for religious purposes was not at that time convenient to be eaten. But now, that these purposes are answered, and these sacrifices are at an end, the reason of our abstinence has ceased; and consequently our abstinence itself is no longer a duty.

A. M. 1657, &c. Ant. Chrif. 2347, &c. from Gen. vii. 20. to the end of ch. ix.

Blood, we allow, had still something more sacred in it: it was a type of the sacrifice of Christ, who was to be offered upon the altar of his cross; but that oblation being now made, the reason of its appropriation, and being with-held from common use, is now no more. And, though the council at Jerusalem made a decree, even subsequent to the sacrifice of Christ, that the *brethren, who were of the Gentiles, should abstain from things strangled, and from blood;* yet before we can determine any thing from this injunction, the occasion, place, time, and other circumstances of it, must be carefully looked into.

The occasion of the decree was this,-----While Paul and Barnabas were preaching the gospel at Antioch, certain persons, converted from Judaism, came down from Jerusalem, and, very probably, pretending a commission from the apostles, declared it their opinion, that whoever embraced the Christian religion, was obliged, at the same time, to be circumcised, and observe the whole law.

The place, where the question arose, was Antioch, where (as Josephus tells us) there was a famous Jewish university, full of *Proselytes of the gate*, (as they were called,) and who, in all probability, were converted by the men of [k] Cyprus and Cyrene, who were among those that were dispersed at the first persecution, which immediately ensued at the martyrdom of Stephen.

The persons who moved this question were [l] *some of the sect of the Pharisees,* converted to Christianity; but still so prejudiced in favour of their old religion, or at least of the divine rite of circumcision, that they thought there was no coming to Christ without entering in at that gate.

The persons to whom the question related, [m] were *Proselytes of the gate,* i. e. Gentiles by birth, but who had renounced the Heathen religion as to all idolatry, and were thereupon permitted to live in Palestine, or wherever the Jews inhabited; and had several privileges allowed them, upon condition, that they would observe the laws of society, and conform to certain injunctions that [n] Moses had prescribed them.

The

[k] Acts xi. 20.   [l] Ch. xv. 5.   [m] Miscellanea sacra, vol. 2.   [n] Lev. xvii.

A. M.
1657. &c.
Ant. Chrif.
2347, &c.
from Gen.
viii. 20. to
the end of
ch ix.

The time when this queſtion aroſe, was not long after the converſion of Cornelius; ſo that this body of proſelytes was, very probably, the firſt large number of Gentiles that were received into the Chriſtian church, and this the firſt time that the queſtion was agitated,—" Whether the " *Proſelytes of the gate*, who (as the zealots pretended) could " not ſo much as live among Jews without circumciſion, " could be allowed to be a part of the Chriſtian church " without it?"

Under theſe circumſtances the council at Jeruſalem conveened, and accordingly made their decree, that the *Proſelytes of the gate* (for it is perſons of this denomination only which their decree concerns) *ſhould* ° *abſtain from the meats offered to idols, and from blood, and from things ſtrangled, and from fornication;* the very things which, ᴾ according to the law of Moſes, they engaged themſelves to abſtain from, when they were firſt admitted to the privilege of ſojourning among the Jews. So that, in effect, the decree did no more than declare the opinion of thoſe who made it, to thoſe to whom it was ſent, *viz.* that Chriſtianity did not alter the condition of the proſelytes, in reſpect of their civil obligations; but that, as they were bound by theſe laws of Moſes before their converſion, ſo they were ſtill; and conſequently, that the ſenſe of St Paul is the ſame with the ſenſe of the council at that time; ᑫ *let every one abide in the calling,* i. e. in the civil ſtate and condition wherein he is called. But ſuppoſing the decree to extend farther than the proſelytes of Antioch, yet there was another reaſon why the council at Jeruſalem ſhould determine in this manner, and that was——the ſtrong averſion which they knew the Jewiſh converts would have conceived againſt the Gentiles, had they been indulged the liberty of eating blood; and therefore, to compromiſe the matter, they laid on them this prudent reſtraint, from the ſame principle that we find St Paul declaring himſelf in this manner: ʳ *Though I am free from all men, yet have I made myſelf a ſervant unto all, that I might gain the more. Unto the Jew, I became as a Jew, that I might gain the Jews;—to the weak became I as weak, that I might gain the weak. I am made all things to all men, that I might by all means ſave ſome.*

Nay, admitted the decree was not made with this view, yet, being founded on laws which concerned the Jewiſh polity

° Acts xv. 29.   ᴾ *Vid.* Lev. xvii. and xviii.   ᑫ 1 Cor. vii. 20.   ʳ Ch. ix. 19, 20, 22.

polity only, it could certainly last no longer than that government lasted; and consequently, ever since the temple-worship has expired, and the Jews have ceased to be a political body, it must have been repealed; and accordingly, if we look into the gospel, say they, we may there find a repeal of it in full form. For therein we are told, ˢ that *the kingdom of God is not meat and drink, but righteousness, and peace, and joy in the Holy Ghost;* ᵗ that *meat commendeth us not unto God;* ᵘ that *what goeth into the mouth defileth not the man;* ˣ that *to the pure, all things are pure;* ʸ that *there is nothing unclean of itself, but only to him that esteemeth it to be unclean, it is unclean; for every creature of God is good, and nothing is to be refused, if it be received with thanksgivings, for it is sanctified with the word of God and prayer* ᶻ; And therefore we are ordered, ᵃ that *whatever is sold in the shambles, even though it be a thing offered to idols, that to eat, asking no questions for conscience sake;* and are told, that ᵇ *whoever commandeth us to abstain from meats, which God has created to be received with thanksgiving of them that believe, and know the truth,* ought to be ranked in the number of seducers.

In a word, the very genius of the Christian religion, say they, is a charter of liberty, and a full exemption from the law of Moses. It debars us from nothing, but what has a moral turpitude in it, or at least what is too base and abject for a man that has the revelation of a glorious and immortal life in the world to come; and as there is no tendency of this kind in the eating of blood, they therefore conclude, that this decree of the apostles either concerned the ᶜ Jewish proselytes only, who, in virtue of the obedience they owed to the civil laws of Palestine, were to abstain from blood; or obliged none, but the Gentiles of Antioch, Syria, and Cilicia, to whom it was directed; was calculated for a certain season only, either to prevent giving offence to the Jews, who were then captious, or to reconcile Gentile and Jewish converts, who were then at some variance; but was to last no longer than till the Jews and Gentiles were formed into one communion. So that now, the prohibition given by God to Noah, the laws given

A M. 1657, &c.
Ant. Chrif. 1347, &c.
from Gen. viii. 10, to the end of ch. ix.

ˢ Rom. xiv. 17.   ᵗ 1 Cor. viii. 8.   ᵘ Matth. xv. 11.
ˣ Tit. i. 15.   ʸ Rom. xiv. 14.   ᶻ Tim. iv. 4, 5.
ᵃ 1 Cor. x. 25. 28.   ᵇ 1 Tim. iv. 1. 3.   ᶜ Miscellanea sacra, vol. 2.

A. M. 1567, &c. Ant. Chrif. 2347, &c. from Gen. viii. 20 to the end of ch. ix.

ven by Moses to the Israelites, and the decree sent by the apostles to the Christians at Antioch, are all repealed and gone, and a full licence given us to eat blood with the same indifference, as any other food; if so be we thereby [d] *give no offence* to our weaker brethren, *for whom Christ died.*

Those who maintain the contrary opinion, *viz.* That the eating of blood, in any guise whatever, is wicked and unlawful, found the chief of their arguments upon the limitation of the grant given to Noah, the reasons that are commonly devised for the prohibition, and the literal sense of the apostolic decree.

The arguments against the eating of blood.

[e] 'When princes give grants of lands to any of their subjects, say they, they usually reserve some royalties (such as the mines, or minerals) to themselves, as memorials of their own sovereignty, and the other's dependence. If the grant indeed be given without any reserve, the mines and minerals may be supposed to be included in it; but when it is thus expressly limited, " You shall have such and such " lordships and manors, but you shall not have the mines " and minerals with the lands, for several good reasons " specified in the patent;" it must needs be an odd turn of thought to imagine, that the grantee has any title to them; and yet this is a parallel case: for when God has thus declared his will to the children of men,—— " You " shall have the flesh of every creature for food, but you " shall not eat the blood with it;" it is every whit as strange an inference, to deduce from hence a general right to eat blood.

The commandment given to Adam is,—— [f] *Of every tree in the garden thou shalt freely eat; but of the tree of knowledge of good and evil, thou shalt not eat.* This is the first law; and the second is like unto it, [g] *Every moving thing, that liveth, shall be meat for you; even as the green herb, have I given you all things; but flesh, with the life thereof, which is the blood thereof, shall you not eat.* This, upon his donation both to Adam and Noah, God manifestly reserves to himself, as an acknowledgment of his right, to be duly paid; and when it was relaxed or repealed, say they, we cannot tell.

Nay, so far from being repealed, that it is not only in his words to Noah, that God has declared this inhibition, but in the law, delivered by his servant Moses, he has explained

[d] 1 Cor. viii. 11, &c.   [e] *Vid.* Revelation examined, vol. 2.
[f] Gen. ii. 16, 17.   [g] Ch. ix. 3, 4.

plained his mind more fully concerning it. '[h] Whatsoever man there is, of the house of Israel, or of the strangers, that sojourn among you, that eateth any manner of blood, I will even set my face *against that soul*, and will cut him off from among his people.' This is a severe commination, say they; and therefore observe, how oft, in another place, he reiterates the injunction, as it were, with one breath. '[i] Only be sure, that thou eat not the blood, for the blood is the life, and thou mayest not eat the life with the flesh. Thou shalt not eat it; thou shalt pour it upon the earth, as water; thou shalt not eat it, that it may go well with thee, and thy children after thee.'

A. M. 1657, &c. Ant. Chris. 2347, &c. from Gen. viii. 20. to the end of ch. ix.

Now, there are several reasons, continue they, why God should be so importunate in this prohibition. For, having appointed the blood of his creatures to be offered for the sins of men, he therefore requires, that it should be religiously set apart for that purpose; and having prohibited the sin of murther under a severe penalty, he therefore guards against it, by previously forbidding the eating of blood, lest that should be an inlet to savageness and cruelty.

The Scythians, (as [k] Herodotus assures us,) from drinking the blood of their cattle, proceeded to drink the blood of their enemies; and were remarkable for nothing so much, as their horrid and brutal actions. The animals, that feed on blood, are perceived to be much more furious than others that do not; and thereupon they observe, that blood is a very hot, inflaming food; that such foods create choler, and that choler easily kindleth into cruelty. Nay, they observe farther, that eating of blood gave occasion to one kind of early idolatry among the Zabii, in the east, *viz.* the worship of dæmons, whose food, as they imagined, was blood; and therefore they, who adored them, had communion with them by eating the same food. Good reason therefore, say they, had God, in the gospel, as well as the law, to prevent a practice which he could not but foresee would be attended with such pernicious effects.

For the apostolic decree, as they argue farther, did not relate to one set of people only, *the proselytes of the gate*, who were lately converted to Christianity; nor was it directed to some particular places only, and with a design to answer some particular ends, the prevention of offence, or the reconciliation of contending parties; to subsist for

[h] Lev. xvii. 10.   [i] Deut. xii. 23, &c.   [k] Lib. 4.

A. M. 1657, &c. Ant. Chrif. 1347, &c. from Gen. viii. 20, to the end of ch. ix.

a determinate time, and then to lose all its obligation: but it concerned all Christians, in all nations, and in all future ages of the church; was enacted for a general use and intent; and has never since been repealed: and to support these assertions, they proceed in this method.

Before the passing of this decree, they say, St Paul preached Christianity to the whole body of the Gentiles at Antioch. For he had not long preached in the synagogues, before the Gentiles [l] besought him, that he would preach to them the same words, *i. e.* the doctrine of Jesus Christ, on the next Sabbath day; and accordingly we are told, that on the 'Sabbath-day, came almost the whole city together to hear the word of God,' which certainly implies a concourse of people more than the 'Proselytes of the gate;' nay, more than the whole body of the Jews, who were but a handful, in comparison of the rest of the inhabitants of that great city; and that this large company was chiefly made up of Gentiles, the sequel of the history informs us. For when the '[m] Jews saw the multitude, they were filled with envy, and spake against those things which were spoken by Paul, contradicting and blaspheming. Then Paul and Barnabas waxed bold, and said, It was necessary that the word of God should first have been spoken to you; but seeing ye put it from you, and judge yourselves unworthy of everlasting life, lo, we turn to the Gentiles. And when the Gentiles heard this, they were glad, and glorified the word of the Lord; and as many as were ordained to eternal life, believed: and the word of the Lord was published throughout all the region.'

Now, this transaction at Antioch, say they, happened seven years before the decree against blood, and things strangled was passed at Jerusalem; and therefore, as the Gentiles, not in Antioch only, but in all the region round about, were no strangers to the doctrine of Jesus Christ, there is reason to suppose that this decree, when passed, was not confined to one particular set of men, but directed to all Gentile converts at large. For hear what the president of the council says upon this occasion; '[n] Wherefore my sentence is, that we trouble not them, who from among the Gentiles are turned to God; but that we write unto them, that they abstain from pollutions of idols, and from fornication, and from things strangled, and from blood: for Moses of old time hath in every city them that preach him, being read in the synagogue every Sabbath-day.'

My

[l] Acts xiii. 42, &c.   [m] Acts xiii. 45. &c.   [n] Acts xv. 19. to 22.

My sentence (says the Apostle) is, that ye write unto the Gentile converts upon these points; *for Moses has these of old in every city that preach him*, i. e. there is no necessity of writing to any Jewish convert, or any proselyte convert to Christianity, to abstain from these things, because all that are admitted into synagogues, (as the proselytes were,) know all these things sufficiently already. And accordingly, upon this sentence of St James, the decree was founded, and directed (according to the nature of the thing) to those whom it was fitting and necessary to inform in these points, i e. to those who were unacquainted with the writings of Moses.

The letter indeed, which contained the decree, was directed to the brethren at Antioch, Syria, and Cilicia; but it would be shocking, and unchristian to think, that the precepts of an apostolic epistle were obligatory to those only to whom the epistle was directed. The purport of it concerned all. It was to apprise the Heathen converts to Christianity, that they were exempted from the observance of the law of Moses, except in four instances laid down in that canon; and as it was of general concern for all converts to know, the apostles, we may presume, left copies of it in all the churches: for so we are told expressly of St Paul, and his companions, that ' ° as they went through the cities, they delivered them the decrees for to keep, which were ordained of the apostles and elders, that were at Jerusalem; and so were the churches established in the faith, and increased in number daily.'

The apostles, say they, out of Christian prudence, might do many things to prevent offence, and to accommodate matters to the people's good-liking: but certainly it looks below the dignity of a synod, to meet, and debate, and determine a question, with the greatest solemnity, merely to serve a present exigence; to leave upon record a decree which they knew would be but of temporary obligation; and yet, could not but foresee, would occasion endless scruples, and disputes in all future ages of the church. If it was to be of so short a continuance, why was not the repeal notified, and why were not so many poor, ignorant people saved, as died martyrs in the attestation of it? But, above all, how can we suppose it consistent with the honour and justice of the apostles, to impose things as necessary, which were but of transient and momentary duration?

Observe the words of the decree, (cry they,) ' It seemed good unto the Holy Ghost, and **to us, to lay** upon you no greater

° Chap. xvi. 4, 5.

A. M.
1657, &c.
Ant. Christ.
1347, &c.
from Gen.
viii. 20. to
the end of
ch. ix.

A. M. 2657, &c.
Ant. Chrif. 2347, &c.
from Gen. viii. 20. to the end of ch. ix.

greater burthen, than those necessary things, *viz.* that ye abstain from meats offered to idols, and from blood, and from things strangled, and from fornication.' If these abstinences were only intended to be enjoined for a season, could they properly be enjoined under the denomination of *necessary things?* Is that the appellation for duties of a transient and temporary observation? Did neither the apostles, nor the Holy Ghost, know the distinction between necessary and expedient? Or, suppose it not convenient to make the distinction at that time, how come things of a temporary, and those of an eternal obligation, to be placed upon the same foot of necessity in the same decree? Or, were fornication and idolatrous pollutions to be abstained from, only for a season, in compliment to the infirmity of the Jews, or in order to make up a breach between some newly initiated converts? These are absurdities, say they, which cannot be avoided, when men will assert the temporary obligation of this decree.

Some general declarations in Scripture, especially in St Paul's epistles, seem indeed like a repeal of it; but then if we consider the scope and occasion of these declarations, we shall soon perceive, that they were intended to be taken in a limited sense, otherwise they are not consistent with the decree itself. Our blessed Saviour, for instance, tells the people, that, not ' that which goeth into the mouth defileth the man, but that which cometh out of it:' but now, if this declaration of his destroys the validity of the apostolic decree it will follow, 1*st*, That this decree was repealed just twenty years before it was made; which is a supposition somewhat extraordinary: and, 2*dly*, That the whole body of the apostles did, after full debate, make a most solemn decree, and that under the influence of the Spirit of God, in direct contradiction to the express declaration of their Lord and Master, which is a little too contiguous to blasphemy; and therefore let us consider the occasion of our Saviour's words.

The Pharisees, it seems, were offended at his disciples, for sitting down to meat before they had washed their hands, as being a violation of one of their traditional precepts. Whereupon our Saviour tells the company, 'Not that which goeth into the mouth defileth the man;' never meaning to give them a permission to eat any thing prohibited by the law, but only to instruct them in this,-----That there was not all that religion, or profanation of religion, as the

Pharisees

Pharisees pretended, in observing or not observing the tradition of the elders, by eating with washed or unwashed hands; that the thing itself was of an indifferent nature; nor could a little soil taken in at the mouth, by eating with dirty hands, defile the man, because nothing of that kind could properly be called a pollution.

A. M. 1657, &c. Ant. Chrif. 2347, &c. from Gen. viii. 20. to the end of ch. ix.

St Paul himself was one of the council of Jerusalem when the prohibition of blood was ratified by the Spirit of God, and imposed on the Gentiles who were converted to the Christian faith; and therefore we can hardly think, that in his epistles, which were written not many years after, he should go about to abolish the observation of those precepts which, after mature deliberation, were enacted by a general assembly of the church. And therefore, when he tells us, that *the kingdom of God*, i. e. the Christian religion, *consisteth not of meat and drink*, and that *meat commendeth us not unto God*, he must be understood, in a comparative sense, *viz*. That it neither consists in, nor commendeth us so much, as holiness and purity of life. When he declares, *That every creature of God is good*, that *nothing is unclean of itself*, and that *to the pure all things are pure*, &c. He must necessarily be understood with this restraining clause,---In case there be no particular statute to the contrary; for where there is one, all the sanctity in the world will not give a man a toleration to break it. And when he complains of some men's commanding us to abstain from certain meats, as an infringement upon our Christian liberty, and a branch of the doctrine of devils, the meats which they forbade must be supposed to be lawful in their kind, and under no divine prohibition, otherwise we bring the apostles who inhibited the use of blood under the like imputation.

It cannot be denied indeed, that P St Paul allows Christians to eat *things offered to idols*, which may seem to invalidate this apostolic decree. But the answer to this is, ———q That the plain intention of the council at Jerusalem, in commanding to abstain from meats offered to idols, was to keep Christians from idolatry, or, as St James expresses it, *from pollutions of idols;* and the true way to effect this, they knew, was by prohibiting all communion with idols, and idolaters in their feasts, which were instituted in honour of their idols, and were always kept in their temples: but how is this command defeated by St Paul's permitting the Corinthians to eat any part of a

creature

P 1 Cor. x. 27. q Revelation examined, vol. 2. p. 66.

A. M. 1657, &c.
Ant. Chrif. 2347, &c.
from Gen. viii. 20. to the end of ch. ix.

creature fold in the fhambles, or fet before them in private houfes, (though that creature might chance to have been flain in honour to an idol,) fince the Chriftian who eat it in this manner did not eat it in honour to the idol, but merely as common food?

To illuftrate this by a parallel inftance. Suppofe that the apoftolic decree had commanded Chriftians to abftain from things ftolen, would not any one conceive, that the defign of this command was to prohibit theft, and all communion with thieves in their villainy? Yes, furely:-----Suppofe then, that any one of the council fhould after this tell the people whom he preached to, that they might buy any meat publicly fold in the fhambles, or fet before them in private houfes, *afking no queftions for confcience fake*, though poffibly the butcher or the hoft might have ftolen the meat; would any one think that this permiffion was intended to invalidate the decree of abftaining from things ftolen? And if fuch a conftruction would be abfurd in the one cafe, why fhould it not be deemed fo in another? especially when St Paul himfelf fo expresfly, fo folemnly deters Chriftians from all participation in idolatrous feafts; ‘ˢ The things which the Gentiles facrifice' (fays he) ‘ they facrifice to devils, not to God; and I would not that ye fhould have fellowfhip with devils. Ye cannot drink the cup of the Lord, and of devils; ye cannot be partakers of the Lord's table, and of devils.'

In a word, (fay they,) whatever the fenfe of certain paffages in St Paul's writings may feem to be, they cannot be fuppofed to contradict the decree at Jerufalem: a decree to which himfelf confented, nay, which he himfelf principally occafioned, and which he himfelf actually carried about, and depofited with the feveral churches. For to imagine, that with his own hands he depofited the decree in one church, under the fanction of a canon ratified by the Spirit of God, and then immediately went to another, and preached againft that very canon, and decried it as inconfiftent with Chriftian liberty, is to charge the Apoftle with fuch an inconfiftency of behaviour, folly, and prevarication, as but badly comports with the character of an *ambaffador of Jefus Chrift*. And therefore, unlefs we are minded to impair the authority, and fap the foundation of revealed religion, we muft allow the decree to be ftill in force; and the command which prohibits the eating of blood, ftill chargeable upon every man's confcience. A command,

ˢ 1 Cor. x. 20, 21.

command given by God himself to Noah, repeated to Moses, and ratified by the apostles of Jesus Christ: given immediately after the flood, when the world, as it were, began anew, and the only one given on that occasion; repeated with awful solemnity to the people whom God had separated from the rest of the world to be his own; repeated with dreadful denunciations of divine vengeance upon those who should dare to transgress it; and ratified by the most solemn and sacred council that ever was assembled upon earth, acting under the immediate influence of the Spirit of God; transmitted from that sacred assembly to the several churches of the neighbouring nations by the hand of no meaner messengers than two bishops and two apostles; asserted by the best writers, and most philosophic spirits of their age, the Christian apologists, and sealed with the blood of the best men, the Christian martyrs; confirmed by the unanimous consent of the fathers, and reverenced by the practice of the whole Christian church for above 300 years, and of the eastern church even to this very day.

A. M.
1657, &c.
Ant. Chrif.
2347 &c.
from Gen.
viii. 20, to
the end of
ch. ix.

These are some of the chief arguments on both sides of the question: and to form a judgement hereupon, we may observe,—— That though this prohibition of eating blood, can hardly be deemed a commandment of moral obligation, yet is it a positive precept, which cannot but be thought of more weight and importance, for being so oft and so solemnly enjoined; that though the reasons alledged for its injunction are not always so convincing, yet the prevention of cruelty and murder, which is immediately mentioned after it, will, in all ages, be ever esteemed a good one; and though the liberty granted in the gospel seems to be great, yet can it hardly be understood without some restriction.

The decision of the question.

It seemed once good to the Holy Ghost, among other necessary things, to prescribe an abstinence from blood; and when it seemed otherwise to him, we are no where, that I know of, instructed. Could it be made appear indeed, that this prescription was temporary and occasional, designed to bind one set of men only, or calculated for the infant-state of the church, the question would be then at an end: but since there are no proper marks in the apostles' decree, to shew the temporary duration of it; and the notion of proselytes of the gate, to whom alone it is said to be directed, (how commodious soever it may be to solve all difficulties,) upon examination is found to be groundless or uncertain, the obligation, I fear, lies upon every good Christian

still

A. M.
1657, &c.
Ant. Chrif.
2347, &c.
from Gen.
viii. 10. to
the end of
ch. ix.

ftill. But as this is not every one's fentiment, ' ⁵ As one believeth that he may eat all things, and another thinketh it *the fafe fide of his duty* to abftain; fo let not him that eateth not, judge him that eateth; but judge this rather, that no man put a ftumbling-block, or an occafion to fall, in his brother's way.'

⁵ Rom. xiv. 2, 3. 13.

CHAP. II.

Of the confufion of languages.

THE HISTORY.

A. M.
1757, &c.
Ant. Chrif.
2347, &c.
from Gen.
xi. to ver.
10.

Reafons for building the tower of Babel.

FOR fome years after the flood, it is highly probable that Noah and his family lived in the neighbourhood of the mountains of Armenia, where the ark refted: that, as they began to multiply and fpread, they thence removed into the countries of Syria; then croffing the Tigris into Mefopotamia, and fo fhaping their courfe eaftward, came at length to the pleafant plain of Babylon, on the banks of the river Euphrates. The fertility of the foil, the delightfulnefs of the place, and the commodioufnefs of its fituation, made them refolve to fettle there, and to build a city, which fhould be the metropolis of the whole earth, and in it a vaft high tower, which fhould be the wonder of the world: for the prefent ufe, a kind of *pharos* or landmark, and to future ages a monument of their great power and might.

By this project they promifed themfelves mighty matters; but that which chiefly ran in their heads, was their keeping together in one body, that, by their united ftrength and counfels, as the world increafed, they might bring others under their fubjection, and make themfelves univerfal lords. But one great difcouragement to this their project was, ——That in the place which they had chofen for the fcene of all their greatnefs, there was no ftone to build with. Perceiving, however, that there was clay enough in the country, whereof to make bricks *, and plenty of a pitchy fubftance,

* The word which our tranflators make *flime*, is in Hebrew *hemar*, in Greek *afphaltos*, in Latin *bitumen*; and that this

plain

Chap. II.   *from the Flood to the Call of Abraham.*   285

substance, called *bitumen* which would serve instead of mortar; with one consent they went to work, and in a short time every hand was employed in making bricks, building the city, and laying the foundation of a prodigious pile, which they purposed to have carried up to an immense height, and had already made a considerable progress in the work, when God, dissatisfied with their proceedings, thought proper to interpose, and at the expence of a miracle, quashed all their project at once; insomuch, that this first attempt of their vanity and ambition became the monument of their folly and weakness.

A. M. 1757, &c. Ant. Chrif. 2247, &c. from Gen. xi. to ver. 10.

The blessing which God had given Noah and his sons, to *increase and multiply, and replenish the earth*, had now, for above an hundred years, exerted itself to good purpose; but though the number of their descendents was very large, yet the language which they all spake was but one, the same which had descended to them † from their great progenitor

And for the confusion of languages.

plain did very much abound with it, which was of two kinds, liquid and solid; that the liquid bitumen here swam upon the waters; that there was a cave and fountain, which was continually casting it out; and that this famous tower, at this time, and no less famous walls of Babylon, were afterward built with this kind of cement, is confirmed by the testimony of several profane authors. For thus Strabo tells us, 'In Babylonia bitumen mul-
'tum nascitur, cujus duplex est genus, authore Eratosthene,
'liquidum et aridum. Liquidum vocant *naphtam* in Susiano agro
'nascens aridum vero, quod etiam congelescere potest, in Baby-
'lonia, fonte propinquo Naphtæ;' lib. 16, Thus Justin, speaking of Semiramis, 'Hæc Babyloniam condidit, (says he) murum-
'que urbis cocto latere circumdedit, arenæ vice bitumine inter-
'strato, quæ materia in illis locis passim è terri exæstuat;' lib 1.
And thus Vitruvius, who is elder than either,' Babylone lacus
'est amplissima magnitudine, habens supranatans liquidum bit-
'umen, quo bitumine, et latere testaceo, structus murum Semi-
'ramis Babyloni circumdedit;' lib. 8. To these we may add some modern testimonies, which tell us, that these springs of bitumen are called *oyum Hit, the fountains of Hit* and that they are much celebrated by the Persians and Arabs. All modern travellers, except Rauwolf who went to Persia and the Indies by the way Euphrates, before the discovery of the Cape of Good Hope, mention these fountains as a very strange and wonderful thing. *Vid.* Biblioth. Biblica, vol. 1, p. 281; Heidegger's Hist patriar. exercit. 21.; and Univers. hist. lib. 1, c. 2.

† That the children of Noah did speak the same language with Adam, is very manifest; because Methuselah, the grandfa-

Vol. I. N° 5.   3 E   ther

A. M. 1757, &c. Ant. Chrif. 2247, &c. from Gen. xi. to ver. 10.

nitor Adam and very probably was pronounced in the fame common manner. To fruftrate their undertaking therefore, God determined with himfelf † to *confound their language*; by which means it came to pafs, that though their tongues ftill retained the faculty of fpeech, yet having loft the pronuciation of their native language, on a fudden they were fo changed, and modified to the expreffion of another, (which was of a found quite different,) that the next ftander-by could not comprehend what his neighbour meant, and this in a fhort time ran them into the utmoft diforder and confufion. For thefe different dialects produced different ideas in the mind of the builders, which, for want of underftanding one another, they employed to improper objects, and fo were obliged to defift from their enterprize. And not only that, but being by this means deprived of the pleafure and **comfort of mutual fociety,** (except with fuch as fpake the fame language,) all thofe who were of one dialect joined themfelves together, and leaving the devoted place, as they then thought it,) departed

ther of Noah, lived a confiderable time with him, and queftionlefs fpake the fame language. And that this language was no other than the Hebrew, is very probable from this argument, —That Shem the fon of Noah, was for fome time contemporary with Abraham, who defcended from him, and whofe family continued the fame language that they both fpoke, until the time of Mofes, who recorded the hiftory of his own nation in his native language; fo that what we have now in the Pentateuch, according to the opinion of all Hebrew and moft Chriftian writers, is the very fame with what God taught Adam, and Adam his pofterity; *Patrick's Commentary.*

† Some commentators, from the word *confound*, are ready to infer, that God did not make fome of thefe builders fpeak new, different languages, only that they had fuch a confufed remembrance of the original language they fpoke before, as made them fpeak it in a qnite different manner: fo that by the various inflections, terminations, and pronounciations of divers dialects, they could no more underftand one another, than thofe who underftand Latin can comprehend thofe who fpeak French, Italian, or Spanifh, though thefe languages do certainly arife from it. But this we conceive to be a great miftake, not only becaufe it makes all languages extant to be no more than fo many different dialects of the fame original, and confequently reducible to it; but becaufe upon examination, it will appear, that there are certain languages in the world fo entirely different from each other, that they agree in no one effential property whatever; and muft therefore, at this time, have been of immediate infufion.

ed in tribes, † as their choice or their chance led them to seek out fresh habitations. Thus God not only defeated their design, but likewise accomplished his own, of having the world more generally and more speedily peopled than it otherwise would have been; and to perpetuate the memory of such a miraculous event, the place which was first called *Babel*, and, with small variation, afterwards *Babylon*, from this confusion of languages, received its denomination.

A. M. 1757, &c. Ant. Christ. 2247, &c. from Gen. xi.-to ver. 10.

This confusion of tongues (if not dispersion of the people) is supposed by most chronologers to have fallen 101 years after the flood; for Peleg, the son of Eber, (who was great grandson to Shem,) was certainly born in that year, and is said to have had the name *Peleg* given him, because that in his time the earth was divided.

THE OBJECTION.

" BUT upon the supposition that the ark rested on the
" mountains of Armenia, and the family of Noah,
" for some time, continued in that coast; how can they,
" with any tolerable propriety, be said to have *journeyed*
" *from the east into the land of Shinar*, when, if by *Shinar*
" we are to understand the land of *Chaldea* or *Babylon*, e-
" very map will inform us, that the mountains of Arme-
" nia lie in a manner quite north of Babylon, and conse-
" quently they must have travelled from the north, and
" not from the east, to have arrived at that place?

" But Moses perhaps might not be so good a geographer
" as he is at the multiplication of mankind. According to
" the Hebrew computation, (which is reckoned true,) the
" new world had now subsisted much about an hundred
" years; and can we suppose, that the descendents of no
" more than three couple (for Noah, we may now suppose,
" was become effete, and unable to beget children) were,
" in so short a time, a number sufficient to set about the

3 E 2 building

† The dispersion of Noah's sons was so ordered, that each family and each nation dwelt by itself; which could not well be done (as Mr Mede observes) but by directing an orderly division, either by casting of lots, or chusing according to their birth-right, after that portions of the earth were set out, according to the number of their nations and families; otherwise some would not have been content to go so far north as Magog did, whilst others were suffered to enjoy more pleasant countries.

A. M. 1757, &c.
Ant. Chrif. 2247, &c.
from Gen. xi. to ver. 10.

"building of a city, which was to be the metropolis of the whole world, and of a 'tower, whose top was to reach up to heaven?'

"Designs of this nature are generally attempted by vast extensive empires that are over-stocked with people, and have multitudes of idle hands to employ: but to suppose a small tribe of men (and who of necessity must some of them be busied in other occupations,) and much more, to suppose a colony or detachment only of them (as most commentators will have it) to have had the hardiness to enterprize so prodigous a fabric as the tower of Babel is represented, is something so romantic, that it puts one in mind of that fabulous stuff of the giants piling one mountain upon another, to scale heaven, and wage war with the Gods.

"But supposing the story to be true, yet where would the harm be in building a town to dwell in, and a tower for its ornament or defence? It is a laudable ambition, one would think, for a people to desire to perpetuate their name; and for a city to be at unity with itself, how joyful a thing is it! What then can we conceive should be the reason that God should be so highly offended at these builders, as himself to interpose in disappointing their design? but to interpose in the manner he did, by subducting the old, and infusing new languages, so as to make them unintelligible to one another, this is a thing so unaccountable that it would tempt one to think, that there was a mistake somewhere in our translation.

"The Hebrew word *shaphah*, which we render *language*, (or lip, as it is in the marginal note,) has, doubtless, very frequently that signification; nor is it to be denied, but that one universal language was spoken by Noah's family. But then it appears from several passages in Scripture, (particularly from Isa. xix. 18.,) that the word does not so properly denote *languages*, as it does an agreement in sentiments and inclinations, which seem every whit as necessary for the building of a city as the greatest similitude of dialect can be. Now, taking the word in this sense, it may be, that what we call *confounding their language*, may mean confounding their minds and raising a spirit of discord among them, which might make them abandon their enterprize, and disperse into different countries; and then, though they might speak all the same language at parting, a considerable

"diversity

"diversity would naturally, and without the intervention
"of a miracle, in a short time ensue.

"We see, in a thousand years, what alterations and
"deviations have been made from the Latin, in France,
"Italy, Spain, and the Subalpine countries. In France,
"the Gascon and Provencial dialects are hardly understood
"at Paris: in Spain, besides the Castilian, there are two
"large idioms, the Portueguese and the Catalan, neither of
"which are readily intelligible by a person that has always
"lived at Madrid: and a man may know all the rest of
"the dialects which are derived from the Latin, and yet
"be wholly to seek in the Grisons language.——All these
"tongues, however, we certainly know, have sprung from
"the Latin within these twelve hundred years, and the
"nations who speak them have constantly maintained a
"mutual commerce and intercourse together. If then such
"alterations are actually visible in dialects (which have
"been formed from languages still extant) in so few
"years, what may we reasonably suppose to have been
"the fate of languages that existed above three thousand
"years ago? especially, when men were so totally di-
"vided from one another, as we may imagine the first in-
"habitants of this globe were after this great dispersion.
"In short, [a] the cause of the variety of languages in
"the world is grounded in reason and nature; in the
"difference of climates, in the unsettled temper of man-
"kind, the necessary mutability of human things, the rise
"and fall of states and empires, and change of modes
"and customs, which necessarily introduce a proportion-
"able change in language, and therefore, supposing the
"Hebrew to be the primitive language, in a proper period
"of time after such a dispersion, all other languages will
"be found as naturally springing from it as so many
"branches from the same stock. It is in vain then to have
"recourse to miracles, when the business may as well be
"done without it; when it is but supposing, that all lan-
"guages now extant sprung originally from one common
"root, and that they are no more than different forms
"and dialects of it, which the force of time, assisted
"with some incidental causes, without the intervention of
"any superior power, naturally produces; otherwise we
"can hardly imagine how dialects that are so near a-kin
"came to be placed so nearly to one another."

Those

---

[a] Vid. *Sentiment de quelques theologiens sur l' historie critique*, p. 435; and a letter to Dr Waterland, p. 28, 29.

A. M. 1757, &c. Ant. Chrif. 2247, &c. from Gen. xi. to ver. 10.	Those who have undertaken to settle the geography of the Holy Scriptures, tell us, that the land of Shinar was all that valley which the river Tygris runs along, from the mountains of Armenia northwards to the Persian gulf; or at least to the southern division of the common channel of the Tygris and Euphrates. ^b So that the country of
Answered, by shewing the proper situation of Ararat, from whence the people so journeyed;	Eden was part of the land of Shinar: and as Eden was probably situate on both sides of the aforementioned channel, so it is not unlikely that the valley of Shinar did extend itself on both sides (but on the western side, without all doubt) of the river Tygris. Now the mountains of Armenia, according to the account of most geographers, lie north, and not east, from Shinar and Assyria; but then it may be supposed ^c either that Moses, in this place, followed the geographical style of the Assyrians, who called all that lay beyond the Tigris the *east country*, though a great part of it, toward Armenia, was really northward; or (as some ^d others will have it) that as mankind multiplied, they spread themselves in the country eastward of Ararat; and so making small removes, (from the time of their descent from the mount to the time of their journeying into the land of Shinar,) they might probably enough be said to have begun their progress from the east. But without the help of these solutions, and taking Moses in a literal sense, he is far from being mistaken. ^e Most geographers indeed have drawn the mountain of Ararat a good way out of its place, and historians and commentators, taking the thing for fact, have been much peplexed to reconcile this situation with its description in Scripture: whereas, by the accounts of all travellers for some years past, the mountain which now goes under the name of *Ararat* lies about two degrees more east than the city of Shinar or Senjar, from whence the plain, in all probability, takes its name; and therefore, if the sons of Noah entered it on the northside, they must of necessity have *journeyed from the east*, or, which is the same thing, have travelled westward from the place where they set out, in order to arrive at the plain of Babylon.
and that all mankind were engaged in the building of Babel.	Historians indeed, as well as commentators, have generally given in to the common opinion, that Shem and his family

^b Well's Geography, vol. 1. p. 210.   ^c Bochart's Phaleg. l. 1. c. 7   ^d Kercher's Turris Babel, 12.
^e Universal history, l. 1. c. 2.

family were not concerned in this expedition; but for what reason we cannot conceive, since there is no fact, in all the Mosaic account, more firmly established than this,——that the whole race of mankind, then in being, were actually engaged in it.

As soon as Moses has brought the three sons of Noah out of the ark, he takes care to inform us, that ' ᶠ of them was the whole earth overspread.' After he has given us the names of their descendents, at the time of their dispersion, he subjoins, and ' ᵍ by these were the nations divided in the earth after the flood :' and then, proceeding to give us an account of this memorable transaction, he tells us, that ' ʰ the whole earth was of one language, and of one speech ;' and that as they, namely the whole earth, ' ⁱ journeyed from the east, they found a plain in the land of Shinar, and dwelt there,' &c. ; ᵏ so that, from the beginning to the end of this transaction, the connection between the antecedent and relative is so well preserved, that there is no room to suppose, that any less than all mankind, were gathered together on the plain of Shinar, and assisted in the building of Babel : nor seems it improbable, that Moses has made these unusual repetitions, to inculcate the certainty of that fact, and to take away all ground for supposing, that any other branch of Noah's posterity was in any other part of the earth at that time.

The time indeed, when this transaction happened, is very differently computed by chronologers, according as they follow the LXX interpreters, who make it 531; the Samaritan copy, who makes it 396 ; or the Hebrew, which allows it to be no more than 101 years from the flood to the confusion of tongues, and less, we may suppose, to the first beginning to build the tower. If we take either of the former computations, the thing answers itself : upon a moderate multiplication, there will be workmen more than enough, even without the posterity of Shem : but if we submit to the Hebrew account of time, we shall find ourselves straitened, if we part with one third of our complement, in so laborious a work. There is no necessity however to suppose, ˡ with some, that every one of these progenitors, as soon as married, (which was very early,) had every year twins by his wife; which, according to arithmetic progression, would amount to no less than

A. M. 1757, &c. Ant. Chrif. 2247 &c. from Gen. xi. to ver. 10.

What the number of them might then probably be.

ᶠ Gen. ix. 19.   ᵍ Ch. x. 32.   ʰ Ch. xi. 1.
ⁱ Ibid. ver. 2.   ᵏ Universf. hist. l. 1. c. 2.   ˡ Temporarius in demonst. chronol. l. 2.

The History of the BIBLE, Book II.

A. M. 1757, &c.
Ant. Chrst. 2247, &c.
from Gen. xi. to ver. 10.

than 1554420 males and females, in the shortest period given. Half the number would be sufficient to be employed on this occasion; and ᵐ half the number will be no unreasonable supposition, considering the strength of constitution men had then, and the additional blessing which God bestowed upon them, and whereby he interested his peculiar providence, "Ut ad incrementum sobolis humanæ,
" ad orbis valetitatem instaurandam, præcipua quædam in
" illis fœcunditas inesset, quæ justam alioquin ætatem an-
" teverteret; ut vel a pueris ipsis, quod nonnulli suspican-
" tur, probabile esset, generandi vim illis et usum potuisse
" suppetere;" ⁿ as Petavius elegantly expresses it."

But after all, there seems to be no occasion for supposing an extraordinary increase of people, or for confining the first undertaking of this great building to the compass of one hundred years after the flood. In the tenth chapter of Genesis, it is said indeed, that *unto Eber were born two sons, and that the name of the one was Peleg*, which being derived from an Hebrew word, that signifies *to divide*, has this reason annexed to it, *for in his days was the earth divided*. Now, by the subsequent account of Peleg's ancestors we find, that he was born in the 101st year after the flood; from whence it is concluded, that the earth began to be divided at his birth. But this is a conclusion that by no means results from the text, which only says that *in his days was the earth divided*; words which can, with no manner of propriety, imply, that this division began at his birth.

His name indeed was called *Peleg*; but it does not therefore follow, that this name was given him at his birth. It might have been given at any time after, from his being a principal agent among his own family, in the division made in his days; as several names have, throughout all ages, been given upon the like accidents, not only to private persons, but to whole families. Or suppose the name to be given at his birth, yet no reason can be assigned, why it might not be given prphetically, as well as that of Noah, from an event then foreseen, though it might not come to pass for some considerable time after the name was given.

ᵐ Usher's Chron. sacra. p. 28.   ⁿ Doct. temp. l. 9.
x 24.

○ Since Peleg then, according to the sacred account, lived two hundred and thirty-nine years, and his younger brother Joktan, and his sons, were a considerable colony in the distribution of the world, it is much more rational to suppose, that this distribution did not begin till a good part of Peleg's life was expended. Suppose it, however, to be no more than an hundred years after his birth; yet we may still retain the Hebrew computation, and have time and hands enough for the carrying on the great work of Babel, before this distribution, since mankind might very well be multiplied to some millions, in the compass of two hundred years.

<small>A M. 1757, &c. Ant. Chrif. 2247, &c. from Gen. xi. to ver. 'O.</small>

Putting all these considerations together then, we can hardly imagine, that there wanted a sufficient number of men to go upon an enterprise, which, though not strictly chargeable with sin, because there was no previous command forbidding it, yet, in the sense of God himself, bold and presumptuous enough: ' ᴾ Behold the people is one, and they have all one language, and now this they begin to do;' this is their first attempt, and after this, ' nothing ‡ will be restrained from them; ' they will think themselves competent for any thing that they shall have a fancy to do. For though God could have no reason to apprehend † any molestation

<small>Why God disliked and defeated their undertaking.</small>

○ Revelation Examined, vol. 2. differt. 3.   ᴾ Gen. xi. 6

‡ The common versions say of the builders of the tower of Babel, *And now nothing* will, or shall, *be restrained from them, which they have imagined to do*. But this is false in fact; because God soon put a stop to their design by confounding them, and *scattering them abroad from thence, over the face of the earth.* We may observe therefore, that the same particle, which is indeed sometimes taken negatively, is evidently here to be taken interrogatively, and is equal to the most express affirmation: and therefore the text should thus be translated, *Shall they not be restrained in all they imagine to do?* Yes, they shall; which accordingly was immediately executed; *Essay for a new translation.*

† What their attempts were, the historian has represented in their own words: *And they said, Go to, let us build us a city, and a tower, whose top may reach unto heaven* Gen. xi. 4. But far be it from any one to imagine, that these builders could be so stupidly ignorant, as ever to think by this, means to climb up to heaven, or that they would not have chosen a mountain, rather than a plain, or a valley, for this, if they could once

lestation from their attempts, (as the poets make heaven all in an uproar upon the invasion of the giants,) yet, since they were contrary to his gracious design of having the earth replenished, it was an act highly consistent with his infinite wisdom and goodness to see them disappointed.

The divine purpose was, that men should not live within the limits of one country only, and so be exposed to perpetual contentions, while every one would pretend to make himself master of the nearest and most fertile lands; but that, possessing themselves of the whole, and cultivating almost every place, they might enjoy a proportionable increase of the fruits of the earth. ᵠ Thorns and briars were springing up every where; woods and thickets spreading themselves around; wild beasts increasing; and all this while the sons of Noah gathering together in a cluster, and designing so to continue; so that it was highly seasonable for God to confound their mis-timed prospects, and disperse them.

Their purpose was to make themselves a name by enslaving others: but God foresaw, ʳ that absolute power and

have entertained so gross an imagination. It is a common hyperbole this in the Sacred Writings, to signify any great and lofty building, as may be seen in Deut. i. 18. Dan. iv. 8. and in several other places; nor is the like manner of expression unusual among profane authors likewise: for Homer, speaking of the island of Calypso, tells us, than in it was a place:

————ὅθι δένδρεα μακρὰ πεφύκει
Κλήθρητ' αἴγειρόστ', ἐλάητ ἡν οὐρανομήκης.
Odyss. i. ver. 238.

By a literal interpretation of the Hebrew idiotism, however, it is a common thing for the greatest absurdities to be received by the unwary for realities; and not at all a wonder, that the misunderstanding the text should give rise to what we are told of the giants in the fable attempting to scale heaven, and of the expedition of Cosigna and his companions, who had contrived ladders for that end; hoping, that so they might make their nearer addresses to the queen of heaven. And thus even the silliest of the Pagan tales may be traced up to their original; for there is generally some foundation for them in truth, either misunderstood or misapplied. *Vid.* Le Clerc's Commentary; Voss. Hist. Græc. lib. 1. cap. 3.; and Bibliotheca Biblica ad locum.

ᵠ Waterland's Scripture vindicated, part 1. ʳ Le Clerc's Dissertation.

Chap. II.   *from the Flood to the Call of Abraham.*   295

and univerſal empire were not to be truſted in any mortal hand; that the firſt kings would be far from being the beſt men; but as they required a ſuperiority by fraud and violence, ſo they would not be backward to maintain it by oppreſſion and cruelty: and therefore, to remedy ſuch public grievances, he determined with himſelf, that there ſhould be a diverſity of governments in the world; that if the inhabitants of any place chanced to live under a tyrannical power, thoſe that were no longer able to endure the yoke, might fly into other countries and dominions, (which they could not do, if the whole was one entire monarchy,) and there find ſhelter from oppreſſion. And as he knew how conducive the bad example of princes would be towards a general corruption of manners, he therefore took care to provide againſt this malady, by appointing ſeveral diſtinct kingdoms and forms of government at one and the ſame time; that if the infection of vice got aſcendency, and prevailed in one place, virtue and godlineſs, and whatever is honourable and praiſe-worthy, might find a ſafe retreat, and flouriſh in another. Thus all the miſchiefs which might poſſibly ariſe from an univerſal monarchy, and all the advantages that do daily accrue from ſeparate and diſtinct governments, were in the divine foreſight and conſideration, when he put a ſurpriſing ſtop to the building of theſe men, and their ambitious ſchemes of empire together.

A. M. 1757, &c. Ant. Chriſ. 2247, &c. from Gen. xi. to ver. 10.

For in what manner ſoever it was that he effected this, † whether it was by diſturbing the memories, or perverting

That this defeat was immediately his work.

† Since Moſes has no where acquainted us, (ſays the learned Heidegger, in his Hiſt. patriar. lib. 1. exercit. 211.) in what manner the confuſion of languages was effected, every one is left to follow what opinion he likes beſt, ſo long as that opinion contains nothing incongruous to the received rule of faith: nay, it may not be inconvenient to produce ſeveral opinions upon this ſubject, to the intent that every one may embrace that which ſeems to him moſt conformable to truth. And therefore he inſtances in the opinions of ſeveral learned men, but in thoſe more particularly of Julius Scaliger, who aſcribes this event to a confuſion of notions which God miraculouſly ſent among the builders; and that of Iſaac Caſaubon, who will needs have all the different languages now extant to be no more than derivatives from the Hebrew. Scaliger's words, as Heidegger quotes them, are theſe: ' Sic enim aiunt (Hebræi ſcilicet) quo impii
' propoſiti opus illud interciperetur atque prohiberetur, factum
                                              ' a Deo

perverting their imaginations; by diversifying their hearing, or new-organizing their tongues; by an immediate infusion of new languages, or a division of the old into so many different dialects; and again, whether these tongues, or dialects of tongues, † were few or more; whether there

'a Deo optimo maximo, ut lapidem petenti alius calcem, alius
'sabulum, alius maltham, alius bitumen, alius aquam, ferret.
'Fortasse etiam non defuisse arbitror, qui sibi dictam putarent
'contumeliam atque propterea manum confererent, ubi maxi-
'ma intercedit occasio subtilitatis; nam si lapidem petenti alius
'aliud, multi multa diversa omnia afferebant, videretur unius
'soni modus, in varias species deductus diversis mentibus sese
'insinuasse. Una igitur prisca adhuc extaret lingua, variæ ve-
'ro significatus.' The words of Casaubon are as follow: 'Si
'in Babele linguæ in totum diversæ factæ sunt, necessario Chal-
'dæi Assyrii ἀλλοκότως illas linguas retinuissent: atqui contra-
'rium videmus accidisse. Est enim verissimum, linguas cæteras
'eo manifestiora et magis expressa originis Hebraica vestigia
'servasse, et nunc servare, quo propius ab antiqua et prima ho-
'minum sede abfuerunt. Nam proximus quisque populus genti
'Hebraicæ proxime ad illius linguam accessit. Longinquitas
'vero alienationem subinde majorem intulit. Clarum hoc, ex
'comparatione linguarum, Syriacæ, Chaldaicæ, Arabicæ Pu-
'nicæ &c. cum Hebraica, clarissimum item, si Græcam linguam
'diligenter species. Græci prima in Asia habitarunt: inde
'Iones, vel, ut Æschylus vocat Hebraico Javones, in Europam
'trajecerunt; in antiquissimis quibusque Græcorum scriptori-
'bus multa propterea vocabula Hebraica, quæ postea vel de-
'sierunt esse in usu, vel admodum sunt mutata: observamus
'etiam Asiaticos Græcos magis ἰουδαίζειν, quam Europæos."
† It is not to be thought, that there were as many several dialects as there were men at Babel, so that none of them understood one another. This would not only have dispersed mankind but utterly destroyed them; because it is impossible to live without society, or to have any society without understanding one another. It is likely therefore that every family had its peculiar dialect, or rather, that some common dialect, or form of speaking, was given to those families whom God designed to make one colony in the following dispersion. Into how many languages the people were divided, it is impossible to determine. The Hebrews fancy seventy, because the descendents of the sons of Noah, as they are enumerated in Scripture, are just so many: the Greek fathers make them seventy-two, because
the

there were only so many originals at first, (as many perhaps as there were either tribes or heads of families,) and all the rest were no more than derivatives from them; the operations of an almighty power are equally visible, and the footsteps of divine wisdom apparent, in the very method of his disappointing these ambitious builders.

^s He could, no doubt, with the same facility have sent down fire from heaven to consume them; but then, that would have been but a momentary judgement, whereof we should have known nothing but what we read in the dead letter of a book: whereas by this means, the remembrance of God's interposition is preserved to all future ages, and in every new language that we hear, we recognize the miracle.

^t It was equally the finger of God, we allow, whether the minds or the tongues of the workmen were confounded; but then, in that case, the miracle does not so plainly and so flagrantly appear, nor would it have had so good an effect upon the builders themselves; because men may quarrel and break off society without a miracle; whereas they cannot speak with new tongues by their own natural strength and ingenuity.

Nor is the formation of a new language only more miraculous, but to the imaginations of the persons upon whom it was wrought, incredibly more surpirsing than any disagreement in opinion, or any quarrel that might thereupon

A. M. 1757, &c. Ant. Christ. 2247, &c. from Gen. xi. to ver. 10.

And [not a confusion of minds but of tongues.]

the LXX version adds two more, (Elisa among the sons of Japhet, and Canaan among the sons of Shem,) and the Latin fathers follow them. But this is all conjecture, and what is built upon a very weak foundation. For in many places, so many people concurred in the use of the same speech, that of the seventy scarce thirty remain distinct, as Bochart has observed: and among these, others have supposed, that the Hebrew, Chaldee, and Arabic, in the east; the Greek and Latin in the west; and the Finnish, Sclavonian, Hungarian, Cantabric, and the ancient Gaulish, in the north; are generally reputed originals: besides some more that might be discovered in Persia, China, the East-Indies, the midland parts of Africa, and all America, if we had but a sufficient knowledge of the history of these people. *Vid,* Patrick's Commentary; and Wotten of the confusion of languages at Babel.

^s Heidegger's Hist. patriar. vol. 1. exercit. 21. ^t Wotten of the confusion of languages at Babel.

A. M.
1757, &c.
Ant. Chrif.
2247, &c.
from Gen
xi. to ver.
10

upon enfue. And therefore I have always thought, that this account of the confufion of tongues which God wrought at Babel, would fcarce have been told fo particularly, and reprefented as God's own act and deed, had it only arifen from a quarrel among the builders, which obliged them to leave off their work, and fcatter themfelves over the face of the earth. For when God is here defcribed as coming down in perfon to view their work, fomething almoft as folemn as the creation, full as folemn as the denuciation of the flood, when Noah was commanded to build the ark, is certainly intended by that expreffion: and therefore, when Mofes acquaints us, that there was but one language at that time, the circumftance would be impertinent, if he did not intimate withal, that very foon after there were to be more.

Ifa. xix. 18. explained.

The prophet Ifaiah indeed, fpeaking of the converfion of fome Egyptians to the Jewifh faith, tells us, that ' in that day fhall five cities in the land of Egypt fpeak the language *(or* lip, *as it is in the margin)* of Canaan, and fwear to the Lord of hofts.' Speaking the language of Canaan, ᵘ is thought by fome to mean no more than being of the fame religion with the Jews, who inhabited the land of Canaan; but why may it not be interpreted literally, as it is in our tranflation? Might not thefe five cities particularly, to fhew the value and reverence that they had for the religion of the Jews, learn their language: efpecially fince they would thereby be better enabled to underftand the books of Mofes and the Prophets, which were written in that tongue? Do not the Mahometans, whatever they are, Turks, Tartars, Perfians, Moguls, or Moors, all learn Arabic, becaufe Mahomet wrote the Alcoran in that language? Why then fhould we be offended at the literal fenfe of the words, when the figurative is fo low and flat in comparifon of it? ˣ In that day Egypt fhall be like a woman; it fhall be afraid and fear, becaufe of the fhaking of the hand of the Lord of Hofts. ʸ The Lord of hofts fhall be a terror unto Egypt, and ᶻ in that day fhall there be an altar to the Lord in the midft of the land of Egypt, *i. e.* they fhall become profelytes to the law of Mofes; and that they may not miftake in underftanding the fenfe of the law which

they

ᵘ Le Clerc's Commentary.   ˣ Ifa. xix. 16.   ʸ Ver. 17.
ᶻ Ver. 19.

Chap. II.   *from the Flood to the Call of Abraham.*

they shall then embrace, they shall agree to learn the language in which it is written. This is an easy and genuine sense of the words: but, instead of that, to fly to a forced and abstruse one, merely to evade the evidence of a miracle, favours of vanity at least, if not of irreligion.

_{A. M. 1757, &c. Ant. Chrif. 2247. &c. from Gen. xi. to ver. 10.}

In short, all interpreters, both Jewish and Christian, understood this confusion of Babel, to be a confusion of languages, not of opinions. They saw the texts, if literally understood, required it; they observed a surprising variety of tongues, essentially different from one another; and they knew that this was not in the least inconsistent with the power of God. They did not question, but that he who made the tongue could make it speak what, and how he pleased; and they acquiesced (as all wise and honest interpreters should) in the literal application, perceiving that nothing unworthy of God, or trifling, or impossible in itself, resulted from it.

But to give this part of the objection a full and satisfactory answer, we shall look a little into the nature of languages in general, and thereby endeavour to shew, that there are some languages, when once established, are not so subject to variation as is pretended; and that in the ages subsequent to this extraordinary event, they could not, in any natural way, undergo all the alterations we now perceive in them, supposing them all descended from one common stock.

_{That from the time of this confusion, there were all along several languages essentially different.}

^a Now, in order to this, we must observe, that every language consists of two things, matter and form. The matter of any language are the words whereby men, who speak the language, express their ideas; and the several ways whereby its nouns are declined, and verbs conjugated, are its form.

The Latins and Greeks vary their nouns by terminations; as *Vir, viri, viro, virum,* ἄνθρωπος, ἀνθρώπου, ἀνθρώπῳ, ἄνθρωπον. We decline by the prepositions *of, to, from, the,* in both numbers; but the Hebrews have no different terminations in the same number, and only vary thus,—— *Ish,* man; *ishim,* men; *ishah,* woman; *ishoth,* women. The rest are varied by prepositions inseparably affixed to the words, as *ha-ish, the man; le-ish, to the man; be-ish, in the man;* &c. which prepositions, thus joined, make

^a Wotten of the confusion of languages at Babel.

A. M.
1757, &c.
Ant. Chrif.
2247, &c.
from Gen.
x¹. to ver.
10.

make one word with the noun to which they are affixed, and are herein different from all those languages which come from a Latin or Teutonic original.

The western and northern people consider every transitive verb, either actively or passively, and then they have done; as *amo*, in Latin, is *I love*; *amor*, *I am loved*; and so in Greek, ἀγαπῶ, ἀγαπῶμαι: but in Hebrew, every word has, or is supposed to have, seven conjugations; in Chaldee and Syriac, six; and in Arabic, thirteen; all differing in their significations.

The western languages abound with verbs that are compounded with prepositions, which accompany them in all their moods and tenses, and therein vary their signification: but in the eastern there is no such thing; for though they have (in Arabic especially) many different significations, some literal, and some figurative, yet still their verbs, as well as nouns, are uncompounded.

In the Greek, both ancient and barbarous, in the Latin, and the dialects arising from it, and in all the branches of what we call the old Teutonic, the possessive pronouns, *my*, *thy*, *his*, *yours*, *theirs*, &c. make a distinct word from the noun to which they are joined, as Πατὴρ ἡμῶν, *pater noster*, *fader vor*, *our father*, &c. But in all the oriental tongues, the pronoun is joined to the end of the noun, in such a manner as to make but one word. Thus *ab*, in Hebrew, is *father*; *abi*, *my father*; *abinu*, *our father*. In Chaldee, from the same root, *abouna* is *our father*; in Syriac, *abun*; in Arabic and Ethiopic the same.

Once more. All western languages mark the degree of comparison in their adjectives by proper terminations, *wise*, *wiser*, *wisest*; *sapiens*, *sapientior*, *sapientissimus*; σοφὸς, σοφώτερος, σοφώτατος: But none of the eastern tongues already mentioned, have any thing in them like this.

These are some of the marks and characters which distinguish the eastern from the western languages; and what is farther observable, these characters have none of them disappeared, or shifted from one to another, for near three thousand years. They appear in every book of the Old Testament, from Moses down to Malachi; in the Chaldee paraphrasts, in the Syriac versions, in the Misna, in the Gemara, and in every other Rabbinical book, down to the Jewish writers of the present age: but on the other hand, if we consider Homer's poems, which are the oldest monuments we have of the Greek language; if we take

Theocritus

Chap. II.   *from the Flood to the Call of Abraham.*   301

Theocritus for the Doric dialect; Euripides, or Thucydides, for the Attic; Herodotus, or Hippocrates, for the Ionic; and Sappho for the Æolic; and so descend to the Greek, which is spoken at this day, we shall see the general marks of western languages running through them all. These idioms shew themselves, at first sight, to be nothing more than dialects manifestly springing from the same common root, which never did, and (as far as we may judge from the practice of above two thousand years) never will conjugate verbs, decline nouns, or compare adjectives, like the Hebrew or Arabic. These languages did always compound verbs and nouns with prepositions, which essentially alter the sense. These languages had never any positive pronouns affixed to their nouns, to determine the person or persons to whom of right they belong; nor do they affix any single letter to their words, which may be equivalent to conjunctions, and connect the sense of what goes before with what follows; which any person but tolerably initiated in the eastern languages must know to be their properties.

A. M. 1757, &c. Ant Chrif. 2247, &c. from Gen. xi. to ver. 10.

And indeed, if we cast but our eye a little forward into the sacred history, it will not be long before we may perceive some instances of this difference between languages. For when Jacob and Laban made a covenant together, they erected a heap of stones, on which they eat, and Laban called it *Jegar-sahadutha*, but Jacob *Gal-ed*, which words signify (those in Chaldee, which are Laban's, and the other in Hebrew, which are Jacob's) *an heap of witnesses*; and in like manner, Pharaoh calls Joseph *Tsophnath-Paaneahh*, which words are neither Hebrew nor Chaldee. So that here we see three distinct dialects formed in Jacob's time; and yet we may observe, that the world was then thin, commerce narrow, and conquests few; so that the people were constrained to converse with those of their own tribe, and consequently could keep their dialect far more entire than it is possible for any nation to do now, when commerce, conquests, and colonies planted in regions already peopled with nations that speak distinct languages, may be supposed to bring in a deluge of new words, and make innumerable changes. But nations seldom trade much abroad, or make invasions upon their neighbours, or send forth plantations into remote countries, until they are pretty well stocked at home, which could hardly be the case of any one country for several ages after the dispersion.

That there could not, in the first ages, be all that alteration in languages that is pretended.

A. M. 1757, &c. Ant. Chrif. 2247, &c. from Gen xi. to ver. 10

It is a miftaken notion which fome have imbibed, that every little thing, be it but the change of air, or difference of climate, (which at moft can but affect the pronunciation of fome letters or fyllables,) can make a diverfity in languages. Small and infenfible alterations, which perhaps will **appear in** an age or two, will undoubtedly happen; but unlefs people converfe much with ftrangers, their language will fubfift, as to its conftituent form, the fame for many generations.

The Roman language, **for** inftance, was brought to a confiderable perfection before Plautus's time; and though now and then fome obfolete words may appear in his writings, yet any man that underftands Latin may read the books that were written in it, from Plautus down to Theodoric the Goth, which was near feven hundred years; and had not the barbarous nations broken into Italy, it might have been an intelligible language for feveral ages more. And in like manner, we may fay, that had not the Turks, when they over-ran Greece, brought darknefs and ignorance along with them, the Greek tongue might have continued even to this day, fince it is manifeft, from Homer's poems, and Euftathius's commentaries upon them, that it fubfifted for above two thoufand years, without any confiderable alteration; for the fpace of time between the poet and his commentator was no lefs.

And that there are more original languages in the world than is imagined.

And if the languages which we are acquainted with remained fo long unchanged to any great degree in times of more commerce **and** action than what could be fubfequent upon the difperfion, there is reafon to believe, that (though it be difficult to define the number of them,) there are many more original languages in the world than fome men imagine. For if we confider their great antiquity, **their** mutual agreement in the fundamentals (which we have defcribed) can be no argument that any one of them is derived from the reft; fince it is natural to fuppofe, that when **God** confounded the fpeech of the builders of Babel, he made the dialects of thofe people who were to live near one another, fo far to agree, that they might, with lefs difficulty, and in a fhorter fpace of time, mutually underftand each other, and fo more eafily maintain an intercourfe together. For though their affociation (confidering the ends that engaged them in it) was certainly culpable, yet perhaps it might not deferve fo fevere a punifhment as an entire feparation **of every** tribe among them from their
neareft

nearest kindred, with whom they had hitherto spent all their time.

To sum up the force of this argument in a few words. If we consider the time since the building of the tower of Babel, not yet 4000 years, and the great variety of languages that are at present in the world; if we consider how entirely different some are from others, so that no art of etymology can reduce them to the least likeness or conformity; and yet, in those early days, when the world was less peopled, and navigation and commerce not so much minded, there could not be that quick progression of languages; and if we examine the alterations which such languages as we are acquainted with, have made in two or three thousand years past, where colonies of different people have not been imported, we shall find the difference between language and language to be so very great, and the alteration of the same language, in a considerable tract of time, to be so very small, that we shall be at a loss to conceive, whence so many and so various languages could have proceeded, unless we take in the account of Moses, which unriddles the whole difficulty, and justly ascribes them to the same Almighty power, which taught our first parents to speak one tongue at the beginning, and, in after-ages, inspired the apostles of Jesus Christ with the gift of many.

A. M.
1757, &c.
Ant. Chr.f.
2247, &c.
from Gen.
xi. to ver.
10.

A recapitulation of the whole argument.

DISSERTATION II.

Of the tower of Babel.

THAT there really was such a building as the tower of Babel, erected some ages after the recovery of the earth from the deluge, is evident from the concurrent testimony of several Heathen writers. For when (besides the particular description which ᵇ Herodotus, the father of the Greek historians, gives us of it) we find Abydenus (as he is ᶜ quoted by Eusebius) telling us, "That the first " race of men, big with a fond conceit of the bulk and " strength of their bodies, built, in the place where Baby- " lon now stands, a tower of so prodigious an height, " that it seemed to touch the skies, but that the winds and " the gods overthrew the mighty structure upon their " heads;" when we find Eupolemus (as he is ᵈ cited

That there really was such a building as the tower of Babel.

by

ᵇ Lib. 1. c. 181.   ᶜ Præparat. evang. l. 9. c. 14.
ᵈ Alex. Polyhist. apud Euseb. Præp. evan. l. 9. c. 18.

A. M. 1757, &c.
Ant. Chrif. 2247, &c.
from Gen. xi. to ver. 10.

by Alexander Polyhistor) leaving it upon record, "That the city of Babylon was first built by giants, who escaped from the flood; that these giants built the most famous tower in all history; and that this tower was dashed to pieces by the almighty power of God, and the giants dispersed, and scattered over the face of the whole earth;" and lastly, when [e] we find Josephus mentioning it as a received doctrine among the Sibyls, "That at a certain time, when the whole world spake all one language, the people of those days gathered together, and raised a mighty tower, which they carried up to so extravagant an height, that it looked as if they had proposed to scale heaven from the top of it; but that the gods let the winds loose upon it, which, with a violent blast, beat it down to the ground, and at the same time struck the builders with an utter forgetfulness of their native tongue, and substituted new and unknown languages in the room of it:" When we find these, and several other authors, I say, that might be produced, bearing testimony to Moses in most of the material circumstances attending the building of this tower, we cannot but conclude, that the representation which he gives us of the whole transaction is agreeable to truth.

The short is, all the remains now extant of the most ancient Heathen historians (except Sanchoniatho) concur in confirming the Mosaic account of this matter; and the sum of their testimonies is,——[f] 'That a huge tower was built by gigantic men at Babylon; that there was then but one language among mankind; that the attempt was offensive to the gods; and that therefore they demolished the tower, overwhelmed the workmen, divided their language, and dispersed them over the face of the whole earth.'

That it was not blown down or destroyed.

There is one circumstance indeed, wherein we find these ancient historians differing with Moses, and that is, in affirming that the tower was demolished by the anger of God, and by the violence of the winds; but as it seems more consistent with the divine wisdom (for the admonition of posterity) to have such a monument of men's folly and ambition for some time standing; so we may observe, that (in confirmation of our sacred penman, who speaks of it as a thing existing in his time) Herodotus, the Greek historian,

[e] Antiq. l. 1. c. 5.   [f] Vid. Josephus's Antiq. l. 1. c. 5. Eusebius's Præpar. evang. l. 9. c. 14. &c.; and Huetius's Quæst. Alnetan. l. 2. p. 189.

Chap. II. *from the Flood to the Call of Abraham.* 305

historian, tells us expressly, that he himself actually saw it, as it was repaired by Belus, or some of his successors; Pliny, the Latin historian, that it was not destroyed in his days; and some modern travellers, (whom by and by we shall have occasion to quote,) that there are some visible remains of it extant even now. And therefore the fancy of its being beat down with the winds is taken up, in pure conformity * to some Persian tales, recorded of Nimrod, whom these historians suppose to be the first projector of it.

<small>A. M. 1657, &c. Ant. Chrif. 2247, &c. from Gen. xi. to ver. 10.</small>

It cannot be denied indeed, but that the generality of interpreters, meeting with the expression of ᵍ *the children of men*, whereby they understand bad men and infidels, as opposed to the children of God, which usually denote the good and the faithful, are apt to imagine, that none of the family of Shem, which retained (as they say) the true worship and religion, were engaged in the work, but some of the worse sort of people only, who had degenerated from the piety of their ancestors: but by *the children*

<small>Who were the builders of it.</small>

---

* The author of the book called *Malem* tells us this story, ——That when Nimrod saw that the fire into which he caused Abraham to be cast, for not submitting to the worshipping of idols, did him no damage, he resolved to ascend into heaven, that he might see that great God whom Abraham revealed to him. In vain did his courtiers endeavour to divert him from this design: he was resolved to accomplish it and therefore gave orders for the building of a tower that might be as high as possible. They worked upon it for three years together: and when he went up to the top, he was much surprised to see himself as far from heaven, as when he was upon the ground; but his confusion was much increased, when they came to inform him, the next morning, that his tower was fallen, and dashed in pieces. He commanded them then, that another should be built which might be higher and stronger than the former: but when this met with the same fate, and he still continued an obstinate persecutor of those who worshipped the true God, God took from him the greatest part of his subjects, by the division and confusion of their tongues, and those, who still adhered to him, he killed by a cloud of flies, which he sent amongst them; *Calmet's Dictionary on the word* Nimrod. The poets, in like manner, having corrupted the tradition of this event with fictions of their own, do constantly bring in Jupiter defeating the attempts of the Titans:

Fulmina de cœli jaculatus arce,
Vertit in authores pondera vasta suos, &c. Ovid.

ᵍ Gen. xi. 5.

children of men in that place, it is evident, that we are to understand all mankind, because in the initial words of the chapter, they are called ʰ *the whole earth;* nor can we well conceive how, in so short a time, after that a-wakening judgement of the deluge, the major part of mankind, even while Noah and his sons were still alive, should be so far corrupted in their principles, as to deserve the odious character of unbelievers.

not Nimrod

ⁱ Josephus indeed, and some other authors, are clearly of opinion, that Nimrod, a descendent from the impious Ham, was the great abettor of this design, and the ringleader of those who combined in the execution of it. But though the undertaking seems to agree very well with the notion which the Scripture gives us of that ambitious prince; yet, besides that, ᵏ others, extremely well versed in all Jewish antiquities, have made it appear, that Nimrod was either very young at the time, or even not yet born, when the project of building the tower and city was first formed, there is reason to believe (even supposing him then alive, and in great power and authority among his people) that he was not in any tolerable condition to undertake so great a work.

The account which Moses gives us of him is.——— That he ˡ *began to be a mighty one in the earth;* which the best writers explain, by his being the first who laid the foundation of regal power among mankind: but it is scarce imaginable, how an empire, able to effect such a work, could be entirely acquired, and so thoroughly, established by one and the same person, as to allow leisure for amusements of such infinite toil and trouble.

ᵐ Great and mighty empires indeed have seemingly been acquired by single persons; but when we come to examine into the true original of them, we shall find, that they began upon the foundations of kingdoms already attained by their ancestors, and established by the care and wisdom of many successive rulers for several generations, and after a long exercise of their people in arts and arms, which gave them a singular advantage over other nations that they conquered. In this manner grew the empires of Cyrus, Alexander, and all the great conquerors in the world: nor can we, in all the records of history, find one large

---

ʰ Ver. 1.   ⁱ Antiq. l. 1. c. 5.   ᵏ Bochart's Phaleg. l. 1. c. 10.   ˡ Gen. 10. 8.   ᵐ Revelation Examined, vol. 2. dissert. 3.

large dominion, from the very foundation of the world, that was ever erected and established by one private person. And therefore we have abundant reason to infer, that Nimrod, though confessedly the beginner of sovereign authority, could, at this time, have no great kingdom under his command.

A. M. 1757, &c. Ant. Chrif. 2241, &c. from Gen. xi. to ver. 10.

But admitting his kingdom to be larger than this supposition; yet, from that day to this, we can meet with no works of this kind attempted, but from a fulness of wealth, and wantonness of power, and after peace, luxury, and long leisure had introduced and established arts: so that nothing can be more absurd, than to attribute such a prodigious work to the power and vanity of one man, in the infancy both of arts and empire, and when we can scarce suppose, that there was any such thing as artificial wealth in the world.

Since then this building was undoubtedly very ancient, as ancient as the Scripture makes it, and yet could not be effected by any separate society, in the period assigned for it, the only probable opinion is, that it was (as we said before) undertaken and executed by the united labours of all the people that were then on the face of the earth. It is not unlikely, however, that after the dispersion of the people, and their leaving the place unfinished, ⁿ Nimrod and his subjects, coming out of Arabia, or some other neighbouring country, might, after their fright was over, settle at Babel, and there building the city of Babylon, and repairing the tower, make it the metropolis (as afterwards it was) of all the Assyrian empire.

Though he might afterwards settle there.

To this purpose, there is a very remarkable passage ᵒ in Diodorus Siculus, where he tells us; "That on the "walls of one of the Babylonian palaces was pourtrayed "a general hunting of all sorts of wild beasts, with the "figure of a woman on horseback piercing a leopard, and "a man fighting with a lion; and that on the walls of "the other palace were armies in battalia, and huntings "of several kinds." Now of this Nimrod, the sacred historian informs us, that he was a great and remarkable hunter, so as to pass into a proverb; and this occupation he might the rather pursue, as the best means of training up his companions to the exploits of war, and of making himself popular, by the glory he gained, and the public good he did, in destroying those wild beasts, **which at that time** infested

ⁿ Bochart's Phaleg. l. 1. c. 10.   ᵒ Lib. 1.

A. M. 1757, &c. Ant. Chrif 2247, &c. from Gen. xi. to ver. 10.

infested the world. And as this was a part of his character, the most rational account that we can give of these ornaments on the Babylonian palaces, is, that they were set up by some of Nimrod's descendents, in their ancestor's imperial city, in memory of the great founder of their family, and of an empire which afterwards grew so famous.

For what purposes it was built.

[p] Eutychius, patriarch of Alexandria, will needs have it, that Nimrod was the first author of the religion of the Magians, the worshippers of fire: and from hence, very probably, [q] a late archbishop of our own has thought, that this tower of Babel (whose form was pyramidal, as he says, and so resembling fire, whose flame ascends in a conic shape) was a monument designed for the honour of the sun, as the most probable cause of drying up the waters of the flood. For, "though the sun," says he, was not "merely a god of the hills, yet the Heathens thought it "suitable to his advanced station, to worship him upon "ascents, either natural, or where the country was flat, "artificial, that they might approach, as near as possibly "they could, the deity they adored." This certainly accounts for God's displeasure against the builders, and why he was concerned to defeat their undertaking; but as there is no foundation for this conjecture in Scripture, and the date of this kind of idolatry was not, perhaps, so early as it is pretended, the two ends which Moses declares the builders had in view, in forming their project, will be motives sufficient for their undertaking it.

For if we consider that they were now in the midst of a vast plain, undistinguished by roads, buildings, or boundaries of any kind, except rivers; that the provision of pasture, and other necessaries, obliged them to separate; and that, when they were separated, there was a necessity of some land-mark to bring them together again upon occasion, otherwise all communication, and with it, all the pleasures of life must be cut off; we can hardly imagine any thing more natural and fit for this purpose, than the erection of a tower, large and lofty enough to be seen at great distances, and consequently sufficient to guide them from all quarters of that immense region; and when they had occasion to correspond, or come together, nothing certainly could be more proper, than the contiguous buildings of a city for their reception, and convenient communication.

I

[p] Calmet's Dictionary on the word *Nimrod*. [q] Tenison, of idolatry.

If we consider likewise, that all the pride and magnificence of their ancestors were now defaced, and utterly destroyed by the deluge, without the least remains, or memorial of their grandeur; that consequently the earth was a clear stage, whereon to erect new and unrivaled monuments of glory and renown to themselves; and that at this juncture, they wanted neither art nor abilities, **neither numbers nor materials, to make themselves masters of** what their vanity projected; we may reasonably suppose, that the affectation of renown was another motive to their undertaking; since it is very well known, that **this is the** very principle which has all long governed the whole race of **mankind, in** all the works and monuments of magnificence, the mausoleums, pillars, palaces, pyramids, and whatever has been errected of any pompous kind, from the foundation of the world to **this** very day. So that, taking their resolution under the **united** light of these two motives, the reasoning of the builders will run thus: "We "are here in a vast plain: † **our dispersion is inevitable:** "our increase, and the necessaries of life demand it. We "are strong and happy when united; but when divided, "we shall be weak and wretched. Let us then contrive "some means of union and friendly society, which may, at "the same time, perpetuate our fame and memory. **And** "what means so proper for these purposes, as a magnificent "city, and a mighty tower whose top may touch the "skies? The tower will be a land-mark to us through "the whole extent of this plain, and a centre of unity, "to prevent our being dispersed; and the city which may "prove the metropolis of the whole earth, will, at all "times afford us a commodious habitation. Since then "we need fear no dissolution **of our** works by any future "deluge, let us erect **something that** may immortalize "our names, and outvie the labours **of** our antediluvian "fathers." And that this seems to have been the reasoning

A. M. 1757. &c. Ant. Chrif. 2247, &c. from Gen. xi. to ver. 10.

---

† Here they speak as if they feared a dispersion; but it is hard to tell for what cause, unless it was this;—That Noah having projected a division of the earth among his posterity, (for it was a deliberate business, as we noted before,) the people had no mind to submit to it; and therefore built a fortress to defend themselves in their resolution of not yielding to his design; but what they dreaded, they brought upon themselves by their own vain attempt to avoid it. *Vid.* Patrick's Comment. and Usher ad A. M. 1757.

ing of their minds, will further appear, if we come now to take a short survey of the dimensions of the building, according to the account which the best histiorians have given us of it.

The dimensions of the tower.

It is the opinion of the learned [r] Bochart, that whatever we read of the tower, inclosed in the temple of Belus, may very properly be applied to the tower of Babel; because, upon due search and examination, he conceives them to be one and the same structure. Now, of this tower [s] Herodotus tells us, that it was a square of a furlong on each side *i. e.* half a mile in the whole circumference, whose height, being equal to its basis, was divided into eight towers, built one upon another; but what made it look as divided into eight towers, was very probably the manner of its ascent. *The passage to go up it,* continues our author, *was a circular, or winding way, carried round the outside of the building to its highest point:* [t] from whence it seems most likely, that the whole ascent was, by the benching-in drawn in a flopping line from the bottom to the top, eight times round it, which would make the appearance of eight towers one above another. This way was so exceeding broad, that it afforded space for horses and carts, and other means of carriage to meet and turn; and the towers, which looked like so many stories upon one another, were each of them seventy-five foot high, in which were many stately rooms, with arched roofs, supported by pillars, which were made parts of the temple, after the tower became consecrated to that idolatrous use; and, on the uppermost of the towers, which was held more sacred, and where their most solemn devotions were performed there was an observatory, by the benefit of which it was, that the Babylonians advanced their skill in astronomy beyond all other nations.

Some authors, † following a mistake in the Latin version of Herodotus, wherein the lowest of these towers is said

---

[r] *Vid.* Phaleg. part 1. l. c. 9.   [s] Lib. 1.   [t] Prideaux's Connection, part 1.

† The words of Herodotus are; Ἐν μέσῳ δὲ τῷ ἱερῷ πύργος στερεὸς οἰκοδόμηται, σταδίου καὶ τὸ μῆκος καὶ ἐπὶ τούτῳ τῷ πύργῳ ἄλλος πύργος ἐπιβέβηκε, καὶ ἕτερος μάλα, ἐπὶ τούτῳ, μέχρις ὀκτὼ πύργων. Now, tho' it be allowed, that the word μῆκος may signify *height*, as well as *length*, yet it is much better to take Herodotus in the latter sense here: otherwise the tower (if every story answers the lowest) will rise to a prodigious height, though nothing near to what Jerom (l. 5,

Chap. II.   *from the Flood to the Call of Abraham.*   311

said to be a furlong thick, and a furlong high, will have each of the other towers to be of a proportionate height, which amounts to a mile in the whole: but the Greek of Herodotus (which is the genuine text of that author,) says no such thing, but only, that it was a furlong long, and a furlong broad, without mentioning any thing of its height; and ᵘ Strabo in his description of it, calling it a *pyramid*, because of its decreasing, or benching-in at every tower,) says of the whole, that it was a furlong high, and a furlong on every side: for to reckon every tower a furlong high, would make the thing incredible, even though the authority of both these historians were for, as they are against it. Taking it only as it is described, by Strabo, it was prodigious enough; since, according to his dimensions only, without adding any farther, it was one of the most wonderful works in the world, and much exceeded the greatest of the pyramids of Egypt.

A. M. 1757, &c. Ant. Chrisſ. 2247, &c. from Gen. xi. to ver. 10.

In this condition continued the tower of Babel, or the temple of Belus, until the time of Nebuchadnezzar; but he enlarged it by vast buildings, which were erected round it, in a square of two furlongs on every side, or a mile in circumference; and inclosed the whole with a wall of two miles and a half in compass, in which were several gates leading to the temple, all of solid brass, which very probably were made of the brazen sea, the brazen pillars, and the other brazen vessels which were carried to Babylon from the temple of Jerusalem: for so we are told, that all the sacred vessels, which Nebuchadnezzar carried from thence, he put ˣ *into the house of his god in Babylon*, i. e. into the house or temple of Bel, (for † that was the name of the great god of the Babylonians,) surrounding it with the pomp

Its subsequent history.

3 H 2   of

Comment. in Esaiam) affirms, from the testimony of Eyewitnesses, as he says, who examined the remains of it very carefully, *viz.* that it was no less than four miles high; *Universal hist. l. c.* 2.

ᵘ Lib. 16.   ˣ 2 Chron. xxxvi. 7. Dan. i. 2.

† Bel is supposed to have been the same with Nimrod, and to have been called *Bel*, from his dominions, and *Nimrod* from his rebellion; for *Bel*, or *Baal* (which is the same) signifies *Lord*, and *Nimrod*, *Rebel*, in the Jewish and Chaldean language; the former was his Babylonish name, by reason of his empire in that place; and the latter his Scripture name, by reason of his rebellion, in revolting from God, to follow his own wicked designs; *Prideaux's Connection, part* 1. *l.* 2.

of these additional buildings, and adorning it with the spoils of the temple of Jerusalem. This tower did not subsist much above an hundred years, when Xerxes coming from his Grecian expedition, wherein he had suffered a vast loss of men and money, out of pretence of religion, († as being himself a Magian, and consequently detesting the worship of God by images,) ʸ but in reality with a design to repair the damages he had sustained, demolished it, and laid it all in rubbish; having first plundered it of all its immense riches, among which were several images, or statues of massy gold, and ᶻ one particularly of forty feet high, which very probably was † that which Nebuchadnezzar ᵃ consecrated in the plains of Dura.

Thus

† The two great sects of religion among the Persians were the Magians and Sabians. The Sabians worshipped God, thro' sensible images, or rather worshipped the images themselves. The Babylonians were the first founders of this sect; for they first brought in the worship of the planets, and afterwards that of images, and from thence propagated it to all other nations where it prevailed. The Magians, on the contrary, worshipped no images of any kind; but God only, together with two subordinate principles, the one, the author and director of all good, and the other, the author and director of all evil. These two sects always had a mortal enmity to each other; and therefore it is no wonder, that Xerxes who had always the Archimagus attending him in his expeditions, with several other inferior Magi, in the capacity of his chaplains, should by them be prevailed on to take Babylon in his way to Susa, in order to destroy all the idolatrous temples there.

ʸ Prideaux's Connection, part 1.   ᶻ Diodorus Siculous, l. 2.

† Nebuchadnezzar's golden image is said indeed in Scripture to have been 60 cubits, i. e. ninety feet high, but that must be understood of the image and pedestal altogether: for that image being said to have been but six cubits broad or thick, it is impossible that the image could have been sixty cubits high; for that makes its height to be ten times its breadth or thickness, which exceeds all proportions of a man, forasmuch as no man's height is above six times his thickness, measuring the slenderest man living at the waist. But where the breadth of this image was measured, it is not said: perhaps it was from shoulder to shoulder, and then the proportion of six cubits breadth will bring down the height exactly to the measure which Diodorus has mentioned. For the usual height of a man being four and an half of his breadth between the shoulders,

ᵃ Dan iii. 1.

Chap. II.   *from the Flood to the Call of Abraham.*   313

Thus fell this great monument of antiquity, and was ne‑ A. M.
ver repaired any more: For although Alexander, at his re‑ 1757, &c.
turn to Babylon, after his Indian expedition, expressed his Ant. Chr.
intentions of rebuilding it, and accordingly set ten thou‑ 2247, &c.
sand men on work to rid the place of its rubbish; yet, be‑ from Gen.
fore they had made any progress therein, that great con‑ xi. to ver.
queror died on a sudden, and has ever since left both the 10.
city and tower so far defaced, that the very people of the
country are at a loss to tell where their ancient situation
was. Since some late travellers however have, in their o‑
pinions, found out the true ruins and remains of this once
renowned structure, we shall not be averse to gratify our
reader's curiosity ᵇ with an account of what one of the
best authority among them has thought fit to communicate
to the public.

" In the middle of a vast and level plain (says he) a‑ The pre‑
" bout a quarter of a league from the Euphrates, (which sent re‑
" in that place runs westward,) appears an heap of ruined mains of it.
" buildings, like a huge mountain, the materials of which
" are so confounded together, that one knows not what to
" make of it. Its figure is square, and rises in form of a
" pyramid, with four fronts, which answer to the four
" quarters of the compass, but it seems longer from north
" to south than from east to west, and is (as far as I could
" judge by my pacing it; a large quarter of a league. Its
" situation and form correspond with that pyramid which
" Strabo calls the tower of *Belus*; but even in his time it
" had nothing remaining of the stairs, and other orna‑
" ments mentioned by Herodotus, for the greatest part of
" it was ruined by Xerxes and Alexander, who designed
" to have restored it to its former lustre, but was prevent‑
" ed by death.

" There

it must, according to this proportion, have been twenty-seven
cubits high, which is forty foot and an half. Nor must it be
forgot what Diodorus further tells us, viz. That this image
contained a thousand Babylonish talents of gold, which, upon
a moderate computation, amounts to three millions and an
half of our money. But now if we advance the height of the
statue to ninety foot without the pedestal, it will increase the
value to a sum incredible; and therefore it is necessary to take
the pedestal likewise into the height mentioned by Daniel;
Prideaux's Connection, part 1. l. 2.

ᵇ *Vid.* Pietro della Valle, part 2. l. 17.

"There appear no marks of ruins round the compass of this rude mass, to make one believe that so great a city as Babylon ever stood here. All that one can discover, within 50 or 60 paces of it, is only the remains here and there of some foundations of buildings; and the country round about it is so flat and level, that one can hardly conceive it should be chosen for the situation of so noble a city, or that there were ever any considerable structures on it. But considering withal, that it is now at least four thousand years since that city was built, and that in the time of Diodorus Siculus, as he tells us, it was almost reduced to nothing, I, for my part, am astonished that there appears so much as there does.

"The height of this mountain of ruins is not in every part equal, but exceeds the highest palace in Naples. It is a mishapen mass, wherein there is no appearance of regularity. In some places it rises in points, is craggy, and inaccessible; in others it is smooth, and of easy ascent.——Whether ever there were steps to ascend it, or doors to enter into it, it is impossible at present to discover: and from hence one may easily judge, that the stairs ran winding about on the outside, and that, being the less solid parts, they were the soonest demolished, so that there is not the least sign to be seen of them now.

"In the inside of it there are some grottos, but so ruined, that one can make nothing of them; and it is much to be doubted, with regard to some of them, whether they were built at the same time with the work, or made since by the peasants for shelter, which last seems to be more likely. It is evident from these ruins, however, that the tower of *Nimrod* (so our author calls it) was built with great and thick bricks, as I carefully observed, causing holes to be dug in several places for that purpose; but they do not appear to have been burnt, but only dried in the sun, which is extremely hot in those parts.

"In laying these bricks, neither lime nor sand was made use of, but only earth tempered and petrified; and in those parts which made the floors, there had been mingled with the earth (which served instead of lime) bruised reeds or hard straws, such as large mats are made of, to strengthen the work. In several other places, especially where the strongest buttresses were to be, there were, at due distances, other bricks of the same size, but more solid, and burnt in kilns, and set in good lime

Chap. II.   *from the Flood to the Call of Abraham.*   315

" or bitumen, but the greater number were such as were
" dried in the sun."

This is the most of what this sedulous traveller could
discover; and yet, upon the foot of these remarks, he
makes no scruple to declare, " That this ruin was the an-
" cient Babel, or the tower of Nimrod, (as he calls it):
" for besides the evidence of its situation, it is so acknow-
" ledged to be, and so called by the inhabitants of the
" country to this very day:" notwithstanding some others
are of a contrary opinion, *viz.* ^c *That this, and some
other ruins not far distant from it, are not the remains of
the original tower, but rather some later structures of the
Arabs.*

We cannot dismiss this subject however, without making
some reflections on the vanity and transitoriness of all sublunary things, as well as the veracity of all God's predictions; since that goodly city, which was once the pride of
all Asia, and the designed metropolis of the whole universe,
according to the words ^d of the prophets, *is fallen, is
fallen low, very low, and become a dwelling-place for dragons, an astonishment, and an hissing without an inhabitant*;
and that stately tower, which once reared its head on high,
and seemed to menace the stars, is brought *down to the
ground, even to the dust;* insomuch, that the place of it is
to be seen no more; or, if by chance found out by some
inquisitive traveller, the whole is now become only a confused heap of rubbish, according to the word of God, by
the same prophet; ^e *I will roll thee down from the rocks,
and make thee as a burnt mountain, and they shall not take of
thee a stone for a corner, nor a stone for foundations, but thou
shalt be an everlasting desolation, saith the Lord.*

^c Universf. hist. l. 1. c. 2.   ^d Isai. xxi. 9.; and Jer. li. 37.
^e Jer. li. 25, 26.

CHAP. III.

Of the Dispersion, and first Settlement of the Nations.

The History.

IN what manner the children of Noah were admitted to
the possession of the several countries they afterwards
came to inhabit, the sacred historian has not informed us;
but

Marginal notes:
A. M. 1757, &c. Ant. Chris. 2247, &c. from Gen. xi. 10 ver. 10.

A moral reflection hereupon.

A. M. 1759, &c. Ant. Chris. 2245, &c. from Gen. x. to the end; and from chap xi. ver. 10. to the end.

The settlement of the sons of Japhet.

A. M. 1759, &c. Ant. Chrif. 2245, &c. from Gen. x. to the end, and from chap. xi. ver 10 to the end.

but this we may depend on, that ᵃ this great division of the earth was not the result of chance, but of mature deliberation; not a confused, irregular dispersion, wherein every one went where he pleased, and settled himself where he liked best, but a proper assignment of such and such places for every division and subdivision of each nation and family to dwell in. Japhet, as we said before, though usually mentioned last, yet was in reality the eldest son of Noah, and accordingly has his descendents here placed in the front of the genealogy. He had † seven sons: Gomer, who seated himself in Phrygia; Magog, in Scythia; Madai, in Media; Javan, in Ionia, or part of Greece; Tubal, in Tibarene; Mashech, in Moschia, (which lies in the north-east parts of Cappadocia); and Tiras, in Thrace, Mysia, and the rest of Europe towards the north.

The sons of Gomer were Ashkanaz, who took possession of Ascania, (which is part of Lesser Phrygia,) Riphah, of the Riphæan mountains; and Togarmagh, of part of Cappadocia and Galatia.

The sons of Javan were Elishah, who seated himself in Peloponnesus; Tarshish, in Spain; Kittim, in Italy; and Dodanim ᵇ (otherwise called *Rhodanim*) in France, not far from the banks of the river Rhosne, to which he seems to have given the name. By these, and the colonies which in some space of time proceeded from them, not only a considerable part of Asia, but all Europe, and the islands adjacent, were stocked with inhabitants; and the several inhabitants were so settled and disposed of, that each tribe or family, who spake the same language, kept together in one body; and (how distant soever in their situation) continued, for some time at least, their relation to the people or nation from whom originally they sprang.

Shem

ᵃ Mede's Disc. 49. 50. l. 1.

† The following account of the plantations of the three sons of Noah and their descendents is extracted from Bochart's Phaleg.; Heidegger's Historia patriarcharum, vol. 1. exercit. 22.; Wells's Sacred geography, vol. 1.: Bedford's Scripture-chronology. l. 2.: Shuckford's Connection. vol. 1.: Parker's Bibliotheca Biblica, vol. 1.; the authors of the Universal history, l. 1; Le Clerc and Patrick's Commentaries; Pool and Ainsworth's Annotations; with other authors of the like nature; from whom we have made use of the most probable conjectures, and to whom we refer the reader, rather than encumber him with a multitude of explanatory notes.

ᵇ 1 Chron. i. 7.

Shem, the second son of Noah, (and from whom the Hebrew nation did descend,) had himself five sons; whereof Elam took possession of a country in Persia, called after himself at first, but in the time of Daniel, it obtained the name of *Susiana*; *Assur*, of *Assyria*; *Arphaxad*, of *Chaldea*; *Lud*, of *Lydia*; and *Aram*, of *Syria*, as far as the Mediterranean sea.

A. M. 1759, &c. Ant. Chrif. 2245, &c. from Gen. x. to the end; all from chap. xi. ver. 10. to the end.

Of Shem.

The sons of Aram were Uz, who seated himself in the country of Damascus; Hull, near Cholobatene in Armenia; Mash, near the mountains Masius; and Gether, in part of Mesopotamia.

Arphaxad had a son named *Salah*, who settled near Susiana, and begat Eber, (the father of the Hebrew nation,) who had likewise two sons; *Peleg*, whose name imports *division*, because in his days mankind was divided into several colonies; and Joktan, who had a large offspring, to the number of thirteen sons, all seated in Arabia Felix, and who, in all probability, were the progenitors of such people and nations as in those parts, in after ages, had some affinity to their several names. For here it was that the Allumœotæ, who took their name from Almodad, the Selapeni from Sheleph, and the Abalitæ from Obal, &c. lived, *viz.* from that part of Arabia which lies between Musa, (a famous sea-port in the red-sea,) and the mountain Climax, which was formerly called *Sephar*, from a city of that name built at the bottom of it and then the metropolis of the whole country.

Ham the youngest son of Noah, had four sons; whereof Cush settled his abode in that part of Arabia which lies towards Egypt; Mizraim, in both Upper and Lower Egypt; Phut, in part of Lybia; and Canaan in the land which was afterwards called by his name, and in other adjacent countries.

And of Ham.

The sons of Cush were Seba, who settled on the southwest part of Arabia; Havilah, who gave name to a country upon the river Pison, where it parts with Euphrates, to run into the Arabian gulf; Sabah, who lived on the same shore (but a little more northward) of the Arabian gulf, Raamah, who, with his two sons Sheba and Dedan, occupied the same coast, but a little more eastward; and Sabtecha, who (we need not doubt) placed himself among the rest of his brethren. But among all the sons of Cush Nimrod was the person who, in these early days, distinguished himself by his bravery and courage. His lot chanced to fall into a place that was not a little infested with wild

A. M.
1759, &c.
Ant. Chrif.
2245, &c.
from Gen.
x. to the
end; and
from chap.
xi. ver. 10.
to the end.

wild beasts, and therefore he betook himself to the exercise of hunting, and drawing together a company of stout young fellows, not only cleared the country of such dangerous creatures, but procured himself likewise great honour and renown by his other exploits, he raised himself at length to the dignity of a king, (the first king that is supposed to have been in the world,) and having made Babylon the seat of his empire, laid the foundation of three other cities, *viz.* Erech, Accad, and Calneth, in the neighbouring provinces; and so passing into Assyria, and enlarging his territories there, he built Nineveh, Rehoboth, Cala, and Resen, (which was afterwards called *Larissa*,) situate upon the Tygris. But to return to the remainder of Ham's posterity.

Mizraim, his second son became king of Egypt, which after his death, was divided into three kingdoms by three of his sons; Ananim, who was king of Tanis, or Lower Egypt, called afterwards *Delta*; Naphtuhim, who was king of Naph, or Memphis, in Upper Egypt; and Pathrusim, who set up the kingdom of Pathros, or Thebes, in Thebais. Ludim and Lehabim peopled Lybia: Caslubim fixed himself at Casiotis, in the entrance of Egypt from Palestine; and having two sons, Philistim and Caphterim, the latter he left to succeed him at Casiotis, and the former planted the country of the Philistines between the borders of Canaan and the Mediterranean sea. The sons of Canaan were Sidon, the father of the Sidonians, who lived in Phœnicia; Heth the father of the Hittites, who lived near Hebron; Emor, the father of the Amorites, who lived in the mountains of Judea; and Arvad, the father of the Arvadites, not far from Sidon. But whether the other sons of Canaan settled in this country, cannot be determined with any certainty and exactness; only we must take care to place them somewhere between Sidon and Gerar, and Admah and Zeboim; for these were the boundaries of their land.

Upon the whole then we may observe, that the posterity of Japhet came into the possession not only of all Europe, but of a considerable portion of Asia: [c] for two of his sons Tiras and Javan, together with their descendents, had all those countries which, from the Mediterranean sea, reach as far as Scandinavia northward; and his other sons from the Mediterranean, extended themselves eastward over almost all Asia Minor, and part of Armenia,

over

[c] Heidegger's Hist. patriar. vol. 1. exercit. 22. sect. 1.

Chap. III.   *from the Flood to the Call of Abraham.*   319

over Media, Iberia, Albania, and those vast regions towards the north, where formerly the Scythians, but now the Tartars, dwell: That the posterity of Ham held in their possession all Africa, and no small part of Asia; [d] Mizraim, both the Upper, Lower, and Middle Egypt, Marmarica, and Ethiopia, both east and west; Phut, the remainder of Africa, Lybia, **Interior and Exterior**, Numidia, Mauritania, Getulia, &c.; Cush, all Arabia that lies between the Red-sea and the Gulf, beyond the Gulf, Carmania, and no small part of Persia, and towards the north of Arabia, (till expelled by Nimrod,) Babylonia, and part of Chaldea; and Canaan, Palestine, Phœnicia, part of Cappadocia, and that large tract of ground along the Euxine sea, even as far as Cholchis; and that the posterity of Shem had in their possession part both of the Greater and Lesser Asia; [e] in the Lesser, Lydia, Mysia, and Caria; and in the Greater, Assyria, Syria Mesopotamia, Armenia, Susiana, Arabia Felix, &c. and perhaps eastward, all the countries as far as China.

A. M. 1759. &c. Ant. Christ. 2245. &c. from Gen. x. to the end; and from chap. xi. ver. 10. to the end.

These are the plantations [f] *of the families of the sons of Noah in their generations*, and after this manner *were the nations divided in the earth after the flood*. And now to descend to a more particular account of the posterity of his son Shem, from whom the Hebrews (who are the proper subjects of our history) were descended.

Two years after the flood, when Shem was 100 years old, he had a son named *Arphaxad*; after which time he lived 500 years: so that the whole of his life was 600.

A. M. 1658.

Arphaxad, when 35, had a son named *Salah*; after which he lived 403 years; in all 438.

A. M. 1693.

Salah, when 30, had a son named *Eber*, (from whom his descendents were called *Hebrews*,) after which he lived 403 years; in all 433.

A. M. 1723.

Eber, when 34, had a son named *Peleg*, in whose time (as we said) the earth came to be divided; after which he lived 430 years; in all 464.

A. M. 1757.

Peleg, when 30, had a son named *Reu*, after which he lived 209 years; in all 239.

A. M. 1787.

Reu, when 32, had a son named *Serug*; after which he lived 207 years; in all 239.

A. M. 1819.

Serug, when 30, had a son named *Nahor*; after which he lived 200 years; in all 230.

A. M. 1849.

Nahor, when 29, had a son named *Terach*; after which he lived 119 years: in all 148. But of all these persons,

A. M. 1878.

[d] *Ibid.* sect. 2.   [e] *Ibid.* sect. 3.   [f] Gen. x. 32.

A. M. 1997, &c.
Ant. Chrif. 2007, &c.
from Gen. x. to the end; and from chap. xi. ver. 10 to the end.

it muft be remarked, that they had feveral other children of both fexes, though not recorded in this hiftory.

Terah, when 70, (for he was not bleffed with children fooner,) had three fons, one after another, Abraham, Nahor, and Haran; whereof Haran, the eldeft, died before his father, in his native country of Ur, leaving behind him one fon, whofe name was *Lot*, and two daughters, whereof the elder, *viz.* Milcah, was married to her uncle Nahor, and the younger († whofe name was *Sarai*) was married to

A. M. 1948. her uncle Abram; but at this time fhe was barren, and had no children.

A. M. 1997. The corruption of mankind was now become general; and idolatry and polytheifm began to fpread like a contagion, * the people of Ur, in particular, ᵍ (as is fuppofed by the fignification of the name) worfhipped the element of fire, which was always thought a proper fymbol of the fun, that univerfal god of the eaft. Terah, the father of Abram, ʰ was certainly a companion (fome fay a prieft) of thofe who adored fuch ftrange gods; nor was Abram himfelf (as it is generally imagined) uninfected. But God being minded to felect this family out of the reft of mankind, and in them to eftablifh his church, ordered Terah to leave the place of his habitation, which was then corrupted

† It is very probable, that Sarai was called *Ifcah* before fhe left Ur; becaufe, in the 29th verfe, we read that Haran had a daughter of that name, and yet we cannot fuppofe, but that, had fhe been a diftinct perfon, Mofes would have given us an account of her defcent, becaufe it fo much concerned his nation to know from whom they came both by the father and mother's fide; *Patrick's Commentary.*

* The city of Ur was in Chaldee, as the Scripture affure us in more places than one; but ftill its true fituation is not fo well known. For fome think it to be the fame as Camarina in Babylonia; others confound it with Orcha, or Orche. in Chaldea; while others again take it to be Ura, or Sura, upon the banks of the river Euphrates. Bochart and Grotius maintain, that it is Ura. in the eaftern part of Mefopotamia, which was fometimes (as it appears from Acts vii. 2. 4.) included under the name *Chaldea*; and this fituation feems the more probable, not only becaufe it agrees with the words of St. Stephen in the above cited place, but with the writings of Ammianus Marcellinus likewife, who himfelf travelled this country, and mentions a city of this name in the place where Bochart fuppofes it, about two days journey from Nifibis; *Wells's Geography, vol.* I.

ᵍ *Vid.* Calmet's Dictionary on the word *Ur.* ʰ Jof. xxiv. 2. 14.

rupted in this manner; which accordingly he did, and taking with him his son Abram and his wife, together with his grandson Lot, left Ur, with an intent to go into Canaan; but in his journey fell sick at * Haran, a city of Mesopotamia, where being forced to make his abode for some time ‖ in the 145th year of his age he there died.

A. M. 1997, &c. Ant. Chrif. 1007, &c. from Gen. x. to the end; and from chap. xi. ver. 10. to the end

The Objection

" BUT how well soever we may think it comports
"   with the character of a good historian, to enter-
" tain us with a dry catalogue of names, and of names
" which never once more appear upon the stage of action;
" to tell us, that such an one, at such a time, begat such
" an one, and then died, aged so and so, without enter-
"   " ing

* Haran; which is likewise called *Charan*, according to the Hebrew, and *Charran*, according to the Greek pronunciation was a city situated in the west, or north-west part of Mesopotamia, on a river of the same name, which very probably runs into the river Chaboras, as that does into the Euphrates. It is taken notice of by Latin writers, on account of the great overthrow which the Parthians gave the Roman army, under the command of Crassus, and, as some think, had its name given by Terah, in memory of Haran his deceased son. But others think it is much better derived from the word *Hharar*, which denotes its soil to be *hot* and *adust*, as it appears to be from a passage out of Plutarch, in the life of Crassus, and several other ancient testimonies. *Vid.* Calmet's Dictionary; Wells's Geography; and Le Clerc's Commentary *in locum*.

‖ St Stephen (in Acts vii. 4.) tells us, that after the death of his father, Abraham removed from Haran, or, as he calls it, *Charran*, to the land of Canaan. In Gen. xii. 4. we are told, that Abraham was *seventy-five years old, when he departed out of Charran*. In Gen. xi. 26. it is said, that Terah was *seventy years old when he begat Abraham*; and yet, in ver. 32. of the same chapter, it is affirmed, that *he died, being two hundred and five years old*. But at this rate Terah must have lived sixty years after Abram's going from Haran: for 75 (the number of Abram's years when he left Haran) being added to 70, the number of Terah's years, when he begat Abram, make 145 years only; whereas the account in Genesis is, that he lived 205. This therefore must certainly proceed from a fault crept into the text of Moses; because of the two hundred and five years which are given to Terah, when he died at Haran, he only lived an hundred and fortyfive, according to the Samaritan version, and the Samaritan chronicle which, without doubt, do agree with the Hebrew copy, from which they were translated; *An Essay for a new translation*.

"ing any further in his story, or acquainting us with one title of the transactions of his life; yet sure we cannot think, that his account of the origin of nations, or the plantations of mankind over the face of the earth, can be either rational or consistent. In little more than the space of an hundred years, to suppose mankind so far increased, as to be able to send out colonies, from the centre of their dispersion, to all the parts of the then known world, is somewhat unaccountable: but then to make infants, mere infants, or persons, who perhaps, at that time, were unborn, the chiefs and leaders of these colonies; to give them countries which they never saw, and these countries names which they never could deserve, is a thing vastly absurd, and what argues, at least, a strange forgetfulness in our author.

"Peleg, for instance, could not have been long born, and Joktan, his younger brother, (much more Joktan's sons,) can scarce be supposed to have been born when the dispersion happened; and yet they are represented both as heads and princes of families; one conducting his people to † the southern parts of Mesopotamia, and the other, with his numerous family, taking possession of † a good share of Arabia Felix. And whereas it is said of the sons of Japhet, that *by them were the isles of the Gentiles divided into their lands*, it is manifest, from the account of Moses himself, that the places which he assigns for their habitation, were all upon the continent; nor were the islands of Europe peopled, till many generations after this period were past and gone.

"The design of Moses, no doubt, is to evince, that all the present inhabitants of the world descended originally from the three sons of Noah; but besides the great
"difficulty

---

† It is not unlikely, that either Peleg, or some of his posterity, gave name to a town upon Euphrates, called *Phalga*, not far from the place where the river Chaboras runs into it; *Pat. Com.*

† The Arabians it is certain, do avowedly derive their original from Jocktan; and herein they may as well be credited, as the Europeans, who pretend to be sprung from Japetus, or Japhet; or the Africans, who will have Ham, or Jupiter Hammon for their founder. There is moreover, in the territories of Mecha, a city which even to this day is called *Baisath Jocktan*, i. e. the *seat and habitation of Jocktan*, very remarkable for the elegancy of its buildings, the pleasure of its situation, and plenty of its fountains; *Patrick* and *Le Clerc's Comment.*

"difficulty of settling the several nations in any tolerable
"manner, according to the chartel which he has given
"us, there muft of neceffity have been people in the
"world, either efcaped from the flood, or felf-originated,
"before this æra of their difperfion.

"Between the flood and this difperfion, the fpace is
"little more than a hundred years: Ninus is placed by
"many chronologers in this firft century: but fuppofe him
"confiderably later, he is far from being the firft founder
"of the Affyrian monarchy. Belus preceded him, and
"feveral kings there were before Belus: but now, how
"can this agree with the propagation of mankind from
"the fons of Noah? Some petty ftates might perhaps be
"erected; but it is impoffible to conceive, that the foun-
"dation of fo great an empire fhould be laid, in fo fmall
"a compafs of time, by the pofterity of three perfons.

"The records, and aftronomical obfervations of fome
"countries, reaching much lower than the Mofaic date
"of the flood; the hiftory of China, and the ftate and
"grandeur of other eaftern nations, in times as ancient
"as any mentioned in profane hiftory, together with the
"maturity of civil difcipline and government, of learning
"and inventions of all kinds, before ever Greece or Italy,
"or any other weftern people, grew to be at all confi-
"derable, are a fufficient argument that thefe people
"were no defcendents of Noah; or that if they were,
"that there muft be a grofs miftake in point of compu-
"tation. For (to take one argument more from Mofes
"himfelf) from the flood to the time of Abraham, (ac-
"cording to the Hebrew account,) were much about 305
"years; and yet, in that patriarch's days, the world was
"fo well replenifhed, and dominions fo well eftablifhed,
"that we read of feveral kings encountering one another;
"by which it is evident, that the earth had been peopled
"fome time before, or otherwife there could not have
"been fuch potent princes as fome of them are reprefent-
"ed to be at that time.

"The difficulties then, in the Mofaic account of the
"origin of nations, being fo many, and fo infuperable, it
"may not perhaps be deemed fo abfurd a thing, that fe-
"veral other nations (as well as the Greeks and Egyp-
"tians) have owned no founder, but profeffed themfelves
"Aborigines, or the firft inhabitants of the countries
"where they lived. And without fome fuch fuppofition,
"what can we fay for the natives of America, a large con-
"tinent,

A. M. 1997, &c. Ant. Chrif. 2007, &c. from Gen. x. to the end; and from chap. xi. ver. 10. to the end.

" tinent, which Moses makes no mention of; and yet, up-
" on its first discovery, was found stocked with a compe-
" tent number of inhabitants, though it apparently has no
" connection, and consequently could have no communica-
" tion with any other parts of the globe? Who was their
" great progenitor? What chief, of all the race of Noah,
" first discovered the passages that have ever since been
" lost, and carried a colony into this new world, which
" could none of them find their way back again? These
" questions we expect to be resolved in, or otherwise we
" may be permitted to conclude, that the inhabitants of
" this part of the world had better fate than those of the
" other, in escaping the rage of the waters, and so survi-
" ving the flood."

Answered by shewing why Moses sets down genealogies

It may seem not a little strange to some perhaps, why Moses, in his account of the times both preceding and subsequent to the flood, should be so particular in setting down the genealogies of the patriarchs; but he who considers that this was the common method of recording history in those days, will soon perceive, that he had reason sufficient for what he did; namely, to give content and satisfaction to the age wherein he wrote. We indeed, according to the present taste, think these genealogies but heavy reading; nor are we at all concerned who begat whom, in a period that stands at so distant a prospect; but the people, for whom Moses wrote, had the things either before their eyes, or recent in their memories. They saw a great variety of nations around them, different in their manners and customs, as well as their denominations. The names whereby they were then called, were not to them so antique and obsolete, as they are to us. They knew their meaning, and were acquainted with their derivation. And therefore it was no small pleasure to them, to observe, as they read along, the gradual increase of mankind; how the stem of Noah spread itself into branches almost innumerable, and how, from such and such a progenitor, such and such a nation, whose history and adventures they were no strangers to, did arise. Nor can it be less than some satisfaction to us, even at this mighty distance, to perceive, that after so many ages, the change of languages, and the alteration of names, brought in by variety of conquests, we are still able to trace the footsteps of the names recorded by Moses; by the help of these can *

discover

* Those who have undertaken to give us an account of the
several

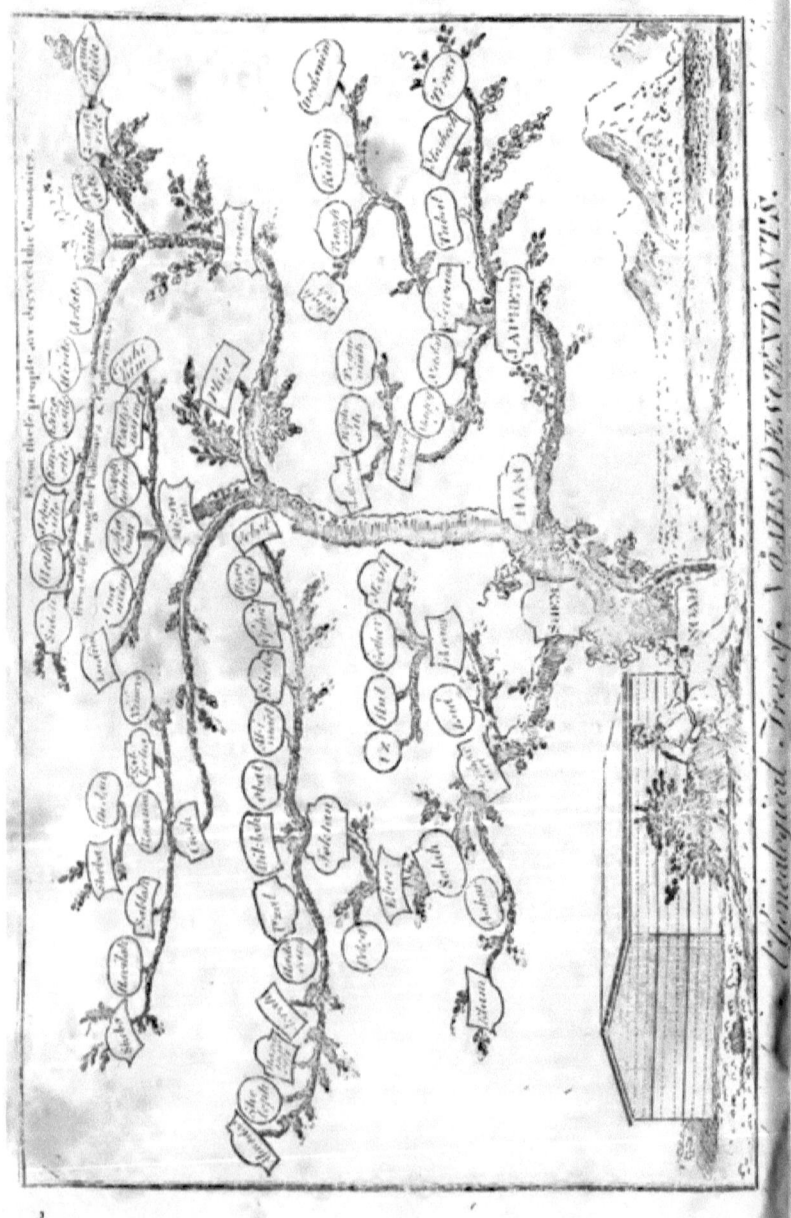

Genealogical Tree of NOAHS DESCENDANTS.

discover those ancient nations which descended from them and, with a little care and application, the particular regions which they once inhabited; whereof the best heathen geographers, without the assistance of these sacred records, were never in a capacity so much as to give us a tolerable guess.

A M 1997, &c. Ant Chrif. 1007. &c. from Gen. x. to the end; and from chap. xi. ver. 10. to the end.

But there is a farther reason for our **historian's** writing in this manner. God had promised to Adam, and in him to all his posterity, a restoration in the person of the Messiah. This promise was renewed to [1] Noah, and afterwards confirmed to Abraham, the great founder of the Jewish nation. Fit therefore it was, in this regard, that he should record exact genealogies, and that all other sacred historians should successively do the same: nor can we sufficiently admire the divine wisdom, in settling such a method, in the beginning of the world, by Moses, and carrying it on by the prophets, as might be of general use as long

several countries assigned to Noah's posterity, have laid down certain rules, as land marks, to direct our inquiry into the original of each particular nation. They tell us, that wherever we find the scripture assigning any portion or tract of land, to any branch of Noah's posterity we may rest assured, that that particular branch, or at least the major part of it, settled itself there: that the families, or tribes of any nation, are continually ranked in that nation; so that wherever we find the nation, there we may expect to find the family likewise, unless there be apparent evidence of their transplantation: That when two or more of these nations are mentioned together, it is highly probable, that they were either both seated together, or lay in a very near neighbourhood to each other: That when two nations or tribes happen to be incorporated into one, the name of one of them is generally swallowed up by the other, and always goes along with the greater: that all original plantations ought to be sought for within a reasonable compass of earth, from the centre of their dispersion, from whence they might, in colonies, afterwards extend themselves into still remoter parts: that the origin of nations, and their cognation and affinity to one another, are to be judged of by the agreement of languages, the remainders of ancient names, the history of nations, monumental inscriptions, and a conformity of manners and customs; and that, lastly, according to these criteria, we shall find that the race of Shem settled chiefly in Asia; those of Ham, part in Asia, and part in Africa; and the greater part of those of Japhet in Europe; so that Shem was situate in the east, with Japhet on the north, and Ham on the south.

[1] *Vid*. Bp Sherlock's Use and intent of prophecy.

A M 1997, &c.
Ant. Chrif 2007, &c.
from Gen. x. to the end; and from chap. xi. ver. 10 to the end.

That the heads of all the nations then exifting are not fet down.

long as the world fhould laft. For as the expectation of the Meffiah put the Jews upon keeping an exact account of all their genealogies; fo when Chrift came into the world, it was evident beyond difpute, that he was of the *feed of Abraham, of the tribe of Judah,* and of the lineage of David, according to the promifes which had, from time to time, been recorded of him.

It is well worth our obfervation, however, that, in the catalogue which Mofes gives us of the defcendents of Noah, he makes mention of no more than fixteen fons of the three brothers, or principal founders of fo many original nations; nor of any more than feven of thefe fixteen, of whom it is recorded, that they had any children; and even of thefe feven, there is one (we may obferve) whofe children are not numbered. [k] But it is not to be imagined, that in two or three hundred years, upon a moderate calculation, or even but in an hundred years at the loweft account, Noah fhould have had no more than fixteen grandfons; and that of thefe too, the majority fhould go childlefs to the grave: it is much more likely, or rather felf-evident, that the nine grandfons, of whom we find nothing in Scripture, were neverthelefs fathers of nations, as well as any of the reft, and not only of original nations, called after their names, but of leffer and fubordinate tribes, called after their fon's names : and (what makes the amount to feem much lefs) there is reafon to fuppofe, that how many foever the grand-children of Noah were, we have, in this tenth chapter of Genefis, the names of thofe only who were patriarchs of great nations, and only of fuch nations as were, in the days of Mofes, known to the Hebrews. For if we read it attentively, we fhall perceive, [l] that the defign of the holy penman, is not to prefent us with an exact enumeration of all Noah's defcendents, (which would have been infinite,) no, nor to determine who were the leading men above all the reft; but only to give us a catalogue, or general account, of the names of fome certain perfons, defcended of each of Noah's children, who became famous in their generations; and fo pafs them by, as having not fpace enough in his hiftory to purfue them more minutely. For we may obferve, that the conftant practice of our author (as it is indeed of all other good authors,) is to cut things fhort that do not properly relate to his

[k] Biblioth. Bibl. vol. 1. Occaf. annot. 17. [l] Shuckford's Connect. l. 3.

his purpose; and when he is hastening to his main point, to mention cursorily such persons as were remarkable (though not the subject he is to handle) in the times whereof he treats.

<small>A M. 1997, &c. Ant. Chrift. 1007, &c. from Gen. x. to the end; and from chap. xi. ver. 10 to the end.</small>

Thus, in the entrance of his history, his business was to attend to the line of Seth; and therefore, when he comes to mention the opposite family of Cain, [m] he only reckons up eight of them, and these the rather because they were the real inventors of some particular arts, which the Egyptians vainly laid claim to. And, in like manner, when he comes to the life of Isaac, Jacob's was the next line wherein his history was to run; and therefore he contents himself with giving us a catalogue of some of Esau's race, but such of them only as were in after-ages, [n] *the Dukes of Edom, according to their habitations in the land of their possession,* as he expresses it. Unless, therefore, we would desire it in an author, that he would be luxuriant, and run wild, we cannot, with any colour of reason, blame the divine historian for stopping short upon proper occasions; for had he pursued all the families descended from Noah, into their several plantations, and there given us the history of all their various adventures, the world, we may almost say, would not have contained the books which he must have written.

What grounds there may be for the supposition, I cannot tell; but to me there seems no reason why we should be obliged to maintain, that all the parts of the habitable world were peopled at once, immediately after the confusion of languages. The historian, indeed, speaking of the persons he had just enumerated, gives us to know, that [o] *by these were the nations divided after the flood:* but how long after the flood, he does not intimate: so that there is no occasion to understand the words, as though he meant, that either by these only, or by these immediately, or by these all at once, was the earth replenished; but only, that among others, (unmentioned, because not so well known to the Jews,) there were so many persons of figure descended from the sons of Noah, who, some at one time, and some at another, became heads of nations, and had, by their descendants, countries called after their names; so that [p] by them the

<small>The world peopled gradually.</small>

---

[m] Gen. iv. [n] Ch. xxxvi. 43. [o] Ch. x. 32.
[p] Shuckford's Connection, vol. 1. l. 3.

A M 1997, &c.
A'c. Chrif. 2007, &c. from Gen. x. to the end; and from chap. xi. ver. 10. to the end.

the *nations were divided*, i. e. people were broken into different nations on the earth, not all at once, or immediately upon the confusion, but at several times, as their families increased and separated after the flood.

For, considering that the number of mankind was then comparatively small, and the distance of these countries, from the place of their dispersion, immensely wide; it is more reasonable to think, that these several plantations were made at different times, and by a gradual progression. Moses indeed informs us, that the earth was portioned out among the children of Noah, after their tongues: supposing then, that the number of languages was, according to the number of the heads of nations, sixteen; these sixteen companies issued out of Babel at separate times, and by separate routs, and so took possession of the next adjacent country, whereunto they were to go. Here they had not settled long, before the daily increase of the people made the bounds of their habitation too narrow; whereupon the succeeding generation, under the conduct of some other leader, leaving the place in possession of such as cared not to move, penetrated farther into the country, and there settling again, and again becoming too numerous, sent forth fresh colonies into the places they found unoccupied; till, by this way of progression on each side, from the centre to every point of the circumference, the whole world came in time to be inhabited, in the manner that we now find it. If then the several parts of the globe were by the sons of Noah gradually, and at sundry times, peopled, there wanted not, all at once, so many; and if several of the sons of Noah, who had their share in peopling the globe, are not taken notice of by Moses, there might possibly be many more to plant and replenish the earth than we are aware of. Let us then see what their number, upon a moderate computation, might, at this time, be supposed to be.

What the number of the people then in the world might possibly be.

To this purpose we are to remember, that we are not to make our computation according to the present standard of human life, which *, since the time of the flood, is vastly

* In the Mosaic history we find, by what degrees the long lives, which preceded the flood, were after it shortened. The first three generations recorded in Scripture after the deluge, Arphaxad, Salah, and Heber, lived above 430 years. Yet not so long as their ancestor Shem, who being born 100 years before the

Chap. III.   *from the Flood to the Call of Abraham.*   329

vastly abbreviated; that the strength of constitution necessary to the procreation of children, which, by a continued course of temperance, and simplicity of diet, then prevailed, is now, by an induction of all manner of riot and excess, sadly impaired; and that the divine benediction, which, in a particular manner, was then poured out upon the children of Noah, could not but prove effectual to the more than ordinary multiplication of mankind; so that length of days, assisted by the blessing of God, and attended with a confirmed state of health, could not but make a manifestly great difference between their case and ours.

A. M. 1997, &c. Ant. Christ. 2007, &c. from Gen. x. 10 to the end; and from chap. xi. ver. 10. to the end.

* Various are the ways which have been attempted by learned men to shew the probable increase of mankind, in that period of time: but for our present purpose, it

the flood, lived above 500 after it. The three next generations, Peleg, Reu, and Serug, lived not much above 230 years; and from their time only Terah lived above 200. All the others after him were below that number. Moses came not to be above 120; and in his days he complains that the age of man was shortened to about seventy or eighty years; and near this standard it has continued ever since; *Millar's Church history, p.* 35.

* Petavius [de Doct. Temp. l. 9. c. 14.] supposes, that the posterity of Noah might beget children at seventeen; that each of Noah's sons might have eight children in eight years after the flood; and that every one of these eight might beget eight more: by this means, in one family (as in that of Japhet 238 years after the flood) he makes a diagram, consisting of almost an innumerable company of men. Temporarius (as the learned Usher, in his Chron. Sacra, ch. 5. tells us) supposes that all the posterity of Noah, when they attained twenty years of age, had every year twins; and hereupon he undertakes to make it appear, that in 102 years after the flood, there would be in all 1,534,400; but without this supposition of twins, there would in that time be 388,605 males, besides females. Others suppose, that each of the sons of Noah had ten sons, and by that proportion in a few generations, the amount will arise to many thousands within a century. And others again insist on the parallel between their increase and the multiplication of the children of Israel in Egypt, and thereupon compute, that if from 72 men, in the space of 215 years, there were procreated 600,000, how many will be born of three men in the space of 100 years? But what method soever we take to come to a probable conjecture, we still have cause to believe, that there was a more than ordinary multiplication in the posterity of Noah after the flood; *Stillingfleet's Orig. Sacr. l.* 3. *c.* 4.

A M 1997, &c. Ant. Chrif. 2007, &c. from Gen. x. to the end; and from chap. xi. ver. 10. to the end.

it will be fufficient to fuppofe, ^q that the firft three couples, *i. e.* Noah's three fons, and their wives, in twenty years time after the flood, might have thirty pair, and by a gradual increafe of ten pair for each couple in forty years time, till the three hundred and fortieth year after the flood, in which Peleg died, there might rife a fufficient number (* as appears by the table under the page) to fpread colonies over the face of the whole earth. And if to thefe, the feveral collateral defcendents of Noah's pofterity were taken in; if the children which Noah himfelf might poffibly have in the 350 years he lived after the flood; which Shem and his two brothers might have in the laft 160; which Salah and his contemporaries might have in the laft 160; and which Heber and his contemporaries might have in the laft 191 years of their lives, (which are not reckoned in the account,) together with the many more grandfons of Noah and their progeny, which, in all probability, (as we obferved before,) are not fo much as mentioned in it; it is not to be imagined how much thefe additions will fwell the number of mankind to a prodigious amount above the ordinary calculation.

That kingdoms at this time were but fmall.

But allowing the number at this time to be not near fo large as even the common computation makes it; yet we are to remember, that at the firft planting of any country, an handful of men (as it were) took up a large tract of ground. ^r At their firft divifion, they were fcattered into fmaller bodies, and feated themfelves at a confiderable diftance from one another, the better to prevent the increafe of the beafts of the field upon them. Thefe fmall companies had each of them one governor, who,

^q Bifhop Cumberland's Origines gentium, tract. 4.; and Millar's Church-hiftory, chap. 1. part 2.

* Years of the world.   Years after the flood.   Pairs of men and women.

Years of the world	Years after the flood	Pairs of men and women
1676	20	30
1716	60	300
1756	100	3,000
1796	140	30,000
1836	180	300,000
1876	220	3,000,000
1916	260	30,000,000
1956	300	300,000,000
1996	340	3,000,000,000

^r Bedford's Script. chron. l. 1. c. 5.

Chap. III.   *from the Flood to the Call of Abraham.*   331

who, in Edom seems to be called [s] *a duke*, and in Canaan, [t] *a king*, (whereof there were no less in that small country than one and thirty at one time:) but of what power or military force these several princes were, we may learn from this one passage in Abraham's life, viz. that [u] when Chedorlaomer, in conjunction with three other kings, had defeated the kings of Sodom and Gomorrah with three kings more that came to their assistance, plundered their country, and taken away Lot and his family, who at this time sojourned in these parts; Abraham, with no more than 318 of his own domestics, pursue the conquerors, engages them, beats them, and, together with his nephew Lot, and all his substance, recovers the spoil of the country which these confederate kings were carrying away. A plain proof this, one would think, that this, multitude of kings which were now in the world were titular, rather than real; and that they had none of them any great number of subjects under their command. For though Canaan was certainly a very fruitful land, and may therefore be presumed to be better stored with inhabitants than any of its neighbouring proivnces; yet we find, that when Abraham and Lot first came into it, though [x] *they had flocks, and herds, and tents, that the land was not able to bear them, that they might dwell together;* yet, as soon as they were seperate, they found no difficulty to settle in any part thereof with the rest of its inhabitants.

How great soever the growth of the Assyrian monarchy became at last, yet we have too little certainty of the time when it began, ever to question, upon that account, the truth of the propagation of the world by the sons of Noah. Ninus (whom profane history generally accounts the first founder of it) is placed [y] by one of our greatest chronologers, in the 2737 year of the world according to the Hebrew computation; so that, living in the time of the Judges, he is supposed to have been contemporary with Deborah; but [z] others think this a date much too early. Nimrod, we must allow, founded a kingdom at Babylon, and perhaps extended it into Assyria; but this kingom was but of small extent, if compared

A M 1997. &c. Ant. Chrift. 1007, &c. from Gen. x. to the end; and from chap. xi. ver. 10. to the end.

The kingdom of Assyria in particular.

---

[s] Gen. xxxvi. to the end.   [t] Jos. xii. 9. to the end.
[u] Gen. xiv.   [x] Gen. xiii. 5, 6.   [y] Usher's Annot. Vet. Test A. M. 2737.   [z] Stillingfleet's Orig. Sacr. l. 3. c. 4. and Sir Isaac Newton's Chron.

A M
1907, &c.
Ant. Chrif.
2007, &c.
from Gen.
x. to the
end; and
from chap.
xi. ver. 10.
to the end.

pared with the empires which arose afterwards; and yet, had it been ever so much greater, it could not have been of any long continuance, because the custom in those early days was for the father to divide his territories among his sons. After the days of Nimrod, we hear no more, in the sacred records, of the Assyrian empire, till about the year 3234, when we find Pul invading the territories of Israel, and making Menahem tributary to him. It is granted indeed, that the four kings, who in the days of Abraham, invaded the southern coast of Canaan, came from the countries where Nimrod had reigned, and perhaps were some of his posterity who had shared his conquests; but of what small significance such kings as these were, we are just now come from relating. Sesac and Memnon, two kings of Egypt, were great conquerors, and reigned over Chaldea, Assyria, and Persia; and yet in all their histories, there is not one word of any opposition they received from the Assyrian monarchy then standing: and though Nineveh, in the time of Joash, king of Israel, was become a large city; yet it had not yet acquired that strength as not to be afraid (according to the preaching of Jonah) of being invaded by its neighbours, and destroyed within forty days. Not long before this, it had freed itself indeed from the dominion of Egypt, and had got a king of its own, but (what is very remarkable) ^a its king was not as yet called *the king of Assyria*, but only ^b *the king of Nineveh*; nor was his proclamation for a fast published in several nations, no, nor in all Assyria, but only in Nineveh, and perhaps the villages adjacent: whereas, when once they had established their dominion at home, secured all Assyria properly so called, and began now to make war upon their neighbouring nations, their kings were no longer called *the kings of Nineveh*, but began to assume the title of *the kings of Assyria*. These, and several more instances which the author I have just now cited has produced, are sufficient arguments to prove that the Assyrians were not the great people some have imagined in the early times of the world; and that if they made any figure in Nimrod's days, it was all extinguished in the reigns of his successors, and never revived, until God, for the punishment of the wickedness of

his

^a Sir Isaac Newton's Chronology, ch. iii.   ^b Jonah iii.

Chap. III.   *from the Flood to the Call of Abraham.*   333

his own people, was pleased to raise them from obscurity, and, as the Scripture expresses it, ^c *stirred up the spirit of Pul, and the spirit of Tiglath-Pilneser, king of Assyria.*

And in like manner we may observe, that whatever notice has been made in the world with the astronomical observations of the Chaldeans, which Aristotle is said to have sent into Greece, and according to which Alexander is thought to have taken at Babylon, the whole is a mere fiction and romance. There is nothing extant (as ^d a very good judge of ancient and modern learning tells us) in the Chaldaic astrology, of older date than the æra of Nabonassar, which begins but 747 years before Christ. By this æra the Chaldeans computed their astronomical observations, the first of which falls about the 27th year of Nabonassar; and all that we have of them are only seven eclipses of the moon, and even these but very coarsely set down, and the oldest not above 700 years before Christ. And to make short of the matter, the same author informs us farther, that the Greeks were the first practical astronomers who endeavoured in earnest to make themselves masters of the sciences: that Thales was the first who could predict an eclipse in Greece, not 600 years, and that Hipparchus made the first catalogue of the fixed stars, not above 650 years before Christ.

What the history of the Egyptians and Chinese, and their boasted antiquity, is, we have had occasion to take notice ^e more than once; and need only here to add, that, bating that strange affectation wherein they both agree, of being thought so many thousand years older than they have any authentic testimonies to produce; there is a manifest analogy between the Scripture-history, and what Berosus has told us of the one, and Martinius of the other: For (to refer the reader to what we have observed from Berosus concerning the Egyptians) ^f the genealogy which the Chinese give us of the family of their first man, Puoncuus seems to carry a nearer resemblance to Moses's patriarchal genealogies; Thienhoang their second king's civilizing the world, answers very well to Seth's settling the principles, and reforming the lives of men;

Vol. I. No. 5.   3 L

---

^c 1 Chron. v. 26.   ^d Wotten's Reflections, ch. 23.
^e *Vid.* Apparatus, p. 78, 79.; and the History, l. 1. c. 5.
^f Biblioth. Bib. in the introduction, p. 77.

A M 1997, &c. Ant.Chrif. 2007, &c. from Gen. x, to the end; and from chap xi. ver. 10. to the end.

men) and Fohi's fourth fucceffor, whom they accufe of deftroying their ancient religion, and introducing idolatry, is plainly copied from the hiftory of Nimrod, who was probably the firft eftablifher of idol-worfhip. So that from thefe, and fome other particulars in their hiftory, we may be allowed to conclude, that the ancient Chinefe (as all other nations did) agreed, in the main, with Mofes in their antiquities; and that the true reafon of their chronological difference is, that the reign of the Chinefe kings (in the very fame manner as the Egyptian dynafties) were not fucceffive, [g] but of feveral contemporary princes, who at one and the fame time, had different and diftinct dominions.

The wild pretences of felf origination confuted.

The want of certain records of ancient times, and confequently, the grofs ignorance which fome nations laboured under as to their original, has thrown feveral into a wild notion and conceit, that they were felf-originated, came never from any other place, and had never any primordial founder or progenitor. But now, whatever hypothefis they are minded to take; whether they fuppofe a beginning or no beginning of human generation; whether they fuppofe men to have fprung out of the fea, or out of the land; to have been produced from eggs caft into the matrix of the earth, or out of certain little *pustulæ* or fungofities on its furface; to have been begotten by the *anima mundi* in the fun, or by an *anima terræ* pervading the body of this terraqueous globe; to have been fent forth into the world filently, and without noife, or to have opened the womb of their common mother with loud claps of thunder: take they which of thefe hypothefes they will, I fay, and when they once come to reafon upon it, they will foon find themfelves hampered and entangled with abfurdities, and impoffibilities almoft innumerable.

All nations to whom the philofophers in fearch after knowledge reforted, had memorials, we find, left among them, of the firft origin of things; but the univerfal tradition of the firft ages was far better preferved among the eaftern than weftern nations, and thefe memorials were kept with greater care by the Phœnicians and Egyptians than by the Greeks and Romans. [h] Among the Greeks however, when they firft undertook to philofophize, the beginning of the world, with the gradual progreffion of its inhabitants, was no matter of difpute; but that being taken for granted, the enquiry was, Out of what material

[g] M. de Loubere's Hift. of Siam, vol. 1. occaf. annot. c. 17.   [h] Bibliotheca Biblica,

terial principles the cosmical system was formed? and Aristotle arrogating to himself the opinion of the world's eternity as a *nostrum*, declared that all mankind before him asserted the world's creation.

From this wild notion of Aristotle, in opposition to an universal tradition, and the consent of all ages, the poets took occasion to turn the histories of the oldest times into fables; and the historians, in requital and courtesy to them, converted the fables which the poets had invented into histories, or rather popular narratives; and most of the famous nations of the earth, that they might not be thought more modern than any of their neighbours, took occasion too of forging certain antiquities, foolish genealogies, extravagant calculations, and the fabulous actions and exploits of gods and heroes, that they might thus add to their nobility by an imaginary anticipation of time, beyond the possible limits that could be made known by any pretence of certainty.

The wiser sort of men however saw into this; and, from the ordinary increase and propagation of mankind, the invention and growth of arts and sciences, and the advancements carried on in civil discipline and government, could discern the folly and superstition of all such romantic pretensions: but then, having lost the true ancient tradition, they were drove to the necessity of a perpetual vicissitude, either of general or particular deluges; by which, when things were come to their crisis and perfection, they were made to begin again, and all preceding memoirs were supposed to be lost in these inundations. But this is all a groundless conjecture, a mere begging of the question, and a kind of prophesying backwards of such alterations and revolutions, as it is morally impossible for them to know any thing of.

Since therefore an eternal succession of generations is loaded with a multitude of insuperable difficulties, and no valid arguments are to be found for making the world older than our sacred books do make it; since the presumed grandeur of the Assyrian, and other monarchies, too soon after the flood, to be peopled by Noah's children, is a gross mistake, and the computations of the Chaldeans and other nations, from their observations of the celestial bodies, groundless and extravagant; since all the pretensions of the several Aborigines are found to be ridiculous, and the more plausible inventions of successive revolutions entirely imaginary;

ginary; since neither the self-originists, nor the revolutionists, even upon their own principles, can account for what is most easily accounted for by the writings of Moses; and (what is a farther consideration) since † there are many customs and usages, both civil and religious, which have prevailed in all parts of the world, and can owe their original to nothing else but a general institution; which institution could never have been, had not all mankind been of the same blood originally, and instructed in the same common notices, before they were divided in the earth: since the matter stands thus, I say, we have all the reason in the world to believe, that this whole narration of Moses concerning the origination of mankind, their destruction by the flood, their renovation by the sons of Noah, their speedy multiplication to a great number, their dispersion upon the confusion of languages, and their settling themselves in different parts of the world, according to their allotments, is true in fact; because it is rational, and consistent with every event; consonant to the notions we have of God's attributes; and not repugnant to any system of either ancient or modern geography that we know of.

Time indeed, and the uncertain state of languages; the different pronunciation of the same word, according to the dialect of different nations; the alterations of names in several places, and substitution of others of the like importance in the vernacular tongue; the disguising of ancient stories in fables, and frequently mistaking the idiom of oriental languages; the inundation of barbarism in many countries, and the conquests and revolutions generally introductive

---

† **Such are,** 1. The numbering by decads. 2. The computing time by a cycle of seven days. 3. The sacredness of the seventh number, and observation of a seventh day as holy. 4. The use of sacrifices, propitiatory, and eucharistical. 5. The consecration of temples and altars. 6. The institution of sanctuaries and their privileges. 7. Separation of tenths and first fruits to the service of the altar. 8. The custom of worshipping the Deity discalceated or bare-footed. 9. Abstinence of husbands from their wives before sacrifice. 10. The order of priesthood, and the maintenance of it. 11. Most of the expiations and pollutions mentioned by Moses in use among all famous nations. 12. An universal tradition of two protoplasts, deluges, and renewing mankind afterwards; *Bibliotheca Biblica, vol.* 1. p. 296.

Chap. III. *from the Flood to the Call of Abraham.*

troductive of new names, which have happened almost in all; these, and several other causes, create some perplexity in determining the places recorded by Moses, and ascertaining the founder of each particular nation: but still notwithstanding these disadvantages, we may, in some measure, trace the foot-steps of the sons of Noah, issuing out from Babel into the different quarters of the world, and in several conntries, perceive the original names of their founders preserved in that of their own.

A M 1997, &c. Ant. Chrif. 2007, &c. from Gen. x. to the end; and from chap. xi. ver. 10 to the end.

For, though the analogy of names be not, at all times, a certain way of coming to the knowledge of things; yet, in this case, I think it can hardly be denied, but that the Assyrians descended from Asiur; the Canaanites, from Canaan: the Sidonians, from Sidon; the Lydians, from Lud; the Medes from Madai; the Thracians, from Tiras; the Elamites, from Elam; the Ionians, from Javan; with several others produced by [k] Grotius, [l] Montanus, [m] Junius, [n] Pererius, and more especially [o] Bochart, that most splendid star of France, (as [p] one calls him upon this occasion,) who, with wonderful learning and industry, has cleared all this part of sacred history, and given a full and satisfactory account of the several places where the posterity of Noah seated themselves after the deluge.

How the large continent of America came to be peopled (since no mention is made of it in the writings of Moses, and so vast a sea separates it from any other part of the known world) is a question that has exercised the wit of every age, since its first discovery. It is worthy our observation however, that though all the great quarters of the world are for the most part separated from each other, by some vast extensive ocean; [q] yet there is always some place or other, where some isthmus, or small neck of land, is found to conjoin them, or some narrow sea is made to distinguish and divide them. Asia and Africa, for instance, are joined together by an isthmus, which lies between the Mediterranean sea and Arabian gulf. Upon the coasts of Spain and Mauritania, Europe and Africa are divided by no larger a sea than the Fretum Herculis, or straits of Gibraltar; and above the Palus Mœotis, Europe has nothing to part it from Asia, but the small river Tanais. America, as it is divided into North and South, is joined together

By what ways and what nations, America might be peopled.

---

[k] *Vid.* Annot. l. 1. De Verit.   [l] Paleg.   [m] In Gen. x.   [n] Ibid.   [o] Phaleg.   [p] Heidegger.
[q] Heidegger's Hist. patriarcharum, vol. 1. excr. 22.

together by a neck of land which, from sea to sea, is not above 18 leagues over: what separates North America from the northern parts of Asia, is only the straits of Anien; or South America from the most southern parts of Asia, is only the straits of Magellan. And therefore, since providence, in the formation of the earth, has so ordered the matter, that the principal continents are, at some place or other always joined together by some little isthmus, and generally separated by some narrow sea; and (what is further to be observed) since most of the capital islands in our part of the hemisphere, such as Sumatra in Asia, Madagascar in Africa, and England in Europe, are generally at no great distance from the continent; we have some reason to presume, that there may possibly be a certain neck of land (though not as yet discovered) which may join some part of Asia, or perhaps some part of Europe, to the main continent of America. Or, if we may not be allowed the supposition, yet [r] why might not there formerly have been such a bridge (as we may call it) between the south-east part of China, and the most southern continent of this new world, though now broken off (as [s] some suppose England to have been from France) by the violent concussions of the sea; as indeed the vast number of islands which lie between the continent of China and Nova Guinea, (which are the most contiguous to each other,) would induce one to think, that once they were all one continued tract of land, though by the irruption of the sea, they are now crumbled into so many little islands?

The difference, however, between the inhabitants of South and north America, is so remarkably great, that there is reason to imagine, they received colonies at first from different countries; and therefore some are of opinion, that as the children of Shem, being now well versed in navigation, might, from the coasts of China, take possession of the southern parts; so might the children of Japhet, either from Tartary, pass over the straits of Anien, or out of Europe, first pass into Norway, thence into Iceland, thence into Greenland, and so into the northern parts of America: and this they think the more probable, because of the great variety of languages which are observed among the natives of this great continent; a good indication, as one would imagine, of their coming thither at different times, and from different places.

We

---

[r] Patrick's Commentary.   [s] *Vid.* The new general Atlas.

Chap. III.   *from the Flood to the Call of Abraham.*

We indeed, according to the common forms of speech, call these places islands, which are, on every side, surrounded by the sea; but the Hebrews were wont to give that name to all maritime countries, such as either had several islands belonging to them, or such as had no island at all, provided they were divided from Palestine or from Egypt by the sea, and could not conveniently be gone to any other way. ᵗ Such are the countries of the Lesser Asia, and the countries of Europe, where the descendants of Japhet were seated; and that these are denoted by the *Isles of the Gentiles**, might be evinced from several parallel passages in Scripture. At present we need only take notice, that as the Lesser Asia was from Babel, the nearest place of Japhet's allotment, it is very probable, that he and his sons continued there for some time, till the increase of their progeny made them send out colonies, which not only peopled the isles of the Mediterranen and Ægean seas, but passing into Europe, spread themselves farther and farther till at length they came to take possession of the very island wherein we now live.

To this purpose the writers on this subject have made it appear, that from their original country, which was Asia Minor, they sent a colony to the Mæotic Lake, on the north of the Euxine sea; and as they were called

Cimmerii

A M 1907, &c. Ant. Chrif. 2007, &c. from Gen. x. to the end; and from chap. xi. ver. 10. to the end.

The isles of the Gentiles

and that of England.

ᵗ Well's Geography of the Old Testament, vol. 1.

* Thus the prophet Isaiah, ch. xi. 10, 11. speaking of the calling of the Gentiles, and of the restoration of the Jews, has these words: *The Lord shall recover the remnant of his people from Assyria, Egypt, Pathros, Cush, Elam, Shinar, Hamah, and from the isles of the sea,* where, by the *isles of the sea* (which is the same with the *isles of the Gentiles*) we must necessarily understand such countries as are distinct from the countries which are expressly named, viz. *Assyria Egypt* &c. and therefore most likely the countries of the Lesser Asia, and Europe. The same prophet, in order to shew God's omnipotence, speaks in this manner *Behold the nations are as a drop in the bucket, and are counted as the small dust of the balance; behold he takes up the isles as a very litile thing,* ch. xl 15. Where, if by the isles we mean those which we call strictly so, the comparison of the disparity is lost, because those which we call *isles*, are indeed very little things; and therefore the proper signification of the word, in this place, must be these large countries which were beyond the sea in regard to Egypt whence Moses came, or Palestine whither he was now going; *Well's Geography, vol.* 1. *p.* 113.

A. M. 1997, &c. Ant. Chrif. 2007, &c. from Gen. x. to the end; and from chap xi. ver. 10 to the end.

Cimerii in Afia, fo they gave the name of *Bofphorus Cimmerius* to the Straits we there meet with; that after this, fpreading farther, they fell down the Danube, and fettled in a country, which† from them was called *Germany*; that from Germany, they advanced ftill farther, till they came into France, for the inhabitants of France, (as ᵘ Jofephus tells us) were anciently called *Gomorites*; and that from France they came into the fouth part of Briton; and therefore we find that the Welfh (the ancient inhabitants of this ifle) call themfelves *Kumero*, or *Cymro*, call a woman *Kumeræs*, and the language they fpeak *Kumerag*; which feveral words carry in them fuch plain marks of the original name from whence they are derived, that if any regard is to be had to etymologies in cafes of this nature, we cannot forbear concluding, that the true old Britons, or Welfh, are the genuine defcendants of Gomer. And fince it is obferved, that the Germans were likewife the defcendants of Gomer, particularly the Cymbri, to whom the Saxons, and efpecially the Angles, were near neighbours, it will hence likewife follow, that our anceftors, who fucceeded the old Britons *

† The people of this country are called *Germars*, and they call themfelves *Germen*, which is but a fmall variation, and eafy contraction of Gomeren, *i. e* Gomerians: For the termination *en* is a plural termination in the German language; and from the fingular number, *Gomer* is formed *Gemren*, by the fame analogy, that from *brother* we form *brethren*; *Well's Geography*, vol. 1. p. 127. and *Bedford's Scripture Chronology* l. 2. c. 4.

ᵘ Antiq. l. 1.

* To fhew how the weftern part of our ifland came likewife to be peopled, the above cited author of Scripture-chronology fuppofes, that when Jofhua made his conqueft in the land of Canaan, feveral of the inhabitants of Tyre, being ftruck with the terror of his arms, left their country; and being fkilled in the art of navigation, failed into Africa, and their built a city, called *Carthage*, or *the city of wanderers*, as he interprets the word: that the Syrians and Phœnicians being always confiderable merchants, and now fettling in a place convenient for their purpofe, began to enlarge their trade; and coafting the fea-fhore of Spain, Portugal, and France, happened at length to chop upon the iflands called *Caffiterides*, now the iflands of Scilly, whereof he gives us a defcription from Strabo; that having here fallen into a trade for tin and lead, it was not long before they difcovered the land's end on the weft fide of Cornwall,

tons in the eastern part of this isle, were in a manner descended from Gomer the first son of Japhet.

Thus we see, [x] that the plantations of the world by the sons of Noah, and their offspring, recorded by Moses in this tenth chapter of Genesis, and by the inspired author of the first book of Chronicles, are not unprofitable fables, or endless genealogies, but a most valuable piece of history, which distinguishes from all other people, that particular nation, of which Christ was to come; gives light to several predictions and other passages in the prophets; shews us the first rise and origin of all nations, their gradual increase, and successive migrations, cities building, lands cultivating, kingdoms rising, governments settling, and all to the accomplishment of the divine benediction: [y] *Be fruitful, and multiply, and replenish the earth: and the fear of you, and the dread of you, shall be upon every* other creature.

A. M. 1997, &c. Ant. Chrif. 2007, &c. from Gen. x. to the end, and from chap. xi. ver. 10. to the end.

DISSERTATION. III.

Of the sacred Chronology, and profane History, Letters, Learning, Religion, and Idolatry, &c. during this period.

BEfore we enter upon the history of the world, as it is delivered in some Heathen authors, from the time of the flood, to the calling of Abraham, it may not be improper to settle the sacred chronology; and that the rather because the difference is very considerable, (as appears by the subsequent table,) according as we follow the computation of the Hebrew text, of the Samaritan copies, or of the Greek interpreters. But before we come to this, we must observe, that in the catalogue which we refer to, Moses takes notice of no other branch of Noah's family, but only that of Shem, and his descendents in a direct line to Abraham, and the different computations [z] relating to them, may be best perceived by the following table.

The difference that is found in the sacred chronology

Now wall, and finding the country much more commodious than Scilly, removed from thence, and here made their settlement. And this conjecture he accounts more feasible, by reason of the great affinity between the Cornish language, and the ancient Hebrew or Phœnician; l. 2. c. 4. p. 195.

[x] Millar's Church History, ch. 1. per. 2.   [y] Gen. ix. 1.
[z] Usher's Chron, sac. cap. 2.

A. M. 1997, &c.
Ant. Chrif 2007, &c.
from Gen. x. to the end; and from chap. xi. ver. 10. to the end.

After the flood Shem was	Heb.	Sam.	Sep	Heb.	Sam.	Sep.	Heb.	Sam.	Sep.
1	2	2	2	500	500	500		600	
2 Arphaxad	35	135	135	403	303	330		438	
0 Cainan	0	0	130	0	0	330		0	
3 Salah	30	130	130	403	303	330		433	
4 Eber	34	134	134	430	270	270		404	
5 Peleg	30	130	130	209	109	209		332	
6 Reu	32	132	132	207	107	207		239	
7 Serug	30	130	130	200	100	200		230	
8 Nahor	29	79	79	119	69	125		148	
9 Terah the father of Abram.	70	70	70				205	145	205
In all	292	942	1072						
	Before they had children.			After they had children.			Before they died.		

Now, whoever cafts his eye into this table, may eafily perceive, that except the variations which may poffibly have been occafioned by the negligence of tranfcribers, [a] the difference between the Samaritan and Septuagint chronology, is fo very fmall, that one may juftly fufpect, that the former has been tranfcribed from the latter, on purpofe to fupply fome defect in its copy; but that the difference between the Greek and Hebrew chronology, is fo very great that the one or other of them muft be egregioufly, wrong becaufe the Septuagint do not only add a patriarch, named *Cainan*, never mentioned in the Hebrew, and fo make eleven generations from Shem to Abraham, inftead of ten; but in the lives of moft of thefe patriarchs, they infert 100 years before they came to have children, *i. e.* they make them fathers 100 years later than the Hebrew text does, though (to bring the matter to a compromife) they generally deduct them again in the courfe of their lives.

On both fides have appeared men of great learning; but they

[a] Shuckford's Connection, vol. 1. l. 3.

they who assert the cause of the Septuagint, are not unmindful to urge the testimony of St Luke, who, [b] between Arphaxad and Salah, has inserted the name of Cainan, which (as he was an inspired writer) he could never have done, had not the Septuagint been right, in correcting the Hebrew Scriptures: besides that, the numbers in the Septuagint give time for the propagation of mankind, and seem to agree better with the history of the first kingdoms of the world.

A M 1997, &c. Ant. Chrif. 2007, &c. from Gen. x. to the end; and from chap. xi ver. 1. to the end.

On the other hand, they who abide by the Hebrew text, cannot think, that the authority of the Septuagint is so sacred, as their adversaries imagine. Upon examination, they find many things added, many things omitted, and, through the whole, so many faults almost every where occuring, "that were a man to recount them all," as [c] St Jerom expresses it, "he would be obliged not only "to write one, but many books;" "nor need we seek for "distant examples of this kind," [d] says Bochart, "since "this very genealogy is all full of anachronisms, vastly dif- "ferent both from the Hebrew and the vulgar version."

The arguments for and against the LXX computation.

Editions moreover there were of an ancient date, which in imitation of the Alexandrian manuscript, preserved by Origen in his Hexapla, had none of this insertion. Both Philo and Josephus, though they make use of the Septuagint version, know nothing of Cainan; Eusebius and Africanus, though they took their accounts of these times from it, have no such person among their postdiluvians; and therefore [e] it is highly reasonable to believe, that this name crept into the Septuagint through the carelessness of some transcriber, who, inattentive to what he was about, inserted an antediluvian name (for such a person there was before the flood) among the postdiluvians; and having no numbers for his name, wrote the numbers belonging to Salah twice over.

Since therefore, the Hebrew text, in all places where we find Noah's posterity enumerated, takes not the least notice of Cainan, but always declares Salah to be the immediate son and successor of Arphaxad; [f] we must either say, that Moses did, or that he did not know of the birth of this pretended patriarch: if he did not, how came the LXX interpreters by the knowledge of what Moses, who lived much nearer the time, was a diligent searcher into

[b] Chap. iii. 36.   [c] On Jeramiah xvii.   [d] Phaleg. l. 2. c. 2.
[e] Heidgger's hist. patriar. vol. 2. exer. 1.   [f] Shuckford's Connection, vol. 1. l. 2.

A M 1957, &c.
Ant. Chrif. 2007, &c.
from Gen. x. to the end; and from chap. xi. ver. 10. to the end.

into antiquity, and had the affiftance of a divine fpirit in every thing he wrote, was confeffedly ignorant of? If he did know it, what poffible reafon can be affigned for his concealing it, efpecially when his infertion or omiffion of it makes fuch a remarkable variation in the account of time from the flood to the call of Abraham; unlefs he was minded to impofe upon us by a falfe or confufed chronology, which his diftinct obfervation of the feries of the other generations, and his juft affignment of the time which belonged to each, will not fuffer us to think?

Rather therefore than impeach, this fervant of God, (who has this teftimony upon record, that [g] *he was faithful in all his houfe*,) either of ignorance or ill-intent, we may affirm (with Bochart and his followers) that St Luke, never put Cainan into his genealogy, (for as much as † it is not to be found in fome of the beft manufcripts of the New Teftament,) but that fome tranfcriber finding it in the Septuagint, and not in St Luke, marked it down in the margin of their copies, as an omiffion in the copies of St Luke, and fo later copies and editors finding it thus in the margin, took it at laft into the body of the text, as thinking perhaps that this augmentation of years might give a greater fcope to the rife of kingdoms, which otherwife might be thought too fudden: whereas (if we will believe a very competent judge of this matter) "[h] Thofe who "contend for the numbers of the Septuagint moft ei-"ther reject (as fome do) the concurrent teftimony of "the Heathen Greeks and the Chriftian fathers concern-"ing the ancient kingdoms of Affyria and Egypt, or muft "remove all thefe monarchies farther from the flood. "Nor muft the teftimony of Varro be overlooked, which "tells us, that there were but 1600 years between the firft "flood and the Olympiads; whereas this number is ex-"ceeded feven or eight hundred years by the Septuagint's "account. Thefe, and feveral other confiderations, (fays "he) incline me to the Hebrew numbers of the patriarchs "generating, rather than to the Seventy's; becaufe, by "the numbers of the Seventy, there muft be about 900 "years between the flood and the firft year of Ninus "which

[g] Heb. iii. 2.

† The ancient manufcripts of the gofpels and Acts, both in Greek and Latin, which Beza prefented to the univerfity of Cambridge, wants it: nor is it to be found in fome manufcripts which Archbifhop Ufher, in his Chron. Sacr. p. 32. makes mention of; *Millar's Hiftory of the Church*, ch. 1. period 2.

[h] Bifhop Cumberland's Origin antiquif. p. 177, &c.

Chap. III.   *from the Flood to the Call of Abraham.*   345

"which certainly is too much distance between a grand- "father and a grandchild's beginning to reign.

Thus it seems reasonable to suppose, that the interpolation of the name of Cainan in the LXX's version might be the work of some ignorant and pragmatical transcriber: and in like manner, the addition and subtraction of several hundred years in the lives of the fathers before mentioned might be effected by such another instrument, who thinking perhaps, that the years of the antediluvian lives were but lunar ones, and computing, that at this rate the six fathers (whose lives are thus altered) must have had their children at 5, 6, 7, 8, years old, (which could not but look incredible,) might be induced to add the 100 years, in order to make them of a more probable age of manhood at the birth of their respective children. Or, if he thought the years of their lives to be solar, yet still he might imagine that infancy and childhood were proportionably longer in men who were to live 7, 8, or 900 years, than they are in us; and that it was too early in their lives for them to be fathers at 60, 70, or 80 years of age; for which reason he might add the 100 years to make their advance to manhood (which is commonly not till one fourth part of our days is near over) proportionable to what was to be the ultimate term of their lives.

A. M. 1759, &c. Ant. Chrif. 2245 &c. from Gen. x. to the end; and from chap. xi. ver. 10. to the end.

This seems to be the only method of reconciling the difference between the LXX version and the Hebrew text, in point of chronology; and now to proceed to what we find recorded in profane history during this period.

After the dispersion of nations, the only form of government that was in use for some time was paternal, when fathers of nations were as kings, and the eldest of families as princes. But as mankind increased, and their ambition grew higher, the dominion which was founded in nature gave place to that which was acquired and established by power.

The profane history during this period.

In early ages, a superiority of strength or stature was the most engaging qualifications to raise men to be kings and rulers. The Ethiopians [k] as Aristotle informs us, made choice of the tallest persons to be their princes; and though Saul was made king of Israel by the special appointment of God, yet it appears to have been a circumstance not inconsiderable in the eyes of the people, [l] that *he was a choice*

The erection of kingdoms.

---

[i] Shuckford's Connection, vol. i. lib. 5. ex Lud. Capell. Chron. sacra. in apparatu Walton ad Bibl. Polyglot.
[k] De Repub. l. 4. c. 4.   [l] 1 Sam. ix. 2.

choice young man, and goodly; and that there was not among the children of Israel a goodlier man than he. But when experience came to convince men, that other qualifications, besides stature and strength, were necessary for the people's happiness, they then chose persons of the greatest wisdom and prudence for their governors. ᵐ Some wise and understanding man, who knew best how to till and cultivate the ground, to manage cattle, to prune and plant fruit-trees, &c. took into their families, and promised to provide for such as would become their servants, and submit to their directions. And thus, in continuance of time, heads of families became kings; their houses, together with the near habitations of their domestics, became cities; their servants, in their several occupations and employments, became wealthy and considerable subjects; and the inspectors and overseers of them became ministers of state, and managers of the public affairs of the kingdom.

In the first beginning of political societies, almost every town (as we may suppose) had its own king, ⁿ who, more attentive to preserve his dominions than to extend them, restrained his ambition within the bounds of his native country; till disputes with neighbours, (which were sometimes unavoidable,) jealousy of a more powerful prince, an enterprizing genius or martial inclination, occasioned those wars which often ended in the absolute subjection of the vanquished, whose possessions falling into the power of the conqueror, enlarged his dominions, and both encouraged and enabled him to push on his conquests by new enterprizes.

The reign of Nimrod. Nimrod was the first man we meet with in Scripture who made invasions upon the territories of others: for he dispossessed Ashur, the son of Shem, who had settled himself in Shinar, and obliged him to remove into Assyria, whilst himself seized on Babylon, and having repaired, and not a little enlarged it, made it the capital of his kingdom.

A description of Babylon. ᵒ This city was situate on both sides of the river Euphrates, having streets running from north to south, parallel with the river, and others from east to west. † The compass

---

ᵐ Shuckford's Connection, vol. ii l. 6.   ⁿ Justin, l. 1. c. 1.
ᵒ Prideaux's Connection.

† It must be observed however, that all this compass of ground was not really built upon; for the houses stood at a considerable distance, with gardens and fields interspersed; so that it was a large city in scheme, rather than in reality; *Prideaux's Connection part* 1. *l.* 2.

Chap. III.   *from the Flood to the Call of Abraham.*   347

compass of the wall, which was surrounded with a vast ditch filled with water, was 480 furlongs, *i. e.* about 60 miles; the height of it 350 feet, and the breadth so vastly great, that carts and carriages might meet on the top of it, and pass one another without danger. Over the Euphrates (which cut the city into two equal parts from north to south) there was a stately bridge; and at each end of the bridge † a magnificent palace, the one of 4, and the other of 8 miles circumference: and belonging to the larger palace were those hanging gardens, which had so celebrated a name among the Greeks. They were made in form of a square of 400 foot on every side, and were carried up aloft into the air in the manner of several large terrasses, one above another, till they came up to the height of the walls of the city. They were sustained by vast arches built upon arches, one above another, and strengthened by a wall on every side that was 22 feet thick; and as they wanted no plants or flowers fit for a garden of pleasure, so there are said to have grown in them trees, which were no less than eight cubits thick in the body, and 50 feet in height. But this, among other pompous things appertaining to this city, was the work of ages subsequent to Nimrod, and built by Nebuchadnezzar, to gratify his wife Amytis, who being the daughter of Astyages, king of Media, and much pleased with the mountainous and woody parts of her own country, was desirous of having something like it in Babylon.

From the Assyrians this great and noble city came into the hands of the Persians, and from them into the hands of the Macedonians. Here it was that Alexander the Great died: but not long after his death, the city began to decline apace, by the building of Seleucia, about forty miles above it, by Seleucus Nicanor, who is said to have erected this new city in spleen to the Babylonians, and to have drawn out of Babylon 500,000 persons to people it; so that the ancient city was, in the time of Curtius the historian, lessened a fourth part; in the time of Pliny, reduced to desolation; in the days of St Jerom turned into a park, wherein the kings of Persia did use to hunt; and according

A. M. 1997, &c. Ant. Chrisf. 2007, &c. from Gen. x. to the end; and from chap. xi. ver. 10. the end.

---

† The old palace (which was probably built by Nimrod) stood on the east-side of the river, and the new one (which was built by Nebuchadnezzar) exactly over-against it, on the west-side; *Prideaux*, ibid.

A. M. 1997, &c. Ant. Chri. 2067, &c. from Gen. x. to the end; and from chap xi. ver. 10 to the end.

ing to the relation * of some late travellers, is now reduced to one tower only, called *the tower of Daniel*, from whence may be seen all the ruins of this once vast and splendid city.

It can hardly be imagined, that the first kings were able, either to make or execute laws with that strictness and rigour, which is necessary in a body of men, so large as to afford numerous offenders: and for this reason it seems to have been a prudent institution in Nimrod, when his city of Babylon began to be too populous to be regulated by his inspection, or governed by his influence, to † lay

* Mr Reuwolf, who in 1574 passed through the place where this once famous city stood, speaks of the ruins of it in the following manner. 'The village of Elugo (says he) is now si-
' tuate where heretofore Babylon of Chaldea stood. The har-
' bour, where people go ashore, in order to proceed by land to
' the city of Bagdad, is a quarter of a league distant from it
' The soil is so dry and barren, that they cannot till it; and
' so naked, that I could never have believed that this powerful
' city, once the most stately and renowned in all the world,
' and situated in the fruitful country of Shinar, could have stood
' there, had I not seen, by the situation of the place, by many
' antiquities of great beauty, which are to be seen round about,
' and especially by the old bridge over the Euphrates, where
' of some piles and arches of incredible strength are still re-
' maining, that it certainly did stand there.—The whole front
' of the village Elugo is the hill upon which the castle stood, and
' the ruins of its fortifications are still visible, though demolish-
' ed. Behind, and some little way beyond, is the tower of Ba-
' bylon, which is half a league diameter, but so ruinous, so
' low, and so full of venomous creatures, which lodge in the
' holes they make in the rubbish, that no one durst approach
' nearer to it than within half a league, except during two
' months in the winter, when these animals never stir out of
' their holes;' *Calmet's Dictionary.*

† The cities which he founded are said to be Erec, Accad, and Calne. Erec was the same that occurs in Ptolemy. under the name of *Arecca*, and which is placed by him at the last, or most southern turning of the common channel of the Tigris and Euphrates. Accad lay northward of Erec, and very probably at the common joining of the Tigris and Euphrates. And Calne (which is said to be the same with Ctesiphon) upon the Tygris, about three miles distant from Seleucia, and was for some time the capital city of the Parthians: for that it was the same with Ctesiphon, seems to be confirmed by the country, which lies about it, being *Chalonitis*, which is evidently derived from

A Plan of the CITY of BABYLON.

Chap. III.   *from the Flood to the Call of Abraham.*   349

lay the foundations of other cities; by which means he dif-   A M
posed of great numbers of his people, and, putting them   1997, &c.
under the direction of such deputies as he might appoint,   Ant Christ.
brought their minds by degrees to a sense of government,   1007, &c.
until the beneficial use of it came to be experienced, and   from Gen.
the force and power of laws settled and confirmed. He is   x. to the
supposed to have begun his reign A. M. 1757, to have   end; and
reigned about 148 years, and to have died A. M. 1905.   from hip.
     About the beginning of Nimrod's reign, Ashur, * one   xi ver. 10.
of the descendents of Shem, being driven from Babel (as   to the end.
most suppose) by the invasion of Nimrod, led his company   Of Ashur.
on the Tygris, and so, settling in Assyria, laid the first foundation of Nineveh, which, in process of time, equalled   A descrip-
even Babylon itself in bigness. For, whereas we observed   tion of Ni-
of Babylon, that it was in circuit 480 furlongs, ᵖ the de-   neveh.
scription which Diodorus gives us of Nineveh, is, that it
was 150 furlongs, *i. e.* near 19 miles in length; 90 furlongs, *i. e.* somewhat above 11 miles in breadth; and 480
furlongs, *i. e.* just 60 miles in circumference; and for this
reason

from *Chalne,* or *Chalno,* whereby we find it called in different
parts of Scripture; *Wells's Geography, vol* 1. *c.* 5.
     * Many authors have imagined that Nineveh was not built
by Ashur, but by Nimrod himself, because they think it not
likely that Moses should give an account of the settlement of
one of the sons of Shem, where he is expressly discoursing of
Ham's family; and therefore they interpret (as the marginal
note directs) Gen. x. 11. *Out of that land went forth Ashur,* he, *i. e.*
Nimrod, went forth into Assyria, which is the explanation that
I have in some measure followed. But others imagine, that
Moses is not so exactly methodical, but that upon mentioning
Nimrod and his people, he might hint at a colony which departed from under his government, though it happened to be
led by a person of another family: That the land of Ashur
and the land of Nimrod are mentioned as two distinct countries
in Micah v. 6.; and that if Nimrod had built Nineveh, and
planted Assyria, Babylon and Assyria would have been but one
empire, nor could the one be said to have conquered the other
with any propriety: whereas we are expressly told by Diodorus, that the Assyrians conquered the Babylonians; and may
thence infer, that before Ninus united them, Babylonia and
Assyria were two distinct kingdoms, and not the plantation of
one and the same founder; *Shuckford's Connection, vol.* 1. *l.* 4.

     ᵖ Wells's Geography.

reason it is ^q called *an exceeding great city of three days journey*, according to the common estimation of 20 miles to a day's journey. And equal to the greatness was the strength of this city: for its walls were 100 feet high, and so very broad, that three carts might go a-breast on the top of them; whereon were raised 1500 turrets, and each of them 200 feet high, and so very strong, that the place was deemed inpregnable, ^r till Nabopollasar, king of Babylon, having made an affinity with Astyages king of Media, entered into a confederacy with him against the Assyrians, and hereupon joining their forces together, they besieged Nineveh, and after having taken the place, and slain the king thereof, to gratify the Medes, they utterly destroyed that ancient city, and from that time Babylon became the metropolis of the Assyrian empire.

Such was the rise and fall of this great city, where Ashur governed his subjects much in the same manner as Nimrod did his in Babylon: For as they increased, he dispersed them in the country, and, † having built some other cities

Margin: A. M. 1997, &c. Ant. Christ. 2007, &c. from Gen. x. to the end; and from chap. xi. ver. 10. to the end.

---

^q Jonah, iii. 3.   ^r Prideaux's Connection, vol. 1.

† The cities which Ashur is said to have built, were Rehoboth, Resen, and Calah. The word *Rehoboth*, in the Hebrew tongue signifies *streets*, and the sacred historian seems to have added the word *city*, on purpose to shew that it was here to be taken as a proper name. Now, as there are no footsteps of this name in these parts, but a town there is, by Ptolemy called *Birtha*, which in the Chaldee tongue denotes the same as does Rehoboth in the Hebrew, in an appellative or common acceptation; it is hence probably conjectured, that Rehoboth and Birtha are only two different names of one and the the same city, which was seated on the Tigris, about the mouth of the river Lycus. Resen is supposed, by most learned men, to be the same city which Xenophon mentions under the name of *Larissa*, and that, not only because the situation of this Larissa well enough agrees with the situation of Resen, as it is described by Moses lying between Nineveh and Calah; but because Moses observes, in the same text, that *Resen was a great city;* in like manner, as Xenophon tells us that Larissa, tho' then ruinated, had been a large city of eight miles circumference, with walls 100 feet high, and 25 feet broad. And whereas Larissa is a Greek name, and in the days of Xenophon there were no Greek cities in Assyria; for this they account, by supposing, that when the Greeks might ask What city those were the ruins of; the Assyrians might answer, Laresen, or of Resen, which Xenophon expressed by Larissa,

Chap. III.   *from the Flood to the Call of Abraham.*   351

cities along the Tigris, he there settled them under the government of deputies or viceroys.

Whilst Nimrod and Ashur were settling their people in their respective countries, Mizraim, the second son of Ham, * and who, by Heathen writers, is constantly called *Menes* seated himself at first near the entrance of Egypt, and there perhaps built the city of Zoan, which was anciently the habitation of the kings of Egypt; but from Zoan he removed farther into the country, and took possession of those parts which were afterwards called *Theibais*, where he built the city of Thebes, and (as Herodotus will have it) the city of Memphis likewise. He reigned 62 years and died A. M. 1943.

Belus succeeded Nimrod, and was the second king of Babylon; but whether he was related to his predecessor or not, is a thing uncertain. It seems most likely, that as Nimrod, though a young man in comparison of many then alive, was advanced, for some merit or other, to the regal dignity: so when he died, Belus might appear to be the most proper person, and for that reason was appointed to succeed him: for he is represented as a prince of study, the inventor of the Chaldean astronomy, and one who spent his time in cultivating his country, and improving his people. He reigned 60 years, and died A. M. 1969.

Ashur, king of Nineveh, dying much about this time, Ninus became the second king of Assyria, and proved a man of an ambitious and enterprizing spirit. Babylonia lay

Marginal notes: A M 1997, &c. Ant. Chrif. 2007, &c. from Gen. x. 10 to the end; and from chap. xi. ver. 10. to the end. Of Menes. Of Belus.

Larissa, a name not unlike several cities in Greece. And lastly, as to Calah, or Calach, since we find in Strabo a country, about the head of the river Lycus, called *Calachene*, it is very probable that the said country took this name from Calach, which was one of the capital cities of it. Ptolemy makes mention likewise of a country called *Calacine* in these parts: And whereas Pliny mentions a people called *Classitæ*, through whose country the Lycus runs, there is some reason to suppose. that Classitæ is a corruption of Calachitæ; *Wells's Geography, vol.* 1.

* The person whom Moses calls *Mizraim*, is, by Diodorus, and other Heathen writers, commonly celled *Menes*; by Syncellus, *Mestraim*. Menes is supposed to be the first king of Egypt by Herodotus, l. 2.; by Diodorus, l. 1.; by Eratosthenes and Africanus from Manetho; by Eusebius and Syncellus in Chro. Eufeb.; and the time of Menes coincides very well with that of Moses's Mizraim, as Sir John Marsham [in his Can. Chron. p. 2.] has pretty clearly evinced; *Shuckford's Connection, vol.* 1. l. 4.

A. M. 1997, &c.
Ant. Chrif. 2007, &c.
from Gen. x. to the end; and from chap. xi. ver. 10. to the end.

lay too near him, not to become the object of his desire; and therefore, making all military preparations for that purpose, he invaded it; and as its inhabitants had no great skill in war, soon vanquished them, and laid them under tribute. His success in this attempt made him begin to think of subjecting other nations: and as one conquest paved the way for another, in a few years, he over-ran many of the infant states of Asia, and so by uniting kingdom to kingdom, made a great accession to the Assyrian empire. His last attempt was upon Oxyartes, or Zoroastres, King of Bactria, where he met with a brisker opposition than he had hitherto experienced; but at length, by the contrivance and conduct of Semiramis, the wife of one Memnon, a captain in his army, he took the capital, and reduced the kingdom: but being hereupon charmed with the spirit and bravery of the woman, he fell in love with her, and prevailed with her husband (by giving him his own daughter in lieu of Semiramis in marriage) to consent to his having her for his wife. By her he had a son named Ninyas; and after a reign of 52 years, he died A. M. 2017.

Ninyas was but a minor when his father died; and therefore his mother, who all along had a great sway in the administration of public affairs during her husband's lifetime, continued in the government with the † consent and approbation of her subjects. She removed her court from Nineveh to Babylon, which she encompassed with the wall we mentioned before, and adorned with many public and magnificent buildings; and having thus finished the

† Justin in his history of this woman, informs us, that upon the death of her husband, she made use of the stratagem of personating her son, to obtain the empire to herself: but Diodorus, with more probability, ascribes her advancement to her conduct, bravery, and magnanimous behaviour. When she took upon her to be Queen, the public affairs were put in the hands, to which Ninus when alive, used generally to commit them; and it is not likely that the people should be uneasy at her governing, who had, for several years together, by a series of actions, gained herself a great credit and ascendant over them; especially if we consider, that when she took up the sovereignty, she still pressed foreward in a course of actions which continually exceeded the expectations of her people, and left no room for any to be willing to dispute her authority; *Shuckford's Connection*, vol. 1. l. 4.

Chap. III.   *from the Flood to the Call of Abraham.*   353

the seat of her empire, and settled all the neighbouring kingdoms under her authority, she raised an army, with an intent to conquer India; but after a long and dangerous war, being tired out with defeats, she was obliged, with the small remainder of her forces, to return home; where, finding herself in disgrace with her people, she resigned the crown and authority to her son, after she had reigned 42 years; and soon after died, A. M. 2059.

<small>A M 1997. &c. Ant. Chrif. 2067. &c. from Gen. x. to the end; and from chap. xi. ver. 10. to the end.</small>

Her son Ninyas began his reign, full of a sense of the errors of his mother's administration, and engaged in none of the wars and dangerous expeditions, wherein she had harrassed and fatigued her people: but though he was not ambitious to enlarge his empire, ⁵ yet he took all due care to regulate, and settle, upon a good foundation, the extensive dominions which his parents had left him. By a wise contrivance of annual deputies over his provinces, he prevented many revolts of distant countries, which might otherwise have happened; and his taking up that state of being difficult of access, (which was afterwards much improved by eastern monarchs,) might perhaps procure him a greater veneration from his subjects. However this be, it is certain, that most authors have represented him as a weak and effeminate prince, which might naturally arise (without any other foundation) from his succeeding a father and mother, who were rather too active to enlarge their dominions, as well as from the disposition in most writers, to think a turbulent and warlike reign, if victorious, a glorious one, and to overlook an administration, that is employed in the silent, but more happy arts of peace and good government.

<small>Ninyas.</small>

In Egypt, Mizraim, after his death, had three sons, who became the kings of the several parts thereof. Ananim, or rather Anan, was king of the Lower Egypt, or Delta; Naphtuhim, or Naph, of Middle Egypt, or the country about Memphis; and Pathrusim, or Patrus, of the Upper Egypt, or the country of Thebais: and agreeably hereunto, from these three kings did these several countries take their ancient denominations. Of the first of these, *viz.* Ananim, we have nothing remaining but only his name and the time of his death: for after he had reigned 63 years, according to Syncellus, he died A. M. 2006.

<small>The kings of Egypt.</small>

Of

⁵ Diodorus Siculus, l. 2.

A M 1997, &c.
Ant. Chrif. 2007, &c.
from Gen. 3. to the end; and from chap. xi. ver. 10. to the end.

Of the second, viz. Naphtuhim, we are told, that he was the author of the architecture of these ages; had some useful knowledge of physic and anatomy; and taught his subjects (as he learned it from his brother Pathrusium) the use of letters: for to this Pathrusium, (whom they call *Thyoth*,) the Egyptians indeed ascribe the invention of all arts and sciences whatever. The Greeks called him *Hermes*, and Latins *Mercurius*; and while his father Mizraim lived, he is supposed to have been his secretary, and greatly assistant to him in all his undertakings. When his father died, he instructed his brothers in all the knowledge he was master of; and as for his own people, he made wholesome laws for their government, settled their religion and form of worship, and enriched their language by the addition of several words, to express several things which before they had no names for.

This is the best account that we can give of the Babylonian or Assyrian empires, and of the kings that ruled Egypt, for some ages next after the dispersion of mankind. Other nations, no doubt, were settled into regular governments in these times: Canaan was inhabited rather sooner than Egypt; and ᵗ according to Moses, Hebron, in Canaan, was built seven years before Zoan in Egypt; but as none of these nations made any considerable figure in the first ages, their actions lie in obscurity, and must be buried in oblivion. The few men of extraordinary note, that were then in the world, lived in Egypt and Assyria; and for this reason, we find little or no mention of any other countries, until one of these two nations came to send out colonies, which by degrees polished the people they travelled to, and instructed them in such arts and sciences, as made them appear with credit in their own age, and (as soon as the use of letters was made public) transmitted their names with honour to posterity.

The use and invention of letters.

The knowledge of letters cannot have been of any long standing among us Europeans, who are settled far from the first seats of mankind, and far from the places which the descendents of Noah first planted. "None of the "ancient Thracians." "says Ælian, "knew any thing of "letters: nay, the Europeans in general, thought it disreputable to learn them, though in Asia they were held "in greater request." The Goths, according to the express

ᵗ Numb. xiii. 22.   ᵘ Universal history, l. 8, c, 6.

Chap. III.   *from the Flood to the Call of Abraham.*   353

press testimony [x] of Socrates, had their letters and writings from Ulphila, their bishop, *anno Dom.* 370. The Sclavonians received theirs from Methodius, a philosopher, about *an. Dom.* 856. The people of Dalmatia had theirs not till St Jerom's, and those of Illyria, not till St Cyril's days.

The Latins (who were more early) received their letters (as most authors agree) from the Greeks, and were taught the use of them, either from some of the followers of Pelasgus, who came into Italy about a hundred and fifty-eight years after that Cadmus came into Greece, or from the Arcadians whom Evander led into those parts, about sixty years after Pelasgus.

Among the Greeks, the Ionians were the first who had any knowledge of letters; and they, in all probability, had them from the Phœnicians, who were the followers of Cadmus, when he came into Greece; but from whom the Phœnicians had them, has been matter of some dispute. Many considerable writers have derived them directly from Egypt, and are generally agreed, that Thyoth, or Mercury, was the inventor of them. In the early ages, when mankind were but few, and these few employed in the several contrivances for life, it could be but here and there one that had leisure, or perhaps inclination, to study letters. The companies that removed from Babel, were most of them rude and uncultivated people: they followed some persons of figure and eminence, who had gained an ascendent over them; and these persons, when they had settled them in distant places, and came to teach them such arts as they were masters of, had every thing they taught them imputed to their own invention, because the poor ignorant people knew no other person that was versed and skilled in them.

Though therefore the Egyptians had confessedly the use of letters very early among them; and though their Thyoth, or Mercury, might be the first who taught others their use, and for that reason be reputed the inventor of them; yet I cannot but think, that Noah and his sons, who had learned them in the old world, taught them to their posterity in the new. For since mankind subsisted 1600 years before the flood, it is not very probable, that they lived all this while without the use of letters. If they did, how came we by the short annals which we have of the antediluvian ages?
But

A M 1997, &c.
Ant. Chrif.
107, &c.
from Gen.
x. to the
end; and
from chap.
xi. ver. 10.
to the end.

[x] Hist. Ecclef. l. 4. c. 33.

A M 1997, &c. Ant. Chrif. 2007, &c. from Gen. x. to the end; and from chap. xi. ver. 10. to the end.

But if they did not, it is not unlikely, that Noah, being well skilled in the knowledge and use of them, might teach them to his children: and if we pursue the enquiry, and ask from whence Noah attained his knowledge, the most proper reply will be, that he had it from the instruction of his parents, as his parents might have it, in their several successions from Adam, and as Adam might have it from God.

Which was originally from God.

And indeed, if we consider the nature of letters, it cannot but appear something strange, that an invention so surprising as that of writing is, should be found out in an age so near the beginning of the world. [y] Nature may easily be supposed to have prompted men to speak, to try to express their minds to one another by sounds and noises; but that the wit of man should, among its first attempts, find out a way to express words in figures or letters, and to form a method, by which they might expose to view all that can be said or thought, and that within the compass of 16, 20, or 24 characters, variously placed, so as to form syllables and words; that the wit of man, I say, could immediately and directly fall upon a project of this nature, is what exceeds the most exalted notions we can possibly form of his capacity; and must therefore remit us to God (in whom are hid all the treasures of infinite wisdom) for the first invention and contrivance of it.

The learning arts and commerce.

As soon as the use of letters, whether of divine or human invention, came generally to be known, it is reasonable to think, that all arts and sciences would from thence receive a powerful assistance, and in process of time begin to take root, and flourish; but this was a period a little too early to bring them to any great perfection. [z] For though Noah and his sons had doubtless some knowledge of the inventions of the antediluvians, and probably acquainted their descendants with such of them as were most obvious and useful in common life; yet it cannot be imagined, that any of the more curious arts, or speculative sciences, were improved to any degree (supposing them to be known and invented) till some considerable time after the dispersion. On the contrary, one consequence of that event seems to have been this —— that several inventions, known to their ancestors, were lost, and mankind gradually degenerated into ignorance and barbarity, till ease and plenty had given them

[y] Shuckford's Connection, vol. i. l. 4. [z] Universal history, l. 1. c. 2.

them leisure to polish their manners, and to apply themselves to such parts of knowledge as are seldom brought to perfection under other circumstances.

The inhabitants of Babylon indeed are supposed to have had a great knowledge in astronomical matters, much about this time; [a] for when Alexander the great took possession of that city, Calisthenes the philosopher, who accompanied him, upon searching into the treasures of the Babylonian learning, found that the Chaldeans had a series of observations for 1903 years backwards from that time; *i. e.* from the 1771st year of the world's creation forwards. But this is a notion that we have already confuted; as indeed the nature of a thing will teach us, that upon the first settlement in any country, a nation could not but find employment enough (at least for some ages) in cultivating their lands and providing themselves houses and other necessaries, for their mutual comfort and subsistence.

Ninus and Semiramis are supposed to have improved vastly the arts of war and navigation about this period: for * we read of armies, consisting of some millions of horse

A M 1997, &c.
Ant. Chris. 2007, &c.
from Gen. 1. to the end; and from chap. xi. ver. 10. to the end.

---

[a] Simplicius de Cœlo. l. 2. com. 46.

* The history of the Assyrian empire, as we have it in Diodorus Siculus, l. 2. c. 1.—22. and in Justin, l. 1. c. 1, 2. is, in the substance of it, to this effect—The first who extended this empire, was Ninus, who being a warlike prince, and desiring to do great things, gathered together the stoutest men in the country, and, having trained them up in the use of arms, entered into an alliance with Ariæus King of Arabia, by whose assistance he subdued the Babylonians, and imposed a tribute on them, after he had taken their King captive, and killed him, with his children. Then having entered Armenia with a great army, and destroyed several cities, he so terrified the rest, that King Barzanes submitted to him. After this, he vanquished Pharnus King of Media in battle; crucified him and his wife, and seven children; and, in the space of seventeen years, overcame all Asia, except India and Bactria; but no author declares the particulars of his victories. Of the maritime provinces, he subdued, according to Ctesias, whom we follow, (says Diodorus) Egypt, Phœnicia, the Lower Syria, Cilicia, Pamphylia, Lycia; and besides these, Caria, and Phrygias, Lydia, Mysia, Troas, together with the Propontis, Bithynia, Cappadocia, and all the barbarous nations, as far as the Tanais; with Persia, Susiana, Caspiana, and many other nations that we need not here enumerate. From this last expedition, as soon as he returned, he built a city, which he called by his own name, *Ninus*, not far from the river Euphrates; and being afterwards enamoured with the beau-

horse and foot; and of fleets, and gallies, with brazen beaks, to transport the forces over a river only, to the number of two thousand; but all that narration of Diodorus and Justin, as it is acknowledged to be taken from Ctesias, (whom † all the best critics of antiquity look upon as an authority and valour of a woman of uncertain birth, named *Semiramis*, he took her to wife, and by her advice and direction governed all things with success. For, having gathered together an army of seventeen hundred thousand foot, and two hundred and ten thousand horse, and six hundred thousand chariots, (numbers incredible in those days!) with these he advanced against Oxyartes, king of Bactria, who met him with an army of four hundred thousand men: but the Bactrians being defeated, and their capital, by the valour and direction of Semiramis, taken, she was thereupon advanced to the honour of being made queen, which occasioned her husband to hang himself. After Ninus had thus settled his affairs in Bactria, his wife Semiramis had a son (whom he named Ninyas) and not long after died, leaving the administration of the kingdom in his wife's hands; who, to raise her own glory, built a stately monument for her deceased husband; built the city of Babylon, and other remarkable places; and then, having brought Egypt, Ethiopia, and Lybia, all the way to the temple of Jupiter Hammon, under her jurisdiction, returned into Asia; where she had not been long, before hearing that Stabrobates, or Staurobates, King of India, governed a rich country, she resolved to take it from him. To this purpose she prepared a great army and fleet: but being told what mighty elephants there were in India, in order to have something like them, she caused three hundred thousand hides of oxen to be dressed, and stuffed with straw, under which there was a camel to bear the machine, and a man to guide it, which at a distance made a kind of resemblance of these vast creatures. Her army consisted of three millions of foot, one million of horse, and an hundred thousand chariots; of an hundred thousand of those that fought on camels; of two hundred thousand camels for the baggage: and two thousand gallies, with brasen heads, to transport her army over the river Indus.—But all this must be false and fabulous; because it is incredible to think either that her own country should supply, or the country whereinto she was marching, should be able to sustain such an immense number of men, and other creatures, as are here related: besides that, it is false in fact, that the kings of Assyria ever governed all Asia, or stretched their conquests over Egypt and Lybia; *Miller's history of the church, chap.* 1. *part* 3.

† This Ctesias was a native of Cnidus, and physician to Artaxerxes Mnemnon. He wrote a Persian history in three and twenty books, of which there remain only a few fragments, preserved

author deferving no credit,) may very juftly be accounted falfe and fabulous. And though it cannot be denied, that the invention of fhipping, which was not before the flood, (for had it been before, more than Noah and his family might have faved themfelves from the waters,) is a great ftep towards the improvement of commerce; yet as the difperfion of mankind made it more difficult to trade with nations who fpake a different language, fo the method whereinto we may fuppofe they entered at firft, extended no farther than this:——That the colonies, who planted new countries, not only perceiving their own wants, from the conveniences they had left behind them, but finding likewife fomething ufeful in their fettelments, which were before unknown to them or their founders, fetched what they wanted from the parts where they formerly dwelt, and, in exchange for that, carried what they had difcovered in their new plantations thither; and this feems to have given the firft rife to traffic and foreign trade, whofe gradual advances we may have occafion to take notice of hereafter. In the mean time, we fhall conclude this book, and this chapter together, with an account of the religion which at this time obtained in the moft famous nations of the world; and obferve withal, by what means it came to degenerate into idolatry, and other wicked and fuperftitious, practices.

A M 1997, &c. A Chrift. 2007, &c. from Gen x. to the end; and from chap. xi ver. 10. to the end.

Now, befides the common notion of a God, which men might either learn from tradition, or collect by their own reflection, the very hiftory of the deluge, which had not fo long ago befallen the world, could not but inftruct and confirm the generations we are now treating of in feveral articles of their religion. If they had the account of this remarkable judgement tranfmited to them in all its circumftances, they could not but entertain thefe conceptions of God:——That he takes cognizance of the things which are

The religion of the ancients.

ferved by Photius; but very valuable authors, who have feen Ctefias, when perfect, give him no commendable character. Plutarch (in Artaxerxes) calls him a fabulous vain man, and a great liar. A. Gellius (Noctes Atticæ, l.9. c. 4.) reckons him among the fabulous writers; and Ariftotle (in his Hiftoria animalium) fays, that he was an author who deferves no credit; as indeed, if we will judge either by the incredible things in his ftory, or by what he fays of the Indian and Perfian affairs, in his fragments that remain, we fhall have reafon to conclude, that thefe great men have not given him this character without good grounds; *Miller's Hiftory, ibid.*

are done here on earth; that he is a lover of virtue, and a severe punisher of vice; that he is infinite in power, by commanding the winds and rains, seas and elements, to execute his will; that he is likewise infinite in mercy, in forewarning the wicked of their ruin (as he did the old world) several years before its execution; and that therefore a being of such a nature and disposition was to be served, and worshipped, and feared and obeyed. So that the sum of religion, in the ages subsequent to the flood, even to the promulgation of the law, must have consisted in the belief of a God, and his sacred attributes; in the devout worship of him, by the oblation of prayers and praises, and such sacrifices as he himself had instituted; and in the observance of those eternal rules of righteousness, of justice and mercy, of sobriety and temperance, &c. which, if not expresly delivered to the sons of Noah, were nevertheless deducible from the nature of things, and the relations wherein mankind stood toward one another.

And now, if we look into the principal nations which were at this time ezisting, we shall find, that [b] the Persians, above all other people, were remarkable for having amongst them a true account of the creation of the world, and its destruction by water, which they strictly adhered to, and made the foundation of their religion; nor have we any reason to think, but that they were for some time very zealous professors of it, though by degrees they came to corrupt it, by introducing novelties, and fancies of their own, into both their faith and practice: We shall find, [c] that many of the Arabians preserved the true worship of God for several ages, whereof Job (who perhaps lived in the days now under consideration) was a memorable instance; as was likewise Jethro, the priest of Midian, in the days of Moses: we shall find, that the Canaanites of old were of the same religion with Abraham; for tho' he travelled up and down many years in their country, yet was he respected by the inhabitants of it, as a person in great favour with God; and Melchisedeck, the king of Salem, who was the priest of the most high God, and consequently of the same religion, received him with this address; [d] *Blessed be Abraham, servant of the most high God, possessor of heaven and earth:* we shall find, from Abimelech's prayer, upon his receiving intimation, that Sarah was Abraham's wife, that among the Philistines there were,

[b] Hyde's Relig. vet. Persarum c. 3. [c] Shuckford's Connection, vol. 1. l. 5. [d] Gen. xiv. 19.

were some true worshippers of the God of heaven; *Lord, Wilt thou slay a righteous nation? Said he not unto me, she is my sister; and she, even she herself, said, he is my brother: in the integrity of my heart, and innocency of my hands have I done this:* we shall find that the Egyptians allowed no mortal creature to be a god; professed to worship nothing but their god *Cneph*, ᶠ whom they affirmed to be without beginning, and without end; and though, in the mythologic times, ᵍ they represented this deity by the figure of a serpent, with the head of an hawk in the middle of a circle, yet they affirmed at the same time, that the God whom they thus represented, was the creator of all things, a being incorruptible and eternal, with several other attributes becoming the divine nature: In short, we shall find, that all the nations then known in the world, not only worshipped the same God, whom they called *the maker and creator of the universe*, but worshipped him likewise in the same form and manner; that they had all the like sacrifices, either expiatory, to make atonement for their sins; precatory, to obtain favours from Almighty God; propitiatory, to avert his judgments; or eucharistical, to return thanks for his extraordinary mercies; and that all these sacrifices were every-where offered upon altars, with some previous purifications, and other ceremonies to be observed by the offerer: So that religion, in every nation, for some time after the flood, both in principle and practice, was the same, till some busy and pragmatical heads, being minded to make some improvements, (as they thought,) added their own speculations to it, and so both destroyed its uniformity, and introduced its corruption.

A. M. 1597 &c. Ant Christ. 1007 &c. from Gen. x to the end; and from chap. xi ver 10. to the end.

When this corruption of religion was first introduced, is not so easy a matter to determine, because neither sacred nor profane history have taken any notice of it. Those ʰ who account idolatry one of the sins of the antediluvian world, suppose that Ham, being married into the wicked race of Lamech, retained a strong inclination for such a false worship; and that after he was cursed by his father Noah, and separated from the posterity of Shem, he soon set it up. Those ⁱ who imagine that the tower of Babel was a monument intended for the honour of the sun, which had dried up the waters from off the face of the

And idolatry of these times, when it began.

ᵉ Gen. xx 5.   ᶠ Plutarch de Iside et Osiride. p. 359.
ᵍ Eusebius's Præp. Evan. l. 1. c. 10.   ʰ Bedford's Scripture-chronology, l. 2. c. 6.   ⁱ *Vid.* Tennison of idolatry.

A M 1997, &c. Ant. Chrif. 2007, &c. from Gen. x. to the end; and from chap. xi. ver. 10 to the end.

the earth, muft fuppofe, that the worfhip of that planet began whilft the remembrance of the deluge was frefh in men's minds: but thofe [k] who are of opinion, that the difference of men's dialects, and the difference of their fentiments concerning God, might not improperly commence together, muft date the firft inftitution of idolatry not a great deal lower than the time of the difperfion.

[l] The generality of Chriftian fathers, as well as oriental writers, are pofitive in their affertions, that the firft appearance of idolatry was in the days of Serug: "Because, as Enoch, fay they, was the feventh from Adam, in whofe time the general impiety, before the flood, is faid to have begun; fo Serug, being in like manner the feventh from Noah, lived at a proper diftance for fuch a corruption of religious worfhip to be introduced, and grow." But this is a reafon too trifling to be taken notice of: nor can I fee (fays our learned Selden) [m] how they can be able to maintain their opinion, who determine fo peremptorily concerning a matter of fo diftant and uncertain a nature.

But whatever the date of idolatry might be, it is certain that it had its firft birth, not in Egypt, (as fome have maintained,) but in Chaldea, as the Moft Reverend author of the Treatife of Idolatry has evinced; [n] and that, becaufe in the days of Abraham we find all other nations and countries, adhering to the true account of the creation and deluge, and worfhipping the God of heaven, according to what had been revealed to them; whereas the Chaldeans had fo far departed from his worfhip, and were fo zealous in their errors and corruptions, that upon Abraham's family refufing to join with them, they expelled them their country, and [o] *caft them out from the face of their gods.*

Celeftial bodies the firft idols in every country.

The Chaldeans indeed, by reafon of the plain and eafy fituation of their country, which gave them a larger profpect of the heavenly bodies than thofe who inhabited mountainous places, had a great conveniency for aftronomical obfervations, and accordingly, were the firft people who took any great pains to improve them. And as they were

[k] Cyril. Alex. contra Julian. l. 1. [l] Heidegger's Hift. patriar. vol. ii. exer. 1. [m] De Diis Syris, proleg. 3. [n] Shuckford's Connection, vol. i. l. 5. [o] Judith v. 8.

were the first astrologers; [p] so learned men have observed, that lying on the ground, or else on flat roofs, all night, to make their observations, they fell in love with the lights of heaven, which, in the clear firmament of those countries, appeared so often, and with so much lustre; and perceiving the constant and regular order of their motions and revolutions, they thence began to imagine, that they were animated with some superior souls, and therefore deserved their adoration; and as the sun excelled all the rest, so the generality of learned men have, with good reason, imagined, that this bright luminary was the first idol in the world.

Among the Egyptians, [q] Syphis, king of Memphis, was the first who began to speculate upon such subjects. He examined what influence the sun and moon had upon the terrestrial globe; how they nourished and gave life and vigour to all things; and thereupon, forgetting what his ancestors had taught him, viz. *that in the beginning God created the heavens, as well as the earth*, the sun and moon, as well as the creatures of this lower world, he concluded, that they were two great and mighty deities, and accordingly, commanded them to be worshipped.

The Persians perhaps [r] were never so far corrupted, as to lose entirely the knowledge of the supreme God. They saw those celestial bodies running their courses, as they thought, day and night, over all the world, and reviving and invigorating all the parts and products of the earth; and though they kept themselves so far right, as not to mistake them for the true God, yet they imagined them to be his most glorious ministers; and not taking care to keep strictly to what their forefathers had taught them, they were led away by their own imaginations to appoint an idolatrous worship for beings that had been created, and by nature were not gods.

What kind of idolatry was current among the Canaanites, Moses sufficiently intimates in the caution he gives the Israelites, just going to take possession of it, viz. that [s] *when they lifted up their eyes to heaven, and saw the sun, and moon, and stars, even all the host of heaven*, they should not, as the inhabitants of the country were, be

A. M. 1991, &c. Ant. Chris. 2007, &c. from Gen. x. to the end; and from chap. xi. ver. 10. to the end.

---

[p] Tennison of idolatry. [q] Diodorus, l. 1. [r] Hyde's Relig. vet. Persarum, c. 1. [s] Deut. iv. 19.

A. M. 1957, &c.
Ant. Chrif 2007, &c.
from Gen x. to the end; and from chap. xi. ver. 10 to the end.

be driven to worship, and to serve them: and that this was the customary worship among the Arabians, the justification which Job makes of himself is a sufficient proof; ᵗ *If I beheld the sun when it shined, or the moon walking in brightness, and mine heart hath been secretly enticed, or my mouth hath kissed my hand,* i. e. if with devotion of soul, or profession of outward respect, I have worshipped those heavenly bodies, which, by their height, motion, and lustre, attract the eye, and ravish the senses, *this also were an iniquity to be punished by the judges; for then I should have denied the God that is above.* And therefore the account ᵘ which the Greek historian gives us of the origin of this kind of idolatry, is more than probable, *viz.* that the most ancient inhabitants of the earth (meaning those who lived not long after the flood, and particularly the Egyptians) contemplating on the world above them, and being astonished with high admiration at the nature of the universe, believed that there were two eternal gods, the sun and the moon; the former of which they called *Osiris*, and the latter *Isis*: since, of later years, upon the discovery of America, though many different idols were found in different places, yet as for the sun, it was the universal deity, both in Mexico and Peru.

Their great multiplicity of idols.

But whatever the first idol might be, it soon multiplied into such a prodigious number, as to fill both heaven and earth with its progeny; insomuch that there are not three parts of the creation, but what, in one nation or other, had their worshippers. ˣ They worshipped universal nature, the soul of the world, angels, devils, and the souls of men departed, either separate and alone, or in union with some star, or other body. They worshipped the heavens; and in them both particular luminaries and constellations; the atmosphere; and in it the meteors and fowls of the air; the earth, and in it beasts, birds, insects, plants, groves, and hills, together with divers fossils and terrestrial fire. They worshipped the water; and in it the sea and rivers; and in them fishes, serpents, and insects, together with such creatures as live in either element. They worshipped men, both living and dead; and in them the faculties and endowments of the

---

ᵗ Job xxxi. 26, 27. ᵘ Diodorus Siculus, l. 1.
ˣ Tennison of idolatry.

Chap. III. *from the Flood to the Call of Abraham.* 365

the soul, as well as the several accidents and conditions of the life. Nay, they worshipped the images of animals, even the most hateful, such as serpents, dragons, crocodiles, &c. and descended at last so low, as to pay a religious regard to things inanimate, herbs and plants, and the most stinking vegetables.

A M 1997, &c. Ant. Chrif. 2007, &c. from Gen. x. to the end; and from chap.

How men came to part with the religion of their ancestors for such trash, and ⁷ *to change the glory of the incorruptible God into the image of corruptible man, and birds, and four-footed beasts, and creeping things,* the Apostle, who remonstrates to the indignity, has in some measure supplied us with a reason, when he tells, that this state of things, how gross and strange soever it was, was introduced under the pretences of wisdom, or by men professing to be wise.

xi. ver. 10, to the end:

How the world came to fall into this state.

It was the wise amongst them that formed the design; and, addressing to the multitude, with a grave appearance, prevailed (as we may conceive) by some such form of arguing as this. ² "We are all aware, ye sons of Noah, "that religion is our chief concern; and therefore it well "becomes us to improve and advance it as much as pos- "sible. We have indeed received appointments from God "for the worship which he requires; but if these ap- "pointments may be altered for his greater glory, there is "no doubt but that it will be a commendable piety so to "alter them. Now our father Noah has instructed us in "a religion, which, in truth, is too simple, and too "unaffecting: It directs us to the worship of God, ab- "stractedly from all sense, and under a confused notion; "under the formality of attributes, as power, goodness, "justice, wisdom, eternity, and the like; an idea fo- "reign to our affections, as well as our comprehensions: "whereas, in all reason, we ought to worship God "more pompously, and more extensively, and not only to "adore his personal and essential attributes, but likewise "all the emanations of them, and all those creatures by "which they are eminently represented. Nor can this "be any derivation from his honour, since his honour is "certainly more amply expressed, when in this manner "we acknowledge, that not only himself, but all his crea- "tures likewise, are adorable. We ought therefore (if "we will be wise) to worship the host of heaven, be-

Vol. I. No. 5.   3 P   "cause

---

⁷ Rom. i. 22, 23.   ² Young's Sermons, vol. ii. sermon 1.

A. M. 1997, &c. Ant. Chrif. 2007, &c. from Gen. x. to the end; and from chap. xi. ver. 10. to the end.

"caufe they are eminent reprefentations of his glory and eternity: we ought to worfhip the elements, becaufe they reprefent his benignity and omniprefence: we ought to worfhip princes, becaufe they fuftain a divine character, and are the reprefentatives of his power upon earth: we ought to worfhip men famous in their generation, even when they are dead, becaufe their virtues are the diftinguifhing gifts and communications of God: nay, we ought to worfhip the ox and the fheep, and whatever creatures are moft beneficial, becaufe they are the fymbols of his love and goodnefs; and with no lefs reafon, the ferpent, the crocodile, and other animals that are noxious, becaufe they are the fymbols of his awful anger."

This feems to be a fair opening of the project; and by fome fuch cunning harangue as this, we may fuppofe it was that the firft contrivers of idolatry drew in the ignorant and admiring multitude. And indeed, confidering the natural habitude of vuglar minds, and the ftrong inclinations they have, in matters of an abftrufe confideration, to help themfelves by fenfible objects, it feems not fo difficult a tafk to have drawn them in.

The motives which engaged men in it.

Thofe who worfhipped univerfal nature, or the fyftem of the material world, perceived firft, that there was excellency in the feveral parts of it, and then (to make up the grandeur and perfection of the idea) they joined them altogether in one divine being. Thofe who laboured under a weaknefs and narrownefs of imagination, diftributed nature into its feveral parts, and worfhipped that portion of it which was accounted of moft general ufe and benefit. Ufefulnefs was the common motive, but it was not the only motive which inclined the world to idolatry: for, upon farther inquiry, we fhall find, that whatever ravifhed with its tranfcendent beauty, whatever affrightened with its malignant power, whatever aftonifhed with its uncommon greatnefs; whatever in fhort, was beautiful, hurtful, or majeftic, became a deity, as well as what was profitable for its ufe. ᵃ The fun, men foon perceived, had all thefe powers and properties united in it: its beauty was glorious to behold; its motion wonderful to confider; its heat occafioned different effects; barrennefs in fome places, and fruitfulnefs in others; and the immenfe globe of light appeared highly exalted, and riding in triumph, as it were, round the

ᵃ Tennifon of idolatry.

Chap. III. *from the Flood to the Call of Abraham.* 367

the world. The moon, they saw, supplied the absence of the sun by night; gave a friendly light to the earth; and, besides the great variety of its phases, had a wonderful influence over the sea, and other humid bodies. The stars they admired for their height and magnitude, the order of their positions, and celerity of their motions, and thence were persuaded, either that some celestial vigour or other resided in them, or that the souls of their heroes and great men were translated into them when they died; and upon these, and such like presumptions, they accounted all celestial bodies to be deities. [b] The force of fire, the serenity of air, the usefulness of water, as well as the terror and dreadfulness of thunder and lightening, gave rise to the consecration of the meteors and elements. The sea, swelling with its proud surface, and roaring with its mighty billows, was such an awful sight, and the earth, bedecked with all its plants, flowers, and fruits, such a lovely one as might well affect a Pagan's veneration; when for the like motives, *viz.* their beneficial, hurtful, delightful, or astonishing properties, beasts, birds, fishes, insects, and even vegetables themselves, came to be adored.

A. M.
1997, &c.
Ant. Chrif.
2007. &c.
from Gen.
x. to the
end; and
from chap.
xi. ver. 10.
to the end.

The pride and pomp of the great, and the low and abject spirits of the mean, occasioned first the flattery, and then the worship of kings and princes as gods upon earth. Men famous for their adventures and exploits, the founders of nations or cities, or the inventors of useful arts and sciences, were reverenced while they lived, and, after death, canonized. The prevailing notion of the soul's immortality made them imagine, that the spirits of such excellent persons, either immediately ascended up into heaven, and settled there in some orb or other; or that they hovered in the air; whence, by solemn invocations, and by making some statue or image resemblant of them, they might be prevailed with to come down and inhabit it.

The rise of image-worship.

Whether the idolarty of image-worship was first begun in Chaldea or in Egypt, we have no grounds from history to determine: but wherever it had its origin, the design of making statues and images at first was certainly such as the author of the book of Wisdom [c] has represented it, *viz.* to commemorate an absent or deceased friend, or to do honour to some great man or sovereign prince; which (whether so intended or no at first) the ignorance

3 P 2 and

[b] Herbert's ancient religion of the Gentiles, [c] Chap. xiv. 15, &c.

and superstition of the people turned in time into an object of religious adoration; "the singular diligence of the artificer," as our author expresses it, "helping to set forward the ignorant to more superstition: for he, peradventure, willing to please one in authority, forced all his skill to make the resemblance of the best fashion, and so the multitude, allured by the grace of the work, took him now for a god, who a little before was but honoured as a man."

A M 1997, &c. Ant. Chrif. 2007, &c. from Gen. x. to the end; and from chap. xi ver. 10. to the end.

We cannot but observe, however, with what elegance and fine satire it is, that the Scripture sets off the stupidity and gross infatuation, both of the artificer and adorer. *The carpenter heweth down cedars, and taketh the cypress and the oak. He stretcheth out his rule; he marketh it out with a line; he fitteth it with planes; he marketh it out with the compass, and maketh it after the figure of a man, according to the beauty of a man. ——— He burneth part thereof in the fire; with part thereof he eateth flesh; he roasteth roast and is satisfied; yea he warmeth himself, and saith Aha! I am warm, I have seen the fire; and the residue thereof he maketh a God, even his graven image. He falleth down unto it, and worshippeth it, and prayeth unto it, and saith, Deliver me, for thou art my god; never considering in his heart, nor having knowledge or understanding to say, I have burnt part of it in the fire; yea also I have baked bread upon the coals thereof: I have roasted flesh, and eaten it; and shall I make the residue thereof an abomination? Shall I fall down to the stock of a tree?*

The gross folly and stupidity of it.

That rational creatures should be capable of so wretched a degeneracy as this amounts to, may justly provoke our wonder and amazement: And yet we may remember, that these people (who may possibly be the object of our scorn and contempt) had the boasted light of nature to be their guide in matters of religion. Nay, they had some advantages that we apparently want: They lived much nearer the beginning of the world; had the terrors of the Lord, in the late judgement in the deluge, fresh in their minds: Had the articles of their religion comprised in a small compass; and what is no bad friend to reason and sober recollection, lived in more simplicity, and less luxury, than these later ages can pretend to; and yet, notwithstanding these advantages, so sadly, so shamefully did they miscarry, that the wit of a man would be at a loss to devise a reason for their conduct, had not the divine wisdom

The insufficiency of reason to guide us in matters of religion.

Chap. III.   *from the Flood to the Call of Abraham.*

wisdom informed us, that [d] *they alienated themselves from the light of God*, and *lightly regarded the counsels of the Most High;* that they *forsook the guide of their youth, and rejected* those revelations, *which at sundry times, and in divers manners* were made to their forefathers, for the rule and measure of their faith and practice. We indeed had we lived in those days, may be apt to think, that we would not have been carried away with the common corruption; that the light of nature would have taught us better, than to pay our devotions to brute beasts, or to look upon their images as our gods. But alas! we little consider, what the power of reason, of mere unassisted reason, is against the force of education, and the prevalence of custom, engaged on the side of a false, but flashy, and popular religion. Aristotle, Plato, and Cicero, were in after ages some of the greatest reasoners that the world has produced; and yet we find them complying with the established worship of their country: what grounds have we then to imagine, that in case we had been contemporaries with them, we had acquited ourselves any better? Our reason indeed now tells us, that we would have died, rather than have submitted to these impious modes of worship; but then we are to remember, that reason is now assisted by the light and authority of a divine revelation; that therefore we are not competent judges, how we should act without this superior aid; but that, in all probability, [e] taking away the direction and restraint of this, reason would relapse into the same extravagancies, the same impiety, the same folly and superstition, which prevailed over it before. And therefore, (to conclude in the words of our blessed Saviour, spoken indeed upon another, but very applicable upon this occasion,) [f] *Blessed are the eyes which see the things which ye see,* a full and perfect rule of faith and manners contained in that Holy Bible which is in every one's hands; *for I tell you, that many prophets and kings have desired to see those things, which ye see, and have not seen them; and to hear those things, which ye hear, and have not heard them.*

A. M. 1997, &c.
Ant. Chrif. 2007, &c.
from Gen. x. to the end; and from chap. xi ver. 10. to the end.

[d] Eph. iv. 18.   [e] Roger's Necessity of a divine revelation.   [f] Luke x. 23, 24.

THE END OF THE FIRST VOLUME.

www.ingramcontent.com/pod-product-compliance
Lightning Source LLC
Chambersburg PA
CBHW021423300426
44114CB00010B/624